Second Canadian Edition

Strategic Management

creating competitive advantages

Gregory G. Dess
University of Texas at Dallas

G. T. Lumpkin
University of Illinois at Chicago

Alan B. Eisner
Pace University

and

Theodore Peridis
Schulich School of Business, York University

McGraw-Hill Ryerson

Toronto Montréal Boston Burr Ridge, IL Dubuque, IA Madison, WI
New York San Francisco St. Louis Bangkok Bogotá Caracas
Kuala Lumpur Lisbon London Madrid Mexico City Milan New Delhi
Santiago Seoul Singapore Sydney Taipei

Dedication

To my family, Margie and Taylor; my parents, Bill and Mary Dess; and Professor Fremont Kast

–Greg

To my wife, Vicki; and my colleagues at the University of Illinois at Chicago

–Tom

To my family, Helaine, Rachel, and Jacob

–Alan

To my mother, for all her sage advice; Diana, Catherine, and Matthew, thank you for making every day interesting

–Theo

McGraw-Hill Ryerson

STRATEGIC MANAGEMENT: CREATING COMPETITIVE ADVANTAGES
Second Canadian Edition

ISBN 13: 978-0-07-097997-0
ISBN 10: 0-07-097997-9

1 2 3 4 5 6 7 8 9 10 TCP 0 9

Printed and bound in Canada

Vice-President, Editor-in-Chief: Joanna Cotton
Senior Sponsoring Editor: Kim Brewster
Managing Editor, Development: Kelly Dickson
Developmental Editors: Rebecca Walker/Arlene May Bautista
Marketing Manager: Cathie Lefebvre
Senior Editorial Associate: Christine Lomas
Manager, Editorial Services: Margaret Henderson
Supervising Editor: Cathy Biribauer
Copy Editor: Julie van Tol
Production Coordinator: Lena Mastromarco
Inside Design: Michelle Losier
Composition: SR Nova Pvt Ltd. Bangalore, India
Cover Design: Michelle Losier
Cover Photo: © Eric Jacobson/Getty Images
Printer: Transcontinental Printing Group

Library and Archives Canada Cataloguing in Publication Data

Strategic management : creating competitive advantages / Gregory G. Dess ... [et al.]. — 2nd Canadian ed.

Canadian ed. written by Gregory G. Dess, G. T. Lumpkin, Theodore Peridis.

Includes bibliographical references and indexes.
ISBN 978-0-07-097997-0

    1. Strategic planning—Textbooks.   I. Dess, Gregory G.

HD30.28.S729 2009   658.4'012   C2008-907246-4

About the Authors

Theodore Peridis   is the Chair of the Policy and Strategic Management Area at the Schulich School of Business, York University, where he is also the Director of the Strategy Field Studies and the Global Leadership programs. His research and teaching interests lie in the areas of strategic management, strategic alliances, as well as mergers and acquisitions with emphasis on the role of knowledge, learning, and communication across cultures. Theo received his PhD from New York University and has taught in Europe, North America, South America, the Middle East, and Asia. Theo has received many academic and teaching awards and recognitions for his work: He was recently named Schulich's "Best in Class" by *Canadian Business* magazine and "Professor of the Year" for the Kellogg-Schulich Executive MBA program.

Gregory G. Dess   is the Andrew R. Cecil Endowed Chair in Management at the University of Texas at Dallas. His primary research interests are in the areas of strategic management, organization-environment relationships, and knowledge management. He has published numerous articles on these subjects in both academic and practitioner-oriented journals. In August 2000, he was inducted into the Academy of Management's Journals Hall of Fame as one of its charter members. Professor Dess has conducted executive programs in the United States, Europe, Africa, Hong Kong, and Australia. During 1994, he was a Fulbright Scholar in Oporto, Portugal. He received his PhD in Business Administration from the University of Washington (Seattle).

G. T. (Tom) Lumpkin   is Associate Professor of Management and Entrepreneurship at the University of Illinois at Chicago. He received his PhD in management from the University of Texas at Arlington and MBA from the University of Southern California. His research interests include entrepreneurial orientation, opportunity recognition, strategy-making processes, and innovative forms of organizing work. He has published numerous research articles and book chapters. He is a member of the Editorial Review Boards of *Entrepreneurship Theory & Practice* and the *Journal of Business Venturing*. Professor Lumpkin also conducts executive programs in strategic and entrepreneurial applications of ecommerce and digital business technologies.

Alan B. Eisner   is Professor of Management and Graduate Management Program Chair at the Lubin School of Business, Pace University. He received his PhD in management from the Stern School of Business, New York University. His primary research interests are in strategic management, technology management, organizational learning, and managerial decision making. He has published research articles and cases in journals such as *Advances in Strategic Management, International Journal of Electronic Commerce, International Journal of Technology Management, American Business Review, Journal of Behavioral and Applied Management*, and *Journal of the International Academy for Case Studies*. He is the Associate Editor of the Case Association's peer-reviewed journal, *The CASE Journal*.

Brief Contents

Contents

Preface

Introduction to the Second Canadian Edition

Welcome to the Second Canadian Edition of *Strategic Management: Creating Competitive Advantages*. We are very pleased with the overwhelmingly positive response to the first edition, and we are most grateful for the constructive and extensive feedback that we have obtained from the many instructors who took the time to review and comment on our work. Their input has been invaluable and has led to what we feel are substantial improvements that make this second edition even more relevant, comprehensive, and student-friendly, while retaining all the valuable elements of the first edition. The textbook in your hands reflects the state-of-the-art thinking in the field of strategic management, while bringing into focus the Canadian business landscape and the uniqueness of our country's economic, political, historical, and social evolution. We have strived to preserve tradition and, at the same time, introduce the topics that today concern practicing managers: globalization, technology, innovation, ethics, corporate governance, and entrepreneurship.

Before embarking on this project we frequently asked ourselves the obvious question: Why do we want to write this book? After all, there are already some good strategy textbooks on the market. However, some soul-searching and a visit to the library convinced us there was still a need for a book that students would find highly relevant and readable as well as rigorous. To this end, we worked hard, both to cover all the traditional bases and to integrate throughout the book key themes that are vital to an understanding of strategic management.

To bring strategy concepts to life, we incorporated hundreds of short examples from business practices to illustrate virtually every concept in the book, and we provided dozens of "Strategy Spotlights"—more detailed examples of actual situations—to drive home the key points. We also developed three separate chapters addressing timely subjects about which all business students should have a solid understanding: the role of intellectual assets and knowledge in value creation; the importance of disruptive technologies such as the Internet, and the resulting digital business strategies that can create competitive advantages in the twenty-first century; and the value of fostering entrepreneurship in established organizations and new venture start-ups.

Most importantly, we considered and reflected on both the traditional bases and the key themes from a uniquely Canadian perspective. Because Canada is so close to the United States—geographically, economically, and technologically—we often forget how our own values and institutions give rise to very distinct and different organizations in the private, public, and not-for-profit sectors. We highlighted such uniqueness by incorporating Canadian introductory cases, Canadian-centred Strategy Spotlights, and more than 120 Canadian examples throughout the text. Every page in this book celebrates

Canadian management achievements, although whenever appropriate, we also recognize weaknesses and situations where Canadian managers have fallen short of strategic management success.

Based on the many useful insights from our reviewers as well as reflection on the changes that have occurred in the field of strategic management and the "real world," we have introduced many improvements to the second Canadian edition. While the book incorporates the uniqueness of Canada as a country and as a place where many diverse organizations operate and thrive, it still retains all the elements that thousands of instructors and students of numerous strategic management courses found very attractive in the original editions.

Key Features of *Strategic Management,* Second Canadian Edition

Among the many exciting features the second Canadian edition offers are the following:

- Crisply written chapters that cover all of the strategy bases and address contemporary topics. We divide the chapters logically into the traditional sequence: **strategic analysis**, **strategic formulation**, and **strategic implementation**. In addition, we provide chapters on timely topics such as digital strategies, intellectual capital, knowledge management, and entrepreneurship. We have added an entire new supplementary appendix on **Analyzing Strategic Management Cases**, for instructors and students who wish to cover this relevant material that provides insights on how to tackle a case and get the most out of this unique pedagogical opportunity. It contains not just the traditional treatment of the subject and instructions about analyzing cases, but it also offers suggestions on how to manage case analysis meetings and avoid distractions and time-wasting activities. Moreover, the section is augmented by two sub-appendices that include a comprehensive overview of financial ratio analysis that should be used in analyzing strategy cases, as well as a very informative source of databases, Web sites and publications where students can find invaluable information about companies, industries, and the environment. This last section covers both global and uniquely Canadian sources, and it represents a very comprehensive guide to a virtual library that students would find useful, not just for their strategy course but for all their academic courses as well as in their subsequent work environment.
- We devote **equal attention to each of the three processes of strategic management**. Strategic analysis commonly receives the most exposure, reflecting on the traditional industrial organization roots of the field. Yet, observing managers in real time and analyzing their ultimate successes has clearly demonstrated that more rests on how decisions are made and executed than on which models are employed in gathering and making sense of the pertinent information. We have strived to balance the coverage of strategic analysis and to give the same emphasis to strategic formulation and strategic implementation, allocating the twelve chapters of the textbook equally among the three strategic management processes.
- **Key strategic concepts** are introduced in a clear and concise manner and are followed by timely and interesting examples from management practice. These concepts include SWOT analysis, five-forces analysis, the resource-based view of the firm, value-chain analysis, competitive advantage, diversification and portfolio analysis, boundaryless organizations, leadership, and corporate governance.
- Extensive use of **Strategy Spotlights** throughout the book provides relevant, interesting illustrations of actual management practices, boosts student interest, and reinforces student learning.

- The text provides a thorough grounding in **ethics, globalization, and technology**. These concepts are central themes throughout the book and form the basis for many of the Strategy Spotlights in the chapters.

- Many of the key concepts are applied to start-up firms and **smaller businesses.** This is particularly important since many students plan to work in such firms.

- Consistent chapter format and features **reinforce learning**. Each chapter begins with a list of the key learning objectives. The opening case describes a situation in which a company's performance was critically affected by specific strategy concepts and provides the foundation for the ensuing discussion. Throughout the text, the learning objectives (LO) are identified in the page margins as they are developed and elaborated upon.

- At the end of each chapter, there are four different types of **questions and exercises** that help students assess their understanding and application of the material: summary review questions, experiential exercises, application questions and exercises, and ethics questions. Each chapter contains at least one exercise that involves the use of the Internet.

- *Strategic Management* features the best chapter **teaching notes** available today. Rather than just summarize key points, we focus on "value-added" material to enhance the teaching and learning experiences. Each chapter includes literally dozens of questions to spur discussion as well as many examples from management practice to provide further illustrations of key points. We have worked hard to provide a complete package that will make classes relevant, rigorous, and rewarding for the instructors and the students.

- The second Canadian edition further builds on these features to enhance the value of our book for both instructors and students. Eleven of the **opening cases** that lead off each of the chapters discuss Canadian organizations, such as Nortel, BCE, Power Corp, and Cott within a Canadian and international context. Canadian organizations face unique challenges, operate within distinct structures and institutions, and management practices reflect our unique history and vast geography. We feel it is often more instructive to analyze things that can go wrong when strategy concepts are not followed than to observe and exalt perfection; therefore, most of these mini-cases address flawed decisions and bad situations that have led to significant erosion of value and destruction of competitiveness.

- We incorporate the key role of **corporate governance** in the strategic management process, reflecting on the most controversial topic and the very heated debate regarding today's business organizations. Corporate governance issues manifest themselves very differently within the Canadian context, due to our unique regulatory environment and the concentration of corporate ownership. Our discussion takes such uniqueness into consideration and highlights its advantages and disadvantages.

Acknowledgements

Strategic Management, Second Canadian Edition, represents far more than just the joint efforts of the four authors. Rather, it is the product of the collaborative inputs and contributions of many individuals. Some of them are academic colleagues, others are the outstanding team of professionals at McGraw-Hill Ryerson, and still others are those closest to us, our family. To all we express our sincere gratitude.

First, we would like to acknowledge the thorough and constructive reviews we received from a superb team of reviewers across the country. Their input in both pointing out errors as well as suggesting areas which needed further development was extremely helpful. We sincerely believe their dedication and professionalism in the task was unparalleled, and the entire team hopes we have done justice in incorporating their ideas to the final product.

Ian Anderson, *Algonquin College*
Shamsud Chowdhury, *Dalhousie University*
Dr. Brooke Dobni, *University of Saskatchewan*
Barbara Gardner, *Southern Alberta Institute of Technology*
Jack Ito, *University of Regina*
Peter Johnson, *McMaster University*
Raymond Leduc, *University of Western Ontario*
Dr. Terrance Power, *Royal Roads University*
Robert Sexty, *Memorial University of Newfoundland*
Mark Simpson, *George Brown College*
Ron Smith, *Ryerson University*
Francis Tapon, *University of Guelph*

In addition, colleagues at the Schulich School of Business provided invaluable feedback as they used the first edition in their classes and gained unique insights from presenting the material to their very demanding students. Moreover, Paul Beamish from the Richard Ivey School of Business responded enthusiastically and put together an exceptional set of cases to accompany this book and help expose the richness of the Canadian corporate landscape.

During the preparation of the first edition, Neeraj Julka provided extensive research and spent hundreds of hours compiling the information for the Canadian examples, while JoAnne Stein and Clara Kan, administrative assistants at Schulich, worked diligently to make up for many missed deadlines and last-minute changes. I would be remiss if I did not acknowledge the ongoing and generous support of the Dean and all my colleagues at the Schulich School of Business, whose encouragement and patience created an environment that allowed me to undertake and complete this project and, at the same time, protected me from the many distractions that crept up daily to derail the completion of both the first and second editions of the book.

The team at McGraw-Hill Ryerson, consisting of Senior Sponsoring Editor Kim Brewster, Developmental Editors Rebecca Walker and Arlene May Bautista, Supervising Editor Cathy Biribauer, and Copy Editor Julie van Tol, should rightly be part of the author list since they did all the real work to bring this effort to fruition. Throughout, they skilfully coached, motivated, guided and, most of all, put up for much too long with a not-so-reliable and quite mercurial author, and made him look good.

Most importantly, I want to acknowledge my family. So frequently throughout this project, they had to be disappointed when yet one more weekend had to be taken from our personal time together and be given instead to pushing forward with the writing of "the book." To all, I am truly grateful.

Theo Peridis
Toronto

A Guided Tour

*S*trategic Management: Creating Competitive Advantages, Second Canadian Edition, has been organized around the traditional sequence of topics and concepts in strategy, while bringing into focus the Canadian business landscape and the uniqueness of our country's economic, political, historical, and social evolution. We have also introduced timely topics that concern managers today, such as globalization, technology and innovation, ethics, corporate governance, and entrepreneurship.

Please take a moment to look through the features below and better acquaint yourself with this text and its pedagogical features.

chapter map

The Chapter Map at the beginning of each section guides instructors and students through the organizational structure of the text.

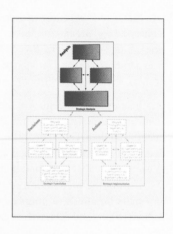

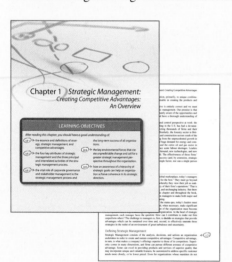

learning objectives

Each chapter begins with a set of Learning Objectives—key learning objectives inform students about what should be understood after reading the chapter. In addition, these Learning Objectives (LO) are identified in the margins of the chapter as they are developed and elaborated upon.

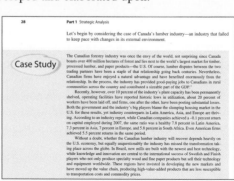

chapter opening cases

The opening case of each chapter describes a situation in which a company's performance was critically affected by specific strategy concepts and asks, "What went wrong?"

strategy spotlights

These detailed and varied examples provide relevant, interesting illustrations of actual management practices that help boost student interest and reinforce learning. Many of these Spotlights are new to the second Canadian edition and illustrate Canada's varied companies.

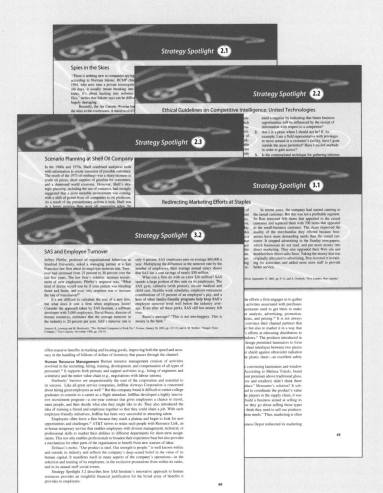

chapter-ending material

The end-of-chapter material challenges students to apply the central strategy concepts emphasized in each chapter. This material includes **Summary Review Questions**, **Experiential Exercises**, **Application Questions and Exercises**, and **Ethics Questions**. Each chapter includes at least one exercise that involves using the Internet.

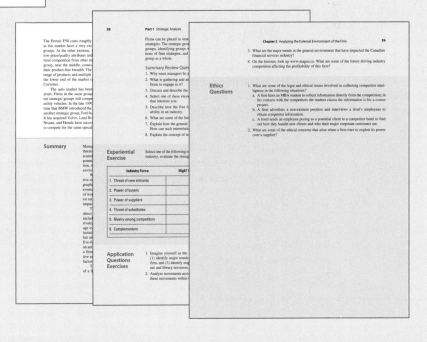

Textbook Supplements

All of the instructor supplements are available through downloading from the Instructor Online Learning Centre, located at: www.mcgrawhill.ca/olc/dess.

Instructor's Manual Written entirely by the text author to ensure clarity and accuracy, this manual provides a matchless resource for instructors.

In addition to summarizing key concepts, the manual provides the following:

- complete lecture outcomes
- discussion questions
- extra Strategy Spotlights/cases
- in-class experiential simulations

Computerized Test Bank A thorough and comprehensive test bank offers, in the easy-to-use EZ Test Software, a minimum of 30 true/false and 40 multiple choice questions for each chapter, using flexible and easy-to-use electronic testing software. Instructors can customize several different test versions for use in their classroom. This test bank, created by Bernard Williams of the University of Lethbridge, is fully electronic, allowing instructors to mix and match whatever questions they choose, or even to create a "random" test. Rich Text Format files are also included, which can be printed out for a test bank on paper.

Microsoft® *PowerPoint*® Presentations A full set of *PowerPoint* presentations will allow instructors to use multimedia to further enhance student learning and, thus, student success. Created by Barb Gardner of Southern Alberta Institute of Technology, these presentations represent the key features in the text.

Videos Chosen by the U.S. author team, the video series that accompanies *Strategic Management: Creating Competitive Advantages*, second Canadian edition, is comprised of 15 programs that enhance and bring to life the chapter material. The videos provide a useful supplement to lectures and text materials that can stimulate class discussions and enrich the learning experience in Canadian classrooms.

Online Learning Centre

The Online Learning Centre (OLC) for the second Canadian edition of *Strategic Management,* at www.mcgrawhill.ca/olc/dess, follows the text, chapter by chapter, with supplemental digital content for students and instructors. As students read the text, they can go online to take self-grading quizzes, review material, and work through interactive exercises.

The instructor's section of the OLC contains useful resource materials, including downloadable versions of the Instructor's Manual, *PowerPoint*® presentations, and Test Bank.

Material on the OLC can be delivered in multiple ways—through the Web site or a course management system.

*i*Learning Services Program

McGraw-Hill Ryerson offers a unique *i*Services package designed for Canadian faculty. Our mission is to equip providers of higher education with superior tools and resources required for excellence in teaching *Strategic Management*. For additional information, visit www.mcgrawhill.ca/highereducation/iservices.

CourseSmart

CourseSmart brings together thousands of textbooks across hundreds of courses in an eTextbook format providing unique benefits to students and faculty. By purchasing an eTextbook, students can save up to 50 percent off the cost of a print textbook; reduce their impact on the environment; and gain access to powerful Web tools for learning, including full text search, notes and highlighting, and e-mail tools for sharing notes between classmates. For faculty, CourseSmart provides instant access to review and compare textbooks and course materials in their discipline area without the time, cost, and environmental impact of mailing print examination copies. For further details contact your *i*Learning Sales Specialist or go to www.coursesmart.com.

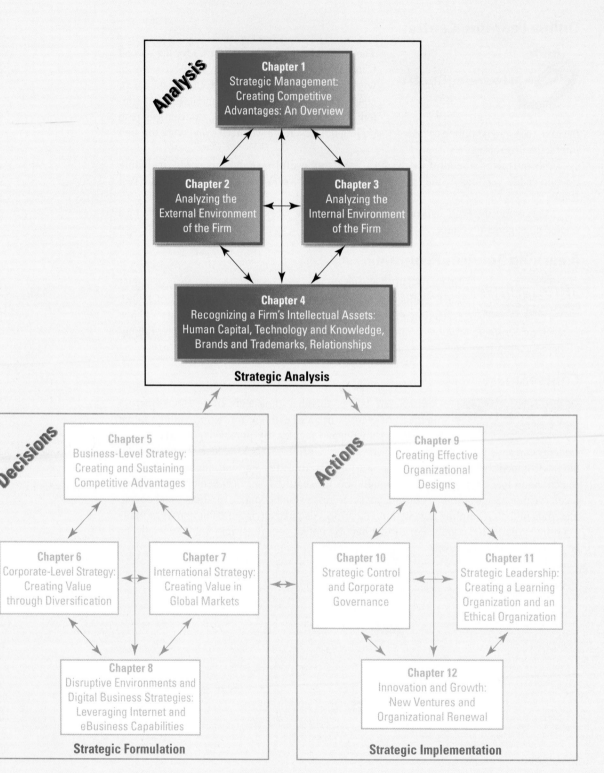

PART 1

Strategic Analysis

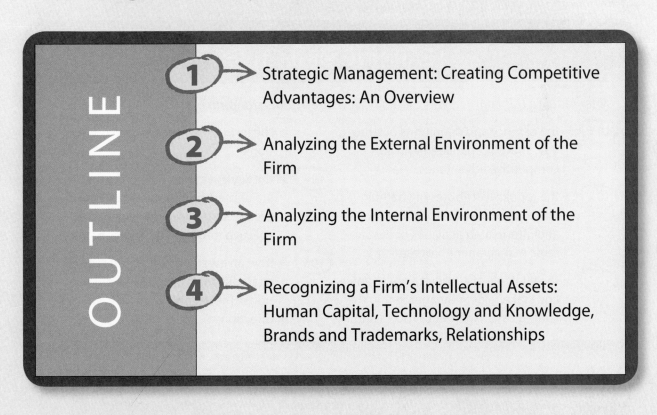

Chapter 1 *Strategic Management: Creating Competitive Advantages: An Overview*

LEARNING OBJECTIVES

After reading this chapter, you should have a good understanding of:

LO 1 the essence and definitions of strategy, strategic management, and competitive advantages.

LO 2 the four key attributes of strategic management and the three principal and interrelated activities of the strategic management process.

LO 3 the vital role of corporate governance and stakeholder management in the strategic management process and the long-term success of all organizations.

LO 4 the key environmental forces that create unpredictable change and call for a greater strategic management perspective throughout the organization.

LO 5 how an awareness of a hierarchy of strategic goals can help an organization achieve coherence in its strategic direction.

One of the things that makes the study of strategic management so interesting is that it tries to answer the question, why do some firms outperform others? How is it that struggling firms can become stars, while high flyers can become earthbound very rapidly? Consider the following examples: When Wal-Mart announced its intention of entering the Canadian retail scene in the mid-1980s, most established companies—large and small alike—were justifiably terrified. Within the next few years and as a direct result of Wal-Mart's aggressive strategy, venerable competitors, such as Eaton's and Kmart, disappeared. Some, such as the Hudson's Bay Company, fell onto the hands of foreign owners, while others were able to face the onslaught head-on and survive or even thrive in the new competitive landscape, as did Canadian Tire. Bombardier has been a Canadian success story of genius and serendipity; it was able to carve a unique place in a range of industries—aerospace, public transit, and outdoor recreational equipment. Following the Internet bubble burst of 2000, many technology firms were particularly ravaged. Let's look at one such firm that experienced a hard fall from grace.

Case Study

In June 2008, another chapter in the long saga of the once behemoth global telecom firm Nortel Networks closed as the RCMP laid criminal charges against several of the company's former top brass, including CEO Frank Dunn. Mr. Dunn was the successor of disgraced CEO John Roth who, after his appointment to the helm of the Brampton, Ontario, firm in 1997, embarked on a three-year journey to transform Nortel from an inefficient bureaucracy into a template for the New Economy. Along the way, Nortel electrified the high-tech industry with a series of lightning-quick manoeuvres and became a major player in the Internet revolution. Roth's efforts earned him Canada's "Outstanding CEO of the Year" award for 2000. He catapulted Nortel beyond its decades-long core business of making telephone equipment and into the red-hot market of fibre-optic networks and other systems for transmitting digital information over the Internet. It also spawned a series of multi-billion dollar acquisitions and new alliances. In 2000, Nortel ranked as North America's number-two maker of telecom products, trailing only Lucent Technologies, and was the second-largest router manufacturer, behind its other chief rival Cisco Systems Inc. In early 2000, Nortel Networks had surpassed $400 billion in market capitalization and accounted for as much as 36 percent of the value of the TSE 300, its stock trading as high as $125 and leading the stock exchange to record trading volumes.

Yet, on February 15, 2001, sales growth expectations were cut in half to 15 percent, earnings growth predictions were reduced from 30 percent to 10 percent, and a first-quarter earnings guidance was revised downward from 16 cents per-share growth to a loss of 4 cents per share. Nortel's stock, which had already been battered along with all high-tech shares during the second part of 2000, lost another third of its value and dropped below $30. The CEO, whose credibility evaporated along with Nortel's market capitalization, was now just another executive scrambling to keep his business intact as the bottom fell out of the high-tech market.

Nortel's shareholders lost a collective $325 billion in value, and the damage wasn't limited to a small, elite class of investors. Through mutual funds, pension plans, retirement savings plans, and other investments, Canadians of all stripes owned a piece of the country's largest, mightiest company.

Roth attempted to explain the sudden change in outlook on the dramatically slowing U.S. economy. He argued that during the four weeks after he first announced 2001 projections on January 18, Nortel customers unexpectedly changed their telecom spending plans, which, for the first time, seriously began to impact sales forecasts of Nortel equipment. Ostensibly, despite earlier warnings from the likes of Cisco, Lucent, and Ericsson, nothing of significance had shown up on Nortel's order books until February 15, 2001. Only then did the bad news flood in—to the tune of U.S.$1.8 billion less in expected revenue for the first quarter.

During the four weeks between forecasts, a number of other events took place. First, two Nortel executives sold approximately $7 million worth of shares. The company's chief technology officer, Bill Hawe, quietly resigned and exercised his own options, worth about U.S.$10 million. On the same day that Hawe resigned, RBC Dominion Securities interviewed Roth for a Webcast, not widely disseminated, during which he commented that customers were "slowing down expenditures of capital like we've never witnessed before!" And finally, Nortel completed an all-stock deal for a JDS Uniphase Corp. subsidiary, worth about U.S.$3 billion at the time but as much as U.S.$1.5 billion less after the stock collapsed.

For many Canadians who had seen their retirement savings disappear, this was a slap in the face—particularly since Roth received $135 million in 2000 from salary, bonus, and proceeds from the sale of Nortel shares. Nortel was knocked off its pedestal—and Roth stood out like the clothing-challenged emperor.[1]

Mr. Dunn, a long-time Nortel employee and a certified management accountant, was brought in to clean up the mess and restore confidence in the corporation. Together with a new management team, he proclaimed a new era of honesty and integrity as well as plant closings, massive layoffs, and substantial curtailing of projects and initiatives. Yet, in 2003, Nortel announced that it was restating financial results for the previous few years. Similar announcements were repeated through the following two years and eventually, in March 2004, Nortel declared, as a part of the ongoing unravelling of its accounting tangle, that it was putting Mr. Dunn, Mr. Beatty its CFO, and its corporate controller Mr. Gollogly on leave. They were fired a month later. The RCMP charged that the three executives actively massaged the books to mask results and manipulate the financial picture of the company to meet analysts' expectations and collect millions in bonuses. During this period, Nortel stock dipped below $1.00.

Who and what might be responsible for Nortel's successes during the 90s and its failures since? Answers to such questions lie at the heart of strategic management and are the subject of this book. Leaders, such as those at Nortel, face a large number of unusual challenges in today's global marketplace. In deciding how much credit (or blame) they deserve, one might consider the *romantic* view of leadership.[2] Here, the implicit assumption is that the leader is the key force in determining an organization's success—or lack thereof. This view dominates the popular press in business magazines, such as *Fortune, BusinessWeek, Forbes*, and *Canadian Business*, wherein the CEO is either lauded for his or her firm's success or chided for the organization's demise. Consider, for example, the credit that has been bestowed on such leaders as Jack Welch, Andrew Grove, Isadore Sharpe, and Frank Stronach for the tremendous accomplishments of their firms: General Electric, Intel, Four Seasons Hotels and Resorts, and Magna International, respectively. In the world of sports, managers and coaches, such as Scotty Bowman or Pat Quinn, get a lot of credit for their teams' outstanding successes in the field and on the ice. On the other hand, when things don't go well, much of the failure of an organization can also, rightfully, be attributed to the leader. After all, Nortel's Roth, in his enthusiasm to pump up revenues, aggressively counted huge contracts that left little margin for error. Such risks are generally not advised, especially as market and economic conditions erode. Nonetheless, he repeatedly ignored negative signals and continued to make rosy forecasts. Profits and the firm's stock price eventually took a big hit.

However, this gives only part of the picture. From another perspective on leadership, *external control* is highlighted. Here, rather than making the implicit assumption that the leader is the most important contributor in determining organizational performance, the focus is on external factors that may positively or negatively affect a firm's success. One doesn't have to look far to support this perspective. Clearly, Nortel was negatively impacted by the worldwide recession that began in 2000, which drastically cut the demand for telecommunication equipment and services. Other rivals, such as Alcatel and Lucent Technologies, were also negatively affected. Furthermore, as we see later on in the book, other perspectives ascribe the success of an organization, primarily, to unique combinations of skills and resources that are rare and invaluable in creating the products and services offered to the market.

The point, of course, is that no single perspective is entirely correct and we must acknowledge multiple angles in the study of strategic management. Our premise is that leaders can make a difference, but they must be constantly aware of the opportunities and threats that they face in the external environment and have a thorough understanding of their firm's resources and capabilities.

Consider a rather dramatic example of the external control perspective at work: the recent financial crisis associated with subprime lending in the U.S. has had a devastating impact on Ontario's manufacturing sector, afflicting thousands of firms and their employees, forcing plant closings and downsizings. Similarly, the forestry sector in British Columbia has suffered from the sluggish housing and construction sectors south of the border. Yet, Alberta and Saskatchewan are prospering from the unprecedented growth in countries such as China and India, which has created huge demand for energy and commodities. Mining companies, oil exploration firms, and the entire oil and gas sector in the western parts of the country are booming and face acute labour shortages. Leaders and entrepreneurs respond and capitalize on shifts in demand, new technologies, and new opportunities that arise in different parts of the world. The effectiveness of those firms' responses highlights the fact that an organization's success (and, by extension, strategic management) cannot be viewed as deriving from a single factor, nor can a single person normally make all the difference in the results.

WHAT IS STRATEGIC MANAGEMENT?

Given the many challenges and opportunities in the global marketplace, today's managers must do more than set long-term strategies and hope for the best.[3] They must go beyond what some have called "incremental management," whereby they view their job as making a series of minor changes to improve the efficiency of their firm's operations.[4] That is fine if their firm is competing in a very stable, simple, and unchanging industry. But there aren't many of those left. As we shall discuss in this chapter and throughout the book, the pace of change is accelerating, and the pressure on managers to make both major and minor changes in a firm's strategic direction is increasing.

Rather than view their role as mere custodian of the status quo, today's leaders must be proactive, anticipate change, continually refine and, when necessary, make significant changes to their strategies. The strategic management of the organization must become both a process and a way of thinking throughout the organization. At the heart of strategic management, each manager faces the question: How can I contribute to make our firm outperform others? The challenge to managers is, first, to **decide** on strategies that provide advantages which can be sustained over time and, second, to effectively **execute** those strategies in the midst of an environment of great turbulence and uncertainty.

Defining Strategic Management

Strategic Management consists of the analysis, decisions, and actions an organization undertakes in order to create and sustain competitive advantages. Competitive advantage, in turn, is what makes a company's offerings superior to those of its competitors. Superiority comes in many dimensions, and firms can pursue different avenues of competitive advantage. Some can excel in providing products and services of superior quality that may incorporate unique and valuable features, be customized to address specific customer needs more closely, or be lower priced. Even for organizations whose mandates do not include making profits, such as government departments and not-for-profit organizations, the concept of competitive advantage is very instructive. Consider, for example, our court system. What is the competitive advantage of a particular court of justice as compared to alternatives such as mediation or arbitration? What elements of its organizing structure, staff, and strategy are responsible for providing resolutions to disputes that are speedier, fairer, or perceived as more just than the alternatives? The answers are important since they can influence whether the populace will trust the court and whether the government will then adequately fund it rather than divert resources to its "competitors."

The above definitions of strategic management and competitive advantage capture two main elements that go to the heart of the field of strategic management. First, the strategic management of an organization entails three ongoing processes: *analysis, decisions*, and *actions*. That is, strategic management is concerned with the *analysis* of strategic goals (vision, mission, and strategic objectives) along with the analysis of the internal and external environment of the organization. Next, leaders must make strategic *decisions*. These decisions, broadly speaking, address two basic questions: What industries should we compete in? How should we compete in those industries? These questions also often involve an organization's domestic as well as its international operations. And last are the *actions* that must be taken. Decisions are of little use, of course, unless they are acted on. Firms must take the necessary actions to implement their strategies. This requires leaders to allocate the necessary resources and to design the organization to bring the intended strategies to reality. Strategic management is, therefore, a process and an evolving managerial responsibility that requires a great deal of interaction among those three subprocesses. It should be noted that although each of the three subprocesses can conceptually be viewed as occurring distinctly and in sequence, effective managers engage in all three, all the time. Their actions provide insights and experiences that further inform their understanding of what is going on in the marketplace as well as what their firm is capable of accomplishing. Such appreciation allows them to continuously refine or drastically change their adopted strategies.

Second, the essence of strategic management is the study of why some firms outperform others.[5] Thus, managers need to determine how a firm is to compete so that it can obtain advantages that are sustainable over a period of time. That means focusing on two fundamental questions, the first being, how should we compete in order to create competitive advantages in the marketplace? For example, managers need to determine if the firm should position itself as the low-cost producer or develop products and services that are unique, which would enable the firm to charge premium prices, or some combination of both. Since managers must also ask how to make such advantages sustainable instead of temporary in the marketplace, the next question is, how can we create competitive advantages in the marketplace that are not only unique and valuable but also difficult for competitors to copy or substitute?[6,7]

Ideas that work are almost always immediately copied by rivals. In the 1980s, American Airlines tried to establish a competitive advantage by introducing the frequent flyer program. Within months, all major airlines in the U.S. as well as in Canada and the rest of the world had similar programs. Overnight, instead of competitive advantage, frequent flyer programs became a necessary tool for competitive parity. The challenge, therefore, is to create a competitive advantage that is sustainable.

Michael Porter argues that sustainable competitive advantage cannot be achieved through operational effectiveness alone.[8] Most of the popular management innovations of the last two decades—total quality, just-in-time, benchmarking, business process re-engineering, outsourcing—are about operational effectiveness. Operational effectiveness means performing similar activities better than rivals. Each of these is important, but none leads to sustainable competitive advantage for the simple reason that everyone is doing them. Strategy is all about being different from everyone else. Sustainable competitive advantage is possible only through performing different activities from rivals or performing similar activities in different ways. Companies such as Wal-Mart, Canadian Tire, and IKEA have developed unique, internally consistent, and difficult-to-imitate activity systems that have provided them with sustained competitive advantage. A company with a good strategy must make clear choices about what it wants to accomplish. Trying to do everything that its rivals does eventually leads to mutually destructive price competition, not long-term advantage.

The Four Key Attributes of Strategic Management

Four attributes distinguish strategic management from the other functions such as accounting, marketing, or operations, which are performed inside an organization.[9] Students of business and commerce have traditionally been exposed to the issues that are pertinent to each of the various functions. More recently, additional emphasis has been placed on such topics as strategic human resource management or strategic marketing, which recognize and address similar strategic attributes within the organizational functions. Exhibit 1.1 states our definition of strategic management and identifies its four attributes.

←(LO 2)

1. Strategic management *is directed toward overall organizational goals and objectives*. That is, effort must be directed at what is best for the total organization, not just a single functional area. Some authors have referred to this perspective as "organizational versus individual rationality."[10] In other words, what might look "rational" or most appropriate for one functional area, such as operations, may not be in the best interest of the overall firm. For example, operations may decide to schedule long production runs of similar products in order to lower unit costs; however, the standardized output may be counter to what the marketing department needs in order to appeal to a sophisticated and demanding target market. Similarly, research and development may "overengineer" the product in order to develop a far superior offering, but the design may make the product so expensive that market demand is minimal. In studying strategic management, we look at cases and strategic issues from the perspective of the whole organization rather than that of the functional areas in which students might have the most training and experience.

2. Strategic management *includes multiple stakeholders in decision making*. Managers must incorporate the demands of many stakeholders when making decisions.[11] Stakeholders are those individuals, groups, and organizations who have a "stake" in the success of the organization, including owners (shareholders in a publicly held corporation), employees, customers, suppliers, the community at large, and so on. Managers will not be successful if they continually focus on a single stakeholder.

Definition: Strategic management consists of the analysis, decisions, and actions an organization undertakes in order to create and sustain competitive advantages.

Key attributes of strategic management:

- directs the organization toward overall goals and objectives
- includes multiple stakeholders in decision making
- incorporates short-term and long-term perspectives
- recognizes trade-offs between efficiency and effectiveness

Exhibit 1.1
Strategic Management Concepts

For example, if the overwhelming emphasis is on generating profits for the owners, employees may become alienated, customer service may suffer, and the suppliers may become resentful of continual demands for pricing concessions. Many organizations have been able to satisfy multiple stakeholder needs simultaneously. In doing so, financial performance may actually increase because employees who are satisfied with their jobs make a greater effort to enhance customer satisfaction, thus leading to higher profits.

3.   Strategic management *incorporates both short-term and long-term perspectives.* Peter Senge, a leading strategic management author at the Massachusetts Institute of Technology (MIT), has referred to this need as a "creative tension."[12] That is, managers must maintain both a vision for the future of the organization as well as a focus on its present operating needs. However, as one descends the hierarchy of the organization from executive to middle-level to lower-level management, a narrower, short-term perspective tends to prevail. Nonetheless, all managers throughout the organization must maintain a strategic management perspective and assess how their actions impact the overall attainment of organizational objectives. For example, laying off several valuable employees may help to cut costs and improve profits in the short term, but the long-term implications for employee morale and customer relationships may suffer—leading to subsequent performance declines.[13]

4.   Strategic management *involves the recognition of trade-offs between effectiveness and efficiency.* Closely related to the third point above, this recognition includes being aware of the need to strive to act effectively and efficiently as an organization. Some authors have referred to this as the difference between "doing the right thing" (effectiveness) and "doing things right" (efficiency).[14] While managers must allocate and use resources wisely, they must still direct their efforts toward the attainment of overall organizational objectives. Managers who are totally focused on meeting short-term budgets and targets may fail to attain the broader goals of the organization. Consider the following anecdote, told by Norman Augustine, formerly CEO of defence giant Martin Marietta (now Lockheed Martin):

> I am reminded of an article I once read in a British newspaper which described a problem with the local bus service between the towns of Bagnall and Greenfields. It seemed that, to the great annoyance of customers, drivers had been passing long queues of would-be passengers with a smile and a wave of the hand. This practice was, however, clarified by a bus company official who explained, "It is impossible for the drivers to keep their timetables if they must stop for passengers."[15]

Clearly, the drivers who were trying to stay on schedule had ignored the overall mission. As Augustine noted, "Impeccable logic but something seems to be missing!"

THE STRATEGIC MANAGEMENT PROCESS

We have identified three ongoing processes—analysis, decisions, and actions—that are central to strategic management. In practice, these three processes—often referred to as strategy analysis, strategy formulation, and strategy implementation—are highly interdependent. Moreover, these three processes do not take place one after the other in a sequential fashion.

Henry Mintzberg, an influential management scholar at McGill University, argues that conceptualizing the strategic management process as one in which analysis is followed by optimal decisions and their subsequent meticulous implementation neither describes the strategic management process accurately nor prescribes ideal practice.[16] In his view, the

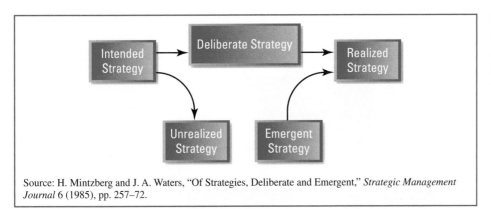

Source: H. Mintzberg and J. A. Waters, "Of Strategies, Deliberate and Emergent," *Strategic Management Journal* 6 (1985), pp. 257–72.

Exhibit 1.2
Realized Strategy and Intended Strategy: Usually Not the Same

business environment is far from predictable, thus limiting our ability for analysis. Further, decisions in an organization are seldom based on optimal rationality alone, given the political processes that occur in all organizations.

Mintzberg proposed an alternative model of strategy development. As depicted in Exhibit 1.2, decisions deriving from analysis constitute the *intended* strategy of the firm. For a variety of reasons, the intended strategy rarely survives in its original form. Unforeseen environmental developments, unanticipated resource constraints, or changes in managerial preferences may result in at least some parts of the intended strategy remaining *unrealized*. On the other hand, good managers will want to take advantage of a new opportunity presented by the environment even if it was not part of the original set of intentions. New federal and provincial legislation promoting renewable energy has attracted many established corporations, such as Siemens, General Electric, and Suncor as well as start-ups, to direct their attention and redeploy their R&D capabilities to develop new technologies and "green" solutions to environmental challenges; such strategic moves do not necessarily constitute parts of the original strategies of firms and can be opportunistic responses to unfolding events, but they are certainly parts of an *emergent* strategy. The final *realized* strategy of any firm is a combination of deliberate and emergent strategies.

Addressing each of the three strategic management processes separately does, nevertheless, serve some useful pedagogical purposes. It allows us to develop a better appreciation of what each entails and to consider the concepts, frameworks, and tools that can be used by managers who engage in each. It serves to demonstrate that effective strategic management poses complex challenges and that sometimes things can go wrong.

Exhibit 1.3 depicts the strategic management process (or at least an unambiguous and systematic reflection of it) and indicates how it ties into the chapters in the book. Consistent with our discussion above, we use two-way arrows to convey the interactive nature of the processes. Next, we briefly elaborate on what each of the three strategic management processes entails.

Strategy Analysis

Strategy analysis may be looked upon as the starting point of the strategic management process. It consists of the "advance work" that must be done in order to effectively formulate and implement strategies. Analysis is about understanding what is going on, why situations have unfolded in particular ways, what issues the organization faces at present and in the future, whether and why the organization has been successful, and what others may be doing and why. Most importantly, analysis is about making sense of the elements and the interactions that formed the organization's world in the past and will continue to be of

Exhibit 1.3
The Strategic Management Process

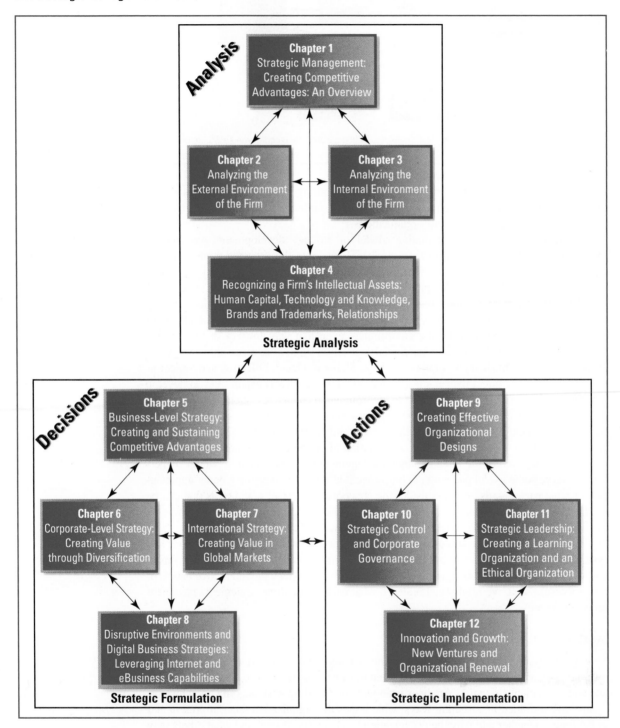

importance in the future. Many strategies fail because managers proceed to formulate and implement strategies without an appreciation of the overarching goals of the organization and without a careful analysis of its external and internal environment.

Strategy analysis starts with an appreciation of the organization's goals and objectives. Various stakeholders have different expectations and aspirations with respect to what an organization should stand for and what it should strive to accomplish. Analyzing organizational goals and objectives (Chapter 1) addresses how organizations reconcile those divergent positions and why organizations must have clearly articulated goals and objectives if they are to channel the efforts of individuals throughout the organization toward common ends. Goals and objectives also provide a means of allocating resources effectively. A firm's vision, mission, and strategic objectives form a hierarchy of goals that range from broad statements of intent and bases for competitive advantage to specific, measurable strategic objectives.

This hierarchy of goals does not emerge in isolation. Rather, it is developed in concert with a rigorous understanding of the ever-changing opportunities and threats in the external environment (Chapter 2) as well as a thorough understanding of the firm's strengths and weaknesses (Chapters 3 and 4). The opening incident in Chapter 1 described how the CEO of Nortel ignored the economic and competitive landscape and set unrealistically high growth targets. The result was an erosion of his firm's competitive position.

As noted, strategy analysis entails an in-depth understanding of the external environment (Chapter 2). Managers monitor and scan the environment as well as analyze competitors. Such information is critical in determining the opportunities and threats in the external environment. Two complementary frameworks are typically employed to provide the structure for analysis of the external environment—one capturing the general environment and the other the industry environment, which encompasses competitors, suppliers, and customers. Strategy analysis of the external environment relies critically on extensive use of tools developed in diverse fields such as macro and microeconomics, political science, marketing, consumer behaviour, operations management, international business, sociology, and psychology. They help managers make sense of the world that surrounds them.

In addition to the external environment, strategy analysis must focus on a firm's internal environment (Chapter 3). What does the firm do? How does it create the products and services it brings to the market? Why does it do things a certain way? Such analysis helps to identify both strengths and weaknesses that can, in part, determine how well a firm will succeed in an industry. Analyzing the strengths and relationships among the activities that constitute a firm's value chain (such as operations, marketing and sales, and human resource management) can be a means of uncovering potential sources of competitive advantage for the firm.

Probably the most important elements within an organization, which contribute vitally to its success, are the knowledge and skills of its workers as well as its intellectual assets such as technology, patents, and trademarks (Chapter 4). In addition to human capital, we address how well the organization creates networks and relationships among its employees, customers, suppliers, and alliance partners.

Strategy Formulation

An organization makes decisions about the strategies it will pursue and the bases for the competitive advantage it will attempt to build. Its overall strategy is developed at several levels. First, business-level strategy addresses the issue of how to compete in given business environments to attain competitive advantage (Chapter 5). The question of how firms compete and outperform their rivals and how they achieve and sustain competitive advantages is the essence of strategic management. Successful firms strive to develop bases for competitive advantage. These can be achieved through cost leadership, differentiation, and by focusing on a narrow or industry-wide market segment. Some advantages can be more sustainable over time, and a firm's business-level strategy changes with the industry life cycle—that is, the stages of introduction, growth, maturity, and decline.

Second, corporate-level strategy focuses on two issues: (1) which businesses to compete in and (2) how businesses can be managed to achieve synergy—the creation of more value by working together rather than operating as stand-alone businesses (Chapter 6). Firms consider the relative advantages and disadvantages of pursuing strategies of related or unrelated diversification and make choices regarding the various means they can employ to diversify—internal development, mergers and acquisitions, and joint ventures and strategic alliances.

Third, a firm must determine the best method for developing international strategies as it ventures beyond its national boundaries (Chapter 7). When firms expand their scope of operations to include foreign markets, they encounter many opportunities and potential pitfalls. They must decide not only on the most appropriate entry strategy but also how they will go about attaining competitive advantages in international markets. Many successful international firms have been able to attain both lower costs and higher levels of differentiated products and services through the successful implementation of a "transnational strategy."

Finally, digital technologies, such as the Internet and wireless communications, are changing the way business is conducted and present both new opportunities and threats for virtually all businesses (Chapter 8). When firms formulate strategies, they should give explicit consideration to how digital technologies add value and impact their performance outcomes. The effective use of the Internet and digital business strategies can help an organization improve its competitive position and its ability to create advantages by enhancing cost leadership, differentiation strategies, or its ability to serve a narrow market segment across geographic boundaries.

Strategy Implementation

Effective strategies are of no value if they are not properly executed. Managers are called to take action and coordinate the activities within their organization to help guide the implementation of the chosen strategies. Moreover, managers align their firm's activities with those of their suppliers, customers, and alliance partners in ways that will achieve desirable outcomes. Strategy implementation encompasses the systems, structures, attitudes, and behaviours that make things happen within organizations.

First, strategy implementation calls on firms to adopt organizational structures and designs that are consistent with their strategies (Chapter 9). Organizational structures define how the various units within an organization relate and interact and how information flows across them. In addition, they establish the appropriate organizational boundaries. These should be sufficiently flexible and permeable to incorporate alliance partners and capitalize on the capabilities of other organizations.

Firms, especially the modern, complex public corporations of today, need to have in place an effective corporate governance structure that aligns the interests of managers with those of the owners of the firm as well as of other stakeholders (Chapter 10). Corporate governance involves not only the board of directors and actively engaged shareholders but also proper managerial reward and incentive systems, along with the strategic control mechanisms that set boundaries on managers' behaviours.

Strategy implementation is, in large part, about leadership (Chapter 11). Today's managers are expected to do much more than manage their troops by telling them what to do. They are called to provide a vision, inspire, and lead ethically and with integrity. Moreover, they recognize that today's successes do not guarantee success in the future. Firms must continuously improve and find new ways to grow and renew. Instilling an entrepreneurial attitude and fostering experimentation throughout the organization help identify new opportunities while specific strategies are being formulated that will enhance the firm's innovative capacity. Chapter 12 looks at both the efforts at organizational renewal within an established corporation and the creation of new ventures. New ventures and small businesses represent a major engine of economic growth. Although the challenges they face are unique, especially for start-up firms entering into business for the first time, many of the concepts that we address in the text are relevant to both corporations and to new ventures and small businesses. Viable opportunities must be recognized, effective strategies must be implemented, and entrepreneurial leadership skills are needed to successfully launch and sustain these enterprises.

THE ROLE OF CORPORATE GOVERNANCE AND STAKEHOLDER MANAGEMENT

Most business enterprises that employ more than a few dozen people are organized as corporations. According to financial theory, the overall purpose of a corporation is to maximize shareholder value, which is reflected in the long-term return to the owners or shareholders. When considering not-for-profit organizations, NGOs, and entities in the public sector, the absence of direct ownership might, on the surface, complicate things. Yet, even there, one may ask, who is really responsible for defining and fulfilling the organization's purpose? Corporate governance is frequently seen as the vehicle to carry out this responsibility. Some have defined corporate governance as "the relationship among various participants in determining the direction and performance of corporations. The primary participants are (1) the shareholders, (2) the management (led by the chief executive officer), and (3) the board of directors."[17]

The board of directors (BOD) consists of the elected representatives of the shareholders. They are charged with overseeing management and ensuring that the interests and motives of management are aligned with those of the owners (i.e., shareholders). In many cases, the BOD is diligent in fulfilling its purpose. For example, Intel Corporation, the giant $36 billion maker of microprocessor chips, is widely recognized as an excellent example of sound governance practices. Its BOD has established guidelines to ensure that its members are independent of the executive management team, and it provides detailed procedures for formal evaluations of both directors and the firm's top officers.[18]

We have, however, also witnessed many scandals concerning poor management and complacent BODs in firms such as WorldCom, Hollinger, Enron, and Tyco.[19] Such malfeasance has led to much criticism and cynicism as well as to the erosion of the public's trust in the governance of corporations. A recent Gallup poll found that 90 percent of Americans felt that people leading corporations could not be trusted to look after the interests of their employees, and only 18 percent thought that corporations looked after their shareholders. Forty-three percent believed that senior executives were in it only for themselves. In Britain, that figure was an astonishing 95 percent.[20]

Notwithstanding these statistics, generating long-term returns for the shareholders is the primary goal of a publicly held corporation. As noted by former Chrysler vice chairman Robert Lutz, "We are here to serve the shareholder and create shareholder value. I insist that the only person who owns the company is the person who paid good money for it."[21]

Despite the primacy of generating shareholder value, managers who focus solely on the interests of the owners of the business will often make poor decisions that lead to negative, unanticipated outcomes. For example, decisions such as mass layoffs to increase profits, ignoring issues related to conservation of the natural environment to save money, and exerting undue pressure on suppliers to lower prices can certainly harm the firm in the long run. Such actions would likely lead to negative outcomes, including alienated employees, increased governmental oversight and fines, and disloyal suppliers.

In addition to *shareholders*, there are other *stakeholders* that must be explicitly taken into account in the strategic management process.[22] A stakeholder can be defined as an individual or group, inside or outside the company, that has an interest in an organization's actions and performance. Stakeholders are affected by what an organization does and can influence, to varying degrees, its performance. Although companies can have different stakeholders, each generally has five prominent stakeholder groups: customers, employees, suppliers (of goods, services, and capital), the community at large, and, of course, the owners.[23]

In essence, stakeholders have a "stake" in how a company competes, how it conducts its affairs, how it uses its own as well as the public's resources, and how it performs. Some stakeholders may be able to exert direct influence on those decisions, while others may only be passive recipients of the consequences. Consider, for example, our public health system and the organizations within it such as hospitals, clinics, ethical and generic pharmaceutical manufacturers, pharmacies, individual doctors and their professional associations, insurance companies, patients and their families, patient advocacy groups, as well as the government and taxpayers who are paying for it all. Each one of those organizations has to consider multiple stakeholders in making critical decisions because each decision has the potential to seriously affect the well-being of a number of individuals and groups. In turn, each stakeholder will attempt to exert whatever degree of influence it can to direct the decisions to serve its own interests.

Alternative Perspectives of Stakeholder Management

The role of stakeholder management in the strategic management process can be considered under different perspectives.[24] In one view, the role of management is to look upon the various stakeholders as competing for the attention and resources of the organization. The gain of one individual or group is the loss of another individual or group. That is, employees want higher wages, which drive down profits; suppliers want higher prices for their inputs and slower, more flexible delivery times, which drive up costs; customers want fast deliveries and higher quality, which drive up costs; the community at large wants charitable contributions, which take money from company goals; and so on. This *zero-sum* thinking is rooted, in part, in the traditional conflict between workers and management, limited resources, and competing priorities of the diverse stakeholders.

Although there will always be some conflicting demands placed on the organization by its various stakeholders, there is value in exploring how the organization can achieve better results through *stakeholder symbiosis*, which recognizes that stakeholders are dependent upon each other for their success and well-being.[25] That is, managers acknowledge the interdependence among employees, suppliers, customers, shareholders, and the community at large and incorporate this understanding in their decisions. Sears, for example, has developed a sophisticated quantitative model that demonstrates symbiosis. With this model, Sears can predict the relationship between employee satisfaction, customer satisfaction, and financial results.[26] The Sears model found that a 5 percent improvement in employee attitudes led to a 1.3 percent improvement in customer satisfaction, which, in turn, will drive a 0.5 percent improvement in revenue.

Social Responsibility: Moving Beyond the Immediate Stakeholders

Increasingly, it is argued that an organization must acknowledge and act upon the interests and demands of stakeholders that lie beyond its immediate constituencies; that is, citizens and society in general, as well as customers, owners, suppliers, and employees. *Corporate Social Responsibility (CSR)* calls on firms to consider the changing relationships between business, society, and government, and to act in a socially responsible manner.[27]

Social responsibility is the expectation that businesses or individuals will strive to improve the overall welfare of society.[28] From the perspective of a business, this means that managers must take active steps to make society better by virtue of the business being in existence. As social norms and values change, a corporation's actions that constitute socially responsible behaviour tend to change as well. In the 1970s, affirmative action was a high priority and firms responded. During the 1990s, the public became increasingly concerned about the quality of the physical environment. Many firms responded by engaging in recycling and reducing waste. Today, in the wake of heightened awareness about climate change, a new kind of priority has arisen—the need to be responsible and protect the environment, reduce emissions, and battle global warming.

The Triple Bottom Line To remain viable in the long run, companies increasingly recognize the imperative of measuring both the deployment and utilization of productive assets, along with the outcomes, more comprehensively than what has been captured by traditional accounting methods. They adopt what is called a triple bottom line, a technique that involves assessing financial as well as environmental and social performance.[29] Shell, NEC, and Procter & Gamble, along with other corporations, have realized that failing to account for the environmental and social costs of doing business poses risks to the company and the community in which it operates.

The first bottom line presents the financial measures with which all leaders are familiar.[30] The second bottom line assesses ecological and material capital. And the third bottom line measures human and social capital. Starting with its 1999 annual report, for example, BP Amoco reports on such performance indicators as annual sales and operating costs (bottom line #1); levels of hydrocarbon emissions, greenhouse emissions, and oil spills compared to the prior year (bottom line #2); and its workforce safety record, employee training, and philanthropic contributions (bottom line #3).

Social responsibility for Suncor Energy of Calgary means accountability to employees and the communities where they work. Suncor reports annually on environmental, social, and economic performance. Given the location of many of its operations, its commitment to be socially responsible means extensive consultations with aboriginal communities and substantial investments in community projects involving the Athabasca Tribal Council and Métis communities. Such activity helps ensure that those communities share the benefits of oil sands development and industry relations agreements with Fort McKay, Athabasca Chipewyan, and Miksew Cree First Nations.[31]

THE STRATEGIC MANAGEMENT PERSPECTIVE: AN IMPERATIVE THROUGHOUT THE ORGANIZATION

Strategic management requires managers to take an integrative view of the organization and assess how all of the functional areas and activities fit together to help the organization achieve its goals and objectives. This cannot be accomplished if only the top managers in the organization take an integrative, strategic perspective of issues facing the firm while everyone else fends for themselves in their independent, isolated functional areas. Marketing and sales will generally favour broad, tailor-made product lines; production will demand standardized products that are relatively easy to make, in order to lower manufacturing costs; research and development will design products to demonstrate technical elegance; and so on. Instead, people throughout the organization need to be striving toward overall goals.

The above argument has always made sense, but the need for such a perspective is accelerating in today's increasingly complex, interconnected, ever-changing global economy. As noted by Peter Senge of MIT, the days when Henry Ford, Alfred Sloan, and Tom Watson (top executives at Ford, General Motors, and IBM, respectively) "learned for the organization" are now over:

> In an increasingly dynamic, interdependent, and unpredictable world, it is simply no longer possible for anyone to "figure it all out at the top." The old model, "the top thinks and the local acts," must now give way to integrating thinking and acting at all levels. While the challenge is great, so is the potential payoff. "The person who figures out how to harness the collective genius of the people in his or her organization," according to former Citibank CEO Walter Wriston, "is going to blow the competition away."[32]

Some Key Driving Forces

Many driving forces are increasing the need for a strategic perspective and greater involvement throughout the organization.[33] Among the most important of these are globalization, technology, and intellectual capital.[34] These forces are inherently interrelated and, collectively, they are accelerating the rate of change and uncertainty with which managers at all levels must deal. The implication of such unpredictable change was probably best captured by former AOL Time Warner chairman Stephen M. Case in a talk to investors and analysts:

> If sometimes feel like I'm behind the wheel of a race car. [O]ne of the biggest challenges is there are no road signs to help navigate. And … no one has yet determined which side of the road we're supposed to be on.[35]

Globalization The defining feature of the global economy is not the flow of goods—international trade has existed for centuries—but the flow of capital, people, and information worldwide. With globalization, time and space are no longer a barrier to making deals anywhere in the world. Digital networks permit instantaneous transactions, and market traders operate around the clock. Markets become more open and free trade agreements bring more foreign firms to domestic markets. Competitive moves in one market can impact firms in other segments of the global economy, creating ripple effects and further challenging competitors to respond.

Along with the increasing speed of transactions and global sourcing of all forms of resources and information, managers must address the paradoxical demand to think globally and act locally. They have to move resources and information rapidly around the world to meet local needs. They also face new challenges: volatile political situations, difficult trade issues, ever-fluctuating exchange rates, unfamiliar cultures, and gut-wrenching social problems.[36] Today, managers must be more literate in the ways of foreign customers, commerce, and competition than ever before. Globalization requires that organizations increase their ability to learn and collaborate and to manage diversity, complexity, and ambiguity. Top-level managers can't do it all alone.

Technology Technological change and diffusion of new technologies are moving at an incredible pace. Such developments accentuate the importance of innovation for firms if they are to remain competitive. David de Pury, former co-chair of the board of Asea

Brown Boveri, claimed that "innovate or die" is the first rule of international competition. Similarly, continuous technological development and change shrink product life cycles. Andrew Grove, chairman of Intel, explained the recent introduction of a sophisticated new product at his company—one in which it had invested considerable funds. However, later in the same year, Intel was forced by competition to introduce a replacement product that would cannibalize its existing product. The firm had only 11 months to recoup that significant investment. Such time-intensive product development involves the efforts and collaboration of managers and professionals throughout the organization. Once again, top-level managers can't do it all alone.

Intellectual Capital Knowledge has become the direct source of competitive advantage(s) for companies selling ideas and relationships (e.g., professional services, software companies, and technology-driven companies) as well as for all companies trying to differentiate themselves from rivals by how they create value for their customers. Merck, the $52 billion pharmaceutical company, has become enormously successful because its scientists discover medicines, not because of their skills in producing pills in an efficient manner; SAP, the German-based business software solutions provider, generates global sales of $16 billion on the basis of less than $6 million in physical inventory.

Creating and applying knowledge to deliver differentiated products and services of superior value for customers requires the acquisition of superior talent as well as the ability to develop and retain that talent.[37] Successful firms create an environment with strong social and professional relationships, and where people feel strong "ties" to their colleagues and their organization.

Technologies are used to leverage human capital and to facilitate collaboration among individuals.[38] The challenge for management is to instill human capital with a strategic perspective and use its talents to effectively help the organization attain its goals and objectives.

Strategy Spotlight 1.1 discusses the global market for talent. It illustrates how forces of globalization, technology, and intellectual capital can be related. Let's now look at what some companies are doing to increase the involvement of employees throughout the organization in the strategic management process.

Enhancing Employee Involvement in the Strategic Management Process

Today's organizations increasingly need to anticipate and respond to dramatic and unpredictable changes in the competitive environment. With the emergence of the knowledge economy, human capital (as opposed to financial and physical assets) has become the key to securing advantages in the marketplace that persist over time.

To develop and mobilize people and other assets in the organization, leaders are needed throughout the organization.[39] No longer can organizations be effective if the top "does the thinking" and the rest of the organization "does the work." Everyone needs to be involved in the strategic management process. Peter Senge noted the critical need for three types of leaders:

- Local line leaders who have significant profit and loss responsibility.
- Executive leaders who champion and guide ideas, create a learning infrastructure, and establish a domain for taking action.
- Internal networkers who, although having little positional power and formal authority, generate their power through the conviction and clarity of their ideas.[40]

Sally Helgesen, author of *The Web of Inclusion: A New Architecture for Building Great Organizations*, made a similar point regarding the need for leaders throughout the organization. She asserted that many organizations "fall prey to the heroes-and-drones

The Global Market for Talent

Globalization today involves the movement of people and information across borders, not just goods and investment. Many technology-strategy consultants operating in North America, and making over $150,000 annually, are blissfully unaware of the challenge posed by the likes of Ganesh Narasimhaiya.

Ganesh is a 30-year-old Indian who enjoys cricket, R&B music, and bowling. He has a bachelor's degree in electronics and communications, and he can spin out code in a variety of languages: COBOL, Java, and UML (Unified Modelling Language), among others. Ganesh has worked on high-profile projects for Wipro, a $903 million Indian software giant, all over the world. He has helped GE Medical Systems roll out a logistics application throughout Southeast Asia. He proposed a plan to consolidate and synchronize security solutions across a British client's ebusiness applications. He developed a strategy for transferring legacy system applications onto the Web for a company in Norway. He works up to 18 or 19 hours a day at a customer site, and for that he may earn as much as $7,000 a month.

When he's home in Bangalore, his pay is about one-quarter of that—$21,000 a year. But by Indian standards, this is a small fortune.

Ganesh is part of Wipro's strategy of amassing a small force of high-level experts who are increasingly focused on specific industries and can compete with anyone for a given consulting project. Wipro's Trojan horse is the incredibly cheap offshore outsourcing solution that it can provide. The rise of a globally integrated knowledge economy is a blessing for developing nations. What it means for the North American and Western European skilled labour forces is less clear. This is something that strategy consultants working for Accenture and EDS in the United States, Canada, or Germany need to think about. Why? Forrester Research has predicted that at least 3.3 million white-collar jobs and $136 billion in wages will shift from the U.S. alone to low-cost countries by 2015. With dramatically lower wage rates and the same level of service, how is the Western technology professional going to compete with Ganesh and his colleagues?

Sources: K. H. Hammonds, "Smart, Determined, Ambitious, Cheap: The New Face of Global Competition," *Fast Company*, February 2003, pp. 91–97; P. Engardio, A. Bernstein, and M. Kripalani, "Is Your Job Next?" *BusinessWeek*, February 3, 2003, pp. 50–60.

syndrome, exalting the value of those in powerful positions while implicitly demeaning the contributions of those who fail to achieve top rank."[41] Cultures and processes in which leaders emerge at all levels, both up and down as well as across the organization, typify today's high-performing firms.[42]

What are some firms doing to increase involvement of employees throughout the organization? Top-level executives are key in setting the tone. Consider Richard Branson, founder of the Virgin Group, whose core businesses include retail operations, hotels, communications, and an airline. He is well known for creating a culture and an informal structure in which anybody in the organization can be involved in generating and acting upon new business ideas. In a recent interview, he stated

> [S]peed is something that we are better at than most companies. We don't have formal board meetings, committees, etc. If someone has an idea, they can pick up the phone and talk to me. I can vote "done, let's do it." Or, better still, they can just go ahead and do it. They know that they are not going to get a mouthful from me if they make a mistake. Rules and regulations are not our forte. Analyzing things to death is not our kind of thing. We very rarely sit back and analyze what we do.[43]

To inculcate a strategic management perspective throughout the organization, many large, traditional organizations often require a major effort in transformational change. This involves extensive communication, training, and development to strengthen a strategic perspective within the organization. Ford Motor Company is one such example.

Ford instituted a major cultural overhaul and embarked on a broad-based attempt to develop leaders throughout the organization. It wanted to build an army of "warrior

Strategy and the Value of Inexperience

Peter Gruber, chairman of Mandalay Entertainment, explained how his firm benefited from the creative insights of an inexperienced intern.

Sometimes life is all about solving problems. In the movie business, at least, there seems to be one around every corner. One of the most effective lessons I've learned about tackling problems is to start by asking not "How to?" but rather "What if?" I learned that lesson from a young woman who was interning on a film I was producing. She actually saved the movie from being shelved by the studio.

The movie, *Gorillas in the Mist*, had turned into a logistical nightmare. We wanted to film at an altitude of 11,000 feet, in the middle of the jungle, in Rwanda—then on the verge of a revolution—and to use more than 200 animals. Warner Brothers, the studio financing the movie, worried that we would exceed our budget. But our biggest problem was that the screenplay required the gorillas to do what we wrote—in other words, to "act." If they couldn't or wouldn't, we'd have to fall back on a formula that the studio had seen fail before: using dwarfs in gorilla suits on a sound stage.

We called an emergency meeting to solve these problems. In the middle of it, a young intern asked, "What if you let the gorillas write the story?" Everyone laughed and wondered what she was doing in the meeting with experienced filmmakers. Hours later, someone casually asked her what she had meant. She said, "What if you sent a really good cinematographer into the jungle with a ton of film to shoot the gorillas. Then you could write a story around what the gorillas did on film." It was a brilliant idea. And we did exactly what she suggested: we sent Alan Root, an Academy Award–nominated cinematographer, into the jungle for three weeks. He came back with phenomenal footage that practically wrote the story for us. We shot the film for $20 million—half of the original budget!

This woman's inexperience enabled her to see opportunities where we saw only boundaries. This experience taught me three things. First, ask high-quality questions, like "what if?" Second, find people who add new perspectives and create new conversations. As experienced filmmakers, we believed that our way was the only way—and that the intern lacked the experience to have an opinion. Third, pay attention to those with new voices. If you want unlimited options for solving a problem, engage the what if before you lock onto the how to. You'll be surprised by what you discover.

Source: P. Gruber, "My Greatest Lesson," *Fast Company* 15 (1998), pp. 88, 90.

entrepreneurs"—people who have the courage and skills to reject old ideas and who believe in change passionately enough to make it happen:

Recently, Ford sent about 2,500 managers to its Leadership Development Center during the year for one of its four programs—Capstone, Experienced Leader Challenge, Ford Business Associates, and New Business Leader—instilling in them not just the mind-set and vocabulary of a revolutionary but also the tools necessary to achieve a revolution. At the same time, through the Business Leaders Initiative, all 100,000 salaried employees worldwide will participate in business-leadership "cascades," intense exercises that combine trickle-down communications with substantive team projects.[44]

Finally, Strategy Spotlight 1.2 demonstrates how sometimes, even inexperience can be a virtue. "Thinking outside the box" and questioning the prevailing wisdom can lead to novel ideas and successful outcomes. It further reinforces the benefits of having broad involvement throughout the organization in the strategic management process.

ENSURING COHERENCE IN STRATEGIC DIRECTION

To be successful, employees and managers throughout the organization must be striving for common goals and objectives. By specifying desired results, it becomes much easier to move forward. Otherwise, without a clear vision of what the firm is striving to accomplish, no one really knows what to work toward. As the old nautical expression puts it, "No wind favours the ship that has no charted course."

Exhibit 1.4
An Organization's
Hierarchy of Goals

Organizations express priorities best through stated goals and objectives that form a *hierarchy of goals*. The hierarchy of goals for an organization includes its vision, mission, and strategic objectives. Exhibit 1.4 depicts the hierarchy of goals and highlights how they serve to connect all parts of the organization both horizontally and vertically. What visions may lack in specificity, they make up for in their ability to evoke powerful and compelling mental images. On the other hand, strategic objectives tend to be more specific and provide a more direct means of determining if the organization is moving toward broader, overall goals.[45]

Organizational Vision

The starting point for articulating a firm's hierarchy of goals is the company vision. It is often described as a goal that is "massively inspiring, overarching, and long-term."[46] A vision represents a destination that is driven by, and evokes, passion. A vision may or may not succeed; it depends on whether everything else happens according to the firm's strategy.

Developing and implementing a vision is one of a leader's central roles. In a survey of 1,500 senior leaders, 870 of whom were CEOs (from 20 different countries), respondents were asked what they believed were the key traits that leaders must have. Ninety-eight percent responded that "a strong sense of vision" was the most important. Similarly, when asked about critical knowledge skills, the leaders cited "strategy formulation to achieve a vision" as the most important skill. Ninety percent also reported a lack of confidence in their own skills and ability to conceive a vision for their organization. For example, T. J. Rogers, CEO of Cypress Semiconductor, an electronic chipmaker that faced some difficulties in 1992, lamented that his own short-sightedness caused the danger: "I did not have the 50,000-foot view, and got caught."[47]

One of the most famous examples of a vision is from Disneyland: "To be the happiest place on earth." Other examples are,

- "Restoring patients to full life." (Medtronic)
- "More! Providing Canadians with a one-stop destination in meeting their food and everyday household needs." (Loblaw)
- "Clear; Simple; First; True; Profitable; Proud" (Bell Canada Enterprises, BCE)
- "The elimination of all workplace fatalities, injuries and illnesses" (Workplace Safety and Insurance Board, WSIB [Ontario])
- "Our vision is to be the world's best quick service restaurant." (McDonald's)

Although it is difficult to accurately measure how well such visions are being achieved, they do provide a fundamental statement of an organization's sense of its own *purpose* and reflect the collective *values* of its stakeholders, their aspirations, and their goals. A good vision statement tells everybody, both inside and outside the organization, what it stands for, what inspires its management and employees, and what gets them going and motivates them to strive to excel. Such visions go well beyond narrow financial objectives and strive to capture both the minds and hearts of employees. An other way to consider a vision is to ask the question, If we were immensely successful in what we do, how would that success look, say, 10 years from now? If someone was talking about our organization in glowing terms, what would we like them to be saying about us?

A vision statement may contain a slogan, diagram, or picture—whatever grabs attention.[48] The aim is to capture the essence of the more formal parts of the vision in a few words that are easily remembered, yet evoke the spirit of the entire vision statement. In its 20-year battle to dominate the photocopy equipment business, Canon's slogan was "Beat Xerox." Motorola's slogan is "Total Customer Satisfaction." Outboard Marine Corporation's slogan is "To Take the World Boating." And Chevron strives "To Become Better than the Best."

Vision statements are not a cure-all. Sometimes they backfire and erode a company's credibility. Visions fail for many reasons, including those discussed in the following paragraphs.[49]

The Walk Doesn't Match the Talk An idealistic vision can arouse employee enthusiasm. However, that same enthusiasm can be quickly dashed if employees find that senior management's behaviour is not consistent with the vision. Often, vision is a sloganeering campaign of new buzzwords and empty platitudes like "devotion to the customer," "teamwork," or "total quality" that aren't consistently backed by management's action.

Irrelevance A vision that is created in a vacuum—unrelated to environmental threats or opportunities or to an organization's resources and capabilities—can ignore the needs of those who are expected to buy into it. When the vision is not anchored in reality, employees will reject it.

Not the Holy Grail Managers often search continually for the one elusive solution that will solve their firm's problems—that is, the next holy grail of management. They may have tried other management fads only to find that these fell short of their expectations. However, they remain convinced that one exists. Visions support sound management, but they require everyone to walk the talk and be accountable for their behaviour. A vision cannot simply be viewed as a magic cure for an organization's illness.

An Ideal Future Irreconciled with the Present Although visions are not designed to mirror reality, they do need to be anchored somehow in it. People have difficulty identifying with a vision that paints a rosy picture of the future but either takes no account of the often hostile environment in which the firm competes or ignores some of the firm's weaknesses. As we will see in the next section, many of these same issues can apply to mission statements.

Mission Statements

A company's mission differs from vision in that it encompasses both the purpose of the company as well as the basis of competition and competitive advantage.

Exhibit 1.5 contains the vision and mission statements of the Workplace Safety and Insurance Board (WSIB), a $3.5 billion entity mandated to administer Ontario's no-fault workplace insurance plan for workers and employers in the province. It insures over $150 billion in annual payroll. Note that while the vision statement is broad, the mission

Exhibit 1.5
Comparing WSIB's
Vision and Mission

Vision
The elimination of all workplace fatalities, injuries and illnesses
Mission

"to lead, prevent, and preserve"

- Lead and partner with others in the creation of healthy and safe workplaces.
- Prevent and respond to fatalities, injuries, and illnesses and measurably lessen their impacts on workers, their families, and workplaces of Ontario when they do occur.
- Preserve a strong and sustainable workplace safety and insurance system that will continue to serve the people of Ontario.

Sources: WSIB Annual Report and publications.

statement is more specific and focused on the means by which the organization will achieve its vision. This includes providing specific avenues that will direct the organization's efforts and identifying key partners, markets, and services that will make it happen.

Effective mission statements incorporate the concept of stakeholder management, suggesting that organizations must respond to multiple constituencies if they are to survive and prosper. Customers, employees, suppliers, and owners are the primary stakeholders, but others may also play an important role in a particular corporation. Mission statements also have the greatest impact when they reflect an organization's enduring, overarching strategic priorities and competitive positioning. Mission statements can also vary in length and specificity. The two mission statements below illustrate these issues:

- "To produce superior financial returns for our shareholders as we serve our customers with the highest quality transportation, logistics, and ecommerce." (Federal Express)
- "To be the very best in the business. Our game plan is status go … we are constantly looking ahead, building on our strengths, and reaching for new goals. In our quest of these goals, we look at the three stars of the Brinker logo and are reminded of the basic values that are the strength of this company … People, Quality and Profitability. Everything we do at Brinker must support these core values. We also look at the eight golden flames depicted in our logo, and are reminded of the fire that ignites our mission and makes up the heart and soul of this incredible company. These flames are: Customers, Food, Team, Concepts, Culture, Partners, Community and Shareholders. As keeper of these flames, we will continue to build on our strengths and work together to be the best in the business." (Brinker International, whose restaurant chains Chili's and On the Border operate across 25 countries ranging from the U.S. and Canada, to Australia, Japan, and Saudi Arabia)[50]

Few mission statements identify profit or any other financial indicator as the sole purpose of the firm. Indeed, most do not even mention profit or shareholder return.[51] Employees of organizations or departments are usually the mission's most important audience. For them, the mission should help to build a common understanding and promote a nurturing of purpose and commitment.

Profit maximization not only fails to motivate people but also does not differentiate between organizations. Every corporation wants to maximize profits over the long term. A good mission statement, thus, must communicate why an organization is special and different. Studies that linked corporate values and mission statements with financial performance found that the most successful firms mentioned values other than profits. The less successful firms focused almost entirely on profitability.[52] In essence, profit is the metaphorical equivalent of oxygen, food, and water, which the body requires. They are not the point of life, but without them there is no life.

Vision statements tend to be quite broad and enduring and often represent an inspiring, overarching, and emotionally driven destination. A firm's mission, on the other hand, tends to be more specific and to address questions concerning the organization's reason for being and the basis of its intended competitive advantage in the marketplace. It should change when competitive conditions change or the firm is faced with new threats or opportunities.

Strategic Objectives

Strategic objectives are used to operationalize the mission statement. That is, they help to provide guidance on how the organization can fulfill or move toward the "higher goals" in the goal hierarchy—the mission and vision. As a result, they tend to be more specific and cover a more well-defined time frame. Objectives are specific and concrete yardsticks that measure the progress toward the organization's mission and vision.[53] If an objective lacks specificity or measurability, it is not very useful, simply because there is no way of determining whether it is helping the organization to move forward.

Exhibit 1.6 lists several strategic objectives of corporations, divided into financial and non-financial categories. While many strategic objectives aim toward generating greater profits and returns for the owners of the business, others are directed at customers or society at large.

| Exhibit 1.6 |
| Strategic Objectives |

Strategic Objectives (Financial)

- Increase sales growth 6% to 8% and accelerate core net earnings growth to 13% to 15% per share in each of the next five years. (Procter & Gamble)
- Generate Internet-related revenue of $1.5 billion. (Automation)
- Increase the contribution of Banking Group earnings from investments, brokerage, and insurance from 16% to 25%. (Wells Fargo)
- Cut corporate overhead costs by $30 million per year. (Fortune Brands)

Strategic Objectives (Non-financial)

- Ensure that a majority of our customers, when surveyed, say they consider Wells Fargo the best financial institution in the community. (Wells Fargo)
- Operate 6,000 stores by 2010—up from 3,000 in the year 2000. (Walgreens)
- Develop a smart card strategy that will help us play a key role in shaping online payments. (American Express)
- Reduce greenhouse gases by 10% (from a 1990 base) by 2010. (BP Amoco)

Sources: Company documents and annual reports.

For an objective to be meaningful, it needs to satisfy several SMART criteria. It must be

- *Specific.* Provide a clear message as to what needs to be accomplished (e.g., market share, new product introductions, customer satisfaction scores).

◆ *Measurable.* Contain indicators that explicitly measure progress toward fulfilling the objective (e.g., 15 percent market share; 3 new product launches; 10 percent increase in customer retention).

◆ *Appropriate.* Connect and be consistent with the vision and mission of the organization.

◆ *Realistic.* Identify an achievable target given the organization's capabilities and opportunities in the environment. It must be challenging but doable.

◆ *Timely.* There needs to be a time frame for accomplishing the objective. Unless there is a timeline for achieving the objective, there is little value in setting goals (e.g., 3 new product launches every 6 months, market leadership in 5 years, employee training goals in 12 months).

When objectives satisfy the above criteria, there are many benefits for the organization. First, they help direct employees throughout the organization toward common goals. This helps to concentrate and conserve valuable resources in the organization and to work collectively in a more timely manner.

Second, challenging objectives can help to motivate and inspire employees throughout the organization to higher levels of commitment and effort. A great deal of research has supported the notion that individuals work harder when they are striving toward specific goals instead of being asked simply to do their best.

Third, as we noted earlier in the chapter, there is always the potential for different parts of an organization to pursue their own goals rather than overall company goals. Although well intentioned, these goals may work at cross-purposes to the organization as a whole. Meaningful objectives, thus, help to resolve conflicts when they arise.

Finally, proper objectives provide a yardstick for rewards and incentives. Not only will they lead to higher levels of motivation by employees, but they will also help to ensure a greater sense of equity or fairness when rewards are allocated.

There are, of course, still other objectives that are even more specific. These are often referred to as short-term objectives—essential components of "action plans" that are critical in implementing a firm's chosen strategy. We will discuss these issues in Chapter 10. Chapter 3 presents a comprehensive approach to measuring progress toward results that is called the "balanced scorecard" and uses accounting and other metrics to monitor business activities from multiple perspectives and to align managerial decisions and actions with the organization's vision.

Summary

We began this introductory chapter by defining strategic management and articulating some of its key attributes. Strategic management is defined as "consisting of the analysis, decisions, and actions an organization undertakes to create and sustain competitive advantages." The issue of how and why some firms outperform others in the marketplace is central to the study of strategic management. Strategic management has four key attributes: it is directed at overall organizational goals, includes multiple stakeholders, incorporates both short-term and long-term perspectives, and incorporates trade-offs between efficiency and effectiveness.

The second section discussed the strategic management process. Here, we adhered to the above definition of strategic management and focused on three core activities in the strategic management process—strategy analysis, strategy formulation, and strategy implementation. We noted how each of these activities is highly interrelated to and interdependent on the others. We also discussed how each of the twelve chapters fits into the three core activities and provided a summary of the opening vignettes in each chapter.

Next, we introduced two important concepts, corporate governance and stakeholder management, that must be taken into account throughout the strategic management process. Governance mechanisms can be broadly divided into two groups: internal and external. Internal governance mechanisms include shareholders (owners), management (led by the chief executive officer), and the board of directors. External control is exercised by auditors, banks, analysts, and an active business press, as well as the threat of takeovers. We identified five key stakeholders in all organizations: owners, customers, suppliers, employees, and society at large. Successful firms go beyond an overriding focus on solely satisfying the interests of owners. Rather, they recognize the inherent conflicts that arise among the demands of the various stakeholders as well as the need to endeavour to attain "symbiosis"—that is, interdependence and mutual benefit among the various stakeholder groups. Managers must also recognize the need to act in a socially responsible manner, as well as to incorporate issues related to environmental sustainability in their strategic actions.

In the fourth section, we discussed three interrelated factors—globalization, technology, and intellectual capital—that have accelerated the rate of unpredictable change that managers face today. These factors, and the combination of them, have increased the need for managers and employees throughout the organization to have a strategic management perspective and to become more empowered.

The final section addressed the need for consistency between a firm's vision, mission, and strategic objectives. Collectively, they form an organization's hierarchy of goals. Visions should evoke powerful and compelling mental images. However, they are not very specific. Strategic objectives, on the other hand, are much more specific and are vital to ensuring that the organization is striving toward fulfilling its vision and mission.

Summary Review Questions

1. How is "strategic management" defined in the text, and what are its four key attributes?

2. Briefly discuss the three key activities in the strategic management process. Why is it important for managers to recognize the interdependent nature of these activities?

3. Explain the concept of "stakeholder management." Why shouldn't managers be solely interested in shareholder management—that is, maximizing the returns for owners of the firm (its shareholders)?

4. What is corporate governance? What are its three key elements, and how can it be improved?

5. How can "symbiosis" (interdependence, mutual benefit) be achieved among a firm's stakeholders?

6. What are some of the major trends that now require firms to have a greater strategic management perspective and empowerment in the strategic management process throughout the firm?

7. What is meant by a "hierarchy of goals"? What are the main components of it, and why must consistency be achieved among them?

Experiential Exercise

Using the Internet or library sources, select four organizations—two in the private sector and two in the public sector. Find their mission statements. Complete the following exhibit by identifying the stakeholders that are mentioned. Evaluate the differences between firms in the private sector and those in the public sector.

	Private Sector #1	Private Sector #2	Public Sector #1	Public Sector #2
Name				
Mission Statement				
Stakeholders (✓ = mentioned)				
1. Customers				
2. Suppliers				
3. Managers/employees				
4. Community at large				
5. Owners				
6. Others?				
7. Others?				

Application Questions Exercises

1. Go on the Internet and look up the history of a company such as BCE, Bombardier, Loblaw, Nortel, Wal-Mart, GE, or Ford. What are some of the key events that would represent the "romantic" perspective of leadership? What are some of the key events that depict the "external control" perspective of leadership?

2. Select a company that competes in an industry in which you are interested. What are some of the recent demands that stakeholders have placed on this company? Can you find examples of how the company is trying to develop "symbiosis" (interdependence and mutual benefit) among its stakeholders? (Use the Internet and library resources.)

3. Provide examples of companies that are actively trying to increase the amount of employee empowerment in the strategic management process throughout the organization. Do these companies seem to be having positive outcomes? Why? Why not?

4. Look up the vision statements and/or mission statements for a few companies. Do you feel that they are constructive and useful as a means of motivating employees and providing a strong strategic direction? Why? Why not? (Note: annual reports, along with the Internet, may be good sources of information.)

Ethics Questions

1. A company focuses solely on short-term profits to provide the greatest return to the owners of the business (i.e., the shareholders in a publicly held firm). What ethical issues could this raise?

2. A firm has spent some time—with input from managers at all levels—in developing a vision statement and a mission statement. Over time, however, the behaviour of some executives is inconsistent with these statements. What kinds of ethical issues might such behaviours raise?

Chapter 2   *Analyzing the External Environment of the Firm*

LEARNING OBJECTIVES

After reading this chapter, you should have a good understanding of:

LO 1 the elements that constitute a firm's general environment and their impact on the firm's strategies and performance.

LO 2 how to define the competitive environment and delineate industry boundaries.

LO 3 why environmental scanning, environmental monitoring, and collecting competitive intelligence are critical inputs to developing forecasts of the business environment.

LO 4 why scenario planning is a useful technique for firms competing in industries characterized by unpredictability and change.

LO 5 how trends and events in the general environment and forces in the competitive environment are interrelated and affect performance.

LO 6 how forces in the competitive environment can affect profitability and how a firm can improve its competitive position by increasing its power vis-à-vis those forces.

LO 7 the concept of strategic groups and their strategy and performance implications.

Let's begin by considering the case of Canada's lumber industry—an industry that failed to keep pace with changes in its external environment.

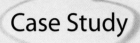

The Canadian forestry industry was once the envy of the world, not surprising since Canada boasts over 400 million hectares of forest and lies next to the world's largest market for timber, processed lumber, and paper products—the U.S. Of course, lumber disputes between the two trading partners have been a staple of that relationship going back centuries. Nevertheless, Canadian firms have enjoyed a natural advantage and have benefited enormously from the relationship. In the process, the industry has provided good-paying jobs to Canadians in rural communities across the country and contributed a sizeable part of the GDP.[1]

Recently, however, over 10 percent of the industry's plant capacity has been permanently shelved, operating facilities have reported historic lows in utilization, about 20 percent of workers have been laid off, and firms, one after the other, have been posting substantial losses. Both the government and the industry's big players blame the slumping housing market in the U.S. for these results, yet industry counterparts in Latin America, Asia, and Europe are thriving. According to an industry report, while Canadian companies achieved a –0.1 percent return on capital employed during 2007, the same ratio was a healthy 7.8 percent in Latin America, 7.3 percent in Asia, 7 percent in Europe, and 5.8 percent in South Africa. Even American firms achieved 5.5 percent returns in the same period.

Without a doubt, whether the Canadian lumber industry will recover depends heavily on the U.S. economy, but equally unquestionably the industry has missed the transformation taking place across the globe. In Brazil, new mills are built with the newest and best technology, while knowledge and innovation are central to the international success of Swedish and Finish players who not only produce specialty wood and fine paper products but sell their technology and equipment worldwide. These regions have invested in developing the new markets and have moved up the value chain, producing high-value-added products that are less susceptible to transportation costs and commodity prices.

What Went Wrong with the Canadian Forestry Industry? *The industry, as well as the government*, missed some key trends. Rather than embracing the shift to new markets, the deployment of new production technologies, and the creation of new products, firms in the industry stuck with traditional methods of harvesting and operating because these had been key to past success. They ignored both the increasing demand for lumber and paper products coming from newer economies such as China, as well as the rules of the global game. The government and the industry as a whole were preoccupied with the North American softwood lumber dispute. Without a doubt this has been a very serious and expensive issue for the Canadian industry, but it has been diverting their attention from developments taking place in the sector. It has delayed necessary investments in new plant and equipment, and to a large degree has fuelled the regional and short-term perspectives espoused within the sector. It has resulted in critical delays in a number of areas: closings of unproductive facilities, rationalization of production in larger and more efficient plants, corporate mergers, and investment in technology and product development. The companies, on the whole, made numerous strategic errors as they continued to develop their products based on traditional principles, those of the customers and technologies in the North American market, without tracking the changing consumer tastes and preferences around the world.

Because they were not willing to respond to changing trends, their actions lacked speed and decisiveness. As a result, they are now lagging in an industry that they once dominated. Entire communities in British Columbia that had historically prospered from the forest industry, today lie devastated, with extremely high levels of unemployment and few alternatives as, one after the other, sawmills close down indefinitely and people lose their job.

To be successful, managers must recognize opportunities and threats in their firm's external environment. They must be aware of what's going on outside their company. If they focus exclusively on the efficiency of internal operations, their firm may degenerate into the world's most efficient producer of buggy whips or carbon paper. A firm's strategy can easily stray away and get out of touch with the evolving realities of the marketplace. Management's assumptions, premises, and beliefs can start diverging from, or become inconsistent with, the actual structure of the relevant industry, the competition, and the customers.

To understand the business environment of a particular firm, managers need to continuously analyze and stay abreast of both the *general environment* and the firm's *industry* and *competitive environment*. The *general environment* consists of a myriad of elements that an organization finds outside its own boundaries and which have some bearing on its ability to exist and thrive. Many factors shape the organization's general environment, and the interrelationships among those factors are typically beyond the control of the managers of any given organization. Factors such as government legislation, general economic trends, globalization, advances in technology, national cultural differences, the general level of education, and an aging population could potentially and critically affect the fortunes of a particular organization; yet, its managers are largely powerless in any significant attempt to influence them.

Within this broad general environment, firms typically compete with other firms in the same industry. An *industry*, or a company's *competitive environment*, is composed of a set of firms that produce similar products or services, sell to similar customers, and use similar methods of production. An industry is commonly viewed from the suppliers' perspective and is defined as a collection of similar producers and firms that employ fairly similar production processes. The beer industry, for example, consists of all the firms that own and operate brewing facilities, whether large or small, with a national or local presence. Under this perspective, Molson, Labatt, Sleeman, Lakeport, Moosehead, and a host of microbrewers such as Yukon, Big Rock, Great Western, Brascal, Brasserie McAuslan, Nelson, Creemore Springs, Fireweed, Fort Garry, Storm Brewing in Newfoundland, and Wellington constitute the beer industry in Canada. A manager defining the industry for a strategy analysis will look to the list of firms, their relative strategies, their product offerings, as well as the various markets and consumers served by those firms. Possible substitute products, such as wines and spirits, will also be considered.

However, such a definition of an industry might not be complete. What about Anheuser-Busch, one of the largest brewers in the world, which sells beer in Canada under licence but does not own any brewing capacity; is it a competitor? What about some strong imports such as Corona and Heineken? They ship their products into Canada from far-off locations. What about global brewers such as InBev and Sapporo that own two of the largest Canadian brewers, Labatt and Sleeman, respectively? What about the forays of some of the Canadian firms overseas, most notably Molson's merger with Coors or its acquisition of Kaiser in Brazil? While questions about market share, market coverage, or competitive behaviour will clearly have to incorporate those additional players, they may have little relevance in discussions about suppliers, production capacity or capacity utilization, or domestic distribution and regulations.

An industry can also be viewed from the market's perspective. Consumers seek to satisfy their needs through the use of products and services. An industry consists of all those producers whose products can satisfy similar consumer needs. Thus, an opera company, the symphony, various theatres, and a professional sports franchise all compete for the entertainment dollars of a city's residents and could rightly belong in the same industry, even though their operations are drastically different. Similarly, fancy chocolates, good wines, and flowers are competing options for consumers looking to express gratitude for a dinner invitation.

Alternative definitions of an industry may arise from identical products offered by very different firms. Consider, for example, a firm that sources from China and supplies accessories for power tools, drill bits, and blades to retailers such as Canadian Tire, Home Depot, and Rona. What is a meaningful definition of its industry? Does it consist of other producers of power tool accessories, such as Stanley or Black & Decker, which produce similar accessories in North America? Or does it consist of other wholesalers, who source small parts and tools from China, Korea, or Vietnam? Should both types be included in the definition of the industry? How can one make comparisons? Understandably, the issues faced by each are drastically different, though they depend on the same markets for their business. Consumers, furthermore, may not really know or care whether the accessories come from one place or the other.

Time is another factor in defining the boundaries of an industry. When the time dimension of a specific issue under consideration is relatively short, direct competitors belong in the same industry, and firms that produce different products for different markets can safely be left out. But when the strategy analysis encompasses a longer timeline, the assumption of strategic distance is no longer safe. Distant firms can find themselves in direct competition in the long run. For example, foreign competitors can enter the market within a long enough time, and the adoption of new technology can allow firms to leapfrog competition.

Technological developments also raise substantial issues about the boundaries of industries. Telecommunications used to be governed by the same federal agency, CRTC, even though telephone providers were separated from television broadcasters and cable companies. The three industries unfolded very differently and faced unique competitive pressures. Today, convergence is the buzzword in the whole sector, and everybody accepts the direct competition among BCE, Rogers, Telus, and Shaw. Moreover, Apple with its iPhone, RIM with the BlackBerry, and Microsoft have entered the fray.

Gathering industry information and understanding competitive dynamics among the different companies in the industry are keys to successful strategic management. The challenge for managers is to define the industry broadly enough to incorporate the relevant issues but not so broadly that their focus is rendered meaningless. In their award-winning book *Competing for the Future*, Gary Hamel and C. K. Prahalad suggest that "every manager carries around in his or her head a set of biases, assumptions, and presuppositions about the structure of the relevant 'industry,' about how one makes money in the industry, about who the competition is and isn't, about who the customers are and aren't, and so on."[2] Environmental analysis requires managers to continually question these assumptions. Peter Drucker labelled these interrelated sets of assumptions the "theory of the business."[3]

A firm's strategy may be good at one point in time, but it may go astray when management's frame of reference gets out of touch with the realities of the actual business situation. This happens when management's assumptions, premises, or beliefs are incorrect or when internal inconsistencies among them render the overall "theory of the business" invalid. As Warren Buffett, investor extraordinaire, colourfully notes, "Beware of past performance 'proofs.' If history books were the key to riches, the Forbes 400, the list of the world's wealthiest people, would consist of librarians." And Arthur Martinez, chairman of Sears, Roebuck & Co. states, "Today's peacock is tomorrow's feather duster."

In the business world, many peacocks have become feather dusters, or at least had their plumage dulled. Consider the high-tech company Novell, which has undergone hard times.[4] Novell went head-to-head with Microsoft and bought market-share loser *WordPerfect* to compete with *Microsoft Word*®. The result—a $1.3 billion loss when Novell sold *WordPerfect* to Corel. And today we may wonder who will be the next Eaton's, Jetsgo, Consumers' Distributing or Encyclopaedia Britannica Inc.

CREATING THE ENVIRONMENTALLY AWARE ORGANIZATION

So how do managers become environmentally aware?[5] They use three important processes—scanning, monitoring, and gathering competitive intelligence—to understand the environment and develop forecasts. Exhibit 2.1 illustrates the relationship between these important activities. In addition to forecasts, managers recognize the importance of scenario planning in anticipating major future changes in the external environment.[6]

Scanning, Monitoring, Competitive Intelligence, Forecasting, and Scenario Analysis

Environmental Scanning Environmental scanning involves surveillance of a firm's external environment to predict future environmental changes and detect changes already under way.[7] Successful environmental scanning alerts the organization to critical trends and events before the changes have developed a discernible pattern and before competitors recognize them.[8,9]

Sir John Browne, chief executive officer of petroleum company BP Amoco, described in a speech the kind of environmental changes his company was experiencing:

> The next element of the change we've experienced is the growth in demand, and the changing nature of that demand. The world uses eight million more barrels of oil and 30 billion more cubic feet of natural gas every day than it did in the spring of 1990. The growth of natural gas in particular has been and continues to be spectacular, and I believe that change can legitimately be seen as part of a wider, longer-term shift to lighter, cleaner, less carbon-intensive fuels.[10]

Consider how difficult it would be for BP Amoco to develop strategies and allocate resources if it did not scan the external environment for such emerging changes in demand.

Companies may frequently benefit from studies conducted by outside experts in a particular industry. In a recent study, A. T. Kearney, a large international consulting company, identified several "key issues" in the automobile industry:[11]

◆ *Globalization.* This is not a new trend but it has intensified, with enormous opportunities opening up in Asia, central and eastern Europe, and Latin America.
◆ *Time to Market.* A gap still exists between product development cycles in the United States and Europe compared to Japan. This gap persists even though Japanese companies continue to move operations to other countries.
◆ *Shifting Roles and Responsibilities.* Design responsibility, purchasing, even project management and systems engineering, are shifting from the original equipment manufacturers to integrators and other suppliers.

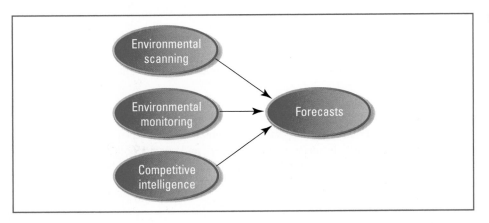

Exhibit 2.1
Inputs to Forecasting

All firms in the industry are affected by such developments, and executives are called to consider them in their strategic responses.

Environmental Monitoring Environmental monitoring tracks the evolution of environmental trends, sequences of events, or streams of activities. These are often uncovered during the environmental scanning process. They may be trends that the firm came across by accident or were brought to its attention from outside the organization. Consider the automobile industry example above. While environmental scanning may make the automobile industry executive aware of these trends, this is not sufficient. Ability to respond to those trends requires close monitoring, which involves closer ongoing scrutiny. For example, managers should closely monitor sales in Asia, central and eastern Europe, and Latin America. They should observe how fast Japanese companies and other competitors bring products to market compared with their own firm. What about escalating oil prices and their implications for consumer attitudes, let alone their wallets? They should also study trends with their own suppliers/integrators in purchasing, project management, and systems engineering. Monitoring enables firms to evaluate how dramatically environmental trends are changing the competitive landscape.

Note the following examples of indicators monitored by executives from several industries. These same indicators would be used as inputs in determining the firm's strategic direction and investment decisions.

- *An Appliance manufacturing executive.* New building construction permits as well as the average square footage of new housing units.
- *A Pier 1 Imports executive.* Net disposable income (NDI), consumer confidence index, and housing starts.
- *A Johnson & Johnson medical products executive.* Percentage of gross domestic product (GDP) spent on health care, number of active hospital beds, and the size and power of purchasing agents (indicates the concentration of buyers).

Competitive Intelligence Competitive intelligence (CI) helps firms better define and understand their industry and also identify rivals' strengths and weaknesses.[12] This includes the intelligence gathering associated with the collection of data on competitors and the interpretation of such data for managerial decision making. Competitive intelligence helps a company avoid surprises by anticipating competitors' moves and decreasing response time.[13]

Examples of competitive analysis are evident in daily newspapers and periodicals such as *The Wall Street Journal, BusinessWeek*, and *Fortune*. For example, banks continually track home loan, auto loan, and certificate of deposit (CD) interest rates charged by competitors in a given geographic region. Major airlines change hundreds of fares daily in response to competitors' tactics. Car manufacturers are keenly aware of announced cuts or increases in rivals' production volumes, sales, and sales incentives (e.g., rebates and low interest rates on financing). They use this information to plan their own marketing, pricing, and production strategies. Exhibit 2.2 provides some insights on what CI is (and what it isn't).

The Internet has dramatically accelerated the speed at which firms can find competitive intelligence. Leonard Fuld, founder of the Cambridge, Massachusetts, training and consulting firm Fuld & Co., specializes in competitive intelligence.[14] His firm often profiles top company and business group managers and considers these issues: What is their background? Style? Are they marketers? Are they cost cutters? Fuld has found that

Exhibit 2.2
What Competitive
Intelligence Is and Is
Not!

Competitive Intelligence Is …	Competitive Intelligence Is Not …
1. **information** that has been analyzed to the point where it is possible to make an appropriate decision.	1. **spying.** Spying implies illegal or unethical activities. It rarely occurs since most corporations do not want to find themselves in court or upsetting shareholders.
2. **a tool** to alert management early to both threats and opportunities.	2. **a crystal ball.** CI gives corporations good approximations of reality, short and long term. It does not predict the future.
3. **a means to deliver reasonable assessments.** CI offers approximations of the market and competition. It is not a peek at a rival's financial books. Reasonable assessments are what modern entrepreneurs need and want on a regular basis.	3. **database search.** Databases offer just that—data. They do not analyze the data in any way. They certainly don't replace human beings, who make decisions by examining the data and applying their common sense, experience, and intuition.
4. **a way of life, a process.** If a company uses CI the way it should be used, it becomes everyone's job—not just the strategic planning or marketing staff's. It is a process by which critical information is available to those who need it.	4. **a job for one smart person.** A CEO may appoint one person as the CI ringmaster, but one person cannot do it all. At best, the ringmaster can keep management informed and ensure that others become trained to apply this tool within their business units.

Sources: G. Imperato, "Competitive Intelligence—Get Smart!" *Fast Company*, April 1998, p. 269; and F. M. Fuld, "What Competitive Intelligence Is and Is Not!" www.fuld.com/whatCI.html.

the more articles he collects and the more biographies he downloads, the better he can develop profiles.

One of Fuld & Co.'s clients needed to know if a rival was going to start competing more aggressively on costs. Fuld's analysts tracked down articles from the Internet and a local newspaper profile of the rival firm's CEO. The profile said the CEO had taken a bus to a nearby town to visit one of the firm's plants. Fuld claimed, "Those few words were a small but important sign to me that this company was going to be incredibly cost-conscious." Another client retained Fuld to determine the size, strength, and technical capabilities of a privately held company. Initially, it was difficult to get detailed information. Then one analyst used Deja News (www.dejanews.com), a unit of Google, to tap into some online discussion groups. The analyst's research determined that the company had posted 14 job openings on one Usenet group. Those postings were a road map to the competitor's development strategy.

At times, a firm's aggressive efforts to gather competitive intelligence may lead to unethical or illegal behaviours.[15] Strategy Spotlight 2.1 tells the story of two well-known rivals who probably crossed the line in their efforts to gather competitive intelligence. Strategy Spotlight 2.2 provides an example of a company, United Technologies (UT), that has set clear guidelines to help prevent unethical behaviour.

Spies in the Skies

"There is nothing new in companies spying on each other," according to Norman Inkster, RCMP chief from 1987 to 1994, who now runs a private investigation firm. "In the old days, it usually meant breaking into rivals' offices; today, it's about hacking into websites and electronic files," tactics that Inkster says can be difficult to detect and hugely damaging.

Recently, the Air Canada–WestJet battle moved from the skies to the courtrooms. A massive civil lawsuit over corporate espionage provided a rare glimpse of the dirty tricks rivals may resort to in the name of competition. The critical battle was also playing out in the court of public opinion: Air Canada, long thought to be a corporate bully, appeared to be the victim, while WestJet, for years the darling of investors and the flying public, was cast as the bad guy.

In its statement of claim, which accused WestJet of "high-handed and malicious" conduct, Air Canada said the company surreptitiously tapped into its employee Web site and set up a "screen scraper," a program designed to automatically lift data off one site and dump it into another. A standard airline perk allows staff to travel almost for free on flights with open seats. Employees receive a personal code so they can check which flights are available. Air Canada found that someone (or something) had used a single access code to enter the system an astounding 243,630 times between May 2003 and March 2004, for an average of 786 hits a day. In one extraordinary day, the site was tapped 4,973 times. The code allegedly belonged to Jeffrey Lafond, a former Canadian Airlines International employee, who had accepted a buyout package soon after Canadian was taken over by Air Canada—a package that included two staff tickets per year for five years. Lafond admitted providing his employee and personal ID numbers to WestJet co-founder Mark Hill but said he didn't think the load-factor information was relevant. Air Canada alleged that WestJet boosted its own profits using the illegally obtained information and claimed a whopping $220 million in damages.

In reply, WestJet dismissed the suit as an attempt to embarrass a rival and, in a counter-suit, accused Air Canada of stealing its confidential information. Allegedly, Air Canada sent investigators to pilfer a WestJet executive's garbage for data!

Eventually, the two sides settled their dispute when WestJet admitted that its conduct was unethical and unacceptable and agreed to pay Air Canada's legal costs plus make a substantial donation to Air Canada's choice of charities.

Sources: K. Macklem, "Spies in the Skies," *Maclean's*, September 20, 2004, pp. 20–24; Reuters, posting 5/30/2006.

A word of caution: Executives must be careful to avoid spending so much time and effort tracking the competitive actions of traditional competitors that they ignore new competitors. Further, broad changes and events in the larger environment may have a dramatic impact on a firm's viability. Peter Drucker, whom many consider the father of modern management, wrote:

> Increasingly, a winning strategy will require information about events and conditions outside the institution: noncustomers, technologies other than those currently used by the company and its present competitors, markets not currently served, and so on.[16]

Consider the fall of the once-mighty Encyclopaedia Britannica.[17] Its demise was not caused by a traditional competitor in the encyclopedia industry. It was caused by new technology. CD-ROMs came out of nowhere and devastated the printed encyclopedia industry. Why? A full set of the *Encyclopaedia Britannica* sells for about $2,000 while an encyclopedia on CD-ROM, such as *Microsoft Encarta®*, sells for about $50. To make matters worse, many people receive *Encarta* free with their personal computers.

A manager typically has at his disposal a plethora of sources for information and insights; the Internet, online services such as D&B, Factiva, Reuters, S&P, and Thompson's, conferences, professional networks, industry analysts' reports, and government publications are but a few of the many sources at hand; the danger may rest less in not being able to find out what is going on around him but in being overwhelmed by too much

Slide 14-16

egy Spotlight 2.2

United Technologies

...atened a supplier by indicating that future ...ness opportunities will be influenced by the ...ipt of information with respect to a competitor?

...I in a place where I should not be? If, for ...mple, I am a field representative with privileges ...ove around in a customer's facility, have I gone ...ide the areas permitted? Have I misled anybody ...rder to gain access?

...he contemplated technique for gathering information evasive? Does it involve sifting through trash or setting up an electronic "snooping" device directed at a competitor's facility from across the street?

of ethics. In the last decade, they have clearly articulated their principles governing business conduct. These include an antitrust guide, an ethics guide when contracting with the U.S. government and foreign governments, a policy on accepting gifts from suppliers, and guidelines for proper usage of email. One such document is the Code of Ethics Guide on Competitive Intelligence. This encourages managers and workers to ask themselves these five questions whenever they have ethical concerns.

1. Have I done anything that coerced somebody to share this information? Have I, for example,

4. Have I misled somebody in a way that the person believed sharing information with me was required or would be protected by a confidentiality agreement? Have I, for example, called and misrepresented myself as a government official who was seeking some information for some official purpose?

5. Have I done something to evade or circumvent a system intended to secure or protect information?

Sources: B. Nelson, "The Thinker," *Forbes*, March 3, 2003, pp. 62–64; and "The Fuld War Room—Survival Kit 010," Code of Ethics (printed 2/26/01).

information and being paralyzed by his inability to process all that seems pertinent and is available from everywhere. Nevertheless, managers must develop the habit of continuous awareness and curiosity and use judgement to shift through the mountains of accessible data and information to make sense of it all. Frameworks and tools such as those presented in this and the next chapter are useful means to assist managers in putting that information to productive use.

Environmental Forecasting Environmental scanning, monitoring, and competitive intelligence are important inputs for analyzing the external environment. However, they are of little use unless they provide raw material that is reliable enough to help managers make accurate forecasts. Environmental forecasting involves the development of plausible projections about the direction, scope, speed, and intensity of environmental change.[18] Its purpose is to predict change. It asks, how long will it take a new technology to reach the marketplace? Will the present social concern about an issue result in new legislation? Are current lifestyle trends likely to continue?

Some forecasting issues are much more specific to a particular firm and the industry in which it competes. Consider how important it is for Motel 6, a low-end hotel chain across North America, to predict future indicators, such as the total number of available rooms in the budget segment of the industry. If its predictions are low, it will build too many units, creating a surplus of room capacity that would drive down room rates. Similarly, if Pier 1 Imports is overly optimistic in its forecast of future net disposable income and housing starts, it will order too much inventory and later be forced to discount merchandise drastically. Since the late 1990s Bombardier had been contemplating future trends in people's

35

travel patterns to help it decide whether to invest in a new-generation aircraft that can carry between 110 and 135 passengers. Eventually it announced its plan for the new aircraft, but only five years after Embraer introduced its own version, which helped the Brazilian firm move into the third spot in global rankings, ahead of its Canadian rival. Bombardier is using the current oil crisis to emphasize the economics of its proposed design that uses state of the art materials and a completely redesigned engine to claim that the aircraft will be 20 percent more efficient than anything else available in the market and justify its late entry and belated response. Within the same industry, Europe's Airbus bet its future on A380, a giant airliner that can carry up to 800 passengers and presumably ease congestion in some of the world's busiest airports. Boeing maintains that the future lies in smaller planes, such as its proposed 787, which can quickly move in and out of busy airports. Each company has bet billions of dollars on its own belief about how the future will turn out.

A danger of forecasting is that managers may view uncertainty as black and white and ignore important grey areas. Either they assume that the world is certain and open to precise predictions, or they assume it is uncertain and completely unpredictable.[19] Under-estimating uncertainty can lead to strategies that neither defend against looming threats nor take advantage of opportunities. In 1977, Kenneth H. Olsen, then president of Digital Equipment Corp., announced, "There is no reason for individuals to have a computer in their home" and directed all his firm's research efforts on mainframe computers and work-stations. The explosion in the personal computer market was not easy to detect in 1977, but it was clearly within the range of possibilities that industry experts were discussing at the time. Similarly, there have been numerous underestimates of the growth potential of new telecommunication services. The electric telegraph was derided by Ralph Waldo Emerson, and the telephone had its skeptics. More recently, an "infamous" McKinsey study in the early 1980s predicted that there would be fewer than one million cellular users in the United States by the year 2000. The actual number was one hundred times larger.[20]

At the other extreme, if managers assume the world is unpredictable, they may abandon the analytical rigour of their traditional planning process and base strategic decisions on gut instinct. Such a "just do it" approach may cause executives to place misinformed bets on emerging products or markets that result in record write-offs. Entrepreneurs and venture capitalists, who took the plunge and invested in questionable Internet ventures in the late 1990s provide many examples.

Scenario Analysis A more in-depth approach to forecasting involves scenario analysis. Scenario analysis draws on a range of disciplines and interests, among them economics, psychology, sociology, and demographics. It usually begins with a discussion of partici-pants' thoughts on ways in which societal trends, economics, politics, and technology may affect the issue under discussion. For example, consider Lego. The popular Danish toy manufacturer has a strong position in its market for "construction toys." But what would happen if its market, broadly defined, should change dramatically? After all, Lego com-petes not only with producers of similar products such as Mega Bloks, Canada's largest toy manufacturer. It competes on a much broader canvas for a share of children's playtime. From this perspective, Lego products have numerous competitors, many of them computer based; still others have not yet been invented. Lego may end up with an increasing share of a narrow, shrinking market, much like IBM in the declining days of the mainframe computer. To avoid such a fate, managers must consider their future in a context wider than their present, traditional markets. They need to lay down guidelines for at least 10 years into the future to anticipate rapid changes. Scenarios represent one technique that can assist managers in coping with the uncertainty and unpredictability of today's rapidly changing world, where competition can appear from anywhere at any time and where the rules of the game can change with little forewarning.

Scenario Planning at Shell Oil Company

In the 1960s and 1970s, Shell combined analytical tools with information to create scenarios of possible outcomes. The result of the 1973 oil embargo was a sharp increase in crude oil prices, short supplies of gasoline for consumers, and a depressed world economy. However, Shell's strategic planning, including the use of scenarios, had strongly suggested that a more unstable environment was coming, with a shift of power from oil companies to oil producers. As a result of the precautionary actions it took, Shell was in a better position than most oil companies when the 1973 embargo occurred. Shell also uses scenario planning to plan major new oil field investments. This is because elements of risk can be identified and explored over a considerable period of time.

The Shell process of scenario planning involves the following stages:

1. Interviews with people both inside and outside the business, using an open-ended questioning technique to encourage full and frank answers.

2. Analysis of interviews by issue in order to build a "natural agenda" for further processing.

3. Synthesis of each agenda so as to draw out underlying areas of uncertainty/dispute and possible interrelationships among issues.

4. A small number of issues workshops to explore key issues to improve understanding and identify gaps for further research. These generate a wide range of options for strategy.

5. A scenario workshop to identify and build a small number of scenarios, which may occur in some 10 to 15 years time or even later.

6. A testing of strategy options against the scenarios in order to assess robustness (i.e., whether or not a given strategy is effective under more than one scenario).

Sources: R. Martin, "The Oracles of Oil," *Business* 2.0, January 2002, pp. 35–39; www.touchstonerenard.co.uk/Expertise/Strategy/Scenario_Planning/scenario_planning.htm; and J. Epstein, "Scenario Planning: An Introduction," *The Futurist*, September 1998, pp. 50–52.

Scenario analysis is different from other tools for strategic planning such as trend analysis or high and low forecasts. The origins of scenario planning lie with the military, which used it during World War II to cope effectively with multiple challenges, limited resources, and great unpredictability in the unfolding of the war.[21] Strategy Spotlight 2.3 provides an example of scenario analysis at Shell Oil Company, one of the earliest adopters of this kind of analysis, which used it to prepare to cope with the uncertainty of extreme volatility in oil prices. Other practitioners of scenario planning include Levi Strauss, which uses it to consider potential impacts of everything from cotton deregulation to the unlikely occurrence of the total disappearance of cotton from this planet. Also, a German insurance company contemplated the fall of the Berlin Wall and made plans to expand in central Europe. And in 1990, when Nelson Mandela was released from a South African prison, he met with a panel that helped him create scenarios to chart the country's possible futures. Scenario planning helps by considering how trends or forecasts could be upset by unpredictable events.

SWOT Analysis

One of the most widely used if not basic techniques for analyzing firm and industry conditions is the SWOT analysis. SWOT stands for Strengths, Weaknesses, Opportunities, and Threats. SWOT analysis provides a framework for analyzing those four elements of a company's internal and external environment. Managers rely on SWOT to stimulate self-reflection and group discussions about how to improve their firm and position it for success. They use it regularly to identify and evaluate the opportunities and threats in the business environment as well as the strengths and weaknesses of their firm's internal environment. SWOT guides managers to develop a basic listing of conditions both inside and surrounding their firm.

The strengths and weaknesses portion of SWOT refers to the areas within the firm where it excels and where its traditional points of power, ability, and capacity (strengths) lie. Conversely, it refers to where there may be disadvantages, and where the firm may be lacking relative to its competitors (weaknesses). Examples of strengths may be superior knowledge, strong brands, state-of-the-art facilities, unique access to certain markets, highly motivated workforce, extensive distribution networks, deep financial pockets, and strong leadership. On the contrary, weaknesses can be found in difficulties in accessing raw materials, wounded brands, high financial leverage, and pending lawsuits. We address strengths and weaknesses more extensively in Chapter 3, through our discussion of an organization's value chain and the resource-based view of the firm.

Opportunities and threats are environmental conditions external to the firm. These could be factors in the general environment, such as improving economic conditions that cause lower borrowing costs or an aging population that demands new services for leisure and convenience. Opportunities can arise from technological developments, such as the Internet and telecommunications, or advances in biotechnology. One can find opportunities almost everywhere, whether identifying new market needs, new and better ways to respond to existing needs, new ways of delivering products and services, new applications of technology, easing regulatory conditions, industry consolidation, or technology convergence. Threats, on the other hand, can mount from formidable competitors, new legislation, an aging population, shifts in tastes and values of consumers, protectionism, terrorism, an oil crisis, increasing commodity prices, or new technology that threatens to make our products obsolete.

Although opportunities and threats are rather subjective interpretations of what is unfolding in a firm's external environment, and two informed individuals can easily come up with different lists of them, it is important that managers systematically consider each area of their general and competitive environment for specific opportunities as well as for looming threats. It is also important not to cast the net too narrowly. Strategists who rely on traditional definitions of their industry and competitive environment often focus their sights too narrowly on current customers, technologies, and competitors. Hence, they fail to notice important changes on the periphery of their environment—changes that may trigger the need to redefine industry boundaries and identify a whole new set of competitive relationships. It is also important not to focus too much on one moment in time. Strategy and competition unfold over time. As circumstances change, a static analysis cannot capture the dynamics of the competitive environment; managers risk missing the changing impact on their strategies and competitiveness.

Not all trends, opportunities, and threats apply equally to all companies within an industry, and one firm's SWOT analysis is not applicable to another. Specific trends may benefit some companies while they harm others. Consider, for example, the heightened awareness about health and fitness, which presents an opportunity to some companies (e.g., health clubs and diet-food producers), but represents a clear threat to others (e.g., tobacco firms and breweries).

It is also worth noting that SWOT analysis is not the unquestionable solution to strategic planning and should not be an end in itself. It is a framework that allows a manager to classify issues and observations in a meaningful and useful way. It does have its limitations. It is simply a starting point for discussion. By listing the firm's attributes, managers identify the raw material needed to perform more in-depth strategic analysis. SWOT analysis cannot, however, yield environmental forecasts nor show managers how to achieve a competitive advantage. SWOT's value lies in providing a systematic framework to initiate discussion among thoughtful managers who are contemplating the challenges and opportunities facing their firm.

THE GENERAL ENVIRONMENT

The general environment is composed of factors that can have dramatic effects on a firm's strategy and critically affect its performance. Yet, typically, a firm has little ability to predict trends and events in the general environment and even less ability to control them. It is difficult to predict future political events such as the ongoing Middle East peace negotiations and tensions on the Korean peninsula. Oil and other commodity prices, SARS, mad cow disease, terrorism, and other shocks could not be anticipated easily, nor could we fathom their financial, social, and economic impact. Who would have guessed the Internet's impact on national and global economies in the past decade or two? In the 1980s, the Internet was little more than a method for academic researchers to exchange computer files. In less than 20 short years, such dramatic innovations in information technology have helped, along with many other factors, to keep inflation in check across the world by lowering the cost of doing business and bringing the world closer together.

←(LO 1)

We divide the general environment into six segments: demographic/psychographic, sociocultural, political/legal, technological, economic, and global. First, we discuss each segment and provide a summary of the segment and examples of how events and trends can impact industries. Second, we address relationships among the general environment segments. Third, we consider how trends and events can vary across industries. Exhibit 2.3 provides examples of key trends and events in each of the six segments of the general environment.

The Demographic/Psychographic Segment

Demographics are the most easily understood and quantifiable elements of the general environment. They are at the root of many changes in society. Demographics include elements such as the aging population,[22] rising or declining affluence, changes in ethnic composition, geographic distribution of the population, and disparities in income level. Psychographics reflect the various attitude and interest differences among individuals and complement the demographic characteristics of the population. Psychographics capture the variance among many different individuals who may belong to a particular group, such as urban professionals, college students, and stay-home fathers, but vary widely in their perceptions, priorities, and the ways they interpret and react to external events.

The impact of a demographic trend, like trends in all segments of the general environment, varies across industries. The aging of the Canadian population might have a positive effect on the real estate and consumer industries but a negative impact on manufacturers of diapers and baby food. Rising levels of affluence in many developed countries bode well for brokerage services as well as upscale pet stores. However, these same trends may have an adverse effect on fast-food chains because people can afford to dine at higher-priced restaurants. Fast-food restaurants depend, for their efficient operation, on minimum-wage employees, but the competition for labour intensifies as more attractive employment opportunities become prevalent, thus threatening the employment base for restaurants. Let's look at the details of some of these trends.

Exhibit 2.3
General
Environment: Key
Trends and Events

Demographic/Psychographic

- aging population
- rising affluence
- changes in ethnic composition
- shifting geographic distribution of population
- growing disparities in income levels
- increasing levels of education
- diminishing sense of loyalty to corporations among urban professionals

Sociocultural

- more women in the workforce
- increased numbers of temporary workers
- greater concern for fitness
- greater concern for environment
- postponement of family formation

Political/Legal

- protection of cultural industries (e.g., CRTC)
- settlements of aboriginal land claims
- deregulation of utilities and other industries
- increases in provincially mandated minimum wages
- changes in taxation at provincial and federal levels
- legislation on corporate governance, reforms in bookkeeping, stock options, etc.

Technological

- genetic engineering
- Internet technology emergence
- computer-aided design/computer-aided manufacturing systems (CAD/CAM)
- synthetic and exotic materials research
- pollution/global warming
- computing technology miniaturization
- wireless communications
- nanotechnology

Economic

- interest rates
- unemployment
- Consumer Price Index
- GDP
- stock market valuations

Global

- global trade
- currency exchange rates
- emerging economies (India and China)
- trade agreements among regional blocs (e.g., NAFTA, EU, ASEAN)
- WTO developments on tariffs

The aging of the population in Canada and other developed countries has important implications. The aging baby boomers, who control an estimated 80 percent of the wealth in Canada, will be reaching retirement in just a few years. It is also projected that by the year 2025, nearly one-fifth of Canadians will be over 65. With the greying of baby boomers, the demand for homes for "active elders" (as home developers refer to retirees) is bound to soar. In the U.S., the National Association of Home Builders estimates that people in the 55–74 age group will buy 281,000 homes in 2010, up from 189,000 in 1995.[23] Of course, these developments will be tempered by the unfolding housing crisis for the bottom part of the market. Parallel trends are predicted for Canada. This may be good news for baby boomers because there is always strength in numbers (especially in the political arena). It's also good news for drugstores, which see older patients seven times more often than younger ones.[24] The life insurance industry also benefits from increasing life expectancies but hospitals find their budgets strained by the more expensive and more intensive health related needs of the aging population.

Another demographic trend is the shift in what constitutes a family. Households are smaller. In 2001, Canada had as many one-person households (2.97 million) as households of four or more people (2.94 million). Two-person households now account for one-third of all households. Smaller family sizes are due in part to the decrease in fertility rates of couples, but there has also been an increase in the number of childless couples and empty nesters—families whose children have moved out. At the same time, more young adults, aged 20 to 29, are continuing to live with their parents. In 2001, 41 percent of the 3.8 million young adults lived with their parents. The baby-boom echo[25]—those born during the 1980s to the baby boomers—are repeating the buying behaviours of their parents as they go through college, rent apartments, and form families of their own.

The Sociocultural Segment

Sociocultural forces influence the values, beliefs, and lifestyles of a society. Examples include a higher percentage of women in the workforce, dual-income families, increases in the number of temporary workers, greater concern for healthy diets and physical fitness, greater interest in the environment, and postponement of having children. Such forces enhance sales of products and services in many industries but depress sales in others. The increased number of women in the workforce has increased the need for business clothing merchandise but decreased the demand for baking product staples (since people have less time to cook from scratch). A greater concern for health and fitness has had differential effects. This trend has helped industries that manufacture exercise equipment and healthful foods but harmed industries that produce snack foods and candy.

Sociocultural norms impact attitudes about entrepreneurship and the start-up activity of firms. Canada, together with the United States and Israel, scored the highest among respondents in terms of their propensity to start a business and the general view that starting a new business was a "respected occupation."[26] Such attitudes have traditionally served countries well in encouraging individuals to take risks and venture on their own, which bodes well for the economic prosperity of the country.

The trend toward increased educational attainment of women in the workplace has led to the increased participation of women in upper management positions. Statistics show that women have become the dominant holders of college degrees. Based on figures of a recent graduating class, women with bachelor's degrees outnumber their male counterparts by 27 percent. For the class of 2006–2007, the gap surged to 38 percent. Additionally, throughout the 1990s, the number of women earning MBAs increased by 29 percent compared to only 15 percent for men.[27] Given these educational attainments, it is hardly surprising that companies owned by women have been one of the key drivers of the economy. In the U.S., these companies number more than 9 million; they account for 40 percent of all businesses and have generated more than $3.6 trillion in annual revenue. Canada boasts one of the highest rates of female employers and persons heading their own business at over 41 percent, compared to 39 percent in the U.S. and fewer than 30 percent in most of Europe.[28]

The Political/Legal Segment

Political processes and legislation define the regulations with which industries must comply.[29] Some important elements of the political/legal arena include environmental regulation, occupational health and safety legislation, immigration policies, deregulation of utilities and other industries, and increases in provincially mandated minimum wages.

Government legislation has a significant impact on corporations. The U.S. Congress passed the Sarbanes-Oxley Act in 2002, and Canada followed soon with similar provisions, which greatly increased the accountability of auditors, executives, members of the board of directors, and corporate lawyers. Those provisions were introduced in response to the widespread perception that existing governance mechanisms had failed to protect the interests of shareholders, employees, and creditors. They were brought about by the embarrassing revelations and criminal activities associated with executives within Enron, Tyco, WorldCom, and Hollinger International. They have significant ramifications for all public and private corporations on both sides of the border as well as for numerous European and Asian companies that trade and have transactions with the North American financial markets.

As with many factors in the general environment, changes that benefit one industry may adversely affect others. Following the events of September 11, 2001, and the precipitous drop in air travel, the U.S. government announced financial assistance to the ailing airline industry to the tune of $5 billion cash and a further $10 billion in loan guarantees. Of course, the hotel and hospitality industries demanded similar treatment but received nothing. Opponents have argued that such schemes only enrich the shareholders of airline stocks at the expense of taxpayers. Related arguments have been raised in Canada regarding financial assistance that has frequently been extended to Bombardier Inc., to enable it to continue assembling planes in Quebec and Ontario. In fact, during the last few years, the government of Quebec has extended loan guarantees to Bombardier that exceed $2.3 billion, in its effort to retain the high-paying jobs in the province.

Since Confederation, subsequent Canadian governments have adopted industrial policies that have been largely both interventionist and protectionist.[30] As a result, more than 700 Crown corporations have been involved in everything from selling liquor to producing nuclear reactors, and every facet of the Canadian economy has been operating within a framework of thousands of regulations. Although the rationale has always been a desire to maintain economic and cultural independence from the U.S., critics argue that such regulations have also been responsible for the relative underperformance of the Canadian economy during the latter part of the twentieth century, as compared to most of the other industrialized nations.

The Technological Segment

Developments in technology lead to new products and services and improve how they are produced and delivered to the end user. Innovations can create entirely new industries and alter the boundaries of existing industries.[31] Examples of technological developments and trends are genetic engineering, Internet technology, computer-aided design/computer-aided manufacturing (CAD/CAM), research in artificial and exotic materials, and, on the downside, pollution and global warming. Firms in the petroleum and primary metals industries incur significant expenses to reduce the amount of pollution they produce. Engineering and consulting firms that work with polluting industries derive financial benefits from solving such problems.

Another important technology development is the combination of information technology (IT) and the Internet. By the end of 2000, productivity in the United States was increasing at an annual rate of 5.7 percent. This represents the fastest pace in 35 years, double the historical average of 2 to 3 percent per year. According to a study conducted jointly by Harvard University and the Federal Reserve, IT is responsible for almost half of the rapid productivity gains in recent years. It has also helped offset the inflationary effects of wage increases.[32] By contrast, during the 1990s, productivity in Canada increased by half as much. Most observers have blamed the disappointing performance on lower investments in technology among governments and corporations alike.

The Internet has reduced the cost of getting information and increased its availability, boosting company profits. How are these costs reduced? Consider two examples. Fidelity Investments has found that it costs $15 to handle a transaction over the phone but less than a cent to perform that same transaction on the Web. Airlines have saved millions of dollars by diverting passengers away from commissioned travel agents and their own telephone operators, which traditionally cost in excess of 5 percent of the price of a ticket. Ticket purchases on the airlines' own Web sites cost pennies and, as an added benefit, they decrease errors and increase loyalty among their customers.

There are downsides to technology development. In addition to ethical issues raised by advances in biotechnology, there are threats to our environment associated with the emission of greenhouse gases. To combat such problems, some firms in the petroleum industry take a proactive approach. BP Amoco plans to decrease its greenhouse gas emissions by giving each of its 150 business units a quota of emission permits and encouraging the units to trade them. If a unit cuts emissions and has leftover permits, it can sell them to other units that are having difficulty in meeting their goals. For example, Julie Hardwick, manager at the Naperville, Illinois, petrochemical division, saved up permits by fast-tracking a furnace upgrade that allowed elimination of a second furnace.[33]

The Economic Segment

The economy has an impact on all industries, from suppliers of raw materials to manufacturers of finished goods and services as well as all organizations in the service, wholesale, retail, government, and non-profit sectors. Key economic indicators include interest rates, unemployment rates, the consumer price index, the gross domestic product (GDP), and net disposable income. Interest-rate increases have a negative impact on the residential home construction industry but a negligible (or neutral) effect on industries that produce consumer necessities such as prescription drugs or common grocery items.

Other economic indicators are associated with equity markets. Perhaps the most watched is the Dow Jones Industrial Average (DJIA), which is composed of 30 large industrial firms. When stock market indexes increase, consumers' confidence and spending increase, and there is often an increased demand for luxury items such as jewellery and automobiles. But when stock valuations decrease, demand for these items shrinks.

The recent unfavourable performance of the stock market and the weakened overall economic conditions in the United States, as well as in Canada and the rest of the world, have been precipitated by the boom in the housing sector that was fuelled mainly by a series of interest rate cuts by central banks, which by mid-2003 led to the lowest mortgage rates since World War II.

The Global Segment

There is an increasing trend for firms to expand their operations and market reach beyond the borders of their "home" country. Globalization provides opportunities to access both larger potential markets and a broader base of factors of production such as raw materials, labour, skilled managers, and technical professionals. However, such endeavours also carry many political, social, and economic risks.

Examples of important elements in the global segment include exchange rates, global trade, the economic emergence of China and India, trade agreements among regional blocs (e.g., North American Free Trade Agreement, European Union, Association of Southeast Asian Nations), and the General Agreement on Tariffs and Trade. Increases in trade across national boundaries provide benefits to cargo and shipping industries but have a minimal impact on service industries such as bookkeeping and medical services. The emergence of China as an economic power has benefited many industries and sectors, including steel, construction, computers, as well as consumer goods. Nonetheless, it has had a negative impact on the clothing sector in North America and has seriously challenged many manufacturers.

Few industries are as global as the automobile industry. Consider just a few examples of how some of the key players expanded their reach into Latin America during the 1990s. Fiat built a new plant in Argentina, Volkswagen retooled a plant in Mexico to launch the New Beetle, DaimlerChrysler built a new plant as a joint venture with BMW to produce engines in Brazil, and General Motors built a new car factory in Brazil. Suppliers to the industry have followed suit. Magna and Dofasco have built facilities in the region to supply components on a just-in-time basis to those plants. Why the interest? In addition to the region's low wage rates and declining trade barriers, the population of 400 million is very attractive. But the real bonus lies in the 9 to 1 ratio of people to cars in the region compared to a 2 to 1 ratio in developed countries. With this region's growth expected to be in the 3 to 4 percent range for the first part of the century, sales should increase at a healthy rate.[34]

Similarly, consider the extent of globalization in the Norwegian shipping industry. Despite a small population of only 4.5 million, Norway developed the world's third-largest merchant fleet. And as the world's second-largest oil exporter, it has the vessels and equipment needed to service oil fields off its storm-swept coast. When the warship *USS Cole* was severely damaged by terrorists on October 12, 2000, it was returned to the United States from Yemen aboard a giant Norwegian-owned transport ship, the *Blue Marlin*. According to Frederik Steenbuch, manager of Oslo-based Offshore Heavy Transport, which owns the *Blue Marlin*, "This has nothing to do with Norway. It is purely international. The *Blue Marlin* was built in Taiwan, flies a Panamanian flag, and has a crew from Latvia. The key machinery on board was built in Korea under a Danish license."[35]

Relationships among Elements of the General Environment

In our discussion of the general environment, we see many relationships among the various elements.[36] For example, two demographic trends, the aging of the population and regional population shifts, have important implications for the economic segment (in terms of tax policies to provide benefits to increasing numbers of older citizens) and the political segment (in terms of the relative priorities set on the government's agenda). Another example is the emergence of information technology as a means to increase the rate of productivity gains across many developed countries. Such use of IT results in lower inflation (an important element of the economic segment) and helps offset costs associated with higher labour rates.

The effects of a trend or event in the general environment vary across industries. Commodity price increases, especially for oil and gas, have boosted the economies of Alberta, Saskatchewan, and Newfoundland and have increased the value of the Canadian dollar by some 50 percent over the last few years. In turn, this has had devastating effects on the manufacturing sector in Ontario and Quebec whose exports to the U.S. have been hammered by the increasing value of the loonie. The housing and financial crises in the U.S. have further hobbled those industries that traditionally rely on a healthy American market. Governmental legislation that permits the importation of prescription drugs from Canada into the U.S. is a very positive development for Canadian drugstores but a very negative event for drug manufacturers in the United States. Exhibit 2.4 provides other examples of how the impact of trends or events in the general environment can vary across industries.

Segment/ Trends and Events	Industry	Positive	Neutral	Negative
Demographic/Psychographic				
Aging population	Health care	✓		
	Baby products			✓
Rising affluence	Brokerage services	✓		
	Fast foods			✓
	Upscale pets and supplies	✓		
Sociocultural				
More women in the workforce	Clothing	✓		
	Baking products (staples)			✓
Greater concern for health and fitness	Home exercise equipment	✓		
	Meat products			✓
Political/Legal				
Environmental legislation	Heavy manufacturing			✓
	Environmental consulting	✓		
	Plastics, chemicals			✓
Technological				
Genetic engineering	Pharmaceutical	✓		
	Publishing		✓	
Pollution/global warming	Engineering services	✓		
	Petroleum			✓
Economic				
Interest rate increases	Residential construction			✓
	Most common grocery products		✓	
Global				
Increasing global trade	Shipping	✓		
	Personal service		✓	
Emergence of China as an economic power	Soft drinks	✓		
	Defence			✓

Exhibit 2.4
The Impact of General Environmental Trends and Events on Various Industries

THE COMPETITIVE ENVIRONMENT

In addition to the general environment, managers must also consider the competitive environment, sometimes referred to as the task or industry environment. The nature of competition in an industry as well as the profitability of a particular firm are more directly influenced by developments in the competitive environment.

LO 6 The competitive environment consists of many factors that are predominantly relevant to a firm's strategy. These include existing or potential competitors, customers, and suppliers. Potential competitors may include a supplier considering forward integration, such as an automobile manufacturer acquiring a rental car company, or a firm in an entirely new industry introducing a similar product that uses a more efficient technology.

In the following sections, we discuss key concepts and analytical techniques that managers should use to assess their competitive environments. First, we examine Michael Porter's five-forces model that illustrates how these forces can be used to explain individual firms' profitability in an industry.[37] Then, we address the concept of strategic groups, which demonstrates that even within an industry it is often useful to group firms on the basis of similarities in their strategies. Firms within a strategic group tend to react similarly to external events, and competition tends to be more intense among firms *within* a strategic group than between strategic groups.

Porter's Five-Forces Model of Industry Competition

The "five forces" model developed by Michael E. Porter has been the most commonly used analytical tool for examining the competitive environment.[38] It describes the competitive environment in terms of five basic competitive forces:

1. The threat of new entrants.
2. The bargaining power of buyers.
3. The bargaining power of suppliers.
4. The threat of substitute products and services.
5. The intensity of rivalry among competitors in an industry.

Each of these forces affects a firm's ability to compete in a given market. Together, they determine the profit potential for a particular industry. The model is shown in Exhibit 2.5. Managers should be familiar with the five-forces model for several reasons. It helps them assess the overall attractiveness of an industry and decide whether their firm should remain in or exit that industry. It provides the rationale for increasing or decreasing resource commitments. The model helps assess how to improve a firm's competitive position with regard to each of the five forces. For example, managers can use insights provided by the five-forces model to create higher entry barriers that discourage new rivals from competing with their firm.[39] Or they may develop strong relationships with their distribution channels to better balance the bargaining power of their buyers.

The Threat of New Entrants The threat of new entrants refers to the possibility that the profits of established firms in the industry may be eroded by new competitors. The extent of the threat depends on existing barriers to entry and the combined reactions from existing competitors. If entry barriers are high and/or the newcomer can anticipate a sharp retaliation from established competitors, the threat of entry is low. These circumstances discourage new competitors. There are six major sources of entry barriers:

- *Economies of Scale* Economies of scale refer to spreading the costs of production and other business activities over a large number of units produced. The per-unit cost of a product typically decreases as the absolute volume produced within a period increases. Larger facilities, automation, fixed overhead costs, and advertising expenses can be some of the typical sources of economies of scale for a traditional manufacturer. For example, research and development costs, commercialization expenses, and legal and regulatory compliance give significant rise to economies of scale in the pharmaceutical industry. The presence of such economies of scale in an industry deters entry by forcing the firm contemplating entry to come in on a large scale and risk strong reaction from existing firms or come in on a small scale and accept a cost disadvantage. Both are undesirable options.

fixed + variable costs

♦ ***Product Differentiation*** When existing competitors have strong brand identification and customer loyalty, differentiation creates a barrier to entry by forcing entrants to spend heavily to overcome existing customer loyalties. Building a brand requires enormous investment, takes time, and is of course fraught with risk.

♦ ***Capital Requirements*** The need to invest large financial resources to compete creates a barrier to entry, especially if the capital is required for risky or unrecoverable upfront advertising or research and development (R&D).

♦ ***Switching Costs*** A barrier to entry is created by the existence of one-time costs that the buyer faces when switching from one supplier's product or service to another. Specialized equipment, nonstandardized technologies, and unique inputs to a specific production process are some of the elements that generate switching costs and make it harder for customers to move away from an established firm to a new entrant.

♦ ***Access to Distribution Channels*** The new entrant's need to secure distribution for its product can create a barrier to entry. Exclusive agreements, restrictive practices, and franchise networks provide preferential access to an incumbent and preclude newcomers from establishing a foothold into a market.

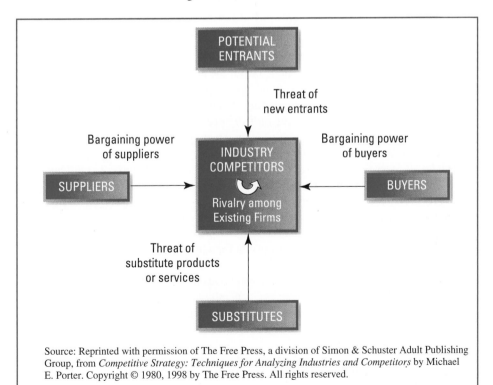

Exhibit 2.5
Porter's Five-Forces Model of Industry Competition

Source: Reprinted with permission of The Free Press, a division of Simon & Schuster Adult Publishing Group, from *Competitive Strategy: Techniques for Analyzing Industries and Competitors* by Michael E. Porter. Copyright © 1980, 1998 by The Free Press. All rights reserved.

◆ ***Cost Disadvantages Independent of Scale*** Some existing competitors may have advantages that are independent of size or economies of scale. These derive from

◆ proprietary products
◆ favourable access to raw materials
◆ government subsidies
◆ favourable government policies

In an industry where few, or none, of these entry barriers are present, the threat of new entry is high. If a new firm can launch its business with little capital investment or can operate efficiently despite its small scale of operation, it is likely to be a serious threat, as new competitors can easily erode the profits of established firms. Industries such as dry cleaning, craft brewing, consulting, and much of retailing present few barriers and experience a constant entry and exit of players as firms can set up operations very easily and compete locally without much regard for global brands or large scale.

The Bargaining Power of Buyers   Buyers threaten an industry by forcing down prices, bargaining for higher quality or more services, and playing competitors against each other. These actions erode industry profitability.[40] The power of each large buyer or buyer group depends on attributes of the market situation and the importance of that group's purchases to the industry's overall business. Loblaw's President's Choice line of products demonstrates how a buyer can exert power over its suppliers by creating conditions to its advantage. Since the President's Choice brand belongs to Loblaw, the producers have little influence on product design, features, or placement, and they must compete on price to attract the business from the powerful supermarket chain. Margins have decreased across the board among major producers in the food industry since Loblaw introduced its private label. Things deteriorated further for producers as the success of Loblaw was followed by many other food retailers' own private labels. Similarly, Wal-Mart absorbs 30 percent of Procter & Gamble's global production and critically affects the performance of one of the world's largest consumer goods corporations. A buyer is powerful under the following conditions:

◆ ***It purchases large volumes relative to a seller's sales.*** If a large percentage of a supplier's sales are purchased by a single buyer, the importance of the buyer's business to the supplier increases. Large-volume buyers, particularly, are powerful in industries with high fixed cost (e.g., automobile manufacturers to the steel industry).
◆ ***The products it purchases from the industry are standard or undifferentiated.*** Confident they can always find alternative suppliers, buyers play one company against the other, as in commodity grain products.
◆ ***The buyer faces few switching costs.*** Switching costs lock the buyer to particular sellers. Specialized components force buyers to deal with specific suppliers and largely accept their terms. Conversely, when buyers can easily switch between suppliers for their needs, they can play one supplier against another. The buyers' power is further enhanced if the seller faces high switching costs—if, for example, it has to commit substantial resources upfront for equipment or product design in order to earn the buyer's business.
◆ ***It earns low profits.*** Low profits create incentives to lower purchasing costs. On the other hand, highly profitable buyers are generally less price sensitive.
◆ ***The buyers pose a credible threat of backward integration.*** If buyers are either partially integrated or pose a credible threat of backward integration, they are typically able to secure concessions.
◆ ***The industry's product is unimportant to the quality of the buyer's products or services.*** When the quality of the buyer's products is not affected by the industry's

product, the buyer is more indifferent to the input's features and concentrates, instead, on negotiating the lowest price.

At times, a firm or set of firms in an industry may increase its buyer power by using the services of a third party. FreeMarkets Online is one such third party.[41] Pittsburgh-based FreeMarkets has developed software enabling large industrial buyers to organize online auctions for qualified suppliers of semi-standard parts such as fabricated components, packaging materials, metal stampings, and services. By aggregating buyers, FreeMarkets increases the buyers' bargaining power. The results are impressive. In its first 48 auctions, most participating companies saved over 15 percent; some saved as much as 50 percent. Even large firms such as United Technologies have been able to achieve substantial savings in their procurement of circuit boards and other computer components.

The Bargaining Power of Suppliers Suppliers can exert bargaining power over participants in an industry by threatening to raise prices, alter the terms of supply, or even lower the number of features and reduce the quality of goods and services they provide to the industry. Powerful suppliers can squeeze the profitability of firms in an industry to the point of taking away all the profits.[42] The factors that make suppliers powerful tend to be the mirror opposite of those that make buyers powerful. A supplier will be powerful in the following circumstances:

- *The supplier industry is dominated by a few companies and is more concentrated (few firms dominate the industry) than the industry it sells to.* Suppliers selling to fragmented industries exert influence over prices, quality, and terms.
- *The industry is not an important customer of the supplier.* When suppliers sell to several industries and a particular industry does not represent a significant fraction of their sales, suppliers are able to exert power.
- *The supplier's product is an important input to the buyer's business.* When such inputs are important to the success of the buyer's manufacturing process or product quality, the bargaining power of suppliers is high.
- *The supplier's products are differentiated or it has built up switching costs for the buyer.* Differentiation or switching costs facing the buyers cut off their options to play one supplier against another. When buyers are unable to substitute among different inputs, their suppliers can exert substantial power in determining prices and terms. (Conversely, even large suppliers can be affected if they have to compete with substitutes.)
- *The supplier group poses a credible threat of forward integration.* This provides a check against the industry's ability to improve the terms by which it purchases.

When considering supplier power, we typically focus on companies that supply raw materials, equipment, machinery, and associated services. But the supply of labour is also an important input to businesses, and labour's power varies over time and across occupations and industries. As we enter the twenty-first century, the outlook is not very good for semi-skilled and unskilled labourers who face numerous substitutes, most notably, technology. Correspondingly, their wages have barely kept up with inflation. Immigration, de-unionization, and globalization have also diminished the relative bargaining power of those sectors of the labour market. On the other hand, workers with the right skills and jobs have enjoyed the spoils of the New Economy and will likely continue to do so in the foreseeable future. Knowledge workers with specialized training and expertise are highly desirable and can command high compensation for their contributions; few viable substitutes currently exist to threaten their clout in the labour market.

The Threat of Substitute Products and Services All firms within an industry compete with industries producing substitute products and services. Substitutes limit the potential returns of an industry by placing a ceiling on the prices which firms in that industry can charge. The more attractive the price/performance ratio of substitute products, the tighter the lid on an industry's profits.

Identifying substitute products involves searching for other products or services that can perform the same function as the industry's offerings or satisfy the same needs of its customers. Flowers, greeting cards, and a box of chocolates have few physical characteristics in common, but they are easy substitutes in the eyes of well-wishing consumers. Identifying substitute products is not always easy; it is a subtle task that can lead a manager into businesses seemingly far removed from the industry. For example, the airline industry might not consider video cameras much of a threat. But as digital technology has improved and wireless and other forms of telecommunication have become more efficient, teleconferencing has become a viable substitute for business travel for many executives.

Teleconferencing can save both time and money, as IBM found out with its "Manager Jam" idea.[43] With over 300,000 employees, including 30,000 managers scattered around six continents, IBM is one of the world's largest businesses. The shift to an increasingly mobile workplace means many managers supervise employees they rarely see face-to-face. To enhance coordination, Samuel Palmisano, IBM's CEO, launched a program exploring the role of the manager in the twenty-first century. Manager Jam, as the project was nicknamed, was a 48-hour real-time Web event in which managers from 50 different countries swapped ideas and strategies for dealing with problems shared by all of them, regardless of geography. Some 8,100 managers logged on to the company's intranet to participate in the discussion forums—without having to leave their offices for a single moment.

The Intensity of Rivalry among Competitors in an Industry Rivalry among existing competitors takes the form of jockeying for position. Firms use tactics like price competition, advertising battles, product introductions, and increased customer service or warranties. Rivalry occurs when competitors sense the pressure or act on an opportunity to improve their position.

Some forms of competition, such as price competition, are typically highly destabilizing and are likely to erode the average level of profitability in an industry. Rivals easily match price cuts, an action that lowers profits for all firms. On the other hand, advertising battles expand overall demand or enhance the level of product differentiation for the benefit of all firms in the industry. Rivalry, of course, differs across industries. In some instances it is characterized as warlike, bitter, or cutthroat, whereas in other industries it is referred to as polite and gentlemanly. Intense rivalry is the result of several interacting factors, including the following:

- *Numerous or equally balanced competitors* When there are many firms in an industry, the likelihood of mavericks is great. Some firms believe they can make moves without being noticed. Even when there are relatively few firms, and they are nearly equal in size and resources, instability results from fighting among companies that have the resources for sustained and vigorous retaliation.

- *Slow industry growth* Slow industry growth turns competition into a fight for market share since firms seeking to expand their sales have to earn those new sales away from their competitors.

- *High fixed costs* High fixed costs create strong pressures for all firms to increase capacity. Excess capacity often leads to escalating price cutting.

- *Lack of differentiation or switching costs* Where the product or service is perceived as a commodity or near commodity, the buyer's choice is typically based on price, service, and well-defined features, resulting in pressures from intense price and service competition. Lack of switching costs has the same effect, as competitors can easily replace each other's product offerings.

- *Capacity augmented in large increments* Where economies of scale require that capacity must be added in large increments, capacity additions can be very disruptive to the industry supply/demand balance.

- *High exit barriers* Exit barriers are economic, strategic, and emotional factors that keep firms competing even though they may be earning low or negative returns on their investments. Some exit barriers are specialized assets, fixed costs of exit, strategic interrelationships (e.g., relationships between the business units and others within a company in terms of image, marketing, shared facilities, and so on), emotional barriers, and government and social pressures (e.g., governmental discouragement of exit out of concern for job loss).

Rivalry between firms is often based solely on price, but it can involve other factors. Consider, for example, the state of the domestic airline industry in early 2005. Air Canada had just come out of a bankruptcy reorganization that effectively wiped out all shareholders' investments in the company. When the reorganization was approved, Air Canada's shares were charitably valued at $0.02. After the reorganization, the original bondholders of its debt became the owners of its parent, ACE Aviation Holdings. Air Canada had been able to shed a substantial portion of its debt burden and was in a better position to face the high fuel costs plaguing the industry and handle heavy labour costs—the legacy of its prosperous past. Air Canada had come out with all of its route network and fleet intact. It still operated extensively cross-border, to the Caribbean, Mexico, Central America, as well as to the five main European capitals and, frequently, to Asia.

Yet, the big competitive battle was still within Canada's borders. Its major competitor, WestJet of Calgary, with a fleet of very efficient workhorses, the Boeing 737s, was flying point to point within Canada and a limited number of routes to the U.S. The competition was intense even though Air Canada held 62 percent of the domestic market and WestJet served some 28 percent. Two smaller players, Jetsgo of Montreal and CanJet Airlines of Halifax, had 8 and 2 percent, respectively. The presence of Jetsgo seemed to be clouding the competitive dynamics. Jetsgo was fighting for its life with load factors that industry analysts speculated were below break-even. It was continuously underpricing the two larger carriers in an effort to attract new customers and was making headlines with One Dollar fares. CanJet followed suit, reducing fares for all overlapping routes. Although they represented a very small slice of the market, they were forcing lower ticket prices on everybody.

To complicate matters further, Fidelity Investments, the largest mutual fund company in the U.S., owned shares, through its various holdings, in Air Canada and WestJet, and it had invested in Jetsgo. Analysts had been questioning the motives of Fidelity and had estimated that the existing state of affairs primarily hurt WestJet shares. If Jetsgo were to disappear, the big beneficiaries would not be the flying public or the employees but rather WestJet owners whose shares would appreciate by some 40 percent. A rational, wealth-maximizing shareholder would be expected to dump Jetsgo and watch his or her holdings in WestJet appreciate overnight. The rivalry among competitors in the domestic airline industry was extremely intense, and the competitive avenues readily expanded beyond the traditional dimensions.

As a postscript, Jetsgo, indeed, filed for bankruptcy in March 2005. Overnight, ACE and WestJet shares went up by 15 and 50 percent, respectively. Consumers complained that, within a day or so, fares also increased by 10 to 20 percent on various domestic routes, although both airlines fervently denied that specific increases had anything to do with the disappearance of a nuisance competitor.

Using Industry Analysis: A Few Caveats For industry analysis to be valuable, a company must collect and evaluate a wide variety of information from many sources. As the trend toward globalization accelerates, information on foreign markets as well as on a wider variety of competitors, suppliers, customers, substitutes, and potential new entrants becomes more critical. Industry analysis helps a firm to not only to evaluate the profit potential of an industry but also to consider various ways to strengthen its position vis-à-vis the five forces.

The five-forces analysis implicitly assumes a zero-sum game, determining how a firm can enhance its position relative to the forces. Yet, such an approach can often be short-sighted; that is, it can overlook the many potential benefits of developing constructive win-win relationships with suppliers and customers. Establishing long-term mutually beneficial relationships with suppliers improves a firm's ability to implement just-in-time inventory systems, which allow it to manage inventories better and respond faster to market demands. Conversely, a company that exploits its powerful position against a supplier will likely face reprisal when the balance of power shifts.[44] By working together as partners, suppliers and manufacturers can provide the greatest value at the lowest possible cost. Later chapters address such collaborative relationships and how they can be made most effective.

The five-forces analysis has also been criticized for being essentially a static analysis. However, this position misses two critical points that are reflective of the dynamic nature of the five-forces model. First, the model should not be used to describe the structure of an industry at a single moment in time. It might represent how various elements align at a single instant, but it does not convey how they got there nor the direction in which they are heading. Similarly, the five-forces analysis depicts an industry that might be converging or diverging, where firms are increasing or withdrawing from their involvement in various activities and where developments are continuous or discontinuous. The analysis requires that managers elaborate on those issues before conclusions can be drawn.

Second, both scholars and practitioners recognize that external forces as well as strategies of individual firms are continually changing the structure of all industries. The search for a dynamic theory of strategy has led to greater use of game theory in industrial organization economics research and strategy research. Based on game-theoretic considerations, Brandenburger and Nalebuff recently introduced the concept of the value net,[45] which, in many ways, is an extension of the five-forces analysis. It is illustrated in Exhibit 2.6. The value net represents all the players in the game and analyzes how their interactions affect a firm's ability to generate and appropriate value. The vertical dimension of the net includes suppliers and customers. The firm has direct transactions with them. On the horizontal dimension are substitutes and complementors, players with whom a firm interacts but may not necessarily transact. The concept of complementors is perhaps the single most important contribution of value net analysis and, hence, is explained in more detail in the next paragraph.

Complementors typically are products or services that have possible impact on the value of a firm's own products or services. Those who produce complements are usually referred to as complementors. Powerful computers are of no value to a user unless there is

Exhibit 2.6
The Value Net

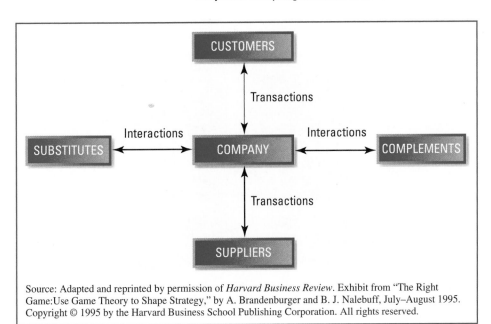

software that runs on them. Similarly, new and better software is possible only if the hardware on which it can be run is available. This is equally true in the video game industry, where the sales of game consoles and video games complement each other. Nintendo's success in the early 1990s was a result of their ability to manage their relationship with their complementors. They built a security chip into the hardware and then licensed the right to develop games to outside firms. These firms paid a royalty to Nintendo for each copy of the game sold. The royalty revenue enabled Nintendo to sell game consoles at close to their cost, thereby increasing their market share, which, in turn, caused more games to be sold and more royalties to be generated.

Industry Dynamics

One of the criticisms often levelled against traditional industry analysis is that it is static, while the competitive landscape undergoes very rapid changes due to technological developments, shifting customer preferences, changes in the regulatory environment, as well as competitive moves of the incumbents. While this does not diminish the value of the five-forces analysis at a given point in time, it does raise awareness of a need for additional tools and frameworks for understanding and analyzing the rapid changes taking place in most industries.[46] For example, consider some of the automobile industry's core activities that have historically generated profits for the industry and which might be threatened with obsolescence by the fact that today consumers can find all the information they need for making automobile purchase decisions—price, performance, reliability, and technical characteristics—by going online. The core selling activities of a car dealership are no longer of great value to the customer. Then again, consider some of the core assets possessed by firms in any industry, such as knowledge, brand names, and the like, that might have historically been critical to building competitive advantages in that industry. In the video rental industry, for example, the core assets were traditionally location and wide selection. In an era of video downloads, location is of no significance and typical rental outlets cannot possibly match the enormous

Exhibit 2.7
Four Evolutionary
Trajectories of
Industry Change

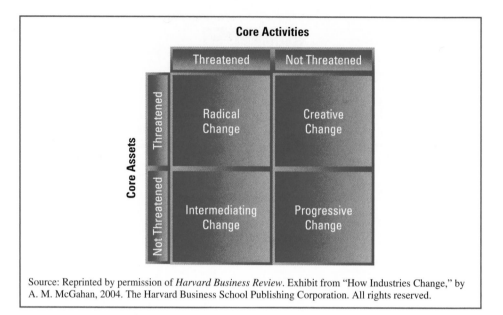

selection offered by firms such as Netflix. An industry whose core activities or core assets face obsolescence will follow one of four change trajectories, as they are depicted in Exhibit 2.7.

Radical change occurs when core activities and core assets both face the threat of obsolescence. For example, the overnight delivery industry is experiencing this problem. The availability of cheap and instantaneous document delivery through fax machines and the Internet has made the core assets (delivery trucks, airplanes, and a central hub) and core activities (document tracking) of firms such as FedEx suddenly less relevant. A similar situation was faced by typewriter manufacturers two decades ago when relatively inexpensive PCs became widely available.

Intermediating change occurs when core assets are not threatened but core activities are. Automobile dealerships are an example of an industry facing intermediating change, as customers can get all the information they need online. Second, as the quality and longevity of cars improve, individual purchases have become less frequent. Moreover, car manufacturers are increasingly sharing the task of customer relations with the dealers, and, in some cases, they have even completely taken over this function. Finally, inventory management and financing are now subject to significant economies of scale that only large, integrated companies can take advantage of.

When core assets are threatened but core activities are not, industries tend to follow the *creative change* trajectory. Some industries undergoing creative change include the film production industry, the pharmaceutical industry, oil and gas exploration, and pre-packaged software. In each of these industries, there is rapid asset turnover but relatively stable relationships with suppliers and customers. For example, in the pharmaceutical industry patents for some drugs expire while new drugs are approved, but the core activities of commercialization and marketing continue to be relevant.

Finally, *progressive change* occurs in industries where neither core assets nor core activities face imminent threat of obsolescence. Change does occur, but it is within the existing framework of the industry. At any given moment incremental changes may be occurring, but over time these events accumulate to result in substantial change. The commercial airline industry and the discount retailing industry are both experiencing progressive change. Their suppliers and the customers have not changed, the core assets and activities have changed only incrementally, but over the last decade both these industries have experienced significant changes.

Each of the above four change trajectories unfolds over many years, sometimes even decades. This gives firms within an industry time to respond to the changes. Resisting change, on the other hand, seldom succeeds. When faced with *radical* or *intermediating changes*, it is wise to aggressively pursue profits in the near term while avoiding investments that could reduce strategic flexibility in the future. Another response is forming alliances, often with rivals, to protect common interests and defend against new competition from outsiders. Diversification can also be an effective solution for firms facing *radical change*. FedEx's acquisition of Kinko's fits into this category. In order to succeed, firms facing *intermediating change* must find unconventional ways to extract profits from their core assets. For example, threatened by eBay, traditional auctioneers have responded by capitalizing on their appraisal expertise; for a fee, they will certify the value of the items being sold online.

Strategies for firms facing *creative change* include spreading the risk of new-project development over a portfolio of assets or outsourcing project management and development tasks. Successful companies in *progressive change* industries carve out distinct positions based on technical or marketing expertise or geography. They might also develop a system of interrelated activities that are a safeguard against competitors. Wal-Mart and Southwest Airlines are excellent examples of this approach. Their strategies are entirely observable and easy to understand, but they are the result of hundreds of incremental changes compounding over time and thus are difficult for rivals to match.

Strategic Groups within Industries

← (LO 7)

In an industry analysis, two assumptions are unassailable: (1) no two firms are totally different and (2) no two firms are exactly the same. The analysis can be enhanced by identifying groups of firms that are mostly similar to each other, which are known as strategic groups.[47] This is important because rivalry tends to be greater among firms that are alike. Canadian Tire is more concerned about Wal-Mart than Holt Renfrew, Mercedes is more concerned about BMW than Hyundai, and the Hudson's Bay Company is more concerned about Sears than Club Monaco.[48]

The strategic groups concept is, however, more complex than these examples may convey. Classifying an industry into strategic groups involves judgment. If it is to be useful as an analytical tool, one must exercise caution in deciding what dimensions to use to map the firms. Dimensions include breadth of product and geographic scope, price/quality, degree of vertical integration, type of distribution (e.g., dealers, mass merchandisers, private label), and so on. Dimensions should also be selected to reflect the variety of strategic combinations in an industry. For example, if all firms in an industry have roughly the same level of product differentiation (or R&D intensity), this would not be a good dimension to select.

What value is the strategic groups concept as an analytical tool? First, strategic groupings help a firm identify barriers to mobility that protect a group from attacks by other groups.[49] Mobility barriers are factors that deter the movement of firms from one strategic position to another. For example, in the chainsaw industry, the major barriers protecting the high-quality, dealer-oriented group are technology, brand image, and an established network of servicing dealers.

The second value of strategic grouping is that it helps a firm identify groups whose competitive position may be marginal or tenuous. One may anticipate that these competitors may exit the industry or try to move into another group. This has been the case in recent years in the retail department store industry, where firms such as J. C. Penney, the Hudson's Bay Company, and Kmart have experienced extremely difficult times because they were stuck in the middle—neither an aggressive discount player like Wal-Mart nor a prestigious upscale player like Holt Renfrew.

Third, strategic groupings help chart the future directions of firms' strategies. Arrows emanating from each strategic group can represent the direction in which the group (or a firm within the group) seems to be moving. If all strategic groups are moving in a similar direction, this could indicate a high degree of future volatility and intensity of competition. In the automobile industry, for example, the competition in the minivan and sport utility segments intensified when many firms entered those product segments.

Fourth, strategic groups are helpful in thinking through the implications of each industry trend. Is the trend decreasing the viability of a group? If so, in what direction should the strategic group move? Is the trend increasing or decreasing entry barriers in a given group? Will the trend decrease the ability of one group to separate itself from other groups? Such analysis can help in making predictions about industry evolution. A sharp increase in interest rates, for example, would tend to have less impact on providers of higher-priced goods (e.g., Porsches) than on providers of lower-priced goods (e.g., Dodge Neons). The Dodge Neon customer base is much more price sensitive.

Exhibit 2.8 provides a strategic grouping of the worldwide automobile industry.[50] In this case, we have identified four strategic groups. In the top left-hand corner are high-end luxury automakers who focus on a very narrow product market. Most of the cars produced by the members of this group cost well over $100,000. Some cost many times that amount.

Exhibit 2.8
The World Automobile Industry: Strategic Groups

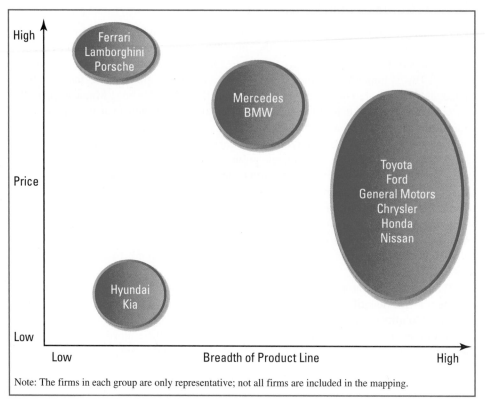

Note: The firms in each group are only representative; not all firms are included in the mapping.

The Ferrari F50 costs roughly $550,000 and the Lamborghini L147 $300,000.[51] Players in this market have a very exclusive clientele and face little rivalry from other strategic groups. At the other extreme, in the lower left-hand corner, is a strategic group that has low-price/quality attributes and targets a narrow market. These players, Hyundai and Kia, limit competition from other strategic groups by pricing their products very low. The third group, near the middle, consists of firms high in product pricing/quality and average in their product-line breadth. The final group, at the far right, consists of firms with a broad range of products and multiple price points. These firms have entries that compete at both the lower end of the market (e.g., the Ford Focus) and the higher end (e.g., Chevrolet Corvette).

The auto market has been very dynamic, and competition has intensified in recent years. Firms in the same group have responded similarly, even though firms from different strategic groups still compete in the same product markets such as minivans and sport utility vehicles. In the late 1990s, Mercedes entered the fray with the M series at the same time that BMW introduced the X5. Porsche also made an entry with the Cayenne. Within another strategic group, Ford has gone on an acquisition binge to attract high-ticket buyers. It has acquired Volvo, Land Rover, Jaguar, and Aston Martin.[52] In similar moves, Toyota, Nissan, and Honda have successfully introduced Lexus, Infiniti, and Acura, respectively, to compete for the same upscale market.

Summary

Managers must continuously analyze the external environment to minimize or eliminate threats and exploit opportunities. This involves a continuous process of environmental scanning and monitoring as well as obtaining competitive intelligence on present and potential rivals. These activities provide valuable inputs for developing forecasts. In addition, many firms use scenario planning to anticipate and respond to volatile and disruptive environmental changes.

We identified two types of environment: the general environment and the competitive environment. The six segments of the general environment are demographic/psychographic, sociocultural, political/legal, technological, economic, and global. Trends and events occurring in these segments, such as the aging of the population, higher percentages of women in the workplace, governmental legislation, and increasing (or decreasing) interest rates, can have a dramatic effect on a firm. A given trend or event may have a positive impact on some industries and a negative or neutral impact on others.

The competitive environment consists of industry-related factors and has a more direct impact than the general environment. Porter's five-forces model of industry analysis includes the threat of new entrants, buyer power, supplier power, threat of substitutes, and rivalry among competitors. The intensity of these factors determines, in large part, the average expected level of profitability in an industry. A sound awareness of such factors—in isolation and in combination—is beneficial not only for deciding what industries to enter but also for assessing how a firm can improve its competitive position. In employing the five-forces analysis, one should remember that it is essentially a static model that assumes an antagonistic view of the world and does not consider complex interrelationships among a firm's web of interactions and transactions. The general environment and the competitive environment are quite interdependent, and changes in one segment can greatly affect factors in another segment.

The concept of strategic groups is also important in analyzing the external environment of a firm. No two organizations are exactly the same, nor are they completely different.

Firms can be placed in strategic groups on the basis of similarities in their resources and strategies. The strategic groups concept is valuable for determining mobility barriers across groups, identifying groups with marginal competitive positions, charting the future directions of firm strategies, and assessing the implications of industry trends for the strategic group as a whole.

Summary Review Questions

1. Why must managers be aware of a firm's external environment?

2. What is gathering and analyzing competitive intelligence, and why is it important for firms to engage in it?

3. Discuss and describe the six elements of the external environment.

4. Select one of these elements, and describe some changes relating to it in an industry that interests you.

5. Describe how the five forces can be used to determine the average expected profitability in an industry.

6. What are some of the limitations (or caveats) in using the five-forces analysis?

7. Explain how the general environment and competitive environment are highly related. How can such interrelationships affect the profitability of a firm or industry?

8. Explain the concept of strategic groups. What are the performance implications?

Experiential Exercise

Select one of the following industries: personal computers, airlines, or automobiles. For this industry, evaluate the strength of each of Porter's five forces as well as complementors.

Industry Force	High? Medium? Low?	Why?
1. Threat of new entrants		
2. Power of buyers		
3. Power of suppliers		
4. Threat of substitutes		
5. Rivalry among competitors		
6. Complementors		

Application Questions Exercises

1. Imagine yourself as the CEO of a large firm in an industry that interests you. Then (1) identify major trends in the general environment, (2) analyze their impact on the firm, and (3) identify major sources of information to monitor these trends. (Use Internet and library resources.)

2. Analyze movements across the strategic groups in the Canadian retail industry. How do these movements within this industry change the nature of competition?

3. What are the major trends in the general environment that have impacted the Canadian financial services industry?

4. On the Internet, look up www.magna.ca. What are some of the forces driving industry competition affecting the profitability of this firm?

Ethics Questions

1. What are some of the legal and ethical issues involved in collecting competitor intelligence in the following situations?
   a. A firm hires an MBA student to collect information directly from the competition; in his contacts with the competitors the student claims the information is for a course project.
   b. A firm advertises a non-existent position and interviews a rival's employees to obtain competitor information.
   c. A hotel sends an employee posing as a potential client to a competitor hotel to find out how they handle new clients and who their major corporate customers are.

2. What are some of the ethical concerns that arise when a firm tries to exploit its power over a supplier?

Chapter 3 *Analyzing the Internal Environment of the Firm*

LEARNING OBJECTIVES

After reading this chapter, you should have a good understanding of:

LO 1 → how managers can use the value-chain analysis to gain insights into a firm's internal environment.

LO 2 → how individual activities within the firm add value and how interrelationships among activities within the firm as well as between the firm and its suppliers and customers create value.

LO 3 → how managers can use the resource-based view of the firm to gain insights into a firm's internal environment.

LO 4 → the four criteria that a firm's resources must possess to maintain a sustainable advantage and how value created can be appropriated by employees.

LO 5 → how financial ratio analysis and other metrics of performance as well as meaningful comparisons across firms inform managers' understanding of the workings of their own organization.

LO 6 → the value of recognizing how the interests of a variety of stakeholders can be interrelated.

Case Study

The automotive sector represents one of Canada's most important economic engines and contributes substantially to Ontario's economic prosperity. Beyond the six automobile manufacturers, namely General Motors, Ford, Chrysler, Toyota, Nissan, and Honda, it includes a broad range of auto parts makers such as Magna, Linamar, Delphi, and Johnson Controls as well as smaller outfits such as ThyssenKrupp Budd and BBi Enterprises.[1] The sector employs over 150,000 Canadians and supports jobs for many more in the surrounding communities and among its suppliers such as the producers of steel and aluminium.

Most of the industry's primary actors are critically intertwined with operations on both sides of the border. Yet, the financial health of each one of them varies tremendously and extends from profits in the hundreds of millions of dollars for Toyota, Magna, Linamar, and Johnson Controls to losses at General Motors, Ford, and Delphi, and bankruptcies at BBi Enterprises and Tower Automotive. How is it that such discrepancies abound within the same industry? How can it be that while one firm is making a billion dollar investment in a new plant, another firm down the street is laying off thousands of workers? An analysis of the activities performed by each of those firms and an appreciation of how effectively and efficiently different firms perform those activities promise to shed light on such questions. For example, a recent study documents that a Chrysler minivan requires some $1,400 in labour costs, while at Honda direct labour amounts to only $929, giving the Japanese firm a potential price advantage of $471 for each of its vans. Elsewhere, Magna has employed an innovative technology of hydroforming, with spectacular results. Hydroforming is a process that uses liquid under high pressure to shape metal tubing and form automobile frames without the need for stamping and welding. Budd does not seem to be able to benefit from its investment in the same technology. Similarly, in spite of their best efforts, the Detroit-based automobile manufacturers are consistently losing market share to the Japan-based and North America-built cars by Toyota, Honda, and Nissan.

The results speak of the uniqueness of individual situations and the need to complement the analysis of the external environment with a detailed assessment of what takes place inside each organization. As we learned in Chapter 2, a SWOT analysis consists of a careful listing of a firm's strengths, weaknesses, opportunities, and threats. While the -OT elements are likely to be rather common across different firms within an industry, the SW- elements are unique and constitute the starting point for a discussion of a firm's competitive advantage. Yet, as we elaborated in Chapter 2, SWOT by itself cannot show managers how to achieve a competitive advantage. Managers need to proceed to an analysis of the system of activities that creates the products and of the resources that are utilized in unique ways to successfully fulfill the customer's wants. SWOT is a very helpful starting point, which can form the basis for evaluating a firm's situation but cannot answer the critical questions about competitive advantage. For that, we need to turn to a more in-depth analysis of the inner workings of the organization and develop insights about the processes that create value within the organization.

VALUE-CHAIN ANALYSIS

Value-chain analysis views the organization as a sequential process of value-creating activities. It is based on the simple notion that a firm engages in a series of activities that combine the various necessary inputs to create the product offering that the firm brings to the marketplace. It disaggregates a firm into its various activities in order to understand the ways all inputs are deployed and costs are incurred in creating a firm's products and services. The value-chain analysis provides the foundation for understanding the building blocks of competitive advantage. This approach was described in Michael Porter's book

Exhibit 3.1
The Value Chain:
Primary and Support
Activities

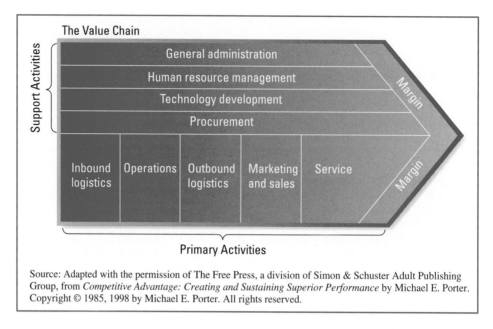

The Value Chain

Support Activities

General administration

Human resource management

Technology development

Procurement

Margin

| Inbound logistics | Operations | Outbound logistics | Marketing and sales | Service |

Margin

Primary Activities

Competitive Advantage.[2] In competitive terms, value is the amount that buyers are willing to pay for what a firm provides them. In reality, value can be measured by total revenue, a reflection of the price a firm's product commands and the quantity it can sell. A firm is profitable to the extent that the value it receives exceeds the total costs involved in creating its product or service. Creating value for buyers that exceeds the costs of production (i.e., margin) is a key concept used in analyzing a firm's competitive position.

Porter described two different categories of activities. First, five primary activities—inbound logistics, operations, outbound logistics, marketing and sales, and service—contribute to the physical creation of the product or service, its sale and transfer to the buyer, and its service after the sale. Second, support activities—procurement, technology development, human resource management, and firm infrastructure—either add value by themselves or add value through important relationships with both primary activities and other support activities. Exhibit 3.1 illustrates Porter's value chain.

To get the most out of value-chain analysis, managers need to view the concept in its broadest context, without regard to the boundaries of their own organization. That is, they must place their organization within a more encompassing value system that includes the firm's suppliers, customers, and alliance partners. For example, steel producers, auto parts makers, vehicle assemblers, and car dealers constitute the automobile value system, and the value chain of one player contributes to the creation of value at another player. In effect, the efficient business operations of an auto parts maker, such as Magna, contribute to the value chain of an assembler that is striving to produce an attractive, reasonably priced car.

Understanding how value is created within the organization is, therefore, not enough; managers must become aware of how value is created for other organizations that are involved in the overall supply chain or distribution channel in which the firm participates.[3] Moreover, they need to appreciate that companies add value by means of relationships among activities within the organization as well as activities outside the organization, such as those activities associated with customers and suppliers.[4] In the following sections, we discuss each of the categories of activities and present examples that highlight those interrelationships, as well as the application of the value chain in both the manufacturing and the service sectors. The value chain is often viewed as primarily relevant to manufacturing operations. Indeed, the basic concepts such as inbound logistics, operations, and procurement draw from the traditional ideas about creating value that have arisen in the physical production of goods. However, we can readily see that operations, the process of transforming inputs into outputs, takes place as much in factories as in accounting or law firms, in airline companies or in retail stores. Moreover, our examples suggest that how the primary and support activities of a given firm are configured and deployed will often depend on industry conditions and the extent to which the company is service or manufacturing oriented.

Primary Activities

Five generic categories of primary activities are involved in competing in any industry, as shown in Exhibit 3.2. Each category is divisible into a number of distinct activities that depend on the particular industry and the firm's strategy.[5]

Exhibit 3.2
The Value Chain: Some Factors to Consider in Assessing a Firm's Primary Activities

Inbound Logistics	Operations	Outbound Logistics	Marketing and Sales	Service
• Location of distribution facilities to minimize shipping times. • Excellent material and inventory control systems. • Systems to reduce time to send "returns" to suppliers. • Warehouse layout and designs to increase efficiency of operations for incoming materials.	• Efficient plant operations to minimize costs. • Appropriate level of automation in manufacturing. • Quality production control systems to reduce costs and enhance quality. • Efficient plant layout and workflow design.	• Effective shipping processes to provide quick delivery and minimize damages. • Efficient finished goods warehousing processes. • Shipping of goods in large lot sizes to minimize transportation costs. • Quality material-handling equipment to increase order-picking efficiency.	• Highly motivated and competent sales force. • Innovative approaches to promotion and advertising. • Selection of most appropriate distribution channels. • Proper identification of customer segments and needs. • Effective pricing strategies.	• Effective use of procedures to solicit customer feedback and to act on information. • Quick response to customer needs and emergencies. • Ability to furnish replacement parts as required. • Effective management of parts and equipment inventory. • Quality of service personnel and ongoing training. • Appropriate warranty and guarantee policies.

Source: Adapted with permission of The Free Press, a division of Simon & Schuster Adult Publishing Group, from *Competitive Advantage: Creating and Sustaining Superior Performance* by Michael E. Porter. Copyright © 1985, 1998 by Michael E. Porter. All rights reserved.

Inbound Logistics Inbound logistics are primarily associated with receiving, storing, and distributing inputs to the product. They include material handling, warehousing, inventory control, vehicle scheduling, and returns to suppliers.

Just-in-time (JIT) inventory systems, for example, were designed to achieve efficient inbound logistics. Toyota epitomizes JIT inventory systems in which parts deliveries arrive at the assembly plants only hours before they are needed. JIT systems play a vital role in fulfilling Toyota's commitment to fill a buyer's new car order in just five days.[6] This standard is in sharp contrast to most competitors that require approximately 30 days' notice to build vehicles. How can Toyota achieve such fast turnaround? Its 360 key suppliers are linked on-line with the company in a virtual assembly line: suppliers load parts onto trucks in the order in which they will be installed; parts are stacked on trucks in the same place each time to help workers unload them quickly; and deliveries are required to meet a rigid schedule, with as many as 12 trucks a day and no more than four hours between trucks.

Operations Operations concern all activities associated with transforming inputs into the final product form, including machining, packaging, assembly, testing, printing, and facility operations.

Creating environmentally friendly manufacturing is one way a firm can use operations to achieve competitive advantage. Shaw Industries (now part of Berkshire Hathaway), a world-class competitor in the floor-covering industry, is well known for its strong concern for the environment.[7] It has been successful in reducing the expenses associated with the disposal of dangerous chemicals and other waste products from its manufacturing operations. Its environmental endeavours have multiple payoffs. Shaw has received numerous awards for its recycling efforts—awards that enhance its corporate reputation.

Examples of Shaw's successes include EcoSolution Q, the industry's first nylon covering containing recycled content and the most successful product launch in the company's history. Shaw's residential staple polyester carpet, made from virtually 100 percent petroleum-based materials, keeps one billion plastic containers out of landfills each year through recycling. Shaw is also pioneering other innovative recycling solutions, including recycled nylon for automotive under-hood applications and ground-up carpet as an ingredient in road materials and fibre-reinforced concrete.

Outbound Logistics The activities of outbound logistics are associated with collecting, storing, and distributing the product or service to buyers. They include finished goods, warehousing, material handling, delivery vehicle operation, order processing, and scheduling.

Campbell Soup Company uses an electronic network to facilitate its continuous-replenishment program with its most progressive retailers, including Loblaw and Wal-Mart.[8] Each morning, retailers electronically inform Campbell of their product needs and of the level of inventories in their distribution centres. Campbell uses that information to forecast future demand and to determine which products require replenishment (based on the inventory limits previously established with each retailer). Trucks leave Campbell's shipping plant that afternoon and arrive at the retailers' distribution centres the same day. The program cuts the inventories of participating retailers from about a four- to a two-weeks' supply. Campbell Soup Company achieved this improvement because it knows the inventories of key retailers and can deploy supplies when they are most needed.

The Campbell Soup example also illustrates the win-win benefits of exemplary value-chain activities. Both the supplier (Campbell) and its buyers (retailers) come out ahead. Since the retailer makes more money on Campbell's products delivered through continuous replenishment, it has an incentive to carry a broader line and give the company greater shelf space. Campbell found that after it introduced the program, sales of its products grew twice as fast through participating retailers as through all other retailers. Not surprisingly, supermarket chains love such programs.

Strategy Spotlight 3.1

Redirecting Marketing Efforts at Staples

On his first day as CEO of Staples Business Depot, one of North America's largest office supply chains, Ron Sargent put on the black pants, black shoes, and red shirt that associates wear and headed to the Staples store in Brighton, Massachusetts. This is Staples's first store (opened in May 1986), and by going there he was trying to rally the Staples troops around a concept called "Back to Brighton." It was a symbolic message to the members of the organization that they were going to improve service and refocus on their core customer base: the small-business customer. After growing rapidly for most of its 16 years, Staples encountered a decline in performance during 2000. To make matters worse, its main rival, Office Depot, was experiencing a competitive rebound. Thus, Staples was forced to reexamine every aspect of its business.

In recent years, the company had started catering to the casual customer. But this was not a profitable segment. So Ron removed 600 items that appealed to the casual customer and replaced them with 700 items that appealed to the small-business customer. The chain improved the quality of the merchandise they offered because businesses have more demanding needs than the casual customer. It stopped advertising in the Sunday newspapers, which businesses do not read, and put more money into direct marketing. They also upgraded their Web site and doubled their direct sales force. Taking the money that was originally allocated to advertising, Ron invested it in training for associates and added more store staff to provide better service.

Sources: M. Roman, "Ronald Sargent: Straightening Out Staples," *BusinessWeek*, September 17, 2001, pp. 9–11; and A. Overholt, "New Leaders, New Agenda," *Fast Company*, June 2002, p. 52.

Marketing and Sales Marketing and sales include the efforts a firm engages in to gather market intelligence and understand its customers, the activities associated with purchases of products and services by end users, and the inducements used to get them to make purchases.[9] They include market research, consumer analysis, advertising, promotion, sales force, quoting, channel selection, channel relations, and pricing.[10] It is not always enough to have a great product. Managers must also convince their channel partners that it is in their best interests not only to carry the product but also to market it in a way that is consistent with their strategy. Consider Monsanto's efforts at educating distributors to improve the value proposition of its line of Saflex windows.[11] The products introduced in the early 1990s had a superior attribute; the window design permitted laminators to form an exceptional type of glass by sandwiching a plastic sheet interlayer between two pieces of glass. Not only is this product stronger and a better shield against ultraviolet radiation than regular glass, but when cracked, it adheres to the plastic sheet—an excellent safety feature for both cars and homes.

Despite these benefits, Monsanto had a hard time convincing laminators and window manufacturers to carry products made with Saflex. According to Melissa Toledo, brand manager at Monsanto, "Saflex was priced at a 30 percent premium above traditional glass, and the various stages in the value chain (distributors and retailers) didn't think there would be a demand for such an expensive glass product." Monsanto's solution? It subsequently reintroduced Saflex as KeepSafe and worked to coordinate the product's value propositions. By analyzing the experiences of all of the players in the supply chain, it was able to create marketing programs that helped each build a business aimed at selling its products. As Toledo reported, "We want to know how they go about selling those types of products, what challenges they face, and what they think they need to sell our products. This helps us a lot when we try to provide them with these needs." Thus, marketing is often a key element of competitive advantage.

Strategy Spotlight 3.1 discusses how Staples Business Depot redirected its marketing efforts.

Service Service consists of the range of activities associated with enhancing or maintaining the value of the product, such as installation, maintenance, support, repair, training, parts supply, and product adjustment.

Internet-based retailers (etailers) provide many examples of how superb customer service is critical for adding value. Nearly all etailers have faced a similar problem: they figured that the Web's self-service model would save them millions in customer service costs. But that was the last place they could afford to shave costs.[12] According to market researcher Datamonitor, 7.8 percent of abandoned online shopping carts could be salvaged through an effective customer service solution—an impressive $6.1 billion in lost annual sales. Bill Bass, senior vice president of ecommerce at catalogue retailer Lands' End, Inc., claimed, "If there's a train wreck to happen, it's going to be around customer service."

At Sephora.com, a customer service representative taking a phone call from a repeat customer has instant access to, for example, what shade of lipstick the customer likes best. This helps the rep cross-sell by suggesting a matching shade of lip gloss. CEO Jim Wiggett expects such personalization to build loyalty and boost sales per customer. Swisschalet.ca guides customers to build personal profiles of their food preferences to make ordering online easier, while Pizza Pizza, an Ontario-based pizza chain, allows online customers to repeat their recent orders with the press of a single button. Exhibit 3.3 shows the value chain for a commercial airline company and identifies specific activities within each generic category.

Support Activities

Support activities might not directly add value to the creation of the product, but they provide for and facilitate the primary activities and ensure that they operate efficiently and effectively. Support activities can be divided into four generic categories, as shown in Exhibit 3.4. As with primary activities, each category is divisible into a number of distinct value activities that are specific to a particular industry. For example, technology development's discrete activities may include component design, feature design, field testing, process engineering, and technology selection. Similarly, procurement may be divided into activities such as qualifying new suppliers, purchasing different groups of inputs, and monitoring supplier performance.

Procurement Procurement refers to the function of purchasing inputs to be used in the firm's value chain. Purchased inputs include raw materials, supplies, and other consumable items as well as assets such as machinery, laboratory equipment, office equipment, and buildings. Note that the issues here refer to the activities relating to purchasing inputs rather than the inputs themselves.

Microsoft has enhanced its procurement process (and the quality of its suppliers) by providing formal reviews to its suppliers. For example, one of Microsoft's divisions has extended the review process used for employees to its outside suppliers.[13] The evaluation system that Microsoft developed has helped clarify its expectations. An executive noted, "We had one supplier—this was before the new system—that would have scored a 1.2 out of 5. After we started giving this feedback, and the supplier understood our expectations, its performance improved dramatically. Within six months, it scored a 4. If you'd asked me before we began the feedback system, I would have said that was impossible."

Technology Development Every value activity embodies technology.[14] The array of technologies employed in most firms is very broad, ranging from technologies used to prepare documents and transport goods to those embodied in processes and equipment or the product itself. Technology development related to the product and its features supports the entire value chain, while other technology development is associated with particular primary or support activities. Shoppers Drug Mart's "HealthWATCH Med Ready"™

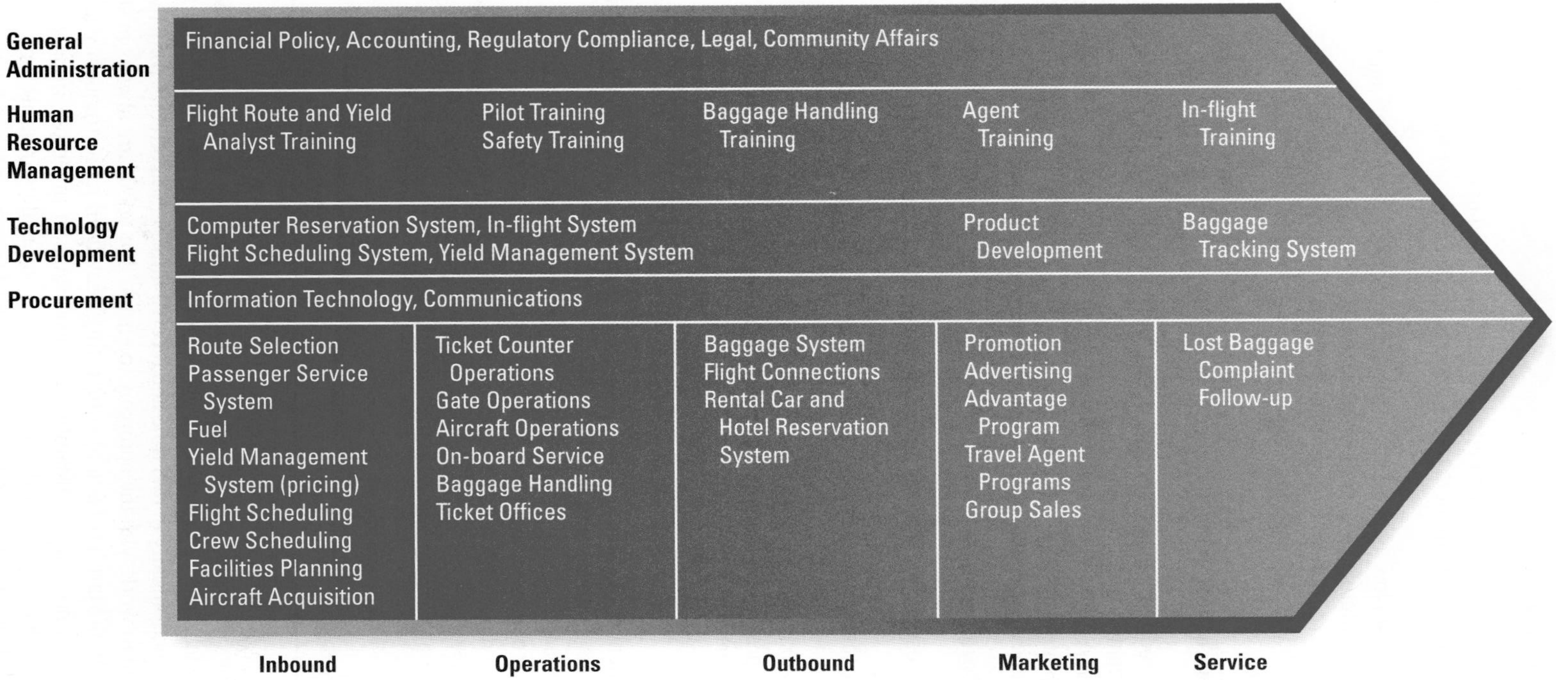

	Inbound	Operations	Outbound	Marketing	Service
General Administration	Financial Policy, Accounting, Regulatory Compliance, Legal, Community Affairs				
Human Resource Management	Flight Route and Yield Analyst Training	Pilot Training Safety Training	Baggage Handling Training	Agent Training	In-flight Training
Technology Development	Computer Reservation System, In-flight System Flight Scheduling System, Yield Management System			Product Development	Baggage Tracking System
Procurement	Information Technology, Communications				
	Route Selection Passenger Service System Fuel Yield Management System (pricing) Flight Scheduling Crew Scheduling Facilities Planning Aircraft Acquisition	Ticket Counter Operations Gate Operations Aircraft Operations On-board Service Baggage Handling Ticket Offices	Baggage System Flight Connections Rental Car and Hotel Reservation System	Promotion Advertising Advantage Program Travel Agent Programs Group Sales	Lost Baggage Complaint Follow-up

Source: Adapted with permission of The Free Press, a Division of Simon & Schuster, Inc., from *Competitive Advantage: Creating and Sustaining Superior Performance* by Michael E. Porter. Copyright © 1985, 1998 by Michael E. Porter. All rights reserved.

Exhibit 3.3
Airline Company Value Chain

Exhibit 3.4
The Value Chain:
Some Factors
to Consider in
Assessing a Firm's
Support Activities

General Administration

♦ Effective planning systems to attain overall goals and objectives.
♦ Ability of top management to anticipate and act on key environmental trends and events.
♦ Ability to obtain low-cost funds for capital expenditures and working capital.
♦ Excellent relationships with diverse stakeholder groups.
♦ Ability to coordinate and integrate activities across the "value system."
♦ High visibility and consistency to inculcate organizational culture, reputation, and values.

Human Resource Management

♦ Effective recruiting, development, and retention mechanisms for employees.
♦ Quality relations with trade unions.
♦ Quality work environment to maximize overall employee performance and minimize absenteeism.
♦ Reward and incentive programs to motivate all employees.

Technology Development

♦ Effective research and development activities for process and product initiatives.
♦ Positive collaborative relationships between R&D and other departments.
♦ State-of-the-art facilities and equipment.
♦ Culture that enhances creativity and innovation.
♦ Excellent professional qualifications of personnel.
♦ Ability to meet critical deadlines.

Procurement

♦ Procurement of raw material inputs to optimize quality and speed and to minimize the associated costs.
♦ Development of collaborative "win-win" relationships with suppliers.
♦ Effective procedures to purchase advertising and media services.
♦ Analysis and selection of alternate sources of inputs to minimize dependence on one supplier.
♦ Ability to make proper lease versus buy decisions.

Source: Reprinted with the permission of The Free Press, a division of Simon & Schuster Adult Publishing Group, from *Competitive Advantage: Creating and Sustaining Superior Performance* by Michael E. Porter. Copyright © 1985, 1998 by Michael E. Porter. All rights reserved.

program serves to protect patients against over or competing medications, as well as increase the filling, re-filling, and transfers of prescriptions by its customers. Wal-Mart invests heavily in technology to support its inbound logistics and its operations. All its suppliers are linked electronically in real time and receive information directly form the stores. They are expected to work with the company to ensure that goods are always in stock and on the shelves.[15] Wal-Mart has been also investing heavily in radio frequency identification (RFID) tags that promise to streamline the processing of inventory in its warehouses and throughout the delivery network. Already, crates and pallets from its larger suppliers such as Procter & Gamble, Kimberly-Clark, and Levi Strauss are tagged with microchips so that electronic readers at the entrances and exits of its massive storage facilities pick up the signals and track the goods electronically as they move in and out. The technology

SAS and Employee Turnover

Jeffrey Pfeffer, professor of organizational behaviour at Stanford University, asked a managing partner at a San Francisco law firm about its employee turnover rate. Turnover had increased from 25 percent to 30 percent over the last few years. The law firm's solution: increase recruitment of new employees. Pfeffer's response was, "What kind of doctor would you be if your patient was bleeding faster and faster, and your only response was to increase the rate of transfusion?"

It's not difficult to calculate the cost of a new hire, but what does it cost a firm when employees leave? Consider the approach taken by SAS Institute, a software developer with 5,000 employees. David Russo, director of human resources, estimates that the average turnover in the industry is 20 percent per year. SAS's turnover rate is only 4 percent. SAS employees earn on average $60,000 a year. Multiplying the difference in the turnover rate by the number of employees, their average annual salary shows that SAS has a cost savings of nearly $50 million.

What can a firm do with an extra $50 million? SAS spends a large portion of this sum on its employees. The SAS gym, cafeteria (with pianist), on-site medical and child care, flexible work schedules, employer retirement contributions of 15 percent of an employee's pay, and a host of other family-friendly programs help keep SAS's employee turnover level well below the industry average. Even after all these perks, SAS still has money left over.

Russo's message? "This is not tree-huggery. This is money in the bank."

Sources: R. Levering and M. Moskowitz, "The 100 Best Companies to Work For," *Fortune*, January 20, 2003, pp. 127–52; and A. M. Webber, "Danger: Toxic Company," *Fast Company*, November 1998, pp. 152–61.

offers massive benefits in tracking and locating goods, improving both the speed and accuracy in the handling of billions of dollars of inventory that passes through the channel.

Human Resource Management Human resource management consists of activities involved in the recruiting, hiring, training, development, and compensation of all types of personnel.[16] It supports both primary and support activities (e.g., hiring of engineers and scientists) and the entire value chain (e.g., negotiations with labour unions).

Starbucks' baristas are unquestionably the soul of the corporation and essential to its success. Like all great service companies, JetBlue Airways Corporation is concerned about hiring great employees as well.[17] But this company found it difficult to entice college graduates to commit to a career as a flight attendant. JetBlue developed a highly innovative recruitment program—a one-year contract that gives employees a chance to travel, meet people, and then decide what else they might like to do. They also introduced the idea of training a friend and employee together so that they could share a job. With such employee-friendly initiatives, JetBlue has been very successful in attracting talent.

Employees often leave a firm because they reach a plateau and begin to look for new opportunities and challenges.[18] AT&T strives to retain such people with Resource Link, an in-house temporary service that enables employees with diverse management, technical, or professional skills to market their abilities to different departments for short-term assignments. This not only enables professionals to broaden their experience base but also provides a mechanism for other parts of the organization to benefit from new sources of ideas.

Dofasco's motto, "Our product is steel. Our strength is people." is well known within and outside its industry and reflects the company's deep-seated belief in the value of its human capital. It manifests itself in many aspects of the company's operations—in the selection and training of its employees, in the exclusive promotions from within its ranks, and in its annual staff social events.

Strategy Spotlight 3.2 describes how SAS Institute's innovative approach to human resources provides an insightful financial justification for the broad array of benefits it provides to employees.

General Administration General administration consists of a number of activities, including general management, planning, finance, accounting, legal and government affairs, quality management, and information systems. Administration typically supports the entire value chain and not individual activities.

Although general administration is sometimes viewed only as overhead, it can be a powerful source of competitive advantage. In a telephone operating company, for example, negotiating and maintaining ongoing relations with regulatory bodies can be among the most important activities for competitive advantage. In a similar vein, effective information systems can contribute significantly to cost position, while in some industries, top management plays a vital role in dealing with important buyers.[19]

Demonstrating strong symbolic leadership, the chief executive officer of BCE Inc., Michael Sabia, declined his bonus for the second time in three years. He did not accept the $1.47 million award, even though the firm did meet its targets. His refusal stemmed from billing glitches that plagued the wireless unit and that led thousands of frustrated customers to complain about the service. Such decisions demonstrate exemplary management of general administration.

Legal services can contribute real value to a firm in many ways. One example is ensuring the protection of a firm's intellectual property through patents, trademarks, and copyrights. Although many companies are not aware of the earnings potential of their patent holdings, Texas Instruments (TI) is one notable exception.[20] In essence, TI began investigating the income-generation potential of its patent portfolio in the mid-1980s, out of desperation, when it faced bankruptcy. Since then, TI has earned an impressive $4 billion in patent royalties; its licensing revenues are estimated to be $800 million per year. In May 1999, TI signed yet another licensing pact for its semiconductor patents with Hyundai, an agreement that is expected to generate a total of $1 billion in additional royalties over seven years.

Strategy Spotlight 3.3 discusses how Gary Kelly, Southwest Airlines's chief financial officer, adds value for his company.

RESOURCE-BASED VIEW OF THE FIRM

To carry out the activities of its value chain, a firm needs resources. A firm's resource base comprises all the inputs necessary for the performance of each of the activities, irrespective of who owns or controls those resources. Frequently, the firm contracts for the use of particular resources, while it owns other resources and can utilize them at will. In either case, the way in which resources are utilized by the organization is a critical decision, and success depends, to a large extent, on the appropriateness of such decisions by the management of the organization. Managers, though, recognize that the ability of a firm's resources to confer competitive advantage(s) cannot be determined without taking into consideration the broader competitive context. To that end, and under the resource-based view (RBV) of the firm, managers combine two perspectives: (1) the internal analysis of phenomena within a company and (2) an external analysis of the industry and its competitive environment.[21] The RBV goes beyond the traditional SWOT analysis by *integrating the* internal and external perspectives. It is a very useful framework for gaining insights on why some competitors are more profitable than others. It is also helpful in developing strategies for individual businesses and diversified firms since it reveals how core competencies embedded in a firm can help it exploit new product and market opportunities.

In the two sections that follow, we discuss the three key types of resources that firms possess: tangible resources, intangible resources, and organizational capabilities. Then, we

How a Firm's General Administration Can Create Value

A firm's general administration can significantly impact its performance. Southwest's chief financial officer, Gary Kelly, is a key contributor to the airline's solid financial performance.

While the rest of the airline industry was laying off workers by the thousands, Southwest did not furlough anyone. Its ability to shine in dire times is a result of its conservative financial culture that values a large cash balance and low debt. Southwest began conserving funds in 2000, when it saw a recession on the horizon. After installing a new computer system and renegotiating contracts with vendors, it managed to boost its cash on hand from $600 million to about $1 billion.

Through the years, Wall Street analysts have criticized Kelly's conservative approach and goaded him to use the extra cash to make acquisitions or buy back stock. Goldman Sachs's airline analyst actually called the balance sheet "too strong." Yet, it is such fiscal preparedness that has kept the company's debt-to-capital ratio at around 40 percent (compared to the industry average of about 70 percent), which allows for more flexibility during tough times.

Kelly has also come up with some creative measures to get through the recent slumping economy and terrorism threats. For example, he rescheduled the delivery of 19 planes from Boeing by developing an arrangement between Boeing and a collection of banks. This arrangement, whereby the banks formed a group called the Amor Trust, allowed the trust to take delivery from Boeing as scheduled and store the planes in the Mojave Desert until Southwest needed them. The idea was to strike a balance between maintaining the good relationship with Boeing, its only supplier of planes, and holding off spending the cash on the planes it does not yet need. Darryl Jenkins, director of the Aviation Institute at George Washington University, attributes Southwest's success to two things: "Consistency, and the fact that they don't listen to other people."

Sources: W. Zellner and M. Arnadt, "Holding Steady," *BusinessWeek*, February 3, 2003; and I. Mount, "Southwest's Gary Kelly: A Tip of the Hat to the CFO at the One Airline Still Making Money," *Business 2.0*, February 12, 2002, pp. 5–7.

address the conditions under which these resources can enable a firm to attain a sustainable competitive advantage.

It is important to note that resources by themselves typically do not yield a competitive advantage. Even if a basketball team recruited an all-star centre, there would be little chance of victory if the other members of the team were continually outplayed by their opponents or if the coach's attitude was so negative that everyone, including the centre, became unwilling to put forth their best efforts. And imagine how many World Series titles Joe Torre would have won as manager of the New York Yankees if none of the players he signed could throw fastballs over 70 miles per hour. Although the all-star centre and the baseball manager are unquestionably valuable resources, they would *not* enable the organization to attain advantages under these circumstances.

The RBV allows managers to build on the insights from their SWOT analysis. SWOT is useful for identifying internal strengths and capabilities but does not reveal how to turn those into a competitive advantage nor how rapidly the environment could change, allowing imitators to come into the market and erode such advantage. A firm's strengths and capabilities, no matter how unique or impressive, may not enable it to achieve a competitive advantage in the marketplace. It is akin to employing a highly creative product designer in a firm that produces low-cost commodity products. If anything, the additional expense could erode the firm's cost advantage. If a firm builds its strategy on a capability that, by itself, cannot create or sustain competitive advantage, it is essentially wasting resources. RBV explicitly directs managers to integrate the internal and external perspectives and helps them develop strategies that build on core competencies and enable the firm to achieve sustainable competitive advantages.

Types of Firm Resources

Resources come in numerous forms. They are the inputs into a firm's production processes, and they range from widely available commodities to extremely scarce and hard-to-develop unique skills that might be responsible for the ultimate success of the firm's products. Resources include all assets, capabilities, organizational processes, information, knowledge, systems, and so forth controlled by a firm, which enable it to develop and implement value-creating strategies. Resources are fundamental to the firm's operations, and each firm possesses a unique bundle of resources. Moreover, resource accumulation is typically constrained and time consuming. A firm's strategic choices are limited by the resources that are available to it at a particular time and by its ability to accumulate additional resources.[22] Below, we define the three major types of resources.

Tangible Resources Assets that are relatively easy to identify, measure, and value are called tangible resources. They include concrete, physical assets such as real estate, cash, production facilities and equipment, raw materials, and components. Their value arises from their physical characteristics such as their location, capacity, and features. They may represent essential inputs to a firm's operations, but only seldom can they provide the basis for competitive advantage, mainly because they are easy to identify, describe, and imitate. Among its tangible resources, a firm can enlist its cash and cash equivalent assets, its accounts receivable, its borrowing capacity, natural resources and raw materials (either in the ground or on hand), components, parts, inventory, plant, machinery and equipment, facilities, and its physical proximity to customers and suppliers.

Intangible Resources Assets that are harder to identify and quantify are called intangible resources. They are not concrete and can be elusive; yet, they are potentially invaluable inputs into a firm's operations. They include brand names, company reputations, knowledge, technology, patents, copyrights and trademarks, trade secrets, expertise, and experience.

Intangible assets are combined with tangible assets to create the firm's product offerings. Interestingly, it is not the relative amount of tangible to intangible inputs that determines the nature or the value of the output. For example, Holt Renfrew the upscale retail store chain and Club Monaco the specialty fashion retailer, utilize real estate, store fixtures, cash machines, a computer network, and merchandise—all tangible assets. These combine with their brand names; experienced staff; marketing campaigns; accumulated reputation for quality, service, and support; management systems; and policies and procedures for ordering, pricing, merchandising, and selling, to produce the value that is desired by their clientele. Although substantial tangible resources are required for the retail value to be produced, all the real value, at least what is most desirable to their customers, is created by the intangibles.

Intangible resources are much more difficult for competitors (and for a firm's own managers) to account for or imitate since they are typically embedded in unique routines and practices that have evolved and accumulated over time. These include human resources (e.g., experience and capability of employees, as well as trust in and effectiveness of work teams), innovation resources (e.g., technical and scientific expertise and ideas), and reputation resources (e.g., brand name, reputation with suppliers for fairness and with customers for reliability and product quality). A firm's culture may also be a resource that provides competitive advantage.[23]

One might not think that motorcycles, clothes, toys, and restaurants have much in common. Yet, Harley-Davidson has entered all of these product and service markets by capitalizing on its strong brand image, a valuable intangible resource.[24] It has used that image to sell accessories, clothing, and toys, and it has licensed the Harley-Davidson Café in New York City to provide further exposure for its brand name and products.

Organizational Capabilities Organizational capabilities are not specific tangible or intangible assets but the competencies and skills that a firm employs to transform those assets into outputs.[25] In short, they refer to what a firm does with the resources under its control. They concern an organization's capacity to make decisions, coordinate the use of tangible and intangible resources, and leverage these to bring about a desired end. Organizational capabilities are, in effect, the processes and routines that arise from numerous exchanges of information and knowledge and which guide the interactions of the firm's employees. Examples of organizational capabilities are lean manufacturing, excellent product development capabilities, superb innovation processes, and flexibility in manufacturing processes.

Gillette's capability to combine several technologies has been one of the keys to its unparalleled success in the wet-shaving industry. Technologies that are central to its product development efforts include its expertise concerning the physiology of facial hair and skin, the metallurgy of blade strength and sharpness, the dynamics of a cartridge moving across skin, and the physics of a razor blade severing the hair—highly specialized areas for which Gillette has unique capabilities. Combining these technologies has helped the company to develop innovative products such as the Excel, Sensor Excel, and MACH 3 shaving systems.

Dell Inc., with annual revenues of $49 billion and net profits of $3 billion, made its mark by competing in a quasi commodity market for personal computers, but it differentiated itself by pioneering a direct sales approach, with user-configurable products to address the diverse needs of the individual, corporate, and institutional customer base. Dell integrated many tangible resources, intangible resources, and organizational capabilities, and it has continued to maintain its competitive advantage by further strengthening its value-chain activities and the interrelationships that are critical to satisfying the largest market opportunities. They achieved this by (1) implementing ecommerce direct sales and support processes that took into account the sophisticated buying habits of the largest markets and (2) matching their operations to the purchase options by adopting flexible assembly processes, while leaving inventory management to the extensive supplier network. They have sustained those advantages by investing in intangible resources such as proprietary assembly methods and packaging configurations that help to protect against the threat of imitation.

Unquestionably, 3M also has developed a competitive advantage utilizing intangible resources that bring innovative products to its markets. Not only does it employ a plethora of highly knowledgeable and curious scientists in its labs, but it frees 15 percent of their time for unrestricted experimentation and tinkering. It encourages the sharing of findings and best practices among all its staff and, finally, sets minimum sales targets that contain at least 30 percent of sales from products less than five years old. As a result, it has one of the highest numbers of patents to its name and has brought almost 50,000 innovations to the market within its 100-year history.[26]

FIRM RESOURCES AND SUSTAINABLE COMPETITIVE ADVANTAGES

As we have mentioned, resources alone are not a basis for competitive advantages, nor are advantages sustainable over time. In some cases, a resource or capability helps a firm to increase its revenues or to lower costs, but the firm derives only a temporary advantage because competitors quickly imitate or substitute for it. Many ecommerce businesses saw their profits seriously eroded because new (or existing) competitors easily duplicated

Exhibit 3.5
Four Criteria for
Assessing Resources
and Capabilities

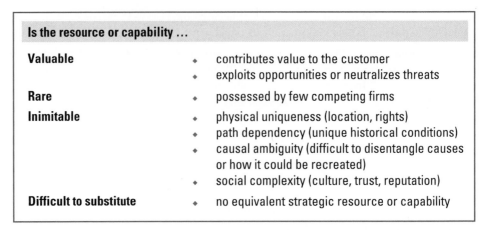

Is the resource or capability ...	
Valuable	◆ contributes value to the customer
	◆ exploits opportunities or neutralizes threats
Rare	◆ possessed by few competing firms
Inimitable	◆ physical uniqueness (location, rights)
	◆ path dependency (unique historical conditions)
	◆ causal ambiguity (difficult to disentangle causes or how it could be recreated)
	◆ social complexity (culture, trust, reputation)
Difficult to substitute	◆ no equivalent strategic resource or capability

their business model. Consider, for example, Priceline.com whose offerings enabled customers to place bids online for airline tickets and a wide variety of other products. Its resources (i.e., its software development knowledge) and its capabilities (i.e., its means to expand from one product line to others) were not sufficient foundations for a sustainable competitive advantage. It was simply too easy for competitors—a consortium of major airlines—to duplicate Priceline's products and services.

For a resource or a capability to provide a firm with the potential for a sustainable competitive advantage, it must meet four criteria.[27] These criteria are summarized in Exhibit 3.5. First, the resource must be valuable in the sense that it exploits opportunities and/or neutralizes threats in the firm's environment. Second, it must be rare among the firm's current and potential competitors. Third, the resource must be difficult for competitors to imitate. Fourth, the resource must have no strategically equivalent substitutes. Let's examine each of these criteria.

Is the Resource Valuable? Resources can be a source of competitive advantage only when they are valuable. They are valuable when they contribute to the fulfillment of customers' needs at a price the customers are willing to pay—that is, when they can be deployed to meet under-served needs better than the competitors can and when their cost of deployment is lower than the value placed on fulfillment of the need by the customer. In those conditions, resources are valuable because they enable a firm to formulate and implement strategies to exploit opportunities, minimize threats, and improve its efficiency and effectiveness.

The fact that firm resources must be valuable in order to be considered as potential sources of competitive advantage reveals an important complementary relationship among environmental models (e.g., SWOT and the five-forces analysis) and the resource-based model. Environmental models isolate those firm resources that exploit opportunities and/or neutralize threats. The resource-based model then suggests what additional characteristics these resources must possess if they are to support a sustained competitive advantage.

Is the Resource Rare? If competitors or potential competitors also possess the same valuable resource, it is not a source of competitive advantage because all of these firms can potentially exploit that resource in the same way. Common strategies based on such a resource would give no single firm an advantage. For a resource to provide competitive advantages, it must be uncommon—that is, rare relative to other competitors.

This argument can apply to bundles of valuable firm resources that are used to formulate and develop strategies. Some strategies require a mix of resources—tangible assets, intangible assets, and organizational capabilities. If a particular bundle of firm resources is not rare, then a number of firms will be able to conceive of and implement the strategies in question. Thus, such strategies will not be a source of competitive advantage, even if the resources in question are valuable.

Can the Resource Be Imitated Easily? Inimitability (difficulty in imitating) is a key to value creation because it constrains competition.[28] If a resource is inimitable, then any advantages generated are more likely to be sustainable. Having a resource that competitors can easily copy generates only temporary value. This has important implications. Since managers often fail to apply this test, they tend to base long-term strategies on resources that are imitable. IBP (Iowa Beef Processors) became the first meat-packing company in North America to modernize by building a set of assets (automated plants located in cattle-producing states) and capabilities (low-cost "disassembly" of carcasses) that earned returns on assets of 1.3 percent in the 1970s. By the late 1980s, however, ConAgra and Cargill had imitated these resources, and IBP's profitability fell by nearly 70 percent, to 0.4 percent.

Monster.com entered the executive-recruiting market by providing, in essence, a substitute for traditional bricks-and-mortar headhunting firms. Although Monster.com's resources are rare and valuable, they are subject to imitation by new rivals—other dot-com firms. Indeed, headhunter.com, jobsearch.com, and hotjobs.com are but a few of the many firms that have entered, and some 30,000 online job boards exist today. It would be difficult for any firm to attain a sustainable advantage in this industry.

But an advantage based on inimitability won't last forever either. Competitors will eventually discover a way to copy most valuable resources. However, managers can forestall this and sustain profits for a while longer by developing strategies around resources that have at least one of the following four characteristics.[29]

Physical Uniqueness   The first source of inimitability is physical uniqueness, which, by definition, is inherently difficult to copy. A beautiful resort location, mineral rights, or Merck & Co.'s pharmaceutical patents simply cannot be imitated. Locations, technologies, patents, monopoly licenses, and exclusive permits are among the resources that convey uniqueness and could possible lead to competitive advantage.

It should be noted that many managers believe that several of their resources may fall into this category, but on close inspection, few do. Moreover, many of those advantages diminish with time as alternative locations are developed, patents and permits expire, and monopolists become regulated.

Path Dependency   A greater number of resources cannot be imitated because of what economists refer to as path dependency. This simply means that resources are unique and, therefore, scarce because of all that has happened in the course of their development and/or accumulation. Competitors cannot go out and buy these resources quickly and easily; they must be built up over time in ways that are difficult to accelerate.

The Gerber Products Co. brand name for baby food is an example of a resource that is potentially inimitable. Recreating Gerber's brand loyalty would be a time-consuming process that competitors could not expedite, even with expensive marketing campaigns. Similarly, the loyalty and trust that Southwest Airlines employees feel for their firm and its co-founder, Herb Kelleher, is the result of a resource that has been built up over a long period of time. Also, a crash R&D program generally cannot replicate a successful technology when research findings cumulate. Clearly, these path-dependent conditions build protection for the original resource. The benefits from experience and learning through trial and error cannot be duplicated overnight.

Causal Ambiguity   Inimitability may also arise because it is impossible to disentangle the causes or possible explanations for either what the valuable resource is or how it can be recreated. What is the root of 3M's innovation process? One can study it and draw up a list of possible factors, but it is a complex, multilayered process that is difficult to understand and would be hard to imitate.

In many cases, causally ambiguous resources are organizational capabilities. They often involve a complex web of social interactions that may even depend on particular individuals. When Continental and United tried to mimic the successful low-cost strategy of Southwest Airlines, the planes, routes, and fast gate turnarounds were not the most difficult aspects for them to copy. Those were all rather easy to observe and, at least in principle, easy to duplicate. However, they could not replicate Southwest's culture of fun, family, frugality, and focus since no one can clearly specify exactly what that culture is or how it came to be.

Social Complexity   A final reason that a firm's resources may be inimitable is that they may reflect a high level of social complexity. Such phenomena are typically beyond the ability of firms to systematically manage or influence. When competitive advantages are based on social complexity, it is difficult for other firms to imitate them.

A wide variety of firm resources may be considered socially complex. Examples include interpersonal relations among the managers of a firm, its culture, or its reputation with its suppliers and customers. In many of these cases, it is easy to specify how these socially complex resources add value to a firm. Hence, there is little or no causal ambiguity surrounding the link between them and competitive advantage. But an understanding that certain firm attributes, such as quality relations among managers, can improve a firm's efficiency does not necessarily lead to systematic efforts to imitate them. Such social engineering efforts are beyond the capabilities of most firms.

Although complex physical technology is not included among the sources of inimitability, the exploitation of physical technology in a firm typically involves the use of socially complex resources. That is, several firms may possess the same physical technology, but only one of them may have the social relations, culture, group norms, and so on to fully exploit the technology in implementing its strategies. Many firms have attempted to replicate IKEA's success but none have been able to come even close to the results achieved by its unique culture and values. If such complex social resources are not subject to imitation (and assuming they are valuable and rare and no substitutes exist), a firm may obtain a sustained competitive advantage from exploiting its physical technology more effectively than other firms.

Are Substitutes Readily Available?   Of course, if competitors can substitute the contributions that a particular resource makes, even if that resource is valuable, rare, and inimitable, its ability to become the source of competitive advantage will diminish. Two valuable resources are strategically equivalent when each one can be exploited separately to implement the same strategies. Substitutability can take different forms. It may be impossible for a firm to imitate exactly another firm's resource, by it may be able to substitute a similar resource that enables it to develop and implement the same strategy. A firm seeking to imitate another firm's high quality top management team would be unable to replicate the team exactly, short of hiring them all away from the competitor. However, it might be able to develop its own unique management team and develop its own strategically equivalent resource. Moreover, very different resources can become strategic substitutes. Online sellers, such as Amazon.ca, diminish the uniqueness of prime retail locations by substituting bricks-and-mortar locations with the convenience of the Internet. Several pharmaceutical firms have, similarly, seen the value of patent protection erode in the face of new drugs that are based on different chemical properties; although they might behave differently, they can be used in similar treatment regimes. Furthermore, radical changes might arise within the pharmaceutical industry in the near future from substitution of chemotherapy with genetic therapies.[30]

Recall that resources and capabilities must be valuable, rare, and difficult to imitate or substitute in order for a firm to attain competitive advantages that are sustainable over time.[31] When a firm's resources and capabilities do not meet any of the four criteria, it will be difficult to develop any type of competitive advantage. The resources and capabilities it possesses will not enable the firm to exploit environmental opportunities or to neutralize environmental threats. When a firm possesses resources and capabilities that are at least valuable, the firm can at the least achieve competitive parity with its competitors. However, if those resources and capabilities are not difficult for competitors to imitate, that parity will only allow a temporary competitive advantage to be eroded sooner or later by imitation or substitution. It is only when all four criteria are satisfied that competitive advantages can be sustained over time.

The Generation and Distribution of a Firm's Profits: Extending the Resource-Based View of the Firm

Many scholars would agree that the resource-based view of the firm has been useful in determining when firms will create competitive advantages and enjoy high levels of profitability. However, it has not been developed to address how a firm's profits will be distributed to a firm's management and employees.[32] This becomes an important issue because a firm may be successful in creating competitive advantages that can be sustainable for a period of time, while much of the profits can be retained (or "appropriated") by its employees and managers—instead of flowing to the owners of the firm (i.e., the shareholders).

For a simple illustration, let's first consider Viewpoint DataLabs International, a company that makes sophisticated three-dimensional models and textures for film production houses, video games, and car manufacturers. This example will help to show how employees are often able to obtain (or "appropriate") a high proportion of a firm's profits.

Walter Noot, head of production, was having trouble keeping his highly skilled Generation X employees happy with their compensation. Each time one of them was lured away for more money, everyone would want a raise. "We were having to give out raises every six months—30 to 40 percent—then six months later they'd expect the same. It was a big struggle to keep people happy."[33] At Viewpoint DataLabs, it is apparent that much of the profits are being generated by the highly skilled professionals working together on a variety of projects. They are able to exercise their power by successfully demanding more financial compensation. In part, management has responded favourably because they are united in their demands and because their work involves a certain amount of social complexity and causal ambiguity.

In general, profits will flow to the owners of the valuable, rare, and inimitable resources that are responsible for the creation of those profits. Four factors help explain the extent to which employees and managers will be able to obtain a proportionately high level of the profits that they generate.[34] These include the following:

♦ ***Employee Bargaining Power.*** If employees are vital to forming a firm's unique capability, they will earn disproportionately high wages. For example, marketing professionals may have access to valuable information that helps them to understand the intricacies of customer demands and expectations, or engineers may understand unique technical aspects of the products or services. Additionally, in some industries, such as consulting, advertising, and tax preparation, clients tend to be very loyal to individual professionals employed by the firm, instead of to the firm itself. This enables them to "take the clients with them" if they leave. This enhances their bargaining power.

◆ *Employee Replacement Cost.* If employees' skills are idiosyncratic and rare (a source of resource-based advantage), they should have high bargaining power, based on the high cost required by the firm to replace them. For example, Raymond Ozzie, the software designer who was critical in the development of Lotus Notes, was able to dictate the terms under which IBM acquired Lotus.

◆ *Employee Exit Costs.* This factor may tend to reduce an employee's bargaining power. An individual may face high personal costs when leaving the organization. Thus, that individual's threat of leaving may not be credible. In addition, some of an employee's expertise may be firm-specific, so it would be of limited value to other firms. A related factor is that of causal ambiguity, which would make it difficult for the employee to explain his or her specific contribution to a given project. A rival firm might then be less likely to pay a high wage premium since it would be unsure of the employee's unique contribution to the firm's success.

◆ *Manager Bargaining Power.* Like other members of the firm, managers' power would be based on how well they create resource-based advantages. They are generally charged with creating value through the process of organizing, coordinating, and leveraging employees as well as other forms of capital such as plant, equipment, and financial capital (issues we address in more detail in Chapter 4). Such activities provide managers with sources of information that may not be readily available to others. Thus, although managers may not know as much about the specific nature of customers and technologies, they are in a position to have a more thorough, integrated understanding of the total operation.

In Chapter 10, we discuss the conditions under which top-level managers (such as CEOs) of large corporations have been, at times, able to obtain levels of total compensation that would appear to be significantly disproportionate to their contributions to wealth generation as well as to top executives in peer organizations. Here, corporate governance becomes a critical control mechanism. Such diversion of profits from the owners of the business to top management is far less likely when the board does not consist of a high proportion of the firm's management and when board members are truly independent outsiders (i.e., do not have close ties to management). In general, given the external market for top talent, the level of compensation that executives receive is based on factors similar to those discussed above, which determine the level of their bargaining power.[35]

EVALUATING FIRM PERFORMANCE

If strategy is about an organization's success, assessing and measuring firm performance becomes a critical input to the analysis of the internal environment of the firm. Two approaches are typically used to evaluate a firm's performance. The first is financial ratio analysis, which, generally speaking, identifies how a firm is performing according to its balance sheet and income statement. When performing a financial ratio analysis, managers must take into account the firm's performance from a historical perspective (not just at one point in time) as well as the way in which it compares with industry norms and key competitors.[36]

The second perspective may be considered a broader stakeholder perspective. Firms must satisfy a broad range of stakeholders, including employees, customers, and owners, to ensure their long-term viability. Central to this discussion is a well-known approach, the balanced scorecard, which has been popularized by Robert Kaplan and David Norton.[37]

Financial Ratio Analysis

← LO 5

The beginning point in analyzing the financial position of a firm is to compute and analyze five different types of financial ratios:

- Short-term solvency or liquidity
- Long-term solvency measures
- Asset management (or turnover)
- Profitability
- Market value

Financial analysis is the staple of the disciplines of accounting and finance. Extensive literature and a plethora of textbooks serve to guide students and managers through the logic, the technical analysis, and the thoughtful interpretation of those analyses. An accompaniment to this section is provided online, containing detailed explanations of definitions and discussion of these types of ratios, as well as examples of how each is calculated.

A meaningful ratio analysis must go beyond the calculation and interpretation of financial ratios.[38] It must include an analysis of how ratios change over time as well as how they are interrelated. For example, a firm that takes on too much long-term debt to finance operations will see an immediate impact on its indicators of long-term financial leverage. The additional debt will also have a negative impact on the firm's short-term liquidity ratio (i.e., current and quick ratios) since the firm must pay interest and principal on the additional debt each year until it is retired. Additionally, the interest expenses must be deducted from revenues, reducing the firm's profitability.

A firm's financial position should not be analyzed in isolation. Important reference points are needed. In order to make financial analysis more meaningful, historical comparisons, comparisons with industry norms, and comparisons with key competitors must be taken into account.

Historical Comparisons When managers evaluate a firm's financial performance, it is very useful to examine changes in its financial position over time. This provides a means of evaluating trends. For example, Home Depot reported revenues of $77.3 billion and net income of $4.2 billion in 2007.[39] This is an impressive performance that many corporations would be extremely happy to be able to declare. But compare those results to the $77 billion in revenues and the $5.6 billion in net income that was achieved in 2005; there is not much to boast about anymore. Moreover, Home Depot had only 2,042 stores in 2005, while it took 2,234 stores to achieve the 2007 results. From the perspective of its history, the company's performance looks much less remarkable. Exhibit 3.6 illustrates a 10-year period of return on sales (ROS) for a hypothetical company. As indicated by the dotted trend lines, the rate of growth (or decline) differs substantially over time periods.

Comparison with Industry Norms When managers evaluate a firm's financial performance, they also compare it with industry norms. A firm's current ratio or profitability may appear impressive at first glance. However, it may pale when compared with industry standards or norms.

By comparing a firm with all other firms in its industry, we can calculate relative performance. Banks and other lending institutions often use such comparisons when evaluating a firm's creditworthiness. Exhibit 3.7 includes a variety of financial ratios for three industries: semiconductors, grocery stores, and skilled-nursing facilities. Why is there such variation among the financial ratios for these three industries? There are several

Exhibit 3.6
Historical Trends:
Return on Sales
(ROS) for a
Hypothetical
Company

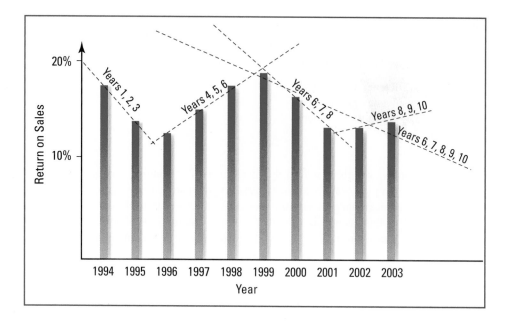

Exhibit 3.7
How Financial
Ratios Differ across
Industries

Financial Ratio	Semiconductors	Grocery Stores	Skilled-Nursing Facilities
Quick ratio (times)	1.9	0.5	1.1
Current ratio (times)	4.0	1.6	1.6
Total liabilities to net worth (%)	30.7	92.0	163.5
Collection period (days)	49.6	2.9	31.2
Assets to sales (%)	187.8	20.2	101.6
Return on sales (%)	5.8	0.8	1.6

Source: Dun & Bradstreet, *Industry Norms and Key Business Ratios, 2003–2004*. One Year Edition,
SIC #2000-3999 (Semiconductors); SIC #5200-5499 (Grocery Stores); SIC #6100-8999 (Skilled-Nursing
Facilities). New York: Dun.

reasons. With regard to the collection period, grocery stores operate mostly on a cash basis, so they have a very short collection period. Semiconductor manufacturers sell their output to other manufacturers (e.g., computer makers) on terms such as 2/15 net 45, which means they give a 2 percent discount on bills paid within 15 days and start charging interest after 45 days. Skilled-nursing facilities would also have a longer collection period than grocery stores because they typically rely on payments from insurance companies.

The industry norms for return on sales also highlight some differences among these industries. Grocers, with very slim margins, have a lower return on sales than either skilled-nursing facilities or semiconductor manufacturers. But how might we explain the differences between skilled-nursing facilities and semiconductor manufacturers? Health care facilities, in general, are limited in their pricing structures by government health regulations and by insurance reimbursement limits, but semiconductor producers have pricing structures determined by the market. If their products have superior performance, semiconductor manufacturers can charge premium prices.

Company (or division)	Sales* ($ billions)	R&D budget ($ billions)
P&G Drug Division	$ 0.8	$0.38
Bristol-Myers Squibb	20.2	1.80
Pfizer	27.4	4.00
Merck	32.7	2.10

*Most recently completed fiscal year. Data: Lehman Brothers, Procter & Gamble.

Source: R. Berner, "Procter & Gamble: Just Say No to Drugs," *BusinessWeek*, October 9, 2000, p. 128; data courtesy of Lehman Brothers and Procter & Gamble.

Exhibit 3.8
Comparison of Procter & Gamble's and Key Competitors' Drug Revenues and R&D Expenditures

Comparison with Key Competitors Recall from Chapter 2 that firms with similar strategies are considered members of a strategic group in an industry. Furthermore, competition tends to be more intense among competitors within groups than across groups. Thus, we can gain valuable insights into a firm's financial and competitive position if we make comparisons between a firm and its most direct competitors. Consider Procter & Gamble's ill-fated efforts to enter the highly profitable pharmaceutical industry. Although P&G is a giant in consumer products, its efforts over two decades have produced nominal profits at best. In 1999, P&G spent $380 million on R&D in drugs—22 percent of its total corporate R&D budget. However, its drug unit produced only 2 percent of the company's $40 billion sales. The reason is that while $380 million is hardly a trivial amount of capital, its key competitors dwarfed P&G. Consider the drug revenues and R&D budgets of P&G compared to its main rivals as shown in Exhibit 3.8. *BusinessWeek*'s take on P&G's chances, in an article entitled "Just Say No to Drugs," was, "Don't bet on it. P&G may be a giant in detergent and toothpaste, but the consumer-products maker is simply outclassed by the competition."[40]

Integrating Financial Analysis and Stakeholder Perspectives: The Balanced Scorecard

In the previous section, we focused on what may be considered a good starting point in assessing a firm's performance. Clearly, it is useful to see how a firm is performing over time in terms of the several ratios. However, such traditional approaches to performance assessments can be a double-edged sword.[41] Many important transactions that managers make—investments in research and development, employee training and development, advertising and promotion of key brands, and new product development—may greatly expand a firm's market potential and create significant long-term shareholder value. But such critical investments are not reflected positively in short-term financial reports. Why? Because financial reports typically measure expenses, not the value created. Thus, managers may be penalized for spending money in the short term to improve their firm's long-term competitive viability!

Now consider the other side of the coin. A manager may be destroying the firm's future value by operating in a way that makes customers dissatisfied, depletes the firm's stock of good products coming out of R&D, or damages the morale of valued employees. Such budget cuts, however, may lead to very good short-term financials. The manager may look good in the short run and even receive credit for improving the firm's performance. In essence, such a manager has mastered denominator management, whereby decreasing investments makes the return on investment (ROI) ratio larger, even though the actual return remains constant or shrinks.

To provide a meaningful integration of the many issues that come into evaluating a firm's performance, Kaplan and Norton developed a *balanced scorecard*.[42] This is a set of measures that provide top managers with a fast but comprehensive view of the business. In a nutshell, it includes financial measures that reflect the results of actions already taken, but it complements these indicators with operational measures of customer satisfaction, internal processes, and the organization's innovation and improvement activities—operational measures that drive future financial performance.

The balanced scorecard enables managers to consider their business from four key perspectives:

- Customer perspective: How do customers see us?
- Internal business perspective: What must we excel at?
- Innovation and learning perspective: Can we continue to improve and create value?
- Financial perspective: How do we look to shareholders?

Customer Perspective   The way in which a company is performing from its customers' perspective is a top priority for management. The balanced scorecard requires that managers translate their general mission statements on customer service into specific measures that reflect the factors that really matter to customers. For the balanced scorecard to work, managers must articulate goals for four key categories of customer concerns: time, quality, performance and service, and cost. For example, lead time may be measured as the time from the company's receipt of an order to the time it actually delivers the product or service to the customer. Also, quality measures may indicate the level of defective incoming products, as perceived by the customer, as well as the accuracy of the company's delivery forecasts.

Internal Business Perspective   Although customer-based measures are important, they must be translated into indicators of what the firm must do internally to meet customers' expectations. Excellent customer performance results from processes, decisions, and actions that occur throughout organizations in a coordinated fashion, and managers must focus on those critical internal operations that enable them to satisfy customer needs. The internal measures should reflect business processes that have the greatest impact on customer satisfaction. These include factors that affect cycle time, quality, employee skills, and productivity. Firms also must identify and measure the key resources and capabilities they need to ensure continued strategic success.

Innovation and Learning Perspective   The customer and internal business process measures on the balanced scorecard identify the parameters that the company considers most critical to success. However, given the rapid rate of change in markets, technologies, and global competition, the criteria for success are constantly changing. To survive and prosper, managers must make frequent changes to existing products and services as well as introduce entirely new products with expanded capabilities. A firm's ability to improve, innovate, and learn is tied directly to its value. Simply put, only by developing new products and services, creating greater value for customers, and increasing operating efficiencies can a company penetrate new markets, increase revenues and margins, and enhance shareholder value.

Financial Perspective   Measures of financial performance indicate whether the company's strategy, implementation, and execution are, indeed, contributing to bottom-line improvement. Typical financial goals include profitability, growth, and shareholder value. Periodic financial statements remind managers that improved quality, response time, productivity, and innovative products benefit the firm only when they result in improved sales, increased market share, reduced operating expenses, or higher asset turnover.

Exhibit 3.9 provides an example of the balanced scorecard for a semiconductor manufacturer, ECI. Its managers saw the scorecard as a way to clarify, simplify, and then operationalize the vision at the top of the firm. The scorecard was designed to focus the attention of top executives on a short list of critical indicators of current and future performance. For example, to track the specific goal of providing a continuous stream of attractive solutions, ECI measured the percent of sales from new products and the percent of sales from proprietary products (customer perspective). After deciding that manufacturing excellence was critical to their success, managers determined that cycle time, unit costs, and yield would be the most viable indicators (internal business perspective). Like many companies, ECI determined that the percent of sales from new products is a key measure of innovation

Exhibit 3.9
ECI's Balanced Business Scorecard

Customer Perspective	
Goals	**Measures**
◆ New products	◆ Percent of sales from new products
◆ Responsive supply	◆ On-time delivery (defined by customer)
◆ Customer partnership	◆ Number of co-operative engineering efforts

Internal Business Perspective	
Goals	**Measures**
◆ Manufacturing excellence	◆ Cycle time
◆ Design productivity	◆ Unit cost
◆ New product introduction	◆ Yield
	◆ Silicon efficiency
	◆ Engineering efficiency
	◆ Actual introduction schedule versus plan

Innovation and Learning Perspective	
Goals	**Measures**
◆ Technology leadership	◆ Time to develop next generation
◆ Manufacturing learning	◆ Process time to maturity
◆ Product focus	◆ Percent of products that equal 80% of sales
◆ Time to market	◆ New product introduction versus competition

Financial Perspective	
Goals	**Measures**
◆ Survive	◆ Cash Flow
◆ Succeed	◆ Quarterly sales growth and operating income by division
◆ Prosper	◆ Increased market share and ROE

Source: Adapted with permission of *Harvard Business Review*. Exhibit from "The Balanced Scorecard: Measures that Drive Performance," by R. S. Kaplan and D. P. Norton, 69, no. 1 (1992). Copyright © 1992 by the Harvard Business School Publishing Corporation. All rights reserved.

and improvement (innovation and learning perspective). Finally, ECI decided on three key financial goals—survive, succeed, and prosper—with the corresponding measures of cash flow, quarterly sales growth/operating income by division, and increased market share and return on equity, respectively.

Before ending our discussion of the balanced scorecard, we would like to provide another example that illustrates the causal relationships among the multiple perspectives in the model. Sears, the huge retailer, found a strong causal relationship between employee attitudes, customer attitudes, and financial outcomes.[43] Through an ongoing study, Sears developed (and continues to refine) what it calls its total performance indicators, or TPI—a set of indicators that shows how well the company is doing with customers, employees, and investors. Sears's quantitative model has shown that a 5 percent improvement in employee attitudes leads to a 1.3 percent improvement in customer satisfaction, which, in turn, drives a 0.5 percent improvement in revenue. Thus, if a single store improved its employee attitude by 5 percent on a survey scale, Sears could predict, with confidence, that if the revenue growth in the district as a whole were 5 percent, the revenue growth in that particular store would be 5.5 percent. Interestingly, Sears' managers consider such numbers as rigorous as any others that they work with every year. The company's accounting firm audits management as closely as it audits the financial statements.

One final implication of the balanced scorecard is that managers do not need to look at their job as primarily balancing stakeholder demands. They need to avoid the mindset that asks, "How many units in employee satisfaction do I have to give up to get some additional units of customer satisfaction or profits?" Instead, when done properly, the balanced scorecard provides a win-win approach, a means of simultaneously increasing satisfaction among a wide variety of organizational stakeholders—employees (at all levels), customers, and shareholders. And, as we shall see in Chapter 4, indicators of employee satisfaction have become more important in a knowledge economy, where intellectual capital (as opposed to labour and financial capital) is the primary creator of wealth.

Summary

In the traditional approaches to assessing a firm's internal environment, the primary goal of managers would be to determine their firm's relative strengths and weaknesses. Such is the role of SWOT analysis, wherein managers analyze their firm's strengths and weaknesses as well as the opportunities and threats in the external environment. In this chapter, we discussed why this may be a good starting point but hardly the best approach to take in performing a sound analysis. There are many limitations to SWOT analysis, including its static perspective, its potential to overemphasize a single dimension of a firm's strategy, and the likelihood that a firm's strengths do not necessarily help the firm create value or competitive advantages.

We identified two frameworks that serve to complement SWOT analysis in assessing a firm's internal environment: value-chain analysis and the resource-based view of the firm. In conducting a value-chain analysis, the first step is to divide the firm into a series of value-creating activities. These include primary activities such as inbound logistics, operations, and service as well as support activities such as procurement and human resource management. The next step is to analyze how each activity adds value as well as how *interrelationships* among value activities in the firm and between the firm and its customers and suppliers add value. Thus, instead of merely determining a firm's strengths and weaknesses per se, we analyze them in the overall context of the firm and its relationships with customers and suppliers, the value system.

The resource-based view of the firm considers the firm as a bundle of resources: tangible resources, intangible resources, and organizational capabilities. Competitive advantages that are sustainable over time generally arise from the creation of bundles of resources and capabilities. For advantages to be sustainable, four criteria must be satisfied: value, rarity, inimitability, and exploitability. Such an evaluation requires a sound knowledge of the competitive context in which the firm exists. The owners of a business may not capture all of the value created by the firm. The appropriation of value created by a firm between the owners and employees is determined by four factors: employee bargaining power, replacement cost, employee exit costs, and manager bargaining power.

An internal analysis of the firm would not be complete unless we evaluate its performance and make the appropriate comparisons. Determining a firm's performance requires an analysis of its financial situation as well as a review of how well it is satisfying a broad range of stakeholders, including customers, employees, and shareholders. We discussed the concept of the balanced scorecard, in which four perspectives must be addressed: customer, internal business, innovation and learning, and financial. Central to the balanced scorecard is the idea that the interests of various stakeholders can be interrelated. We provided examples of how indicators of employee satisfaction lead to higher levels of customer satisfaction, which, in turn, lead to higher levels of financial performance. Thus, improving a firm's performance does not need to involve making trade-offs among different stakeholders. Assessing the firm's performance is also more useful if it is evaluated in terms of how it changes over time, compares with industry norms, and compares with key competitors.

Summary Review Questions

1. SWOT analysis is a technique to analyze the internal and external environment of a firm. What are its advantages and disadvantages?
2. Briefly describe the primary and support activities in a firm's value chain.
3. How can managers create value by establishing important relationships among the value-chain activities both within their firm and between the firm and its customers and suppliers?
4. Briefly explain the four criteria for the sustainability of competitive advantages.
5. Under what conditions are employees able to appropriate some of the value that is created by their firm?
6. What are the advantages and disadvantages of conducting a financial ratio analysis of a firm?
7. Summarize the concept of the balanced scorecard. What are its main advantages?

Experiential Exercise

Dell Computer is a leading firm in the personal computer industry, with annual revenues of $61 billion during its 2007 fiscal year. Dell has created a very strong competitive position via its "direct model," whereby it manufactures its personal computers to detailed customer specifications.

Below we address several questions that focus on Dell's value chain activities and interrelationships among them as well as whether they are able to attain sustainable competitive advantage(s). In preparation for this exercise, you should do some online research to familiarize yourself with Dell's strategy and operations.

1. Where in Dell's value chain are they creating value for their customer?

Value-Chain Activity	Yes/No	How Does Dell Create Value for the Customer?
Primary:		
Inbound logistics		
Operations		
Outbound logistics		
Marketing and sales		
Service		
Support:		
Procurement		
Technology development		
Human resource management		
General administration		

2. What are the important relationships among Dell's value-chain activities? What are the important interdependencies? For each activity, identify the relationships and interdependencies.

	Inbound logistics	Operations	Outbound logistics	Marketing and sales	Service	Procurement	Technology development	Human resource management	General administration
Inbound logistics									
Operations									
Outbound logistics									
Marketing and sales									
Service									
Procurement									
Technology development									
Human resource management									
General administration									

3. What resources, activities, and relationships enable Dell to achieve a sustainable competitive advantage?

Resource/Activity	Is It Valuable?	Is It Rare?	Is It Inimitable?	Is It Exploitable?
Inbound logistics				
Operations				
Outbound logistics				
Marketing and sales				
Service				
Procurement				
Technology development				
Human resource management				
General administration				

Application Questions Exercises

1. Using published reports, select two CEOs who have recently made public statements regarding a major change in their firm's strategy. Discuss how the successful implementation of such strategies requires changes in the firm's primary and support activities.
2. Select a firm that competes in an industry that you are interested in. Drawing on published financial reports, complete a financial ratio analysis. Based on changes over time and a comparison with industry norms, evaluate the firm's strengths and weaknesses in terms of its financial position.
3. How might exemplary human resource practices enhance and strengthen a firm's value-chain activities?
4. Using the Internet, look up your university or college. What are some of its key value-creating activities that provide competitive advantages? Why?

Ethics Questions

1. What are some of the ethical issues that may arise when a firm tries to improve each if its primary activities?
2. What are some to the ethical dilemmas that may arise when companies impose their own value systems on their suppliers?
3. What are some of the ethical issues that may arise when a firm becomes overly zealous in advertising its products?
4. What are some of the ethical issues that may arise from a firm's procurement activities? Are you aware of any of these issues from your personal experience or from businesses you are familiar with?

Chapter 4 Recognizing a Firm's Intellectual Assets:
Human Capital, Technology and Knowledge, Brands and Trademarks, Relationships

LEARNING OBJECTIVES

After reading this chapter, you should have a good understanding of:

LO 1 → the increasing value of intellectual assets for today's corporations and for the prosperity of a country.

LO 2 → why the management of knowledge and knowledge professionals is so critical in today's organizations.

LO 3 → the importance of recognizing the interdependence between attracting, developing, and retaining human capital.

LO 4 → the key role of social capital in leveraging human capital within and across an organization.

LO 5 → the vital role of technology in leveraging knowledge and human capital.

LO 6 → how protecting intellectual property is central to sustainable competitive advantage.

Technology, knowledge, human capital, as well as brand names and trademarks, all make critical contributions to a firm's competitive advantage and represent an increasingly important proportion of a company's wealth. Peter Drucker identified that the "knowledge workers" and the knowledge they possess are the primary resource of the economy overall, arguing that these are far more valuable than material or financial resources for the long term prosperity of a country and its firms.[1] Even in resource-based economies similar to Canada's, success depends on the ability of individual firms to create technological innovations that transform raw materials to value-added goods.

The management of top talent and the existence of mechanisms that leverage human capital to innovate and develop products and services that create value have become critical factors. Silicon Valley in California has been the breeding ground for much talent in a range of technology-intensive industries. Individual firms within the Valley find new talent by tapping into the social contacts of existing owners and employees. New firms develop out of workers' previous experience; experience involves contact with former employers and co-workers. Intricate networks of relationships facilitate the screening and selection of suitable candidates for new and existing firms alike. Individuals often have more loyalty to their peers, including those in competing firms, than they do to their current employer. This makes the social network even more crucial. Individuals typically do not work for the same company for a lifetime. In fact, job changes are frequent and common. John Doerr of venture capital firm Kleiner Perkins Caufield & Byers (KPCB) is fond of saying that Silicon Valley is the only place where you can change jobs and keep your parking space![2]

The Waterloo region in southern Ontario is another such case. A traditional manufacturing centre that produced Segram's whisky, Bauer skates, Hush Puppies shoes, and Schneiders meats, the area has seen many of those product lines disappear, taking numerous manufacturing jobs with them. Yet, the region is thriving and adding jobs as the likes of Open Text Corporation and Research in Motion Ltd. (RIM) are creating world-leading products and establishing new firms for the New Economy.[3] Tom Jenkins, chairman and chief strategy officer of Open Text, is quoted as saying that the ongoing success of the region does not depend on erecting barriers that would keep existing companies there and foreign competition out; instead, creating an environment promoting education and rewarding entrepreneurship will ensure that new firms will continue to spawn.

Some companies excel at leveraging their human capital. Strong human capital often leads to useful relationships among others within the firm, promoting a social infrastructure that is vital for gaining consensus on major decisions, integrating multiple administrative levels, promoting co-operation, and sharing information across departmental boundaries. Other companies, however, fail miserably to take advantage of their human capital and social relationships. Consider, for example, Xerox, the company that invented xerography, the principal technology underlying the ubiquitous photocopier.

Case Study

Xerox Corporation's Palo Alto Research Center, in the heart of the Silicon Valley, has been legendary within the high-tech sector for the many technological breakthroughs that have emanated from within its labs over the last 50 years.[4] Some of its early computer innovations are the mouse, the graphical user interface that lies at the heart of the Apple Macintosh operating system and Microsoft's Windows®, as well as the Macintosh computer itself. Yet, Xerox has not always been able to capitalize on such revolutionary ideas and has, in fact, underperformed its peers. At the same time, Steven Jobs, who left Xerox's research centre to co-found Apple Computer Inc., and numerous others have built multi-billion dollar corporations on the foundations of leading-edge technologies first developed at Xerox.

Xerox's problems did not end in the labs either. During the 1980s, Xerox lost its market leadership position in photocopiers to Canon. After numerous attempts to revive the brand and introduce new products, many of its sales reps had, by late 2000, quit to join other firms and had taken with them valuable product knowledge, which often took years to acquire, as well as their relationships with customers. Xerox's stock price was about the same in late 2003 as it was in 1961.

Despite the company's phenomenal success during its early years, one built on the foundation of the original patent and some subsequent breakthroughs, Xerox seemed to struggle to integrate its human resources in bringing new technologies to market. While one might expect that a company whose fortunes were based on technological advances and risk taking would encourage its employees to challenge the status quo in executive discussions and invite disagreements when problems arose, this is not how people were taught to behave at Xerox. Senior management had little imagination and had instituted a bureaucratic style and formality reminiscent of military barracks.

Consider, for example, some of the recent adventures within Xerox. In 1999, Rick Thoman, who had been brought to Xerox after years of experience at Intel and IBM, was made chief executive officer, successor to Paul Allaire who was named chairman. Thoman immediately set about to fix a number of problems. Barry Romeril, the chief financial officer, had done a poor job overseeing corporate finances. "Creative accounting" made Xerox's Mexican subsidiary look stellar until someone noticed just how creative this had been! The result—a $119 million write-off from a subsidiary with only $400 million in revenues. The Securities and Exchange Commission had launched a lawsuit against Xerox for overstating earnings by $3 billion between 1997 and 2000. The company was also facing a downgrade of its bonds to junk status, along with numerous shareholder lawsuits. Romeril had also dangerously exposed the company to the turbulent Brazilian economy by failing to hedge against currency exchange rates. After Xerox incurred a 13 percent loss in net worth in 1999, Thoman wanted Romeril fired. But subtle politics were working behind the scenes to derail his plans. Romeril was an old friend of Allaire who did not want to get rid of Romeril.

Thoman also wanted to restructure Xerox's global sales division to better compete with the Japanese firms. Dolan, president of Xerox's global sales, disagreed. Dolan was also a friend of Allaire and was able to wield Allaire's power over Thoman and block the restructuring. And, as it turned out, another member of the executive group, Anne Mulcahy, was Dolan's sister.

Such infighting did not remain within the executive suite for long. The sales force eventually began to feel the impact of the negative relationships and lack of direction. It had previously served as a team of experts on one or just a few of Xerox's products, selling to a wide market. Thoman's vision included a sales force that was limited geographically but had broad product knowledge. Rather than service a wide market, the sales force would concentrate on developing strong relationships with customers. Customers would benefit by having closer access to the expertise of the sales reps.

However, the uncertainty surrounding their job duties had a negative impact on how the reps viewed the company. It became increasingly difficult for them to portray the positive image of the firm that's so necessary to increase sales revenues. As the reps began considering their options, many of them quit to join other firms that had more stability. Although new reps could be trained, many of the client relationships were permanently scarred.

With Xerox's stock tumbling, one would have thought that a strong leader like Thoman would be valued. But not at Xerox. In May 2001, Thoman was fired. Mulcahy was promoted to president and chief operating officer. Romeril kept his job. For a while, Xerox was facing possible Chapter 11 bankruptcy. But at least Allaire, Romeril, Dolan, and Mulcahy were still friends.

What Went Wrong at Xerox? The Xerox case addresses many key issues for today's organizations. Historically, Xerox hasn't suffered from a shortage of talent or technological innovation. Rather, it has experienced problems leveraging its talent and technologies into successful products and services. Also, the dysfunctional organizational politics at the top of the organization eroded human and social capital throughout the company. As we see below, in today's knowledge economy, the key question is not how big a company's stock of resources is—whether it be top-level talent, physical resources such as buildings and machinery, or financial capital. Rather, the question becomes, How good is the company in attracting top talent and leveraging that talent to produce a stream of products and services valued by the marketplace?

THE CENTRAL ROLE OF INTELLECTUAL CAPITAL IN TODAY'S ECONOMY

For most of the twentieth century, managers were primarily concerned with tangible resources such as land, equipment, and money as well as intangibles such as brands, image, and customer loyalty. Most efforts were directed more toward the efficient allocation of labour and capital—the two traditional factors of production.

Today, more than 50 percent of the gross domestic product (GDP) in developed economies is knowledge-based; that is, it is based on intellectual assets and intangible people skills.[5] Intellectual and information processes create most of the value for firms in large service industries (e.g., software, medical care, communications, and education), which provide 65 percent of Canada's GDP. In the manufacturing sector, intellectual activities like R&D, process design, product design, logistics, marketing, or technological innovation produce the preponderance of value added.[6] Consider the perspective of Gary Hamel and C. K. Prahalad, two leading writers in strategic management:

> The machine age was a physical world. It consisted of things. Companies made and distributed things (physical products). Management allocated things (capital budgets); management invested in things (plant and equipment).
>
> In the machine age, people were ancillary, and things were central. In the information age, things are ancillary, knowledge is central. A company's value derives not from things, but from knowledge, know-how, intellectual assets, competencies—all embedded in people.[7]

In the knowledge economy, wealth is increasingly created through the effective management of intellectual assets and knowledge workers instead of by the efficient control of physical and financial assets. The growing importance of knowledge, coupled with the move by labour markets to reward knowledge work, tells us that someone who invests in a company is, in essence, paying for a set of talents, capabilities, skills, and ideas—intellectual capital—not physical and financial resources.

The following examples should illustrate this point. People don't buy Microsoft's stock because of its software factories; it doesn't own any. Rather, the value of Microsoft rests on the company's ability to set standards for personal-computing software, exploit the value of its name, and forge alliances with other companies. Similarly, Merck didn't become the "Most Admired" company for seven consecutive years in *Fortune*'s annual survey because it can manufacture pills, but rather because its scientists can discover medicines. P. Roy Vagelos, who was CEO of Merck during its long run atop the "Most Admired" survey said, "A low-value product can be made by anyone anywhere. When you have knowledge no one else has access to—that's dynamite. We guard our research even more carefully than our financial assets."[8] RIM, Biovail, and Cognos have generated billions of dollars in market value from the creation and application of technology developed in the fields of telecommunications, biotechnology, and software. Their facilities, plants, and equipment represent a small fraction of the total value ascribed to them by the financial markets.

Consider for example RIM, whose 2007 sales of $7.2 billion and income of $1.6 billion support a market value of $74.2 billion out of a book value of $4.5 billion. Its ratio of market-to-book value of 16 compares to a Canadian average of 3 for all publicly traded firms, and an average of 3.5 for U.S. firms. The ratio for General Motors is currently less than 1 and Magna International's is 1.4. As one might expect, the gap between a firm's market value and its book value is far greater for knowledge-intensive corporations than it is for firms with strategies based primarily on tangible assets. In firms where knowledge and the management of knowledge workers are key contributors to developing products and services—and where physical resources are less critical—the ratio of market-to-book value tends to be much higher. Many writers have defined intellectual capital as the difference between a firm's market value and book value— that is, a measure of the value of a firm's intangible assets.[9] This admittedly broad definition includes assets such as reputation, employee loyalty and commitment, customer relationships, company values, brand names, and the experience and skills of employees.[10]

How do companies create value in the knowledge-intensive economy? The answer rests on their ability to manage their intellectual assets and attract and effectively leverage human capital through mechanisms that create products and services of value. Thus, for us to understand and appreciate the sources of a firm's competitive advantage, we must first take a close look and analyze how that firm handles its intellectual capital. But before we further develop the role of intellectual assets and human capital in wealth creation, let's delineate some of the basic concepts as they are presented in Exhibit 4.1

First, consider intellectual capital. Intellectual capital consists of intangible assets, such as human capital, social capital, intellectual property, and brands and trademarks, which all contribute to a firm's ability to create value through new knowledge and its useful applications. Innovation rests at the heart of economic development, and the management of intellectual capital is arguably the only source of sustainable competitive advantage. According to James Conley, managing intellectual assets entails the whole life cycle of creation, codification, valuation, protection, and leveraging of such assets.[11]

Second, human capital consists of the "*individual* capabilities, knowledge, skills, and experience of the company's employees and managers." This concerns knowledge that is relevant to the task at hand and the capacity to add to the reservoir of knowledge, skills, and experience through learning.[12]

Third, social capital involves "the network of relationships that individuals have throughout the organization." Such relationships are critical in sharing and leveraging knowledge and in acquiring resources. Social capital extends beyond the organizational boundaries to include relationships between the firm and its suppliers, customers, and alliance partners.[13]

Exhibit 4.1
Types of Intellectual Capital (Intellectual assets)

Human Capital	Social Capital	Intellectual Property
Individuals' ◆ capabilities ◆ knowledge, both tacit and explicit ◆ skills ◆ experiences	Relationships ◆ formal and informal ◆ personal and professional ◆ organizational Networks	Copyrights Trademarks Patents

Fourth is the concept of "knowledge," which comes in two different forms. On the one hand, there is explicit knowledge that is codified, documented, easily reproduced, and widely distributed. Examples include engineering drawings, software code, sales collateral, and patents. The other type of knowledge is tacit knowledge.[14] This is knowledge that is, in essence, in the minds of employees and is based on their experiences and backgrounds. Tacit knowledge is shared only with the consent and participation of the individual.

Fifth is the concept of intellectual property. Ideas, innovations, and creations contribute to sustainable competitive advantage only when a firm is able to protect its exclusive right to extract value from them for a long period of time and prevent others from copying or imitating them for their own benefits. As Conley and Szobocsan have pointed out, the careful and purposeful management of copyrights and trademarks is the single most important reason Disney has been able to maximize the economic life of its animation classics over many years; *Snow White*, after all, is almost 70 years old, and it still sells briskly when the Disney folks periodically offer another round of videos, compact disks, and toys for sale.[15]

New knowledge is constantly being created in organizations. It involves the continual interaction of explicit and tacit knowledge. Consider, for example, two software engineers working together on a computer code. The computer code itself is the explicit knowledge. However, through their sharing of ideas based on each individual's experience—that is, their tacit knowledge—new knowledge is created as they make modifications to the existing code. Another important issue is the role of "socially complex processes," which include leadership, culture, and trust.[16] These processes play a central role in the creation of knowledge. They represent the "glue" that holds the organization together and helps to create a working environment where individuals are more willing to share their ideas, work in teams, and, in the end, create products and services of value.

Numerous books have been written on the subject of knowledge management and the central role that it has played in creating wealth in organizations and countries throughout the developed world.[17] Here, we focus on the central resource itself, human capital, and some guidelines on how it can be attracted, developed, and retained. Tom Stewart, editor of the *Harvard Business Review*, noted that organizations must also carry out significant efforts to protect their human capital. A firm may "diversify the ownership of vital knowledge by emphasizing teamwork, guard against obsolescence by developing learning programs, and shackle key people with golden handcuffs."[18] In addition, people are less likely to leave an organization if there are effective structures to promote teamwork and information sharing, strong leaders to encourage innovation, and cultures that demand excellence and ethical behaviour. Such issues are also central to the topic of this chapter. We provide more detail in later chapters as we discuss organizational structure and design in Chapter 9; organizational controls (culture, rewards, and boundaries) in Chapter 10; and a variety of leadership and entrepreneurship topics in Chapters 11 and 12.

← LO 2

HUMAN CAPITAL: THE FOUNDATION OF INTELLECTUAL CAPITAL

To be successful, organizations must recruit talented people—employees at all levels with the proper sets of skills and capabilities coupled with the right values and attitudes. Such skills and attitudes must be continually developed, strengthened, and reinforced, and each employee must be motivated and focused on the organization's goals and objectives.

The rise to prominence of the knowledge worker as a vital source of competitive advantage is changing the balance of power in today's organization. Knowledge workers place professional development and personal enrichment (financial and otherwise) above company loyalty. Attracting, recruiting, and hiring the "best and the brightest," is a

Exhibit 4.2
Human
Capital: Three
Interdependent
Activities

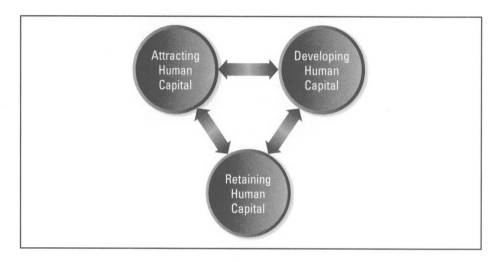

critical first step in the process of building intellectual capital. At a symposium for CEOs, Bill Gates said, "The thing that is holding Microsoft back … is simply how [hard] we find it to go out and recruit the kind of people we want to grow our research team."[19]

But hiring is only the first of three vital processes in which all successful organizations must engage to build and leverage their human capital. Firms must also *develop* employees at all levels and specialties so that they fulfill their potential and, in doing so, maximize their joint contributions. Finally, firms must provide the working environment and intrinsic and extrinsic rewards to *retain* their best and brightest; without employee retention, the first two processes are rendered meaningless.

These three activities are highly interrelated. They constitute a three-legged stool (see Exhibit 4.2).[20] If one leg is weak or broken, the stool collapses. Poor hiring impedes the effectiveness of development and retention processes. In a similar vein, ineffective retention efforts place additional burdens on hiring and development. Jeffrey Pfeffer likened the activity of stepping up recruitment efforts in order to compensate for poor retention to a doctor who responds to a bleeding patient with increases in the speed of transfusion.[21] Although there are no simple, easy-to-apply answers, we can learn from what leading-edge firms are doing to attract, develop, and retain human capital in today's highly competitive and rapidly changing marketplace. Let's begin by discussing hiring and selection practices.

Attracting Human Capital

"All we can do is bet on the people we pick. So my whole job is picking the right people."

Jack Welch, former chairman, General Electric Company[22]

The first step in the process of building superior human capital is input control: attracting and selecting the right person. Many human resource professionals still approach employee selection from a "lock and key" mentality—that is, fit a key (a job candidate) into a lock (the job). Such an approach involves a thorough analysis of both the person and the job. Only then can the right decision be made as to how well the two will fit together. How can you fail, the theory goes, if you get a precise match of knowledge, ability, and skill profiles? Frequently, however, the precise matching approach places its primary emphasis on task-specific skills (e.g., motor skills, specific information gathering and processing capabilities, and communication skills) and puts less emphasis on the broad general knowledge and experience, social skills, values, beliefs, and attitudes of employees.

Many have questioned the precise matching approach. They argue that firms can identify top performers by focusing on key employee mindsets, attitudes, social skills, and general orientations that lead to success in nearly all jobs. It is believed that if firms get these elements right, the task-specific skills can be learned in relatively short order. (This does not imply, however, that task-specific skills are unimportant; rather, it suggests that the requisite skill sets must be viewed as a necessary but not sufficient condition.) This leads us to a phrase that is popular with many organizations today and serves as the heading of the next section.

"Hire for Attitude, Train for Skill" Organizations are increasingly placing their emphasis on the general knowledge and experience, social skills, values, beliefs, and attitudes of employees. Consider Southwest Airlines' hiring practices, which involve a strong focus on employee values and attitudes. Given its strong team orientation, SWA uses an "indirect" approach. For example, the interviewing team asks a group of employees to prepare a five-minute presentation about themselves. During the presentations, the interviewers observe which candidates are enthusiastically supporting their peers and which candidates are focused on polishing their own presentations while the others are presenting.[23] The former are, of course, favoured.

Social skills are also important. Being pleasant and collegial are requirements of Rosenbluth International, a travel-management company based in Philadelphia, with annual revenues over $4 billion. Here, job applicants are asked to play a trial game of softball with the company team. Potential executives are frequently flown to the firm's North Dakota ranch to help repair fences or drive cattle. Do athletic ability or ranching skills matter? Not at all. According to Keami Lewis, Rosenbluth's diversity manager, "You can teach a person almost anything. But you can't teach him or her how to be nice."[24] Or, as Tom Stewart has suggested, "You can make a leopard a better leopard, but you can't change its spots."[25]

Many have argued that the most common—and fatal—hiring mistake is to select individuals with the right skills but the wrong mindset on the assumption that "we can change them." According to Alan Davidson, an industrial psychologist, "The single best predictor of future behaviour is past behaviour. Your personality (largely reflecting values, beliefs, attitudes, and social skills) is going to be essentially the same throughout your life."[26]

Sound Recruiting Approaches and Networking Companies that take hiring seriously must also take recruiting seriously. The number of jobs that successful knowledge-intensive companies must fill is astonishing. Ironically, many companies still have no shortage of applicants. Southwest Airlines typically gets 150,000 resumés a year, yet hires only about 5,000. Netscape reviews 60 resumés for every hire.[27] The challenge becomes having the right job candidates, not the greatest number of them.

Few firms are as thorough as Microsoft when it comes to recruiting. Each year, the firm scans the entire pool of 25,000 U.S. and 2,000 Canadian computer-science graduates and identifies the 8,000 in which they are interested. After further screening, 2,600 are invited for on-campus interviews at their universities. Out of these, only 800 are invited to the company's Redmond, Washington, headquarters. Of this group, 500 receive offers, and usually 400 accept. These massive efforts, however, provide less than 20 percent of the company's hiring needs. To find the other talent, Microsoft maintains a team of 300 recruiting experts whose full-time job is to locate the best and brightest in the industry.[28] Other firms, such as GE Medical Systems and RIM of Waterloo, Ontario, have found that current employees are the best source for new ones. When someone refers former colleagues or friends for a job, his or her own reputation is also on the line. Employees tend to be careful in recommending people for employment unless they are reasonably confident that these people will turn out well. This provides a good "screen" for the firm in deciding whom to hire. After all, hiring the right people makes things a lot easier: fewer rules and regulations, less need for monitoring and hierarchy, and greater internalization of organizational norms and objectives.

Developing Human Capital

It is not enough to hire top-level talent and expect that the skills and capabilities of those employees remain current throughout the duration of their employment. Rather, training and development must take place at all levels of the organization. For example, Solectron assembles printed circuit boards and other components for its Silicon Valley clients. Its employees receive an average of 95 hours of company-provided training each year. Chairman Winston Chen observed, "Technology changes so fast that we estimate 20 percent of an engineer's knowledge becomes obsolete each year. Training is an obligation we owe to our employees. If you want high growth and high quality, then training is a big part of the equation."[29] Although the financial returns on training may be hard to calculate, most experts believe it is not only real but also essential. One company that has calculated the benefit from training is Motorola. This high-technology firm has calculated that every dollar spent on training returns $30 in productivity gains over the following three years. Dofasco Inc. of Hamilton, Ontario, not only hires locally and predominantly on the basis of its own employees' referrals but also has in place a two-year orientation plan for each of its new employees. Dofasco invests substantial time and resources in developing new employees because it expects them to stay for most or all of their working life; indeed, it enjoys the lowest turnover in the industry.

In addition to training, the effective development of human capital throughout the organization entails widespread involvement, monitoring of progress, and continuous evaluation and feedback.

Encouraging Widespread Involvement The development of human capital requires the active involvement of leaders at all levels throughout the organization. It won't be successful if it is viewed only as the responsibility of the human resource department. Each year at General Electric (GE), 200 facilitators, 30 officers, 30 human resource executives, and many young managers actively participate in GE's orientation program at the firm's impressive Crotonville training centre outside New York City. Topics include global competition, winning on the global playing field, and personal examination of each new employee's core values vis-à-vis GE's values. As a senior manager once commented, "There is nothing like teaching Sunday school to force you to confront your own values."

The "cascade approach" is another way that managers at multiple levels in an organization become actively involved in developing human capital. For example, Robert Galvin, former chairman of Motorola, requested a workshop for more than 1,000 Motorola senior executives to help them understand the market potential of selected Asian countries. However, rather than bringing in outside experts, participants were asked to analyze the existing competition and determine how Motorola could compete in these markets. After researching their topics, the executives travelled around the world to directly observe local market developments. Then, they taught the concepts of globalization to the next level of 3,000 Motorola managers. By doing so, they not only verified their impressions through first-hand observations, but they also reinforced their learning and shared it by teaching others.

Monitoring Progress and Tracking Development Whether a firm uses on-site formal training, off-site training (e.g., universities), or on-the-job training, tracking individual progress—and sharing this knowledge with both the employee and key managers—becomes essential. At Citibank, a talent inventory program keeps track of roughly 10,000 employees worldwide—how they're doing, what skills they need to work on, and where else in the company they might thrive. Larry Phillips, head of human resources, considers the program critical to the company's global growth.[30]

GlaxoSmithKline, the global pharmaceutical giant, places increasingly greater emphasis on broader experiences over longer periods of time. Dan Phelan, senior vice president and director of human resources, explained, "We ideally follow a two-plus-two-plus-two formula in developing people for top management positions." The formula reflects the belief that SmithKline's best people should gain experience in two business units, two functional units (such as finance and marketing), in two countries.

Evaluating Human Capital In today's competitive environment, collaboration and interdependence have become vital to organizational success. Individuals must share their knowledge and work together constructively to achieve collective, not just individual, goals. To address the "softer" dimensions of communications and social skills, the values, beliefs, and attitudes that go beyond technical skills, organizations have begun to use 360-degree evaluation and feedback systems.[31] In these systems, superiors, direct reports, colleagues, and even internal and external customers rate a person's skills. Managers also rate themselves in order to have a personal benchmark. The 360-degree feedback system complements teamwork, employee involvement, and organizational flattening. Moreover, as organizations continue to push responsibility downward, traditional top-down appraisal systems become insufficient. A manager who previously managed the performance of three supervisors might now be responsible for ten, and is less likely to have the in-depth knowledge needed to appraise and develop each sufficiently and fairly.

To assist its managers in the task of appraisal, GE's 360 leadership assessment evaluates all managers on ten distinct characteristics—namely, vision, customer/quality focus, integrity, accountability/commitment, communication/influence, shared ownership/boundary-less, team building/empowerment, knowledge/expertise/intellect, initiative/speed, and global mindset. Each of these characteristics has four performance criteria, and those around a manager are asked to rate that person on those criteria. With respect to vision, for example, the four criteria are (1) the ability to develop and communicate a clear, simple, customer-focused vision/direction for the organization; (2) the ability to be forward-thinking, stretch horizons, challenge imaginations; (3) the ability to inspire and energize others to commit to vision, capture minds, and lead by example; and (4) as appropriate, the ability to update vision to reflect constant and accelerating change affecting the business.

Finally, evaluation systems must ensure that a manager's success does not come at the cost of compromising the organization's core values. It is understood that such conduct leads only to short-term wins for both the manager and the organization. The organization typically suffers long-term losses in terms of morale, turnover, productivity, and so on. Accordingly, Merck's former chairman, Ray Gilmartin, told his employees, "If someone is achieving results but not demonstrating the core values of the company, at the expense of our people, that manager does not have much of a career here."

Retaining Human Capital

It has been said that talented employees are like "frogs in a wheelbarrow."[32] They can jump out at any time. Today's leaders can either provide the work environment and incentives to keep productive employees and management from wanting to bail out, or they can rely on legal means such as employment contracts and non-compete clauses.[33] Automotive industry supplier Magna International has a keen focus on cultivating the creative potential of its workforce and retaining their talent. Its strategy—to foster the entrepreneurial spirit—is relatively simple. Each division within the $26 billion multinational firm operates as a separate "Automotive Systems Corporation," with its own profit centre. According to Magna's corporate constitution, 10 percent of pre-tax profits are allocated to employees, and up to 6 percent may be distributed to senior managers. In addition, no less than 20 percent of after-tax profits must be distributed to shareholders. This "Fair Enterprise

System" is designed to keep good employees prospering within the Magna family and the corporation prospering because of them.[34]

An individual's identification with the organization's mission and values, challenging work and a stimulating environment, and financial and non-financial rewards and incentives all play a critical role in retaining a firm's human capital.

Identifying with an Organization's Mission and Values People who identify with and are committed to the core mission and values of the organization are less likely to stray or bolt to the competition. Consider BC Biomedical Laboratories of Surrey, British Columbia. It was recently named Canada's "Best Employer" for the third year running. BC Biomedical's CEO, Doug Buchanan, attributes it squarely to the fact that management and employees share the same goals and attitudes; all are driven by their desire to be able to help others in times of need. A flat organization allows every employee to be in direct contact with patients and to have a clear image of where the business is going. For the last four years, BC Biomedical has recorded a mere 1 percent turnover among its 412 employees.[35]

Employees form strong bonds with organizations that create simple and straightforward missions—strategic intents—that channel efforts and generate intense loyalties.[36] Examples include Canon's passion to "beat Xerox" and Honda's early commitment to build fuel efficient and environmentally friendly cars, even when those were not popular. Likewise, leaders can arouse passions and loyalty by reinforcing the firm's quest to "topple Goliath" or by constantly communicating a history of overcoming adversity and life-threatening challenges.[37] For example, CEO Richard Branson of the Virgin Group constantly uses the David and Goliath imagery, pitting his company against such powerful adversaries as British Airways and Coca-Cola.

Challenging Work and a Stimulating Environment Arthur Schawlow, winner of the 1981 Nobel Prize in physics, was once asked what he believed made the difference between highly creative and less creative scientists. His reply, "The labour of love aspect is very important. The most successful scientists often are not the most talented. But they are the ones impelled by curiosity. They've got to know what the answer is."[38]

Such insights highlight the importance of intrinsic motivation: the motivation to work on something because it is interesting, exciting, satisfying, or personally challenging. Consider Jorgen Wedel's perspective on the relative importance of pay compared with the meaningfulness of work: "I get calls from headhunters who offer bigger salaries, signing bonuses, and such. But the excitement of what I am doing here is equal to a 30 percent pay raise." Wedel is executive vice president of Gillette's international division.

To keep competitors from poaching talent, organizations must keep employees excited about the challenges and opportunities available. Scott Cook, chairman of Intuit, understands this reality: "I wake up every morning knowing that if my people don't sense a compelling vision and a big upside, they'll simply leave."[39]

Financial and Non-Financial Rewards and Incentives Without a doubt, financial rewards are a vital organizational control mechanism. Money—whether in the form of salary, bonus, or stock options—can mean many different things to people. For some, it might mean security; to others, recognition; and to still others, a sense of freedom and independence.

Nevertheless, most surveys show that money is not the most important reason why people take or leave jobs and that money, in some surveys, is not even in the top ten.[40] Consistent with these findings, Tandem Computers (now part of Hewlett-Packard) never used to tell people being recruited what their salaries would be. People who asked were told that their salaries were competitive. If they persisted along this line of questioning, they would not be offered a position. Why? Tandem realized a rather simple idea:

people who come for money will leave for money. Clearly, money can't be ignored, but it shouldn't be the primary mechanism to attract and retain talent.

Without the proper retention mechanisms, organizations can commit time and resources to inadvertently helping the competition develop their human capital.[41] And, given the importance of networking and teams, losses tend to multiply and intensify. The exodus of talent can erode a firm's competitive advantages in the marketplace.

In Toronto, the departure of David Kassie from the top job at CIBC World Markets and his overtures to other high-flying investment bankers and equity traders created tremors; their loyalty appeared to be directed more toward their former boss and his promise of big bonuses and partnerships in an upstart investment firm than it was to their current employers.[42]

At various firms, rewards and incentives may include an impressive array of amenities aimed at retaining employees, such as on-site stores, dry-cleaning services, banks, ATMs, excellent cafeterias, and athletic facilities. Non-financial rewards even involve accommodating working families with children. Coping with the conflicting demands of family and work is a problem at some point for virtually all employees. Whirlpool Canada offers additional "work/life balance" days to each employee. CIBC estimated that it saved more that 6,800 employee days and enjoyed savings of $1.4 million by providing emergency babysitting services to staff in its Toronto locations through a two-year pilot project. It plans to roll out the program across Canada. In a recent study, 13 percent of women with preschoolers indicated that they would work more hours if additional or better child care were provided.[43]

Similar initiatives are developed to address and capitalize on the increasing diversity of the workforce, but also to deal with the cultural differences of an increasingly heterogeneous population and customer base. Gender, race, ethnicity, and nationality are but the most recognized dimensions of diversity. Organizations that compete globally recognize the benefits of effectively managing a diverse workforce in the atmosphere of enhanced creativity, diversity of ideas and solutions, greater flexibility, and better attraction of people and resources that directly impact the nurturing of competitive advantages.

THE VITAL ROLE OF SOCIAL CAPITAL

Successful firms are well aware that the attraction, development, and retention of talent are *necessary but not sufficient conditions* for creating competitive advantage. In the knowledge economy, it is not the stock of human capital that is important but the extent to which it is combined and leveraged that is. In a sense, developing and retaining human capital becomes less important as key players (talented professionals, in particular) take the role of "free agents" and bring with them the requisite skill, in many cases. Instead, the development of social capital (that is, the friendships and working relationships among talented individuals) becomes increasingly important as it helps tie knowledge workers to a given firm.[44] Knowledge workers often exhibit greater loyalties to their colleagues and their profession than to their employing organization, which may be "an amorphous, distant, and sometimes threatening entity."[45] Thus, a firm must find ways to create "ties" among its knowledge workers.

 ← LO 4

To illustrate, let's look at a hypothetical example. Two pharmaceutical firms are fortunate enough to hire Nobel Prize–winning scientists to work in their laboratories.[46] In one case, the scientist is offered a very attractive salary, outstanding facilities and equipment, and told to "go to it!" In the second case, the scientist is offered approximately the same salary, facilities, and equipment, but he or she will be working in a laboratory with ten highly skilled and enthusiastic scientists. Part of the job is to collaborate with these peers and jointly develop promising drug compounds. There is little doubt as to which

How Nucor Shares Knowledge within and between Its Manufacturing Plants

A key aspect of Nucor's strategy is to develop strong social relationships and a team-based culture throughout the firm. It is effectively supported by a combination of work-group, plant-level, and corporate-wide financial incentives and rewards, wherein knowledge and best practices are eagerly shared by everyone in the organization. How does Nucor do it?

Within-Plant Knowledge Transfers. Nucor strives to develop a social community within each plant that promotes trust and open communication. People know each other very well throughout each plant, and they are encouraged to interact. To accomplish this, the firm's policy is to keep the number of employees at each plant between 250 and 300. Such a relatively small number, combined with employees' long tenure, fosters a high degree of interpersonal familiarity. Additionally, each plant's general manager regularly holds dinner meetings for groups of 25 to 30, inviting every employee once a year. The format is open and includes a few ground rules: All comments are to remain business-

related and are not to be directed to specific individuals. In turn, managers guarantee that they will carefully consider and respond to all suggestions and criticisms.

Between-Plant Knowledge Transfers. Nucor uses several mechanisms to transfer knowledge among its plants. First, detailed performance data on each mill are regularly distributed to all of the plant managers. Second, all general managers of the plants meet as a group three times a year to review each facility's performance and develop formal plans on how to transfer best practices. Third, plant managers, supervisors, and machine operators regularly visit each other's mills. These visits enable operations personnel to go beyond performance data in order to understand first-hand the factors that make particular practices superior or inferior. After all, they are the true possessors of process knowledge. Fourth, given the inherent difficulties in transferring complex knowledge, Nucor selectively assigns people from one plant to another on the basis of their expertise.

Source: A. K. Gupta and V. Govindarajan, "Knowledge Management's Social Dimension: Lessons from Nucor Steel," *Organizational Dynamics*, Fall 2000, pp. 71–80.

scenario will lead to a higher probability of retaining the scientist. The interaction, sharing, and collaboration are likely to create a situation in which the scientist will develop firm-specific ties and be less likely to "bolt" for a higher salary offer. Such ties are critical because knowledge-based resources tend to be more tacit in nature, as we mentioned earlier in this chapter. Therefore, they are much more difficult to protect against loss (i.e., the individual quitting the organization) than other types of capital such as equipment, machinery, and land.

Recall the resource-based view of the firm that we discussed in Chapter 3. Competitive advantages tend to be harder for competitors to copy if they are based on "unique bundles" of resources.[47] If employees are working effectively in teams, sharing their knowledge, and learning from each other, not only will they be more likely to add value to the firm, but they also will be less likely to leave the organization, because of the loyalties and social ties that they develop over time. Strategy Spotlight 4.1 discusses how Nucor, a highly successful steel manufacturer, develops social capital among its employees and managers. This promotes the sharing of ideas within and across its manufacturing plants. Nucor does not utilize any unique or proprietary technology in its mills, yet it has consistently outperformed competitors and is one of the most efficient steel producers in the world.

How Social Capital Helps Attract and Retain Talent

The importance of social ties among talented professionals is creating an important challenge (and opportunity) for organizations today. Writers describe the increasing prevalence of a "Pied Piper effect," in which teams or networks of people are leaving one company for another.[48] The trend is to recruit job candidates at the pinnacle of social networks in organizations, particularly if they are seen as having the potential to bring with them a raft of valuable colleagues. This is a process that is referred to as "hiring via personal networks." The corollary, of course, of this human capital mobility is the emigration of talent from an organization to form start-up ventures. Northern Telecom labs are credited with having supplied the inspiration and the key personnel for scores of technology and telecommunications firms in the Ottawa region during the 1980s and 1990s.[49] Microsoft is perhaps the best-known example of this phenomenon.[50] Professionals have frequently left Microsoft—en masse—to form venture capital and technology start-ups built around teams of software developers. One example is Ignition Corporation of Belleview, Washington, which was formed by Brad Silverberg, a former Microsoft senior vice president. Eight former Microsoft executives, among others, founded the company. Exhibit 4.3 provides a partial listing of other companies that have been formed by groups of former Microsoft employees.

The importance of the Pied Piper effect for today's firms is rather self-evident. Leaders must be aware of social relationships among professionals as important recruiting and retention mechanisms.[51] Social networks can provide an important mechanism for obtaining both resources and information from individuals and organizations outside the boundary of a firm.[52] Also, to be a valued member of a social network, one typically has to have the requisite human capital—that is, knowledge and capabilities that can add value to other members of the network.

The Potential Downside of Social Capital

Some companies have been damaged by high social capital that breeds "groupthink"—a tendency not to question shared beliefs.[53] When people identify strongly with a group, they sometimes support ideas that are suboptimal or simply wrong. An excess of "warm and fuzzy" feelings among group members prevents people from challenging one another with tough questions and discourages them from engaging in the "creative abrasion" that Dorothy Leonard of Harvard University described as a key source of innovation.[54] Two firms well known for their collegiality, strong sense of employee membership, and humane approach—Digital Equipment (now part of Hewlett-Packard) and Polaroid—suffered

Company	What It Does	Defectors from Microsoft
Crossgain	builds software around XML computer language	23 of 60 employees
ViAir	makes software for wireless providers	unwilling to specify
CheckSpace	builds online payment services for small businesses	"a good chunk" of its 30 employees
digiMine	sells data mining services	about 15% of 62 employees in addition to the 3 founders
Avogadro	builds wireless notification software	8 of 25 employees
Tellme Networks	offers information such as stock quotes and scores over the phone	about 40 of 250 employees; another 40 from the former Netscape

Source: R. Buckman, "Tech Defectors from Microsoft Resettle Together," *The Wall Street Journal*, Eastern Edition, 2000. Copyright © 2000 by Dow Jones & Company, Inc. Reproduced with permission of Dow Jones & Company, Inc. via Copyright Clearance Center."

Exhibit 4.3
Companies Formed by Former Microsoft Employees

greatly from market misjudgments and strategic errors. The aforementioned aspects of their culture contributed to their problems.

Additionally, some have argued that socialization processes, whereby individuals are "socialized in the norms, values, and ways of working inherent to the workgroup and the organization," can be potentially expensive in terms of financial resources and managerial commitment.[55] Such expenses may represent a significant opportunity cost that should be evaluated in terms of the overall potential costs and benefits.

In general, however, the effects of high social capital are strongly positive. Engagement, collaboration, loyalty, persistence, and dedication are important benefits.[56] Firms such as United Parcel Service, Hewlett-Packard, Four Seasons Hotels and Resorts, and Tim Hortons have made significant investments in social capital that enable them to attract and retain talent and help them to do their best work. Such companies rarely face any imminent danger from an overdose of a good thing.

USING TECHNOLOGY TO LEVERAGE HUMAN CAPITAL AND KNOWLEDGE

Sharing knowledge and information throughout the organization can be a means of conserving resources, developing products and services, and creating new opportunities. Technology can be used to leverage human capital and knowledge within organizations as well as with customers and suppliers beyond their boundaries. Examples range from simple applications, including the use of email and networks for product development, to more sophisticated uses that enhance the competitive position of knowledge-intensive firms in industries such as consulting, health care, and personal computers, and that help firms retain employees' knowledge, even when they leave.

Consider email—an effective means of communicating a wide variety of information across various parts of an organization and with suppliers and customers. It is quick, easy, and almost costless. Of course, it can become a problem when employees use it excessively or for personal reasons. Nevertheless, email can be an effective means for top executives to communicate information efficiently, share ideas, and relate decisions. Employees use email extensively to relate information, coordinate tasks, contribute to a discussion, and participate in decisions.

The use of technology also enables professionals to work as part of virtual teams to enhance the speed and effectiveness with which products are developed. For example, Microsoft has concentrated much of its development around virtual teams that are networked together throughout the company.[57] This helps accelerate design and testing of new software modules that use the Windows-based framework as their central architecture. Microsoft is able to foster specialized technical expertise while rapidly sharing knowledge throughout the organization. This helps the firm learn how its new technologies can be applied rapidly to new business ventures such as cable television, broadcasting, travel services, and financial services.

Codifying Knowledge for Competitive Advantage

We have identified two different kinds of knowledge. Tacit knowledge is embedded in personal experience and shared only with the consent and participation of the individual. Explicit (or codified) knowledge, on the other hand, is knowledge that can be documented, widely distributed, and easily replicated. One of the challenges of knowledge-intensive organizations is to capture and codify the knowledge and experience that, in effect, resides in the heads of its employees. Otherwise, they will have to constantly "reinvent the wheel," which is both expensive and inefficient. Also, the "new wheel" may not necessarily be superior to the "old wheel."[58]

Once a knowledge asset (e.g., a software code or processes/routines for a consulting firm) is developed and paid for, it can be reused many times at very low cost, assuming that it doesn't have to be substantially modified each time. Let's take the case of the consulting company Accenture.[59] Since the knowledge of its consultants has been codified and stored in electronic repositories, it can be employed in many jobs by a huge number of consultants. Additionally, since the work has a high level of standardization (i.e., there are strong similarities across the numerous client engagements), there generally tends to be a rather high ratio of some 30 consultants to partners. As one might expect, there must be extensive training of the newly hired consultants for such an approach to work. The recruits are trained at Accenture's Center for Professional Education, a 150-acre campus in St. Charles, Illinois. Using the centre's knowledge-management repository, the consultants work through many scenarios designed to improve business processes. In effect, the information technologies enable the consultants to be "implementers, not inventors."

Access Health, a call-in medical centre, also uses technology to capture and share knowledge. When someone calls the centre, a registered nurse uses the company's "clinical decision architecture" to assess the caller's symptoms, rule out possible conditions, and recommend a home remedy, doctor's visit, or trip to the emergency room. The company's knowledge repository contains algorithms of the symptoms of more than 500 illnesses. According to CEO Joseph Tallman, "We are not inventing a new way to cure disease. We are taking available knowledge and inventing processes to put it to better use." At Access Health, the codified knowledge is in the form of software algorithms. They were very expensive to develop, but the investment has been repaid many times over. The first 300 algorithms that Access Health developed have each been used an average of 8,000 times a year. Further, the company's paying customers—insurance companies and provider groups—save money because many callers would have made expensive trips to the emergency room or the doctor's office had they not been diagnosed over the phone.

The use of information technology to codify knowledge can also help a firm to integrate its internal value-chain activities with its customers and suppliers. Dell Computer Corporation uses a sophisticated knowledge-management system to assemble and sell over 11 million personal computers per year. It uses some 40,000 possible configurations, as compared to about 100 for its competitors.[60] Dell employs an army of talented engineers and invests heavily upfront to determine the necessary configurations and then to develop and codify the process of assembly for each configuration. Although each configuration is used, on average, only about 275 times each year, the investment pays off in the cost containment that is passed on to consumers. Dell's knowledge-management system integrates its processes with the assembly activities of its suppliers, giving customers the flexibility to order PCs to their desired specifications and itself an edge in the intensely competitive PC market.

Retaining Knowledge When Employees Leave

All organizations suffer the adverse consequences of voluntary turnover. However, many leading firms are devising ways to minimize the loss of knowledge when employees leave.

Information technology can often help employers cope with turnover by saving some tacit knowledge that the firm would otherwise lose.[61] Customer relationship software, for example, automates sales and provides salespeople with access to client histories, including prior orders and complaints. This enables salespeople to quickly become familiar with client accounts (about which they might otherwise know nothing). Similarly, groupware applications such as Lotus Notes can standardize interactions and keep records of decisions and crucial contextual information, providing something like an electronic record of employee knowledge. Other programs, such as Waterloo-based Open Text's Livelink, enable all employees to track and share documents on their firm's intranet. New simulation software for team-based project management, such as Thinking Tools's Project Challenge, enables new teams to learn how to work together much more rapidly than on-the-job experience alone would permit.

A key issue in such knowledge-management systems becomes one of motivation—in particular, the incentives for people to contribute their knowledge. Some organizations have found that such systems work best when they are incorporated into the firm's evaluation and reward system. For example, Bruce Strong, founder and CEO of Context Integration, a Web consulting firm, decided to develop a knowledge-management system to help employees unlock their thoughts and, collectively, be more productive.[62] Six months and a half-million dollars later, he unveiled IAN (Intellectual Assets Network). The objective was to provide a medium for his consultants to share ideas, ask questions, and trace earlier journeys on similar projects. Strong was quickly disappointed with the lack of involvement by his employees. This is not surprising. Carla O'Dell, president of the American Productivity and Quality Center, said that of the companies trying knowledge management, fewer than 10 percent have succeeded in making it part of their culture. Consultants themselves identified many reasons for not embracing IAN. Depositing notes and product reports into the database was seen as one more task in a busy day. They didn't see any urgency in the task. Moreover, they resented management trying to impose what they perceived as a rigid structure on their work. In response, Strong, began to reinforce the many benefits of the system, including the potential for better and more consistent service. He also publicly recognized people who stood out as strong IAN contributors, and he made this part of everyone's job description. Perhaps most important, he began rewarding people to use it. He assigned points when people used the system—for example, one point for posting a resumé on the system, five points for creating a project record, and so on. The results were tallied every three months, and the score accounted for 10 percent of a consultant's quarterly bonus. Within a two-month period, overall IAN usage almost doubled. Many consultants became enthusiastic converts once they had a positive experience with IAN. Not only does IAN continue to help many of them to provide excellent service to their clients, but some of their knowledge also remains in the firm when they leave.

Exhibit 4.4 poses a series of questions managers should consider in determining (1) how effective their organization is in attracting, developing, and retaining human capital and (2) how effective they are in leveraging human capital through social capital and technology.

PROTECTING THE INTELLECTUAL ASSETS OF THE ORGANIZATION: INTELLECTUAL PROPERTY AND DYNAMIC CAPABILITIES

In today's dynamic and turbulent world, unpredictability and fast change dominate the business environment. Economic prosperity rests upon the useful application of knowledge, and access to the underlying information—in terms of technology, human capital, or research and design networks—is fairly even among firms. Developing dynamic capabilities is the only avenue providing firms with the opportunity to reconfigure their knowledge and activities in order to achieve sustainable competitive advantage. What would give a sustainable competitive advantage to firms and then prevent others from copying their valuable ideas?[63] Protecting a firm's intellectual capital requires a concerted effort on the part of the firm. After all, employees become disgruntled and patents expire. The management of intellectual property involves contracts with confidentiality and non-compete clauses, copyrights, patents, and the development of trademarks.

Exhibit 4.4
Issues to Consider in Creating Value through Human Capital, Social Capital, and Technology

Human Capital

Recruiting "Top-Notch" Human Capital

- Does the organization assess attitude and "general makeup" instead of focusing primarily on skills and background in selecting employees at all levels?
- How important are creativity and problem-solving ability? Are they properly considered in hiring decisions?
- Do people throughout the organization engage in effective networking activities to obtain a broad pool of worthy potential employees? Is the organization creative in such endeavours?

Enhancing Human Capital through Employee Development

- Does the development and training process inculcate an "organizationwide" perspective?
- Is there widespread involvement, including top executives, in the preparation and delivery of training and development programs?
- Is the development of human capital effectively tracked and monitored?
- Are there effective programs for succession at all levels of the organization, especially the top-most levels?
- Does the firm effectively evaluate its human capital? Is a 360-degree evaluation used? Why? Why not?
- Are mechanisms in place to assure that a manager's success does not come at the cost of compromising the organization's core values?

Retaining the Best Employees

- Are there appropriate financial rewards to motivate employees at all levels?
- Do people throughout the organization strongly identify with the organization's mission?
- Are employees provided a stimulating and challenging work environment that fosters professional growth?
- Are valued amenities provided (e.g., flex time, child-care facilities, telecommuting) that are appropriate given the organization's mission, strategy, and how work is accomplished?
- Is the organization continually devising strategies and mechanisms to retain top performers?

Social Capital

- Are there positive personal and professional relationships among employees?
- Is the organization benefiting (or being penalized) by hiring (or by voluntary turnover) en masse?
- Does an environment of caring and encouragement, rather than of competition, enhance team performance?
- Do the social networks within the organization have the appropriate levels of closure and bridging relationships?
- Does the organization minimize the adverse effects of excessive social capital, such as excessive costs and "groupthink"?

Technology

- Has the organization used technologies such as email and networks to develop products and services?
- Does the organization effectively use technology to transfer best practices across the organization?
- Does the organization use technology to leverage human capital and knowledge both within the boundaries of the organization and among its suppliers and customers?
- Has the organization effectively used technology to codify knowledge for competitive advantage?
- Does the organization try to retain some of the knowledge of employees when they decide to leave the firm?

Source: Adapted from G.G. Dess and J.C. Picken, *Beyond Productivity* (New York: AMACON, 1999), pp. 63–64.

The management of intellectual property and intellectual property rights has its conceptual roots in individual rights, especially the right to own property. Such rights can be found in many societies, going back centuries. Simply put, if those rights are not reliably protected by the state, no individual will build private long-term assets and make investments, the foundation of a growing economy. Property rights have been enshrined in constitutions and rules of law in many countries. In the information era, though, adjustments need to be made to accommodate the new realities of knowledge. Knowledge and information are fundamentally different assets from the physical ones that property rights have been designed to protect.

Intellectual property typically has no diminishing returns; much of production is characterized by constant if not zero marginal costs. Indeed, it may take a substantial investment to develop a software program, an idea, or a digital music tune. Once developed, though, their reproduction and distribution cost may be almost zero, especially if the Internet is used. Effective protection of intellectual property is necessary before any investor will finance such an undertaking. Appropriation of their returns is harder to police since possession and deployment are not as readily observable. Unlike physical assets, intellectual property can be stolen simply by broadcasting it; recall Napster and MP3 as well as all the debates about counterfeit software, music CDs, and DVDs coming from developing countries such as China. Part of the problem is that using an idea does not prevent others from simultaneously using it for their own benefit, something that is impossible with physical assets. Also, new ideas are frequently and easily built on old ideas and, thus, are not easily traceable. Strategy Spotlight 4.2 describes the problems that RIM faced early on and the obstacles these issues presented to the success of the BlackBerry. The legal wrangling exposed many of the issues that arise from the limitations of the prevailing legislative environment as it attempts to address the complexities of intellectual properties, and it highlighted the importance of effective intellectual property management.

Economists and jurists alike admit that many of those issues have not been resolved yet, and our current thinking still mainly rests on relatively archaic principles. Politicians have attempted to legislate new patent regulations for very important new pharmaceutical compounds, new research fields such as stem cell research and biotechnology, or the protection of Canadian culture through the awarding of restrictive licences for such services as satellite radio. The relative effects of intellectual property rights and economic growth need to be analyzed. However, a firm that is faced with this challenge today cannot wait for the legislators to resolve the political and economic issues. It has to embark on the next technological development, drug, software solution, electronic game, online service, or any of a myriad other products and services that contribute to our economic prosperity and the creation of wealth for those entrepreneurs who have the idea first and risk bringing it to the market.

Related to the above, dynamic capabilities entail the capacity to build and protect a competitive advantage, which rests on knowledge, assets, competencies, and complementary assets and technologies as well as the ability to sense and seize new opportunities, generate new knowledge, and reconfigure existing assets and capabilities. According to David Teece, dynamic capabilities are related to the entrepreneurial side of the firm and are built within a firm through its environmental and technological "sensing" apparatus, its choices of organizational form, and its collective ability to strategize. Dynamic capabilities are about the ability of an organization to challenge the conventional wisdom within its industry and market, learn and innovate, adapt to the changing world, and continuously adopt new ways to serve the evolving needs of the market while protecting itself against the dynamic and uncertain competitive environment.

Trouble with the BlackBerry

RIM (Research in Motion) is a Waterloo, Ontario, company that is best known for developing the BlackBerry, a wireless device that integrates the functionalities of a cellphone with wireless information services and email capabilities. During its brief history, RIM has become one of the fastest growing companies in North America. Founded in 1984 by Mike Lazaridis, a former University of Waterloo student, RIM was a competent but obscure technology firm until 1999 when the first BlackBerry was released. Through the development of integrated hardware, software, and services that support multiple wireless network standards, the BlackBerry has enabled RIM to grow from less than $50 million in sales revenue in 1999 to $7.2 billion by 2007. Even more impressive, by 2007 the company could boast a market capitalization in excess of $26 billion. RIM's commitment to their slogan "always on, always connected" has won them a legion of dedicated followers around the globe.

Interestingly, legal challenges have been the biggest obstacles that RIM has faced in the eight years since the introduction of the first BlackBerry. In 2002, Virginia-based NTP sued the company alleging patent infringement. Although RIM tried to demonstrate that NTP's patents were invalid because wireless email technology existed prior to NTP's filing of patent applications, the court found them guilty of willfully infringing NTP's patents. While the appeal process dragged on through higher courts, the fear that the court might issue an injunction against BlackBerry greatly slowed the growth of RIM's subscriber base. Given the need to allay the anxieties of the subscribers, who could not imagine life without their BlackBerries, RIM decided to settle its dispute with NTP in March, 2006. The settlement amount was a staggering $612.5 million in "full and final settlement of all claims"!

In a bizarre postscript to the settlement with NTP, in May 2006, RIM was sued by California-based Visto for infringement of its patents. Visto has a history of suing, and occasionally winning, patent infringement lawsuits against companies such as Good Technology, Microsoft, and Seven Networks. It is interesting to note that NTP holds an equity stake in Visto!

Sources: A. Hesseldahl, "RIM's latest patent problem," *BusinessWeek -Online*, May 2, 2006; "Settlement reached in BlackBerry patent case," np, 2006.

Summary

Firms throughout the industrial world are recognizing that the knowledge worker is the key to success in the marketplace. However, we also recognize that human capital, although vital, is still only a necessary but not sufficient condition for creating value. We began the first section of the chapter by addressing the importance of human capital and how it can be attracted, developed, and retained. We then discussed the role of social capital and technology in leveraging human capital for competitive success. We pointed out that intellectual capital—the difference between a firm's market value and its book value—has increased significantly over the past few decades. This is particularly true for firms in knowledge-intensive industries, such as software development, where there are relatively few tangible assets.

The second section of the chapter addressed the attraction, development, and retention of human capital in more detail. We viewed these three activities as a "three-legged stool"—that is, it is difficult for firms to be successful if they ignore or are unsuccessful in any one of these activities. Among the issues we discussed in *attracting* human capital were "hiring for attitude, training for skill" and the value of using social networks to attract human capital. In particular, it is important to attract employees who can collaborate with others, given the importance of collective efforts, teams, and task forces. With regard to *developing* human capital, we discussed the need to encourage widespread involvement throughout the organization, monitor progress and track the development of human capital, and evaluate human capital. Among the practices that are widely acknowledged in evaluating human capital is the 360-degree evaluation system. Employees are evaluated by their superiors, peers, direct reports, and even internal and external customers. Finally, some mechanisms for *retaining* human capital are employees' identification with the organization's mission and values, providing challenging work and a stimulating environment, financial and non-financial rewards and incentives, and providing flexibility and amenities. A key issue here is that a firm should not overemphasize financial rewards. After all, if individuals join an organization for money, they are also likely to leave for money. With money as the primary motivator, there is little chance that employees will develop firm-specific ties to keep them with the organization.

The third section of the chapter discussed the importance of social capital in leveraging human capital. Social capital refers to the network of relationships that individuals have throughout the organization as well as with customers and suppliers. Such ties can be critical in obtaining both information and resources. With regard to recruiting, for example, we saw how some firms are able to hire, en masse, groups of individuals who are part of social networks. Social relationships can also be very important in the effective functioning of groups. Finally, we discussed some of the potential downsides of social capital. These include the expenses that firms may bear when promoting social and working relationships among individuals as well as the potential for "groupthink," wherein individuals are reluctant to express divergent (or opposing) views on an issue because of social pressures to conform.

The fourth section addressed the role of technology in leveraging human capital. We discussed relatively simple means of using technology, such as email and networks, through which individuals can collaborate. We also addressed more sophisticated uses of technology such as management systems. Here, knowledge can be codified and reused at very low cost, as we saw in the examples of firms in the consulting, health care, and high-technology industries. Also, given that there will still be some turnover—voluntary or involuntary—even in the most desirable places to work, technology can be a valuable means of preserving knowledge when individuals terminate their employment with a firm.

The final section addressed the importance of the protection of intellectual property, through the utilization of patents, copyrights, and trademarks, and it considered the development of dynamic capabilities for supporting a sustainable competitive advantage.

Summary Review Questions

1. Explain the role of knowledge in today's competitive environment.

2. Why is it important for managers to recognize the interdependence of factors in the attraction, development, and retention of talented professionals?

3. What are some of the potential downsides for firms that engage in a "war for talent"?

4. Discuss the need for managers to use social capital in leveraging their human capital both within their firm and across firms.

5. Discuss the key role of technology in leveraging knowledge and human capital.

Experiential Exercise

Johnson & Johnson, a leading health care firm with $61 billion in 2007 revenues, is often rated as one of *Fortune*'s "Most Admired Firms." It is considered an excellent place to work and has generated high return to shareholders. Clearly, the firm values its human capital. Using the Internet and/or library resources, identify some of the actions/strategies Johnson & Johnson has taken to attract, develop, and retain human capital. What are their implications?

Activity	Actions/Strategies	Implications
Attracting human capital		
Developing human capital		
Retaining human capital		

Application Questions Exercises

1. Look up successful firms in a high-technology industry as well as two successful firms in more traditional industries such as automobile manufacturing and retailing. Compare their market values and book values. What are some implications of these differences?
2. Select a firm for which you believe its social capital—both within the firm and among its suppliers and customers—is vital to its competitive advantage. Support your arguments.
3. Choose a company with which you are familiar. What are some of the ways in which it uses technology to leverage its human capital?
4. Using the Internet, look up a company with which you are familiar. What are some of the policies and procedures that it uses to enhance the firm's human and social capital?

Ethics Questions

1. Recall an example of a firm that recently faced an ethical crisis. How do you think the crisis and the management's handling of it affected the firm's human capital and social capital?
2. Based on your experiences or what you have learned in your previous classes, are you familiar with any companies that used unethical practices to attract talented professionals? What do you feel were the short-term and long-term consequences of such practices?
3. Who does/should own the knowledge created within a firm? Research outcomes, new processes or even client feedback and insights are frequently possessed by individuals but the firm pays their salaries and provides the resources to make things happen. Should individual employees have ownership rights to such valuable assets?
4. New legislation within the European Union gives artists who have sold their creations subsequent rights to future price appreciation of their work. Is full ownership not transferred with the sale of an artistic piece? Is selling a painting different than selling a music CD? Is selling a CD different than assigning patent rights to an invention?

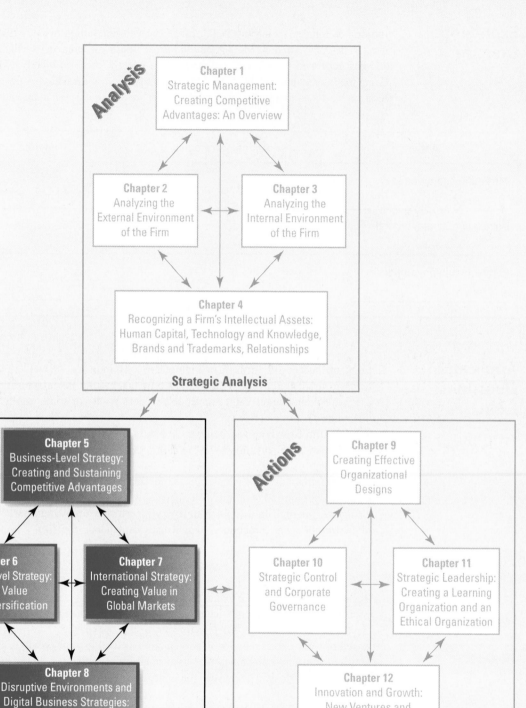

PART 2

Strategic Formulation

Chapter 5 Business-Level Strategy:
Creating and Sustaining Competitive Advantages

LEARNING OBJECTIVES

After reading this chapter, you should have a good understanding of:

LO 1 the central role of competitive advantage in the study of strategic management.

LO 2 the two generic strategy choices: market focus and cost leadership or differentiation.

LO 3 how the successful attainment of generic strategies can improve a firm's relative power vis-à-vis the five forces that determine an industry's average profitability.

LO 4 the pitfalls managers must avoid in striving to attain generic strategies.

LO 5 how a firm can succeed by developing unique strategies that combine elements of generic strategies.

LO 6 the importance of considering the industry life cycle to determine a firm's business-level strategy and its relative emphasis on functional area strategies and value-creating activities.

Success doesn't breed success. Success begets failure because the more you know a thing works, the less likely you are to think that it won't work. When you've had a long string of victories, it's harder to foresee your own vulnerabilities.

Leslie Wexner, CEO, The Limited, Inc.[1]

Cott is not a new name in the beverage market and most people consume its products, even though few may readily recognize the firm.[2] Beginning in the 1950s, Cott soda pop was sold, in a range of fruit flavours, in New Hampshire and Quebec. For some 35 years, it remained a local firm with a largely local following. Dozens of similar regional beverage manufacturers served local markets across North America, and none ever posed a threat to two of the world's savviest and most sophisticated marketing companies, Coca-Cola Co. and PepsiCo, which sold over 80 percent of all non-alcoholic carbonated beverages. Something happened, however, in 1989 that not only revolutionized the beverage industry but forever changed the global retail food industry. That year, Sam and Gerry Pencer, the sons of the Canadian owner of Cott, secured a contract to supply the line of President's Choice soft drinks, the premium private label of Loblaw Companies Ltd. Loblaw itself had recently turned the corner as an ailing food retailer and had launched its President's Choice line of products to improve customers' perceptions of the supermarket chain's quality, build customer loyalty, and increase margins.

Soon, the President's Choice soft drinks surpassed the combined sales of Coke and Pepsi products within Loblaw stores. Cott's success drew new customers from Canada and the U.S. By 1993, the client roster consisted of all major Canadian chains, including, along with Loblaw, A&P, Shoppers Drug Mart, and Sobeys as well as the large American retailers Wal-Mart, Safeway, Price Club, and 7-Eleven. On the supply side, Cott had secured a long-term agreement with RC Cola, which provided Cott with the only reliable alternative source of cola syrup. Cott also capitalized on the presence of substantial excess bottling capacity in the U.S. and enlisted many independent bottlers to help it meet demand. The recipe was simple: produce a quality product at or exceeding the leading national brands, eliminate marketing and distribution costs by adopting the retailer's brand and utilizing the retailer's own distribution and warehousing capacity, and price the product at a substantially lower point in order to provide the retailer with a better margin than the powerful national brands.

Success practically arrived overnight. Cott Corporation mesmerized both Wall Street and Bay Street with its meteoric rise from obscurity to stardom. In late 1993, the stock was trading at $43—an 80 P/E ratio that reflected analysts' expectations of stratospheric growth. Canada's largest supplier of private label soft drinks had only recently entered the U.S. market and, although its sales had grown from $40 million in 1990 to over $300 million in 1993, it had only captured 1 percent of the beverage market. Clearly, the sky was the limit!

In 1993, Cott brought on board its new president, Heather Reisman, a strategic change consultant with strong connections in the Canadian corporate world. Reisman's mission: Convert the small beverage firm to a global powerhouse that would develop "total product service bundles" for major retailers and champion the private label movement in changing food retailing around the world. As part of the plan, Cott acquired a controlling interest in The Watt Group, a world-known corporate design house that was responsible for the creation of many successful corporate images and product designs for firms such as Nestlé and Kraft. Cott and Watt also founded Retail Brands Inc., a consulting firm that would guide retailers through the development and active marketing of their private labels. Cott acquired interests in the manufacturers of snack foods, pet foods, and beer in an effort to replicate the success of the soft drinks and broaden its product offerings. Cott moved its headquarters from Mississauga, Ontario, into plush downtown offices at Toronto's lakefront. Reisman also pushed to spread the retail revolution around the world, and Cott started partnering with and acquiring independent bottlers in Europe, Latin America, and Asia. Along the way, Cott's shares hit $48.

Whether it was the pressure to deliver impressive growth and the expectation of higher and higher free cash flows that led to aggressive accounting practices or simply that senior managers

Case Study

ended up stretched too thin as they embarked on a global endeavour to preach the retail revolution and offer a range of marketing and merchandising consulting services, Cott found itself embroiled in a number of controversies. Analysts started questioning its financial results, and operational problems appeared in many of its facilities. The market punished Cott harshly; its stock fell to just above $3, taking away millions of dollars from its shareholders.

Sales in 1998 declined by 8.5 percent from the previous year, and the firm experienced a net loss of almost $30 million. New management, led by Frank Weise, was brought in to clean house. The first order of business was to focus the company on the premium soft drink business in three markets (Canada, the U.S., and the UK), close down small facilities in far away markets such as Norway and New Zealand, divest non-core businesses, and prune the company's extensive product line. Production efficiencies were introduced throughout the corporation, with an emphasis on streamlining operations, directing production toward the most efficient plants, and simplifying operations by eliminating costly auxiliary services. Over the next two years, the company divested its operations in many markets in Europe, Latin America, and the Pacific and sold its prized corporate design outfit, The Watt Group, along with its marketing and merchandising advisor firm, Retail Brands Inc. The firm soon returned to its roots as an efficient supplier of premium private-label soft drinks for major retailers.

Annual sales in 2003 reached $1.6 billion, and the stock price climbed back to the mid-$40 range. This turn of events occurred in response to the concerted efforts of the new management and strong endorsement by major shareholders, who invested additional capital to fund the firm's growth plans. The summer of 2004 saw very healthy demand and an expanding range of customers, requiring a greater assortment of products. Each of the firm's plants was making a broad range of products for its local market.

However, by the end of the summer, Cott had again started to experience operational problems. The firm's capacity was stretched, and it was unable to handle the increasing demand. It had to resort to the costly move of outsourcing its products to other bottlers. By January 2005, the stock had fallen to below $28, reflecting the market's disappointment with management. A new CEO, John Sheppard, found himself busy assuring analysts and shareholders that the company had not lost its focus and that it would start to rationalize production, streamline operations, put more emphasis on its core products, stop production of less-popular items, and even introduce external audits of the efficiency of its plants.

John seemed to have stopped the tide, and soon he was looking, again, to introduce new product lines, add customers, and enhance services. In pursuit of the energy drink rage that had swept the market, Cott launched Red Rain and Red Rave to compete with the highly successful Red Bull drink. Ready-to-drink teas, sports drinks and flavoured waters followed. Brent Willis, an experienced executive from the beer industry, took over as the CEO to lead the company in its new direction. Only a few months later, though, he had to acknowledge that the company's operations were suffering from "growing pains," supply-chain problems and higher costs for some of its raw materials. The stock took another beating and continued its slide; by 2008 it traded as low as $2 and a new CEO, David Gibbons, a veteran of the consumer packaged goods business, was brought in to turn the company around.

What Went Wrong at Cott? It is hard to imagine the impact on a firm of the kind of roller coaster ride that Cott has experienced during the last 20 years. If the stock price is a reflection of what has taken place inside this company, consider that $3 in 1990 became $48 in 1994, fell back to $3 in 1998, rose to $10 before hitting $46 in 2004, settled for a while at $28 in early 2005, but then ended up at $2.50 in 2008. Not surprisingly, these ups and downs closely reflect the company's strategic choices to align with its commitment to a simple line of core products and efficient operations or their decisions to move toward an ambitious strategy of expansion, product differentiation, and consulting to mass merchants around the world.

Referring back to the value-chain concept in Chapter 3, Cott's success derived from breaking up the traditional value chain of the industry and its customers and reducing costs in the upstream activities of inbound logistics and operations. Moving into the downstream activities of its customers provided little value, as it required the firm to spend precious resources and time in areas that were far from its own strengths.

Cott's ups and downs show that a single-minded commitment to the source of competitive advantage is necessary for success. At the same time, pursuing a poorly defined source of competitive advantage is, as the example shows, often disastrous and certainly insufficient to guarantee success. This is why the topic of competitive advantage is so central to our comprehension of strategy and so crucial for effective strategic management.[3] Without competitive advantages, firms are only able to earn, at best, "economic profits"— the level of normal returns that they could expect from any investments that have the same level of risk. Over time, firms that perform below that level will have difficulty attracting and maintaining the level of investments needed to continue operations, as investors can achieve similar returns by putting their money in the bank or buying bonds.

Since all firms endeavour to enjoy above-average returns, and since only half may do so at any given time, the question of how management should go about achieving this is a core issue in strategic management. Strategy formulation, the second main aspect of strategic management, is about the processes and the decisions managers make to address (1) the choices of businesses in which to compete and (2) how to compete in these businesses. The former is primarily addressed in a firm's corporate strategy.

Business-level strategy is essentially about the particular ways a firm competes in its chosen business. A firm presumably chooses to compete in certain ways in order to create superior value as compared to competitors. The superiority is manifested in the marketplace's response to its products and services. Do buyers rush to buy what the firm has to offer, such as Apple's iPhone, RIM's BlackBerry, or Toyota's Prius? A firm also strives to sustain such superiority over a long period of time. Sustainability usually results from the ongoing relevance and robustness of the competitive advantage against the assaults of competitors, including their attempts to bypass or imitate it, and the firm's ability to continuously outpace them. For not-for-profit organizations, the key issues are, again, sustainability, accomplishing objectives, attracting the support of external constituencies, and generating the resources to pursue the organization's mission.

The business strategy choices available to organizations depend largely on what one views as the important considerations and how one views the process by which managers choose their strategies. Different schools of strategic management emphasize different perspectives of strategy and highlight formal or informal processes, all with different fundamental principles.[4] The design and the planning schools, among the most established, articulate formal processes of external and internal analyses followed by systematic conclusions and recommendations, which incorporate various elements of managerial values and responsibilities. Other schools regard managers as protagonists or members of teams who continuously experiment, learn, perceive, react, or negotiate with others in their efforts to further their businesses.

The two most dominant schools are arguably the positioning school and the resource-based school. The former views business strategy and the corresponding role of managers as identifying and striving to occupy the most attractive competitive positions in the marketplace. It is an outside-in perspective that emphasizes the importance of external analysis and alignment of the firm's activities in order to pursue a desirable position against external forces. The latter school starts with the resources within the firm, the uniqueness of those resources, and it views the choices for exploitation of those resources as the firm's

Exhibit 5.1
Types of Generic
Strategies

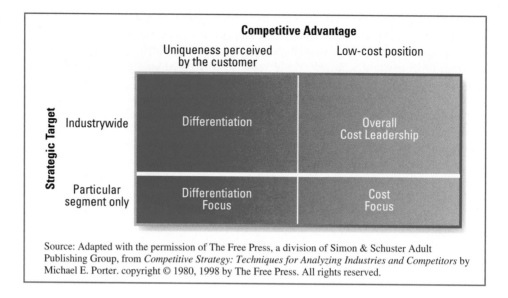

Source: Adapted with the permission of The Free Press, a division of Simon & Schuster Adult Publishing Group, from *Competitive Strategy: Techniques for Analyzing Industries and Competitors* by Michael E. Porter. copyright © 1980, 1998 by The Free Press. All rights reserved.

strategy. It is, by contrast, an inside-out perspective. Both perspectives provide invaluable insights for managers and reveal different but largely complementary facets of business strategies. They also suggest alternative bases of competitive advantage. Those who have studied how managers arrive at their strategic choices frequently report that, in reality, managers strive to reconcile a combination of perspectives.

For pedagogical purposes, we choose to utilize the outside-in perspective, but with a twist. We start with identifying attractive competitive positions but also emphasize how internal resource bundles and activities are utilized to achieve sustainable competitive advantage. The dominant writings of the outside-in perspective derive from the work of Michael Porter of Harvard Business School, who observed that avenues of competitive advantage may take several forms but, at their core, they are all about two choices: target market and type of competitive advantage.[5] The first is essentially about focusing on a narrow strategic target versus going after the whole industry, while the second is about pursuing a low-cost strategy versus uniqueness and differentiation. Those choices create four generic strategies, as shown in Exhibit 5.1. It should be noted that Porter, as well as many writers following his work, prefers to view only three generic strategies—namely, overall low cost, differentiation, and focus. In their writings, a generic focus strategy is simply subdivided into cost focus and differentiation focus. We follow this convention but emphasize the distinct choices that need to be made. Moreover, we consider how firms can successfully combine multiple strategies.

TYPES OF COMPETITIVE ADVANTAGE AND SUSTAINABILITY

 As noted, Michael Porter presented three generic strategies that a firm can use to overcome the five forces and achieve competitive advantage. Each of Porter's generic strategies has the potential to allow a firm to outperform rivals within the same industry. The first, *overall cost leadership*, is based on creating a low-cost position relative to a firm's peers. With this strategy, a firm must manage the relationships throughout the entire value chain and be devoted to lowering costs throughout the entire chain. On the other hand, *differentiation* requires a firm (or business unit) to create products and/or services that are unique and valued as such in the eyes of its customers. Here, the primary emphasis is on "non-price"

Exhibit 5.2
Competitive Advantage and Business Performance

	Competitive Advantage					
	Differentiation and Cost	**Differentiation**	**Cost**	**Differentiation Focus**	**Cost Focus**	**Stuck in the Middle**
Performance						
return on investment (%)	35.5	32.9	30.2	17.0	23.7	17.8
sales growth (%)	15.1	13.5	13.5	16.4	17.5	12.2
gain in market share (%)	5.3	5.3	5.5	6.1	6.3	4.4
Sample size	123	160	100	141	86	105

attributes for which customers will gladly pay a premium. Finally, a firm following a *focus* strategy must direct its attention (or "focus") toward narrow product lines, buyer segments, or targeted geographic markets. A firm emphasizing a focus strategy must attain advantages either through differentiation or a cost leadership approach. Whereas the overall cost leadership and differentiation strategies strive to attain advantages industrywide, focusers build their strategy with a narrow target market in mind.

Before moving on to each generic strategy, it is important to make a couple of observations. First, firms that identify with one or more of the forms of competitive advantage that Porter identified outperform those that do not. There has been a rich history of strategic management research addressing this topic. One study analyzed 1,789 strategic business units and found that businesses combining multiple forms of competitive advantage (differentiation and overall cost leadership) outperformed businesses that used only a single form. The lowest performers were those that did not identify with even a single type of advantage. They were classified as "stuck in the middle"—that is, unable or unwilling to make choices about how to compete, having tried to do everything and accomplishing nothing particularly well. Results of this study are presented in Exhibit 5.2.[6]

Second, when a firm decides to pursue one type of competitive advantage (e.g., low cost), it must attain parity on the basis of the other competitive advantages (e.g., differentiation) relative to competitors. To generate above-average performance, a firm following an overall cost leadership position needs to be able to stay "on par" with competitors with respect to differentiated products.[7] Parity on the basis of differentiation permits a cost leader to translate cost advantages into higher profits than competitors and earn above-average returns.[8] In effect, a supermarket chain, such as No Frills or Price Chopper, which pursues overall cost leadership positions, still needs to pay attention to updating and enlarging current stores, offering extended operating hours, improving shoppers' convenience, and experimenting with new ideas such as organics and green products.

Overall Cost Leadership

The first generic strategy is overall cost leadership. Cost leadership requires a tight set of interrelated efforts that include the following:

- aggressive construction of efficient-scale facilities
- vigorous pursuit of cost reductions from experience

- tight cost and overhead control
- avoidance of marginal customer accounts
- cost minimization in all activities in the firm's value chain, such as R&D, service, sales force, and advertising

Exhibit 5.3 draws on the value-chain concept (see Chapter 3), to provide examples of how a firm can attain an overall cost leadership strategy in its primary and support activities. Contrast this list with Cott's activities in the opening case of this chapter. The value chain can be used as an analytical tool to identify specific activities and the costs and assets associated with them. As Porter explains, analyzing the behaviour of specific cost drivers and assessing the relative costs of competitors for each activity can demonstrate areas where a firm can develop sustainable cost advantages.

Two important concepts related to the overall cost leadership strategy are economies of scale and the experience curve. Economies of scale refer to the decline in per unit costs that usually come with larger production runs, larger facilities, and allocating

Exhibit 5.3
Value-Chain Activities: Examples of Overall Cost Leadership

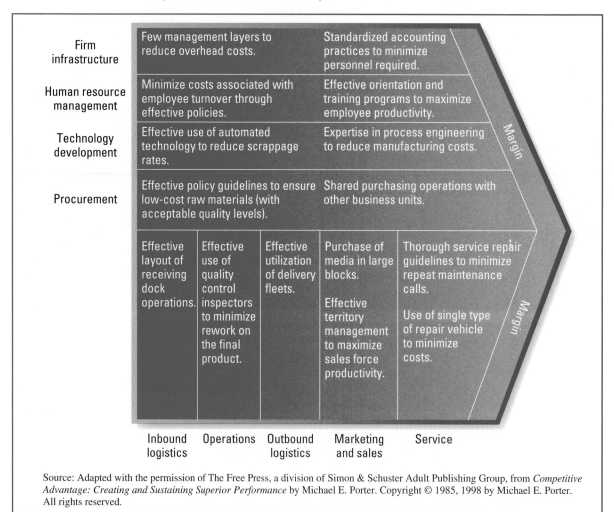

The Experience Curve

The experience curve, as articulated by the Boston Consulting Group in 1968, is a way of looking at efficiencies developed through a firm's cumulative experience. In its basic form, the experience curve relates production costs to production output. As cumulative output doubles, costs decline by 10 to 30 percent. For example, if it costs $10 per unit to produce the first 100 units, the per unit cost could decline to between $9 and $7 in the production of the next 100 units.

What factors account for this increased efficiency? It takes time to learn new tasks, people get better at the same task as they repeat it, and firms continuously introduce product modifications and changes in the manufacturing processes.

Each time the accumulated output doubles, a firm can expect per unit costs to decline. Of course, as output accumulates, it takes longer for the total output to double again, making further gains from experience harder to register. Early stages of a product's life cycle are typically characterized by rapid gains in technological advances in production efficiency. Most experience curve gains come early in the product life cycle.

The technology inherent to the product offers opportunities for enhancement through gained experience. High-tech products give the best opportunity for gains in production efficiencies. As technology is developed, "value engineering" of innovative production processes is implemented, driving down the per unit costs of production.

A product's sensitivity to price strongly affects a firm's ability to exploit the experience curve. Cutting the price of a product with high demand elasticity—where demand increases substantially with modest price decreases—creates significant new consumer purchases of the new product. By cutting prices, a firm can increase demand for its product. The increased demand, in turn, increases product manufacture, thus increasing the firm's experience in the manufacturing process. So by decreasing price and increasing demand, a firm gains manufacturing experience in that particular product, which drives down per unit production costs.

The Japanese automobile manufacturers Toyota and Nissan used the lessons of the experience curve early on in their entry into the North American market. They aggressively priced their cars, with an eye on the cost structures they would enjoy after having traversed lower on the curve. Their long-term orientation paid off handsomely, as buyers responded to the lower prices and happily bought huge volumes of cars, which allowed the manufacturers to ride the experience curve to lower costs even faster.

In an article in the *Harvard Business Review*, Pankaj Ghemawat recommended answering several questions when considering an experience curve strategy:

♦ Does my industry exhibit a significant experience curve?

♦ Have I defined the industry broadly enough to take into account interrelated experience?

♦ What is the precise source of cost reduction?

♦ Can my company keep cost reductions proprietary?

♦ Is demand sufficiently stable to justify using the experience curve?

♦ Is cumulated output doubling fast enough for the experience curve to provide much strategic leverage?

♦ Do the returns from an experience curve strategy warrant the risks of technological obsolescence?

♦ Is demand price-sensitive?

♦ Are there well-financed competitors who are already following an experience curve strategy or likely to adopt one if my company does?

Whether to base strategy on the experience curve depends on what, specifically, causes the decline in costs. For example, if costs drop from economies of scale or efficient production facilities, the experience curve is not helpful. The experience curve can help managers analyze costs when efficient learning, rather than efficient machinery, is the source of cost savings.

Sources: P. Ghemawat, "Building Strategy on the Experience Curve," *Harvard Business Review*, March–April 1985, pp. 143–49; M. E. Porter, *On Competition* (Boston: Harvard Business Review Press, 1996); S. M. Oster, *Modern Competitive Analysis*, 2nd ed. (New York: Oxford University Press, 1994).

fixed costs (such as marketing and research and development) across more units produced. The experience curve refers to how a business "learns" to lower costs as it gains experience with production processes. In most industries, with experience, unit costs of production decline as output increases. The experience curve concept is discussed in Strategy Spotlight 5.1 and illustrated in Exhibit 5.4.

Exhibit 5.4
Comparing
Experience Curve
Effects

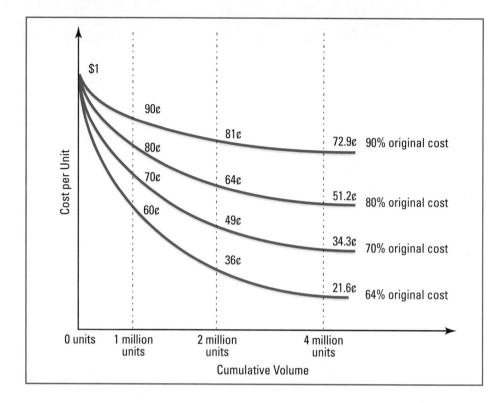

Stephen Sanger, CEO of General Mills, the company that owns many brands, such as Cheerios, Lucky Charms, Betty Crocker, Pillsbury, Yoplait, Häagen Dazs, and Green Giant, recently came up with an idea that helped his firm cut costs.[9] To improve productivity, he sent technicians to watch pit crews during a NASCAR race. That experience inspired the techies to figure out how to reduce, from five hours to 20 minutes, the time it takes to switch a plant line. Sanger knew that interesting benchmarking examples can take place far outside of one's industry. Often, process improvements involve identifying the best practices in other industries and adapting them for implementation in one's own firm. After all, when firms benchmark competitors in their own industry, the end result is often copying and playing catch-up.[10]

IKEA, a global furniture retailer based in Sweden, achieves competitive advantage in different ways and at different points in its value chain. A business that strives for a low-cost advantage must attain an absolute cost advantage relative to its rivals. This is typically accomplished by offering a no-frills product or service to a broad target market using standardization to derive the greatest benefits from economies of scale and experience. However, such a strategy may fail if a firm is unable to attain parity on important dimensions of differentiation such as quick responses to customer requests for design changes. Strategy Spotlight 5.2 describes how IKEA achieves a successful cost leadership strategy. At the same time, it counters perceptions of poor quality or "cheap" merchandise—thus achieving relative parity on differentiation.

Overall Cost Leadership: Improving Competitive Position vis-à-vis the Five Forces An overall low-cost position enables a firm to achieve above-average returns despite strong competition. It protects a firm against rivalry from competitors because

IKEA's Successful Overall Cost Leadership Strategy

IKEA began in 1943 as a one-person mail-order company in a small farming village in the southern part of Sweden. The founder, Ingvar Kamprad, only a 17-year-old boy at the time, initially arranged for the local county milk van to transport the goods to the nearby train station. This cost-effective way of thinking has guided IKEA's success. Today, through its unique, low-cost strategy, IKEA Group has 70,000 employees and revenues of $11 billion. And Interbrand, a marketing research firm, recently rated IKEA 44th on its list of the top 100 most valuable global brands, ahead of Pepsi, Harley-Davidson, and Apple.

Everything at IKEA is done with an eye to cutting costs, reducing waste, and simplifying activities to achieve a successful cost leadership strategy. Even its decision to enter the North American marketplace was driven by the same cost leadership considerations. IKEA chose to come first into Canada, which required a lower investment, lower marketing costs, less risk, and less expensive modifications to its product lines, before embarking on the more expensive and risky entry into the larger U.S. market. IKEA honed its skills for five years in Canada before opening its first store in the U.S. It learned how to operate efficiently on a different continent where cities are further apart, people own larger homes, and the labour force is much more diverse and heterogeneous.

How does IKEA achieve parity on differentiation? Most traditional furniture stores are found in downtown locations, have elaborate showrooms with expensive display samples, several salespeople likely on commission, and they source products from third-party manufacturers who may require up to eight weeks to deliver an order. IKEA takes a totally different approach. It serves customers who are happy to trade off some of that complexity and service for lower prices. Rather than have a salesperson follow customers around the store, IKEA uses a self-service model based on clear in-store displays. IKEA does not rely on third-party manufacturers. Instead, it designs its own low-cost, modular, ready-to-assemble furniture, and it contracts out manufacturing capacity to mass produce in high volume and supply over 200 stores in 35 countries. Within each store, IKEA displays every product in roomlike settings. Thus, customers do not need a decorator to help them imagine what the pieces would look like together. Next to the finished showrooms is a warehouse containing the products in boxes on pallets. Customers do their own pickup and delivery. They can even rent an IKEA van or a roof rack for their car to help them take their purchases home right away. Delivery can also be arranged at a price.

What is central to IKEA's strategy? Good quality at a low price. They sell furniture that is well designed and well made, cheap but not "cheapo," at prices that are generally 30 to 50 percent below the competition. IKEA's emphasis on lowering costs across the whole value chain means that while rivals' prices may have risen over time, IKEA is able to reduce its retail prices by some 20 percent over a four-year period. At IKEA, the process of driving down costs starts the moment a new item is conceived and continues relentlessly throughout its production run.

Sources: K. Kling and I. Goteman, "IKEA CEO Anders Dahlvig on International Growth and IKEA's Unique Corporate Culture and Brand Identity," *Academy of Management Executive* 17, no. 1 (2003), pp. 31–37; L. Margonelli, "How Ikea Designs Its Sexy Price Tags," *Business 2.0*, October 2002, pp. 45–50; and M. E. Porter, "What Is Strategy?" *Harvard Business Review* 74, no. 4 (1996), p. 65.

---

lower costs allow a firm to earn returns even if its competitors eroded their profits through intense rivalry. A low-cost position also protects firms against powerful buyers. Buyers can exert power to drive down prices only to the level of the next most efficient producer. Also, a low-cost position provides more flexibility to cope with demands from powerful suppliers for input cost increases. The factors that lead to a low-cost position also provide substantial entry barriers from economies of scale and cost advantages. Finally, a low-cost position puts the firm in a favourable position with respect to substitute products introduced by new and existing competitors.

A few examples will illustrate these points. IKEA's close attention to costs helps to protect the firm from both buyer power and intense rivalry of competitors. They design

ING Direct: A Highly Successful Low-Cost Strategy

ING Direct, considered the fast-food chain of the financial services industry, is a perfect if not extreme example of a low-cost strategy. This company has been enormously successful in an industry that is losing huge amounts of money. From its humble beginnings in Canada in 1997, it now serves 17 million clients in nine countries with assets exceeding $300 billion.

ING Direct offers a limited lineup of financial services, including savings accounts, GICs, mutual funds, and mortgages. It attracts people who need very little hand holding and are looking for higher interest rates on their savings. The company's Orange Savings Account recently was paying 2.6 percent on the entire balance, compared to the .56 percent average rate for a money-market account at a bank. It is able to offer such enticing rates because 75 percent of its transactions occur online, and it avoids amenities such as chequing accounts or a branch network service. A unique aspect of ING Direct's approach to driving down costs is that it typically "fires" about 0.2 percent of its clients each year. It saves about $1 million annually by getting rid of customers who are too time-consuming, thereby ruthlessly driving down its costs per account to about one-third of the industry average. CEO Arkadi Kuhlmann provides an interesting perspective on how ING Direct gets rid of its overly demanding customers:

> The difference between us and the rest of the financial industry is like the difference between take-out food and a sit-down restaurant. The business isn't based on relationships; it's based on a commodity product that is high-volume and low-margin. We need to keep expenses down, which doesn't work well when customers want a lot of empathetic contact.
>
> If the average customer phone call costs us $5.25 and the average account revenue is $12 per month, all it takes is 100,000 misbehaving customers for costs to go through the roof. So, when a customer calls too many times or wants too many exceptions, our sales associated can basically say, Look this doesn't fit you. You need to go back to your community bank and get the kind of contact you are comfortable with. Of course, we have to use judgment. In some cases, people have legitimate questions. But often, it's customers with large balances who are used to special treatment. They like premiums, platinum cards, and special rates. But you don't get that kind of stuff at the take-out window.

Sources: Stone, A., 2005 Bare bones, plump profits, *BusinessWeek*, March 14: 88; Esfahani, E., 2004, How to get tough with bad customers, *Business 2.0*, October 52; and www.ingdirect.ca

their own furniture and order in large quantities. Thus, they are able to drive down unit costs and enjoy relatively strong power over their suppliers. By increasing its productivity and lowering unit costs, General Mills enjoys greater scale economies and erects higher entry barriers for others who want to enter the industry. Rona, a building and home-improvement retailer based in Quebec, has aligned itself with ITM, one of the world's largest distributors of hardware, giving Rona's 600 stores across Canada enormous purchasing power and the ability to compete head-on with Home Depot from Atlanta. Strategy Spotlight 5.3 discusses ING Direct, a financial services company that provides no-frills service but very generous rates on savings accounts and other services.

Potential Pitfalls of Overall Cost Leadership Strategies There are many benefits from following a strategy of overall cost leadership. However, there are some pitfalls to avoid:

♦ ***Too much focus on one or a few value-chain activities.*** Would you consider a person wise if he or she cancelled a valued newspaper subscription and quit eating out to save money but then "maxed out" several credit cards, leading to hundreds of dollars a month in interest charges? Of course not. Similarly, firms need to pay attention to all activities in the value chain to manage their overall costs. Too often, managers make big cuts in operating expenses but don't question year-to-year spending on capital projects. Or managers may decide to cut selling and marketing expenses but leave manufacturing expenses untouched. Managers should explore *all* value-chain activities—including relationships among them—as possibilities for cost reductions.

♦ *A common input or raw material among rivals.* Firms that compete on overall low-cost strategies are vulnerable to price increases in the factors of production. Since they're competing on the basis of offering low costs, they are less able to pass on price increases because customers can easily take their business to competitors who have lower prices. Consider the hardship experienced by fertilizer producers in early 2001 when energy prices spiked.[11] The dramatic increase—a quadrupling of prices to $10 per thousand cubic feet of natural gas—forced firms to shut down nearly half of their production capacity. Why? Natural gas accounts for over 70 percent of the fertilizer's cost. According to Betty-Ann Hegge, senior vice president of Potash Corporation of Saskatchewan Inc., North America's second largest producer, "Many companies are not even covering their cash costs at these prices." Similarly, Jetsgo, a low-frills airline based in Montreal, had to file for bankruptcy as a result of rising fuel costs. Although such costs had burdened all airlines, they had a devastating effect on a company that had staked its strategy on being the low-cost provider.

♦ *A strategy that is imitated too easily.* One of the common pitfalls of a cost leadership strategy is that a firm's strategy may consist of value-creating activities that are easy to imitate.[12] Such was the case with online brokers in recent years.[13] As of early 2001, there were about 140 online brokers, hardly indicative of an industry where imitation might be difficult. According to Henry McVey, financial services analyst at Morgan Stanley, the market could profitably support between five and ten online brokers. Why? First, although online brokers were geared up to handle 1.2 million trades a day by early 2001, volume had shrunk to about 834,000—a 30 percent drop. Thus, competition for a smaller pool of business was extremely intense. Second, when the stock market is down, many investors trust their instincts less and seek professional guidance from brokerages that offer differentiated services. Eric Rajendra of A. T. Kearney, an international consulting company, claimed, "The current (online broker) model is inadequate for the pressures the industry is facing now."

♦ *A lack of parity on differentiation.* As noted earlier, firms endeavouring to attain cost leadership advantages need to obtain a level of parity on differentiation. Consider, for example, organizations providing online degree programs to adults working full-time. Although such firms may offer low prices, they may not be successful unless they can offer instruction that is perceived as comparable to traditional providers. For them, parity can be achieved on differentiation dimensions such as reputation and quality and through signalling mechanisms such as national and regional accreditation agencies.

♦ *Erosion of cost advantages when the pricing information available to customers increases.* This is becoming a more significant challenge as the Internet dramatically increases the volume of information available to consumers about pricing and cost structures. Life insurance firms offering whole life insurance provide an interesting example.[14] One study found that for each 10 percent increase in consumer use of the Internet, there is a corresponding reduction in insurance prices to consumers of 3 to 5 percent. Recently, the U.S. nationwide savings (or, alternatively, reduced revenues to providers) was between $115 and $125 million annually.

Differentiation

The strategy of differentiation consists of creating differences in the firm's product or service offering by creating something that is perceived *industrywide* as unique and valued by customers. Differentiation can take many forms:

- Prestige or brand image (BMW, Roots clothes, Holt Renfrew retail).
- Quality (Toyota, President's Choice, Pusateri's food).
- Technology (Martin guitars, Marantz stereo components, North Face camping gear).
- Innovation (Medtronic medical equipment, Nokia, 3M, Cirque du Soleil).
- Features (Cannondale bicycles, Honda Goldwing motorcycles, Mountain Equipment Co-op).
- Customer Service (Nordstrom retail, Four Seasons Hotels and Resorts).
- Dealer Network (Lexus, Caterpillar, Canadian Tire).

Exhibit 5.5 draws on the concept of the value chain as an example of how firms may differentiate themselves in primary and support activities. The value chain provides an

Exhibit 5.5
Value-Chain Activities: Examples of Differentiation

Firm infrastructure	Superior MIS—to integrate value-creating activities to improve quality.		Facilities that promote firm image.	Widely respected CEO enhances firm reputation.	
Human resource management	Programs to attract talented engineers and scientists.		Provide training and incentives to ensure a strong customer service orientation.		
Technology development	Superior material handling and sorting technology.		Excellent applications engineering support.		
Procurement	Purchase of high-quality components to enhance product image.		Use of most prestigious outlets.		
	Superior material handling operations to minimize damage. Quick transfer of inputs to manufacturing process.	Flexibility and speed in responding to changes in manufacturing specifications. Low defect rates to improve quality.	Accurate and responsive order processing. Effective product replenishment to reduce customer's inventory.	Creative and innovative advertising programs. Fostering of personal relationship with key customers.	Rapid response to customer service requests. Complete inventory of replacement parts and supplies.
	Inbound logistics	Operations	Outbound logistics	Marketing and sales	Service

Margin

Source: Adapted with the permission of The Free Press, a division of Simon & Schuster Adult Publishing Group, from *Competitive Advantage: Creating and Sustaining Superior Performance* by Michael E. Porter. Copyright © 1985, 1998 by Michael E. Porter.

analytical tool, which highlights the fact that differentiation, as a strategy, is more than simply being different or having different products and different marketing strategies. It also emphasizes that differentiation can derive from anywhere in the value chain.

Firms may differentiate themselves along several different dimensions at once. For example, BMW is known for its high-prestige, superior engineering, and high-quality automobiles. Another example is Harley-Davidson, which differentiates itself on image and dealer services.[15]

Firms achieve and sustain differentiation advantages and attain above-average performance when their price premiums exceed the extra costs incurred in being unique.[16] For example, both BMW and Harley-Davidson charge higher prices to offset higher manufacturing costs and added marketing expenses. A differentiator will always seek out ways of distinguishing itself from similar competitors to justify price premiums greater than the costs incurred for differentiating. Clearly, a differentiator cannot ignore costs. After all, its premium prices would be eroded by a markedly inferior cost position. Therefore, it must attain a level of cost *parity* relative to competitors. Differentiators can do this by reducing costs in all areas that do not affect differentiation. Porsche, for example, invests heavily in engine design—an area in which its customers demand excellence—but it is less concerned about and spends fewer resources in the design of the instrument panel.[17]

Many companies successfully follow a differentiation strategy.[18] For example, some firms have been able to appeal to a very upscale and discriminating segment of the market by offering products with an excellent image and strong brand identification. Holt Renfrew, a purveyor of fashion clothing, caters to the affluent and all those who are willing to pay top dollars for the latest designer outfits. Ferrari's lower-priced model, the 360 Modena, posts a price tag of $200,000. Recently, there was a 50-person, 18-month waiting list for the all-aluminum, 400-horsepower V8-powered model.[19]

Siebel Systems, a leader in customer relationships management (CRM) software, is well known for its own customer service.[20] No software is written until the customer has significant input. Outside consultants routinely poll clients on satisfaction; the compensation of managers and technical professionals is heavily based on such reports. How successful is Siebel? In just seven years from its founding, its sales exceeded $1 billion—faster growth than any other software maker, including Microsoft. CEO Tom Siebel is confident the firm will sustain its growth rate as long as the company "shows respect for the customer."

FedEx's CEO and founder, Fred Smith, claims that the key to his firm's success is innovation.[21] He contends his management team didn't understand their real goal when they started the firm in 1971: "We thought that we were selling the transportation of goods; in fact, we were selling peace of mind." To that end, they now provide each driver with a hand-held computer and a transmitting device that makes it possible for customers to track their packages right from their desktop PCs.

Lexus, a division of Toyota, provides an example of how a firm can strengthen its differentiation strategy by achieving integration at multiple points along the value chain.[22] Although the luxury car line was not introduced until the late 1980s, by the early 1990s the cars had already soared to the top of J. D. Power & Associates's customer satisfaction ratings.

One of Lexus's competitors hired Custom Research Inc. (CRI), a marketing research firm, to find out why Lexus owners were so satisfied. CRI conducted a series of focus groups in which Lexus drivers eagerly offered anecdotes about the special care they experienced from their dealers. It became clear that, although Lexus was manufacturing cars with few mechanical defects, it was the extra care shown by the sales and service staff that resulted in satisfied customers. Such pampering is reflected in the feedback from one customer who claimed she never had a problem with her Lexus. However, upon further probing, she said, "Well, I suppose you could call the four times they had to replace the

VoodooPC: A Successful Canadian Differentiation Strategy

When one thinks of personal computers, commodity products driven by low costs and competitive pricing usually come to mind. This is clearly not the case with VoodooPC, a highly successful computer company based in Alberta that competes at the high end of the market. As one of its employees notes, "We have an unconventional position in a market saturated by big boring giants." VoodooPC Ltd. is a world leader in the design and manufacture of high performance and stylish personal computer entertainment systems. The company has won the prestigious Ultimate Gaming Machine Award three years in a row.

Each VoodooPC is unique and custom made for each customer. To buy a Voodoo computer, you order what you think you need through the Voodoo Web site. Then, a company engineer will contact you to ensure that your Voodoo will exactly match your unique requirements. Ninety-five percent of all orders are further refined after customers talk with Voodoo's engineers.

In a sense, VoodooPCs are works of art. Each computer case has 11 coats of European automobile paint for maximum gloss and colour richness. Desktop models have art cut into the side of the computer tower and they are illuminated from the inside, casting a mysterious glow. Even the inside of the computers look different, each with beautifully folded wires that they call "origami

cabling". Similar to designers of Mercedes-Benz cars, the creators of each VoodooPC sign their names on the inside of the case.

Obviously, VoodooPCs don't compete on price. While there are some lower-end models, the typical prices are between $4,000 and $5,000. Some clientele are willing to pay $19,000 for dual processors, two video chips, and a liquid cooling system. The company even sold a 22-karat-gold-plated desktop for $52,000.

VoodooPC was founded by brothers Rahul and Ravi Sood, who branded Voodoo as the PC company for the hard-core game geek. The strategy has worked. Its sales have surpassed $20 million, and while the profit margins on a typical PC fall around 10 percent, the Sood's machines generally get about 30 percent.

Voodoo prides itself on its custom design capabilities and customer service. It makes sure that the machine fits the buyer like an expensive, custom-made suit. Their approach builds trust and positive buzz in the tight-knit gaming community. Voodoo also claims that it will literally go to the end of the earth to service its machines. In fact, in 2002, it sent a tech-support employee all the way to Sydney, Australia, to fix a PC. The word-of-mouth generated by that single visit more than justified the plane ticket.

Sources: O. Malik, "The 22-Karat PC," *Business2.0*, May 2004, P. 78; "VoodooPC," *Cool Companies*, Calgary and Edmonton Edition, 2005, p. 120–121.

windshield a 'problem.' But frankly, they took care of it so well and always gave me a loaner car, so I never really considered it a problem until you mentioned it now." An insight gained in CRI's research is that perceptions of product quality (design, engineering, and manufacturing) can be strongly influenced by downstream activities in the value chain (marketing and sales, service).

Let's take a closer look at the Lexus example to reiterate some of the key points of a successful differentiation strategy.[23] The example illustrates how strong relationships among value activities reinforce and strengthen the customer's total perception of value. Value activity integration creates value for the end user. Clearly, Lexus must establish and maintain close ties with its dealers by providing resources such as advertising materials, training, parts, supplies, and automobile inventories. Yet, one could easily imagine the futility of Lexus's superb marketing, sales, and service efforts if the company could not maintain high production quality or if procurement were unable to acquire high-quality components. Superb marketing and service alone would be inadequate to support Lexus's strategy. Thus, successful differentiation requires attention to and integration with all parts of a firm's value chain.

Strategy Spotlight 5.4 provides the example of a Canadian company that has succeeded in what is generally considered to be a commodity industry—personal computers.

Like Lexus, its success can be partially explained by its excellence in downstream activities such as customer service, as well as by its reputation for product excellence.

Differentiation: Improving Competitive Position vis-à-vis the Five Forces Achieving differentiation is a viable strategy for earning above-average returns by creating a defensible position for overcoming Porter's five competitive forces. Differentiation provides protection against rivalry since brand loyalty lowers customer sensitivity to price and raises customer switching costs. Lexus has enjoyed enhanced power over buyers because its top J. D. Power ranking makes buyers more willing to pay a premium price. Differentiation reduces buyers' power because buyers lack comparable alternatives. Higher entry barriers result from differentiation because of customer loyalty and the firm's ability to provide uniqueness in its products or services. As well, differentiation provides higher margins that enable a firm to deal with supplier power. Supplier power, like buyers' power, is decreased because there is a certain amount of prestige associated with being the supplier to a producer of highly differentiated products and services. The prestige associated with upper-crust brand names, such as Holt Renfrew and Ferrari, along with the suppliers' desire to be associated with prestige brands, reduces their ability to drive up prices. Finally, a firm that uses differentiation will enjoy high customer loyalty and experience less threat from substitutes than its competitors. The loyalty and "peace of mind" associated with firms such as VoodooPC and Holts make these firms less vulnerable to rivalry from other firms or to pressures from substitute products and services.

Potential Pitfalls of Differentiation Strategies Along with the benefits of differentiation, there are also pitfalls:

- *Uniqueness that is not valuable.* A differentiation strategy must provide unique bundles of products and/or services that customers value highly. It's not enough just to be "different." An example is Gibson's Dobro bass guitar. Gibson came up with a unique idea: design and build an acoustic bass guitar with sufficient sound volume so that amplification wasn't necessary. The problem with other acoustic bass guitars was that they did not project enough volume because of the low-frequency bass notes. By adding a resonator plate on the body of the traditional acoustic bass, Gibson increased the sound volume. Gibson believed this product would serve a particular niche market—bluegrass and folk artists who played in small group "jams" with other acoustic musicians. Unfortunately, Gibson soon discovered that its targeted market was content with their existing options: an upright bass amplified with a microphone or an acoustic electric guitar. Thus, Gibson developed a unique product, but it was not perceived as valuable by its potential customers.[24]

- *Too much differentiation.* Firms may strive for quality or service that is higher than customers desire, leaving themselves vulnerable to competitors who provide an appropriate level of quality at a lower price. Consider for example, the high-end Mercedes-Benz S-Class series, which ranges in price from $85,000 to $150,000. *Consumer Reports* recently described these cars as sumptuous, quiet, luxurious, and a delight to drive. The magazine also considered these to be the least reliable sedans available. According to David Champion, who runs the testing program at *CR*, the problems are electronic. "The engineers have gone a little wild" he says. "They have put in every bell and whistle that they think of, and sometimes they don't have the attention to detail to make those systems work." Consider some features of these models: a computer-driven suspension that reduces body roll as the vehicle whips around a corner, cruise control that automatically slows the car if it gets close to another car, seats that are adjustable 14 ways and that are ventilated by a system that uses eight fans to whisk away perspiration, and memory settings for a number of adjustments depending on who drives the car. Perhaps it is not too surprising that an executive at Mercedes, Sephan Wolfsried, told a symposium in Germany that he eliminated 600 functions from the vehicles, "functions that nobody needed and nobody knew how to use." Drivers who responded to *CR*'s surveys cited "serious" problems with the vehicles electrical and electronic systems, power equipment, and accessories. Sales of the S-Class have been down, although the high-end Lexus cars are doing very well.

- *Too high a price premium.* Customers may desire the product, but they may also be repelled by the price premium compared to that of competitors. For example, Duracell (a division of Gillette) recently charged too high a price for batteries.[25] The firm tried to sell consumers on its superior quality products, but the mass market wasn't convinced. Why not? The price differential was simply too high. At a CVS Drugstore, just one block from Gillette's headquarters, a four-pack of Energizer AA batteries was on sale at $2.99 compared with a Duracell four-pack at $4.59. Not only did Duracell lose market share, but its profits declined over 30 percent. Clearly, the price/performance proposition Duracell offered customers was not being accepted.

- *Differentiation that is easily imitated.* As we noted in Chapter 3, resources that are easily imitated cannot lead to sustainable advantages. Firms may strive for, and even attain, a differentiation strategy that is successful for a time; however, the advantages are eroded through imitation. Consider the frequent flyer programs of airlines and loyalty credit cards that are aligned with automobile manufacturers (such as TD Canada Trust GM Visa), which allow holders to accumulate points toward the purchase of vehicles. The ease of imitation by competitors significantly undermines the value of such differentiation strategies.

- *Dilution of brand identification through product-line extensions.* Firms may erode their quality brand image by adding products or services with lower prices and less quality. Although this can increase short-term revenues, it may be detrimental in the long-run. Profits don't necessarily follow revenues. The case of Gucci illustrates this point.[26] In the 1980s, Gucci was determined to capitalize on its prestigious brand name by launching an aggressive strategy of revenue growth. It added a set of lower-priced canvas goods to its product line. It also pushed goods heavily into department stores and duty-free channels, and it allowed its name to appear on a host of licensed items such as watches, eyeglasses, and perfumes. In the short term, this strategy worked. Sales soared. However, the strategy carried a high price. Gucci's indiscriminate approach to expanding its products and channels tarnished its sterling brand. Sales of its high-end goods (with higher profit margins) fell, causing profits to decline.

- *Perceptions of differentiation that vary between buyers and sellers.* The issue here is that "beauty is in the eye of the beholder." Companies must realize that although they may perceive their products and services as differentiated, their customers may view them as commodities. Indeed, in today's marketplace, many products and services have been reduced to commodities.[27] Thus, a firm could overprice its offerings and lose margins altogether if it has to lower prices to reflect market realities.

Many products and services that used to be differentiated are now sold at online auctions, such as FreeMarkets (an online business-to-business auction house), where several competing sellers fight for big pieces of business purely on price. Personal computers, servers, data storage capacity, hotel rooms, band width, generic drugs, and ocean shipping have been traded at online auctions featuring readily available information about competing products and services. This does not mean that it is impossible for a firm to achieve differentiation strategies in these industries, but certainly differentiation is becoming more difficult.

Focus

← LO 2

Focus is based on the choice of a narrow competitive scope within an industry. A firm following this strategy selects a segment or group of segments and tailors its strategy to serve them. The focuser achieves competitive advantages by dedicating itself to these segments exclusively. The essence of focus is the exploitation of a particular market niche that is unique within the industry. As one might expect, narrow focus itself (like merely "being different" as a differentiator) is simply not sufficient for above-average performance. The focus strategy, as indicated in Exhibit 5.1, has two variants: cost focus and differentiation focus.

Cost Focus In a cost focus generic strategy, a firm strives to create a cost advantage in its target segment and serve customers within that segment with a lower price than rivals who may either target the whole industry or be unable to match the lower-cost position. It exploits differences in cost behaviour in a particular segment and takes advantage of potentially lower costs that arise from purposefully limiting the firm's customer base to a well-defined segment.

Staples Business Depot, Canada's reigning retailer of office supplies, is deliberately limiting its selection to shed customers.[28] Recently, there has been an onslaught of retailers, such as Wal-Mart, Costco, Canadian Tire, and Loblaw, fighting to take a piece of the profitable stationery and office supplies business. In response, Staples Business Depot has aggressively targeted the small-business and home-office clients by increasing the number of private label items it carries, offering jumbo-size packs and passing on the savings of its bulk buying power by cutting prices. At the same time, its collection of single-pack highlighters and Britney Spears backpacks and binders has all but disappeared from its stores' shelves. Staples Business Depot has succeeded in retaining its dominant position in the highly competitive marketplace and continues to open new stores across the country.

Network Appliance (NA) has developed a more cost-effective way to store and distribute computer files.[29] Its larger rival, EMC Corporation, makes mainframe-style products priced over $1 million that store files and Internet traffic. NA makes devices that cost under $200,000 for particular storage jobs such as caching (temporary storage) of Internet content. Focusing on such narrow segments has certainly paid off for NA; it has posted a remarkable 20 straight quarters of revenue growth.

Differentiation Focus A firm pursuing a differentiation focus strategy will seek to differentiate itself within a narrow segment. The dimensions of differentiation are similar to those presented earlier; in this case, the firm aims to provide better service, prestige, image, or quality to a well-defined segment.

The Keg Steakhouse & Bar has developed a simple operating formula that serves it with a stable business, and its customers with perfect steaks, every time.[30] The Keg has purposefully limited its menu and has stayed away from food fashions and fads such as nachos and pizzas; it targets young families and the après-work crowd. Suppliers of meats and vegetables are monitored extremely closely and are expected to meet very specific standards. Cooks follow head office's detailed preparation instructions; service, food quality, and portion size are precisely maintained. Customers have rewarded The Keg with their frequent visits and praises. The Keg was the only chain not to be affected by the "perfect storm" that so greatly impacted the food-services sector in Canada with SARS in 2002, a mad-cow case in Alberta in the spring of 2003, and a blackout in Northeastern North America in August 2003. The industry's sales plunged more than 13 percent, while The Keg's sales slid only 2.4 percent in that period and completely rebounded soon after.

Porsche: Winning through Differentiation Focus

After nearly filing for bankruptcy in the 1990s, Porsche has emerged as a company in a class by itself. It embodies the essence of a differentiation focus strategy. Porsche has one manufacturing plant in Stuttgart, Germany, and the entire company employs only 8,200 employees—fewer than just two or three Detroit automobile factories. And the worst thing (or best?) is that no one *needs* a Porsche.

What's their secret? The answer lies in Porsche's very specific market niche. In fact, their Cayenne, a new sport utility vehicle that was introduced in late 2002, is a "very expensive toy that caters to the person who wants everything," according to Ron Pinelli, an analyst with Autodata Corporation in Woodcliff Lake, New Jersey. Target marketing to a focal segment is Porsche's key to success. Sales for 2002 of 40,000 cars paled in comparison to the Big Three automakers. To illustrate, General Motors stopped making the Pontiac Fiero when sales fell below

40,000. By contrast, Porsche's sales of 40,000 units gave it enough room to profitably restructure its operations and pull itself out of potential bankruptcy without merging or being acquired by a larger firm. With a break-even point of only 12,000 to 14,000 unit sales, Porsche certainly has a comfortable cushion. Further, with growth in its traditional products and the successful launch of the Cayenne, it hoped to increase annual sales to about 80,000 by 2006.

Their differentiation focus strategy has successfully positioned the company as a producer of highly sought-after luxury sports cars. As noted by CEO Wendelin Wiedekig, "Porsche wants to grow and we want to have exclusive products. That means we will keep following the niche strategy." A research report from Deutsche Bank states, "It is the design, the technology, and the brand that make a Porsche stand out."

Sources: A. Taylor, III, "Porsche's Risky Recipe," *Fortune*, February 17, 2003, pp. 90–94; A. Curry, "Dude, Where's My Porsche," *U.S. News & World Report*, November 25, 2002, p. D8; J. Suhr, "Porsche Has High Hopes for SUV in '02," *Lexington (KY) Herald-Leader*, February 2001, p. B10; and J. Healey, "Groomed so as Not to Marry," *USA Today*, August 6, 1999, pp. B1–B2.

Hermès, the upscale French design house, has for years catered to an exclusive clientele with its line of leather goods and silk scarves and ties. It has retained an exclusive image, has religiously guarded the quality and design of its products, and has succeeded in maintaining the allure of rarity and glamour in spite of its presence in 40 countries and more than 300 store locations around the world. Strategy Spotlight 5.5 presents the case of Porsche, another well-known company that has successfully pursued a differentiation focus strategy. Porsche thrives by making products that nobody needs but everyone seems to want!

Focus: Improving Competitive Position vis-à-vis the Five Forces As we have seen, firms pursuing a focus strategy can earn above-average returns. Focus requires that a firm have either a low-cost position with its strategic target, a high differentiation, or both. As we discussed with regard to cost and differentiation strategies, these positions provide defences against each competitive force. Focus is also used to select niches that are the least vulnerable to substitutes or wherein competitors are weakest.

Let's look at our previous examples to illustrate some of these points. First, The Keg and Porsche experienced less rivalry and lower bargaining power among buyers by providing products and services to a targeted market segment that was less price-sensitive. New rivals would have difficulty attracting customers away from these firms based only on lower prices. Similarly, the brand image and quality that these brands evoked heightened the entry barriers for rivals trying to gain market share. Additionally, one could reasonably speculate that these two firms enjoyed some protection against substitute products and services because of their relatively high reputation, brand image, and customer loyalty. With regard to the strategy of cost focus, Network Appliances, the successful rival to EMC in the computer storage industry, was better able to absorb pricing increases from suppliers as a result of its lower-cost structure. Thus, the effects of supplier power were lessened.

Potential Pitfalls of Focus Strategies   Along with the benefits, managers must be aware of the pitfalls of a focus strategy:

- ◆ ***Erosion of cost advantages within the narrow segment.*** The advantages of a cost focus strategy may be fleeting if the cost advantages are eroded over time. For example, Dell's pioneering direct selling model in the personal computer industry—while still the industry standard—is constantly being challenged by competitors as other computer makers gain experience with Dell's distribution method. Similarly, other firms have seen their profit margins drop as competitors enter their product segment.
- ◆ ***Possible competition from new entrants and from imitation.*** Some firms adopting a focus strategy may enjoy temporary advantages because they select a small niche with few rivals. However, their advantages may be short-lived as rivals invade their market niche. A notable example is the multitude of dot-com firms that specialize in very narrow segments such as pet supplies, ethnic foods, and vintage automobile accessories. The entry barriers tend to be low, there is little buyer loyalty, and competition becomes intense. And since the marketing strategies and technologies employed by most rivals are largely non-proprietary, imitation is easy. Over time, revenues fall, profit margins are squeezed, and only the strongest players survive the shakeout.
- ◆ ***Too much focus to satisfy buyer needs.*** Some firms attempting to attain competitive advantages through a focus strategy may have too narrow a product or service. Examples include many retail firms. Hardware chains, such as True Value, are losing market share to rivals, such as Rona and Home Depot, who offer a full line of home and garden equipment and accessories. Similarly, many specialty ethnic and gourmet food stores may see their sales and profits shrink as large, national grocers, such as Loblaw, expand their already broad product lines to include similar items. And given the enormous purchasing power of the national chains, it would be difficult for such specialty retailers to attain parity on costs.

Combination Strategies: Integrating Overall Low Cost and Differentiation

There has been ample evidence—in the popular press and in research studies—about the strategic benefits of combining generic strategies. In the beginning of this section, we provided some evidence from nearly 1,800 strategic business units (see Exhibit 5.2) to support this assertion. The highest performers were businesses that attained both cost and differentiation advantages, followed by those that had either one or the other. Those strategic business units that had the lowest performance identified with neither generic strategy; that is, they were "stuck in the middle." Results from other studies concerning a wide variety of industries, including paints and allied products, Korean electronics, apparel, and screw machine products, are consistent with these findings.[31]

Perhaps the primary benefit to be enjoyed by firms that successfully integrate low-cost and differentiation strategies is that it is generally harder for competitors to duplicate or imitate. An integrated strategy enables a firm to provide two types of value to customers: differentiated attributes (e.g., high quality, brand identification, reputation) and lower prices (because of the firm's lower costs in value-creating activities). The goal becomes one of providing unique value to customers in an efficient manner.[32] Some firms are able to attain both types of advantages simultaneously. For example, superior quality can lead to lower costs because of less need for rework in manufacturing, fewer warranty claims, a reduced need for customer service personnel to resolve customer complaints, and so forth. Thus, the benefits of combining advantages can be additive, instead of merely involving trade-offs. Next, we consider three approaches to combining overall low-cost and differentiation competitive strategies.

Automated and Flexible Manufacturing Systems Given the advances in manufacturing technologies such as CAD/CAM (computer aided design and computer aided manufacturing) as well as information technologies, many firms have been able to manufacture unique products in relatively small quantities at lower costs—a concept known as "mass customization."[33]

Let's consider the case of Andersen Windows—a $1 billion manufacturer of windows for the building industry.[34] Until about 15 years ago, Andersen was a mass producer, in small batches, of a variety of standard windows. However, to meet changing customer needs, Andersen kept adding to its product line. The result was catalogues of ever-increasing size and a bewildering set of choices for both homeowners and contractors. Over a six-year period, the number of products tripled, price quotes took several hours, and the error rate increased—not only damaging the company's reputation but also adding to its manufacturing expenses.

To bring about a major change, Andersen developed an interactive computer version of its paper catalogues that it sold to distributors and retailers. Salespersons can now customize each window to meet the customer's needs, check the design for structural soundness, and provide a price quote. The system is virtually error free, customers get exactly what they want, and the time to develop the design and furnish a quotation has been cut by 75 percent. Each showroom computer is connected to the factory, and customers are assigned a code number that permits them to track the order. The manufacturing system has been developed to use some common finished parts (e.g., mullions, the vertical or horizontal strips separating window panes and sashes), but it also allows considerable variation in the final products. Despite its huge investment in time and money, Andersen has found that the new system has lowered costs, enhanced quality and variety, and improved its response time to customers.

Exploiting the Profit Pool Concept for Competitive Advantage A profit pool can be defined as the total profits in an industry at all points along the industry's value chain.[35] Although the concept is relatively straightforward, the structure of the profit pool can be complex. The potential pool of profits will be deeper in some segments of the value chain than in others, and the depths will vary within an individual segment. Segment profitability may vary widely by customer group, product category, geographic market, or distribution channel. Additionally, the pattern of profit concentration in an industry is very often different from the pattern of revenue generation.

Consider the automobile industry profit pool in Exhibit 5.6. Here we see little relationship between the generation of revenues and the capturing of profits. While manufacturing generates most of the revenue, this value activity is far smaller, profit-wise, than other value activities such as financing and extended warranty operations. Thus, while a car manufacturer may be under tremendous pressure to produce cars efficiently, much of the profit (at least proportionately) can be captured in the aforementioned downstream operations. It's no wonder all car manufacturers and dealers today happily arrange lease financing for their customers. A carmaker would be ill-advised to focus solely on manufacturing while leaving downstream operations to others through outsourcing.

The profit pool concept helps explain U-Haul's success in the truck rental business. Its 10 percent operating margin is far superior to the industry average of less than 3 percent. U-Haul's largest competitor, Ryder, even abandoned the consumer rental business and sold off its fleet in 1996.

What is the key to U-Haul's outstanding performance? Unlike its competitors, U-Haul looked past its core truck rental business and found an untapped source of profit. That source was the accessories business—the sale of boxes and insurance, rentals of trailers

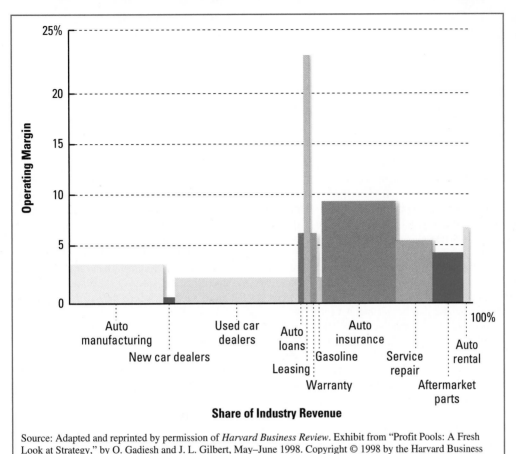

Exhibit 5.6
The U.S. Auto Industry's Profit Pool

and storage space—all the ancillary products and services customers need to complete the moving job that begins when they rent the truck. Profit margins for moving-truck rentals are small; customers shop for the lowest daily rate. But accessories are a different story. With virtually no competition in this part of the value chain, the accessories business enjoys attractive margins. And once a customer signs a rental agreement for a truck, his or her comparison shopping ends. Although the accessories business requires a greater variety of offerings, customers are largely "a captive market" and are, therefore, less price sensitive. U-Haul's strategy became one of tightly managing its costs and prices to consumers in the low-profit truck rental part of the business. This enabled them to attract more customers to whom they sold high-margin accessories.

Coordinating the "Extended" Value Chain by Way of Information Technology
Many firms have achieved success by integrating activities throughout the "extended value chain" and using information technology to link their own value chain with the value chains of their customers and suppliers. As noted in Chapter 3, this approach enables a firm to add value through its own value-creating activities and to pass this value to its customers and suppliers.

Such a strategy often necessitates redefining the industry's value chain. A number of years ago, Wal-Mart took a close look at its industry's value chain and decided to reframe the competitive challenge.[36] Although its competitors were primarily focused on

How Wal-Mart Combines Advantages

One of the most successful retailers of all time, Wal-Mart has trounced its competitors by combining competitive advantages. With net income of $12 billion from total revenues of $374 billion in 2008, Wal-Mart continued to post very impressive performance numbers. During a five-year period from 1998 to 2002, it experienced annual growth rates in revenues and net income of 16 percent and 17 percent, respectively, while the rest of the retail sector had to settle for gains in the 5 percent range. Wal-Mart has broadened its product offerings in recent years and now offers a diverse product line, including groceries, deli items, pharmaceuticals, and fast food. It has expanded internationally by exporting its data systems and models of efficiency to international markets, including Canada, Mexico, China, Indonesia, the United Kingdom, and Brazil.

Much of Wal-Mart's success can be attributed to its strategic focus, emphasis on key value-chain activities, and combination of competitive advantages. The value chains of merchandise retailers, such as Kmart and Target, have been much like that of grocery retailers. These value chains focused on cost control, efficiency in distribution and purchasing, and low-overhead facilities. Rivalry in this sector has centred around store location, pricing, and promotion.

Over the past decade, Wal-Mart has left its competitors behind by differentiating itself. In addition to the diverse product lines previously mentioned, Wal-Mart has distinguished itself from competitors by offering optical shops and photofinishing. By moving into such non-traditional areas, Wal-Mart challenges competitors in industries other than traditional discount retailers. Grocery chains, optical shops, fast-food restaurants, photofinishing stores, and pharmacies must now be concerned with the impact on market share each time Wal-Mart opens a new store in their town.

What is Wal-Mart's secret? A central feature of Wal-Mart's strategy is the logistics technique of cross-docking. Goods are continuously delivered to the company's warehouses, where they are selected, repacked, and then distributed to stores, often without placement in inventory. Instead of wasting valuable time in warehouses, merchandise moves across one loading dock to another in 48 hours or less. This lets Wal-Mart achieve economies associated with full-truckload purchasing.

Sophisticated software automatically determines the precise loading of trucks to minimize handling of individual items and maximize the speed at which goods will be placed on the store shelves, where they can be seen and bought by customers. Wal-Mart is well aware that every single item of the hundreds of millions of products in the system each day can only generate value when it is available to its customers and not sitting in transit. Sophisticated software is also utilized to manage its inventory and distribution systems; at any given point, computers know exactly where each product can be found across Wal-Mart's vast operations and can automatically direct it to the next destination. By avoiding the usual inventory and handling costs, it reduces associated costs by an impressive 20 percent, which translates to a 2 percent reduction in its total cost of sales compared to its competitors.

The benefits to Wal-Mart and its customers multiply. Lower costs help make possible the retailer's everyday low prices. This, in turn, saves money with less frequent promotions. Stable prices lead to more predictable sales,

retailing—merchandising and promotion—Wal-Mart determined that it could unleash more value in the logistics and communications parts of its business than in the retailing part. Here, linkages in the extended value chain became central. That became Wal-Mart's chosen battleground. By redefining the rules of competition such that they played to its strengths, Wal-Mart has attained competitive advantages and dominates its industry.

Strategy Spotlight 5.6 provides some details of how Wal-Mart was able to use technology and overall cost leadership to become the dominant retailer in the world. We also discuss why the company's strategy is highly sustainable; competitors would have a very difficult time imitating it or finding substitutes.

Integrated Overall Low-Cost and Differentiation Strategies: Improving Competitive Position vis-à-vis the Five Forces Firms that successfully integrate both differentiation and cost advantages create an enviable position relative to industry forces. For example, Wal-Mart's integration of information systems, logistics, and transportation helps it to drive down costs and provide outstanding product selection. This dominant competitive position, along with its excellent reputation, serves to erect high entry barriers to potential competitors that have neither the financial nor physical resources to compete head-to-head.

thus reducing stockouts and excess inventory. Fewer stockouts increase customer loyalty, while inventory control allows quick response to changing customer preferences. Everyday low prices bring in more customer traffic, which leads to more sales.

These economies allow Wal-Mart to staff stores with greeters and additional checkout clerks and to reward employees with stock ownership through a profit-sharing plan. Loyal, dedicated employees and enhanced customer service are elements of differentiation that translate into more customer loyalty and increased sales.

Despite the value of cross-docking, it's not easily copied by competitors. If it were, Wal-Mart's advantage would have long since vanished. The key is that cross-docking is complicated to manage. Wal-Mart made strategic investments in a variety of interlocking support systems that are difficult to imitate. The systems involve

- continuous contact between Wal-Mart's distribution centres, suppliers, and every point of sale in each store so that orders can be executed within hours.

- fast, responsive transportation, including 19 distribution centres serviced by nearly 2,000 company-owned trucks.

- fundamental changes in managerial control that allow the stores to pull products when and where they need them rather than having suppliers push products into the system. With less centralized control, a premium

is placed on frequent, informed co-operation between stores, distribution centres, and suppliers.

- information systems that provide store managers with detailed information about customer behaviour, and a fleet of airplanes that regularly ferry store managers to Wal-Mart's Bentonville, Arkansas, headquarters for training on market trends and merchandising.

- a video link connecting each store.

- profit sharing for employees, to encourage high customer responsiveness.

The cross-docking logistics strategy and sophisticated information systems reduce costs in a number of ways. By reducing inventories and shortening procurement cycle times, Wal-Mart can increase its flexibility and responsiveness to changing customer preferences. Wal-Mart has understood the business as a process and expanded its boundaries to include customers and suppliers. It has identified its strengths, added value to multiple activities in new and innovative ways, and leveraged its capabilities to enhance the flexibility of operations through close integration and coordination of interdependent activities. As the company broadens its product offerings and expands into new markets, it's likely that the benefits will only grow, entrenching Wal-Mart as the dominant player in the retail merchandise market and preserving the sustainability of its competitive edge.

Sources: J. Useem, "One nation under Wal-Mart. *Fortune*, March 3, 2003, pp. 65–78; G. G. Dess and J. C. Picken, "Creating Competitive (Dis)Advantage: Learning from Food Lion's Freefall," *Academy of Management Executive* 13, no. 3 (1999), pp. 97–111; and R. Berner, "Too Many Retailers, Not Enough Shoppers," *BusinessWeek*, February 12, 2001, pp. 36–42.

Wal-Mart's size, $374 billion sales in 2008, provides the chain with enormous bargaining power over suppliers. Its low pricing and wide selection reduce the power of buyers (its customers) because there are relatively few competitors that can provide a comparable cost/value proposition. This reduces the possibility of intense head-to-head rivalry and protracted price wars. Finally, Wal-Mart's overall value proposition makes potential substitute products (e.g., Internet competitors) a less viable threat.

Pitfalls of Integrated Overall Cost Leadership and Differentiation Strategies

Firms that attain both types of competitive advantage enjoy high returns. However, as with each generic strategy taken individually, there are some pitfalls to avoid:

- *Failing to attain both strategies and ending up "stuck in the middle."* A key issue in strategic management is the creation of competitive advantages that enable a firm to enjoy above average returns. Some firms may become "stuck in the middle" if they try to attain both cost and differentiation advantages. Eaton's, Canada's original department store, was known for its famous pledge of "goods satisfactory or money refunded." It was the first company to sell from a catalogue and build large open-concept stores, and it subsequently became the purveyor of choice for generations of Canadians. In the early 1980s, Eaton's lost direction in a highly competitive retail market as it tried to achieve differentiation and cost control at the same time but succeeded in neither. It struggled to fend off discounters such as Wal-Mart on one front, department stores such as the Bay on another, and the more popular specialty clothing stores such as Club Monaco, Gap, and Roots on a third. Eaton's had to file for bankruptcy and folded after 100 years because it could not identify with and succeed in any one strategy, while other retailers around it adapted and prospered.

♦ *Underestimating the challenges and expenses associated with coordinating value-creating activities in the extended value chain.* Successfully integrating activities across a firm's value chain with the value chain of suppliers and customers involves a significant investment in financial and human resources. Managers must not underestimate the expenses linked to technology investment, managerial time and commitment, and the involvement and investment required by the firm's customers and suppliers. The firm must be confident that it can generate a sufficient scale of operations and revenues to justify all associated expenses.

♦ *Miscalculating sources of revenue and profit pools in the firm's industry.* Firms may fail to accurately assess sources of revenue and profits in their value chain. This can occur for several reasons. For example, a manager's bias may be due to his or her functional area background, work experiences, and educational background. If the manager's background is in engineering, he or she might be more inclined to perceive that proportionately greater revenue and margins were being created in manufacturing, product, and process design than a person whose background is in a "downstream" value-chain activity such as marketing and sales. Also, politics could make managers "fudge" the numbers and put their area of operations in a more favourable light. This would make them responsible for a greater proportion of the firm's profits, thus improving their bargaining position for their share of the firm's internal resources.

A related problem is directing an overwhelming amount of managerial time, attention, and resources to value-creating activities that create the greatest margins—to the detriment of other important, though less profitable, activities. For example, an automobile manufacturer may focus too much on downstream activities, such as warranty fulfillment and financing operations, to the detriment of differentiation and the cost of the automobiles themselves. Or, as described earlier in the case of the truck rental industry, management might let the quality of rental trucks deteriorate while directing greater attention to the more profitable accessory side of the business.

While the generic strategies model presented here has tremendous advantages, which derive mainly from simplicity, determinism, formality, and tight analytical prescriptions, it also falls short on a number of fronts. Some writers have criticized the model for focusing too narrowly on economic analysis and not enough on the social, political, and cognitive.[37] Moreover, the strategic choices are largely restricted to a very short list of options, discouraging the creation of truly unique strategies.

The model itself lacks dynamism, although industry evolution and realignment of strategic choices are not excluded from its conceptualization. It emphasizes stability—identifying and staying in an attractive position rather than analyzing how one gets there. Managers must think outside the model if they are to identify the tools and choices that will ultimately move their firm to a new competitive position or allow them to respond to the complexity and unpredictability of the business environment that is typical today.

In an attempt to address at least some of these criticisms, we look at the industry life-cycle concept and discuss its implications for strategic decisions. Finally, we explore turnaround strategies—that is, strategies that are necessary in order to reverse performance erosion and regain a competitive position.

INDUSTRY LIFE-CYCLE STAGES: STRATEGIC IMPLICATIONS

The life cycle of an industry refers to the stages of introduction, growth, maturity, and decline that occur over the life of an industry. In considering the industry life cycle, it is useful to think in terms of broad product lines such as personal computers, photocopiers, or long-distance telephone service. Yet, the industry life-cycle concept can be explored from several levels, from the life cycle of an entire industry to the life cycle of a single variation or model of a specific product or service.

Why is it important to consider industry life cycles? The emphasis on various generic strategies, functional areas, value-creating activities, and overall objectives varies over the course of an industry life cycle. Managers must become even more aware of their firm's strengths and weaknesses in many areas to attain competitive advantages. For example, firms depend on their research and development (R&D) activities in the introductory stage of the life cycle. R&D is the source of new products and features that everyone hopes will appeal to customers. Firms develop products and services to stimulate consumer demand. Later, during the maturity phase, the functions of the product have been defined, more competitors have entered the market, and competition is intense. Managers then place greater emphasis on production efficiencies and process (as opposed to the product) engineering in order to lower manufacturing costs. This helps to protect the firm's market position and extends the product life cycle because the firm's lower costs can be "passed on" to consumers in the form of lower prices, which make the product more appealing to price-sensitive customers.

Exhibit 5.7 illustrates the four stages of the industry life cycle and how factors such as generic strategies, market growth rate, intensity of competition, and overall

Stage / Factor	Introduction	Growth	Maturity	Decline
Generic strategies	differentiation	differentiation	differentiation overall cost leadership	overall cost leadership focus
Market growth rate	low	very large	low to moderate	negative
Number of segments	very few	some	many	few
Intensity of competition	low	increasing	very intense	changing
Emphasis on product design	very high	high	low to moderate	low
Emphasis on process design	low	low to moderate	high	low
Major functional area(s) of concern	research and development	sales and marketing	production	general management and finance
Overall objective	increase market awareness	create consumer demand	defend market share and extend product life cycles	consolidate, maintain, harvest, or exit

Exhibit 5.7

Stages of the Industry Life Cycle

objectives change over time. As we noted earlier, managers must strive to emphasize the key functional areas during each of the four stages and attain a level of "parity" in all functional areas and value-creating activities. For example, even though controlling production costs may be a primary concern during the maturity stage, managers should not totally ignore other functions such as marketing and R&D. If they do, they can become so focused on lowering costs that they miss market trends or fail to incorporate important product or process designs. In such cases, the firm may attain low-cost products that have limited market appeal.

It is important to note that while the life-cycle idea is clearly analogous to a living organism (i.e., birth, growth, maturity, and death), the comparison does have limitations.[38] Products and services go through many cycles of innovation and renewal. For the most part, only fad products have a single life cycle. Maturity stages of an industry can be "transformed" or followed by a stage of rapid growth if consumer tastes change, technological innovations take place, or new developments occur in the general environment. The cereal industry is a good example. When medical research indicated that oat consumption reduced a person's cholesterol, sales of Quaker Oats increased dramatically.[39]

Strategies in the Introduction Stage

In the introduction stage, products are unfamiliar to consumers.[40] Market segments are not well defined, and product features are not clearly specified. The early development of an industry typically involves low sales growth, rapid technological change, operating losses, and the need for strong sources of cash to finance operations. Since there are few players and not much growth, competition tends to be limited.

Success in the introduction stage requires an emphasis on research and development and marketing activities to enhance awareness of the product or service. The challenge involves (1) developing the product and finding a way to get users to try it and (2) generating enough exposure so that the product emerges as the standard by which all other competitors' products are evaluated.

There's an advantage to being the "first mover" in a market.[41] Consider Coca-Cola's success in becoming the first soft-drink company to build a recognizable global brand. Moving before others enabled Caterpillar to get a lock on overseas sales channels and service capabilities. Being a first mover in the mid-1990s allowed RIM of Waterloo, Ontario, to establish BlackBerry as the global standard for personal digital assistants (PDAs).

However, there can also be a benefit to being a "late mover." The retailer Target carefully thought out the decision to delay its Internet strategy. Compared to its competitors Wal-Mart and Kmart, Target was definitely the industry laggard. Target patiently waited to learn from the mistakes of the first movers and made sure it understood how to attract online customers before it launched its own Web site. The wait paid off, and, today, Target has a larger online market share than either of its competitors.

Examples of products currently in the introductory stages of the industry life cycle include electric vehicles, voice-over IP telephony, and high-definition television (HDTV).

Strategies in the Growth Stage

The second stage of the industry life cycle, growth, is characterized by strong increases in sales. The potential for strong sales (and profits) attracts other competitors who also want to benefit. During the growth stage, the primary key to success is to build consumer preferences for specific brands. This requires strong brand recognition, differentiated products, and the financial resources to support a variety of value-chain activities such as marketing and sales, customer service, and research and development. Whereas marketing and sales initiatives were mainly directed, in the introduction stage, at spurring *aggregate* demand—that is, demand for all such products—efforts in the growth stage are directed toward stimulating *selective* demand—that is, demand for a firm's product offerings instead of those of its rivals.

Revenues in the growth stage increase at an accelerating rate because (1) new consumers are trying the product and (2) a growing proportion of satisfied consumers are making repeat purchases.[42] In general, as a product moves through its life cycle, the proportion of repeat buyers to new purchasers increases. Yet, new products and services often fail if there are relatively few repeat purchases. This is especially true of many consumer products that are characterized by relatively low price and infrequent purchases. For example, Alberto-Culver introduced Mr. Culver's Sparklers, which were solid air fresheners that looked like stained glass. Although the product quickly went from the introductory to the growth stage, sales then plummeted. Why? Unfortunately, there were few repeat purchasers because buyers treated them as inexpensive window decorations, left them there, and felt little need to purchase new ones. Examples of products currently in the growth stage of the industry life cycle include Internet servers, digital cameras, and personal digital assistants such as RIM's BlackBerry.

Strategies in the Maturity Stage

In the third stage, maturity, aggregate industry demand begins to slow. Since markets are becoming saturated, there are few opportunities to attract new adopters. It's no longer possible to "grow around" the competition, so direct competition becomes predominant.[43] With few attractive prospects, marginal competitors begin to exit the market. At the same time, rivalry among existing competitors intensifies because there is often fierce price competition as expenses associated with attracting new buyers rise. Advantages based on efficient manufacturing operations and process engineering become more important for keeping costs low as customers become more price sensitive. It also becomes more difficult for firms to differentiate their offerings once users have a greater understanding of products and services.

An article in *Fortune* magazine that addressed the intensity of rivalry in mature markets was aptly titled "A Game of Inches." It stated, "Battling for market share in a slowing industry can be a mighty dirty business. Just ask laundry soap archrivals Unilever and Procter & Gamble."[44] These two firms have been locked in a battle for market share since 1965. Why is the competition so intense? There is not much territory to gain. In 2000, total sales for the industry were flat at $6 billion a year. A Lehman Brothers analyst noted, "People aren't getting any dirtier." Thus, the only way to win is to take market share from the competition. To increase its share, Procter & Gamble (P&G) spends $100 million a year promoting its Tide brand on television, billboards, subways, buses, magazines, and the Internet. But Unilever isn't standing still. Armed with a new $80 million budget, it launched a soap tablet product named Wisk Dual Action Tablets. On January 7, 2001, it delivered samples of this product to 24 million U.S. homes in Sunday newspapers, followed by a series of TV ads. P&G launched a counteroffensive: Tide Rapid Action Tablets ads showed side-by-side comparisons of the two products dropped into beakers of water. In the promotion, P&G claimed that its product is superior because it dissolves faster than Unilever's product. A minor point, but Unilever is challenging P&G in court. And the battle goes on.

Many product classes and whole industries, such as beer, automobiles, televisions, furniture, home renovations, and airlines, are in the maturity stage.

Strategies in the Decline Stage

Although all decisions in the phases of an industry life cycle are important, they become particularly critical in the decline stage. Difficult choices must be made, and firms must face up to the fundamental strategic choices of either exiting or staying and attempting to consolidate their position in the industry.[45]

The decline stage occurs when industry sales and profits begin to fall. Typically, changes in the business environment are at the root of an industry or product group entering this stage.[46] Changes in consumer tastes or a technological innovation can push a product into decline. Typewriters entered into the decline stage because of the word processing capabilities of personal computers. Compact disks forced cassette tapes into decline in the pre-recorded music industry, and digital video disks (DVDs) may soon replace compact disks. About 20 years earlier, of course, cassette tapes had led to the demise of long-playing records (LPs).

When a product enters the decline stage, it often consumes a large share of management time and financial resources relative to its potential worth. As sales and profits decline, competitors may start drastically cutting their prices to raise cash and remain solvent in the short term. The situation is further aggravated by the wholesale liquidation of assets, including inventory, of some of the competitors that have failed. This further intensifies price competition.

In the decline stage, a firm's strategic options become dependent on the actions of rivals. If many competitors decide to leave the market, sales and profit opportunities increase. On the other hand, prospects are limited if all competitors remain.[47] If some competitors merge, their increased market power may erode the opportunities for the remaining players. Managers must carefully monitor the actions and intentions of competitors before deciding on a course of action.

Four basic strategies are available in the decline phase: maintaining, harvesting, exiting, or consolidating.[48]

- *Maintaining* refers to keeping a product going without significantly reducing marketing support, technological development, or other investments, in the hope that competitors will eventually exit the market. Many offices still use typewriters for filling out forms and carrying out functions that cannot be completed on a personal computer. In some rural areas, rotary (or dial) telephones persist because of the older technology used in central switching offices. Thus, if a firm remains in the business and others exit, there may still be the potential for revenues and profits.

- *Harvesting* involves taking as much profit as possible from the business and making absolutely minimal investments. It requires that sales volume be maximized and costs be reduced quickly. Managers must review all of the firm's value-creating activities in order to cut associated budgets and wring out as much profit as possible. All value-chain activities should be considered for cost cutting, including primary activities such as operations and sales and marketing as well as support activities such as procurement, information systems, and technology development.

- *Exiting the market* involves dropping the product from a firm's portfolio. Since a residual core of consumers may still use the product, eliminating it should be considered carefully. If the firm's exit involves product markets that affect important relationships with other product markets in the corporation's overall portfolio, an exit could have repercussions for the whole corporation. For example, it may involve the loss of valuable brand names or human capital with a broad variety of expertise in many value-creating activities such as marketing, technology, and operations.

◆ ***Consolidation*** involves one firm acquiring a number of its competitors in a declining industry. The surviving firm enhances its market power and acquires valuable assets. It retains the best facilities and effectively rationalizes its operations. It takes production capacity out of the system in an orderly fashion and prevents a bloody price war that could severely hurt its profits. Certain firms in the North American steel industry undertook an ambitious strategy of consolidation during the late 1990s and created fewer but better positioned players with much more competitive cost structures. Another example of consolidation took place in the U.S. defence industry at about the same time. As the cliché goes, "peace broke out" at the end of the Cold War, and overall U.S. defence spending levels plummeted.[49] Many companies saw more than 50 percent of their market disappear. Only one-quarter of the 120,000 companies that once supplied the Department of Defense were around by 2001; the others shut down their defence business or dissolved altogether. But one key player, Lockheed Martin, became a dominant rival by pursuing an aggressive strategy of consolidation. During the 1990s, it purchased 17 independent entities, including General Dynamics' tactical aircraft and space systems divisions, GE Aerospace, Goodyear Aerospace, and Honeywell ElectroOptics. These combinations enabled Lockheed Martin to emerge as the top provider to three governmental customers: the Department of Defense, the Department of Energy, and NASA. Even before the defence and security buildup that followed the September 11, 2001, terrorist attacks, the firm was ranked among the largest 25 industrial concerns in the United States and was posting healthy profits.

Examples of products currently in the decline stage of the industry life cycle include automotive spark plugs (replaced by electronic fuel ignition), video cassette recorders (replaced by digital video disk recorders), 35mm photographic equipment (replaced by digital cameras), and personal computer zip drives (replaced by compact disk read-write drives).

Relating Generic Strategies to Stages of the Industry Life Cycle: The Personal Computer Industry

The personal computer (PC) industry provides an example of how a firm's generic strategies can vary over stages of the industry life cycle. In the introduction and growth stages, there were many players, such as IBM, Compaq, and others, who endeavoured to create brand recognition and build loyal followings for their entries. To do so required well-developed and well-executed differentiation strategies. Apple was further differentiated because it was the only player to have a graphical user interface (GUI). However, well within a decade, the market matured, particularly when the "Wintel" standard (Microsoft's *Win*dows operating system and In*tel*'s microprocessor units) was widely adopted. This, in effect, eroded Apple's unique feature. Price competition then quickly intensified. Why? Consumer awareness and sophistication with personal computers accelerated, and the market became saturated with similar products. Here, overall low-cost strategies became the dominant form of competition. However, some firms, such as Dell, were still able to make differentiation a key part of their business-level strategy by offering superior service and rapid fulfillment of customer orders. It now appears that many Web appliances, such as Oracle TalkBack and Intel's Dot.Station (each priced at approximately $200), may become viable substitute products. These products provide many features similar to those of personal computers: Internet access, email delivery, and personal calendars. Demand for these products may drive the personal computer industry into the decline stage by significantly lowering aggregate consumer demand. In response, the personal computer companies will have to intensify their cost-reduction initiatives as well as develop focus strategies in order to seek out niches in the market that may prove more viable than exiting the industry altogether. Some of the early reactions have been Compaq's sale to HP and IBM's departure from the market and sale of its entire personal-computer business to Lenovo, China's biggest PC maker.

Turnaround Strategies

One problem with the life-cycle analogy is that we tend to think that decline is inevitably followed by death. In the case of businesses, however, decline can be reversed by strategies that lead to turnaround and rejuvenation. Such a need for turnaround may occur at any stage in the life cycle. However, it is more likely to occur during the maturity or decline stage.

Most successful turnarounds start with a careful analysis of the external and internal environments. The external analysis leads to identification of market segments or customer groups that may still find the product attractive. Internal analysis points to opportunities for reduced costs and higher efficiency. Typically, a firm needs to undertake a mix of both internally and externally oriented actions to effect a turnaround.

A study of 260 mature businesses in need of a turnaround identified three strategies used by successful companies:[50]

- *Asset and cost surgery.* Very often, mature firms tend to have accumulated assets that do not produce any returns. These include real estate, buildings, or fine art pieces; even equipment, such as airplanes, needs to be considered. Outright sales or sale and leaseback free up considerable cash and improve returns. Investment in new plants and equipment can be deferred. Firms in turnaround situations try to aggressively cut administrative expenses and inventories and speed up collection of receivables. Costs can also be reduced by outsourcing production of various inputs for which market prices may be cheaper than in-house production costs.

- *Selective product and market pruning.* Most mature or declining firms have many product lines that are marginally profitable or losing money. The famous 80-20 rule usually applies. It roughly states that a firm generally derives 80 percent of its profit from 20 percent of its products, clients, and markets. One strategy is to discontinue the unsuccessful product lines, cut off the unprofitable and usually difficult clients, and focus all resources on a few core profitable areas. For example, in the early 1980s, faced with possible bankruptcy, Chrysler Corporation sold off all its non-automotive businesses as well as all its production facilities abroad. Focus on the North American market and identification of a profitable niche—namely, minivans—were keys to Chrysler's eventual turnaround.

- *Piecemeal productivity improvements.* There are hundreds of ways in which a firm can eliminate costs and improve productivity. Although individually these are small gains, they cumulate over a period of time to yield substantial gains. Improving business processes by re-engineering them, benchmarking specific activities against industry leaders, encouraging employee input to identify excess costs, reducing R&D and marketing expenses, increasing capacity utilization, and improving employee productivity lead to a significant overall gain.

The turnaround of software maker Intuit is an interesting case of a quick but well-implemented turnaround strategy. After stagnating and stumbling during the dot-com boom, Intuit, which is known for its Quickbooks and Turbotax software, hired Stephen

M. Bennett, a 22-year GE veteran, in 1999. He immediately discontinued Intuit's online finance, insurance, and bill-paying operations, which were losing money. Instead, he focused on software for small businesses that employ less than 250 people. He also instituted a performance-based reward system that greatly improved employee productivity. By the end of 2002, Intuit was once again making substantial profits, and its stock was up 42 percent.[51]

Even when an industry is in overall decline, pockets of profitability remain. These are segments with customers who are relatively price insensitive. For example, the replacement demand for vacuum tubes affords its manufacturers an opportunity to earn above normal returns although the product itself is technologically obsolete. Surprisingly, within declining industries, there may still be segments that are either stable or growing. Cigars and chewing tobacco are examples of profitable segments within the tobacco industry. Although fountain pens ceased to be the writing instrument of choice a long time ago, the fountain pen industry has successfully reconceptualized the product as a high margin luxury item that signals accomplishment, success, and appreciation of the finer things in life. Every business has the potential for rejuvenation. But it takes creativity, persistence, and, most of all, a clear strategy to translate that potential into reality.

Summary

How firms succeed and why they outperform each other goes to the heart of strategic management. In this chapter, we identified three generic strategies and discussed how firms are able not only to attain advantages over competitors but also to sustain such advantages over time. Why do some advantages become long lasting, while others are quickly imitated by competitors?

The generic strategies—overall cost leadership, differentiation, and focus—form the core of this chapter. We began by providing a brief description of each generic strategy (or competitive advantage) and furnished examples of firms that have successfully implemented these strategies. Successful generic strategies invariably enhance a firm's position vis-à-vis the five forces of that industry—a point that we stressed and illustrated with examples. However, there are pitfalls to each of the generic strategies. Thus, the sustainability of a firm's advantage is always challenged because of imitation or substitution by new or existing rivals. Such competition erodes a firm's advantage over time.

We also discussed the viability of combining (or integrating) overall cost leadership and differentiation generic strategies. If successful, such integration can enable a firm to enjoy superior performance and improve its competitive position. However, this is challenging, and managers must be aware of the potential downside risks associated with this kind of initiative.

The concept of the industry life cycle is a critical contingency that managers must take into account in striving to create and sustain competitive advantages. We identified the four stages of the industry life cycle—introduction, growth, maturity, and decline—and suggested how these stages can affect the decisions that managers must make at the business level. These decisions include overall strategies as well as the relative emphasis on functional areas and value-creating activities.

When a firm's performance severely erodes, turnaround strategies are needed to reverse its situation and enhance its competitive position. We discussed three approaches —asset and cost surgery, selective product and market pruning, and piecemeal productivity improvements.

Summary Review Questions

1. Explain why the concept of competitive advantage is central to the study of strategic management.

2. Briefly describe the three generic strategies: overall cost leadership, differentiation, and focus.

3. Explain the relationship between the three generic strategies and the five forces that determine the average profitability within an industry.

4. What are some of the ways in which a firm can attain a successful turnaround strategy?

5. Describe some of the pitfalls associated with each of the three generic strategies.

6. Can firms combine the generic strategies of overall cost leadership and differentiation? Why or why not?

7. Explain why the industry life-cycle concept is an important factor in determining a firm's business-level strategy.

Experiential Exercise

1. What are some examples of primary and support activities that enable Dofasco, a $10 billion integrated steel manufacturer, to achieve success? How do they contribute to Dofasco's business strategy?

Value-Chain Activity	Yes/No	How Does Dofasco Create Value for the Customer?
Primary:		
Inbound logistics		
Operations		
Outbound logistics		
Marketing and sales		
Service		
Support:		
Procurement		
Technology development		
Human resource management		
General administration		

2. Look for up-to-date information on Cott. Use the Internet and the company's own Web site. Has the company been able to sustain its business strategy? What elements have they had to change recently? How have they adjusted their business strategy?

Application Questions Exercises

1. Go to the Internet and look up www.CanadianTire.ca. How has this firm been able to combine overall cost leadership and differentiation strategies?

2. Choose a firm in your local business community with which you are familiar. Is the firm successful in following its generic strategies? Why or why not? What do you think are some of the challenges it faces in implementing these strategies in an effective manner?

3. Think of a firm that has attained a differentiation focus or cost focus strategy. Are its advantages sustainable? Why or why not? (*Hint:* Consider its position vis-à-vis Porter's five forces.)

4. Think of a firm that has successfully achieved a combination of overall cost leadership and differentiation strategy. What can be learned from this example? Are these advantages sustainable? Why or why not? (*Hint:* Consider its competitive position vis-à-vis Porter's five forces.)

Ethics Questions

1. Can you think of a company that suffered ethical consequences as a result of an over-emphasis on a cost leadership or differentiation strategy? What do you think were the financial and non-financial implications?

2. In the introductory stage of the product life cycle, what are some of the unethical practices that managers could engage in to enhance their firm's market position? What could be some of the long-term implications of such actions?

3. Detractors of Wal-Mart and other low-cost competitors argue the processes that set them apart also create major social, environmental, and personal problems for thousands of communities, local businesses, and individuals. The *high cost of low price* and the *high price of low cost* are two positions taken by a range of sceptics to the proliferation of Wal-Marts and easyJets. On the Internet, search those two statements and their associated positions. What issues do they raise? Do you have an opinion?

Chapter 6

Corporate-Level Strategy: *Creating Value through Diversification*

LEARNING OBJECTIVES

After reading this chapter, you should have a good understanding of:

LO 1 ▸ why firms engage in diversification efforts and how managers can create value through diversification initiatives.

LO 2 ▸ how corporations can use related diversification to achieve synergistic benefits through economies of scope and market power.

LO 3 ▸ how corporations can use unrelated diversification to achieve synergistic benefits through corporate restructuring, parenting, and portfolio analysis.

LO 4 ▸ the various means of engaging in diversification: mergers and acquisitions, strategic alliances and joint ventures, internal development.

LO 5 ▸ the value of real options analysis (ROA) in making resource allocation decisions under conditions of high uncertainty.

LO 6 ▸ the reasons for the failure of many diversification efforts.

Bell Canada Enterprises (BCE) had ended 1998 as Canada's second-largest corporation, with total assets of $32 billion, 58,000 employees, revenues of $27 billion, and a net income of $4.6 billion.[1] Fast-forward to eight years later; BCE reported 2006 revenues under $18 billion and a net income of less than $2 billion while thousands of its employees had been laid off. Many of its most successful ventures were under significant competitive pressures; some of its traditional lines of business—those in which BCE used to be the dominant player—had lost their lustre and were unable to generate either the cash or profits that were once as predictable as government bonds. BCE stock was trading for one-half the value it had in 1999. BCE's CEO, Jean Monty, who had earlier been called one of the smartest business people in Canada, was ousted, and Michael Sabia was brought in to pick up the pieces and pull off one of Canada's biggest corporate makeovers. Yet, few things seemed to go BCE's or Sabia's way. Everything took too long to be decided, and the decisions that were made ended up being flops. Yellow Pages was sold off for what looked like a reasonable price; yet, the buyers managed to extract tremendous additional value by restructuring and streamlining the business, tripling its value in a short two years. The wireless and Internet parts of the business, supposedly the engines of growth, somehow could never be as good as those of BCE's competitors, Rogers and Telus. Some of its largest corporate accounts defected and there was a very embarrassing operational glitch that stalled the wireless billing system. Bell continued to lose land-line customers to the cable operators. The stock went nowhere for five years, angering investors who had relied on their BCE holdings for dividends and growth.

Case Study

What Went Wrong at BCE? BCE was a diversified corporation with a number of holdings in the telecommunications sector. Its subsidiary, Bell Canada, operated across most of Canada. BCE used to own part of a thriving telephone equipment manufacturing operation, Northern Telecom, which later became Nortel Networks. Among its other business holdings were a long-distance telephone service provider and a number of small ventures that were set to take advantage of new technologies and position BCE for the increasingly deregulated marketplace of telecommunications. Jean Monty was a rather conservative CEO, as befitting the head of a very successful corporation, who spent as much time lobbying the government to maintain control of its regulated destiny as he did contemplating developments and challenges arising from the new technologies.

BCE, by its own admission, was slow to develop a cohesive Internet strategy and to fully appreciate the potential threat posed by cable companies. As it was readying to sever ties with Nortel, many wondered whether the parent of Nortel didn't have just as much reason to be an international powerhouse of its own. It seems that this got Jean Monty and the BCE board as motivated as did the financial markets' acquisition madness of the early months of 2000.

The company had amassed a war chest of over $6 billion dollars with which Monty planned to expand BCE's presence in Canada, the United States, and overseas. Analysts also expected them to off-load the 20 percent stake on Teleglobe Inc., a long-distance carrier based in Montreal that was controlled by Monty's long-time friend, Charles Sirois. The sale would have added another $2.7 billion dollars. Monty believed in the popular notion of the late 1990s regarding convergence—namely, that the pipe and the content had to be brought under one roof if a firm wanted to capitalize on the technological revolution that was to bring together telephone, television, communications, video, radio, movies, programming, news, media, electronic commerce, and the Internet.

Monty decided, instead, to acquire the rest of Teleglobe, paying some $6.4 billion for it. Another billion went toward acquiring a controlling interest in a national newspaper and a television network. Sympatico, the provider of the Bell Canada Internet service that the company offered to its local customers and which most senior managers within BCE did not truly appreciate, did not get much attention.

By 2003, Teleglobe was practically worthless, and BCE had to write it off completely, to the tune of about $8 billion. Results for 2004 showed that revenues from long-distance services were declining by 8 to 10 percent per year. Competition from Internet-based technology and other providers that reacted more aggressively to deregulation were shrinking Bell's top and bottom lines. Local phone service, Bell's bread and butter, was facing an onslaught from cable operators, who could offer voice services over high-speed Internet connections, and from other service providers following the deregulation of the sector. BCE was barely holding its revenue lines but had to compete more aggressively to retain its customers, who departed at a rate of about 200,000 per year. Sympatico subsequently began growing by 15 to 20 percent, and Bell Mobility, a wireless services company, had 4.7 million subscribers and was making healthy profits. But even those two businesses were not able to reach the performance levels of their peers.

BCE is not alone in having a disappointing experience with its diversification moves and many of its acquisitions. Other larger multinational firms and big acquirers—including AOL-Time Warner, Daimler-Benz, and HP/Compaq—have also failed to effectively integrate their acquisitions, paid too high a premium for the target's common stock, or were unable to understand how the acquired firm's assets would fit with their own business lines. Many high-flying firms have been grounded, largely because of ill-fated deals that were developed by some of Wall Street and Bay Street's top investment banking firms. Studies have frequently shown that some 50 percent of mergers and acquisitions are later divested with loss, giving corporate marriages a divorce rate that is comparable to that of people.[2]

Canadian Tire and La Senza are only two among many well-known Canadian retailers that have tried, not always successfully, to establish a footprint and expand into the U.S. market. Some of those corporate ventures were "greenfield," whereby a company opened its own stores in chosen locations; other ventures took the form of an acquisition, whereby a company acquired a local player with existing stores and retained or changed the name on the marquee; and finally, others took some form of a strategic alliance, whereby the Canadian corporation worked closely with a local partner to jointly pursue the venture. The decisions made by corporations to enter new markets and diversify their businesses, the choices of means by which to undertake those entries, as well as the decisions about the linkages among those businesses lie at the heart of corporate strategy. While the decision to diversify might be justified on very legitimate grounds, the execution of that strategy and the choice of method for carrying out diversification can easily get managers into trouble. Even where the track record of non-acquisition-based diversification moves is slightly better, there have been many similar spectacular failures.

In contrast to BCE's recent history, firms such as IBM, Microsoft, Rogers Communications, Onex, The Keg, and Couche-Tard have had much better luck with their diversification moves. IBM has successfully developed its service business and, during the last 10 years, has transformed itself from a mainframe computer manufacturer to a business solutions powerhouse. Moreover, in the early 1980s, IBM successfully developed, from scratch, a completely different line of business and, for a time, dominated the personal computer market. In addition to greenfield development, many acquisitions in the oil industry, such as British Petroleum PLC's purchases of Amoco and Arco, have performed well, as is the merger of Exxon and Mobil. The Newmont Mining–Franco Nevada merger of American and Canadian gold mining powerhouses yielded both operational and financial benefits. Leading high-tech firms, such as Microsoft, Cisco, IBM, and Intel, have dramatically increased their revenues, profits, and market values through a wide variety of diversification moves, including mergers and acquisitions, strategic alliances and joint ventures, and internal development.

So, the question becomes, why do some diversification efforts pay off and others produce extremely disappointing results? Whereas Chapter 5 focused on business-level strategy—that is, how to achieve sustainable advantages in a given business or product market—this chapter addresses corporate-level strategy—that is, the choice of businesses a corporation should compete in and how those businesses should be managed to jointly create more value than if they were free-standing units. Getting answers to this general question requires us to look at the various types of diversification that can potentially be considered (related and unrelated diversification), the rationale for contemplating each type of diversification, as well as the means to achieve diversification.

MAKING DIVERSIFICATION WORK: AN OVERVIEW

Diversification initiatives—whether through mergers and acquisitions, strategic alliances and joint ventures, or internal development—must be justified by the creation of value for shareholders. But this is not always the case. For example, as noted earlier, acquiring firms typically pay high premiums when they acquire a target firm. However, individuals, as private investors, can diversify their own portfolios of stocks. Moreover, with the advent of the intensely competitive online brokerage industry, they can acquire hundreds of shares for a transaction fee of as little as $10.00, a far cry from the 30 to 40 percent (or higher) premiums that corporations typically must pay to acquire companies.[3]

← (LO 1)

Given the seemingly high inherent downside risks and uncertainties, it might be reasonable to ask why companies should even bother with diversification initiatives. The answer, in a word, is *synergy*, derived from the Greek word *synergos*, which means "working together."[4] Synergy can be achieved in many different ways. First, a firm may diversify into *related* businesses. Here, the primary potential benefits to be derived come from sharing intangible resources (e.g., sales forces, brand names, technologies) and tangible resources (e.g., production facilities, distribution channels) across multiple businesses that can utilize the same resources and spread their costs over a larger revenue base. Maple Leaf Foods has built a successful corporation in processed meats, prepared foods, and baked goods—all businesses benefiting from a common sales and distribution network. Additionally, firms can enhance their market power by increasing dominance in a market, becoming a more critical supplier to their customers, or by increasing their hold on the business through vertical integration. It should be noted that firms can simultaneously enjoy multiple benefits from their related diversification moves, including shared costs and increased market power.

Second, a corporation may diversify into *unrelated* businesses. In these instances, the primary potential benefits derive largely from value created by the corporate office. Examples include leveraging some of the support activities in the value chain such as information systems or human resource practices. Onex Corporation, a $17 billion conglomerate based in Toronto, has followed a successful strategy of unrelated diversification. There are few similarities in the products it makes or the industries in which it competes. Its businesses include Sky Chefs, an airline catering business with operations across the world; plants that make wings, fuselages, and struts for Boeing jets in Kansas and Oklahoma; Emergency Medical Services, a U.S. ambulance and emergency room service company; Celestica, an electronics manufacturer with facilities around the world; Cineplex-Galaxy and Famous Players, two major movie theatre chains; J. L. French Automotive, an auto parts supplier for the major automobile manufacturers; and a fragrance manufacturer based in New Jersey. Moreover, through the personal investments of the

CEO, Gerry Schwartz, it controls Indigo Books and Music, the parent company of book-sellers Indigo, Chapters, and Coles, along with a small stake in Vincour, a winery with holdings in North America and Australia. The corporate office adds value through such activities as planning, performance evaluation, and budgeting systems.

It is important to note that the benefits derived from related and unrelated relation-ships are not mutually exclusive. Many firms that diversify into related areas benefit from information technology expertise in the corporate office, and firms diversifying into unrelated areas often benefit from "best practices" of sister businesses even though their products, markets, and technologies may differ dramatically.

RELATED DIVERSIFICATION: ECONOMIES OF SCOPE AND REVENUE ENHANCEMENT

Related diversification enables a firm to benefit from relationships across different busi-nesses within the diversified corporation by leveraging core competencies and sharing activities (e.g., production facilities and distribution facilities). This enables a corporation to benefit from *economies of scope*. Economies of scope are cost savings from leverag-ing core competencies, sharing resources, or sharing related activities among businesses within the corporation. A firm can also enjoy greater revenues if two businesses, com-bined, attain higher levels of sales than either company could attain independently.

For example, a sporting goods store may build or acquire other stores in different locations, cities, or even countries. This enables it to leverage, or reuse, many of its key resources such as reputation, expert staff and management skills, or efficient purchasing operations, which constitute the basis of its competitive advantage(s) over a larger number of stores.[5]

Leveraging Core Competencies

The concept of core competencies can be illustrated by the imagery of the diversified corporation as a tree.[6] The trunk and major limbs represent core products; the smaller branches are business units; and the leaves, flowers, and fruit are end products. The core competencies are represented by the root system, which provides nourishment, sustenance, and stability to the whole tree. Managers often misread the strength of competitors by looking only at their end products, just as one can fail to appreciate the strength of a tree by looking only at its leaves or counting how many flowers have bloomed. Core compe-tencies may also be viewed as the "glue" that binds existing businesses together or as the engine that fuels new business growth.

Core competencies reflect the collective learning in organizations—how to coordi-nate diverse production skills, integrate multiple streams of technologies, and market and merchandise diverse products and services. The theoretical knowledge necessary to put a radio on a chip does not in itself assure a company of the skill needed to produce a min-iature radio approximately the size of a business card. To accomplish this, Casio, a giant electronic-products producer, must synthesize know-how in miniaturization, microproces-sor design, material science, and ultra-thin precision castings. These are the same skills that it applies in its miniature card calculators, pocket TVs, and digital watches.

For a core competence to create value and provide a viable basis for synergy among the businesses in a corporation, it must meet three criteria:[7]

1. ***The core competence must enhance competitive advantage(s) by creating superior customer value.*** It must enable the business to develop strengths relative to the competition. Every value-chain activity has the potential to provide a viable basis

for building on a core competence. At Gillette, for example, scientists developed the Mach 3 and Sensor Excel after the introduction of the tremendously successful Sensor System and through a thorough understanding of several phenomena that underlie shaving. These include the physiology of facial hair and skin, the metallurgy of blade strength and sharpness, the dynamics of a cartridge moving across skin, and the physics of a razor blade severing hair. These innovations are possible only with an understanding of such phenomena and the ability to combine technologies into innovative products. Customers have consistently been willing to pay more for such technologically differentiated products.

2. ***Different businesses in the corporation must be similar in at least one important way related to the core competence.*** It is not essential that the products or services themselves be similar. Rather, at least one element in the value chain must require similar skills in creating competitive advantage if the corporation is to capitalize on its core competence. At first glance, one might think that motorcycles, clothes, and restaurants have little in common. But at Harley-Davidson, they do.[8] Harley-Davidson has capitalized on its exceptionally strong brand image as well as its merchandising and licensing skills to sell accessories, clothing, and toys; it has also licensed the Harley-Davidson Café in New York City. Loblaw Companies Ltd. operates a range of food stores under the banners of Provigo, No Frills, Fortinos, Loblaws, and Zehrs. Even though each caters to a different customer group, they all rely on the intimate knowledge of the Canadian consumer and the merchandising skills of the parent company. Moreover, it has developed the very successful private label line of President's Choice, which reflects much of the corporation's knowledge about consumer tastes. Finally, Loblaw uses the enhanced negotiating power that arises from its larger scale to extract preferential terms from its suppliers.

3. ***The core competence must be difficult for competitors to imitate or find substitutes for.*** As we discussed in Chapter 5, competitive advantages will not be sustainable if the competition can easily imitate or substitute them. Similarly, if the skills associated with a firm's core competencies are easily imitated or replicated, they are not a sound basis for sustainable advantages. Consider Sharp Corporation, a $17 billion consumer electronics giant.[9] It has a set of specialized core competencies in optoelectronics technologies that are difficult to replicate and that contribute to its competitive advantages in its core businesses. Its most successful technology has been liquid crystal displays (LCDs), which are critical components in nearly all of Sharp's products. Its expertise in this technology enabled Sharp to succeed in video cassette recorders (VCRs), with its innovative LCD viewfinder, and led to the creation of its Wizard, a personal electronic organizer.

Sharing Activities

As we saw above, leveraging core competencies involves transferring accumulated skills and expertise across business units in a corporation. When carried out effectively, this leads to advantages that can become quite sustainable over time. Corporations can also achieve synergy by sharing tangible activities across their business units. These include value-creating activities such as common manufacturing facilities, distribution channels, and sales forces. As we will now see, sharing activities can potentially provide two primary payoffs: cost savings and revenue enhancements.

Deriving Cost Savings through Sharing Activities Typically, this is the most common type of synergy and the easiest to estimate. Peter Shaw, head of mergers and acquisitions at the British chemical and pharmaceutical company ICI, refers to cost savings as "hard synergies" and contends that the level of certainty of their achievement is quite high. Cost savings come from many sources, including elimination of jobs, facilities, and related expenses that are no longer required when functions are consolidated, or from economies of scale in purchasing. Cost savings are generally highest when one company acquires another from the same industry in the same country. Rogers Wireless was able to obtain immediate savings from its acquisition of Microcell through consolidation of back office operations and technical support as well as through higher capacity utilization of its infrastructure. At the same time, the clients of Fido, Microcell's main retail brand name, instantly gained broader market coverage and better reception for their phones.

It is important to note that sharing activities inevitably entails costs that the benefits must outweigh. One often overlooked cost is that involved in the coordination required to manage a shared activity. Even more important is the need to compromise the design or performance of an activity so that it can be shared. For example, a salesperson handling the products of two business units must operate in a way that is usually unlike what either unit would prescribe were it independent. If the compromise erodes the unit's effectiveness, then sharing may reduce rather than enhance competitive advantage.

Enhancing Revenue and Differentiation through Sharing Activities Often two businesses may achieve a higher level of sales growth together than either one could on its own. Shortly after Gillette acquired Duracell, it confirmed its expectation that selling Duracell batteries through Gillette's existing channels for personal care products would increase sales, particularly internationally. Gillette sold Duracell products in 25 new markets in the first year after the acquisition and substantially increased sales in established international markets. In a similar vein, a target company's distribution channel can be used to escalate the sales of an acquiring company's product. This was the case when Gillette acquired Parker Pen. Gillette estimated that it could gain an additional $25 million in sales of its own Waterman pens by taking advantage of Parker's distribution channels.

Firms can also enhance the effectiveness of their differentiation strategies by means of sharing activities among business units. A shared order-processing system, for example, may permit new features and services that a buyer will value. Also, sharing can reduce the cost of differentiation. For instance, a shared service network may make more advanced, remote service technology economically feasible. To illustrate the potential for enhanced differentiation through sharing, consider the $5.1 billion VF Corporation—producer of such well-known brands as Lee, Wrangler, Vanity Fair, and Jantzen.

VF's acquisition of Nutmeg Industries and H. H. Cutler provided it with several large customers that it didn't have before, increasing its plant utilization and productivity. But more importantly, Nutmeg designs and makes licensed apparel for sports teams and organizations, while Cutler manufactures licensed brand-name children's apparel, including Walt Disney kid's wear. Such brand labelling enhances the differentiation of VF's apparel products. According to VF president Mackey McDonald, "What we're doing is looking at value-added knitwear, taking our basic fleece from Basset-Walker (one of its divisions), embellishing it through Cutler and Nutmeg, and selling it as a value-added product." Additionally, Cutler's advanced high-speed printing technologies will enable VF to be more proactive in anticipating trends in the fashion-driven fleece market. Claims McDonald, "Rather than printing first and then trying to guess what the customer wants, we can see what's happening in the marketplace and then print it up."[10]

As a cautionary note, managers must keep in mind that sharing activities among businesses in a corporation can have a negative effect on a given business's differentiation. For example, with the merger of Chrysler and Daimler-Benz, many consumers may lower their perceptions of Mercedes's quality and prestige if they feel that common

American Idol: Far More than Just a Television Show

American Idol is one of several of FremantleMedia's hit television shows. FremantleMedia (FM) is a division of German media giant Bertlemann, which has approximately $20 billion in revenues. Some of FM's other well-known television shows are *The Apprentice, The X Factor*, and game shows such as *The Price is Right* and *Family Feud*.

FM created *Pop Idol* in Britain in 2001, followed the next year by a tremendously successful launch of *American Idol*. There are 41 idols today, such as the *Belgium Idool, Portugal Idolos*, and *SuperStar KZ* (Kazakshstan). Although the show may be crass and occasionally cruel, it is undeniably brilliant. FM has become extremely successful at creating truly global programming. In part, that is due to the creative minds in FM; it has some of the best professionals in the business, who have talent for developing shows that appeal to huge populations with different backgrounds and circumstances.

The real key to FM's success is not just adapting its television hits to other countries, but systematically leveraging its core product, television shows, to create multiple revenue streams. This enables the company to use its core competence in making products of mass appeal and then in customizing them for places with widely varying languages, cultures, and mores. FM then extracts every penny from their hit shows through tie-ins, spinoffs, innovative uses of technology, and marketing masterstrokes.

The *Idol* franchise has created a wide variety of new revenue streams for its corporate parent:

- Products. Brand extensions range from videogames and fragrances to a microphone-shaped soap-on-a-rope.

- TV Licensing. Ads and lucrative sponsorships accompany the show's broadcasts in the various markets.

- Compact Discs. The most successful performers of the *Idol* contests have sold millions of CDs and more than one-third of the revenue goes to BMG, which is another affiliate of Bertelsmann.

- Concerts. Although artists and their managers get the bulk of the revenues from live events, those venues also sell records and merchandise, as well as promote the next *Idol* show.

FM has also introduced slot machines in Las Vegas and recently completed a deal with the Ontario Lottery and Gaming Corporation (OLG) to sell scratch-cards. Both ideas are based on the format of *The Price is Right*, initiating another avenue of product lines.

Sources: P. Sloan, "The reality factory," *Business 2.0*, August 2004, pp. 74-82; J. Cooney "In the news, *License!*" March 2004, p. 48; "Fox on top in Feb; NBC languishing at the bottom," www.indiantelevision.com, March 2, 2005; and www.fremantlemedia.com

production components and processes are being used across the two divisions. And the Jaguar division of Ford Motor Company may be adversely affected as consumers come to understand that it shares many components with its sister divisions at Ford, including Lincoln.

Strategy Spotlight 6.1 discusses how FremantleMedia leverages its hit television show *American Idol* through its core competencies and shared activities to create multiple revenue streams.

Market Power

Similar businesses working together or the affiliation of a business with a strong parent can strengthen an organization's bargaining position in relation to suppliers and customers as well as enhance its position vis-à-vis competitors. Compare, for example, the position of an independent food manufacturer with the same business within Nestlé. Being part of Nestlé Corporation provides the business with significant clout—greater bargaining power with suppliers and customers—since it is part of a firm that makes large purchases from suppliers and provides a wide variety of products to their customers. Access to the parent's deep pockets increases the business's strength relative to rivals. Further, the Nestlé unit enjoys greater protection from substitutes and new entrants. Not only would rivals perceive the unit as a more formidable opponent, but the unit's association with Nestlé would also provide greater visibility and an improved image.

Consolidating an industry can also increase a firm's market power. This has been a trend in the multimedia industry.[11] Several blockbuster deals have been completed, most notably the merger of Time Warner Inc. with America Online Inc. In Canada, Globemedia brought together the assets of a national newspaper (*The Globe and Mail*) and a television network (CTV) under the joint ownership of the world's largest information company (The Thomson Corporation, based in Toronto) and the country's largest telephone company (BCE, based in Montreal). Its competitor, CanWest, of Winnipeg, owns its own newspapers (including the *National Post*, Montreal's *The Gazette*, and *The Vancouver Sun*), a television network (Global), radio stations, along with radio and television stations in Australia and New Zealand. All of these strategic moves have a common goal: to control and leverage as many news and entertainment channels as possible. In 2000 alone, more than $261 billion in mergers and acquisitions in the media industry were announced. The enhanced scale and scope of each company was seen as critical in order to compete more effectively and grow more rapidly in two consolidating industries—newspaper and television broadcasting. The combined company would increase its power by providing a "one-stop shop" for advertisers desiring to reach consumers through multiple media in enormous markets such as New York, Los Angeles, Toronto, London, and Sydney. It would also increase its power relative to its suppliers. A company's enhanced size could be expected to lead to increased efficiencies when purchasing newsprint and other commodities.[12]

When acquiring related businesses, a firm's potential for pooled negotiating power vis-à-vis its customers and suppliers can be very enticing. However, managers must carefully evaluate how the combined businesses may affect relationships with actual and potential customers, suppliers, and competitors. For example, when PepsiCo diversified into the fast-food industry with its acquisitions of Kentucky Fried Chicken, Taco Bell, and Pizza Hut (since spun off as Tricon Inc.), it clearly benefited from its position over these units that served as a captive market for its soft-drink products. However, some of its customers, such as McDonald's, have since refused to consider PepsiCo as a supplier of its own soft-drink needs because of competition with Pepsi's divisions in the fast-food industry. Simply put, McDonald's did not want to patronize the enemy! Thus, although acquiring related businesses can enhance a corporation's bargaining power, it must be aware of the potential for retaliation by others.

It is also important to recognize that managers have limits on their ability to use market power for diversification because government regulations can sometimes restrict the ability of a business to gain very large shares of a particular market.

When General Electric (GE) announced a $41 billion bid for Honeywell, the European Union stepped in. GE's market clout would have expanded significantly as a result of the deal, with GE supplying over one-half the parts needed to build several aircraft engines. The commission's concern, causing it to reject the acquisition, was that GE could use its increased market power to dominate the aircraft engine parts market and crowd out competitors.[13] When Air Canada acquired Canadian Airlines, the federal government imposed numerous restrictions regarding routes, fares, and potential layoffs. They were intended to ensure that the overwhelming power, which was to be accumulated under one firm, could not be abused and that the airline would continue to serve the Canadian public with competitive fares while retaining most of its employees. While managers need to be aware of the strategic advantages of market power, they must, at the same time, be aware of regulations and legislation.

Vertical Integration at Canfor

Canfor Corporation, based in Vancouver, British Columbia, is the world's largest SPF lumber producer and a global leader in the forest products industry. Early in its corporate development, Canfor made the strategic choice to diversify into most aspects of the industry and expand both across stages of the value chain and across markets. Its senior management was convinced that such moves would allow it to better control its destiny and shield the company from the cyclical nature of various parts of the business. It has followed a very successful strategy of vertical integration. It has pursued both backward and forward integration through internal development as well as through acquisitions. Canfor recognized that prudent forest management is as critical to the economics of the business as building strong relationships with the communities where the corporation operates.

Today, it owns or controls vast amounts of timberland that provide the raw materials for its downstream businesses and a valuable supply of fibre. At the same time, it has pursued sustainable forest management certifications in all its woodlands operations and has built partnerships with local aboriginal communities. Further upstream, Canfor operates nurseries and seed orchards to feed those timberlands with new stock. At the other end of its business, it has a marketing and distribution arm that sells high-performance packaging, craft, and other specialty papers to markets around the world. In between, Canfor has built and acquired sawmills, panel and plywood production facilities, pulp and paper mills, and remanufacturing operations. Canfor sees its vertical and horizontal integration strategic moves as an effective response to the realities of the global forestry industry that is facing increasingly larger customers who also operate globally, are getting more dominant, and are exerting more pressure on their suppliers.

Sources: W. Stueck, "Confident Canfor has an eye for acquisitions," *The Globe and Mail*, May 4, 2007, p. B5; Canfor Corporation Annual Reports,; and www.canfor.ca.

Vertical Integration

Vertical integration represents an expansion or extension of the firm by integrating preceding or successive productive processes.[14] That is, the firm incorporates more processes toward the original source of raw materials (backward integration) or toward the ultimate consumer (forward integration). For example, an automobile manufacturer might supply its own parts or make its own engines to secure sources of supply. Or it might control its own system of dealerships to ensure retail outlets for its products. Similarly, an oil refinery might secure land leases and develop its own drilling capacity to ensure a constant supply of crude oil. Or it could expand into retail operations by owning or licensing gasoline stations to guarantee customers for its petroleum products.

Vertical integration can be a viable strategy for many firms. Strategy Spotlight 6.2 discusses Canfor Corporation, a significant player in the international forest products sector. It has attained a dominant position in the industry via a strategy of vertical integration. Canfor has successfully implemented strategies of both forward and backward integration. Similarly, Aber Diamonds Corporation, part owner of the Diavik diamond mine in the Northwest Territories, acquired Harry Winston Inc., an upscale chain of American-based jewellery stores, and saw immediate benefits in enhanced revenues and profits.[15]

Benefits and Risks of Vertical Integration Although vertical integration is a means for an organization to reduce its dependence on suppliers or its channels of distribution to end users, it represents a major decision that an organization must carefully consider. The benefits associated with vertical integration—backward or forward—must be carefully weighed against the risks.

The *benefits* of vertical integration include (1) a secure source of raw materials or distribution channels that cannot be "held hostage" to external markets where costs can fluctuate over time, (2) protection and control over assets and services required to produce and deliver valuable products and services, (3) access to new business opportunities and new forms of technologies, and (4) improved coordination of activities across the value chain.

The *risks* of vertical integration include (1) the costs associated with increased overhead and capital expenditures to provide facilities, raw material inputs, and distribution channels inside the organization; (2) a loss of flexibility resulting from the inability to respond quickly to changes in the external environment, as the huge investments in vertical integration activities are generally not easily deployed elsewhere; (3) problems associated with unbalanced capacities or unfilled demand along the value chain; and (4) additional administrative costs associated with managing a more complex set of activities.

In making decisions about vertical integration, four questions should be considered:[16]

1. *Is the value provided by present suppliers and distributors satisfactory?* If the performance of organizations in the vertical chain—both suppliers and distributors—is satisfactory, it may not, in general, be appropriate for the firm to perform these activities. Firms in the athletic footwear industry, such as Nike and Reebok, have traditionally outsourced the manufacture of their shoes to countries like China and Indonesia where labour costs are low. Since the strengths of these companies are typically in design and marketing, it would be advisable for them to continue to outsource production operations and focus on where they can add the most value.

2. *Are there activities in the industry value chain presently being outsourced or performed independently by others that are a viable source of future profits?* Even if a firm is outsourcing value-chain activities to companies that are doing a credible job, it may be missing out on substantial profit opportunities. To illustrate, consider the automobile industry's profit pool. As noted in Chapter 5, there has been much more potential profit in many downstream activities (e.g., leasing, warranty, insurance, and service) than in the manufacture of automobiles. Not surprisingly, carmakers, such as Ford and General Motors, have undertaken forward integration strategies to become bigger players in these high-profit activities.

3. *Is there relative stability in the demand for the organization's products?* High demand or sales volatility would not be conducive to a vertical integration strategy. Substantial fixed costs in plant and equipment as well as operating costs that typically accompany vertical integration can strain resources in times of high demand and result in unused capacity in times of low demand. The cycles of "boom and bust" in the automobile industry are a key reason why the manufacturers have increased the level of outsourcing in recent years.

4. *Is there a source of core competence in the activity that is considered for outsourcing or vertical integration?* Unlike most other retailers, Wal-Mart has fully integrated all the upstream logistics of the handling, warehousing, transportation, and distribution of the goods it sells in all its stores. It's no wonder that those activities are what sets Wal-Mart apart from the competition and are the contributors to its success. Similarly, Intel both designs and manufactures all its microchips. Numerous writers have cautioned firms to be mindful of outsourcing their core competencies while, thereby, effectively helping to establish their own formidable competitors.[17]

Analyzing Vertical Integration: The Transaction Cost Perspective Another approach that has proven very useful in understanding vertical integration is the *transaction cost perspective*.[18] According to this perspective, every market transaction involves some *transaction costs*. First, a decision to purchase an input from an outside source leads to *search* costs (i.e., the cost to find where it is available, the level of quality, etc.). Second, there are costs associated with *negotiating*. Third, a *contract* needs to be written, spelling out future possible contingencies. Fourth, parties in a contract have to *monitor* each other. Finally, if a party does not comply with the terms of the contract, there are *enforcement* costs. Many of these transaction costs can be avoided by internalizing the activity—in other words, by producing the input in-house.

A related problem with purchasing a specialized input from outside is the issue of *transaction-specific investments*. For example, when an automobile company needs an input specifically designed for a particular car model, its supplier may be unwilling to make the investments in plant and machinery necessary to produce that component for two reasons. First, the investment may take many years to recover, but there is no guarantee the automobile company will continue to buy from them after the contract expires, typically in one or two years. Second, once the investment is made, the supplier has no bargaining power; that is, the automobile company knows that the supplier has no option but to supply at ever-lower prices because the investments were so specific that they cannot be used to produce alternative products. Given the reluctance of the supplier to undertake the investments, vertical integration may be the only option.

Finally, vertical integration also gives rise to *administrative costs*. Coordinating different stages of the value chain now internalized within the firm causes administrative costs to go up. Decisions about vertical integration are, therefore, based on a comparison of transaction costs and administrative costs. If transaction costs are lower than administrative costs, it is best to resort to market transactions and avoid vertical integration. For example, McDonald's may be the world's biggest buyer of beef, but they do not raise cattle. The market for beef has low transaction costs and requires no transaction-specific investments. On the other hand, if transaction costs are higher than administrative costs, vertical integration becomes an attractive strategy. Most automobile manufacturers produce their own engines because the market for engines involves high transaction costs and transaction-specific investments.

Vertical Integration: Further Considerations As many companies would attest, successfully executing strategies of vertical integration can be very difficult. For example, Unocal, a major petroleum refiner that once owned retail gas stations, was slow to capture the potential grocery and merchandise side business that might have resulted from customer traffic to its service stations. Unocal lacked the competencies to develop a separate retail organization and culture. The company eventually sold the assets and brand to Tosco (now part of Phillips Petroleum Co.). Eli Lilly, the pharmaceutical firm, tried to achieve forward integration by acquiring a pharmaceutical mail-order business in 1994, but it was unsuccessful in increasing market share because it failed to integrate its operations. Two years later, Lilly wrote off the venture.

Again, managers must carefully consider the impact that vertical integration may have on existing and future customers, suppliers, and competitors. After Lockheed Martin, a dominant defence contractor, acquired Loral Corporation, an electronics supplier, for $9.1 billion, it had an unpleasant and unanticipated surprise. Loral, as a captive supplier of Lockheed, is now perceived and treated as a competitor by many of its previous customers. McDonnell Douglas (MD), for example, announced that it would switch its business from Loral to other suppliers of electronic systems such as Litton Industries or Raytheon. Thus, before Lockheed Martin can realize any net synergies from this acquisition, it must make up for the substantial lost business resulting from MD's (now part of Boeing) decision to switch suppliers.

UNRELATED DIVERSIFICATION: FINANCIAL SYNERGIES AND PARENTING

With unrelated diversification, potential benefits can be gained from the creation of synergies from the interaction of the corporate office with the individual business units. There are two main sources of such synergies. First, the corporate office can contribute to "parenting" and restructuring of (often acquired) businesses. Second, the corporate office can add value by viewing the entire corporation as a family or "portfolio" of businesses and allocating resources to optimize corporate goals of profitability, cash flow, and growth. Additionally, the corporate office enhances value by establishing appropriate human resource practices and financial controls for each of its business units.

Corporate Parenting and Restructuring

So far, we have discussed how corporations can add value through related diversification by exploring sources of synergy *across* business units. In this section, we discuss how value can be created *within* business units as a result of the expertise and support provided by the corporate office.

The positive contributions of the corporate office have been referred to as the *parenting advantage*.[19] Many firms have successfully diversified their holdings without strong evidence of the more traditional sources of synergy (i.e., across business units). Diversified public corporations such as Brascan, Power Corporation, and Onex, and leveraged buyout firms such as Kohlberg, Kravis, Roberts & Company and Clayton, Dublilier & Rice are a few examples.[20] These parent companies create value through management expertise. How? They improve plans and budgets and provide especially competent central functions such as legal, financial, human resource management, procurement, and the like. Additionally, they help subsidiaries to make wise choices in their own acquisitions, divestitures, and new internal development decisions. Such contributions often help business units to substantially increase their revenues and profits.

Consider Onex Corporation's record. It acquired Sky Chefs from American Airlines in 1984 for $99 million. Onex took over the airline catering business that had only one captive customer; it established high quality standards, tightened operations, introduced management incentives, and started attracting outside customers. By the time Onex sold Sky Chefs to Lufthansa for $1.8 billion in 2001, it boasted over 200 airlines and other commercial customers. In 1996, Onex acquired Celestica, one of IBM's manufacturing divisions, for $262 million. It introduced closely monitored and controlled management processes throughout the operations and pushed to expand the customer base. The concerted efforts have yielded spectacular results for the company; even after the technology meltdown of 2000, Celestica's value is estimated at $2 billion. Recently, Onex purchased three of Boeing's facilities, and analysts expect the same disciplined management intervention to yield long-term results.[21]

Restructuring is another means by which the corporate office can add substantial value to a business.[22] Here, the corporate office tries to find either poorly performing firms with unrealized potential or firms in industries on the threshold of significant, positive change. The parent intervenes, often selling off parts of the business, changing the management, reducing payroll and unnecessary sources of expenses, changing strategies, and infusing the company with new technologies, processes, reward systems, and so forth. When the restructuring is complete, the firm can either "sell high" and capture the added value or keep the business in the corporate family and enjoy the financial and competitive benefits of the enhanced performance.[23]

For the restructuring strategy to work, the corporate management must have the insight to detect undervalued companies (otherwise the cost of acquisition would be too high) or businesses competing in industries with a high potential for transformation.[24] Additionally, of course, they must have the requisite skills and resources to turn the businesses around, even if they may be in new and unfamiliar industries.

Restructuring can involve changes in assets, capital structure, or management. *Asset restructuring* involves the sale of unproductive assets or even whole lines of businesses that are peripheral. In some cases, it may involve acquisitions that strengthen the core business. *Capital restructuring* involves changing the debt-equity mix, or the mix between different classes of debt and equity. Although the substitution of equity with debt is more common in buyout situations, occasionally the parent may provide additional equity capital. *Management restructuring* typically involves changes in the composition of the top management team, organizational structure, and reporting relationships. Tight financial control, rewards based strictly on meeting short- to medium-term performance goals, and reduction in the number of middle-level managers are common steps in management restructuring. In some cases, parental intervention may even result in changes in strategy as well as infusion of new technologies and processes. KKR, a venerable New York private equity firm acquired Shoppers Drug Mart in 2000 for $2.7 billion and worked with management to design and execute a plan that would improve its operations, sales and marketing, as well as provide for expansion. KKR did an IPO just fifteen months later for almost double the value; recently Shoppers' market value exceeded $10 billion as it opened its 1,000th store. Similarly, its leveraged buy-out of Yellow Pages from BCE in 2002 was restructured to generate top-line growth, achieve cost optimization, and improve capital allocation. A short two years later, Yellow Pages had tripled in value.[25]

Portfolio Management

During the 1970s and early 1980s, several leading consulting firms developed the concept of portfolio matrices to achieve a better understanding of the competitive position of an overall portfolio (or family) of businesses, to suggest strategic alternatives for each of the businesses, and to identify priorities for the allocation of resources. Several studies have reported widespread use of portfolio analysis techniques among firms.[26]

The key purpose of portfolio models was to assist a firm in achieving a balanced portfolio of businesses.[27] This consisted of businesses whose profitability, growth, and cash flow characteristics would complement each other and add up to a satisfactory overall corporate performance. Imbalance could be caused either by excessive cash generation with too few growth opportunities or by insufficient cash generation to fund the growth requirements in the portfolio.

The Boston Consulting Group's (BCG) growth/share matrix is among the best known of the portfolio planning approaches.[28] In the BCG approach, each of the firm's strategic business units (SBUs) is plotted on a two-dimensional grid in which the axes are relative market share and industry growth rate. The grid is broken into four quadrants. Exhibit 6.1 depicts the BCG matrix. The following are a few clarifications:

- Each circle represents one of the corporation's business units. The size of the circle represents the relative size of the business unit in terms of revenues.
- Relative market share, measured by the ratio of the business unit's size to that of its largest competitor, is plotted along the horizontal axis.

Exhibit 6.1
The Boston
Consulting Group
(BCG) Portfolio
Matrix

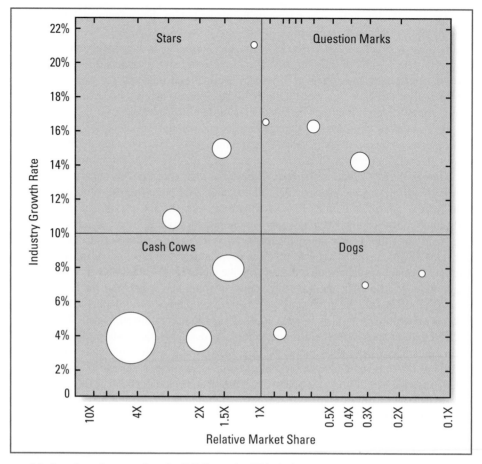

- ◆ Market share is central to the BCG matrix. This is because high relative market share leads to unit cost reduction (due to experience and learning curve effects) and, consequently, superior competitive position.

Each of the four quadrants of the grid has different implications for the SBUs that fall into that section or category:

- ◆ *Stars* are SBUs competing in high-growth industries with relatively high market shares. These firms have long-term growth potential and should continue to receive substantial investment funding.
- ◆ *Question marks* are SBUs competing in high-growth industries but having relatively weak market shares. Resources should be invested in them to enhance their competitive positions and help them increase their relative market share to become "stars"; otherwise, they are destined to become "dogs" and should be divested when the industry matures.
- ◆ *Cash cows* are SBUs with high market shares in low-growth industries. These units have limited long-run potential but represent a source of current cash flows to fund investments in "stars" and "question marks."
- ◆ *Dogs* are SBUs with weak market shares in low-growth industries. Because they have weak positions and limited potential, most analysts recommend that they be divested.

Another portfolio matrix that gained prominence is commonly known as the GE matrix. It is based on the same principles as the BCG matrix, with a few modifications.

In the GE matrix, the vertical axis goes beyond the industry growth rate and looks at the overall attractiveness of the industry, emerging opportunities, intensity of competition, resource requirements, and uncertainty. The various business units are assessed as high, medium, or low on their industry attractiveness. The horizontal axis expands on the business unit's market position and competitive strength and includes such aspects as relative market share, relative costs, capabilities, relative product attributes, relative image, and reputation. SBUs are assessed as strong, average, or weak compared to competitors. The result is a matrix with nine cells. Similar to the BCG matrix, diversified corporations are expected to plot their businesses on the matrix and follow particular strategies corresponding to each of the cells.

In using portfolio strategy approaches, a corporation tries to create synergies and shareholder value in a number of ways.[29] Since the businesses are unrelated, synergies that develop are those that result from the actions of the corporate office with the individual units instead of among business units. First, portfolio analysis provides a snapshot of the businesses in a corporation's portfolio; therefore, the corporation is in a better position to allocate resources among the business units according to prescribed criteria (e.g., the use of cash flows from the "cash cows" to fund promising "stars"). Second, the expertise and analytical resources in the corporate office provide guidance in determining what firms may be attractive (or unattractive) acquisitions. Third, the corporate office is able to provide financial resources to the business units on favourable terms that reflect the corporation's overall ability to raise funds. Fourth, the corporate office can provide high-quality review and coaching for the individual businesses. Fifth, portfolio analysis provides a basis for developing strategic goals and reward/evaluation systems for business managers. For example, managers of "cash cows" would have lower targets for revenue growth than managers of "stars," but the former would have higher threshold levels of profit targets on proposed projects than the managers of "star" businesses. Compensation systems would also reflect such realities: "Cash cows" would, understandably, be rewarded more on the basis of cash that their businesses generated than would managers of "star" businesses. Similarly, managers of "star" businesses would be held to higher standards for revenue growth than managers of "cash cow" businesses.

To see how companies can benefit from portfolio approaches, consider Ciba-Geigy (now called Novartis). In 1994, Ciba-Geigy adopted portfolio planning approaches to help it manage its business units, which competed in a wide variety of industries, including chemicals, dyes, pharmaceuticals, crop protection, and animal health.[30] It placed each business unit in a category corresponding to the BCG matrix. The business unit's goals, compensation programs, personnel selection, and resource allocation were strongly associated with the category within which the business was placed. For example, business units classified as "cash cows" had much higher hurdles for obtaining financial resources (from the corporate office) for expansion than "question marks" since the latter were businesses for which Ciba-Geigy had high hopes for accelerated future growth and profitability. Additionally, the compensation of a business unit manager in a "cash cow" would be strongly associated with its success in generating cash to fund other businesses, whereas a manager of a "question mark" business would be rewarded on his or her ability to increase revenue growth and market share. The portfolio planning approach appears to have worked. In 2001, Ciba-Geigy's revenues and net income stood at $18.5 billion and $4.0 billion, respectively. This represented an increase of 22 percent in revenues and 95 percent in net income over a five-year period.

Despite the potential benefits of portfolio models, there are also some notable downsides. First, they compare SBUs on only two dimensions, making the implicit but erroneous assumption that (1) those are the only factors that really matter and (2) that every unit can be accurately compared on that basis. Second, the approach views each SBU as a stand-alone entity, ignoring common core business practices and value-creating activities that may hold promise for synergies across business units. Third, portfolio models do not explicitly incorporate an SBU's core competencies in the analysis, and they ignore the importance of nurturing and protecting those for the long-term viability and success of a business. Decisions informed exclusively by portfolio models can be misleading and dangerous since they are unlikely to be based on an appreciation of the role of core competencies in building a successful business. Fourth, unless care is exercised, the process can become largely mechanical, substituting an oversimplified graphical model for the important contributions of the CEO's (and other corporate managers') experience and judgment. Fifth, a strict reliance on the rules regarding resource allocation across SBUs can be detrimental to a firm's long-term viability. For example, according to one study, over one-half of all the businesses that should have been cash users (based on the BCG matrix) were instead cash providers.[31] Finally, while colourful and easy to comprehend, the imagery of a portfolio matrix can lead to some troublesome and overly simplistic prescriptions. As one author noted:

> The dairying analogy is appropriate (for some cash cows), so long as we resist the urge to oversimplify it. On the farm, even the best-producing cows eventually begin to dry up. The farmer's solution to this is euphemistically called "freshening" the cow: The farmer arranges a date for the cow with a bull, she has a calf, the milk begins flowing again. Cloistering the cow—isolating her from everything but the feed trough and the milking machines—assures that she will go dry.[32]

To see what can go wrong, consider Cabot Corporation, which supplies carbon black for the rubber, electronics, and plastics industries. Following the BCG matrix, Cabot moved away from its "cash cow," carbon black, and diversified into "stars," such as ceramics and semiconductors, in an overaggressive effort to create more revenue growth for the corporation. Cabot's return on assets declined as the firm shifted away from its core competence to unrelated areas. The portfolio model failed in that it pointed the company in the wrong direction in an effort to spur growth—away from their core business. Recognizing its mistake, Cabot Corporation returned to its mainstay carbon black manufacturing and divested unrelated businesses. Fortunately, the company was able to regain a leadership position in its field, with $1.6 billion in 2002 revenues.[33]

Caveat: Is Risk Reduction a Viable Goal of Diversification?

Analysts and academics have suggested that one of the purposes of diversification is to reduce the risk that is inherent in a firm's variability in revenues and profits over time. In essence, the argument is that if a firm enters new products or markets that are affected differently by seasonal or economic cycles, its performance over time will be more stable. For example, a firm manufacturing lawn mowers may diversify into snow blowers to even out its annual sales. Or a firm manufacturing a luxury line of household furniture may introduce a lower-priced line since affluent and lower-income customers are affected differently by economic cycles.

At first glance, such reasoning may make sense, but there are some problems with it. First, a firm's shareholders can diversify their portfolios at a much lower cost than a corporation. As we noted in this chapter, individuals can purchase shares with almost no premium (e.g., only a small commission is paid to a discount broker), and they don't have to worry about integrating the acquisition into their portfolio. Second, economic cycles and their impact on a given industry (or firm) are difficult to predict with any degree of accuracy.

Nevertheless, some firms have benefited from diversification by lowering the variability (or risk) in their performance over time. Consider Emerson Electric, a $16 billion manufacturer that has enjoyed an incredible run—43 consecutive years of earnings growth![34] It produces a wide variety of products, including measurement devices for heavy industry, temperature controls for heating and ventilation systems, and power tools sold at Home Depot. Recently, many analysts questioned Emerson's purchase of companies that sell power systems to the volatile telecommunications industry. Why? This industry is expected to experience, at best, minimal growth. However, CEO David Farr maintained that such assets could be acquired inexpensively because of the aggregate decline in demand in this industry. Additionally, he argued that the other business units, involving the sales of valves and regulators to the now-booming oil and natural gas companies, were able to pick up the slack. Therefore, while net profits in the electrical equipment sector (Emerson's core business) sharply decreased, Emerson's overall corporate profits increased 1.7 percent.

In summary, risk reduction in and of itself is rarely a viable way to create shareholder value. It must be undertaken with a view of a firm's overall diversification strategy.

THE MEANS TO ACHIEVE DIVERSIFICATION

So far, we have addressed the types of diversification (e.g., related and unrelated) that a firm may undertake to achieve synergies and create value for its shareholders. Next, we address the means by which a firm can go about achieving diversification and these desired benefits.

We address three basic means. First, through mergers or acquisitions, corporations can directly acquire the assets and competencies of other firms. Second, corporations may agree to pool the resources of other companies with their resource base. This approach is commonly known as a strategic alliance or joint venture. Although these two forms of partnerships are similar in many ways, there is an important difference. Unlike strategic alliances, joint ventures involve the formation of a third-party legal entity, whereupon the two (or more) firms each contribute equity. Third, corporations may diversify into new products, markets, and technologies through internal development. This approach—sometimes called corporate entrepreneurship, greenfield, or organic growth—involves the leveraging and combining of a firm's own resources and competencies to create synergies and enhance shareholder value. All three approaches are valuable strategic alternatives, and managers consider all three as means to pursue their strategies. Although mergers and acquisitions tend to command the lion's share of publicity, firms typically engage in any combination of the three in order to address different situations and achieve different results. Each one has its advantages and disadvantages, those mainly relating to speed and timing, risk, investment and cost requirements, ease of execution, control, and flexibility.

Mergers and Acquisitions (M&A)

Growth through mergers and acquisitions has played a critical role in the success of many corporations in a wide variety of economic sectors, including resources and energy, manufacturing, services, as well as the high-technology and knowledge-intensive industries. Canada recently experienced a dramatic increase in such activity, emanating from aggressive global firms that found Canadian assets attractive and relatively undervalued. During the last few years, Canadian corporate icons—such as Alcan, Inco, Falconbridge, and Dofasco—changed ownership and are now subsidiaries and divisions of American, European, or Asian corporations. The shareholders of those firms reaped great financial gains, but the headquarters of these firms and the strategic decisions have effectively

Exhibit 6.2

Some of the Biggest Mergers and Acquisitions of All Time and Their Effect on Shareholder Wealth

Deal	Year	Value of the deal ($ billion)	Value created since combination ($ billion)	Value destroyed since combination ($ billion)
Manulife/ John Hancock*	2003	36	12.7	—
AOL/Time Warner	2001	350	—	148
Vodafone/Mannesmann	2000	340	—	299
Pfizer/Warner-Lambert	2000	200	—	78
Glaxo/SmithKline	2000	150	—	40
Chase/J. P. Morgan	2000	80	—	26
Exxon/Mobil	1999	80	8	—
SBC/Ameritech	1999	60	—	68
WorldCom/MCI	1998	200	—	94
Travelers/Citicorp	1998	140	109	—
Daimler/Chrysler	1998	80	—	36

*As of December 10, 2004. All other values as of July 1, 2002.

Sources: K. H. Hammonds, "The Numbers Don't Lie," *Fast Company*, September 2002, p. 80; and Thomson DataStream.

moved overseas, taking with them senior management positions and, some would argue, Canada's ability to control its economic destiny.[35] Of course, Canadian firms have themselves always been active acquirers, both domestically and internationally. Bombardier's global success is, in part, the outcome of acquisitions: Canadair, de Havilland, Learjet (U.S.), Short (Ireland) and Skyjet (U.S.) aerospace firms; Lohnerwerke (Austria), Alco (U.S.), BN (Belgium), ANF (France), CNCF (Mexico), Waggonfabrik Tablot (Germany), and Adtranz (Germany) in rail transportation. Yet, not many acquisitions end up creating the promised value. Exhibit 6.2 lists some of the largest mergers and acquisitions in recent business history and reports the estimated dismal results in terms of the erosion of the acquiring firm's shareholder value that have followed a major acquisition transaction.

Motives and Benefits While the motivations for such moves may vary, managers ascribe similar reasons for their proposed acquisitions. Market and technology changes can occur very quickly and unpredictably; therefore, speed—speed to market, speed to positioning, and speed to becoming a viable company—is critical in some industries. For example, Alex Mandl, AT&T's president in the early 1990s, was responsible for the acquisition of McCaw Cellular. Although many industry experts felt the price was too steep, he believed that cellular technology was a critical asset for the telecommunications business and that it would have been extremely difficult to build that business from the ground up. Mandl claimed, "The plain fact is that acquiring is much faster than building."[36]

Mergers and acquisitions can also be a means of obtaining valuable resources that can help an organization expand its product offerings and services. For example, Cisco Systems, a dominant player in networking equipment, acquired more than 70 companies from 1993 to early 2000.[37] They provided Cisco with access to the latest in networking equipment. But Cisco also learned the importance of integrating acquired companies efficiently and effectively.[38] It used its excellent sales force to market the acquired technology to its corporate customers and telephone companies, and it put in place strong incentives for the staff of acquired companies to stay on.

Merger and acquisition activity can also lead to consolidation within an industry and give firms instant scale to respond to external pressures. In the pharmaceutical industry, the patents for many top-selling drugs have started to expire; one of the observed consequences is heightened M&A activity.[39] Although health care providers and patients are happy about the lower-cost generic options that arrive upon expiry of drug patents, pharmaceutical firms are being pressed to make up for lost revenues and are required to undertake major and risky investments to develop new drugs.

Combining top firms such as Pfizer Inc. and Warner-Lambert Co., as well as Glaxo Wellcome and SmithKline Beecham, has many potential long-term benefits. They not only promise significant post-merger cost savings, but the increased size of the combined companies also brings greater research and development possibilities.

Molson Inc. of Montreal, Quebec, and Adolph Coors Co. of Golden, Colorado, merged their operations in an attempt to create a firm that could stand up to the continuing consolidation in the global beer industry. The intended synergies rest on rationalizing production across the two countries, improving the effectiveness of marketing efforts, and cross-selling brands in Europe and Latin America, where the two firms have local operations.[40] Molson, in part, was responding to its archrival Labatt's acquisition by InBev of Belgium and to the subsequent purchase of Sleeman's by Sapporo of Japan.

Corporations can also enter new markets and new market segments by way of acquisitions. The Loblaw Companies—with a strong presence in Ontario and the West but with no footprint in the Quebec grocery market—acquired Provigo, that province's second largest chain, to gain entry into the highly competitive market.

Mergers and acquisitions provide a firm with many potential benefits. They enable a firm to quickly enter new product markets and acquire new skills and competencies as well as a wide variety of value-creating activities through sales forces, distribution channels, and manufacturing operations.

Potential Limitations However, there are also many potential downsides associated with mergers and acquisitions. Among these are the expensive premiums that are frequently paid to acquire a business; premiums of 20, 30, or even 80 percent are not uncommon, and the acquiring firm must create enough value to recoup the investment. Although synergies and economies of scale, which should result in increased sales and market gains, may indeed materialize, the performance hurdle has already been set quite high. Other difficulties relate to integrating the activities and resources of the acquired firm into the corporation's own operations as well as identifying "synergies" that may be quickly imitated by the competition.

Moreover, managers' egos and credibility can sometimes get in the way of sound business decisions. Size is not always important for the success of a business, but senior managers may be preoccupied with the personal prestige of leading the largest firm in their industry, even if that means paying excessive amounts of money to accumulate enough entities to become the biggest player. At other times, if the acquisition does not perform as planned, managers who pushed for the deal find their reputation at stake. In order to protect their credibility, and in spite of better business judgment, these managers might funnel more resources and escalate their commitment toward an inevitably doomed venture. Finally, there are many cultural issues that may bring calamity to a well-intended M&A endeavour.

Consider, for example, the insights of Joanne Lawrence who played an important role, as vice president and director of communications and investor relations at Smith-Kline Beecham, in the merger between SmithKline and the Beecham Group, a diversified consumer-oriented group headquartered in the United Kingdom:

> The key to a strategic merger is to create a new culture. This was a mammoth challenge during the SmithKline Beecham merger. We were working at so many different cultural levels, it was dizzying. We had two national cultures to blend—American and British—that compounded the challenge of selling the merger in two different markets with two different shareholder bases. There were also two different business cultures: One was very strong, scientific, and academic; the other was much more commercially oriented. And then we had to consider within both companies the individual businesses, each of which has its own little culture.[41]

Strategic Alliances and Joint Ventures

Strategic alliances and joint ventures are assuming an increasingly prominent role in the strategy of leading firms, both large and small.[42] Such co-operative relationships have many potential advantages. Among these are entering new markets; reducing purchasing, manufacturing, and other costs in the value chain; and developing and diffusing new technologies.

Entering New Markets Often, a company that has a successful product or service wants to introduce it into a new market. However, it may not have the requisite marketing expertise because it does not understand customer needs, know how to promote the product, or have access to the proper distribution channels.

Couche-Tard of Quebec, which also operates Mac's convenience stores in Ontario, has partnered with Convenience Retail Asia, an established chain of convenience stores in Hong Kong and mainland China, to embark on an aggressive growth strategy in China.[43] Its Circle K banner has been employed to expand aggressively into the U.S. and Mexican markets, using partnerships with large integrated oil companies that provide it with ready access to prime locations and market knowledge of local customers. Already, Couche-Tard has over 5,000 stores and $11 billion in revenue.

In other situations, a company may be prevented from entering a new market due to regulatory, reputational, or legal barriers. High-flyer Nortel used joint ventures, during its 1990s meteoric growth, to enter many markets in Asia and Latin America. Partners provided capital, but more importantly, local knowledge, along with legitimacy and access to governments for the telecommunications infrastructure projects that were the bread and butter of Nortel's telecommunications systems.

Reducing Costs in the Value Chain Strategic alliances often enable firms to pool capital, value-creating activities, or facilities in order to reduce costs. For example, Molson Companies and Carling O'Keefe Breweries formed a joint venture to merge their brewing operations. While Molson had a modern and efficient brewery in Montreal, Carling's was outdated. However, Carling had the better facilities in Toronto. In addition, Molson's Toronto brewery was located on the waterfront and had substantial real estate value. Overall, the synergies gained by the efficient use of their combined facilities added $150 million of pre-tax earnings during the initial year of the venture. Economies of scale were realized and facilities were better utilized.

Developing and Diffusing New Technologies Strategic alliances may also be used to build on the technological expertise of two or more companies in order to develop products that are technologically beyond the capability of the companies acting independently. STMicroelectronics (ST) is a high-tech company based in Geneva, Switzerland, that has thrived—largely due to the success of its strategic alliances.[44] The firm develops and manufactures computer chips for a variety of applications: mobile phones, set-top boxes, smart cards, and flash memories. In 1995, it teamed up with Hewlett-Packard (HP) to develop powerful new processors for various digital applications that are now nearing completion. It also formed a strategic alliance with Nokia to develop a chip that would give Nokia's phones a longer battery life. Here, ST produced a chip that tripled standby time to 60 hours—a breakthrough that gave Nokia a huge advantage in the marketplace. The firm's CEO, Pasquale Pistorio, was among the first in the industry to form R&D alliances with other companies. Now, ST's top 12 customers, including HP, Nokia, and Nortel, account for 45 percent of revenues. According to Pistorio, "Alliances are in our DNA." Such relationships help ST keep better-than-average growth rates, even in difficult times. That's because close partners are less likely to defect to other suppliers. ST's financial results have been consistently impressive. Magna International, the Aurora, Ontario, based global automobile parts manufacturer, has entered into an alliance with IBM to explore new systems designs, software development, and engineering that would lead to advanced driver information systems. Magna knows cars and IBM knows software; together they can address technological challenges that would eventually allow cars to respond to road signs or take evasive action to avoid a crash, even when the driver is distracted.[45]

Potential Limitations Despite their promise, many alliances and joint ventures fail to meet expectations for a variety of reasons. First, without the proper partner, an alliance can be unproductive, even if formed for the best of reasons. Each partner should bring the desired complementary strengths to the partnership. Ideally, the strengths contributed by the partners are unique so that synergies created can be more easily sustained and defended over the longer term. The goal must be to develop synergies between the contributions of the partners, which would ultimately result in a win-win situation for both. Second, partners must usually share control over the direction of their strategic alliance and defer to others over important decisions. In many cases the partner is geographically quite distant, or the joint venture's operations might reside within the partner's own facilities. The consequences of a limited ability to control critical decisions may be compounded by the divergent goals of the partners and their different perspectives on the alliance. Goal alignment and monitoring of progress frequently impose significant tension on an alliance. Moreover, the partners must be compatible and willing to trust each other. Often, however, little attention is given to nurturing the close working relationships and interpersonal connections that bring together the partnering organizations. The human or people factors are not carefully considered or, at worst, dismissed as unimportant.

Tim Hortons and Wendy's worked very hard to assure compatibility of the partners. Although the companies' cultures were, indeed, quite similar, the executives of both firms spent literally thousands of hours in each other's operations.[46] Proceeding cautiously at first, they created working teams and cross-functional task forces consisting of members from both sides. They initially opened a few joint locations in Prince Edward Island and across Ontario's highways to serve motorists with Tim Hortons doughnuts, muffins, and its famous coffee as well as with Wendy's sandwich fare and fries, thereby utilizing the facilities around the clock. Their success encouraged them to move forward and expand to city locations. After some further collaboration, the two firms merged to create a new corporation that has consistently delivered financial and market performance. Analysts attributed the firm's success to the ongoing effort by all managers to build on the unique cultures of the initial partners. Interestingly, with the changing of the guard at the very top of the combined firm, the two sides grew apart and some claimed that the success of Tims started to bother the top brass in the U.S. Wendy's spun off Tim Hortons into an independent entity in 2006.

Lululemon athletica's recent seaweed-clothing scandal emanated from its German supplier's claims about the health benefits of the fabrics used in its top line of t-shirts. Special seaweed blend cotton shirts were supposed to not only contain health-promoting substances that support blood flow and stimulate skin regeneration but also to secrete vitamins, minerals, and amino acids that had stress-reducing and detoxifying properties.[47] Independent labs announced test results that challenged those claims. To complicate things further, the t-shirts were not even made by the German firm, which supplied the fibre to Asian manufacturers. Lululemon's health claims were based on the assurances of its partners but its own stock took the fallout with losses of about 10 percent of its value on the news.

Internal Development

Firms can also diversify by means of corporate entrepreneurship and new venture development. In today's economy, internal development is such an important means by which companies expand their businesses that we have devoted a whole chapter to it (see Chapter 12). Sony and the Minnesota Mining & Manufacturing Co. (3M) are among the companies best known for their dedication to innovation, R&D, and cutting-edge technologies. For example, 3M has developed its entire corporate culture to support its ongoing policy of generating at least 25 percent of total sales from products created within the most recent four-year period. During the 1990s, 3M exceeded this goal by achieving about 30 percent of sales per year from new internally developed products.

Many companies use some form of internal development to extend their product lines or add to their service offerings. This approach to internal development is used by many large, publicly held corporations as well as small firms.

Compared to mergers and acquisitions, firms that engage in internal development are able to capture the value created by their own innovative activities without having to "share the wealth" with alliance partners or face the difficulties associated with combining activities across the value chains of several companies or merging corporate cultures. Another advantage is that firms can often develop new products or services at a relatively lower cost and, thereby, rely on their own resources rather than turning to external funding. Moreover, internal development is fully customized to fit the company's existing culture, systems, and core competencies. There are also potential disadvantages. Internal development may be time consuming; thus, firms may forfeit the benefits of speed that growth through mergers and acquisitions or strategic alliances can provide. This may be especially important among high-tech or knowledge-based organizations and in fast-paced environments where being an early mover is critical. Firms that choose to grow and diversify through internal development must, therefore, develop capabilities that allow them to move quickly from initial opportunity recognition to market introduction.

REAL OPTIONS ANALYSIS: A USEFUL TOOL

In discussing the means of diversification, we briefly explore some recent developments in *real options analysis (ROA)*, which has its roots in the field of finance and has slowly entered the tool kit of consultants and executives who aim to support strategic decision making in firms. What does ROA consist of, and how can it be appropriately applied to the investments required to initiate strategic decisions? To understand *real* options, it is first necessary to have a basic understanding of what *options* are.

An option gives its owner the right but not the obligation to engage in a specific transaction. The most common is the stock option. A stock option grants the holder the right to buy (call option) or sell (put option) shares of the stock at a fixed price (strike price) at some time in the future.[48] In essence, a call option gives its holder the right to buy a stock at a predetermined price at a given point in time, no matter what the price of the stock will be at that time. If the stock does trade at a price above the strike price, the holder will only have to pay the strike price and can immediately pocket the difference by selling the stock in the open market. For the privilege, the holder has invested a very small amount in acquiring the option. On the other hand, if the stock trades at a price below the strike price at the given point in time, the option is worthless, and the holder will allow it to expire, having lost the modest investment. An important aspect of stock options is that the investment to be made immediately is relatively small, whereas the investment to be made in the future can be substantial. For example, an option to buy a rapidly rising stock at a strike price of $50 might cost as little as $.50.[49] An important point to note is that owners of such a stock option have limited their losses to $.50 per share, while the upside potential is unlimited. This aspect of options is attractive because they offer the prospect of high gains with relatively small upfront investments that represent limited losses. At the same time, it should be understood that options can become totally worthless. The holder who invested $.50 to acquire an option will lose all the investment if the stock's value falls even $.01 below the strike price, while the holder of the stock will still be able to trade the stock for the going price.

The phrase "real options" applies to situations in which options theory and valuation techniques are applied to real assets, or physical things, as opposed to financial assets. Some of the most common applications of real options concern property and insurance. A real estate option grants the holder the right to buy or sell a piece of property at an established price some time in the future. The actual market price of the property may rise above the established (or strike) price—or the market value may sink below the strike price. If the price of the property goes up, the owner of the option is likely to buy it. If the market value of the property drops below the strike price, the option holder is unlikely to execute the purchase. In the latter circumstance, the option holder has limited the loss to the cost of the option but during the life of the option, retains the right to participate in whatever the upside potential might be. Casualty insurance is another variation of real options. With casualty insurance, the owner of the property has limited the loss to the cost of the insurance, while the upside potential is the actual loss, ranging, of course, up to the limit of the insurance.[50]

Applications of Real Options Analysis to Strategic Decisions The concept of options can also be applied to strategic decisions in which management has flexibility; that is, the situation will permit management to decide whether to invest additional funds to grow or accelerate the activity, delay in order to learn more, shrink the scale of the activity, or even abandon it. The initial alliance between Tim Hortons and Wendy's can be evaluated as an option that provided both firms with the opportunity to learn more about each other and assess their initial investment before proceeding with a full merger. Decisions to invest in business activities such as R&D, motion pictures, exploration and production of oil wells, and the opening and closing of copper mines often have similar flexibility.[51] Some important issues to note include the following:

♦ Real options analysis is appropriate to use when investments can be staged; in other words, a smaller investment up front can be followed by subsequent investments. In short, real options can be applied to an investment decision that gives the company the right, but not the obligation, to make follow-up investments.

♦ The strategic decision-makers have "tollgates" or key points at which they can decide whether to continue, delay, or abandon the project. In short, the executives have flexibility. There are opportunities to make other go or no-go decisions associated with each phase.

♦ It is expected that there will be increased knowledge about outcomes at the time of the next investment and that additional knowledge will help inform the decision makers about whether to make additional investments (i.e., whether the option is in the money or out of the money).

Many strategic decisions tend to bear a series of options. This phenomenon is called "embedded options," a series of investments in which, at each stage of the investment, there is a go/no-go decision. For example, pharmaceutical companies have successfully used real options analysis in evaluating decisions about investments in R&D projects and in forming alliances with start-up biotechnology firms.[52] Pharmaceuticals have at least four stages of investments: basic research yielding compounds and the three federally mandated phases of clinical trials. Generally, each phase is more expensive to undertake than the previous phase. However, as each phase unfolds, management knows more about the underlying drug and the many sources of uncertainty, including the technical difficulties with the drugs themselves, as well as external market conditions such as the results of competitors' research. Management can make the decision to invest more with the intent of speeding up the process, delay the start of the next phase, reduce investment, or even abandon the R&D.[53] Merck famously applied real options analysis to its relationship with Biogen, one of the earlier biotechnology firms that was developing technology which Merck didn't really understand and couldn't assess. Eli Lilly used it to proceed cautiously but eventually to acquire Hybritech when it established that, indeed, the drugs under development had real potential in the marketplace.[54]

HOW MANAGERIAL MOTIVES CAN ERODE VALUE CREATION

Thus far in the chapter, we have implicitly assumed that CEOs and top executives are "rational beings" who act in the best interests of shareholders to maximize long-term shareholder value. The real world and agency theory have shown, however, that this is not the case. Frequently, they may act in their own self-interest. Below, we address some managerial motives that can serve to erode, rather than enhance, value creation. These include "growth for growth's sake," excessive egotism, and the introduction of a wide variety of anti-takeover tactics to protect the entrenchment of current management.

Growth for Growth's Sake

There are huge incentives for executives to increase the size of their firm, and many of these are hardly consistent with increasing shareholder wealth. Top managers, including the CEO, of larger firms typically enjoy more prestige, higher rankings for their companies on various corporate lists such as the Fortune 500 and Report on Business 1000 (which are based on revenues, not cash flows or profits), greater incomes, more job security, and so on. There is also the excitement and associated recognition of making a major acquisition. As noted by Harvard's Michael Porter, "There's a tremendous allure to mergers and acquisitions. It's the big play, the dramatic gesture. With one stroke of the pen you can add billions to size, get a front-page story, and create excitement in markets."[55]

At times, executives' overemphasis on growth can result in a plethora of ethical lapses, which can have disastrous outcomes for their companies. A good example of bad practice is Joseph Bernardino's leadership at Andersen Worldwide. Bernardino had a chance, early on, to take a hard line on ethics and quality in the wake of earlier scandals at clients such as Waste Management and Sunbeam. Instead, according to former executives, he put too much emphasis on revenue growth. The firm's reputation quickly eroded when it audited and signed off on the highly flawed financial statements of such infamous firms as Enron, Global Crossing, Qwest Communications, and WorldCom. WorldCom, in fact, is recognized as the biggest financial fraud of all time. Bernardino ultimately resigned in disgrace in March 2002, and his firm was dissolved later that year.[56]

Egotism

Most would agree that there is nothing wrong with ego, per se. After all, a healthy ego helps make a leader confident, clear-headed, and able to cope with change. CEOs, by their very nature, are often fiercely competitive people in the office as well as on the tennis court or golf course. However, when pride is at stake, individuals will sometimes go to great lengths to win—or at least to not back down.

Few executives (or lower-level managers) are exempt from the potential downside of too much ego. GEl's former CEO, Jack Welch, considered by many to be the world's most admired executive, admitted to his regrettable decision for GE in acquiring Kidder Peabody.[57] According to Welch, "My hubris got in the way in the Kidder Peabody deal. [He was referring to GE's buyout of the soon-to-be-troubled Wall Street firm.] I got wise advice from Walter Wriston and other directors who said, 'Jack, don't do this.' But I was bully enough and on a run to do it. And I got whacked right in the head." In addition to poor financial results, Kidder Peabody was wracked by a widely publicized trading scandal that tarnished the reputations of both GE and Kidder Peabody. GE eventually divested Kidder and registered a multi-billion dollar loss.

The business press has included many stories of how egotism and greed have infiltrated organizations. Some incidents are considered rather astonishing, such as Tyco's former CEO Dennis Kozlowski's well-chronicled purchase of a $6,000 shower curtain and vodka-spewing, full-size replica of Michaelangelo's David.[58] Other well-known examples of egos and power grabs include executives at Enron; the Regis family who defrauded Adelphia of roughly $1 billion; Bernie Ebbers, the former CEO of WorldCom, originally from Alberta, who granted himself a $408 million personal loan from the company while orchestrating accounting fraud to inflate profits; and Ross Johnson, CEO of Nabisco, originally from Winnipeg and the protagonist in *Barbarians at the Gate*. Frank Dunn of Nortel, Conrad Black of Hollinger International, and Miles Nadal of MDC are among executives who have allegedly tested the limits of the law and the pockets of their shareholders.

Few would argue that Frank Stronach is not the soul and the genius behind the tremendous global success that is Magna International, a company he founded in Aurora, Ontario, back in 1957 and led to become one of the world's largest and most profitable automobile parts manufacturers. Yet, Frank will continually be haunted by Magna's ventures into gaming and horseracing; the creation of Magna Entertainment Corp., and the millions of dollars that have been thrown into a black hole that just does not seem to know how to make a profit, does provide for Frank's personal love of horses and thoroughbred racing.[59]

Anti-Takeover Tactics

Unfriendly or hostile takeovers can occur when a company's stock becomes undervalued. A competing organization can buy the outstanding stock of a takeover candidate in sufficient quantity to become a large shareholder. It then makes a tender offer to gain full control of the company. If the shareholders accept the offer, the hostile firm buys the target company and either fires the target firm's management team or strips them of their power.

A number of anti-takeover tactics can be utilized to preserve the corporate status quo. Among the most common are poison pills, frequently put in place but seldom exercised;

greenmail, a well-known tactic in the U.S. that is prohibited in Canada; controlling share-holders; staggered boards; lock-up agreements; white knights; and golden parachutes. Although such tactics have been defended by management and boards of directors as pro-tecting the rights of shareholders, many students of takeover activity have questioned the motives inherent in these tactics and have argued that, by and large, they entrench senior management and protect the jobs of board members.[60] We briefly comment on each one below.

Poison pills, or shareholder rights plans, allow existing shareholders, under certain conditions, to have the option to buy additional shares at a discount to the current market price. This action is typically triggered when a new shareholder accumulates more than a set percentage of ownership, usually 20 percent. Managers fear that the new shareholder might be masterminding a takeover of the company. In the name of protecting existing sharehold-ers, newly issued stock is offered at a steep discount to all shareholders, except the alleged aggressor. As the existing shareholders buy the discounted shares, the stock is diluted significantly since there are now more shares, each with a lower value. If there has been a takeover bid at a set price per share, the overall price offered for the company immediately goes up by a substantial amount since there are now more shares outstanding. This assures shareholders of receiving a high price for the company. Of course, the takeover bidder is aware of the poison pill provision and is likely to stop just short of accumulating shares beyond the trigger level. The senior management and the board will usually negotiate better terms before removing the poison pill. Often, however, the board will also negotiate keep-ing the senior management and itself in place as part of the deal to remove the pill.

Greenmail is an effort by the target firm to prevent an impending takeover. When a hos-tile firm buys a large block of outstanding target company stock and the target firm's manage-ment feels that a tender offer is impending, they offer to buy the stock back from the hostile company at a higher price than the unfriendly company paid for it. The positive side is that this often prevents a hostile takeover. On the downside, the same price is not offered to pre-existing shareholders. Greenmail is illegal in Canada because it deprives shareholders of the right to make a choice on whether or not to tender their shares to the bid. There is also some-thing morally suspect when the senior managers and the directors of a public company use the existing shareholders' money to buy out a potential acquirer to protect their own jobs.

Controlling shareholders could be members of a founder's family or others in a privileged ownership position. Either through majority ownership or ownership of special classes of shares involving multiple voting rights, they can effectively block any unwanted takeover attempt. Ted Rogers at Rogers Communications Inc. and Laurent Beaudoin at Bombardier Inc. own relatively small percentages of those public companies but, through dual-share structures, can effectively dictate the strategic decisions made by their boards. At Bombardier, in particular, institutional shareholders are calling for corporate reforms in light of the federal and provincial governments' involvement in funding development of the next generation of passenger jets.[61]

Staggered boards limit the number of board members that are elected each year, usu-ally to one third of all seats. This effectively delays any unwanted suitor from controlling the board for at least two years, even after gaining control of voting shares.

Lock-up agreements and break-up fees are commitments that senior managers and boards make to friendly firms in order to consummate transactions with them, even if a superior offer were to come forth. Allegedly, such fees serve to cover the friendly suitor's expenses for its troubles in getting involved; in essence, they make the superior offer that much more expensive for the unwanted offering party, which will have to pay the penal-ties upon completion of the deal. Creo of Vancouver, British Columbia, signed a break-up fee of $32 million to signal its support for Kodak's offer of $980 million. A few years ago, Canadian Airlines signed an operating agreement with American Airlines for over $100 million in its attempt to block Air Canada's hostile bid.

White knights represent firms that are invited by the target firm's management to step in during a hostile bid and offer a higher price for the firm in exchange for the co-operation of management. Springfield served as a white knight for Schneider's when the family-controlled firm wanted to block the attempt by Maple Leaf Foods to acquire the largest hog producer and manufacturer of processed meat products in Canada.

Golden parachutes are pre-arranged employment contracts between companies and their managers, specifying that, in the event of a hostile takeover, the firm's managers will be paid a significant severance package. Although top managers may lose their jobs, the golden parachute provisions protect their income.

Clearly, anti-takeover tactics often raise serious ethical issues and highlight the divergence of interests between individual shareholders and the managers who undertake diversification moves—supposedly on their behalf.

Summary

A key challenge for today's managers is to create "synergy" when engaging in diversification activities. As we discussed in this chapter, corporate managers do not, in general, have a very good track record in creating value in such endeavours, particularly mergers and acquisitions. Among the factors that serve to erode shareholder values are paying an excessive premium for the target firm, failing to integrate the activities of the newly acquired businesses into the corporate family, and undertaking diversification initiatives that are too easily imitated by the competition.

We addressed two major types of corporate-level strategy: related and unrelated diversification. With *related diversification* the corporation strives to enter into areas in which key resources and capabilities of the corporation can be shared or leveraged. Synergies come from relationships between business units. Cost savings and enhanced revenues can be derived from three major sources. First, economies of scope can be achieved from the leveraging of core competencies and the sharing of activities. Second, market power can be attained from greater negotiating power, and third, benefits can be derived from vertical integration.

When firms undergo *unrelated diversification*, they enter product markets that are dissimilar to their present businesses. Thus, there is generally little opportunity to either leverage core competencies or share activities across business units. Here, synergies are created from relationships between the corporate office and the individual business units. With unrelated diversification, the primary ways to create value are through corporate restructuring and parenting as well as the use of portfolio analysis techniques.

Corporations have three primary means of expanding their activities and diversifying their product markets. These are mergers and acquisitions, strategic alliances and joint ventures, and internal development. There are key trade-offs associated with each of these. For example, mergers and acquisitions are typically the quickest means to enter new markets and provide the corporation with a high level of control over the acquired business. However, with the high premiums that often need to be paid to the shareholders of the target firm and the challenges associated with integrating acquisitions, they can also be quite expensive. Strategic alliances between two or more firms, on the other hand, may be a means of reducing risk since they involve the sharing and combining of resources. But such joint initiatives also provide a firm with less control (than it would have with an acquisition) since governance is shared between two independent entities. In addition, there is a limit to the potential upside for each partner because returns must be shared as well. Finally, through internal development, a firm is able to capture all of the value from its initiatives (as opposed to sharing it with a merger or alliance partner). However, diversification by means of internal development can be very time-consuming—a disadvantage that becomes even more critical in fast-paced competitive environments.

Traditional tools, such as net present value (NPV) analysis, are not always very helpful in making resource allocation decisions under uncertainty. Real options analysis (ROA) is increasingly used to make better-quality decisions in such situations.

Finally, some managerial behaviours may serve to erode shareholder returns. Among these are "growth for growth's sake," egotism, and anti-takeover tactics. As we discussed, some of these issues—particularly anti-takeover tactics—raise ethical considerations because the managers of the firm may not be acting in the best interests of the shareholders.

Summary Review Questions

1. Discuss how managers can create value for their firm through diversification efforts.

2. What are some of the reasons that many diversification efforts fail to achieve desired outcomes?

3. How can companies benefit from related diversification? Unrelated diversification? What are some of the key concepts that can explain such success?

4. What are some of the important ways in which a firm can restructure a business?

5. Discuss some of the various means that firms can use to diversify. What are the pros and cons associated with each of these?

6. Discuss some of the actions that managers may engage in to erode shareholder value.

Experiential Exercise

Rogers Communications is a firm that follows a strategy of related diversification. Evaluate their success (or lack thereof) with regard to how well they have (1) built on core competencies, (2) shared infrastructures, and (3) increased market power.

Rationale for Related Diversification	Successful/Unsuccessful?	Why?
1. Build on core competencies		
2. Share infrastructures		
3. Increase market power		

Application Questions Exercises	1. What were some of the largest mergers and acquisitions over the last two years? What was the rationale for these actions? Do you think they will be successful? Explain.
	2. Discuss some examples from business practice in which an executive's actions appear to be in the interest of him- or herself rather than that of the corporation.
	3. Discuss some of the challenges that managers must overcome in making strategic alliances successful. What are some strategic alliances with which you are familiar? Were they successful or not? Explain.
	4. Use the Internet to select a company that has recently undertaken diversification into new product markets. What do you feel were some of the reasons for this diversification (e.g., leveraging core competencies, sharing infrastructures)?

Ethics Questions	1. In recent years, there has been a rash of corporate downsizing and layoffs. Do you feel that such actions involve ethical considerations? Why or why not?
	2. What are some of the ethical issues that arise when managers act in a manner that is counter to their firm's best interests? What are the long-term implications for both the firms and the managers themselves?
	3. Consider lululemon's predicament reported on page 168. What are some of the issues that arise from the company standing by its supplier's claims? How can a partner in a strategic alliance be committed to the partnership as well as retain its independence?

Chapter 7　International Strategy:
Creating Value in Global Markets

LEARNING OBJECTIVES

After reading this chapter, you should have a good understanding of:

LO 1 ▸ the importance of international expansion as a viable diversification strategy.

LO 2 ▸ the sources of national advantage—that is, why an industry in a given country is more (or less) successful than the same industry in another country.

LO 3 ▸ the motivations (or benefits) and the risks associated with international expansion.

LO 4 ▸ the two opposing forces—cost reduction and adaptation to local

markets—that firms face when entering international markets.

LO 5 ▸ the advantages and disadvantages associated with each of the four basic strategies for achieving competitive advantage in global markets: international, global, multidomestic, and transnational.

LO 6 ▸ the six basic types of entry strategies and the relative benefits and risks associated with each of them.

Back in 2004, Molson Inc., a venerated brewer with a long history in Canada and a strong presence among imports in the U.S., announced its proposed merger with another icon of the North American brewing scene, Adolph Coors Co. of Colorado, to create MolsonCoors, the world's fifth-largest brewer.[1] Although this was presented as a deal made in heaven, analysts contended that it was a desperate move by two firms that were left out of the global consolidation which was taking place and who had missed much of the growth in developing markets such as China, India, Eastern Europe, and Latin America. At the same time, competition at home was intensifying from discounters at the bottom end and premium imports and craft brews at the high end. Indeed, subsequent performance vindicated, for the most part, the analysts as the new firm was not able to turn the tide, reporting both market share and financial losses as well as the departure of some of its most senior executives. The stock price took a dive and disgruntled shareholders responded with lawsuits. MolsonCoors has struggled to keep up with the competition, especially after InBev of Belgium bought Labbatt and Sapporo of Japan bought Sleeman, bringing with them vast financial resources, global brands, and international operations.

This was not Molson's first attempt at internationalization. On the contrary, Molson's had been selling beer in the U.S. for decades and Molson Canadian was the second largest import after Heineken. Molson had also acquired U.S. firms in chemical distribution and sanitation supplies. But, frankly, those moves were half-hearted; Molson had essentially missed the globalization that had been sweeping the brewing industry since the late 1980s, creating global powerhouses such as InBev and SabMiller of South Africa. The global brands of these companies were sold across the world and complemented their local labels while capitalizing on economies of scale in marketing and operations. Molson had tried to go global. In March 2002, it had paid $1.2 billion for Cervejarias Kaiser Brasil SA, Brazil's second largest brewer. The Brazilian market was quite fragmented, with many small players competing for the attention of 173 million potential consumers. Brazil was already the world's fourth-largest market for beer and was growing faster than any of the mature markets in North America, Europe, or Australia. Only China showed more potential than Brazil, which was promising to soon surpass Germany and become the third-largest market in the world behind the U.S. With strong competition in its home market and stagnant sales in the U.S., Molson saw in Brazil the opportunity to grow.

Molson has been brewing beer since 1786 but has recently faced some challenges. A merger with Canada's third-largest brewer, Carling O'Keefe, in the late 1980s did not yield any significant accomplishments, and the merged companies soon had a combined market share that was less than Molson's own market share before the merger. Molson's flagship brand, Molson Canadian, was struggling and needed heavy advertising and aggressive pricing strategies to retain its domestic market position. The only bright spot was Coors Light, which Molson was brewing under license from Coors and which commanded over 50 percent of the "light" segment of the beer market in Canada. Molson had hoped that its foray in Brazil would allow it to assert itself and get back on the globalization bandwagon. As part of this goal, it sold 20 percent of Kaiser to Heineken NV, a Dutch brewer, for $294 million. The sale would bring the two old brewers together, give Heineken a toehold in Brazil, and maybe lead to future collaboration in other markets. Kaiser's brand, Bavaria, at the time controlled 18 percent of the market, and the combination of two strong brewers from Europe and North America was seen as a sure sign of strategy success.

What Went Wrong at Molson? After 2002, Brazil's currency, the real, declined sharply against both the Canadian dollar and the euro, diminishing the value of the partners' initial investment. The competition in Brazil intensified once InBev and SABMiller focused on the growing market and started a price war that only their deep pockets could sustain. After Molson's purchase of Kaiser, Bavaria's market share started to fall and Molson had to pump additional cash to sustain operations. Kaiser's management was replaced, but the new management was not able to show positive results. Molson's position in Brazil fell to third place, and its market share shrunk to 9 percent. Heineken announced in late 2004 that it would write down the full value of its investment in the Brazilian brewery. In 2006, MolsonCoors sold most of its stake in Kaiser to Mexico's FEMSA for $128 million, including some $60 million in Kaiser debt. In the meantime, back in Canada, the conglomerate was trying to sort itself out and put on the block many of its unrelated U.S. and Canadian businesses in chemicals, retail, and supplies, which had distracted management for the last twenty years without producing any financial results.

THE GLOBAL ECONOMY: A BRIEF OVERVIEW

Molson is not the first company to face problems in its international expansion. Many firms have taken the plunge only to discover that competing internationally is much harder than some of the fiercest battles at home. Yet, the foreign markets can provide many opportunities for firms to increase their revenue base and their profitability. Bombardier, CAE of Montreal, SNC Lavalan, and Aldo are some of the Canadian firms that have prospered internationally. How do these firms create value and achieve competitive advantages in the global marketplace? What factors can explain the success of a particular industry in a particular country? How can firms become successful when they diversify and expand the scope of their business to include international operations? International strategy choices present unique sets of challenges to executives who consider foreign markets for further expansion of their current business operations and for diversification opportunities.

Today's managers face many opportunities and risks when they venture abroad. Opportunities abound. Trade among nations has increased dramatically in recent years. It is estimated that by 2015, the trade *across* nations will exceed the trade within nations. In a variety of industries, such as semiconductors, automobiles, commercial aircraft, telecommunications, computers, and consumer electronics, it is virtually impossible to survive unless firms scan the world for competitors, customers, human resources, suppliers, and technology.[2]

The rise of globalization and market capitalism around the world has contributed to the economic boom in the New Economy, where knowledge is the key source of competitive advantage and value creation. It is estimated that globalization has brought phone service to about 300 million households in developing nations and a transfer of nearly $2 trillion from rich countries to poor countries through equity, bond investments, and commercial loans.[3]

At the same time, there have been extremes in the effects of global capitalism on national economies and poverty levels around the world. The economies of East Asia have attained rapid growth, but there has been comparatively little progress in the rest of the world. For example, income in Latin America grew by only 6 percent in the past two decades—just as the continent was opening up to global capitalism. Average incomes in sub-Saharan Africa and the old Eastern European bloc have actually declined. Indeed, the World Bank estimates that the number of people living on $1 per day has *increased* to 1.3 billion over the past decade.

Such disparities in wealth among nations raise an important question: Why do some countries—and their citizens—enjoy the fruits of global capitalism while others are mired in poverty? Stated differently, why do some governments make the best use of inflows of foreign investment and know-how and others do not? There are many explanations. Among these are the need of governments to have track records of business-friendly policies to attract multinationals as well as local entrepreneurs to train workers, invest in modern technology, and nurture local suppliers and managers. Also, it means carefully managing the broader economic factors in an economy, such as interest rates, inflation, unemployment, and so on, as well as having a good legal system that protects property rights, strong educational systems, and a society where prosperity is widely shared.

Marketing to the "bottom of the pyramid"

Many executives wrongly believe that profitable opportunities to sell consumer goods exist only in countries where income levels are high. Even when they expand internationally, they often tend to limit their company's marketing to only the affluent segments within the developing countries. Such narrow conceptualizations of the market lead them to ignore the vast opportunities that exist at the "bottom of the pyramid," according to the University of Michigan professor C. K. Prahalad. The bottom of the pyramid refers to the nearly 5 billion people who inhabit the developing countries. Surprisingly, this group represents $14 trillion in purchasing power, and they are looking for products and services that can improve the quality of their lives. Multinationals are missing out on growth opportunities if they ignore this vast segment of the world market

How can the poor buy if they don't have the money? The key is to bring the cost structures of the companies and their product offerings within the reach of the low-income customers. Unilever started marketing single serve sachets of shampoo to the poor in India several years go. Selling for about a penny each, single sales account for 60 percent of the total value of shampoo sold in India today. A 500 ml bottle of shampoo may cost more than a farm worker's daily income and thus may be out of her reach. But the need for shampoo is almost universal. The challenge is to sell it in a way in which the poor can satisfy their need for shampoo and the company can still make a profit.

Grameen Bank in Bangladesh is very different from the money-centre banks of London or New York. Pioneers of the concept of micro-credit, Grameen Bank extends small loans, sometimes as small as $20, to the thousands of struggling microbusiness entrepreneurs who have no credit histories or collateral to offer. Not only are their loan recovery rates comparable to those of the big banks, but they are also changing the lives of thousands of people who are now able to start and finance their own small businesses.

Casas Bahias, the Brazilian retailer, has built a $2.5 billion-per-year chain selling to the poor who live in the *favelas*, the illegal shanty towns in the outskirts of the cities. Aravind Eye Care, an Indian hospital that specializes in cataract surgeries, has become the largest eye-care facility in the world, performing more than 200,000 procedures per year. The surgeries cost only about $25, compared to some $3,000 in the North America. And, best of all, Aravind has a return on equity of more than 75 percent.

As the above examples demonstrate, in order to sell to the bottom of the pyramid, managers must rethink their costs, quality, scale of operations, and even their use of capital. What prevents managers from selling to this vast market? Often they are the victims of their own false assumptions. First, they think that the poor have no purchasing power. But $14 trillion can buy a lot. Second, they assume that poor people have no use for new technologies. We only have to see the demand for cellphones from entrepreneurs who run microbusinesses in villages in India to dispel this myth. Third, they assume that the poor have no use for their products and services. Shampoo and detergents for cleanliness and banks offering financial services satisfy needs that all people have, not just the affluent. Fourth, they assume that managers may not be excited about working in these markets. Recent experience shows that this may be a more exciting environment than the dogfights for fractions of market share in the mature markets of the developed countries.

Sources: C. C. Miller, "Easy money," *Forbes*, November 27, 2006, p. 134–8; C. K. Prahalad, "Why selling to the poor makes for good business," *Fortune*, 150(9), 2004, p. 32–33; A. Overholt, "A new path to profit," *Fast Company*, January, 2005, p. 23–26; and C. K. Prahalad, *The Fortune at the Bottom of the Pyramid: Eradicating Poverty through Profits* (Philadelphia: Wharton School Publishing, 2005).

The above policies are the type that East Asia—in locations such as Hong Kong, Taiwan, South Korea, and Singapore—has employed to evolve from the sweatshop economies of the 1960s and 1970s to industrial powers today. On the other hand, many countries have moved in the other direction. Consider, for example, Guatemala, a country in Central America. Here, only 52 percent of males complete fifth grade and an astonishing 39.8 percent of the population subsists on less than $1 per day.[4] By comparison, the corresponding numbers for South Korea are 98 percent and less than 2 percent, respectively. Moreover, 70 percent of the land rests in the hands of only 2 percent of the population, in a country that is still predominantly agricultural. Taxes and decades of ill-designed economic policies have kept the country's masses in poverty. Yet, as Strategy Spotlight 7.1 reports, marketing to the "bottom of the pyramid" allows multinational firms to target their goods and services to the nearly 5 billion poor people in the world who inhabit developing countries. Collectively, they represent a very large market with $14 trillion in purchasing power.

In the next section, we address in more detail the question of why particular industries of some nations are more competitive. This discussion establishes an important context for the remainder of the chapter; after we discuss why some *nations and their industries* outperform others, we can better address the various strategies that *firms* can take to create competitive advantage when they expand internationally.

FACTORS AFFECTING A NATION'S COMPETITIVENESS

Michael Porter of Harvard University conducted a four-year study in which he and a team of 30 researchers looked at the patterns of competitive success in 10 leading trading nations. He concluded that there are four broad attributes of nations that individually, and as a system, constitute what is termed "the diamond of national advantage." In effect, the following attributes, together, determine the playing field that each nation establishes and operates for its industries:

- *Factor conditions.* The nation's position in factors of production, such as skilled labour or infrastructure, necessary to compete in a given industry.
- *Demand conditions.* The nature of home-market demand for the industry's product or service.
- *Related and supporting industries.* The presence or absence in the nation of supplier industries and other related industries that are internationally competitive.
- *Firm strategy, structure, and rivalry.* The conditions in the nation governing how companies are created, organized, and managed as well as the nature of domestic rivalry.

We briefly discuss each of these factors.[5] Then, we provide an integrative example— the Indian software industry—to demonstrate how these attributes interact and account for India's high level of competitiveness in this industry.

Factor Conditions[6]

Classical economics suggests that factors of production, such as land, labour, and capital, are the building blocks that create usable consumer goods and services.[7] But this tells only part of the story when we consider the global aspects of economic growth. Companies in advanced nations seeking competitive advantage over firms in other nations *create* many of the factors of production. For example, a country or industry dependent on scientific innovation must have a skilled human resource pool to draw upon. This resource pool is not inherited; it is created through investment in industry-specific knowledge and talent. The supporting infrastructure of a country—that is, its transportation and communication systems as well as its banking system—are also critical.

To achieve competitive advantage, factors of production that are industry and firm specific must be developed. In addition, the pool of resources a firm or a country has at its disposal is less important than the speed and efficiency with which these resources are deployed. Thus, firm-specific knowledge and skills created within a country and that are rare, valuable, difficult to imitate, and rapidly and efficiently deployed are the factors of production that ultimately lead to a nation's competitive advantage.

The island nation of Japan, for example, has little land mass, making the warehouse space needed to store inventory prohibitively expensive. But by pioneering just-in-time inventory management, Japanese companies managed to create a resource from which they gained advantage over companies in other nations that spent large sums to warehouse inventory.

Demand Conditions

Demand conditions refer to the demands that consumers place on an industry for goods and services. Consumers who demand highly specific, sophisticated products and services force firms to create innovative, advanced products and services to meet the demand. This consumer pressure presents challenges to a country's industries. But in response to these challenges, improvements to existing goods and services often result, creating conditions necessary for competitive advantage over firms in other countries.

Demanding consumers push firms to move ahead of companies in other countries where consumers are less demanding and more complacent. Countries with demanding consumers drive firms in that country to meet high standards, upgrade existing products and services, and create innovative products and services. The conditions of consumer demand then influence how firms view a market, with more demanding consumers stimulating advances in products and services. This, in turn, helps a nation's industries to better anticipate future global demand conditions and proactively respond to product and service requirements before competing nations are even aware of the need for such products and services.

Denmark, for instance, is known for its environmental awareness. Demand from consumers for environmentally safe products has spurred Danish manufacturers to become leaders in water pollution control equipment—products it successfully exports to other nations. Canada's vast landmass has always created unique challenges in bringing people and goods together and has sprung a global industry for telecommunications. Similarly, the wealth of metals and mineral resources has not only created a world renowned mining industry but has also provided the conditions for the rise of mining engineering, exploration and drilling, and other specialized industries that today can successfully compete around the world.

Related and Supporting Industries

Related and supporting industries enable firms to manage inputs more effectively. For example, countries with a strong supplier base benefit by adding efficiency to downstream activities. A competitive supplier base helps a firm obtain inputs using cost-effective, timely methods, thus reducing manufacturing costs. Also, close working relationships with suppliers provide the potential to develop competitive advantages through joint research and development and the ongoing exchange of knowledge, helping both suppliers and manufacturers.

Related industries offer similar opportunities through joint efforts among firms. In addition, related industries create the probability that new entrants will appear on the market, increasing competition and forcing existing firms to become more competitive through efforts such as cost control, product innovation, and novel approaches to distribution. Combined, these give the home country's industries a source of competitive advantage over less competitive nations.

The supporting industries in the Italian footwear industry show how such industries can lead to national competitive advantage. In Italy, shoe manufacturers are located near their suppliers. The manufacturers have ongoing interactions with leather suppliers and learn about new textures, colours, and manufacturing techniques while a shoe is still in the prototype stage. The manufacturers are able to project future demand and gear their factories for new products long before companies in other nations become aware of the new styles. Similarly, the geographic proximity of industries related to the pharmaceutical industry in Switzerland (e.g., the dye industry) has given that nation a leadership position in this market, with firms such as Ciba-Geigy, Hoffman LaRoche, and Sandoz using dyes from local manufacturers in many pharmaceutical products.

India and the Diamond of National Advantage

Consider the following facts:

- SAP, the German software company, has developed new applications for notebook PCs at its 500-engineer Bangalore facility.

- General Electric plans to invest $100 million and hire 2,600 scientists to create the world's largest research and development lab in Bangalore, India.

- Microsoft plans to invest $400 million in new research partnerships in India.

- Over one-fifth of Fortune 1000 companies outsource their software requirements to firms in India.

- McKinsey & Co. projects that the Indian software and services industry will be an $87 billion business by 2008; $50 billion of this will be exported.

- For the past decade, the Indian software industry has grown at a 50 percent annual rate.

- More than 800 firms in India are involved in software services as their primary activity.

- Software and information technology firms in India are projected to employ 2.2 million people by 2008.

What is causing such global interest in India's software services industry? Porter's diamond of national advantage helps clarify this question. See Exhibit 7.1.

First, *factor conditions* are conducive to the rise of India's software industry. Through investment in human resource development with a focus on industry-specific knowledge, India's universities and software firms have literally created this essential factor of production. For example, India produces the second largest annual output of scientists and engineers in the world, behind only the United States. In a knowledge-intensive industry, such as software, development of human resources is fundamental to both domestic and global success.

Second, *demand conditions* require that software firms stay on the cutting edge of technological innovation. India has already moved toward globalization of its software industry; consumer demand conditions in developed nations, such as Germany, Denmark, parts of Southeast Asia, and the United States, created the consumer demand necessary to propel India's software makers toward sophisticated software solutions.*

Third, India has the *supplier base as well as the related industries* needed to drive competitive rivalry and enhance competitiveness. Information technology (IT) hardware prices declined rapidly in the 1990s. Furthermore, rapid technological change in IT hardware meant that latecomers like India were not locked into older-generation technologies. Thus, both the IT hardware and software industries could "leapfrog" older technologies. In

Sources: M. Kripalani, "Calling Bangalore: Multinationals are making it a hub for high-tech research," *BusinessWeek*, November 25, 2002, p. 52–4; D. Kapur and R. Ramamurti, "India's emerging competitive advantage in services," *Academy of Management Executive*, 15(2), 2001, p. 20–33; World Bank, *World Development Report* (New York: Oxford University Press, Reuters, 2001); "Oracle in India push, taps software talent," *Washington Post Online*, July 3.

* Although India's success cannot be explained in terms of its home market demand (according to Porter's model), the nature of the industry enables software to be transferred among different locations simultaneously by way of communications links. Thus, competitiveness of markets outside India can be enhanced without a physical presence in those markets.

Firm Strategy, Structure, and Rivalry

Rivalry is particularly intense in nations with conditions of strong consumer demand, strong supplier bases, and high new entrant potential from related industries. This competitive rivalry, in turn, increases the efficiency with which firms develop, market, and distribute products and services within the home country. Domestic rivalry thus provides a strong impetus for firms to innovate and find new sources of competitive advantage.

Interestingly, this intense rivalry forces firms to look outside their national boundaries for new markets, setting up the conditions necessary for global competitiveness. Among all the points on Porter's "diamond" of national advantage, domestic rivalry is, perhaps, the strongest indicator of global competitive success. Firms that have experienced intense domestic competition are more likely to have designed strategies and structures that allow them to successfully compete in world markets. In the U.S., for example, intense rivalry has spurred companies, such as Dell Computer, to find innovative ways to produce and distribute their products. This is largely a result of competition from IBM and Hewlett-Packard.

It should be noted that Porter's diamond does not imply that one managerial style is best across industries; different strategies and different organizational structures have

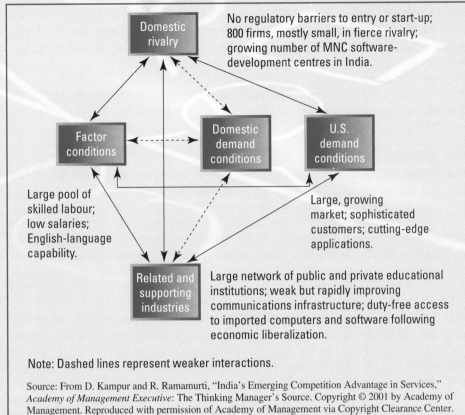

Exhibit 7.1
India's Virtual
Diamond in Software

Domestic
rivalry

No regulatory barriers to entry or start-up;
800 firms, mostly small, in fierce rivalry;
growing number of MNC software-
development centres in India.

Factor
conditions

Domestic
demand
conditions

U.S.
demand
conditions

Large pool of
skilled labour;
low salaries;
English-language
capability.

Large, growing
market; sophisticated
customers; cutting-edge
applications.

Related and
supporting
industries

Large network of public and private educational
institutions; weak but rapidly improving
communications infrastructure; duty-free access
to imported computers and software following
economic liberalization.

Note: Dashed lines represent weaker interactions.

Source: From D. Kampur and R. Ramamurti, "India's Emerging Competition Advantage in Services," *Academy of Management Executive*: The Thinking Manager's Source. Copyright © 2001 by Academy of Management. Reproduced with permission of Academy of Management via Copyright Clearance Center.

addition, relationships among knowledge workers in these IT hardware and software industries offer the social structure for ongoing knowledge exchange, promoting further enhancement of existing products. Further infrastructure improvements are occurring rapidly.

Fourth, with over 800 firms in the software services industry in India, *intense rivalry forces firms to develop competitive strategies and structures*. Although firms like TCS, Infosys, and Wipro have become large, they were quite small only five years ago. And dozens of small and mid-sized companies are aspiring to catch up. This intense rivalry is one of the primary factors driving Indian software firms to develop overseas distribution channels, as predicted by Porter's diamond of national advantage.

been instrumental in creating world-class competitors. Small- and medium-sized family-owned firms dominate the Italian footwear industry, while large multinationals have given Switzerland its leadership position in the pharmaceutical industry.

Strategy Spotlight 7.2 discusses India's software industry. It provides an integrative example of how the insights from Porter's diamond can help to explain the relative degree of success of an industry in a given country.

Concluding Comments on Factors Affecting a Nation's Competitiveness

Porter based his conclusions on case histories of firms in more than 100 industries. Despite the differences in strategies employed by successful global competitors, a common theme did emerge: firms that succeeded in global markets had first succeeded in intense competition in their home markets.

Competitive advantage for global firms typically grows out of relentless, continuing improvement, innovation, and change. Within this framework, governments act as facilitators or inhibitors, through their policies on education, innovation, standards, regulations, taxation, and the removal of obstacles to firms' competitiveness. At the same time, chance can always play a determinant role in the development of globally competitive industries. Nortel's initial success as a global telecommunications powerhouse and the spectacular domestic industry it fostered across Canada has its roots in the Baby Bells—the local telephone companies that were spun off from AT&T in the early 1980s, with the goal of finding alternative equipment suppliers to lessen their dependence on the technology championed by their old parent.

The case of Nortel points to Canada's unique circumstances, which call for some modifications to the diamond analogy. Canada's international trade is responsible for some 70 percent of GDP, one of the highest levels among industrialized nations. More than $1 billion of goods cross the border between Canada and the United States each day. It is impossible to consider Canada's automotive sector without acknowledging the role of the American market in every factor. The same applies to the lumber, pulp and paper, agriculture, minerals, and metals industries. For example, while most of the automobile manufacturers, such as GM, Ford, Chrysler, Honda, and Toyota, have operations in both countries, their strategic and tactical decisions are made on a North American basis; the integration of the industry is such that many of their parts suppliers, such as Magna, are responsible for moving components and subassemblies back and forth multiple times during the various stages of the value chain. It is quite possible for a simple stamped material from Canada to be shipped south of the border for refinement and be brought up again to become part of a subassembly. The subassembly could be shipped south to be installed on a component that crosses the border again for an assembly plant in Canada where it could then become part of a car that is likely sold to a dealer in the south! Our notion of a national diamond and of the associated factors has to incorporate demand and factor conditions in both countries, rivalry among global players, related and support industries, as well as the role of two independent governments in assessing the viability and future prospects of the members of the industry.

Having highlighted the important role that nations play in international strategy, we turn next to the level of the individual firm. In the following section, we discuss a company's motivations for and the risks associated with international expansion.

INTERNATIONAL EXPANSION: A COMPANY'S MOTIVATIONS AND RISKS

 ### Motivations for International Expansion

As one would expect, there are many motivations for a company to pursue international expansion. The most obvious one is to *increase the size of potential markets* for a firm's products and services.[8] The world's population exceeds 6.6 billion, with Canada representing less than 0.5 percent. Exhibit 7.2 lists the population of Canada compared to other major markets abroad and contrasts their per capita purchasing power.

Many multinational firms are intensifying their efforts to market their products and services to countries, such as India and China, where the ranks of the middle class have increased over the past decade. Procter & Gamble has successfully achieved a 50 percent share in China's shampoo market, and PepsiCo has made impressive inroads in the Indian soft-drink market.[9] Strategy Spotlight 7.3 discusses the opportunities that are presented by China's emerging middle class.

China's Emerging Middle Class

For many years, Western companies have dreamed of selling to China's 1.3 billion people, only to find that not enough Chinese could afford foreign goods. However, China's middle class has finally attained a critical mass—between 35 and 200 million people, depending on which definition of middle class is being used. The larger estimates are based on a family income limit of $10,000, which is reasonable given the GDP (PPP) per capital is $5,300.

China's middle-class population are primarily found in the coastal areas where the economy has been able to develop rapidly and where the big cities such as Shanghai, Guangzhou, and Beijing are situated. These citizens tend to be owners of small and medium private enterprises but also include the high-tech specialists and professionals. The central government's emphasis on science and technology has encouraged the rapid development of higher education, the incubator of the middle class.

What is happening in China may be viewed as an example of economies of scale. Many Western companies already have factories in China and are exporting goods.

Now that there is a domestic market to go along with the export market, those factories can increase their output with little additional cost. That is one reason why many foreign companies' profits in China have been so strong in recent years.

Consider the example of Kodak. This company invested $1.2 billion in China in 1998, at the time planning on a 10 to 12 year payback period. However, Kodak initially overestimated the Chinese market. In the early years, domestic demand for cameras and film was well below company forecasts and China operations were in the red. Since then things have turned around with Kodak's sales in China climbing from very little to a first-place position in the market. In fact, revenues grew 40 percent in the first half of 2004 and the company declared that it was ahead of its plan to recoup its investment, with China's profit margins on par with those worldwide. Not surprisingly, manufacturing in China has greatly helped on the cost side; 95 percent of Kodak's digital cameras are made there, some by contract manufacturers but most in its Shanghai factory which runs three shifts a day.

Sources: R. Meredith, "Middle kingdom, middle class," *Forbes*, November 15, 2004, p. 188–192; and "Middle class becomes rising power in China," www.chinadaily.com, November 6.

Exhibit 7.2

Populations and Per Capita GDP of Selected Nations

Country	Population*	Per Capita GDP (PPP, $)**
China	1,330,044,605	5,300
India	1,147,995,898	2,700
United States	303,824,646	45,800
Indonesia	237,512,355	3,700
Brazil	191,908,598	9,700
Japan	127,288,419	33,600
Germany	82,369,548	34,200
Canada	33,212,696	38,400
Norway	4,644,457	53,000
Ireland	4,156,119	43,100
Luxembourg	486,006	80,500
The World	6,677,593,921	10,000

* as of July 2008;

** PPP (purchasing power parity) estimates range from 2006 to 2008

Sources: www.geohive.com/earth; and *The World FactBook*, CIA publications, 2008.

Yet, it is not only multinationals that are seeking to increase the size of their potential markets. Small firms might also be tempted or forced to look overseas for new customers. Lingo Media of Toronto, in spite of its small base as a Canadian publisher, has successfully penetrated the Chinese market, selling over 75 million units of English language educational material; today, it serves 65 percent of the Chinese EELS primary textbook market. Many successful Canadian firms have frequently looked to the neighbouring U.S. market for growth. Nortel sold its first switches outside Canada to local telephone companies in the U.S.; Molson has been selling beer to American consumers for almost a century; most of our forestry and energy firms have typically served American customers; and many Canadian retailers, such as Loblaw, Jean Coutu, Couche-Tard, Canadian Tire, Aldo, La Senza, and Future Shop, have looked first to the U.S. for opportunities, albeit with varying degrees of success.

Expanding a firm's global presence also automatically increases its scale of operations, providing it with a larger revenue and asset base. As we noted in Chapter 5, in discussing overall cost leadership strategies, an increase in revenues and asset base potentially enables a firm to *attain economies of scale*. This provides multiple benefits. One advantage is the spreading of fixed costs, such as research and development, over a larger volume of production. Examples would include the sale of Bombardier aircraft and Microsoft's operating systems in many foreign countries. IMAX knows very well that every new theatre that it opens somewhere in the world lowers the cost of production of its unique movies—a cost that has to be borne by each of the existing theatres in the chain. The Toronto firm has built some 245 special theatres in 36 countries around the world, and each new theatre adds to the firm's capacity to produce more films for all the theatres in the chain. At the same time, some IMAX theatres recently withdrew a film on volcanoes, which management thought might offend certain religious groups in the Southern United States where IMAX does have a number of screens. Attaining global economies of scale does not come without complications and additional ethical questions.

Another advantage would be *reducing the costs of research and development as well as operating costs*. Recall, for example, the establishment of software development operations by Microsoft and other firms in talent-rich India (see Strategy Spotlight 7.2). A final advantage would be the attainment of greater purchasing power by pooling purchases. As Cott increases the number of facilities it has all over the world, it is able to place larger orders for equipment and supplies, thus increasing its bargaining power with suppliers.

International expansion can also *extend the life cycle of a product* that is in its maturity stage in a firm's home country but has greater demand potential elsewhere. As we noted in Chapter 5, products (and industries) generally go through a four-stage life cycle of introduction, growth, maturity, and decline. During much of the 1990s, Nortel frequently sold its earlier generation telephone switches to developing countries, at lower costs, and used the revenues to fund further research and development. Volkswagen continued to produce its original Beetle in Brazil long after it had stopped selling it in Europe and North America.

Finally, international expansion can enable a firm to *optimize the physical location for every activity in its value chain*. Recall from our discussions in Chapters 3 and 5 that the value chain represents the various activities in which all firms must engage to produce products and services. They include primary activities, such as inbound logistics, operations, and marketing as well as support activities, such as procurement, research and development, and human resource management. All firms have to make critical decisions as to where each activity will take place.[10] Optimizing the location for every activity in the value chain can yield one or more of three strategic advantages: performance enhancement, cost reduction, and risk reduction.

Child Labour: How Two Companies Have Addressed This Issue

The issue of child labour has been raised since the early 1990s, when the proliferation of goods from China and Southeast Asia started hitting the North American retail shelves, although experts will explain that children have been exploited for centuries in sweat shops and factories producing goods for local consumption and export. How have companies responded to those concerns? Consider Nike, one of the first to be publicly criticized for the practice. The company initially tried to distance itself from the issue by pointing the finger at its independent subcontractors. Nike has revised its code of conduct a number of times since 1992, making changes that include increasing the minimum age from 14 to 18 for footwear factory workers and from 14 to 16 for equipment and apparel workers. Both of these standards are quite a bit higher than the codes of other companies and of the International Labor Organization's (ILO) convention. The company also has started an internal compliance program, supplemented with external monitoring. These actions, however, do not seem to have silenced the critics. Nike's Web site reflects the way in which the company tries to openly address this critique, providing ample information about the monitoring of facilities and the dilemmas the company faces after introducing its latest code.

On the other hand, Chiquita Banana almost completely follows the SA 8000 standard, including all references to international conventions, but with appropriate modifications to account for workplace issues specific to agriculture. The SA 8000 standard was developed by the Council on Economic Priorities Accreditation Agency and is widely recognized and accepted; it is based on ILO and United Nations conventions. The company's strict child labour provisions do not apply to family farms or to small-scale holdings in the seasonal, non-banana business that do not regularly employ hired workers. This is also meant to allow for employment of a farmer's own children in seasonal activities. Chiquita tries to address the problem associated with children working in supplier factories by giving support to enable them to remain in school until they are old enough to work.

Source: A. Kolk and R. V. Tulder, "Ethics in international business: multinational approaches to child labor," *Journal of World Business*, 39, 2004, p. 49–60.

Performance Enhancement Microsoft's decision to establish a corporate research laboratory in Cambridge, England, is an example of a location decision that was guided mainly by the goal of building and sustaining world-class excellence in selected value-creating activities.[11] This strategic decision provided Microsoft with access to outstanding technical and professional talent. Location decisions can affect the quality with which any activity is performed in terms of the availability of needed talent, speed of learning, and the quality of external and internal coordination.

Cost Reduction Two location decisions founded largely on cost-reduction considerations are Nike's decision to source the manufacture of athletic shoes from Asian countries, such as China, Vietnam, and Indonesia, and the decision of many multinational companies to set up production operations just south of the United States–Mexico border to access lower-cost labour. These operations are called *maquiladoras*. Such location decisions affect the cost structure and are based on the availability of local manpower and other resources, transportation and logistics, and government incentives and the local tax structure.

Performance enhancement and cost-reduction benefits parallel the business-level strategies (discussed in Chapter 5) of differentiation and overall cost leadership. They can, at times, be attained simultaneously. Consider our example, in the previous section, on the Indian software industry. When Oracle set up a development operation in that country, the company benefited from lower labour costs and operational expenses as well as from performance enhancements realized through the hiring of superbly talented professionals.

Managing across borders though also raises challenging ethical dilemmas. One issue that has received a good deal of attention is child labour. Strategy Spotlight 7.4 discusses the approaches of two multinationals in addressing this issue.

Risk Reduction Given the erratic swings in the exchange ratios between the U.S. dollar and the Japanese yen (in relation to each other as well as other major currencies), an important basis for cost competition between Ford and Toyota has been their relative ingenuity at managing currency risks. One of the ways for such competitors to manage currency risks has been to spread the high-cost elements of their manufacturing operations across a few select and carefully chosen locations around the world. Location decisions such as these can affect the overall risk profile of the firm with respect to political, economic, and currency risks.[12]

Potential Risks of International Expansion

When a company expands its international operations, it does so to increase its profits or revenues. As with any other investment, however, there are potential risks to accompany the anticipated returns.[13] To help companies assess the risk of entering foreign markets, rating systems have been developed to evaluate political, economic, and financial and credit risks. *Euromoney* magazine publishes a semi-annual "Country Risk Rating" that evaluates political, economic, and other risks that entrants potentially face. Exhibit 7.3 depicts a sample of country risk ratings, published by the World Bank, from the 178 countries that *Euromoney* evaluates. In the exhibit, note that the lower the score, the higher the country's expected level of risk. Firms contemplating international expansion typically consider four types of risk—namely, political, economic, currency, and management risk.

Exhibit 7.3

A Sample of International Country Risk Rankings

Rank	Country	Total Risk Assessment	Economic Performance	Political Risk	Total of Debt Indicators	Total of Credit and Access to Finance Indicators
1	Norway	99.45	25.00	24.69	20.00	29.77
2	Switzerland	99.15	24.38	25.00	20.00	29.77
3	Luxembourg	99.10	24.43	24.90	20.00	29.77
4	United States	96.93	22.81	24.12	20.00	30.00
12	Canada	92.76	18.43	24.56	20.00	29.77
13	Japan	91.86	20.52	23.62	20.00	27.72
27	Greece	79.05	12.10	20.22	20.00	26.73
51	China	61.21	10.45	17.00	19.68	14.08
60	India	56.34	8.77	15.33	19.25	13.00
61	Russia	53.51	8.63	13.53	18.87	12.48
71	Philippines	48.69	7.17	13.21	18.61	9.70
89	Pakistan	40.34	6.16	8.60	18.99	6.59
141	Argentina	31.98	6.35	4.88	17.37	3.39
183	Afghanistan	3.66	2.10	0.73	0.00	0.83
185	Iraq	1.85	0.47	0.55	0.00	0.83

Source: *Euromoney*, March 2005, 36, no. 431, p. 136.

Political and Economic Risk Generally speaking, the business climate in Canada is very favourable. Other countries around the globe, though, present elevated levels of political risk. Forces such as social unrest, military turmoil, demonstrations, and even violent conflict and terrorism can pose serious threats.[14] Consider, for example, the ongoing tension and violence in the Middle East or the social and political unrest in Thailand and Indonesia.[15] Because such conditions increase the likelihood of destruction of property as well as non-payment for goods and services, countries that are viewed as bearing high political and economic risk are less attractive for most types of business. Nevertheless, firms that choose to operate in those environments, such as Canadian firms in Afghanistan and American firms in Iraq, would expect substantially higher returns from their operations there to compensate for the additional risk.

Political risk can also arise from boycotts directed toward the home government of a corporation and its policies. Many U.S. firms have suffered overseas as a result of the American government's stance in the Middle East, and Canadian firms around the world were the targets of animal rights groups that did not approve of seal hunting in Newfoundland and the Canadian Arctic.

The laws, as well as the enforcement of laws, associated with the protection of intellectual property rights can be another significant potential risk in entering new countries. Microsoft, for example, has lost billions of dollars in potential revenue through piracy of its software products in many countries, including China. Other areas of the globe, such as the former Soviet Union and some eastern European nations, have piracy problems as well. Firms rich in intellectual property have encountered financial losses as imitations of their products have grown through a lack of law enforcement of intellectual property rights.[16]

Currency Risks Currency fluctuations can pose substantial risks. A company with operations in several countries must constantly monitor the exchange rate between its own currency and that of the host country. Even a small change in the exchange rate can result in a significant difference in the cost of production or net profit when doing business overseas. When the dollar appreciates against other currencies, Canadian goods can be more expensive to consumers in foreign countries. Many Canadian firms started reporting reduced profits since 2004 from their American operations, simply because of the appreciation of the loonie. Gold and oil companies, on the other hand, benefited enormously from the decline of the U.S. dollar and the simultaneous global price increases of their commodities, even if those prices were marked in American dollars.

It is important to note that even when government intervention is well intended, the macroeconomic effects of such action can be very negative for multinational corporations. Such was the case in 1997 when Thailand suddenly chose to devalue its currency, the baht, after months of trying to support it at an artificially high level. This, in effect, made the baht worthless compared to other currencies. And in 1998, Russia not only devalued its ruble but also elected not to honour its foreign debt obligations. Of course, ten years later, flush with cash from its oil and gas exports, Russia paid back its debt with depressed dollars.

Management Risks Management risks reflect the challenges that managers face when they must respond to the inevitable differences that they encounter in foreign markets. These concern a variety of factors: culture, customs, language, income levels, customer preferences, distribution systems, and so on.[17]

Differences in cultures across countries pose unique challenges for managers. Cultural symbols can evoke deep feelings.[18] For example, in a series of advertisements aimed at Italian vacationers, Coca-Cola executives turned the Eiffel Tower, Empire State

---

France:

♦ Most English-speaking French have studied British-style English, which can lead to communication breakdowns with speakers of American-style English. For example, in the United States, a presentation that "bombs" has failed, but in England it has succeeded.

♦ Words in French and English may have similar roots but different meanings or connotations. For example, a French person might "demand" something because in French *demander* means "to ask."

Hong Kong:

♦ Negotiations occur over cups of tea. Always accept an offer of tea whether you want it or not. When you are served, wait for the host to drink first.

♦ Chinese negotiators commonly use teacups as visual aids. One cup may be used to represent your company, another cup to represent the Hong Kong company. The position of the cups will be changed to indicate how far apart the companies are on the terms of an agreement.

♦ Also, avoid any gifts of knives, scissors, or cutting tools; these suggest the severing of a friendship to the Chinese. If you're giving flowers, give an even number of them; an odd number would be very unlucky.

Ecuador:

♦ Dinner at an Ecuadorian home lasts for many hours. Expect drinks and appetizers around 8:00 P.M., with dinner not served until 11:00 P.M. or midnight. You will dismay your hosts if you leave as early as 1:00 A.M. A party at an Ecuadorian home will begin late and end around 4:00 A.M. or 5:00 A.M. Late guests may sometimes be served breakfast before they leave.

Sources: T. Morrison, W. Conaway, and G. Borden, *Kiss, Bow, or Shake Hands* (Avon, MA: Adams Media Corporation, 1994); and www.executiveplanet.com/business-culture/112565157281.html.

Building, and the Tower of Pisa into the familiar Coke bottle. So far, so good. However, when the white marble columns of the Parthenon that crowns the Acropolis in Athens were turned into Coke bottles, the Greeks became outraged. Greeks refer to the Acropolis as the "holy rock," and a government official said the Parthenon is an "international symbol of excellence" and that "whoever insults the Parthenon insults international culture." Coca-Cola apologized for the ad. Exhibit 7.4 highlights how cultures vary across countries and some of the implications for the conduct of business across national boundaries.

Let's now look at how firms can attain competitive advantages when they move beyond the boundaries of their home nation.

ACHIEVING COMPETITIVE ADVANTAGE IN GLOBAL MARKETS

We begin this section by discussing the two opposing forces that firms face when they expand into global markets: cost reduction and adaptation to local markets. Then, we address the four basic types of international strategies that they may pursue: international, global, multidomestic, and transnational. The selection of one of these four types of strategies is largely dependent on a firm's relative pressure to address each of the two forces.

Two Opposing Pressures: Reducing Costs and Adapting to Local Markets

Pressures to lower costs derive from the standardization or even commoditization of many products; meaningful differences among producers' diverse offerings may be difficult to discern, and price then becomes the main competitive weapon. Pressure further intensifies when competition arises from producers located in low-cost countries. Standardization promotes substantial economies of scale; supplying global markets with standard products allows for global manufacturing decisions and the adoption of global marketing efforts. Both promise significant savings. In response, Theodore Levitt advocated strategies that favour global products and brands. He suggested that firms should standardize all of their products and services for all of their worldwide markets. Such an approach would help a firm lower its overall costs by spreading its investments over as large a market as possible. Levitt's thesis rests on extensive observations about our world.[19] Television, newspapers, global publications, inexpensive travelling, and the Internet have brought people closer together than ever before. Most luxury brands from France (Louis Vuitton, Hermès, Channel, Dior), Italy (Gucci, Armani, Dolce & Gabbana), Germany (Hugo Boss), as well as the United States (Ralph Lauren, Calvin Klein) are well recognized and have set up stores in the high-fashion streets of each of dozens of metropolises around the world. Aldo, the successful Montreal-based fashion shoe company operates 850 stores in over 40 countries on five continents, selling identical designs of shoes and accessories. Club Monaco, another Canadian fashion icon, owns three stores in its founding city, Toronto, and has already opened two stores in Beijing. Coca-Cola, McDonald's, Levi's, Sony, Apple, and Microsoft are among many brands used daily by hundreds of millions of consumers around the world. Industrial customers of commodities such as steel, aluminium, oil, and gold have identical needs and shop globally for supplies. Levitt also argues that people around the world are willing to sacrifice idiosyncratic preferences in product features, functions, and design for lower prices at high quality.

While pressures for cost reductions might, indeed, direct firms toward standardized global products, one cannot ignore the opposite reality that is also prevalent in the world's markets today.[20] Countless local firms thrive by offering products that cater to the specific needs of local consumers. Many global firms customize their products and services to target local market segments. In Japan, Coca-Cola markets Georgia (a tonic drink) as well as Classic Coke and Hi-C. McDonald's serves wine in France and lamb-based hamburgers in India. Couche-Tard uses the banner Circle K in the U.S., and the range of products in its convenience stores differs markedly from its Quebec and Ontario stores. While many consumers might be willing to sacrifice product attributes for lower prices, many more are likely to want more features, higher product quality, and enhanced services.

Transportation costs and other diseconomies of scale put a damper on the ability of firms to build very large facilities in the most cost-efficient locations in order to supply distant markets. Moreover, flexible factory automation technologies enable economies of scale to be attained at lower levels of output and do not require production of a single standardized product. Sales, service, and distribution are inherently localized activities and increasingly represent a substantial part of a product's total value to consumers.

While Harley-Davidson motorcycles, Bombardier planes, and some of Coca-Cola's soft-drink products are rightly designed to be the same for all markets throughout the world, managers must also strive to tailor their products to the culture of the country in which they are attempting to do business. Few would argue that "one size fits all" generally applies.

Look at what happened when Ford took this approach with the launch of its Escort automobile in Europe in the 1980s. According to the company's then CEO, Jacques Nasser:

> The Escort, which was intended to be our first global product, was engineered on two continents—North America and Europe. Obviously, that made it impossible for us to capitalize on global sourcing for components. And it was launched individually in every country. Not only did every country come up with its own positioning for the car, but each devised its own advertising message and hired its own advertising agency to get that message across. So you had one car and a substantial number of value propositions. One market was saying, "Yeah, this car's a limousine." And another market was saying it was a sports vehicle. That made it impossible for us to get customers' input into the product after it was out there.[21]

Managers face two opposing pressures when they compete in markets beyond their national boundaries, and these pressures place conflicting demands on their firms as they strive to be competitive.[22] On the one hand, competitive pressures require that firms do what they can to lower unit costs so that consumers will not perceive their product and service offerings as too expensive. This may lead them to consider locating manufacturing facilities where labour costs are low and to develop products that are highly standardized across multiple countries.

In addition to responding to pressures to lower costs, managers must strive to be responsive to local pressures and to tailor their products to the demand of the local market in which they do business. This requires differentiating their offerings and strategies from country to country to reflect consumer tastes and preferences as well as making changes to reflect differences in distribution channels, human resource practices, and governmental regulations. However, since the strategies and tactics to differentiate products and services to local markets can involve additional expenses, a firm's costs will tend to rise.

The two opposing pressures result in four different basic strategies that companies can use to compete in the global marketplace: international, global, multidomestic, and transnational. The strategy that a firm selects depends on the degree of pressure that it is facing with respect to cost reductions and the need to adapt to local markets. Exhibit 7.5 shows the conditions under which each of these strategies would be most appropriate.

Exhibit 7.5
Opposing Pressures and Four Strategies

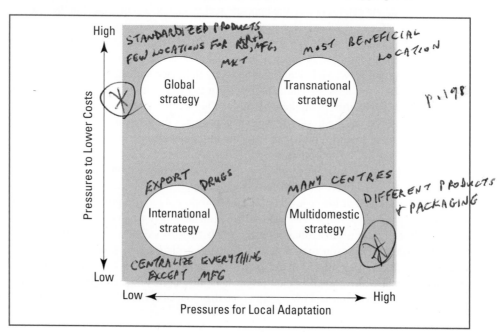

73%

As one would expect, there are advantages and disadvantages associated with each of these strategies. In the following sections, we consider each of the strategies in their basic, or pure, form. In reality, though, firms frequently employ a mix of the elements of all four strategies.

International Strategy

There are a small number of industries in which pressures for both local adaptation and lowering costs are rather low. An extreme example of such an industry is the "orphan" drug industry, which produces medicines for diseases that are severe but affect only a small number of people (for example, the Gaucher disease and Fabry disease). Companies such as Genzyme and Oxford GlycoSciences are active in this segment of the drug industry. There is virtually no need to adapt their products to the local markets. And the pressures to lower costs are low; even though only a few thousand patients are affected, the revenues and margins are significant because patients are charged up to $100,000 per year.

An international strategy is based on diffusion and adaptation of the parent company's knowledge and expertise to foreign markets. Country units are allowed to make some minor adaptations to products and ideas coming from the head office, but they enjoy little independence and autonomy. The primary goal of the strategy is worldwide exploitation of the parent firm's knowledge and capabilities. All sources of core competencies are centralized.

For most of its history, Ericsson, a Swedish telecommunications firm, has followed this strategy. Because its home market (Sweden) was too small to support the R&D effort necessary in the industry, Ericsson built its strategy on its ability to transfer and adapt its innovative products and process technologies to international markets. This strategy of sequential diffusion of innovation that it developed at home helped it to compete successfully against NEC, which followed a global strategy, and ITT, which followed a multidomestic strategy.[23]

The majority of large multinational firms pursued the international strategy in the decades following World War II. These companies centralized R&D and product development but established manufacturing facilities as well as marketing organizations abroad. Companies such as McDonald's and Kellogg are examples of firms still following such a strategy. Although these companies do make some local adaptations, these are of a very limited nature. With increasing pressures to reduce costs due to global competition, especially from low-cost countries, opportunities to successfully employ international strategy are becoming more limited. This strategy is most suitable in situations where a firm has distinctive competencies that local companies in foreign markets lack.

Certain challenges and risks are associated with an international strategy:

♦ Different activities in the value chain typically have different optimal locations. That is, R&D may be optimally located in a country that has an abundant supply of scientists and engineers, whereas assembly may be better conducted in a low-cost location. Nike, for example, designs its shoes in the United States, but all the manufacturing is done in countries like China and Thailand. The international strategy, with its tendency to concentrate most of its activities in one location, fails to take advantage of the benefits of an optimally distributed value chain.

♦ The international strategy is susceptible to higher levels of political risk and currency risk. The company is often too closely identified with a single country. An increase in the value of the currency may suddenly make the product unattractive abroad.

♦ The lack of local responsiveness may result in the alienation of customers. Worse still, the firm's inability to be receptive to new ideas and innovation from its foreign subsidiaries may lead to missed opportunities.

Global Strategy

As indicated in Exhibit 7.5, a firm whose emphasis is on lowering costs tends to follow a global strategy. Competitive strategy is centralized and controlled to a large extent by the corporate office. Since the primary emphasis is on controlling costs, the corporate office strives to achieve a strong level of coordination and integration across the various businesses.[24] Firms following a global strategy strive to offer standardized products and services as well as to locate manufacturing, R&D, and marketing activities in only a few locations.[25]

Bombardier follows a global strategy for its airplanes as well as its public transit systems. Although each individual airline customer may require some customization in terms of fitting the interior of the planes with certain colours and configurations, the planes are, for the most part, standardized and produced in a single location for worldwide distribution. Bombardier also provides its customers with technical support, spare parts, and maintenance, which adhere to global standards.

A global strategy emphasizes economies of scale due to the standardization of products and services and the centralization of operations in a few locations. One advantage of this may be that innovations, which come about through efforts of either a business unit or the corporate office, can be transferred more easily to other locations. Although costs may be lower, the firm following a global strategy may, in general, have to forgo opportunities for revenue growth since it does not invest extensive resources in adapting product offerings from one market to another.

A global strategy is most appropriate when there are strong pressures for reducing costs and comparatively weak pressures for adaptation to local markets. Identifying potential economies of scale becomes an important consideration.[26] Advantages to increased volume may come not only from larger production plants or runs but also from more efficient logistics and distribution networks. Worldwide volume is also especially important in supporting high levels of investment in research and development. As we would expect, many industries requiring high levels of R&D, such as pharmaceuticals, semiconductors, and jet aircraft, follow global strategies.

Another advantage of a global strategy is that it can enable a firm to create a standard level of quality throughout the world. Here is what Tom Siebel, chairman of Siebel Systems, the $2 billion developer of ebusiness application software, has to say about global standardization:

> Our customers—global companies like IBM, Zurich Financial Services, and Citicorp—expect the same high level of service and quality, and the same licensing policies, no matter where we do business with them around the world. Our human resources and legal departments help us create policies that respect local cultures and requirements worldwide, while at the same time maintaining the highest standards. We have one brand, one image, one set of corporate colors, and one set of messages, across every place on the planet. An organization needs central quality control to avoid surprises.[27]

Strategy Spotlight 7.5 discusses the benefits made use of by Gildan, a Canadian firm that markets and manufactures activewear around the world.

There are, of course, some risks associated with a global strategy.[28]

- ♦ A firm can enjoy scale economies only by concentrating scale-sensitive resources and activities in one or few locations. Such concentration, however, becomes a "double-edged sword." For example, if a firm has only one manufacturing facility, it must export its output (e.g., components, subsystems, or finished products) to other markets,

A Global Company with Local Roots: Gildan Activewear

Check the label! Chances are, your school t-shirt and fleece are made by Gildan; across North America and Europe over 50 percent of all decorated activewear sold by and on behalf of thousands of colleges, schools and universities, sports franchises, entertainment venues, summer camps, as well as corporate imprinted promotional golf shirts, are made by this Montreal-based company that Greg and Glenn Chamandy founded some twenty years ago.

From its humble beginnings, Gildan has become a billion dollar, global firm that sources, manufactures, markets, sells, and distributes across the world. The company has become the leading supplier of basic, quality branded activewear for the wholesale imprinted sportswear market. Essentially, it sells blank t-shirts, sports shirts, and fleece in large quantities to wholesalers who have them emblazoned with designs and logos by screenprinters. Consumers purchase Gildan's products in schools, sports events, corporate functions, and travel and tourism destinations. Gildan has also ventured into supplying athletic socks, underwear, and activewear to mass-market retailers in North America and overseas. Having Wal-Mart as one of its major customers has taken Gildan to Latin America, Central America, Europe, and Asia, besides its traditional markets in North America.

Although its headquarters are still in Montreal, few of Gildan's 19,000 employees can be found there as little of the spinning, cutting, sewing, assembly, or manufacturing take place in Canada. While all the strategic decisions are made near Mount Royal, most of the raw materials come from the U.S. and Asia while the spinning takes place in

the southern U.S. and in Central America. The bulk of the manufacturing work is spread across some ten facilities in the Caribbean and Central America. Sales and distribution offices are strategically located in North America, Europe, and Asia. Consider the following figures: 75 percent of Gildan's fixed assets are located in the Caribbean Basin and in Central America, 5 percent can be found in Canada, and approximately 15 percent are in the U.S. The U.S. accounts for 85 percent of sales, in part because the headquarters of Wal-Mart and of other global customers are in the U.S. and thus their sales are booked in that country to be distributed and sold around the world. Canada accounts for just over 4 percent of total sales. Gildan's gross margins are continually affected by the differential exchange rates across its multiple facilities in different countries, as well as by the different levels of efficiency achieved in the various locations. Gildan is a proud Canadian company whose little label adorns millions of college students' favourite activewear, across the world. In the process, Gildan has rewarded its shareholders with continuous earnings growth and three stock splits over the last seven years.

As a postscript to Gildan's global strategy, it is also worth mentioning that the company has come under criticism for closing Canadian, American, and Mexican facilities in order to move operations to Haiti, Honduras, Nicaragua, and the Dominican Republic—all countries that have been frequently connected with sweatshop and unethical labour practices. In response to such criticism, Gildan has committed to adhering to the Fair Labor Association's labour compliance program.

Sources: B. Marotte, "Gildan CEO reducing stake; stock split set," *The Globe and Mail*, May 4, 2007, p. B4; "Gildan Activewear beats expectations, boosts guidance," *The Globe and Mail*, August 4, 2006, p. B5; Maquila Solidarity Network at www..en.maquilasolidarity.org; company annual reports, financial statements and proxy circular; www.gildan.com.

some of which may be a great distance from the operation. Thus, decisions about locating facilities must weigh the potential benefits from concentrating operations in a single location against the higher transportation and tariff costs that result from such concentration.

- ◆ The geographic concentration of any activity may also tend to isolate that activity from the targeted markets. Such isolation could be risky since it may hamper the facility's ability to quickly respond to changes in market conditions and needs.
- ◆ Concentrating an activity in a single location also makes the rest of the firm dependent on that location. Dependency on a sole source implies that, unless the location has world-class competencies, the firm's competitive position can be eroded if problems arise. A European executive of Ford Motor Co., reflecting on the firm's concentration of activities during a global integration program in the mid-1990s, lamented, "Now if you misjudge the market, you are wrong in 15 countries rather than only one."

Multidomestic Strategy

A firm whose emphasis is on differentiating its product and service offerings to adapt to local markets follows a multidomestic strategy. In contrast to a global strategy, whereby decision-making authority tends to be highly centralized in the corporate office, decisions evolving from a multidomestic strategy tend to be more decentralized to permit the firm to tailor its products and respond rapidly to changes in demand. This enables a firm to expand its market and to charge different prices in different markets. For firms following this strategy, differences in language, culture, income levels, customer preferences, and distribution systems are only a few of the many factors that must be considered. Even in the case of relatively standardized products, at least some level of local adaptation is often necessary. Consider Honda motorcycles. Although one could argue that a good product knows no national boundaries, there are subtle differences in ways that a product is used and in what customers expect of it. While Honda uses a common basic technology, it must develop different types of motorcycles for different regions of the world. For example, North Americans primarily use motorcycles for leisure and sports; thus, aggressive looks and high horsepower are key. In Southeast Asia, motorcycles are a basic means of transportation; thus, they require low cost and ease of maintenance. And, in Australia and New Zealand, shepherds use motorcycles to herd sheep; therefore, they demand low-speed torque, rather than high speed and maintenance.[29]

In addition to the products themselves, the way they are packaged must sometimes be adapted to local market conditions. Some consumers in developing countries are likely to have packaging preferences very different from consumers in the West. For example, single-serve packets, or sachets, are very popular in India.[30] They permit consumers to purchase only what they need, experiment with new products, and conserve cash at the same time. Products as varied as detergents, shampoos, pickles, and cough syrup are sold in sachets in India. It is estimated that they make up between 20 and 60 percent of the total volume sold in their categories. In China, sachets are also spreading as a marketing device for such items as shampoos. This brings to the fore the importance of considering all activities in a firm's value chain when determining where local adaptations may be advisable.

Maple Leaf Foods, for example, customizes its prepared meats recipes to meet local tastes in each of the countries in which it sells processed foods. Similarly, La Senza adapts its customer service processes to match the different perceptions about lingerie in each of the 23 countries in which it operates.

Cultural differences may also require a firm to adapt its personnel practices when it expands internationally.[31] Dofasco had to seriously review its famous "Our strength is people" motto and its unique policy of extending empowerment to all employees as it embarked on its venture in Mexico. Mexican workers typically expect more hierarchical structures and are more comfortable under managers who will supervise and make the decisions on all aspects of the daily work life. Dofasco's highly successful strategy and organizational design in Canada is far removed from those principles and has embraced empowerment and delegation of responsibility to the lowest possible levels of the organization. Dofasco had to revisit some of its policies, as well as spend additional resources in the training of its local employees, in order to establish a successful operation in Mexico.

Strategy Spotlight 7.6 describes how multinationals have adapted to the problem of bribery in various countries while adhering to strict federal laws on corrupt practices at home.

Dealing with Bribery Abroad

Most multinational firms experience difficult dilemmas when it comes to the question of adapting rules and guidelines, both formal and informal, while operating in foreign countries. The Foreign Corrupt Practices Act, in fact, makes it illegal for U.S. companies to bribe officials to gain business or facilitate approvals and permissions. Although Canada does not currently have equivalent legislation (except that payments constituting bribes cannot be deducted for tax purposes), the recently introduced Sarbanes-Oxley Act in the U.S. effectively makes these rules applicable to all foreign firms whose shares trade in American stock exchanges.

Unfortunately, in many parts of the world, bribery is a way of life with large payoffs to government officials and politicians necessary to win government contracts. At a lower level, goods won't clear customs unless notionally illegal, but routine and well-accepted, payments are made to officials. What is a foreign company to do in such situations?

Intel follows a strict rule-based definition of bribery as "a thing of value given to someone with the intent of obtaining favorable treatment from the recipient." The company strictly prohibits payments to expedite a shipment through customs if the payment did not "follow applicable rules and regulations, and if the agent gives money or payment in kind to a government official for personal benefit." Texas Instruments, on the other hand, follows a middle approach. They require employees to "exercise good judgment" in questionable circumstances "by avoiding activities that could create even the appearance that our decisions could be compromised." And Analog Devices has set up a policy manager as a consultant to overseas operations. The policy manager does not make decisions for country managers. Instead, the policy manager helps country managers think through the issues and provides information on how the corporate office has handled similar situations in the past.

Source: T. M. Begley and D. P. Boyd, "The Need for a Corporate Global Mind-set," *MIT Sloan Management Review*, Winter 2003, pp. 25–32.

As one might expect, there are some risks associated with a multidomestic strategy. These are listed below.

- Typically, local adaptation of products and services will increase a company's cost structure. In many industries, competition is so intense that most firms can ill afford any competitive disadvantages on the dimension of cost. A key challenge of managers is to determine the trade-off between local adaptation and its cost structure. For example, cost considerations led Procter & Gamble to standardize its diaper design across all European markets. This was done despite research data indicating that Italian mothers, unlike those in other countries, preferred diapers that covered the baby's navel. Later, however, P&G recognized that this feature was critical to these mothers, so the company decided to incorporate this feature for the Italian market despite its adverse cost implications.

- At times, local adaptations, even when well intentioned, may backfire. When the American restaurant chain TGI Fridays entered the South Korean market, it purposely incorporated many local dishes, such as kimchi (hot, spicy cabbage), into its menu. Company analysis of the weak market acceptance indicated that Korean customers anticipated a visit to TGI Fridays as a visit to America. Thus, finding Korean dishes was inconsistent with their expectations.

- Consistent with other aspects of global marketing, the optimal degree of local adaptation evolves over time. In many industry segments, a variety of factors, such as the influence of global media, greater international travel, and declining income disparities across countries, may lead to increasing global standardization. On the other hand, in other industry segments, especially where the product or service can be delivered over the Internet (such as music), the need for even greater customization and local adaptation may increase over time. Firms must recalibrate the need for local adaptation on an ongoing basis; excessive adaptation extracts a price as surely as underadaptation.

Transnational Strategy

Let's briefly review global and multidomestic strategies before we discuss how a transnational strategy can be a vehicle for overcoming the limitations of each of these strategies and, in effect, "getting the best of both worlds."[32]

With a *global strategy*, resources and capabilities are concentrated at the centre of the organization. Authority is highly centralized. Thus, a global company achieves efficiency primarily by exploiting potential scale economies in all of its value-chain activities. Since innovation is highly centralized in the corporate office, there is often a lack of understanding of the changing market needs and production requirements outside the local market, and there are few incentives to adapt.

The *multidomestic strategy* can be considered the exact opposite of the global strategy. Resources are dispersed throughout many countries in which a firm does business, and a subsidiary of the multinational company can more effectively respond to local needs. However, such fragmentation inevitably carries efficiency penalties. Learning also suffers because knowledge is not consolidated in a centralized location and does not flow among the various parts of the company.

A multinational firm following a *transnational strategy* strives to optimize the trade-offs associated with efficiency, local adaptation, and learning.[33] It seeks efficiency not for its own sake but as a means to achieve global competitiveness. It recognizes the importance of local responsiveness but as a tool for flexibility in international operations.[34] Innovations are regarded as an outcome of a larger process of organizational learning that includes the contributions of everyone in the firm.[35] Additionally, a core tenet of the transnational model is that a firm's assets and capabilities are dispersed according to the most beneficial location for a specific activity. Thus, managers avoid the tendency to either concentrate activities in a central location (as with a global strategy) or disperse them across many locations to enhance adaptation (as with a multidomestic strategy). Peter Brabeck, CEO of Nestlé, the giant food company, provides such a perspective:

> We believe strongly that there isn't a so-called global consumer, at least not when it comes to food and beverages. People have local tastes based on their unique cultures and traditions— a good candy bar in Brazil is not the same as a good candy bar in China. Therefore, decision making needs to be pushed down as low as possible in the organization, out close to the markets. Otherwise, how can you make good brand decisions? That said, decentralization has its limits. If you are too decentralized, you can become too complicated—you get too much complexity in your production system. The closer we come to the consumer, in branding, pricing, communication, and product adaptation, the more we decentralize. The more we are dealing with production, logistics, and supply-chain management, the more centralized decision making becomes. After all, we want to leverage Nestlé's size, not be hampered by it.[36]

The Nestlé example illustrates a common approach in determining whether or not to centralize or decentralize a value-chain activity. Typically, primary activities that are "downstream" (e.g., marketing, sales, and service) or closer to the customer tend to require more decentralization in order to adapt to local market conditions. On the other hand, primary activities that are "upstream" (e.g., logistics and operations) or further away from the customer tend to be centralized. This is because there is less need for adapting these activities to local markets and the firm can benefit from economies of scale. Additionally, many support activities, such as information systems and procurement, tend to be centralized in order to increase the potential for economies of scale.

A central philosophy of the transnational organization is enhanced adaptation to all competitive situations as well as flexibility by capitalizing on communication and knowledge flows throughout the organization.[37] A principal characteristic is the integration of unique contributions of all units into worldwide operations. Thus, a joint innovation by headquarters and by one of the overseas units can potentially lead to the development of relatively standardized and yet flexible products and services that are suitable for multiple markets.

Asea Brown Boveri (ABB) is a firm that successfully follows a transnational strategy. ABB, with its home bases in Sweden and Switzerland, illustrates the trend toward cross-national mergers that lead firms to consider multiple headquarters in the future. It is managed as a flexible network of units, and one of management's main functions is the facilitation of information and knowledge flows between units. ABB's subsidiaries have complete responsibility for product categories on a worldwide basis. Such a transnational strategy enables ABB to benefit from access to new markets and the opportunity to utilize and develop resources wherever they may be located.

As with the other strategies, there are some unique risks and challenges associated with a transnational strategy:

◆ The choice of a seemingly optimal location cannot guarantee that the quality and cost of factor inputs (i.e., labour, materials) will be optimal. Managers must ensure that the relative advantage of a location is actually realized, not squandered because of weaknesses in productivity and the quality of internal operations. Ford Motor Co., for example, has benefited from having some of its manufacturing operations in Mexico. While some have argued that the benefits of lower wage rates will be partly offset by lower productivity, this does not always have to be the case. Since unemployment in Mexico is higher than in the United States, Ford can be more selective in its hiring practices for its Mexican operations. And, given the lower turnover among its Mexican employees, Ford can justify a high level of investment in training and development. Thus, the net result could be not only lower wage rates but also higher productivity than in the United States.

◆ Although knowledge transfer can be a key source of competitive advantages, it does not take place "automatically." In order for knowledge to be effectively transferred from one subsidiary to another, it is important for the source of the knowledge, the target units, and the corporate headquarters to recognize the potential value of such unique know-how. Given that there can be significant geographic, linguistic, and cultural distances separating subsidiaries, the realization of knowledge transfer can become very difficult to achieve. Firms must create mechanisms to systematically and routinely uncover the opportunities for knowledge transfer.

Exhibit 7.6
Strengths and
Limitations of
Various Strategies

Strategy	Strengths	Limitations
International	◆ Leveraging and diffusion of parent's knowledge and core competencies. ◆ Lower costs because of less need to tailor products and services. ◆ Greater level of world-wide coordination.	◆ Limited ability to adapt to local markets. ◆ Inability to take advantage of new ideas and innovations occurring in local markets.
Global	◆ Strong integration across various businesses. ◆ Standardization leading to higher economies of scale, which lowers costs. ◆ Potential to create uniform standards of quality throughout the world.	◆ Limited ability to adapt to local markets. ◆ Concentration of activities leading to increased dependence on a single facility. ◆ Potential for higher tariffs and transportation costs from single locations.
Multidomestic	◆ Ability to adapt products and services to local market conditions. ◆ Ability to detect potential opportunities for attractive niches in a given market, enhancing revenue.	◆ Less ability to realize cost savings through scale economies. ◆ Greater difficulty in transferring knowledge across countries. ◆ Potential for "overadaptation" as conditions change.
Transnational	◆ Ability to attain economies of scale. ◆ Ability to adapt to local markets. ◆ Ability to locate activities in optimal locations. ◆ Ability to increase knowledge flows and learning.	◆ Unique challenges in determining optimal locations of activities to ensure cost and quality. ◆ Unique managerial challenges in fostering knowledge transfer.

Exhibit 7.6 summarizes the relative advantages and disadvantages of international, global, multidomestic, and transnational strategies.

Having discussed the types of strategies that firms pursue in international markets and their relative advantages and disadvantages, let's now turn to the types of entry modes that companies may use to enter international markets.

ENTRY MODES OF INTERNATIONAL EXPANSION

A firm has many options available to it when it decides to expand into international markets. Because of the challenges associated with such entry, many firms first start on a small scale and then increase their level of investment and risk as they gain greater experience with the overseas market in question.[38]

Exhibit 7.7 illustrates a wide variety of modes of foreign entry, including exporting, licensing, franchising, strategic alliances, joint ventures, and wholly owned subsidiaries.[39] As the exhibit indicates, the various types of entry form a continuum that ranges from exporting (low investment and risk, low control) to a wholly owned subsidiary (high investment and risk, high control).[40]

Admittedly, there can, at times, be frustrations and setbacks as a firm evolves its international entry strategy from exporting to more expensive types, including wholly owned subsidiaries. According to the CEO of a large U.S. specialty chemical company,

> In the end, we always do a better job with our own subsidiaries; sales improve, and we have greater control over the business. But we still need local distributors for entry, and we are still searching for strategies to get us through the transitions without battles over control and performance.[41]

Exporting

Exporting consists of producing goods in one country to sell in another. This entry strategy enables a firm to invest the least amount of resources in terms of its product, its organization, and its overall corporate strategy. Not surprisingly, many host countries dislike this entry strategy because it provides less local employment than other modes of entry.[42]

Multinationals often stumble onto a stepwise strategy for penetrating markets, beginning with the exporting of products. This often results in a series of unplanned actions to increase sales revenues. As the pattern recurs with entries into subsequent markets, this approach, named a "beachhead strategy," becomes official policy in many organizations.

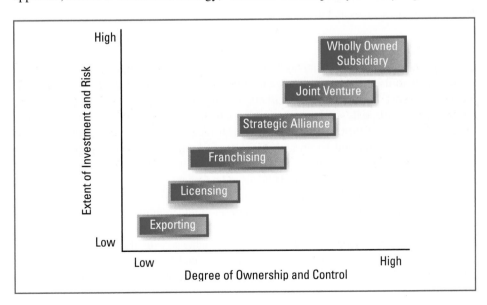

Exhibit 7.7
Entry Modes for International Expansion

Such an approach definitely has its advantages. After all, firms start from scratch in sales and distribution when they enter new markets. Because many foreign markets are nationally regulated and dominated by networks of local intermediaries, firms need to partner with local distributors to benefit from their valuable expertise and knowledge of their own markets. Multinationals generally recognize that they cannot master local business practices, meet regulatory requirements, hire and manage local personnel, or gain access to potential customers without some form of local partnership.

In addition to the need to partner with local firms, multinationals also want to minimize their own risk. They do this by hiring local distributors and investing very little in the undertaking. In essence, the firm gives control of strategic marketing decisions to the local partners—much more control than they would be willing to give up in their home market.

As one might expect, exporting is a relatively inexpensive way to enter foreign markets. However, it can still have significant downsides. In a study of 250 instances in which multinational firms used local distributors to implement their exporting entry strategy, the results were dismal. In the vast majority of the cases, the distributors were bought (to increase control) by the multinational firm or fired. By contrast, successful distributors shared two common characteristics:

- They carried product lines that complemented, rather than competed with, the multinational's products.
- They behaved as if they were business partners with the multinationals. They shared market information with the corporations, they initiated projects with distributors in neighbouring countries, and they suggested initiatives in their own or nearby markets. Additionally, these distributors took on risk themselves by investing in areas such as training, information systems, and advertising and promotion in order to increase the business of their multinational partners.

The key point is the importance of developing collaborative, win-win relationships.

To ensure more control over operations without incurring significant risks, many firms have used licensing and franchising as a mode of entry. Let's now discuss these and their relative advantages and disadvantages.

Licensing

Licensing as an entry mode enables a company to receive a royalty or fee in exchange for the right to use its trademark, patent, trade secret, or other valuable item of intellectual property.[43] In international markets, the advantage is that the firm granting the licence incurs little risk since it does not have to invest any significant resources into the country itself. In turn, the licensee (the firm receiving the licence) gains access to the trademark, patent, and so on and is able to potentially create competitive advantages. In many cases, the country also benefits from the product being manufactured locally. For example, Yoplait yogurt is licensed by General Mills from Sodima, a French co-operative, for sale in the United States, and it is produced and sold by Ultima Foods in Canada. Licensing technology is very common in telecommunications, software, and pharmaceuticals.

There are, of course, some important disadvantages with this type of entry. For example, the licensor gives up control of its product and forgoes potential revenues and profits. Furthermore, the licensee may eventually become so familiar with the patent and trade secrets that it may become a competitor; in effect, the licensee may make some modifications to the product and manufacture and sell it independently of the licensor without having to pay a royalty fee. This situation is aggravated in countries that have relatively weak laws to protect intellectual property. Additionally, if the licensee selected by the multinational firm turns out to be a poor choice, the brand name and reputation of the product may be tarnished.[44]

Franchising

Although licensing and franchising are both forms of contractual arrangements, franchise contracts generally include a broader range of factors in an operation and involve a longer time period. Franchising has the advantage of limiting the risk exposure that a firm has in overseas markets while expanding the revenue base of the parent company. The other side of the coin is that the multinational firm receives only a portion of the revenues, in the form of franchise fees, instead of the entire revenue—as would be the case if the firm set up the operation itself (e.g., a restaurant) through direct investment.

As a vehicle for international expansion, franchising remains an overwhelmingly American form of business, although some notable examples from Canada include Tim Hortons, La Senza, and The Keg. La Senza, as a case in point, operates some 280 corporate stores in Canada but has resorted to franchising for its international expansion. It has established relationships with master franchisees in each of 23 countries, who have built and operate some 230 stores according to La Senza's directions. Today, the company sells its collection of lingerie products through those stores—from the UK to Indonesia. This strategic choice has allowed La Senza to expand internationally and enter all those countries much faster and with significantly less capital requirements as compared to attempting to do it all on its own. According to a recent survey, more than 400 U.S. franchisers have international exposure.[45] This is greater than the combined totals of the next four largest franchiser home countries—France, the United Kingdom, Mexico, and Austria.

Strategic Alliances and Joint Ventures

Strategic alliances can take many forms, including joint research and development, joint exploration initiatives, joint production, or co-distribution of two partners' products. Frequently, a multinational will engage in a strategic alliance with a local firm to produce a product for the local market, utilizing the multinational's technology and brand name but the local firm's management and market knowledge. Unlike licensing, though, the multinational retains substantially more control over the strategic and operational decisions. Joint ventures are a unique form of strategic alliance in that they entail the creation of a third legal entity, owned by the partners, with a clear mandate and a separate organizational structure.

As we discussed in Chapter 6, strategic alliances have been effective in helping firms to increase revenues and reduce costs as well as to enhance learning and diffuse technologies. They enable firms to share the risks as well as the potential returns. Also, by gaining exposure to new sources of knowledge and technologies, such partnerships can help firms develop core competencies that can lead to competitive advantages in the marketplace.[46] Finally, entering into partnerships with host country firms can provide

Microsoft's Partnerships in East Asia

Microsoft is forming strategic alliances and joint ventures with companies in East Asia. Rather than competing with existing firms, Microsoft has entered several countries by co-operating with these firms. It has entered the Japanese and Taiwanese markets by joining efforts with mobile phone operator NTT DoCoMo, which has already established itself as a successful provider of cellular phone service through its Mobimagic service. By teaming with Microsoft, both companies stand to profit by integrating Microsoft's software applications, such as email, into the existing service of cellphone subscribers. Akio Fujii, head of new product development for Microsoft Japan, envisions adding a Web browser to these cellphone services.

Another partner, GigaMedia, has 100,000 broadband subscribers offering sports, music, news, video-on-demand, as well as online karaoke. By hooking up with Microsoft, GigaMedia is now able to move its services from personal computers (PCs) to televisions, with the television serving as the monitor and a set-top box similar to a cable television box functioning as the PC. In exchange for its contribution, Microsoft gleans 2 percent of GigaMedia's broadband subscriber fees and significant revenue from

GigaMedia's ecommerce sales. In a similar move, the Koos Group, owner of KG Telecom, the second largest cellphone operator in Taiwan, has joined ranks with Microsoft to integrate Internet capabilities on the televisions and cellphones of subscribers.

Microsoft has taken strategic moves to blunt competition from Palm by joining forces in an alliance with Psion in London, one of Palm's chief rivals. Microsoft has also reduced Palm's competitive threat in the cellphone market by partnering with Stockholm's Ericsson, a leading manufacturer of mobile phones.

Microsoft has utilized forward-thinking vision to achieve win-win relationships through several joint ventures and strategic alliances throughout the globe. By doing so, it is successfully exporting its influence from an entrenched position in the United States to a global presence. This is good not only for Microsoft and its shareholders; the shareholders of other firms around the world stand to prosper from the co-operative agreements Microsoft has forged with their firms. In addition, the added competition from a powerhouse like Microsoft forces other international firms to compete for efficiencies, thus increasing the potential for overall economic prosperity.

Source: N. Chowdhury, "Gates & Co. Attack Asia," *Fortune.com*, April 17, 2000; and G. Mariano, "Palm to Groove with Liquid Audio Music," *New York Times Online*, April 11, 2001.

very useful information on local market tastes, competitive conditions, legal matters, and cultural nuances.[47] Strategy Spotlight 7.7 discusses how Microsoft has used a variety of partnerships to strengthen its position in East Asia.

Despite the potential benefits, managers must be aware of the risks associated with strategic alliances and joint ventures and how they can be minimized.[48] First, there must be well-articulated goals to guide the strategic alliance, and the partners must agree on a set of related, clearly defined criteria to measure progress. A well-defined strategy must be strongly supported by the organizations that are party to the partnership. Otherwise, the firms may work at cross-purposes and not achieve any of their goals. Second, there must be a clear understanding of the capabilities and resources that will be central to the partnership. Without such understanding, there will be fewer opportunities for learning and developing the competencies that could lead to competitive advantages. Third, trust is a vital element. Phasing in the relationship between alliance partners permits them to get to know each other better and develop trust. According to Philip Benton, Jr., former president of Ford Motor Co. (which has been involved in multiple international partnerships over the years), "The first time two companies work together, the chances of succeeding are very slight. But once you find ways to work together, all sorts of opportunities arise." Without trust, one party may take advantage of the other by, for example, withholding its fair share of resources and gaining access to privileged information through unethical (or illegal) means. Fourth, cultural issues, which could potentially lead to conflict and dysfunctional behaviours, need to be addressed. An organization's culture is the set of values, beliefs, and attitudes that influence the behaviour and goals of its employees. Thus, recognizing cultural differences as well as striving to develop elements of a "common culture" for the partnership is vital. Without a unifying culture, it will become difficult to combine and leverage the kinds of resources that are increasingly important in knowledge-intensive organizations (as discussed in Chapter 4).[49]

As we know, not all partnerships are successful, for a variety of reasons. One of the most famous unsuccessful partnerships in recent business history was the joint venture formed by General Motors (GM) and Daewoo Motor Co. GM sought cheap labour in Korea while Daewoo wanted to export automobiles. The two companies joined forces in 1986 to manufacture one of GM's new designs, the Pontiac LeMans. Things did not work out as planned. The first cars had quality problems. LeMans sales did not achieve their expected targets and Korea's cheap labour quickly vanished with economic prosperity. The dollar declined and there were increasingly strong demands by the newly formed labour unions. Daewoo management was convinced that the car's problems could be solved if sales would improve, believing in the benefits of the experience curve and being willing to take a longer-term perspective. GM wanted immediate results. GM also refused to allow Daewoo to sell cars in Europe, another long term objective of the Korean company. GM saw this as competition to its Opel division that was already covering the market there. The partnership was dissolved in 1990. It clearly had failed from the start, due to minimal understanding of each other's objectives and a lack of effort to re-evaluate plans when problems appeared. [50]

The success of a firm's alliance should not be left to chance.[51] To improve their odds of success, many companies have carefully documented alliance-management knowledge by creating guidelines and manuals to help them manage specific aspects of the entire alliance life cycle (such as partner selection and alliance negotiation and contracting). For example, Lotus Corp. (part of IBM) created what it calls its "35 rules of thumb" to manage each phase of an alliance, from formation to termination. Hewlett-Packard developed 60 different tools and templates, which it placed in a 300-page manual, for guiding decision making in specific alliance situations. The manual included such items as a template for making the business case for an alliance, a partner evaluation form, a negotiations template outlining the roles and responsibilities of different departments, a list of the ways to measure alliance performance, and an alliance termination checklist.

Wholly Owned Subsidiaries

A wholly owned subsidiary is a business in which a multinational company owns 100 percent of the stock. There are two means by which a firm can establish a wholly owned subsidiary. It can either acquire an existing company in the home country or it can develop a totally new operation. The latter is often referred to as a "greenfield venture." Establishing a wholly owned subsidiary is the most expensive and risky of the various entry modes. However, as expected, it can also yield the highest returns. In addition, it provides the multinational company with the greatest degree of control over all activities, including manufacturing, marketing, distribution, and technology development.[52]

Stantec Inc., an Edmonton-based engineering and architectural firm, is growing by acquiring design firms in second-tier markets in the U.S. in preparation for a major push into primary centres such as New York City and Chicago.[53] Stantec's CEO, Tony Franceschini, is betting on a global consolidation that will see a handful of giant firms offering a range of services to clients around the world and is determined to be among the top ten global design firms in a decade. Opening offices in different markets would simply take too long.

Wholly owned subsidiaries as well as direct investment in greenfield ventures are most appropriate when a firm already has the necessary knowledge and capabilities to leverage across multiple locations in many countries. Examples range from restaurants to semiconductor manufacturers. To lower costs, for example, Intel Corporation builds semiconductor plants throughout the world—all of which use virtually the same blueprint. In establishing wholly owned subsidiaries, knowledge can be further leveraged by the hiring of managers and professionals from the firm's home country, often seeking out talent from competitors.

As noted, wholly owned subsidiaries are typically the most expensive and risky of the various modes for entering international markets. With franchising, strategic alliances, or joint ventures, the risk is shared with the firm's partners. In the case of wholly owned subsidiaries, the entire risk is assumed by the parent company. The risks associated with doing business in a new country (i.e., political, cultural, and legal) can be lessened by hiring local talent.

One should not consider entry strategies as a clear-cut progression from exporting through to the creation of wholly owned subsidiaries. Many firms, such as La Senza or The Keg, follow rather unique entry paths. For example, The Keg belongs in the casual dining restaurant segment, where one finds mostly franchise operations, especially those that move internationally; yet the company has chosen to only open own stores in the U.S. Although this decision has certainly slowed its expansion, it has ensured that the company can maintain the atmosphere, unique service, and knowledgeable staff that have allowed it to develop a loyal following in its Canadian operations. Moreover, international expansion is not the exclusive purview of large firms that have first succeeded in their local markets. Many medium and small Canadian firms, such as Lingo Media and Hydrogenics, with little local presence at home, have directed all their efforts to overseas markets.

Summary

We live in a highly interconnected global community where many of the best opportunities for growth and profitability lie beyond the boundaries of a company's home country. Along with the opportunities, of course, there are many risks associated with diversification into global markets.

The first section of the chapter addressed the factors that determine a nation's competitiveness in a particular industry. The framework was developed by Michael Porter of Harvard University and was based on a four-year study that explored the competitive success of ten leading trading nations. The four factors, collectively termed the "diamond of national advantage," are factor conditions; demand conditions; related and supporting industries; and firm strategy, structure, and rivalry.

The discussion of Porter's "diamond" helped, in essence, to set the broader context for exploring competitive advantage at the firm level. In the second section, we discussed the primary motivations and the potential risks associated with international expansion. The primary motivations include increasing the size of the potential market for the firm's products and services, achieving economies of scale, extending the life cycle of the firm's products, and optimizing the location for every activity in the value chain. On the other hand, the key risks include political and economic risks, currency risks, and management risks. Management risks are the challenges associated with responding to the inevitable differences that exist across countries such as customs, culture, language, customer preferences, and distribution systems.

Next, we addressed how firms can go about attaining competitive advantage in global markets. We began by discussing the two opposing forces—cost reduction and adaptation to local markets—which managers must contend with when entering global markets. The relative importance of these two factors plays a major part in determining which of the four basic types of strategies to select: international, global, multidomestic, or transnational. The chapter covered the benefits and risks associated with each type of strategy.

The final section discussed the six types of entry strategies that managers may undertake when entering international markets. The key trade-off in each of these strategies is the level of investment or risk versus the level of control. The strategies include (in order of their progressively greater investment, risk, and control) exporting, licensing, franchising, strategic alliances and joint ventures, and wholly owned subsidiaries. The relative benefits and risks associated with each of these strategies were addressed.

Summary Review Questions

1. What are some of the advantages and disadvantages associated with a firm's expansion into international markets?

2. What are the four factors described in Porter's diamond of national advantage? How do the four factors explain why some industries in a given country are more successful than others?

3. Explain the two opposing forces—cost reduction and adaptation to local markets—that firms must deal with when they go global.

4. There are four basic strategies for achieving competitive advantage in global markets—international, global, multidomestic, and transnational. What are the advantages and disadvantages associated with each?

5. Describe the basic entry strategies that firms have available when they enter international markets. What are the relative advantages and disadvantages of each?

Experiential Exercise

1. Canada is considered a world leader in the mining industry. Using Porter's "diamond" framework for national competitiveness, explain the success of this industry.

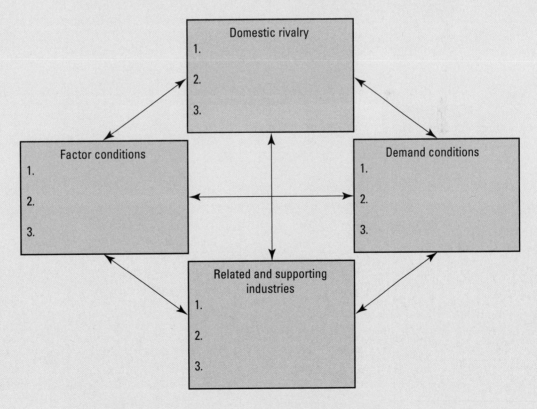

2. What elements of your analysis of the mining industry do not fit neatly inside the diamond? What adjustments to the framework would you suggest?

Application Questions Exercises

1. Data on the "competitiveness of nations" can be found on www.imd.ch/wcy/ranking/. This Web site provides a ranking on a variety of criteria for 49 countries. How might Porter's diamond of national advantage help to explain the rankings for some of these countries for certain industries that interest you?
2. The Internet has lowered the entry barriers for smaller firms that wish to diversify into international markets. Why is this so? Provide an example.
3. Many firms fail when they enter into strategic alliances with firms that link up with companies based in other countries. What are some reasons for this failure? Provide an example.

Ethics Questions

1. Over the past few decades, many North American and European firms have relocated their operations to countries that pay lower wages, such as Mexico, India, and China. What are some of the ethical issues that such actions may raise?
2. As shareholders, pensioners, and mutual fund holders, Canadians, Americans, and Europeans want the firms whose stock they own to maximize profits and pay dividends. As employees and members of the local community, they also want to keep the factories and offices in their own countries. What contradictions and challenges do these positions raise for the executives and managers of global firms?
3. Business practices and customs vary throughout the world. What are some of the ethical issues concerning payments that must be made in a foreign country to obtain business opportunities?

Chapter 8 Disruptive Environments and Digital Business Strategies:
Leveraging Internet and eBusiness Capabilities

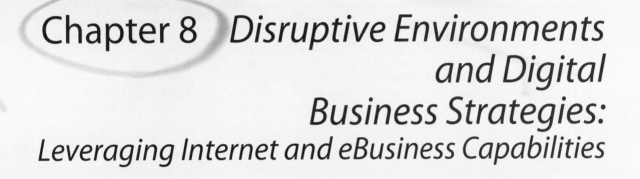

LEARNING OBJECTIVES

After reading this chapter, you should have a good understanding of:

LO 1 → how the Internet is disrupting industry structures and how Internet technologies are affecting the five competitive forces.

LO 2 → why use of Internet technologies is more important to achieving competitive advantage than the technologies themselves.

LO 3 → how firms are using Internet technologies to add value and achieve unique advantages.

LO 4 → how firms can improve their competitive position by effectively deploying ebusiness strategies.

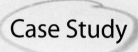

On both sides of the northwest corner of the border between the U.S. and Canada, and almost at the same time in 1995, two separate revolutions took place that would forever change the way books are bought and sold in the world.[1] On the south side, from his garage in Seattle, Washington, Jeff Bezos founded Amazon.com on the idea that a book is a standard product whose content does not change. The wide variety of books and their different subject categories are easy to promote; books can be readily viewed online, and customers do not need to touch or try on a book to decide if it is to their liking; and books are easy to handle, package, and mail. Bezos set up his online bookstore and, within months, thousands of titles could be viewed and bought online with the click of a mouse by anyone, anywhere. The books were shipped instantly to arrive at the customer's doorstep within a few days, even overnight if preferred—and all of this at better than local bookstore prices. In effect, the Internet brought a bookstore with unlimited shelf space to every home. Customers could browse at their leisure, read reviews, and compare titles without leaving their home. They were no longer constrained by the physical boundaries, inventory capacity, or personal tastes of their local bookseller. Amazon grew to become the largest online retailer, surpassing $15 billion in sales of books, along with sales of CDs, DVDs, and toys.

On the other side of the border in Victoria, British Columbia, the proprietor of Timeless Books, Cathy Waters, had a different headache. Her clients wanted hard-to-find titles that her little bookstore could neither afford to stock nor easily find. At most, Timeless Books carried 4,000 titles, not atypical of a neighbourhood store that had to juggle both popular titles that paid the rent and those rare requests. Her solution: place a half-page advertisement in an industry publication, asking if fellow book dealers happened to have any of those hard-to-find titles in stock. Soon, the responses started coming in, and before long her desk was drowning in notes and postcards. Luckily for Cathy, both her husband Keith and their friends Rick and Vivian Pura were well-versed in computers and information technology. They soon designed a program that would automatically match the eager customer on the one side with the willing vendor on the other side to close the deal. Thus, the first book-listing service was created. Advanced Book Exchange, or Abebooks as it came to be called, was launched in early 1996. Sellers were allowed to list their titles and set their own prices. At first, just five local booksellers listed their titles but soon the service claimed over two million rare and used books listed, and shortly thereafter the 1,000th bookseller was signed up. While business was brisk from the start, it took an article in a U.S. national newspaper to turn the venture into an overnight success. The servers couldn't cope with the volume: thousands of hits per day and over 12 million titles listed from over 5,000 dealers. Abebooks had completely transformed the used and rare books industry.

Very much like Amazon.com, it survived and prospered beyond the burst of the tech bubble in 2000. Today, Abebooks completes over $200 million in transactions between sellers and buyers across the globe, and it lists and cross-lists over 100 million titles in an ever-expanding virtual supply of rare, antique, new, and used books, available to the broadest customer base from around the world.

Abebooks and Amazon revolutionized a mature industry that had changed little since the original invention of the printing press, back in 1450. Until about 10 years ago, bookstores had been very stable and predictable businesses, with reasonable margins, few entry and exit barriers, fairly strong suppliers, and limited substitutes. Stores would offer a limited assortment of titles that shopkeepers felt would be of interest. The industry had few bases for consolidation or significant economies of scale, making it a prime example of a fragmented service business. Independent stores on main streets, in shopping malls, and in every neighbourhood's shopping district had dutifully catered to local clients. Even a few big, national chains that had appeared, such as Barnes & Noble and Borders in the U.S. as well as Coles in Canada, controlled less than 10 percent of the market. On the publishers' side, the big firms dominated the industry and very much dictated the terms of the game. Based on Porter's five-forces model of industry analysis, one would readily acknowledge the strength of the suppliers' power and the intensity of rivalry among the fragmented booksellers. Yet, in a short period of time, the Internet succeeded in completely changing the industry. Not only did online sales produce a $25 billion business dominated by a couple of companies with instant presence across the world, but traditional bookselling also changed drastically. The more efficient, bricks-and-mortar booksellers developed parallel online businesses and moved aggressively to assert their power with publishers, developing business models that would allow them to compete on selection and price both online and on the main street. Since then, large, "big box" bookstores, such as Chapters and Indigo, have come to dominate the industry, pushing most independents out of the business. With only a few exceptions, such as Toronto's Book City which has found its niche in appealing to bibliophiles, thousands of neighbourhood bookstores have disappeared and the industry has consolidated. Today, Amazon, Barnes & Noble, and Indigo control over 70 percent of bookselling both online and offline. Abebooks dominates the used and rare online book sales based on the self-reinforcing principle that has also made eBay and other virtual markets so successful. The more sellers and buyers one can bring to a Web site, the more attractive it becomes for additional sellers and buyers to join the same site.

The Internet had other unintended consequences on book publishing and selling. By going online, bookstores broke free of the tight grip of publishers, while publishers could by-pass booksellers and go directly to customers. By using the Internet to appeal to niche markets, 63,000 small publishers with revenues of less than $50 million each generated $14.2 billion in sales in 2005—over half of the industry's total sales. At the same time, while many booksellers tried to emulate Amazon's online success, the dot-com crash of 2000 saw most of them disappear; many were too small to be noticed and specialty bookstores, by focusing on unique categories of books, were not able to achieve the scale that would give them the negotiating power and price advantages necessary to compete with the depth of listings offered by Amazon.

← **LO 1**

The carnage among traditional and online booksellers and the unique success of Amazon and Abebooks amply illustrate both the new opportunities and the pitfalls of doing business in the digital economy. Entry into the fast-moving Internet economy does not guarantee success. Nevertheless, the business world has embraced the Internet and other digital technologies at breathtaking speed. The revolution in information and communication technologies has altered the structure of the world economy.[2]

The growth in Internet use has been especially rapid compared with the adoption rate of other technologies. It took decades for radio, television, and other popular twentieth-century technologies to be adopted, but the Internet boasted 50 million users in less than five years. Penetration rates have surpassed 80 percent in North America and Western Europe while there exist over 1.5 billion users worldwide, a penetration rate of approximately 22 percent.[3] On the retail side, revenues from business-to-consumer (B2C) ecommerce have been steadily growing. According to a study by Shop.org and Forrester Research, online retail sales reached $76 billion in 2002 and topped the $100 billion mark in 2004, representing 4.5 percent of total retail sales.[4] During the 2004 holiday season alone, 3.5 million Canadians spent over $800 million on clothes, books, and DVDs. Overall, some 44 percent of all Canadians have tried ecommerce, and the numbers show that most first-time buyers go back for more. However, the real impact of the Internet is in business-to-business (B2B) ecommerce, which grew to $4.3 trillion worldwide in 2005, according to International Data Corporation (IDC). Moreover, business process outsourcing (BPO), consisting of services ranging from online order management to online payroll and benefits administration, has grown worldwide to over $250 billion. Giga Information Group Inc. reported that the global cost savings from business use of ecommerce would grow beyond $1.25 trillion by the end of the decade.

The impact of the information and communications technologies revolution goes beyond the Internet.

At a more basic level, it is the shift from analogue to digital technologies that is responsible for so many new IT capabilities. Analogue was once the primary technology for conveying information such as music recordings, voice communications, and television signals. It represents a type of physical information that requires large amounts of storage and often works only with hard-wired equipment. By contrast, digital technologies use information in the form of bits—that is, electronic signals expressed as either on or off, one or zero. These bits can be stored in tiny chips, easily reproduced and transferred rapidly and wirelessly.[5] Many technologies have made the switch from analogue to digital—phones, photographs, television signals, information storage, and even books. Digital technology capabilities have become a major driver in today's economy.

All of these technology-driven initiatives—the Internet, wireless communications, and other digital technologies—are having a significant impact on the economy. They are doing so by changing the ways businesses interact with each other and with consumers. This has not only created an environment in which businesses must perform at a higher level—faster, smarter, cheaper—but it has also created many new business opportunities. Strategy Spotlight 8.1 describes two revolutionary ways that companies have employed the Internet within very traditional industries, and the tremendous results they achieved.

In response to such innovative applications and the revolutions they have created, some writers have claimed that familiar business terms, such as "competitive advantage," "industry analysis," and "long-term customer relations," are relics of a bygone era, icons of the "Old Economy."[6] Others, however, contend that the Internet has created a new climate for business in which sound principles of strategic management are *more*, not less, important.[7] It appears that the transformative power of the Internet is, in fact, being felt unevenly across the economy. Information-intensive industries, such as financial services, entertainment, health care, and education, could be radically transformed. In other sectors, such as automobile manufacturing, steel, and pulp and paper, the changes are more measured. Ecommerce spending continues to grow in several other categories, including travel services, clothing, computer hardware and software, and electronics. Even within those categories, though, big changes are not happening overnight, in part because of institutional and regulatory barriers, vested interests, inertia, as well as human nature.

Among the most fundamental shifts that have arisen from the ubiquity of the Internet are changes in competitive practices and interaction between consumers and the companies they do business with, things that critically influence the decisions and choices companies make about product design, services, and features.[8] Manufacturing systems are more flexible, databases can be updated instantaneously, and alternative choices can be evaluated in real time. As a result, customers can be involved, from the beginning, in developing products and are able to personally experience and influence the value creation process in what has come to be called a *co-creation process*, a process that blurs the lines between suppliers, customers, and the firm. Boeing designed its latest planes in collaboration with its suppliers and its major customers. Teams of engineers from all three sides worked together to finalize specifications, select components and materials, make choices about features, and resolve trade-offs. Deere&Company, the farm machinery manufacturer, has equipped its tractors with global positioning systems and biosensors that monitor soil conditions, analyze crops, and diagnose equipment problems in advance. Its service and maintenance teams can be dispatched before the farmer even knows that there might be something wrong with the equipment.

Early Internet Applications in Traditional Industries

Goldcorp, among the world's largest gold mining companies and headquartered in Toronto, credits the Internet for its most successful mine, one of the lowest-cost producers in the world. According to conventional wisdom, the Red Lake mine in Northern Ontario was all but depleted of any ore worth mining. Robert McEwen, Goldcorp's CEO, took a gamble in 1995 by posting the mine's geological data on the Web and inviting geologists from around the world to analyze the information and propose ideas about its prospects and the most likely positions of higher-grade gold. A pair of Australian engineers offered what amounted to a brilliant insight and a novel analysis of the data, which pointed to new, valuable high-grade zones of gold mineralization. They were awarded a prize of half a million dollars, and the mine soon started producing gold at below $100 dollars cash cost per ounce, making Goldcorp an instant force in the global gold mining industry.

Another resource based firm, British Petroleum (BP) has also used the Internet and digital technologies to transform its business. Led by John Leggate, BP's group vice-president for digital business, the company has pursued an aggressive policy of implementing Internet-based capabilities. The effort has paid off in several key areas:

- **Finding Crude.** Instead of sending teams to far-off exploration targets, BP scientists now gather in any of 15 data centres around the globe to view digital 3-D images of drilling sites sent over the Web. *Payoff:* Up to $250 million in annual savings.

- **Buying Gear.** BP's divisions used to bid separately for everything from hard hats to drill bits. In 2001, BP bought 4 percent of its $25 billion in purchases online. *Payoff:* $100 million in savings by identifying low-cost suppliers.

- **Getting Smarter.** All employees have personalized Web pages listing their areas of expertise. This helps managers tap into BP's reservoir of knowledge. *Payoff:* In one case, engineers in the Caribbean saved $600,000 by adopting a drilling process developed in Norway just days earlier.

- **Selling Stuff.** BP is spending $200 million to link service stations to the Net. Web-linked gas pumps and in-store ekiosks let customers check traffic and weather or get free driving directions. *Payoff:* BP hopes that, within five years, this will help generate half of its service station retail sales from goods other than fuel, up from 20 percent of its $2.6 billion in total sales in 2000.

Sources: From a presentation by Robert McEwen to the Schulich School of Business, York University, Toronto, Ontario, November 16, 2004; Goldcorp Inc.'s annual report and Web site; W. Echikson, "When oil gets connected," *BusinessWeek e.biz*, December 3, 2001, EB28–EB30; and British Petroleum, "BP unveils Chicago's gas station of the future," May 14, 2002, www.bp.com.

The changes caused by the Internet and the digital economy have made strategizing more challenging. Rapid improvements in technology as well as globalization, shifting patterns of demand, and uncertainty about costs and revenues point to the importance of strategy formulation. Successful implementation may be even more difficult in the Internet era because of the rapid changes and uncertainty surrounding the new technologies. The Internet phenomenon has heightened the need for effective strategic management. However, the keys to success involve more than just putting up a Web site or creating a dot-com enterprise. Digital business success requires a new strategic perspective that builds on the possibilities provided by information technologies and permits Internet connectivity to transform the way business is conducted. The dot-com crash provides an important lesson about the strategic implications of the Internet: it is the actual use of the Internet for profitable transactions, not the technology itself, that matters to a company's bottom line. Yet, it is the technology that is making it possible to conduct new types of transactions and enhance interactions with nearly every important stakeholder—customers, suppliers, employees, shareholders, competitors, government regulators, and others. Thus, the Internet presents a new strategic challenge: how to make the best use of the new technology without losing sight of important business fundamentals.

HOW THE INTERNET IS AFFECTING THE FIVE COMPETITIVE FORCES

The Threat of New Entrants

In most industries, new entrants are a bigger threat now because information and communication technologies have lowered barriers to entry. For example, it is relatively inexpensive for a new firm to create a Web presence that is as impressive as the Web site of a larger or more established competitor. Unlike the traditional "main street" businesses, where customers could assess the firm's size and quality by walking in the door, those businesses that exist in cyberspace can create an image that makes them seem like strong competitors, regardless of their actual size or the quality of their operations. In effect, scale economies may be less important in this context, and new entrants can go to market with lower capital costs. Strategy Spotlight 8.2 demonstrates how the Internet can serve to diminish the scale economies associated with advertising and marketing costs. Virtual presence is now possible in multiple markets as there is no need for bricks-and-mortar investments, and a single Web site can serve markets across the world as instant translations remove even the traditional language barriers.

Beyond appearances, businesses launched on the Internet may enjoy savings on other traditional expenses such as office rent, sales-force salaries, printing, and postage. A new cyber-entrant can use the savings provided by the Internet to charge lower prices and compete on price, despite the incumbents' scale advantages. As well, because Internet technologies make it possible for young firms to provide services that are equivalent or superior to an incumbent, a new entrant may be able to serve a market more effectively, with more personalized services and greater attention to product details. A new firm may be able to build a reputation in its niche and charge premium prices. By so doing, it can capture small pieces of an incumbent's business and erode profitability.

Another potential benefit of Web-based business is access to distribution channels. Manufacturers or distributors that can reach potential outlets for their products more efficiently by means of the Internet may be encouraged to enter markets that were previously closed to them.

The Bargaining Power of Buyers

The Internet and wireless technologies may increase buyer power by providing customers with more information to make buying decisions, giving them more choices and lowering switching costs. By the same token, such technologies diminish the power of traditional intermediaries such as wholesalers and distributors. The Internet likely increases the power of end users of products and services for several reasons. First, a large amount of consumer information is readily available on the Internet. Consumers can access information around the clock and compare offerings from across the world without moving from their homes and offices. This gives end users the information they need to shop for quality merchandise and bargain for price concessions. The automobile industry provides an excellent example of this phenomenon. For a small fee, agencies such as Consumers Union (publishers of *Consumer Reports*) provide customers with detailed information about actual automobile manufacturer costs.[9] This information, available online, can be used to bid down dealers' profits.

Second, an end user's switching costs are lower because of the Internet. Switching may involve only a few clicks of the mouse to find and view a competing product or service online. As a result, according to Web strategist David Siegel, businesses must be willing to listen to customers more often and respond to them more quickly. "E-customers aren't loyal to a brand," says Siegel. "They may be attracted to a specific business proposition, but their memories are very short. ... Companies must earn their networked

Affordable Ad Campaigns for Smaller Firms

The Internet allows small firms, such as Mr. Case Inc., to compete head-on with large retailers, in spite of their limited advertising budgets. The small, Toronto-based grocery delivery company uses pay-per-click (ppc) ads on Google, Yahoo, and other Internet search engine providers. Unlike traditional online advertising banners that are priced on a per viewer basis and can cost thousands of dollars if placed on high-traffic sites (but cannot guarantee results), a fee is charged only when someone actually clicks on the ppc advertisement. This translates into real savings for a small firm, since the ads incur a charge only when there is an actual customer. The ppc ads have enabled Mr. Case to increase its sales of cases of brand name groceries to consumers, offices, and food service businesses without risking a major investment in advertising, which otherwise would have been necessary in order for it to challenge its much larger competitors. Its advertising cost goes up, but only in line with the traffic it generates.

Sources: MrCase.com; R. Pierce, "Visa Business Card Simplifies Operations for Mr, Case," BizLaunch.ca, August 2007; and P. Lima, "Pay-per-Click Ads Pushing the Right Buttons," *The Globe and Mail*, January 27, 2005, p. B13.

customers' loyalty with *every* new deal."[10] In this environment, buyers are likely to have much more bargaining power.[11]

The bargaining power of distribution channel intermediaries may, on the other hand, decrease because it is much easier and less expensive for producers to reach end users directly. This is especially valuable for specialized companies that can focus their promotional efforts on segments that are easily identified via the Internet.

An important challenge that the Internet has also given rise to is channel conflict, the problem that occurs when end users can access the same products through several different outlets. The more outlets there are from which a product can be purchased, the lower the potential profitability for any single outlet will be.

The Bargaining Power of Suppliers

Use of the Internet and digital technologies to speed up and streamline the process of acquiring supplies is already benefiting many sectors of the economy. But the net effect of the Internet on supplier power will depend on the nature of competition in a given industry.

On the one hand, Internet technologies make it possible for suppliers to access more of their business customers at a relatively lower cost per customer. Suppliers may also be able to create Web-based purchasing arrangements that make purchasing easier and discourage their customers from switching. Ariba, a leading vendor of B2B software, develops online procurement systems that suppliers can install on the computer systems of their customers, thus creating a direct link that reduces transaction costs and paperwork.[12] On the other hand, suppliers may not be able to hold onto these customers because buyers can do comparative shopping and price negotiations so much faster on the Internet and can turn to other suppliers with a few clicks of the mouse. At the same time, the Internet is creating new intermediaries, such as the venerable online booksellers Amazon and Abebooks and auction house eBay, as well as new opportunities for astute incumbents like Ritchie Bros. Auctioneers of Richmond, British Columbia, featured in Strategy Spotlight 8.3.

Finally, suppliers will have greater power to the extent that they can reach end users directly, without intermediaries. Previously, suppliers often had to work through intermediaries who brought their products or services to market for a fee. The Internet is eliminating the need for organizations and business processes that are responsible for intermediary steps in the value chain of many industries.[13] Complex transactions have become simpler, and middlemen who do not add value relative to the open market end up being pushed aside.[14]

A Canadian Auctioneer for the Big Guns

Ritchie, one of the world's leading auctioneers of giant cranes and other types of industrial equipment, started out as a traditional auctioneer almost 50 years ago in Kelowna, British Columbia. Through its commitment to principled auctions in a field that could harbour many shabby operators, the company succeeded in dominating the U.S. and Canadian markets for industrial used equipment. Ritchie became known for its "unreserved auctions" with no minimum pricing and for a solid reputation that, indeed, the best outside bid would win the auction without interference or manipulation from the seller. Although working in a very traditional sector, Ritchie saw the advantages of the Internet and adopted its use with a vengeance. The Internet expanded the auctioneer's reach and added substantially to its business by allowing it to list all the equipment for view online before each auction and by allowing registrants to participate online in its live auctions. Buyers from Europe and Asia can now be part of its regular registrant lists. Building on its success, Ritchie moved into industrial and recreational real estate, golf courses, and housing developments. Last year, it generated over $2 billion in gross auction revenues in 11 countries and it has plans for further expansion. Its live auctions can accommodate participants from over 50 countries, thus generating the highest possible bids for its listings and making Ritchie a very attractive auction house for sellers listing their assets.

Sources: P. Kennedy, "Ritchie moves into real estate auctions," *The Globe and Mail*, July 20, 2006, B4; P. Kennedy, "Auctions going through roof at Ritchie," *The Globe and Mail*, June 20, 2005, B5; www. rbauction.com.

Just as the Internet is eliminating some business functions, it is creating opportunities for new functions. These new activities are entering the value chain by a process known as *reintermediation*, the introduction of new types of intermediaries. Strategy Spotlight 8.4 shows how Canadian Internet pharmacies have become the new intermediaries for American patients. Many of the new functions are affecting traditional supply chains. In consumer markets, for example, delivery services are enjoying a boom because of the Internet. Consumers are choosing to have products delivered to their door, rather than going out to pick them up. Electronic delivery is also becoming common. Utility bills, credit card statements, and other invoices arrive electronically, while bar-code printing technology allows customers to print out their own tickets to movies, concerts, and sporting events, as well as check-in online for their flights.[15] The emergence of ecommerce has created the need for new types of financial intermediaries that can perform clearing functions for purchases made online. New products (e.g., online credit cards) and new services (e.g., online escrow services) have been introduced as use of the Internet has grown.

The Threat of Substitutes

Along with traditional marketplaces, the Internet has created a new marketplace; along with traditional channels, it has become a new channel. In general, the threat of substitutes is heightened because the Internet introduces new ways to accomplish the same tasks.

Consumers will generally choose to use a product or service until a substitute that meets the same need becomes available at a lower cost or offers more benefits. The economies created by Internet technologies have led to the development of numerous substitutes for traditional ways of doing business.

Another example of substitution exists in the realm of electronic storage. With expanded use of desktop computing capabilities during the last 20 years, the need to store information electronically has increased dramatically. Until recently, the trend has been to create increasingly larger desktop storage capabilities and techniques for compressing information, using compacting and "zipping" methods that create storage efficiencies. But

Reintermediation in the Prescription Drugs Business

Internet pharmacies have blossomed in Canada as a result of the difference between the prices of prescription drugs in Canada and those in the United States. American patients are having their prescriptions filled online by Canadian pharmacies. The business used to be restricted to Americans who made the trip across the border for their medications. They were taking advantage of Canada's quasi-regulated prescription drug price regime and the lower exchange rate that, together, generally resulted in prices as much as 50 percent lower than what the same drugs would cost in the United States. Through the Internet, the trips are now unnecessary as prescriptions can be filled online, a fact that has resulted in the creation of a $1 billion industry which, in 2004, employed 4,000 people.

However, some of these online pharmacy operations have begun to cross a line separating convenience from illegitimacy; prescriptions not signed by doctors or filled without a doctor ever having seen the patient began

appearing. Under pressure from the U.S. government, Canada introduced legislation to police such practices. Undeterred by a government crackdown on their domestic operations, the larger of the Internet pharmacies moved parts of their operations overseas to countries such as the UK, Israel, Germany, Hong Kong and Taiwan. The Internet makes this exceedingly easy, since the move requires little more than setting up another Web site. Of course, the Internet does not recognize borders or continents, and the lucrative business has attracted pharmacies from other countries as well. New operators are sourcing even cheaper medicines from countries where a lack of control on the pharmaceutical industry has resulted in the appearance of counterfeit drugs and bogus medicines that will do little to provide the expected benefit or might possibly even harm the patient. Both the Canadian and American governments are working to curb the abuse by establishing regulations and oversight that will reassure and protect consumers.

Source: A. Hutchinson, "Regulation of Rogue Internet Pharmacies Overdue," *Security Debrief*, October 2008, www.securitydebrief.adfero.com; K. T. Rost, "Policing the Wild West World of Internet Pharmacies," *Food and Drug Law Journal*, vol. 55 (2000), pp. 619–639; L. Zehr, "Internet Pharmacies Forced to Open Shop Overseas," *The Globe and Mail*, February 7, 2005, p. B3; "O, no Canada," Consumer Reports, vol. 73, no. 12, December 2008, p. 75.

a viable substitute has recently emerged. Companies such as My Docs Online are providing Web-based storage that firms can access simply by going online. Rather than purchasing more megabytes of storage space, firms can now lease cyberspace. Since these storage places are virtual, they can be accessed anywhere the Web can be accessed. This makes it possible for a traveller to access important documents and files without transporting them physically from place to place. Cyberstorage is cheaper and more convenient than purchasing and carrying additional hard drives.[16]

Substitution is also evident in market research, which was traditionally conducted through mailed questionnaires and test marketing. These can be expensive to plan and administer. Questionnaires must be designed, printed, and mailed—all activities that have a hard cost. New products were often rolled out one city at a time to test the responses of a typical group of a few shoppers before a major launch. But Web technologies have reduced the time and cost of marketing. Insight Express is an online market research firm that can survey 300 people for around $1,000. Initially launched to conduct test marketing for mom-and-pop operations, the company is now test-marketing new names, logos, product ideas, and even business concepts for major online players such as E-Trade and Yahoo![17]

Products can be tested more quickly in cyberspace. This is driven in part by the Internet's ability to capture detailed information using electronic "cookies," records stored on the user's own hard drive that indicate which Web sites the user has visited. Other information can also be captured: how long a visitor views a Web page, whether he or she clicks through a banner ad, and whether a purchase is made.[18] Such detailed information is invaluable to marketers trying to determine how to target their advertising. It also has enormous ethical implications for consumer privacy. Without their knowledge or consent and without knowing when, consumers' personal buying habits may be monitored; moreover, this information may also be sold to businesses that want to target them with direct marketing ads.

The Intensity of Competitive Rivalry

Because the Internet creates more tools and means for competing, rivalry among competitors is likely to be more intense. Only those competitors that can use the Web to give themselves a distinct image, create unique product offerings, or provide "faster, smarter, cheaper" services are likely to capture greater profitability with the new technology. Such gains are hard to sustain, however, because, in most cases, the new technology can be imitated quickly. Thus, the Internet tends to increase rivalry by making it difficult for firms to differentiate themselves and by shifting customer attention to issues of price.

As we saw in Chapter 2, rivalry is more intense when switching costs are low and product or service differentiation is minimized. Because the Internet makes it possible for consumers to shop around with a few clicks of the mouse, it has "commoditized" products that might previously have been regarded as rare or unique. Since the Internet eliminates the importance of location, products that once had to be sought out in geographically distant outlets are now readily available online. This makes competitors in cyberspace seem more equally balanced, which, in turn, intensifies rivalry.

The problem is made worse for competitors by the presence of shopping "bots" and infomediaries. Infomediaries have taken it upon themselves to provide online shoppers with information that allows them to make better purchase decisions. Consumer Web sites like mySimon and PriceSCAN seek out all the Web locations that sell similar products and then provide price comparisons.[19] Some shopping infomediaries, such as BizRate and CNET, not only search for the lowest prices on many different products but also rank the customer service quality of different sites that sell similarly priced items.[20] This is important because research indicates that customer service is three times more significant than price in terms of repeat online sales.[21] Such infomediary services are good for consumers because they give them the chance to compare services as well as price. For businesses, however, they increase rivalry by consolidating the marketing message, which consumers use to make a purchase decision, to a few key pieces of information over which the selling company has little control.

Recognizing that this phenomenon is part of the new Internet reality, many companies willingly participate in such services.[22] For example, BestBookBuys.com is a site that searches for the best prices among the Web sites of 24 different booksellers, including major ones such as Amazon and Barnes & Noble.[23] The booksellers featured on the site are member participants. They have agreed to have their prices included because it provides another kind of access to consumers.

Exhibit 8.1 summarizes many of the ways the Internet is affecting industry structure. These influences also change how companies develop and deploy strategies to generate above-average profits and sustainable competitive advantage.

HOW THE INTERNET ADDS VALUE

As we noted earlier, the Internet and other digital technologies become strategically significant only when their practical applications add value and create competitive advantages. With respect to the basic business exchange, we can consider four related activities that are being revolutionized by the Internet—search, evaluation, problem solving, and transaction.[24]

Exhibit 8.1
How the Internet Influences Industry Structure

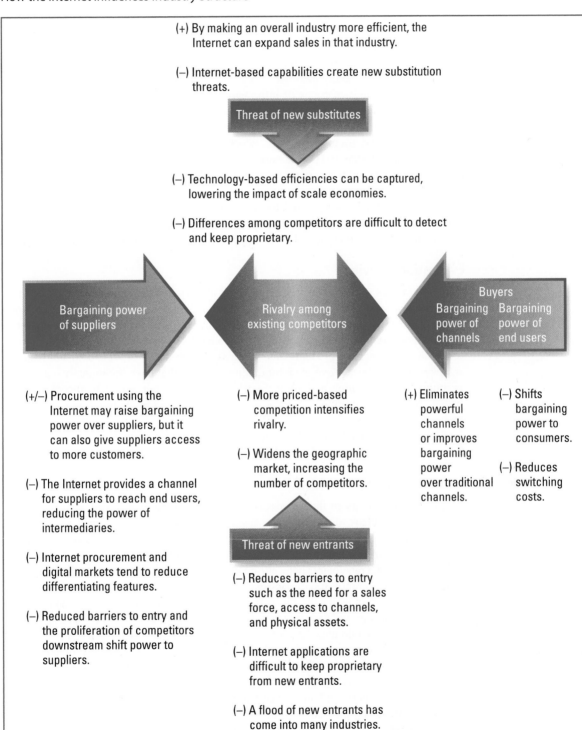

(+) By making an overall industry more efficient, the Internet can expand sales in that industry.

(−) Internet-based capabilities create new substitution threats.

Threat of new substitutes

(−) Technology-based efficiencies can be captured, lowering the impact of scale economies.

(−) Differences among competitors are difficult to detect and keep proprietary.

Bargaining power of suppliers

Rivalry among existing competitors

Buyers
Bargaining power of channels   **Bargaining power of end users**

(+/−) Procurement using the Internet may raise bargaining power over suppliers, but it can also give suppliers access to more customers.

(−) The Internet provides a channel for suppliers to reach end users, reducing the power of intermediaries.

(−) Internet procurement and digital markets tend to reduce differentiating features.

(−) Reduced barriers to entry and the proliferation of competitors downstream shift power to suppliers.

(−) More priced-based competition intensifies rivalry.

(−) Widens the geographic market, increasing the number of competitors.

Threat of new entrants

(−) Reduces barriers to entry such as the need for a sales force, access to channels, and physical assets.

(−) Internet applications are difficult to keep proprietary from new entrants.

(−) A flood of new entrants has come into many industries.

(+) Eliminates powerful channels or improves bargaining power over traditional channels.

(−) Shifts bargaining power to consumers.

(−) Reduces switching costs.

Source: Adapted from M. E. Porter, "Strategy and the Internet," *Harvard Business Review*, March 2001, pp. 63–78.

Search Activities

Search refers to the process of gathering information and identifying purchase options. The Internet has enhanced both the speed of information gathering and the breadth of information that can be accessed. This enhanced search capability and the concomitant decrease in the cost of search are among the key reasons the Internet has lowered switching costs. These efficiency gains have greatly benefited buyers. Suppliers also have benefited. Small suppliers that had difficulty getting noticed can more easily be found, and large suppliers can publish thousands of pages of information for a fraction of the cost that hard-copy catalogues once required. Additionally, online search engines have accelerated the search process to incredible speeds. Consider the example of Google, a search engine developed as a project by two graduate students, which became the number one search service in just a few years. Using 10,000 networked computers, it searches 3 billion Web pages in an average of 500 milliseconds. To do the same search manually, by thumbing through 3 billion pages at the rate of one minute per page, would take 5,707 years. This ability has made Google an essential tool for many businesses. As a result, Google has built a powerful advertising business. Thousands of small, medium, and large firms now spend a significant portion of their advertising budgets on Google and other search engines.[25]

Evaluation Activities

Evaluation refers to the process of considering alternatives and comparing the costs and benefits of various options. Online services that facilitate comparative shopping, provide product reviews, and catalogue customer evaluations of performance have made the Internet a valuable resource. For example, BizRate.com offers extensive product ratings that can help consumers evaluate products. Sites such as CNET, which provide comparative pricing, have helped lower prices even for quality products that have traditionally maintained premium prices. Opinion-based sites, such as ePinions.com and PlanetFeedback.com, provide reports of consumer experiences with various vendors. Future Shop, along with many other retailers such as Sears and Best Buy, provides extensive technical information on all the products it sells and allows consumers to compare multiple brands on price and features—again, with the click of a mouse.

Problem-Solving Activities

Problem solving refers to the process of identifying problems or needs and generating ideas and action plans to address those needs. Whereas evaluation is primarily product-related, problem solving is typically used in the context of services. Customers usually have unique problems, which must be handled one at a time. For example, online travel services, such as Travelocity, help customers on an individual basis select from many options to form a unique travel package. Furthermore, problem solving often involves providing answers immediately. Firms in industries such as medicine, law, and engineering are using the Internet and digital technologies to deliver many new solutions. Some of these are quite remarkable. Eli Lilly, as a case in point, has used the Internet to form a virtual platform where top scientists help drug companies solve complex problems.[26]

Many products involve both a service and a product component; therefore, both problem solving and evaluation may be needed. Dell Computer's Web site is an example of a site that has combined both. By creating a Web site that allows for customization of individual computers, they address the unique concerns of customers, "one computer at a time." As well, the site features a strong evaluative component because it allows users to compare the costs and features of various options. Shoppers can even compare their customized selection to refurbished Dell computers that are available at a substantially lower cost.

Transaction Activities

Transaction refers to the process of completing the sale and includes negotiating and agreeing contractually, making payments, and taking delivery. Numerous types of Internet-enabled activities have contributed to lowering overall transaction costs. Auctions of various sorts, from raw materials used in manufacturing to collectibles sold on eBay, facilitate the process of arriving at mutually agreed-on prices. Services such as Paypal provide a third-party intermediary that facilitates transactions between parties who have never met and probably never will. Amazon.com's One-Click technology allows for very rapid purchases, and Amazon's overall superiority in managing order fulfillment has made its transactions process efficient and reliable.[27]

Other Sources of Competitive Advantage

There are other factors that derive from the Internet and digital technologies that can potentially become sources of competitive advantage. One of them is content. Digitization and information technologies make it possible to capture vast amounts of content at a very low cost.[28] The Internet can improve a firm's value proposition by providing expertise, customer feedback, or entertainment programming much more readily and at substantially lower cost than alternatives. Firms that can capture this value in unique ways and build a sustainable business around it can potentially reap great benefits.

Moreover, the Internet has emerged as a tremendously important learning tool. Over 50 percent of users compare the Internet to a library.[29] Web sites that provide new knowledge or unbiased information are highly valuable. The expertise function is not limited to consumer sites, nor does it always emanate from the company toward its customers. B2B sites that facilitate the sharing of expert knowledge are seen as helping to build community in industry and professional groups and are valued by practitioners as much as B2C sites with help centres, extensive information, and resources for consumers. Buyers often trust what other buyers say more than a company's promises. Being able to interact with like-minded customers by reading about their experiences or learning how they have responded to a new product offering builds a sense of belonging that is otherwise hard to create. The Internet makes this possible by eliminating physical and temporal distances.

Finally, more and more people are using the Internet as an entertainment medium. With technologies such as streamed media, which allow the Internet to move television-like images and sound at very high speeds, computers can provide everything from breaking news to video games and online movies. Over the last few years, TV viewing has decreased, and online activity has increased dramatically. Because of interactive technology, viewers are not restricted to passive participation but can use the Web to engage, create, and control their involvement with the content and customize their entertainment.

Business Models

The Internet provides a unique platform for business activity, which has become, in some ways, like a new marketplace. How do firms conduct business in this new arena? One way of addressing this question is by describing various Internet business models. A business model is a method and a set of assumptions that explain how a business creates value and earns profits in a competitive environment. Some of these models are quite simple and traditional even when applied in an Internet context. Others have features that are unique to the digitally networked, online environment. In this section, we discuss seven Internet business models that account for the vast majority of business conducted online.[30]

- *Commission-based* models are used by businesses that provide services for a fee. The business is usually a third-party intermediary, and the commission charged is often based on the size of the transaction. The most common type is a brokerage service such as a stockbroker (e.g., TD Waterhouse) or real estate broker (e.g., Remax.ca). This category also includes auction companies such as eBay. In exchange for putting buyers and sellers together, eBay earns a commission.

- *Advertising-based* models are used by companies that provide content and/or services to visitors and sell advertising to businesses that want to reach those visitors. It is similar to the broadcast television model in which viewers watch shows produced with advertising dollars. A key difference is that online visitors can interact with both the ads and the content. Large portals such as Yahoo.com fall into this category as well as specialty portals such as iNest.com, a portal that provides services for buyers of newly constructed homes.

- *Markup-based* models are used by businesses that add value in marketing and sales (rather than production) by acquiring products, marking up the price, and reselling them at a profit. Also known as the merchant model, it applies to both wholesalers and retailers. Amazon.com is the most well-known example in this category. It also includes bricks-and-mortar companies such as Sears, which has a very successful online operation, and vendors whose products are purely digital such as Fonts.com, which sells downloadable fonts and photographs.

- *Production-based* models are used by companies that add value in the production process by converting raw materials into value-added products. Thus, it is also referred to as the manufacturing model. The Internet adds value to this model in two key ways. First, it lowers marketing costs by enabling direct contact with end users. Second, such direct contact facilitates customization and problem solving. Dell's online ordering system is supported by a state-of-the-art customized manufacturing process. Travelocity uses its rich database of travel options and customer profiles to identify, produce, and deliver unique solutions.

- *Referral-based* models are used by firms that steer customers to another company for a fee. One type is the affiliate model in which a vendor pays an affiliate a fee each time a visitor clicks through the affiliate's Web site and makes a purchase from the vendor. Many name brand companies use affiliate programs. For example, WeddingChannel.com provides a bridal registry where wedding guests can buy gifts from companies such as Tiffany's, Macy's, or Crate & Barrel, and it receives a fee each time a sale is made through its Web site. Another referral-based example is Yesmail.com, which generates leads using email marketing.

- *Subscription-based* models are used by businesses that charge a flat fee for providing either a service or proprietary content. Internet service providers are one example of this model. Companies such as America Online and Earthlink supply Internet connections for fees that are charged whether buyers use the service or not. Subscription-based models are also used by content creators such as *The Economist* and *The Globe and Mail*'s "Insider Edition." Although these recognizable brands often provide free content, only a small portion is available free. *The Economist*, for example, advertises that 70 percent of its content is available only to subscribers.

- *Fee-for-service-based* models are used by companies that provide ongoing services similar to a utility company. Unlike the commission-based model, the fee-for-service model involves a pay-as-you-go system. Activities are metered, and companies pay only for the amount of service used. Application service providers fall into this category. For example, Daptiv provides virtual workspace where people in different physical locations can collaborate online. Users essentially rent Internet space, along with a host of tools that make it easy to interact, for a fee based on their usage.

Exhibit 8.2 summarizes the key features of each Internet business model and addresses how the four value-adding activities—search, evaluation, problem solving, and transaction—can be sources of competitive advantage. It is important to keep in mind that many companies combine these models to achieve competitive advantages.

Type	Features and Content	Sources of Competitive Advantage
Commission-based	Commissions charged for brokerage or intermediary services. Adds value by providing expertise and/or access to a wide network of alternatives.	Search Evaluation Problem solving Transaction
Advertising-based	Web content paid for by advertisers. Adds value by providing free or low-cost content—including customer feedback, expertise, and entertainment programming—to audiences that range from very broad (general content) to highly targeted (specialized content).	Search Evaluation
Markup-based	Reselling marked-up merchandise. Adds value through selection, distribution efficiencies, and by leveraging brand image and reputation. May use entertainment programming to enhance sales.	Search Transaction
Production-based	Selling manufactured goods and custom services. Adds value by increasing production efficiencies, capturing customer preferences, and improving customer service.	Search Problem solving
Referral-based	Fees charged for referring customers. Adds value by enhancing a company's product or service offering, tracking referrals electronically, and generating demographic data. Expertise and customer feedback are often included with referral information.	Search Problem solving Transaction
Subscription-based	Fees charged for unlimited use of service or content. Adds value by leveraging strong brand name, providing high-quality information to specialized markets, or providing access to essential services. May consist entirely of entertainment programming.	Evaluation Problem solving
Fee-for-service-based	Fees charged for metered services. Adds value by providing service efficiencies, expertise, and practical outsourcing solutions.	Problem solving Transaction

Sources: A. Afuah, and C. L. Tucci, *Internet Business Models and Strategies*, 2nd ed. (Burr Ridge, IL: McGraw-Hill, 2003); M. Rappa, "Business Models on the Web," digitalenterprise.org/models/models.html; and P. Timmers, *Electronic Commerce* (New York: Wiley, 1999).

Exhibit 8.2
Internet Business Models

HOW THE INTERNET IS AFFECTING COMPETITIVE STRATEGIES

As we have seen, the Internet is sweeping across the economy and affecting, in many ways, how business is conducted. It is a resource that companies around the world can access. Thus, to stay competitive, firms must update their strategies to reflect the new possibilities and constraints that this phenomenon represents. In this section, we revisit the competitive strategies introduced in Chapter 5—overall cost leadership, differentiation, and focus (i.e., cost and differentiation)—and address how the Internet and digital technologies can be used to enhance firm performance. We consider two major effects that the Internet is having on business: lowering transaction costs and enabling mass customization. Finally, we briefly discuss the pitfalls associated with using the new technologies and address the role of combination strategies in achieving competitive advantages.

Overall Cost Leadership

An overall-low-cost leadership strategy involves managing costs in every activity of a firm's value chain and offering products that are an exceptional value at the best possible price. The Internet and digital technologies provide new opportunities to manage costs, achieve greater efficiencies, and even change the cost structures of certain industries. The Internet can lower transaction costs and transform business. It applies not just to buy/sell transactions but to the costs of interacting with every part of a firm's value chain, within and outside the firm. Hiring new employees, meeting with customers, ordering supplies, addressing government regulations—all of these exchanges have some costs associated with them. Because business can be conducted differently on the Internet, new ways of saving money are changing the competitive landscape.

Earlier in the chapter, we saw how BP used the Internet to manage costs by lowering procurement costs and creating efficient methods for petroleum engineers to collaborate. General Electric (GE) also used online capabilities to streamline its purchasing operations. Potential suppliers obtain specifications, prepare, and then submit bids to GE electronically. After only one year, GE reported savings of hundreds of thousands of dollars, having cut related labour costs by 30 percent, reduced the cycle time of the bidding process by half, and decreased paperwork requirements of key employees by 60 percent. The process also benefited suppliers by lowering their costs of sales, streamlining the bidding process, and shortening the selling cycle.[31]

Other factors also help to lower transaction costs. The Internet reduces the costs of travelling to a location to search for a product or service, whether it is a retail outlet (as in the case of consumers) or a trade show (as in the case of business-to-business shoppers). Not only is the need for travel eliminated but so too is the supplier's need to maintain a physical address, whether it's a permanent retail location or a temporary presence at a trade show.

The Internet is clearly creating new opportunities for firms to achieve low-cost advantages.[32] While the same potential benefits are available to all companies, some companies have adopted these capabilities more rapidly or implemented them more efficiently. The following cost-saving measures are available throughout a firm's value chain in both primary and support activities:

- Direct access to progress reports and the ability for customers to periodically check work in progress is minimizing rework.

- Online bidding and order processing are eliminating the need for sales calls and minimizing sales-force expenses.
- Online purchase orders are making many transactions paperless, reducing the costs of procurement and paper.
- Collaborative design efforts using Internet technologies that link designers, materials suppliers, and manufacturers are reducing costs and speeding the process of new-product development.
- Human resource departments are using online testing and evaluation techniques in the hiring process and in online training after they hire.

Potential Internet-Related Pitfalls for Low-Cost Leaders As Internet technologies become more widespread, the cost advantages that early movers enjoyed may be available to many firms. One of the biggest threats to low-cost leaders is imitation. This problem is intensified for business conducted by way of the Internet. Most of the advantages associated with contacting customers directly, even capabilities that are software driven (e.g., customized ordering systems or real-time access to the status of work in progress, which lowers the cost of rework), can be duplicated quickly and without threat of infringement on proprietary information.

Another major pitfall for low-cost providers is the availability of information online that allows consumers to comparison shop much more easily. Also, companies that become overly enamoured with the Internet and its ability to cut costs may suffer if they place too much attention on one business activity and ignore others. They may jeopardize customer relations, as in the case of channel conflict, or neglect other cost centres, such as providing services or controlling turnover and recruiting expenses, which then undermine their cost advantages.

Differentiation

A differentiation strategy involves providing unique, high-quality products and services that promote a favourable reputation and strong brand identity, and usually command a premium price.

Among the most striking trends that the new technologies foster are new ways to interact with consumers. In particular, the Internet is creating new ways of differentiating by enabling mass customization, which improves the response of companies to customer wishes. Mass customization is not a new phenomenon; it has been growing for years as flexible manufacturing systems have made manufacturing more adaptable, and electronic data interchange has made communications more direct. But the Internet has generated a giant leap forward in terms of the amount of control customers can have in influencing the process. This is now changing the way companies develop unique product and service offerings, form their reputation, and preserve their brand image. The new technologies may affect the structure of entire industries. In the old days, manufacturers built products and waited for customers to respond. Now, they are taking directions from customers before manufacturing any products. Consider the following examples:

- Dell Computer has strengthened its leadership position by creating an online ordering system that allows customers to configure their own computers before they are built.[33]
- Boeing is designing its newest airliner, the 7E7, in collaboration with its main suppliers and major customers. Online capabilities allow the collaboration to happen in real

time, saving thousands of man-hours and millions of dollars. Moreover, information technologies and sophisticated software facilitate virtual testing of designs without the costly building of prototypes.

- 7-Eleven, the convenience store operator, has created a finely tuned feedback system that monitors subtle shifts in customer demand and recommends revisions to its product offerings on a daily basis.
- Footwear giant Nike lets customers choose the colour of their shoes and add a personal name or nickname through its NIKEiD program. Customers can view their selection at the Nike.com Web site before finalizing the order.[34]

Methods like mass customization, which are changing the way companies go to market, are challenging some of the tried-and-true techniques of differentiation. Traditionally, companies reached customers in various ways—the high-end catalogue, the showroom floor, the personal sales call—and used numerous means to make products more inviting—prestige packaging, celebrity endorsements, charity sponsorships. All of these avenues are still available and may still be effective, depending on a firm's competitive environment. But many consumers now judge the quality and uniqueness of a product or service by their ability to be involved in planning and design, combined with the speed of delivery and reliability of results. Internet capabilities are changing the way differentiators make exceptional products and offer superior service. And these improvements are being made at a reasonable cost, allowing firms to achieve parity on cost relative to competitors.

Opportunities to differentiate using Internet technologies are available in all parts of a company's value chain. Some of the techniques firms are using to achieve competitive advantage are fast becoming industry norms; successful differentiators need to remain attentive to the evolving capabilities of the new technologies. The following capabilities are evident in both primary and support activities:

- Internet-based knowledge management systems that link all parts of the organization are shortening response times and accelerating organization learning.
- Personalized online access provides customers with their own "site within a site" from which their prior orders, status of current orders, and requests for future orders are processed directly on the supplier's Web site.
- Quick online responses to service requests and rapid feedback to customer surveys and product promotions are enhancing marketing efforts.
- Online access to real-time sales and service information is being used to empower the sales force and continually update R&D and technology development efforts.
- Automated procurement and payment systems provide both suppliers and customers with access to detailed status reports and purchasing histories.

Potential Internet-Related Pitfalls for Differentiators As Internet technologies become part of the mainstream, it will become harder to use the Web to differentiate. Internet-based gains from differentiation will not materialize if companies offer differentiating features that customers don't want or create a sense of uniqueness that customers don't value. This has been the case with some of the personalization and customization software that early dot-com companies added to their sites at great expense. Users did not care about these features, and that led to a failed value proposition—the value companies thought they were offering did not translate into sales.

Other problems can result from overpricing products and services or developing brand extensions that dilute a company's image or reputation. Consider, for example, the efforts of Dow Jones & Company to establish an online version of the *Wall Street Journal*.

Golf Balls on the Net

In just 10 years, GCW Inc. has become the top choice for millions of golfers around the world who have been looking for a reliable and inexpensive source of golf balls to satisfy their insatiable passion. From a small wholesaler serving golfers in southern Ontario in the mid-1990s, the Markham-based operation has become a world-known direct supplier to avid golfers who use the firm's Web site, Knetgolf.com, as well as the firm's listings on eBay, to purchase recycled golf balls. Its business model is based on the simple fact that golfers purchase hundreds of golf balls each season; they lose very much the same number of golf balls during each one. GCW employs crews to "harvest" lost and abandoned golf balls at hundreds of golf courses in North America. It cleans, sorts, and packages the balls and sells them through its Web site for half the cost of new balls. "Although we can't keep track, I suspect we have sold the same golf ball to the same person more than once,"

says Gary Sheinfeld, GCW's president. They annually ship some five million balls worldwide, with over 95 percent of the orders placed electronically.

Knetgolf.com does not sell new golf balls, even though their margins could be very attractive. It concentrates on one product and has perfected the cycle that allows it to service its clientele with speed and reliability. Millions of golfers turn to Knetgolf.com where, with the click of a mouse, they can purchase brand name, recycled golf balls at a fraction of the retail price. The site posts hundreds of brands and sets prices that reflect the condition of the balls, ranging from mint to fair. The Internet has also allowed GCW to overcome the relatively short golf season in Ontario. Its customers come from all over the world, including from places such as Arizona, Florida, or Singapore where they golf year round.

Sources: Knetgolf.com; and P. Lima, "Net Golf Ball Business Keeps Cash Rolling In," *The Globe and Mail*, February 24, 2005, P. B9.

Internet users had grown accustomed to getting their online information for free. The company has faced resistance in developing a subscriber base for the online version. Print subscribers typically pay over $100 a year, but the *Journal* has had trouble getting online subscribers to pay $79 for a service that is arguably more customizable, more up to date, and more complete. By 2003, WSJ.com had about 664,000 paying subscribers but was still not profitable and was also a long way from repaying the $140 million its parent company, Dow Jones, had plowed into it since 1995.[35] Nevertheless, other newspapers, such as *The Globe and Mail*, have gone down the same path and are slowly making a business out of their online services.

Focus (Cost and Differentiation)

A focus strategy involves targeting a narrow market segment with customized products and/or specialized services. For companies that pursue focus strategies, the Internet offers new avenues by which to compete, because they can access markets less expensively (low cost) and provide more services and features (differentiation). Some claim that the Internet has opened up a new world of opportunities for niche players who seek to access small markets in a highly specialized fashion.[36] Many of these small players have benefited from waiting and watching as the high-flying dot-coms came and went. Now, a small but growing army of niche players is on the march. According to market researcher Keenan Vision Inc., the number of small emerchants in the United States grew from 70,000 in 1999 to 525,000 in 2001 and was expected to reach 2.6 million by 2004—a full third of all small businesses.[37] Among all Canadian small- and medium-sized businesses, 34 percent are already relying on the Internet for part of their sales. Strategy Spotlight 8.5 profiles a successful firm that uses the Internet to expand its reach globally, while retaining its focused strategy.

Even though the Internet presents some exciting new possibilities, the same problems that low-cost leaders and differentiators face in an ebusiness environment will affect focusers as well. Achieving competitive advantage will depend on how effectively firms use Internet technologies and deploy focus strategies.

To create focus strategies that work, firms must consider how best to deploy their resources throughout every value-creating activity. Both primary and support activities can be enhanced using the kind of single-mindedness that is characteristic of a focus strategy. Companies that have adapted their strategies to serve specialized markets, however, may enjoy only a temporary advantage, unless they seize the following kinds of capabilities that the Internet provides for focusers:

- Permission marketing techniques are focusing sales efforts on specific customers who opt to receive advertising notices.
- Chat rooms, discussion boards, and member functions that create community for customers with common interests are increasing Web-site usage.
- Niche portals that target specific groups are providing advertisers with access to viewers with specialized interests.
- Virtual organizing and online "officing" are being used to minimize firm infrastructure requirements.
- Procurement technologies that use Internet software to match buyers and sellers are highlighting specialized buyers and drawing attention to smaller suppliers.

Potential Internet-Related Pitfalls for Focusers Many aspects of the Internet economy seem to favour focus strategies because niche players and small firms can often implement Internet capabilities as effectively as their larger competitors. However, the same technologies—and the same cost savings—that are creating new opportunities for focusers are also available to major players. Focusers must, therefore, use the new technologies to provide the kinds of advantages that have been the hallmark of a focus strategy in the past: specialized knowledge, rapid response, and strong customer service.

These advantages may be challenged if focusers misread the scope and interests of their target markets. This can cause them to focus on segments that are too narrow to be profitable or to lose their uniqueness by going after overly broad niches, making them vulnerable to imitators or new entrants.

What happens when an ebusiness focuser tries to overextend its niche? Efforts to appeal to a broader audience—by carrying additional inventory, developing additional content, or offering additional services—can cause it to lose the cost advantages associated with a limited product or service offering. Conversely, when focus strategies become too narrow, the ebusiness may have trouble generating enough activity to justify the expense of operating the Web site. So far, Waterloo-based Research In Motion seems to have been able to achieve this balance as it has turned the technology into market dominance in the rapidly growing market for PDAs (personal digital assistants) with its world-known BlackBerry.[38]

ARE INTERNET-BASED ADVANTAGES SUSTAINABLE?

The Internet provides many ways to achieve above-average returns, but it may create even more possibilities for eroding unique advantages. So what's the bottom line? Strategy is about achieving competitive advantage and sustaining it. Does the Internet contribute to or detract from a firm's efforts to attain sustainable competitive advantages?

On the one hand, it appears that the Internet and the achievements in digital technologies that it makes possible are creating new opportunities for strategic success.

A few business models—those like eBay's auction system, which offer capabilities unique to the Internet—seem to be providing strong, *lasting* opportunities for above-average profitability. Such new applications have also created opportunities for companies that supply equipment to run the Internet, such as Cisco Systems and Sun Microsystems, and companies that provide software applications management and online fulfillment services, such as Jupiter Networks and SAP. Many of these companies are thriving because of the ebusiness revolution launched by the Internet.

On the other hand, failures of many firms resulted from the fact that business fundamentals were ignored and basic economic requirements were overlooked. Another major reason was that the service or capability they offered could easily be imitated. This was especially damaging for the young start-ups and "pure plays" (i.e., firms that exist only in cyberspace and have no other physical outlets). Larger firms with greater resources could observe what was working over time and bring more resources and talent to bear on an effective imitation strategy.

ARE COMBINATION STRATEGIES THE KEY TO EBUSINESS SUCCESS?

Because of the changing dynamics presented by the Internet and Internet-based technologies, new strategic combinations that make the best use of the competitive strategies just described may hold the greatest promise for future success. Several things are clear in this regard. First, the Internet, in general, is eroding opportunities for sustainable advantage. Many experts agree that the net effect of the Internet is fewer rather than more opportunities for sustainable advantages.[39] This means strategic thinking is even more important in the Internet age.

More specifically, the Internet has provided all companies with greater tools for managing costs. So it may be that cost management and control will increase in importance as a management tool. This may be good if it leads to an economy that makes more efficient use of its scarce resources. However, for individual companies, it may also shave critical percentage points off profit margins and create a climate that makes it impossible to survive, much less achieve sustainable above-average profits.

Many differentiation advantages are also diminished by the Internet. The ability to comparison shop—to check product reviews and easily inspect different choices—is depriving some companies, such as auto dealers, of the unique advantages that were the hallmark of their success in a previous time. Differentiating is still an important strategy, of course. But how firms achieve it may change, and the best approach may be to combine a differentiation strategy with other competitive strategies.

Perhaps the greatest beneficiaries are the focusers, who can use the Internet to capture a niche that previously may have been inaccessible. Even in this case, however, the same factors that make it possible for a small niche player to be a contender may make that niche attractive to a big company. In other words, an incumbent firm that previously thought a niche market was not worth the effort may use Internet technologies to enter that segment at a lower cost than in the past. The larger firm can then bring its market power and resources to bear in a way that a smaller competitor cannot match.

Firms using combination strategies may also fall short if they underestimate the demands of combining strategic approaches and get "stuck in the middle." This can lead to inaccurately assessing the costs and benefits of a strategy that combines differentiating and low-cost features: firms may believe they can keep prices and costs low but still offer high-end services that are expensive to provide.

Another potential pitfall for companies using combination strategies relates to the difficulty of managing complex strategies. Managers tend to develop a bias in favour of the functional areas with which they are most familiar. Furthermore, companies, in general, tend to fall into the trap of believing that there is "one best way" to accomplish organizational goals. A combination strategy, by definition, challenges a company to carefully blend alternative strategic approaches and remain mindful of the impact of different decisions on the firm's value-creating processes and its extended value-chain activities. Strong leadership is needed to maintain a bird's-eye perspective on a company's overall approach and to coordinate the multiple dimensions of a combination strategy.

Indeed, the key to effectively implementing any ebusiness strategy is for the leaders of today's firms to recognize that the Internet has forever changed the way business is conducted and to adopt practices that use the advantages it has to offer, without ignoring business fundamentals. Companies will increasingly need to adapt to the Internet and implement the capabilities that make ebusiness possible because, as Intel chairman Andy Grove expressed it, "The world now runs on Internet time."[40]

Summary

New technologies often unleash forces in the economy that are highly disruptive. The innovations that flow from such technologies can radically change the competitive landscape. Under such conditions, innovation-driven competition creates new strategic capabilities that alter the rules of competition. Few technologically driven phenomena have been as disruptive or as rich with opportunities as the Internet, wireless communications, and other digital technologies. The Internet is constantly changing the way business is conducted. The new technologies allow businesses to interact with each other and customers in faster, smarter, cheaper ways that are forever changing the competitive landscape. As Internet-based capabilities and related information technologies become more widespread in all parts of the globe, strategic managers need to increasingly integrate the Internet into their strategic plans.

In terms of a firm's competitive environment, most of the changes brought about by the Internet can be understood in the context of Porter's five-forces model of industry analysis. The threat of new entrants is expected to increase as Internet technologies reduce many barriers to entry. The process of disintermediation has enhanced the power of some suppliers by simplifying supply chains, but it may also shift bargaining power to customers. Buyer power has increased for many end users due to lower switching costs, but in some industries the Internet has become a new source of channel conflict. The threat of substitutes will generally be higher because Internet technologies are providing new methods for achieving old tasks. Finally, the Internet heightens the intensity of rivalry among similar competitors, as competition tends to be more price-oriented and technology-based advantages are easily imitated.

The Internet and digital technologies have created new opportunities for firms to add value. Four value-adding activities that have been enhanced by Internet capabilities are search, evaluation, problem solving, and transaction. Search activities include processes for gathering information and identifying purchase options. Evaluation activities concern the process of considering alternatives and comparing the costs and benefits of various options. Problem-solving activities include identifying problems or needs and generating ideas and action plans to address those needs. Transaction activities involve the process of completing a sale, including negotiating and agreeing contractually, making payments, and arranging delivery. These four activities are supported by three different types of content that Internet businesses often use—customer feedback, expertise, and entertainment programming. Strategic use of these attributes can help build competitive advantages and contribute to profitability. Seven business models, which are proving successful for use by Internet firms, were identified. These include commission, advertising, markup, production, referral, subscription, and fee-for-service-based models. Firms have also found that combinations of these business models can contribute to greater success.

The way companies formulate and deploy strategies is also changing because of the impact of the Internet on many industries. Overall low-cost strategies may be more important as some firms use Internet technologies to lower transaction costs and increase the efficiency of their operations. Differentiation strategies may be harder to achieve for many firms because the Internet is eroding some of their most unique features. Further, Internet technologies are enabling the mass customization capabilities of greater numbers of competitors. Focus strategies are likely to increase in importance because the Internet provides highly targeted and lower-cost access to narrow or specialized markets. These strategies are not without their pitfalls, however, and firms need to understand the dangers as well as the potential benefits of Internet-based approaches.

Thus, while promising to provide new opportunities for creating value and fostering firm growth, the Internet may make the competitive landscape more challenging for many incumbent firms. In this chapter, we addressed both the possibilities and the pitfalls of the rapidly expanding presence of the Internet in today's economy.

Summary Review Questions

1. How do Porter's five competitive forces affect companies that compete primarily on the Internet? Provide an example.

2. What effects does the Internet have on the three competitive strategies—overall low-cost, differentiation, and focus? How do these effects relate to a firm's competitive advantage?

3. What effect does ecommerce have on the profitability an industry is able to achieve? How can companies use ecommerce to enhance their own profitability?

4. Explain the difference between the effective use of technology and the technology *itself*, in terms of achieving and sustaining competitive advantages.

5. Describe how the three competitive strategies can be combined to create competitive advantages when firms compete primarily by means of ecommerce.

Experiential Exercise

Using the Internet, identify two firms—one a traditional bricks-and-mortar company and the second an Internet pure play—that have a strong Internet presence. Consider how each of these firms is adding value by using the Internet and digital technologies.

1. Bricks-and-mortar firm: _____
   Which of the following Internet-based activities is the company using to add value?

Value-Adding Activity	Examples of How the Company Uses the Activity	Is It Creating Value? (Yes/No)
Type:		
Search		
Evaluation		
Problem solving		
Transaction		
Content		

2. Internet pure-play firm: _____
   Which of the following Internet-based activities is the company using to add value?

Value-Adding Activity	Examples of How the Company Uses the Activity	Is It Creating Value? (Yes/No)
Type:		
Search		
Evaluation		
Problem solving		
Transaction		
Content		

3. How do the two firms compare? Is one adding more value than the other? What is the pure play doing that might help the bricks-and-mortar firm? What is the bricks-and-mortar firm doing that could benefit the pure play?

Application Questions Exercises

1. Select a company that has implemented an Internet strategy. Look up the company on the Internet, and discuss how it has increased (or decreased) its competitive advantage vis-à-vis Porter's five forces.
2. Choose an Internet firm that is competing with a bricks-and-mortar company. What are the relative advantages and disadvantages of the Internet firm? Do you think it will be successful in the long term?
3. Select a small firm that has used the Internet to its advantage in entering international markets. Do you believe such advantages will be sustainable over time? Explain.
4. How can a firm use an Internet strategy to enhance its overall cost leadership or differentiation competitive advantages? Provide examples.

Ethics Questions

1. Discuss the ethical implications of the use of cookies, adware, or spyware by ecommerce companies to track customer visits to Web sites and customer surfing patterns on the Internet. Don't forget to acknowledge the convenience of working with cookies.
2. What are the ethical implications of online music file sharing among individuals when there is no money exchanging hands in association with such sharing?
3. How can Internet companies that provide free access to other users' computers to download copyrighted material (e.g., Morpheus) guard against infringing on the rights of the artists who develop the material?

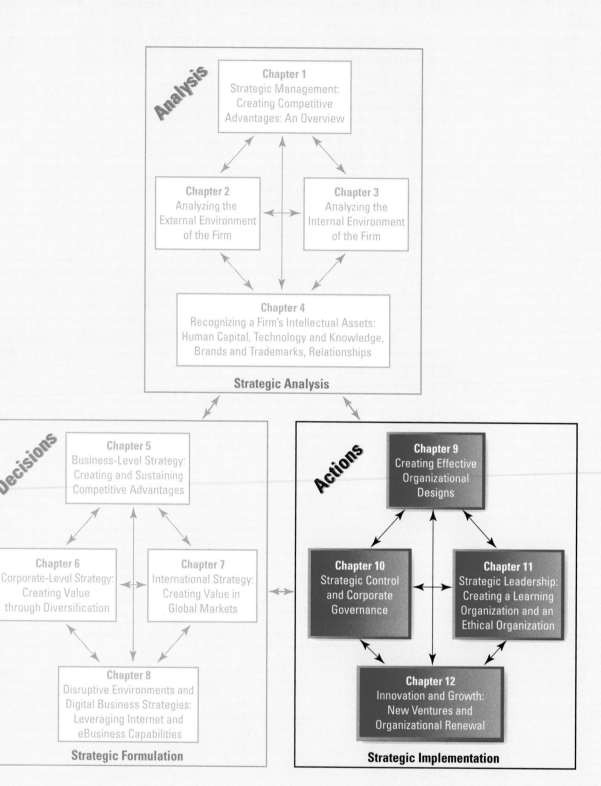

PART 3

Strategic Implementation

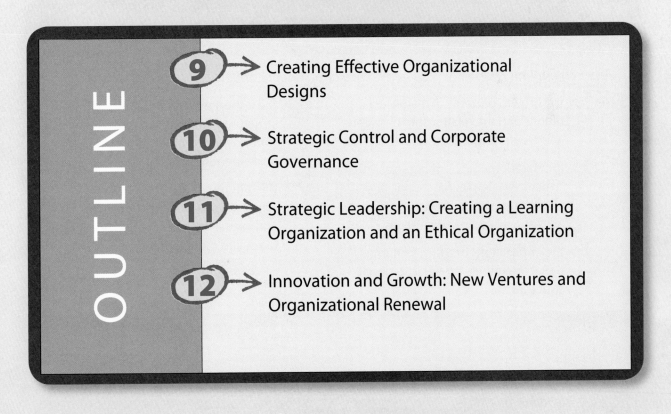

Chapter 9

Creating Effective Organizational Designs

LEARNING OBJECTIVES

After reading this chapter, you should have a good understanding of:

LO 1 → the growth patterns of major corporations and the relationship between a firm's strategy and its structure.

LO 2 → the traditional types of organizational structure—simple, functional, divisional, and matrix—and their relative advantages and disadvantages.

LO 3 → the implications of a firm's international operations for organizational structure.

LO 4 → the importance of organizational structure and the concept of the "boundaryless" organization in implementing strategies.

LO 5 → the different types of boundaryless organizations—barrier-free, modular, and virtual—and their relative advantages and disadvantages.

Power Corporation of Canada has its roots in 1925 and the early days of electrification, when a group of astute Montreal financiers saw the opportunities in hydroelectric power facilities. There was profit to be made from the growing demand for industrial and domestic electricity across the country.[1] The foresight of its founders, A. J. Nesbitt and P. A. Thomson, paid off handsomely, and by the 1950s, the firm was recognized as one of the stewards of Canadian domestic energy as well as an innovative power developer. At the same time, it was generously rewarding its shareholders with consistent financial results. Throughout the early years of its history, Power Corp. owned electricity generating facilities in British Columbia, Alberta, Manitoba, Ontario, Quebec, Newfoundland, and the North as well as interests in utilities, operating in such places as New York, Tokyo, Brazil, and France. From the very beginning, Power Corp. shied away from being an operator itself but recognized the benefits of executive consolidation. Accordingly, it brought expert management advice to its operating affiliates and provided extensive technical services through an engineering and construction department that was responsible for some of the most innovative power development projects in the country.

The industrial boom that followed World War II produced a tremendous appetite for energy around the world, but it also imposed pressures on many governments to better control the energy sources. It made privately owned power companies vulnerable to political pressures, expropriations, and nationalizations. Many utilities changed hands during that period, and many more ended up in the hands of governments. Power Corp. was able to easily adapt to those shifts because each of its operating affiliates was run independently, and the compensation from each expropriation was plowed back into acquiring other private energy companies. During a fifteen-year period, Power Corp. made numerous investments in hydroelectric utilities and other sources of energy, as various governments sought to nationalize other properties belonging to the corporation. It also recognized the challenges such pressures presented and looked for new opportunities to capitalize on the expertise of its management and the strengths of the company.

By 1968, Power Corp.'s portfolio consisted of a small number of large investments in pulp and paper, media, financial services, travel, and transportation. The strategic shift seemed to be working at first, but soon problems beset many of the company's major holdings, and corporate management lacked the knowledge and skills to guide them out of their misfortunes. The deterioration forced its board to accept a share exchange that transferred the leadership of the company to Paul Desmarais, a successful financier from Sudbury, Ontario, who had transformed an ailing bus business into a multi-million dollar company with interests in transportation, life insurance, communications, and real estate. Power Corp.'s 1968 annual report stated that "in addition to economies of scale, the proposed acquisition would further strengthen the Corporation's operating base and management skills. It would also add significantly to earning power and would cause Power Corp. to become essentially an operating company—albeit with a sizable investment portfolio—rather than primarily an investment holding company."

Within a year, Power Corp. had gained majority control or divested a number of businesses to the point that two-thirds of Power's assets were in operating subsidiaries, as opposed to less than 40 percent before. What remained was reorganized into four groupings that included financials (Laurentide Financial, Imperial Life, Great-West Life, Investors Group, and Montreal Trust), industrials (Canada Steamship Lines, Consolidated-Bathurst, Dominion Glass), real estate (Canadian Urban Properties, Trans-Canada Realties, Blue Bonnets Raceways), and communications (Gesca, La Presse, Les Journaux Trans-Canada, Quebec Telemedia). Power Corp. relied on a team of head office executives, a talented pool of autonomous managers, and the strong leadership of its controlling shareholder to start producing results in each of its operating groups.

Financial performance improved, and the company continued to restructure itself in response to external pressures and opportunities. The financial grouping gradually grew in importance and, by 1981, the company had completely reinvented itself one more time. Its organizational structure now reflected five holding units: Pargesa Holding S.A. owned a major interest in Banque de Paris et des Pays-Bas and later acquired interests in a number of financial and industrial companies in Europe and Asia; the Investors Group held Great-West Life, Montreal Trust, as well as its own management and distribution of mutual funds and other managed asset products; Canadian Pacific Ltd. was a rail, shipping, oil, and real estate conglomerate; Gesca Ltée published Montreal's prestigious daily newspaper La Presse as well as other Quebec and Ontario dailies; finally, Consolidated-Bathurst toiled in the pulp and paper sector.

The 1980s and 1990s provided opportunities to consolidate its position, strengthen its balance sheet, and further improve its financial results. Power Corp. sold off a number of its operating holding units at a substantial profit, and by 2005, under the second generation of Desmarais—Paul Jr. and Andre at the helm—it had restructured itself into two groups: the publisher Gesca Ltée and Power Financial Corporation, which, in turn, held Pargesa Holding, Great-West Lifeco Inc., and IGM Financial Inc. Through cross-holdings, the latter two own all of Great-West Life and Annuity Insurance, Great-West Life Assurance, London Life Insurance, Canada Life Assurance, Investors Group, and Mackenzie Financial. The latest structure allowed the company to exploit substantial marketing synergies and cost savings across its various financial holdings by bringing together Canada's largest insurance sales and financial advice network.

Power Corporation of Canada has had a rich and eventful history that, in many respects, has reflected the many transformations of Canada over the same period. Through its evolution from a power utility to a multi-billion dollar financial, industrial, and communications holding company that spans the world, it restructured itself numerous times, always intending to better align its diverse holdings to achieve results. While the company's guiding principles did not change much during those eighty years, the strategies to pursue those principles changed drastically, and the organizational structure that would execute those strategies had to be changed accordingly.

The best conceived strategy will remain just that, a dream and an idea, unless an organization is put in place to make it happen. Lots of great ideas have been left on the drawing board or, even worse, were converted to major disasters because the managers failed in the execution. Executing strategy is normally the biggest challenge facing managers of large and small firms alike. Execution requires commitment, perseverance, and a solid capacity to lead, motivate, direct, and inspire an entire organization to deliver on the dream. Like Power Corp., today's managers are faced with two ongoing and vital challenges in organizing their companies to execute their strategies. First, they must decide on the most appropriate type of organizational structure. This points to the demands on managers to organize the many diverse and specialized activities within their firm in ways that will achieve the best possible results, recognizing that diversity necessitates dividing tasks into meaningful groupings.

Second, they need to devise ways to coordinate and integrate those activities and assess what mechanisms, processes, and techniques are most helpful in enhancing the permeability of the internal and external boundaries of their organization. Clearly, the more diverse the tasks, the more complex the coordination and integration requirements become. And, the more essential the interaction across departments and with suppliers and customers is to the firm's strategy, the more critical achieving effective permeability of the organization's boundaries becomes.

This chapter first explores the traditional forms of organizational structure and their advantages and disadvantages. We then discuss organizing forms that permit more fluid boundaries and allow today's organizations to better respond to rapidly changing and unpredictable environments.

TRADITIONAL FORMS OF ORGANIZATIONAL STRUCTURE

Organizational structure refers to the formalized patterns of interactions that link the tasks, technologies, and people of a firm.[2] Structures are designed to ensure that resources are used most effectively toward accomplishing an organization's mission. Structure provides managers with a means of balancing two conflicting forces: a need for the division of tasks into meaningful groupings and the need to integrate such groupings in order to ensure organizational efficiency and effectiveness. Structure identifies the executive, managerial, and administrative organization of a firm and indicates responsibilities and hierarchical relationships. It also influences the flow of information as well as the context and nature of human interactions.

Most organizations begin very small and either die or remain small. Those few that survive and prosper embark on strategies designed to increase the overall scope of operations and enable them to enter new product-market domains. Such growth places additional pressure on executives to control and coordinate the firm's increasing size and diversity. The most appropriate type of structure depends on the nature and magnitude of growth in a firm.

Patterns of Growth of Large Corporations

Much like Power Corp.'s evolution, a firm's strategy and structure change as it increases in size, diversifies into new product markets, and expands its geographic scope.[3] Exhibit 9.1 illustrates some of the common growth patterns that firms may follow, and their corresponding organizational structures.

A new firm with a *simple structure* typically increases its sales revenue and volume of outputs over time. It may also engage in some vertical integration to secure sources of supply (backward integration) as well as channels of distribution (forward integration). After a time, the simple-structure firm implements a *functional structure* to concentrate efforts on both increasing efficiency and enhancing its operations and products. This structure enables the firm to group its operations into functions, departments, or geographic areas. As its initial markets mature, a firm looks beyond its present products and markets for possible expansion. Such a strategy of related diversification requires a need to reorganize around product lines or geographic markets. This leads to a *divisional structure*. As the business expands in terms of sales revenues, and as domestic growth opportunities become somewhat limited, a firm may seek opportunities in international markets. At this time, a firm has a wide variety of structures to choose from. These include *international division, geographic area, worldwide product division, worldwide functional,* and *worldwide matrix*. As we see later in this section, deciding upon the most appropriate structure when a firm has international operations depends on three primary factors: the extent of international expansion, the type of strategy (global, multidomestic, or transnational), and the degree of product diversity.[4]

There are some other common growth patterns. For example, some firms may find it advantageous to diversify into several product lines rather than focus their efforts on strengthening distributor and supplier relationships through vertical integration. Thus, they would organize themselves according to product lines by implementing a divisional structure. Also, some firms may choose to move into unrelated product areas, typically by acquiring existing businesses. Frequently, their rationale is that acquiring assets and competencies is more economical or expedient than developing them internally. Such an unrelated, or conglomerate, strategy requires relatively little integration across businesses and little sharing of resources. In this case, a *holding company structure* becomes appropriate.

The above paths of growth are not unique, although they do represent typical, traditional patterns of evolution among Western corporations. Frequently, firms follow different trajectories for their development. Moreover, some firms bypass a number of

Exhibit 9.1

Dominant Growth Patterns of Large Corporations (examples of Canadian corporations in parentheses)

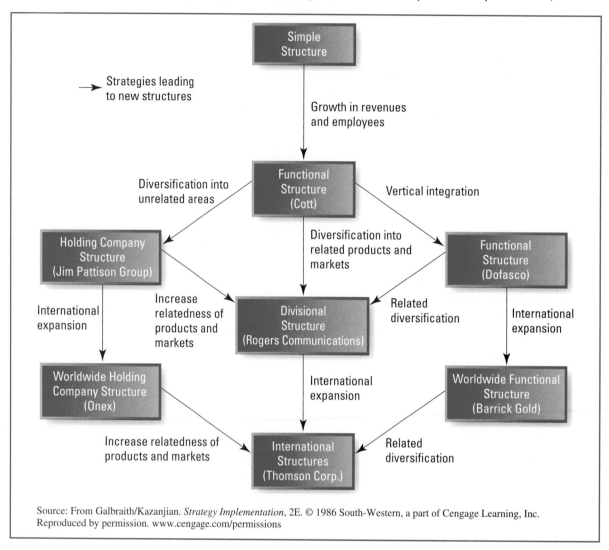

Source: From Galbraith/Kazanjian. *Strategy Implementation*, 2E. © 1986 South-Western, a part of Cengage Learning, Inc. Reproduced by permission. www.cengage.com/permissions

those stages or pursue international strategies very early in their history because of attractive opportunities overseas arising from the globalization of markets, coupled with lower communication and transportation costs. Most commonly, young firms do not engage in many vertical integration activities and, instead, create networks with other independent firms, which have expertise in upstream or downstream activities that complement their own core competencies. Their independence provides tremendous flexibility and agility to respond to the unpredictability of the new environments. Moreover, independent firms require substantially lower investments and fewer resources, which younger firms most likely do not possess.

Simple Structure

LO 2

As one might expect, the simple structure is the oldest and most common organizational form. After all, most organizations are small and have a single or very narrow product line in which the owner-manager (or top executive) makes almost all of the decisions. In effect, the owner-manager controls all activities, and the staff serve as an extension of the top executive's personality.

The simple structure is highly informal, and the coordination of tasks is accomplished by direct supervision. Decision making is highly centralized, there is little specialization of tasks, there are few rules and regulations, and often any evaluation and reward system is informal. Although the owner-manager is intimately involved in almost all phases of the business, a manager is often employed to oversee day-to-day operations.

A small firm with a simple structure may often foster creativity and individualism since there are generally few rules and regulations. However, such "informality" may lead to problems. Employees may not clearly understand their responsibilities, which can lead to conflict and confusion. Also, employees may take advantage of the lack of regulations and act in their own self-interest. Such actions can erode motivation and satisfaction as well as lead to the possible misuse of organizational resources. Further, small organizations have flat structures (i.e., few vertical, hierarchical levels) that limit opportunities for upward mobility. Without the potential for future advancement, recruiting and retaining talent may become very difficult.

Functional Structure

When an organization is small (15 employees or less), it is not necessary to have a variety of formal arrangements and grouping of activities. However, as it grows, increasing demands are placed on the owner-manager to obtain and process all of the information necessary to run the business. Chances are the owner will not have the skill level in all areas (e.g., accounting, engineering, production, marketing) that is necessary to run a growing business. Thus, he or she will need to hire specialists in the various functional areas. The complexity of the business necessitates a functional structure, wherein the major functions of the firm are separated and led by specialists. The coordination and integration of the functional areas becomes one of the most important responsibilities of the chief executive of the firm. Exhibit 9.2 presents a diagram of a functional structure.

Functional structures are generally found in organizations whose strategies entail a single or closely related product or service, high production volume, and some vertical integration. The functional structure provides for a high level of centralization that helps to ensure integration and control over the related product-market activities or multiple primary activities in the value chain.

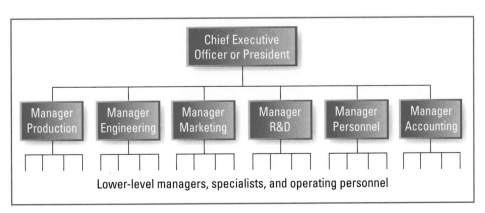

Exhibit 9.2
Functional
Organizational
Structure

Many firms use a functional structure successfully. One example is Sharp, the consumer electronics giant. Sharp Corporation is a global player in the consumer electronics industry, with approximately $17 billion in annual sales. The firm is organized into functional units, allowing coordination of tasks involving research and development, production, marketing, and management. Key components, such as LCDs (liquid crystal displays), are developed and produced in single functional units using the talents of each of these specialties. By using a centralized, functional structure, Sharp is able to achieve economies of scale with its applied research and manufacturing skills. It would be much more expensive if such skills and resources were distributed over many different, relatively autonomous business units. To make sure that these units are not completely sealed off from the other business units in the firm, product managers have the responsibility of coordinating similar products in multiple functional areas throughout the organization.[5]

By bringing together specialists into functional departments, a firm is able to enhance coordination and control within each of the functional areas. The structure ensures that decision making in the firm will be centralized at the top of the organization. This enhances an organizational-level perspective across the various functions in the organization. In addition, the functional structure provides for a more efficient use of managerial and technical talent since expertise is pooled in single departments, such as marketing or engineering, instead of being spread across a variety of areas. Finally, career paths and professional development in specialized areas are facilitated.

There are also some significant disadvantages associated with the functional structure. First, the differences in values and orientations among functional areas may impede communication and coordination. Edgar Schein of MIT has argued that shared assumptions, often based on similar backgrounds and experiences of members, form around functional units in an organization. This leads to what are often called "stove pipes" or "silos," in which departments view themselves as isolated, self-contained units with little need for interaction and coordination with other departments. This erodes communication because functional groups may not only have different goals, personalities, and shared assumptions but also differing meanings of words and concepts.[6]

Furthermore, this silo mentality may lead to short-term thinking—based largely upon what is best for the functional area, not for the organization as a whole. For example, in a manufacturing firm, sales may want to offer a wide range of customized products to appeal to the firm's customers, research and development may over-design products and components to achieve technical elegance, and manufacturing may favour no-frills products that can be produced at low cost by means of long production runs. In addition, functional structures may overburden the top executives in the firm because conflicts among functions have a tendency to be "pushed up" to the top of the organization for resolution. Finally, functional structures make it difficult to establish uniform performance standards across the whole organization. Whereas it may be relatively easy to evaluate production managers on the basis of production volume and cost control, or marketing and sales on market results, establishing performance measures for engineering, research and development, and accounting could be more problematic.

Divisional Structure

The divisional structure (sometimes called the multidivisional structure or M-form) is organized around products, projects, or markets. Each of the divisions, in turn, includes its own functional specialists who are typically organized into departments. A divisional structure encompasses a set of relatively autonomous units governed by a central

Exhibit 9.3
Divisional Organizational Structure

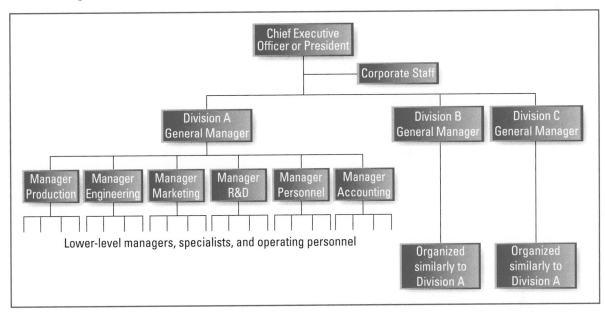

corporate office. The operating divisions are relatively independent, and their scope consists of products and services that are different from those of the other divisions. Corporate-level executives, in conjunction with divisional executives, determine the product-market and financial objectives for each division as well as its contribution to overall corporate performance.[7] Rewards are based largely on measures of financial performance such as net income and revenue. Exhibit 9.3 illustrates a divisional structure.

General Motors was among the earliest firms to adopt the divisional organization structure.[8] In the 1920s, the company formed five major product divisions (Cadillac, Buick, Oldsmobile, Pontiac, and Chevrolet) as well as several industrial divisions. Since then, many firms have discovered that as they diversified into new product-market activities, their functional structures were unable to manage the diverse needs of different product lines and markets and the increased complexity of the entire business. Operational decision making in a large business places excessive demands on the firm's top management. In order to attend to broader, longer-term organizational issues, top-level managers must delegate decision making to lower-level managers. Between the middle and end of the twentieth century, the percentage of Fortune 500 firms that became diversified and the number of firms that adopted the divisional structure rapidly increased.[9]

There are many advantages associated with the divisional structure. By creating separate divisions to manage individual product markets, there is a separation of strategic and operating control. That is, divisional managers can focus their efforts on improving operations in the product markets for which they are responsible, and corporate officers can devote their time to overall strategic issues for the entire corporation. The focus on a division's products and markets—by the divisional executives—provides the corporation with an enhanced ability to respond quickly to important changes in the external environment. Finally, because there are multiple levels of general managers (that is, executives responsible for integrating and coordinating all functional areas), the development of

The Changing Structure at Rogers Communications

Rogers Communications has three main divisions that correspond to its three lines of business: cable, wireless, and media. Each one operates in a very different environment and has a distinct history. Cable, Rogers's traditional business (although Rogers did initially start with an FM radio station), has been a utility with a very stable cash flow and a monopoly licence from the Canadian Radio and Television Commission for some of Canada's major markets. Cable markets are mature, and much of the investment has already been sunk in the ground in miles of coaxial cable. Wireless, a business that Rogers entered in 1985 as a partnership with AT&T, operates in an extremely competitive market with three equally strong players, boasts substantial growth potential, and requires marketing savvy and customer service excellence to prevent customers from switching to competitors. Finally, media is the side business that Rogers acquired when, in 1994, it won a hostile bid for Maclean Hunter, the fourth largest cable operator in Canada; with it came a host of Canadian magazine titles in a variety of fields. Canadian magazines must continuously define themselves as distinct from their American competitors who are much better endowed, have a tenfold larger market to cover journalistic costs, can draw on a much larger pool for advertising dollars, and with minor editorial changes to their American version can cheaply publish duplicate editions in Canada. Each business within Rogers operates with a different philosophy, follows a different strategy, and has developed a very different culture. The divisional structure has allowed the firm to nurture each of the businesses and facilitate their responsiveness to the very different environments.

The challenge facing Rogers today is the convergence of telephone, Internet, and television as the three distinct technologies are coming together. Some cable companies now offer local and long-distance telephone services, while Bell Canada and Telus offer television signals over satellites and are working toward doing the same through advanced technology embedded in their telephone networks. To top it all, it is anticipated that future revenues to the wireless business will come from instant messaging, downloading television programming, and the Internet. Although Rogers is already preparing for the battle, its three divisions certainly face difficulties in aligning their cultures and management ranks. They have purposefully been kept apart for too long to be able to easily communicate and co-operate.

Sources: D. DeCloet, "Ted Tomorrow," *Report on Business Magazine*, March 2005, pp. 29–35; and R. Blackwell, "Mr. Rogers Walks the High Wire in Telecom's Big Top," *The Globe and Mail*, October 9, 2004, pp. B1–B4.

general management talent is enhanced. Strategy Spotlight 9.1 discusses the divisional structure of Rogers Communications and speculates on the advantages and disadvantages the structure brings to the company.

As one would expect, a divisional structure also has disadvantages. First, there are increased costs due to the duplication of personnel, operations, and investment, as each division must staff multiple functional departments. There can also be dysfunctional competition among divisions, since each division tends to become concerned solely about its own operations. Furthermore, divisional managers are often evaluated on common measures, such as return on assets and sales growth. Thus, if goals are conflicting, there can be a sense of a "zero-sum" game that would discourage a sharing of ideas and resources among the divisions for the common good of the corporation. Ghoshal and Bartlett, two leading scholars in strategic management, note the following:

> As their label clearly warns, divisions divide. The divisional model fragmented companies' resources; it created vertical communication channels that insulated business units and prevented them from sharing their strengths with one another. Consequently, the whole of the corporation was often less than the sum of its parts.[10]

Another potential disadvantage is that, with many divisions providing different products and services, there is the chance that differences in image and quality may occur across divisions. For example, one division may offer no-frills products of lower quality, which may erode the brand reputation of another division that has top quality, highly differentiated offerings. Finally, since each division is evaluated in terms of financial measures, such as return on investment and revenue growth, there is often an urge to focus on short-term performance. For example, if corporate management uses quarterly profits as the key performance indicator, divisional management may tend to put significant emphasis on "making the numbers" and in doing so minimize activities such as advertising, maintenance, and capital investments, which would detract from short-term performance measures.

Before moving on, we discuss two variations of the divisional form of organizational structure: the strategic business unit (SBU) and holding company structures.

Strategic Business Unit (SBU) Structure Corporations that are highly diversified—such as George Weston Ltd., a $30 billion food producer and retailer—may consist of dozens of different divisions.[11] If Weston were to use a purely divisional structure, it would be nearly impossible for the corporate office to plan and coordinate activities because the span of control would be too large. Instead, to attain synergies, Weston has put its diverse businesses into three primary SBUs: fisheries (Heritage Salmon and fish farms), bakeries (Bestfoods Baking Co., Entenmann's, Thomas' English Muffins), and retail (Loblaws, No Frills, Fortinos, Zehrs).

With an SBU structure, divisions with similar products, markets, and/or technologies are grouped into homogenous groups in order to achieve some synergies such as leveraging core competencies, sharing infrastructures, and consolidating market power. Generally speaking, the more related businesses are within a corporation, the fewer SBUs will be required. Each of the SBUs in the corporation operates as a profit centre.

The major advantage of the SBU structure is that it makes the task of planning and control by the corporate office more manageable. Also, since the structure provides greater decentralization of authority, individual businesses can react more quickly to important changes in the environment than if all divisions had to report directly to the corporate office.

There are also some disadvantages of the SBU structure. Since the divisions are grouped into SBUs, it may become difficult to achieve synergies across SBUs. That is, if divisions that are included in different SBUs have potential sources of synergy, it may become difficult for them to be realized. The additional level of management increases the number of personnel and overhead expenses, while the additional hierarchical level removes the corporate office further from the individual divisions. Thus, the corporate office may become unaware of key developments that could have a major impact on the corporation.

Holding Company Structure The holding company structure (sometimes referred to as a *conglomerate*) is another variation of the divisional structure. Whereas the SBU structure is often used when similarities exist between the individual businesses (or divisions), the holding company structure is appropriate when the businesses in a corporation's portfolio do not have much in common and when the potential for synergies is, therefore, limited.

Holding company structures are most appropriate for firms that follow a strategy of unrelated diversification. Companies such as the Jim Pattison group, Onex Corporation, and Brascan have relied on the holding company structure to implement their unrelated diversification strategies. Since there are few similarities across the businesses, the corporate offices in these companies provide a great deal of autonomy to operating divisions and rely on financial controls and incentive programs to obtain high levels of performance from the individual businesses. As one would expect, corporate staffs at these firms tend to be small because their involvement in the overall operation of their various businesses is limited.[12]

An important advantage of the holding company structure is the savings associated with fewer personnel and the lower overhead resulting from a small corporate office and fewer levels in the corporate hierarchy. In addition, the autonomy of the holding company structure increases the motivational level of divisional executives and enables them to respond quickly to market opportunities and threats. Finally, new businesses can be added, while underperforming businesses can be dropped relatively easily and with little disruption to the rest of the corporation.

The primary disadvantage of the holding company structure is the inherent lack of control and dependence that corporate-level executives have on divisional executives. Major problems could arise if key divisional executives leave the firm, since the corporate office has very little "bench strength"—that is, additional managerial talent ready to fill key positions on short notice. And, if problems arise in a division, it may become very difficult to turn around individual businesses because of limited staff support in the corporate office.

Matrix Structure

At times, managers may find that none of the structures that we have described above fully meet their needs. In most cases, those structures encourage a silo mentality, whereby a division has little incentive or reason to communicate, co-operate, or interact with other parts of the organization. Frequently, this leads to missed market opportunities, duplication of activities, and missed opportunities to explore synergies throughout the organization because information that is generated and used in one part of the organization does not get transferred to another, where it could be of further use. One approach that tries to overcome the inadequacies inherent in the other structures is the matrix structure. It is, in effect, a combination of the functional and divisional structures. Most commonly, functional departments are combined with product groups on a permanent or on a project basis. For example, a product group may want to develop a new addition to its line; for this project, it obtains personnel from functional departments such as marketing, production, and engineering. These personnel work under the manager of the product group for the duration of the project, which can vary from a few weeks to an open-ended period of time. The individuals who work in a matrix organization become responsible to two managers: the product manager and the manager of their functional area. Exhibit 9.4 illustrates a matrix structure.

In addition to the product-function matrix, other bases may be related in a matrix. Some large multinational corporations rely on a matrix structure to combine product groups and geographical units. Product managers have global responsibility for the development, manufacturing, and distribution of their own line, while managers of geographical regions have responsibility for the profitability of the businesses in their regions.

Global firms, such as ABB and Texas Instruments have adopted matrix structures under the premise that it facilitates more effective utilization of specialized personnel, equipment, and facilities. Rather than duplicating functions, as would be the case in a divisional structure based on products, the resources are shared as needed. Individuals with high expertise can divide their time among multiple projects at one time. Such resource sharing and collaboration enable a firm to use resources more efficiently and to respond more quickly and effectively to changes in the competitive environment. In addition, the flexibility inherent in a matrix structure provides professionals with a broader range of responsibility, and the experience enables them to develop their skills and competencies.

There are also many potential disadvantages associated with matrix structures. The dual-reporting structures can result in uncertainty and lead to intense power struggles and

Exhibit 9.4
Matrix Organizational Structure

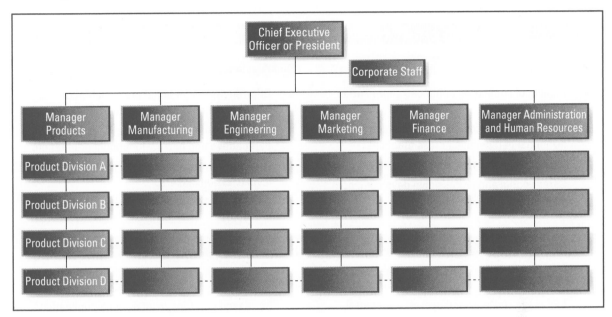

conflict over the allocation of professional personnel and other resources. Additionally, working relationships become more complicated. This may result in excessive reliance on group processes and teamwork, along with a diffusion of responsibility, which, in turn, may erode timely decision making. Exhibit 9.5 summarizes the advantages and disadvantages of the functional, divisional, and matrix organizational structures.

International Operations: Implications for Organizational Structure

Today's managers must maintain an international outlook on their firm's businesses and competitive strategies. To be successful in the global marketplace, managers must ensure consistency between their strategies (at the business, corporate, and international levels) and the structure of their organization. As firms expand into foreign markets, they generally follow a pattern of change in structure that parallels the changes in their strategies. Three major contingencies that seem to influence the structure adopted by firms with international operations are (1) the type of strategy that is driving a firm's foreign operations, (2) product diversity, and (3) the extent to which a firm is dependent on foreign sales.[13]

As international operations become an important part of a firm's overall operations, managers must make changes that are consistent with their firm's structure. The following are the primary types of structures used to manage a firm's international operations:[14]

- International division
- Geographic-area division
- Worldwide functional
- Worldwide product division
- Worldwide matrix

As we discussed in Chapter 7, multidomestic strategies are driven by political and cultural imperatives that require managers within each country to respond to local conditions.

Exhibit 9.5
Functional, Divisional, and Matrix Organizational Structures

Functional Structure

Advantages

- Pooling of specialists enhances coordination and control.
- Centralized decision making enhances an organizational perspective across functions.
- Efficient use of managerial and technical talent.
- Career paths and professional development in specialized areas are facilitated.

Disadvantages

- Differences in functional area orientation impede communication and coordination.
- Tendency for specialists to develop short-term perspective and narrow functional orientation.
- Functional area conflicts may overburden top-level decision makers.
- Difficult to establish uniform performance standards.

Divisional Structure

Advantages

- Increases strategic and operational control, permitting corporate-level executives to address strategic issues.
- Quick response to environmental changes.
- Increased focus on products and markets.
- Minimizes problems associated with sharing resources across functional areas.
- Facilitates development of general managers.

Disadvantages

- Increased costs incurred through duplication of personnel, operations, and investment.
- Dysfunctional competition among divisions may detract from overall corporate performance.
- Difficulty in maintaining uniform corporate image.
- Overemphasis on short-term performance.

Matrix Structure

Advantages

- Increases market responsiveness through collaboration and synergies among professional colleagues.
- Allows more efficient utilization of resources.
- Improves flexibility, coordination, and communication.
- Increases professional development through a broader range of responsibility.

Disadvantages

- Dual-reporting relationships can result in uncertainty regarding accountability.
- Intense power struggles may lead to increased levels of conflict.
- Working relationships may be more complicated and human resources duplicated.
- Excessive reliance on group processes and teamwork may impede timely decision making.

The structures that would be consistent with such a strategic orientation are the *international division* and *geographic-area division* structures. Here, local managers are provided with a high level of autonomy to manage their operations within the constraints and demands of their geographic market. As a firm's foreign sales increase as a percentage of its total sales, it will likely change from an international division structure to a geographic-area division structure. And, as a firm's product and/or market diversity becomes large, it is more likely to benefit from a *worldwide matrix* structure.

Global strategies, on the other hand, are driven by economic pressures that require managers to view operations in different geographic areas as only a component of a larger operation that must be managed for overall efficiency. The structures consistent with the efficiency perspective are the *worldwide functional* and *worldwide product division* structures. Here, division managers view the marketplace as homogeneous and devote relatively little attention to local market, political, and economic factors. The choice between these two types of structures is guided largely by the extent of product diversity. Firms with lower levels of product diversity may opt for a worldwide product division structure. However, when a firm has significant product-market diversity resulting from a series of highly unrelated international acquisitions, a worldwide holding company structure is likely to be implemented. Such firms are characterized by very little commonality among products, markets, or technologies and have little need for integration.

Global Start-ups

Our discussions of dominant patterns of growth earlier in the sections suggested that international expansion occurs rather late in the history of most corporations—typically after possibilities of domestic growth have been exhausted. Increasingly, though, we are seeing two interrelated phenomena. First, many firms now decide to expand internationally relatively early in their history. Second, some firms are "born global," in the sense that from the very beginning they were global in their activities. For example, Logitech Inc., the leading producer of "mouse" for personal computers, was global in its operations from day one.[15] Founded in 1982 by a Swiss national and two Italians, the company was headquartered both in California and in Switzerland. R&D and manufacturing were also conducted in both locations, and as the company grew, they expanded those functions into Taiwan and Ireland. The success of companies such as Logitech challenges the conventional wisdom that a company must first build up assets, internal processes, and experience before venturing into far away lands. It also raises a number of questions: What exactly is a global start-up? Under what conditions should a company start out as a global firm? What does it take to succeed as a global start-up?

A global start-up can be defined as a business organization that from its inception seeks to derive significant competitive advantages from the use of resources and the sale of its products and services in multiple countries. That is, right from the beginning, it uses inputs from around the world and sells to customers around the world. Geographical boundaries of nation-states are by and large irrelevant for a global start-up.

There is no reason for every start-up to be global. Being global necessitates higher communication, coordination, and transportation costs; therefore, from the outset it is important to identify the circumstances under which going global is advantageous. First, if the required human resources are globally dispersed, going global may be the best way to access those resources. For example, a start-up company for fine office furniture may find it necessary to employ designers in Germany, leather craftsmen in Italy, and a sales and distribution organization in North America in order to capitalize on unique skills that can be found dispersed in different countries and global regions. Second, in many cases, foreign financing may be easier to obtain and more suitable for the project than local financing: traditionally, U.S. venture capitalists have shown greater willingness to bear risk, but they have shorter time horizons in their expectations for return; and a Canadian software company may find a more receptive investor in the U.S., while a U.S. start-up

Israel: Home of the Global Start-Ups

Israel may be a minor player in the world of international commerce, but, surprisingly, the country has been home base for a disproportionately large number of global start-ups. Blue chip venture capital firms and private equity firms from the U.S. have funded literally thousands of start-ups in Israel over the last ten years. As a result of the success of these, Israel is third in the ranking of countries with the most companies listed on Nasdaq, the stock exchange that specializes in high-tech firms. Here are some examples:

Gal Bachum and Amir Peleg, the founders of Cash-U Mobile Technologies, initially thought they would develop games for cellphones, but they soon realized that it was difficult to come up with game that has universal appeal. Instead, they now supply a software platform that helps other companies develop games for cellphones. Once they had created the product in their lab outside Tel Aviv, they opened sales offices in London and Singapore. Today, their customers include firms such as Vodafone and Telephonica, and their revenues are growing by about 75 percent annually.

Baradok Pridor and Yonatan Aumann, founders of ClearForest, developed an innovative software program that can analyze unstructured electronic data, such as a Web page or a video clip, as if it were already in a spreadsheet or database. With few applications in Israel, they immediately embarked on presentations to potential clients around the world. The company's customers include Dow Chemical, Thomson Financial, and the FBI. They have raised $33 million over three rounds of venture financing from U.S. venture capitalists. While most of their 83 employees are still located in Israel, the company's headquarters are now in Boston.

Why is Israel home to so many global start-ups? First of all, as a country with a population of only six million people, the home market is too small to support the growth of domestic companies, especially in the high-tech sector. A second reason is that the political uncertainties of the region encourage entrepreneurs to diversify their risk by establishing an international presence. Third, the Israeli culture is one that encourages risk taking, as well as displays of an independent and entrepreneurial spirit. Fourth, many younger generation Israelis have international networks, either due to education or to travel. More importantly, the country has a highly educated workforce, boasting the highest percentage of engineers among the population when compared to other countries, and, in general, Israelis exhibit a strong work ethic.

Sources: M. V. Copeland, "The start-up oasis," *Business 2.0*, August 2004, pp. 46–48; E. Brown, "Global start-up," *Forbes*, November 29, 2007, pp. 150–161.

that is looking for patient capital may be better off looking overseas. Third, the target customers in many specialized industries are located in other parts of the world. Fourth, in many industries, a gradual move from domestic markets to foreign markets is no longer possible, because if a product is successful, foreign competitors will immediately imitate it; pre-emptive entry into foreign markets may, therefore, be the only option. Finally, because of high up-front development costs, a global market may be necessary in order to recover the investment. This is particularly true for start-ups based in smaller nations without large domestic markets.

Successful management of a global start-up presents many challenges. Communication and coordination across time zones and cultures are always problematic. Given that most global start-ups have far fewer resources and less management depth than well-established corporations, one key for success is internalizing a minimal proportion of activities and outsourcing the rest. It is also vital that managers have considerable prior international experience so that they are able to successfully deal with the inevitable communication problems and cultural conflicts. Another key consideration is keeping communication and coordination costs low. The only way to achieve this is by creating less costly administrative mechanisms. The boundaryless organization designs discussed in the next section are particularly suitable for global start-ups because of their flexibility and low cost. Strategy Spotlight 9.2 discusses a number of global start-ups based in Israel.

How an Organization's Structure Can Influence Strategy Formulation

Generally speaking, discussions of the relationship between strategy and structure strongly imply that structure follows strategy. That is, the strategy that a firm chooses (e.g., related diversification) dictates such structural elements as the division of tasks, the appropriate patterns of information flow, the need for integration of activities, and authority relationships within the organization. However, we must also recognize the role that an existing structure can play in strategy formulation. For example, once a firm's structure is in place, it is very difficult and expensive to change.[16] Executives may not be able to modify their duties and responsibilities greatly, or they may not welcome the disruption associated with a transfer to a new location. Further, there may be costs associated with hiring, training, and replacing executive, managerial, and operating personnel. Thus, strategy cannot be formulated without considering structural elements.

The type of organizational structure can also strongly influence a firm's strategy, day-to-day operations, and performance.[17] For example, as we discussed earlier, Sharp's functional structure enables the company to achieve economies of scale with its applied research and manufacturing skills. Also, managers have the responsibility to coordinate similar products in multiple functional areas throughout the organization. Because of lower costs, such structural arrangements should help increase operating performance and enable Sharp to enter new product markets through its applied research. These opportunities would likely not be realized if Sharp had extensive redundant manufacturing resources throughout its divisions and did not effectively coordinate functional area operations across its divisions. The history of success of Sharp's functional structure also suggests that the company is unlikely to consider diversification—a strategy that would require it to move away from the functional structure. Finally, having a holding company structure already in place is likely to make it easier to consider further diversification options. Compared to a firm with a functional structure, one with a holding company structure would more readily pursue additional diversification initiatives or shed underperforming units without disrupting the rest of the organization.

BOUNDARYLESS ORGANIZATIONAL DESIGNS

The term *boundaryless* may bring to mind a chaotic organizational reality in which "anything goes." This is not the case. As Jack Welch, GE's former CEO, has suggested, boundaryless does not imply that all internal and external boundaries vanish completely. Although boundaries may continue to exist in some form, they become more open and permeable.

We can consider four distinct types of boundaries that have traditionally defined an organization.[18] Such boundaries typically keep interaction among individuals within their borders and prevent information from being exchanged with individuals outside the boundaries. First, *vertical boundaries* exist between the various levels inside the organization. Hierarchies set barriers on the interaction among individuals and on the movement of ideas up and down the organization. Often, only formal channels of communication can be used to pass information up to senior managers or to bring direction down to the operating units from the more senior ranks. Second, *horizontal boundaries* exist between the various divisions, departments, and functions within an organization. They typically hinder information generated within one department from being passed to another department or division of the organization. Third, *geographic boundaries* between locations, cultures, and markets act to keep interaction from transcending those boundaries. People naturally turn to those with whom they are in close physical proximity, with whom they are more familiar, and with whom they can speak the same language or

← LO 4

exchange information and ideas. Fourth, *external boundaries* exist between the firm and its customers and suppliers. The interaction can be substantially restricted to arm's length exchanges governed by strict rules of confidentiality, an antagonistic attitude, and an "us versus them" mindset.

Boundaryless structures make those boundaries more permeable and enhance the interactions among individuals, the transfer of information, and the joint decision making across boundaries. They do not replace the traditional forms of organizational structure; rather, they complement them. For example, Sharp Corp. has implemented a functional structure in order to attain economies of scale with its applied research and manufacturing skills. However, to bring about this key objective, Sharp has relied on several integrating mechanisms and processes—key attributes of the boundaryless concept.

To prevent functional groups from becoming vertical chimneys that obstruct product development, Sharp's product managers have responsibility—but not authority—for coordinating the entire set of value-chain activities. And the company convenes enormous numbers of cross-unit and corporate committees to ensure that shared activities, including the corporate R&D unit and sales forces, are optimally configured and allocated among the different product lines. Sharp invests in such time-intensive coordination to minimize the inevitable conflicts that arise when units share important activities.[19]

Others use different devices to enhance the permeability of their boundaries. Smith-Kline Beecham asks employees at different hierarchical levels to jointly brainstorm ideas for managing clinical trial data. Wal-Mart integrates its IT systems with its suppliers and shares point of sale information. These moves allow SmithKline Beecham to significantly cut the new product approval time and Wal-Mart to speed its logistics operations and bring products to its stores' shelves faster than any of its competitors.

LO 5 → We discuss three approaches to making boundaries more permeable and facilitating the widespread sharing of knowledge and information across both the internal and external boundaries of the organization. We begin with the *barrier-free* type, which involves making all organizational boundaries—internal and external—more permeable. We place particular emphasis on team concepts because we view teams as a central building block for implementing the boundaryless organization. Then, we address the *modular* and *virtual* types of organizations, which focus on the need to create seamless relationships with external organizations, such as customers or suppliers. While the modular type emphasizes the outsourcing of non-core activities, the virtual organization is a network of independent organizations and focuses on alliances among independent entities formed to exploit specific market opportunities.

The Barrier-Free Organization

The "boundary" mindset is deeply ingrained in bureaucracies. It is evidenced by such clichés as "That's not my job," "I'm here from corporate to help," or by endless battles over transfer pricing. In the traditional company, boundaries are clearly delineated in the design of an organization's structure. These boundaries are rigid. Their basic advantage is that the roles of managers and employees are simple, clear, well-defined, and long-lived. At the same time, they can be divisive and lead to territorial fights.

Today, such structures are being replaced by fluid, ambiguous, and deliberately ill-defined tasks and roles. Just because work roles are no longer defined by traditional structures, however, does not mean that differences in skills, authority, and talent disappear.

A barrier-free organization enables a firm to bridge real differences in culture, function, and goal in order to find common ground that facilitates information sharing and other forms of co-operative behaviour. Eliminating the multiple boundaries that stifle productivity and innovation can enhance the potential of the entire organization.

Creating Permeable Internal Boundaries For barrier-free organizations to work effectively, the level of trust and shared interests among all parts of the organization must be raised. Similarly, the organization needs to develop among its employees the skill level needed to work in a more democratic organization. Barrier-free organizations also require a shift in the organization's philosophy and corresponding concerns—from investments in high-potential individuals to investments in leveraging the talents of all individuals.

Teams can be an important aspect of barrier-free structures. Jeffrey Pfeffer, author of several insightful books, including *The Human Equation*, suggests that teams have three primary advantages.[20] First, teams substitute hierarchical control with peer-based control of work activities. In essence, employees control themselves, reducing the time and energy management needs to devote to controlling others.

Second, teams frequently develop more creative solutions to problems because they encourage the sharing of the tacit knowledge held by individual team members.[21] Brainstorming, or group problem solving, involves the pooling of ideas and expertise to enhance the chances that at least one group member will think of a way to solve the problems at hand.

Third, by substituting hierarchical control with peer-based control, teams permit the removal of layers of hierarchy and allow the absorption of administrative tasks previously performed by specialists. This prevents the cumbersome costs of having people whose sole job is to watch the people who watch other people do the work. As Norman Augustine wisely pointed out in *Augustine's Laws*, "If a sufficient number of management layers are superimposed on top of each other, it can be assured that disaster is not left to chance!"[22] Teams can both eliminate layers of supervisors and produce better results.

Effective barrier-free organizations must go beyond achieving close integration and coordination within divisions in a corporation. Past research on the multidivisional type of organization has pointed to the importance of interdivisional coordination and resource sharing.[23] The means to this end include interdivisional task forces and committees, reward and incentive systems that emphasize interdivisional co-operation, and common training programs.

A study of professional service firms provides some additional insights.[24] The most important assets of these firms were not the individual technical expertise of their members. That was merely a precondition. Rather, the collective wisdom of multidisciplinary teams was what set them apart. Further, the researchers found that the average performers excelled at using the combined knowledge of boundary-crossing teams to solve especially complex problems with a speed and efficiency that competitors could not match. The competitor of a top-performing investment bank lamented:

> They are the team to beat. Why? They don't slow themselves down with the clutter of bureaucracy. They overwhelm the problem. That could yield inefficiency, but it doesn't. They are smart and quick and work seamlessly together.

The capacity to work together rested on an individual willingness to learn and a belief that no single person had all the answers.[25] A partner in a law firm made the following observation:

> One thing that I look at in a prospective partner is the ability to recognize when you don't know the answer. None of us are expected to be experts across the board. Our practice is highly sophisticated, so that we have to bring to bear front-line and top-level expertise in different categories. I need to be smart enough to recognize that there's an issue and go to my partners for assistance.

> Work is so interdisciplinary that I just can't imagine doing my work without substantial help from others. Right at the top of the firm, everybody's convinced that we are stronger than we are as individuals.

Given the importance of collaboration and collective efforts, what makes a good team becomes of critical importance. Frank Carruba (former head of Hewlett-Packard's labs) provides some interesting insights.[26] He discovered that the difference between mediocre teams and good teams was generally varying levels of motivation and talent. But what explained the difference between good teams and truly superior teams? Carruba found that the key difference—and this explained a 40 percent overall difference in performance— was the way members treated each other or, more precisely, the degree to which they believed in one another and created an atmosphere of encouragement rather than competition. In other words, vision, talent, and motivation could carry a team only so far. What clearly stood out in the "super" teams were higher levels of authenticity and caring, which allowed the full synergy of their individual talents, motivation, and vision to be expressed without barriers.

Developing Effective Relationships with External Constituencies In barrier-free organizations, managers must also create flexible, porous organizational boundaries and establish communication flows and mutually beneficial relationships with internal constituencies (e.g., employees) and external constituencies (e.g., customers). Michael Dell, founder and CEO of Dell Computer, is a strong believer in fostering close relationships with his customers. In an interview, he explained:

> We're not going to be just your PC vendor anymore. We're going to be your IT department for PCs. Boeing, for example, has 100,000 Dell PCs, and we have 30 people that live at Boeing, and if you look at the things we're doing for them or for other customers, we don't look like a supplier, we look more like Boeing's PC department. We become intimately involved in planning their PC needs and the configuration of their network.
>
> It's not that we make these decisions by ourselves. They're certainly using their own people to get the best answer for the company. But the people working on PCs together, from both Dell and Boeing, understand the needs in a very intimate way. They're right there living it and breathing it, as opposed to the typical vendor who says, "Here are your computers. See you later."[27]

Thus far, we have argued that barrier-free organizations create successful relationships with both internal and external constituencies. However, there is one additional constituency—competitors—with whom some organizations have benefited as they developed co-operative relationships. After years of seeing its empty trucks return from warehouses back to production facilities after deliveries, General Mills teamed up with 16 of its competitors.[28] The network of competitors formed an ecommerce business, allowing the companies to find carriers with empty cargo trailers to piggyback freight loads to distributors near the production facilities. This increases revenue for all network members and reduces wasted carrier miles.

Risks, Challenges, and Potential Downsides In spite of its potential benefits, many firms are discovering that creating and managing a barrier-free organization is a frustrating experience.[29] For example, Puritan-Bennett Corporation, a Lenexa, Kansas, manufacturer of respiratory equipment, found that its product development time more than doubled after it adopted team management. Roger J. Dolida, director of R&D, attributed this failure to lack of top management commitment, high turnover among team members, and infrequent meetings. Similarly, efforts at Jerome Goods, a turkey producer in Baron, Wisconsin, to switch to entrepreneurial teams have largely stalled due to a failure to link executive compensation to team performance. Very often, managers trained in rigid hierarchies find it difficult to make the transition to the more democratic, participative style that teamwork requires.

Christopher Barnes, now a consultant with PricewaterhouseCoopers in Atlanta, previously worked as an industrial engineer for Challenger Electrical Distribution (a subsidiary of Westinghouse, now part of CBS) at a plant in Jackson, Mississippi, which produced circuit-breaker boxes. His assignment was to lead a team of workers from the plant's troubled final-assembly operation with the mission, "Make things better." Not surprisingly, that vague notion set the team up for failure.

After a year of futile efforts, the team was disbanded. In retrospect, and after several successes with teams, Barnes identified several reasons for the debacle in Jackson: (1) limited personal credibility—he was viewed as an "outsider"; (2) a lack of commitment to the team—everyone involved was forced to be on the team; (3) poor communications—nobody was told why the team was important; (4) limited autonomy—line managers refused to give up control over team members; and (5) misaligned incentives—the culture rewarded individual performance over team performance. Barnes's experience has important implications for all types of teams, whether composed of managerial, professional, clerical, or production personnel.[30] The pros and cons of barrier-free structures are summarized in Exhibit 9.6.

The Modular Organization

As Charles Handy, author of *The Age of Unreason*, has noted:

> Organizations have realized that, while it may be convenient to have everyone around all the time, having all of your workforce's time at your command is an extravagant way of marshalling the necessary resources. It is cheaper to keep them outside the organization, employed by themselves or by specialist contractors, and to buy their services when you need them.[31]

Pros	Cons
◆ Leverages the talents of all employees.	◆ Difficulties in overcoming political and authority boundaries inside and outside the organization.
◆ Enhances co-operation, coordination, and information sharing among functions, divisions, SBUs, and external constituencies.	◆ Requires strong leadership and common vision; otherwise, can lead to coordination problems.
◆ Enables a quicker response to market changes through a single-goal focus.	◆ Includes time-consuming and difficult-to-manage democratic processes.
◆ Can lead to coordinated win-win initiatives with key suppliers, customers, and alliance partners.	◆ Requires high levels of trust, which can impede performance.
	◆ Difficulties in assigning individual responsibility and allocating individual incentives and rewards.

Exhibit 9.6
Pros and Cons of Barrier-Free Structures

To capture Handy's vision, the modular organization outsources non-vital functions, tapping into the knowledge and expertise of "best in class" suppliers of goods and services, but retains strategic control. Outsiders may be used to manufacture parts, handle logistics, or perform accounting activities. As we discussed in Chapters 3 and 5, the value chain can be used as a framework to identify the key primary and support activities performed by a firm to create value. The key question becomes, which activities should be kept "in-house" and which activities should be outsourced to suppliers? In effect, the organization becomes a central hub surrounded by networks of outside suppliers and specialists, and, much like Lego blocks, parts can be added or taken away. Both manufacturing and service units may be modular.[32]

In the personal computer industry, the shift to the modular structure has been pioneered by relative newcomers like Dell and Gateway as well as by workstation innovators like Sun Microsystems. These companies either buy their products ready-made or purchase all the parts from suppliers and perform only the final assembly. Their larger, more established competitors—IBM and Hewlett-Packard—produce most of their parts in-house. As a result, the smaller modular companies are often ahead of their older rivals in profitability.[33]

Apparel is another industry in which the modular type of structure has been widely adopted. Nike and Reebok, for example, have succeeded by concentrating on their strengths: designing and marketing high-tech, fashionable footwear. Nike has very limited production facilities and Reebok owns no plants. These two companies contract virtually all their footwear production to suppliers in Taiwan, South Korea, and other countries with low-cost labour. By being modular, Nike and Reebok can keep pace with changing tastes in the marketplace because their suppliers have become expert at rapidly retooling for the manufacture of new products.

In a modular company, outsourcing the non-core functions offers three advantages:

1. It can decrease overall costs, stimulate new product development by the hiring of suppliers whose talent may be superior to that of in-house personnel, prevent idle capacity, realize inventory savings, and prevent the company from becoming locked into a particular technology.
2. It enables a company to focus scarce resources on the areas where it holds a competitive advantage. These benefits can translate into more funding for research and development, hiring the best engineers, and providing continual training for sales and service staff.
3. By enabling an organization to tap into the knowledge and expertise of its specialized supply-chain partners, it adds critical skills and accelerates organizational learning.[34]

The modular type enables a company to leverage relatively small amounts of capital and a small management team to achieve seemingly unattainable strategic objectives. Freed from the need to make big investments in fixed assets, the modular company can achieve rapid growth. Certain preconditions must exist or be created, however, before the modular approach can be successful. First, the company must work closely with suppliers to ensure that the interests of each party are being fulfilled. Companies need to find loyal, reliable vendors who can be trusted with trade secrets. They also need assurances that suppliers will dedicate their financial, physical, and human resources to satisfy strategic objectives such as lowering costs or being first to market. Second, the modular company must make sure that it selects the proper competencies to keep in-house. An organization

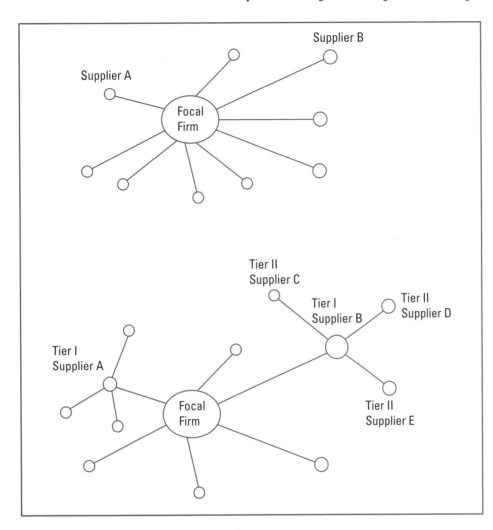

Exhibit 9.7
Examples of Modular Organizations

must be wary of outsourcing critical components of its business that may compromise long-term competitive advantages.

Firms applying the modular concept should identify core competencies and areas that are important for future development and then attempt to outsource non-critical functions. For Nike and Reebok, the core competencies are design and marketing, not shoe manufacturing; for Honda, the core competence is engine technology. These firms are unlikely to outsource any activity that involves their core competence. Exhibit 9.7 presents examples of modular structures from the computer and automobile manufacturing industries. In each case, the focal organization is connected with others in the value-creation process and relies on them for delivering some of the primary and support activities.

Strategic Risks of Outsourcing While adopting the modular form clearly has some advantages, managers must also weigh associated risks. The main strategic concerns are (1) loss of critical skills or developing the wrong skills, (2) loss of cross-functional skills, and (3) loss of control.[35]

Too much outsourcing can result in a firm "giving away" too much skill and control. Outsourcing relieves companies of the requirement to maintain skill levels needed to manufacture essential components. Over time, skills that were once part of the knowledge base of the company disappear. At one point, semiconductor chips seemed like a simple technology to outsource. But now, they have become a critical component of a wide variety of products. Companies that have outsourced the manufacture of these chips run the risk of losing the ability to manufacture them as the technology has rapidly escalated. Thus, they may become increasingly dependent upon their suppliers.

Cross-functional skills refer to the skills acquired through the interaction of individuals in various departments within a company. Often, such interaction assists a department in solving problems as employees interface with others across functional units. However, if a firm outsources key functional responsibilities, such as manufacturing, communication across departments can become more difficult. This is because a firm and its employees must now integrate their activities with a new, outside supplier. This typically brings about new challenges in the coordination of joint efforts.

Another serious drawback can occur when the outsourced products give suppliers too much power over the manufacturer. This can happen when the manufacturer is dependent on a single supplier, or just a few suppliers, for critical components. Suppliers that are key to a manufacturer's success can, in essence, hold the manufacturer "hostage." Nike manages this potential problem by sending full-time "product expatriates" to work at the plants of its suppliers. Also, the company often brings top members of supplier management and technical teams to Nike headquarters. This way, Nike keeps close tabs on the pulse of new developments, builds rapport and trust with suppliers, and develops long-term relationships with suppliers to prevent hostage situations. Exhibit 9.8 summarizes the pros and cons of modular structures.[36]

Exhibit 9.8
Pros and Cons of
Modular Structures

Pros	Cons
• Directs a firm's managerial and technical talent to the most critical activities.	• Inhibits common vision through reliance on outsiders.
• Maintains full strategic control over most critical activities—core competencies.	• Diminishes future competitive advantages if critical technologies or other competencies are outsourced.
• Achieves "best in class" performance at each link in the value chain.	• Increases the difficulty of bringing back into the firm activities that add value due to market shifts.
• Leverages core competencies by outsourcing with smaller capital commitment.	• May lead to an erosion of cross-functional skills.
• Encourages information sharing and accelerates organizational learning.	• Decreases operational control and, potentially, control over a supplier.
• Increases flexibility and reduces resource commitments.	

The Virtual Organization

The virtual organization is viewed as a continually evolving network of independent companies—suppliers, customers, even competitors—linked together to share skills, costs, and access to one another's markets.[37] The members of a virtual organization, by pooling and sharing the knowledge and expertise of each of the component organizations, simultaneously "know" more and can "do" more than any one member of the group could do alone. By working closely together in a co-operative effort, each gains in the long run from the resulting individual and organizational learning that takes place.[38] The term *virtual*, meaning "being in effect but not actually so," is commonly used in the computer industry. A computer's ability to appear to have more storage capacity than it really possesses is called virtual memory. Similarly, by assembling resources from a variety of entities, a virtual organization may seem to have more capabilities than it really possesses.[39]

The virtual organization consists of a grouping of units of different organizations that have joined in an alliance to exploit complementary skills while pursuing common strategic objectives. A case in point is Lockheed Martin's use of specialized coalitions between and among three entities—the company, academia, and government—to enhance competitiveness. According to CEO Norman Augustine:

> The underlying beauty of this approach is that it forces us to reach outward. No matter what your size, you have to look broadly for new ideas, new approaches, new products. Lockheed Martin used this approach in a surprising manner when it set out during the height of the Cold War to make stealth aircraft and missiles. The technical idea came from research done at the Institute of Radio Engineering in Moscow in the 1960s that was published, and publicized, quite openly in the academic media.
>
> Despite the great contrasts among government, academia and private business, we have found ways to work together that have produced very positive results, not the least of which is our ability to compete on a global scale.[40]

Virtual organizations need not be permanent. Participating firms may be involved in multiple alliances at any one time. Virtual organizations can involve different firms performing complementary value activities, or different firms involved jointly in the same value activities, such as production, R&D, advertising, and distribution. The percentage of activities that are jointly performed with alliance partners may vary significantly from alliance to alliance.[41]

How does the virtual type of structure differ from the modular type? Unlike the modular type, in which the focal firm maintains full strategic control, the virtual organization is characterized by participating firms that give up part of their control and accept interdependent destinies. Participating firms pursue a collective strategy that enables them to cope with uncertainty in the environment through co-operative efforts. The benefit is that, just as virtual memory increases storage capacity, the virtual organizations enhance the capacity, or competitive advantage, of participating firms. Strategy Spotlight 9.3 addresses the variety of collaborative relationships in the biotechnology industry. Exhibit 9.9 presents an example of a virtual organization from the oil exploration field.

Each company that links up with others to create a virtual organization contributes only what it considers its core competencies. It will mix and match what it does best with the best of other firms by identifying its critical capabilities and the necessary links to other capabilities.[42]

Challenges and Risks Despite their many advantages, networks of independent firms often fail to meet expectations. For example, the alliance between IBM and Microsoft

Collaborative Relationships in Biotechnology

Collaboration in biotechnology has benefited a variety of firms. Amgen collaborates with a number of smaller firms, including ARRIS, Envirogen, GlycoNex, and Interneuron, among others. The companies work on joint marketing projects and bring R&D scientists together to explore opportunities for new pharmaceutical product development. In exchange for the expertise of the scientists and marketers at the smaller companies, Amgen provides financial clout and technical assistance when new-product opportunities are identified.

Another biotech company that utilizes collaborative relationships with competitors is Biogen. This large pharmaceutical firm once outsourced clinical testing of its new drugs. Now the company brings experts from other firms to Biogen laboratories to work with Biogen scientists.

Chiron, with its more than 7,500 employees, is one of the largest pharmaceutical firms. This company makes extensive use of collaborative efforts with its competitors and currently collaborates with over 1,400 companies, tapping into the knowledge base of R&D experts with a wide variety of skill and expertise in the field. Chiron considers this network one of its core competencies.

Sources: W. W. Powell, "Learning from Collaboration: Knowledge and Networks in the Biotechnology and Pharmaceutical Industries," *California Management Review*, 40, no. 3 (1998), pp. 228–40; E. Williams and R. Langreth, "A Biotech Wonder Grows Up," *Forbes*, September 3, 2001, p. 118.

Exhibit 9.9
Example of a Virtual Organization

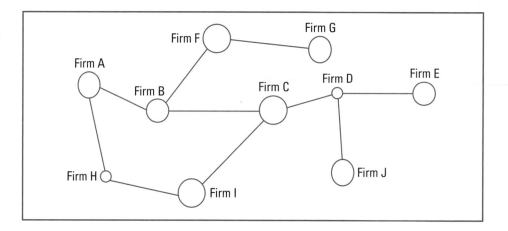

soured in early 1991 when Microsoft began shipping *Windows* in direct competition with *OS/2*, which was jointly developed by the two firms. The runaway success of *Windows* frustrated IBM's ability to set an industry standard. In retaliation, IBM entered into an alliance with Microsoft's archrival, Novell, to develop network software to compete with Microsoft's LAN Manager.

The virtual organization demands a unique set of managerial skills. Managers must build relationships with other companies, negotiate win-win deals for all parties involved, find partners with compatible goals and values, and provide the temporary organization with the right balance of freedom and control. In addition, information systems must be designed and integrated to facilitate communication with current and potential partners.

An ever-changing pattern of alliances, which is constantly being formed and dissolved, does not necessarily imply mutually exploitative arrangements or lack of long-term relationships. The key is for managers to be clear about the strategic objectives while forming alliances. Some objectives are time bound, and those alliances need to be dissolved once the objective is fulfilled. Some alliances may have relatively long-term objectives and will need to be clearly monitored and nurtured to produce mutual commitment and to avoid bitter fights for control. Multiple temporary alliances among the producers of hardware, operating systems, and software are the result of short life cycles in the personal computer industry. Those alliances between Dell and its suppliers are a clear example. By contrast, Renault and Nissan or Ford and Mazda envision long-term benefits from their respective alliances, which transcend multiple product lines, and they make every effort to maintain relative stability in their relationships.[43]

Shared risks, shared costs, and shared rewards are the facts of life in a virtual organization.[44] When virtual organizations are formed, they involve tremendous challenges for strategic planning. As with the modular corporation, it is essential to identify core competencies. However, for virtual structures to be successful, a strategic plan is also needed to determine the effectiveness of combining core competencies.

The strategic plan must address the diminished operational control and overwhelming need for trust and common vision between the partners. This new structure may be appropriate for firms whose strategies require merging technologies (e.g., computing and communication) or for firms exploiting shrinking product life cycles that require simultaneous entry into multiple geographical markets. Further, it may be effective for firms that desire to be quick to the market with a new product or service; an example is the recent profusion of alliances among airlines, primarily motivated by the need to provide seamless travel for the full-fare-paying business traveller. Exhibit 9.10 summarizes the advantages and disadvantages, or pros and cons, of virtual structures.

Boundaryless Organizations: Making Them Work

Designing an organization that simultaneously supports the requirements of its strategy, is consistent with the demands of the environment, and can be effectively implemented by the people around the manager is a tall order for any manager.[45] Many times, the most effective solution is a combination of organizational types; that is, a firm may

Pros	Cons
◆ Enables the sharing of costs and skills.	◆ Difficulties in determining where one company ends and another begins, due to close interdependencies among players.
◆ Enhances access to global markets.	
◆ Increases market responsiveness.	◆ Leads to potential loss of operational control among partners.
◆ Creates a "best of everything" organization, since each partner brings core competencies to the alliance.	◆ Results in loss of strategic control over emerging technology.
◆ Encourages both individual and organizational knowledge sharing and accelerates organizational learning.	◆ Requires new and difficult-to-acquire managerial skills.

Exhibit 9.10
Pros and Cons of Virtual Structures

outsource parts of its value chain to reduce costs and increase quality, engage simultaneously in multiple alliances to take advantage of technological developments or penetrate new markets, and break down barriers within the organization to enhance flexibility.

Regardless of the form of organization ultimately chosen, achieving the coordination and integration necessary to maximize the potential of an organization's human capital involves much more than simply creating a new structure. Techniques and processes designed and implemented to ensure the necessary coordination and integration of an organization's key value-chain activities are critical. Teams are key building blocks of the new organizational forms, and teamwork requires new and flexible approaches to coordination and integration.

As noted earlier, managers trained in rigid hierarchies often find it difficult to make the transition to the more democratic, participative style that teamwork requires. Douglas K. Smith, co-author of *The Wisdom of Teams*, pointed out, "A completely diverse group must agree on a goal, put the notion of individual accountability aside and figure out how to work with each other. Most of all, they must learn that if the team fails, it's everyone's fault."[46] Within the framework of an appropriate organizational design, managers must select a mix and balance of tools and techniques to facilitate the effective coordination and integration of key activities. Some of the factors that must be considered include the following:

- Common culture and shared values
- Horizontal organizational structures
- Horizontal systems and processes
- Communications and information technologies
- Human resource practices

Common Culture and Shared Values Shared goals, mutual objectives, and a high degree of trust are essential to the success of boundaryless organizations. It is neither feasible nor desirable to attempt to "control" suppliers, customers, or alliance partners in the traditional sense. In the fluid and flexible environments of the new organizational architectures, common cultures, shared values, and carefully aligned incentives are often less expensive to implement and often a more effective means of strategic control than rules, boundaries, and formal procedures.

Horizontal Organizational Structures Horizontal organizational structures group similar or related business units under common management control, facilitate the sharing of resources and infrastructures to exploit synergies among operating units, and help to create a sense of common purpose. Consistency in training and the development of similar structures across business units facilitates job rotation and cross training and enhances understanding of common problems and opportunities. Cross-functional teams and interdivisional committees and task groups represent important opportunities to improve understanding and foster co-operation among operating units.

Horizontal Systems and Processes Organizational systems, policies, and procedures are the traditional mechanisms for achieving integration among functional units. Too often, however, existing policies and procedures do little more than institutionalize the barriers that exist from years of managing within the framework of the traditional model. The concept of business re-engineering focuses primarily on these internal processes and procedures. Beginning with an understanding of basic business processes in the context of "a collection of activities that takes one or more kinds of input and creates an output that is of value to the customer," Michael Hammer and James Champy's 1993 best-selling *Reengineering the Corporation* outlined a methodology for redesigning internal systems and procedures—a methodology that has been embraced, in its various forms, by many organizations.[47] Proponents claim that successful re-engineering lowers costs, reduces inventories and cycle times, improves quality, speeds response times, and enhances organizational flexibility. Others advocate similar benefits through the reduction of cycle times, total quality management, and the like. General Electric and others have used benchmarking and adopted "best practices" from leading companies around the world in an effort to streamline their internal systems and procedures.

Communications and Information Technologies Improved communications through the effective use of information technologies can play an important role in bridging gaps and breaking down barriers between organizations. Electronic mail and video conferencing can improve lateral communications across long distances and multiple time zones and, by short-circuiting vertical structures, tend to circumvent many of the barriers of the traditional model. Information technology can be a powerful ally in the redesign and streamlining of internal business processes and in improving coordination and integration between suppliers and customers. Internet technologies have eliminated the paperwork of purchase order and invoice documentation in many buyer-supplier relationships, enabling co-operating organizations to reduce inventories, shorten delivery cycles, and reduce operating costs. Some have argued that information technology must be viewed more as a prime component of an organization's overall strategy than simply in terms of its more traditional role as administrative support. The close relationships that must exist between technology and other value-creating activities were addressed in Chapters 3 and 4.

Human Resource Practices Change, whether in structure, process, or procedure, always involves and impacts the human dimension of organizations. As we noted in Chapter 4, the attraction, development, and retention of human capital are vital to value creation. As boundaryless structures are implemented, as processes are re-engineered, and as organizations become increasingly dependent on sophisticated information technologies, the skills of workers and managers alike must be upgraded to realize the full benefits.

Summary

Successful organizations must ensure that they have the proper type of organizational structure. Furthermore, they must ensure that their firms carry out the necessary integration and processes so that the internal and external boundaries of their firms are flexible and permeable. This is increasingly important as the environments of firms become more complex, changeable, and unpredictable.

In the first section of the chapter, we discussed the growth patterns of large corporations. Although most organizations remain small or die, some firms continue to grow in terms of revenues, vertical integration, and diversity of products and services.

In addition, their geographical scope may increase to include international operations. We traced the dominant pattern of growth, which generally involves progression from a simple structure to a functional structure as a firm grows in size and increases its level of vertical integration. After a firm expands into related products and services, its structure changes from a functional to a divisional form of organization. Finally, when the firm enters international markets, its structure is altered again to accommodate the change in strategy.

We also addressed the different types of organizational structure—simple, functional, divisional (including two variations, strategic business unit and holding company), and matrix—as well as their relative advantages and disadvantages. We closed the section with a discussion of the implications for structure when a firm enters international markets. The three primary factors to take into account when determining the appropriate structure are type of international strategy, product diversity, and the extent to which a firm is dependent on foreign sales.

The second section of the chapter introduced the concept of the boundaryless organization. We did not suggest that the concept of the boundaryless organization replaces the traditional forms of organizational structure; rather, it should complement them. This complementarity is necessary to cope with the increasing complexity of and change in the competitive environment. We addressed three types of boundaryless organizations. The barrier-free type focuses on the need for the internal and external boundaries of a firm to be more flexible and permeable. The modular type emphasizes the strategic outsourcing of non-core activities. The virtual type centres on the strategic benefits of alliances and the forming of network organizations. We discussed both the advantages and disadvantages of each type of boundaryless organization and suggested some techniques and processes that are necessary to successfully implement them. These include common culture and values, horizontal organizational structures, horizontal systems and processes, communications and information technologies, and human resource practices.

Summary Review Questions

1. Why is it important for managers to carefully consider the type of organizational structure that they use to implement their strategies?

2. Briefly trace the dominant growth pattern of major corporations from simple structure to functional structure to divisional structure. Discuss the relationship between a firm's strategy and its structure.

3. What are the relative advantages and disadvantages of the types of organizational structure—simple, functional, divisional, matrix—discussed in the chapter?

4. When a firm expands its operations into foreign markets, what are the three most important factors to take into account in deciding what type of structure is most appropriate? What are the types of international structures discussed in the text, and what are the relationships between strategy and structure?

5. Briefly describe the three different types of boundaryless organizations: barrier-free, modular, and virtual.

6. What are some of the key attributes of effective groups? of ineffective groups?

7. What are the advantages and disadvantages of the three types of boundaryless organizations: barrier-free, modular, and virtual?

Experiential Exercise

Many firms have recently moved toward a modular structure. For example, they have increasingly outsourced many of their information technology (IT) activities. Identify three such organizations. Using secondary sources, evaluate (1) the firm's rationale for IT outsourcing and (2) the implications for performance.

Firm	Rationale	Implication(s) for Performance
1.		
2.		
3.		

Application Questions Exercises

1. Select an organization that competes in an industry in which you are particularly interested. From the Internet, determine what type of organizational structure this organization has. In your view, is it consistent with the strategy that it has chosen to implement? Why? Why not?

2. Choose an article from *Canadian Business*, *Fortune*, *Fast Company*, or any other well-known publication, that deals with a corporation that has undergone a significant change in its strategic direction. What are the implications for the structure of this organization?

3. On the Internet, look up some of the public statements or speeches an executive in a major corporation has made about a major initiative, such as entering into a joint venture or launching a new product line. What do you feel are the implications for making the internal and external barriers of the firm more flexible and permeable? Does the executive discuss processes, procedures, integrating mechanisms, or cultural issues that should serve this purpose? Or are other issues discussed that enable the firm to become more boundaryless?

4. In the publications listed in question 2 above, look up a recent article that addresses a firm's involvement in outsourcing (modular organization) or in strategic alliance or network organizations (virtual organization). Was the firm successful or unsuccessful in this endeavour? Why? Why not?

Ethics Questions

1. If a firm has a divisional structure and places extreme pressures on its divisional executives to meet short-term profitability goals (e.g., quarterly income), could this raise some ethical considerations? Why? Why not?

2. A firm participating in a strategic alliance will normally refrain from exercising direct control and expressing opinions about the management and treatment of its partner's employees (in terms of culture, compensation, rewards and incentives, boundaries). What ethical issues could this stance raise? What could be the potential long-term and short-term downside for the firm?

3. A matrix structure is said to be, potentially, quite stressful to some employees who can't handle the ambiguity of roles and divided responsibilities. What is the ethical obligation of the corporation toward those employees?

Chapter 10   *Strategic Control and Corporate Governance*

LEARNING OBJECTIVES

After reading this chapter, you should have a good understanding of:

LO 1 → the value of strategic control systems in effective strategy formulation and implementation.

LO 2 → the differences between financial and strategic controls and the role they play in the success of organizations.

LO 3 → the benefits of having a proper balance among the three levers of behavioural control: culture, rewards and incentives, and boundaries.

LO 4 → why there is no "one best way" to design strategic control systems and how the most effective systems are contingent on situational factors and the organization's specific strategic choices.

LO 5 → the role of corporate governance mechanisms in ensuring that the interests of managers are aligned with those of shareholders.

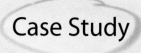

Hollinger International Inc. was a Delaware-incorporated, Chicago-based media company that owned newspapers across much of North America as well as a few overseas spreads, most notably the *Telegraph* in London and the *Jerusalem Post*.[1] Its roots are found in Canada, as it was the brainchild of Lord Conrad Black who was born in Canada in the late 1940s. For a quarter of a century, as a media baron, Black controlled extensive holdings of Canadian newspapers and made a name for himself with his business acumen and media expertise as much as he did for his passion for history. Others commented on his excesses and pomposity. He renounced his Canadian citizenship in order to acquire the Lordship title from the Queen of England. His company, Hollinger, was a force in the North American media scene, amassing and successfully running a range of papers. Among its accomplishments, it boasted the launch of the *National Post*, Canada's second national paper (sold to CanWest Global), the *Chicago Sun Times*, and many regional papers that still serve hundreds of Canadian and American communities.

Yet, for all the many activities and accomplishments that the firm would like to be known for, its publicly traded shares returned little to its shareholders during the last 10 years, and it managed to frequently make the news itself. A report by a special committee of the Hollinger International board filed with the Securities and Exchange Commission in Washington, D.C., in the fall of 2004, alleged that Lord Black, his wife Barbara Amiel, and his top deputy David Radler systematically looted the company while the complacent board rubber-stamped their illegal actions.

What Went Wrong at Hollinger? A board of directors has, above all, the fiduciary duty to closely monitor top management to ensure that it acts in the shareholders' best interest. Hollinger International was 18 percent owned by Hollinger Inc., a Canadian entity that, in turn, was 78 percent owned by Ravelston Corp. Ltd., Lord Black's private holding company. However, a dual-class share structure gave Lord Black, through Ravelston, control over 68 percent of the votes of Hollinger International and the ability to appoint the directors and senior management of the operating firm. During the last few years, the members of the board, hand-picked by Lord Black himself, included internationally known personalities such as former secretary of state Henry Kissinger, former assistant defence secretary and insider to the Bush administration Richard Perle, former governor of Illinois James Thompson, and former U.S. ambassador Richard Burt; all were friends and acquaintances of the Blacks.

The special committee report made a series of allegations about improprieties and related party transactions that were either unreported or misleadingly presented and approved, without much discussion, by a complacent board. It was said that in one sitting, the audit committee approved hundreds of millions of dollars in transactions "in the time needed to consume a tuna sandwich." Examples of alleged misuse of funds included paying $218 million in management fees to Lord Black and other insiders without or with incomplete approval by the board; directing $51.8 million from a non-compete payment on the sale of Hollinger papers to CanWest Global Communications to the personal accounts of Lord Black and Mr. Radler; using company money to make charitable donations in Black's and Radler's names to well-known Canadian institutions and universities; engaging in real estate transactions with Lord Black that favoured him to the detriment of the company; selling company assets below market prices to private firms controlled by Radler and his family; and covering costs for a lavish birthday party for Lord Black's wife on the basis that it was a corporate function. The report also alleged that Perle, though a member of the board, was provided with Hollinger funds to invest through Hollinger Digital Inc. in defence, homeland security, and Internet technologies—again, with little scrutiny from the board. In three years, Perle, Black, and Radler received $15.5 million in bonuses for those investments, while the ventures themselves lost more than $49 million.

Lord Black was forced to step down from his roles as chairman and CEO at Hollinger. Radler and most of his lieutenants were excused and most of the board members resigned. A new board was struck to oversee the affairs of the corporation and attempt to recover the money paid out or lost. Subsequently, Lord Black tried to acquire all the remaining shares of Hollinger Inc. and take it private. The courts blocked his move, deeming it an effort by Black and his holding company, Ravelston, to silence much of the litigation. It is worth noting that an email from Lord Black allegedly commented, with respect to the head of the investment firm GMP Securities hired to provide an independent evaluation of Hollinger (for the purpose of advising the board whether to accept Ravelston's offer), "he won't get his million dollars unless he produces something that works for the company." Observers claimed it was a clear intent to influence the evaluation by the independent firm. In 2007, a Chicago court convicted Lord Black of theft of money and other property from Hollinger by misrepresentations and misleading omissions amounting to fraud and misuse of his position for private gain; moreover, it found him guilty of obstruction of justice with respect of the removal of boxes with papers from the company's headquarters after the official investigation had started. The appeals court rejected all the arguments and even commented on some of the agreements that involved Hollinger subsidiaries and netted the men $5.5 million, characterizing them as "ridiculous." Lord Black is serving a six-and-a-half-year sentence in a Florida jail.

Unfortunately, Lord Black and Hollinger are not isolated and rare incidents. Newspaper headlines pointing to management abuses are a rather common occurrence, and similar events have frequently been associated with U.S. firms such as Enron, Tyco, Sunbeam, and WorldCom. Canada's public companies have not remained unscathed either. Nortel and Royal Group Technologies are among the names that newspapers have frequently cited in regard to lax corporate controls and accounting irregularities. The hand picking of board members, the complacency of corporate boards, the aggressive tactics of management that have sometimes crossed the lines to criminal behaviours, as well as the vanity and excesses of executives have triggered many new government regulations designed to curb abuses and protect shareholders. The U.S. Congress introduced the Sarbanes-Oxley Act in 2002 to ensure better governance of public corporations in the United States. Similar provisions have been put into place by the Canadian government and the various provincial securities commissions, although Canada relies as much on voluntary guidelines as it does on compulsory rules. *The Globe and Mail's* Report on Business has initiated an annual review of the boards of Canada's largest companies, and it reports on progress made in the practice of corporate governance as well as on the mechanisms in place to protect the investing public from abuses.[2] The complexities of today's corporations—cross-ownerships, operations in multiple jurisdictions, listings in multiple stock exchanges, and the reality of management in a highly turbulent and competitive world—bring to the fore the critical role that strategic control plays in ensuring that the organization and its executives do perform their duties for the shareholders who have entrusted them with their money.

Organizations must have effective strategic controls if they are to successfully develop and implement their strategies. This means having systems that allow the organization to effectively respond to environmental changes as well as balance and align the organization's culture, rewards, and boundaries. Overriding this is the goal of the firm's owners (shareholders) and their elected representatives (board of directors) to ensure that the firm's executives (management team) strive to fulfill their fiduciary duty and maximize the long-term value of the firm. A list of controls that are, or are supposed to be, in place for the functioning of each individual corporation and to ensure the presence of trust in the entire institution of public corporations includes effective

◆ corporate governance aligning managerial and shareholder interests,
◆ *informational controls* ensuring that the organization is informed and that its strategies and goals remain aligned with the changing environment—that the organization does the right things—, and
◆ *behavioural controls* ensuring that all the members of the organization behave consistently and in coordination, to achieve desirable outcomes—that the organization does things right.[3]

 Complementing these controls are *financial and operating controls*; that is, quantitative measures which ensure that the firm's performance on multiple dimensions meets previously established targets. Among them are a range of finance and accounting measures, market-based measures, operating performance measures, and benchmarks against competitors.

In this chapter, we first briefly discuss financial and operating controls as feedback-based control systems that measure outcomes after a sufficient time has elapsed and that serve only to guide corrective action subsequent to the implementation of strategy and achievement of results. We then elaborate on informational and behavioural controls—the main strategic control systems at managers' disposal. We highlight their forward-looking nature as contrasted with feedback controls. We expand on their potential to inform and steer action concurrently with strategy formulation and execution. Finally, in the last part of this chapter, we focus on corporate governance and the mechanisms that guide managers to behave in the interests of shareholders.

FEEDBACK CONTROL SYSTEMS

Traditional control mechanisms rely on measuring outcomes. Managers set targets and devise specific metrics to measure the achievement of those targets. The targets are established to match specific objectives and organizational goals. An appropriate time frame is also established that allows pursuit of those objectives and the delivery of results. Performance is measured against the targets. Targets can take the form of accounting metrics, such as ROI, ROA, ROE, budgets, or adherence to financial audit standards such as GAAP. Other targets correspond to market-based outcomes and take the form of sales quotas, market share figures, customer satisfaction scores, product introduction rates, brand coverage, and the like. Operating targets, such as production schedules, tolerance levels, waste rates, utilization, and productivity are also used.

Feedback control systems are placed at the end of a sequential process that starts with strategy formulation and proceeds to goal setting, strategy implementation and action, performance measurement, evaluation and feedback, and, if needed in response to that evaluation, the organization proceeds with steering and corrective action. There is usually no action taken to revise strategies, goals, and objectives until the end of the time period in question, often tied to a firm's annual planning cycle.

 Such financial and operating control systems serve a number of essential functions within organizations and represent valuable management tools. Above all, they facilitate the articulation of clear, unambiguous, explicit, and concrete goals for the organization as a whole and for individual units within it. Each department knows exactly what is expected of it and the time frame within which its task is expected to be accomplished. They provide direct links between individual goals and organizational goals. A feedback-based control system communicates exactly what individual managers are accountable for. Specific results can be compared across units and provide the basis for corrective action. Finally, managers can look back to the actions that have led to the results and draw conclusions about cause and effect; they can use this understanding to inform their subsequent decisions, adjust plans, and take corrective action.

The power of financial and operating controls and feedback control systems, in general, rests on some simple premises that are linked to their very nature. First, there is a fundamental assumption that goals and objectives can be measured with a high level of certainty. Second, the environment is thought to be stable enough and simple enough that a well-managed company can move forward in accordance with detailed and precise plans, which can be set out well in advance of their execution. Third, it is believed that there is a clear and unambiguous connection between original plans and eventual outcomes. The appropriateness of the business strategy or standards of performance is seldom questioned.[4]

Many writers, though, have questioned the plausibility of those premises. Most notably, McGill University's Henry Mintzberg has written about leaders "crafting" a strategy.[5] Drawing on the parallel between the strategist and the potter at her wheel, Mintzberg pointed out that the potter begins work with some general idea of the artifact she wishes to create, but the details of design—even possibilities for a different design—emerge as the work progresses. For businesses facing complex and turbulent business environments, the craftsperson's method seems more appropriate than that provided by the traditional, more rational planner. It helps us deal with the uncertainty about how a design will work out in practice and allows for a creative element.

Mintzberg's observations cast doubt on the value of rigid planning and goal-setting processes. Fixed strategic goals become meaningless for firms competing in highly unpredictable competitive environments, where strategies need to change frequently and opportunistically. An inflexible commitment to predetermined goals and milestones can prevent the very adaptability that is often required of a good strategy. Grant designs with precise and carefully integrated plans seldom work. Rather, most strategic change proceeds incrementally, one step at a time.[6] A leader can best serve the organization by introducing some sense of direction and logic in incremental steps and not hampering its progress with elaborate financial controls that would constrain the managers' ability to anticipate the future. Even organizations that have been extremely successful in the past can become complacent. Often, they may fail to anticipate important changes in their environment and adapt their goals and strategies to the new conditions.

INFORMATIONAL CONTROL: RESPONDING EFFECTIVELY TO ENVIRONMENTAL CHANGE

Adapting to and anticipating both internal and external environmental change is an integral part of strategic control. The relationships between strategy formulation, implementation, and control are not sequential but highly interactive, as suggested by Exhibit 10.1. Informational control is primarily concerned with whether or not the organization is "doing the right things." It deals with the internal environment as well as with the external strategic context. It addresses the assumptions and premises that provide the foundation for an organization's strategy.[7] The key question addressed by informational control is, do the organization's goals and strategies still "fit" within the context of the current strategic environment?

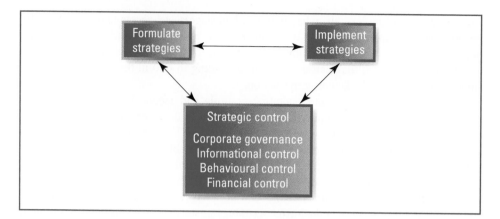

Informational control is part of an ongoing process of organizational learning in which the assumptions that underlie the organization's strategy are continuously being updated and challenged. In such "double-loop" learning, the organization's assumptions, premises, goals, and strategies are regularly monitored, tested, and reviewed.[8] The benefits of continuous monitoring are evident—time lags are dramatically shortened, changes in the competitive environment are detected earlier, and the organization's ability to respond with speed and flexibility is enhanced.

The question that ensues is, how is this done? Informational control systems must have four characteristics to be effective.[9]

1. They must focus on constantly changing information that top managers identify as having potential strategic importance.
2. The information is important enough to demand frequent and regular attention from operating managers at all levels of the organization.
3. The data and information generated by the control system are best interpreted and discussed in face-to-face meetings among superiors and subordinates.
4. The control system is a key catalyst for an ongoing debate about underlying data, assumptions, and action plans.

Strategic control systems track the strategic uncertainties that may keep senior managers awake at night. Depending on the type of business, such uncertainties may relate to changes in technology, customer tastes, government regulation, and industry competition. Since control systems must be designed to gather information that might challenge the strategic visions of the future, they are, by definition, hot buttons for senior managers.

An executive's decision to use the control system interactively, as outlined above—in other words, to invest time and attention to review and evaluate new information on an ongoing basis—sends a clear signal to the whole organization about what is important. The dialogue and debate that emerges from such an interactive process can often lead to new strategies and innovations. Strategy Spotlight 10.1 discusses how executives at *USA Today*, Gannett Co.'s daily newspaper, review information delivered each Friday.

BEHAVIOURAL CONTROL: BALANCING CULTURE, REWARDS, AND BOUNDARIES

Behavioural control is focused on implementation—doing things right. Whereas financial and operating controls assess the results of implementing a strategy at the end of the time period allocated for its execution, behavioural controls recognize the potential costs, lost

USA Today's Interactive Control System

Top managers at Gannett-owned *USA Today* meet each Friday to discuss ongoing strategy. Every week, they review information ranging from day-to-day operations information to year-to-date data. This information enables top management to check the pulse of the industry on a frequent basis, and it minimizes the surprises that often beset other companies that don't keep close tabs on available information. Senior managers frequently meet with operations-level managers for intensive analysis of the weekly information. The results of these high-level meetings on information control allow managers from the operating core of the newspaper to respond to industry trends and events on nearly a real-time basis.

By controlling information, *USA Today* managers

- compare projected advertising volume with actual volume.
- assess new advertising revenues by client type to better target client markets.

- discover revenue shortfalls before major problems arise.
- become aware of unexpected successes that have often led to innovations.

These weekly meetings have returned significant rewards for *USA Today*. Innovations that have been implemented as a result of high information control include

- a new market survey service targeted at the automobile industry (a potential source of high-volume advertising).
- the addition of fractional page colour advertising (increasing the number of advertisers that use colour, thereby increasing advertising revenue).
- expanding the job function of circulation employees to include regional sales of advertising space.
- developing a program of advertising inserts targeted toward specific customers and products.

Sources: R. Simons, "Control in an Age of Empowerment," *Harvard Business Review* 73, no. 2 (1995), pp. 80–88; D. Caney, "Gannett, Knight Rider Walloped by Ad Slump," Reuters, July 17, 2001.

opportunities, and risks associated with withholding intervention until the predetermined strategy and its execution do produce outcomes. A number of reasons compel organizations to develop alternatives to the feedback systems described earlier. First, the competitive environment is increasingly complex and unpredictable, demanding both flexibility and quick response to its challenges. Organizations are frequently called upon, midstream, to make iterative adjustments in direction, alter management priorities in the face of new information and developments, and modify resource allocations during a plan's execution. Moreover, employees do not connect with an organization to the same degree that they did in the past, as professional careers now take very different forms, lateral moves are much more common, and employees move in and out of an organization more frequently.[10] The implicit long-term contract between an employee and the organization has been eroded. Young managers are conditioned to see themselves as free agents and view a career as a series of opportunities and challenges across multiple organizations. At the same time, work does not occur in neat and well-defined ways. Tasks are cross-functional and carried out by teams of workers and, while less repetitive, do not necessarily begin and end in the same time dimensions as the plan. Feedback control systems are rendered less useful in such circumstances because the individuals who set the plan and initiated its execution may not be around to witness the results and receive the feedback at the end.

Behavioural controls then become extremely useful since they leverage the organization's culture, rewards, and incentives, and they define the boundaries of individuals and units. In doing so, they guide behaviour while strategy is unfolding, and they direct individuals' efforts toward desirable outcomes, which may, in fact, be continuously redefined. In effect, behavioural control systems utilize the three levers of culture, rewards, and boundaries in a balanced and consistent manner to achieve results.

Building a Strong and Effective Culture

Consistent with our discussion in Chapter 4, organizational culture is a system of shared values (what is important) and beliefs (how things work) that influence a company's people to produce behavioural norms (the way we do things around here). Over the years, numerous best-sellers, including *Theory Z, Corporate Cultures, In Search of Excellence,* and *Good to Great,*[11] have emphasized the powerful influence of culture on what goes on within organizations and how they perform.

Collins and Porras argued, in *Built to Last,* that the key factor in sustained exceptional performance is a cult-like culture.[12] You can't touch it, you can't write it down, but it's there—in every organization—and its influence is pervasive. It can work for you or against you.[13] Effective leaders understand its importance and strive to shape and use it as one of their important levers of strategic control.[14]

Culture wears many different hats, each woven from the fabric of those values that sustain the organization's primary source of competitive advantage. For example, Federal Express and Four Seasons focus on customer service; Lexus and Hewlett-Packard emphasize product quality; Cirque du Soleil and 3M place a high value on innovation; and Nucor (steel) and Wal-Mart are concerned, above all, with operational efficiency.

Culture sets implicit boundaries—that is, unwritten standards of acceptable behaviour—in dress, ethical matters, and the way an organization conducts its business.[15] By creating a framework of shared values, culture encourages individual identification with the organization and its objectives. Thus, culture acts as a means of reducing monitoring costs.[16]

A firm's culture reflects the historical choices about the business and guides the way in which the firm conducts its business. It defines, for all individuals within the firm, how they should conduct business and how they should relate to customers, suppliers, and others. By encapsulating the organization's norms, values, beliefs, assumptions, symbols, and behaviours, culture delineates what would be appropriate and what the bases should be for the firm's competitive advantages. Consequently, a unique culture not only represents a powerful control mechanism that guides individual behaviour but also becomes the source of the organization's sustainable performance.

Sustaining an Effective Culture Powerful organizational cultures don't just happen overnight, however, and they don't remain in place without a strong commitment, in deeds as well as in words, by leaders throughout the organization. Also, an organization's culture cannot simply be built or assembled; instead, it must be cultivated and encouraged. Storytelling is one way effective cultures are strengthened and sustained. Many are familiar with the story of how Art Fry's failure to develop a strong adhesive led to 3M's enormously successful Post-it Notes. Perhaps less familiar is the story of Francis G. Okie.[17] In 1922, Okie came up with the idea of selling sandpaper to men as a replacement for razor blades. The idea obviously didn't pan out, but this did not stop Okie and his colleagues. The same technology developed by Okie led 3M to its first blockbuster product: waterproof sandpaper that became a staple of the automobile industry. Such stories highlight the importance of risk taking, experimentation, freedom to fail, and innovation—all vital elements of 3M's culture.

Rallies or "pep talks" by top executives also serve to reinforce a firm's culture. The late Sam Walton was well known for his pep rallies at local Wal-Mart stores. Four times a year, the founders of Home Depot—Bernard Marcus and Arthur Blank—used to don orange aprons and stage Breakfast with Bernie and Arthur, a 6:30 a.m. pep rally, broadcast live over the firm's closed-circuit TV network to most of its 45,000 employees.[18]

Legend Group: Providing Incentives at All Levels

One of the key tasks of management is to keep the employees motivated. Designing the right kind of incentives that meet the expectations of employee groups at all the different levels in the hierarchy is a big challenge. Here is how Liu Chuanzhi, chairman of Legend Group, a global personal computer manufacturer based in Beijing, China, dealt with this issue:

> Our executive team needs a sense of ownership in the company. Many state-owned enterprises in China face a special challenge: They cannot give their senior executives stock. But we took an untraditional approach; we reformed our ownership structure to make Legend a joint stock company, enabling us to give all our executive team members stock.

In addition, senior executives need recognition, so we provide them with opportunities to speak to the media. To date, we've lost no senior executives to other companies.

Midlevel managers want to become senior managers, so they respond best to challenges—to opportunities to display and hone their talents. We set very high performance standards for our middle managers, and we let them participate in strategic processes, in designing their own work, and in making and executing their own decisions. If they get good results, they are handsomely rewarded.

Line employees need a sense of stability. If they take responsibility and are conscientious, they earn a predictable bonus. We also tie team performance to company or unit performance, and individual performance to team performance. For example, we might let the team decide how to allocate a percentage of their team bonus to individuals, with some general guidelines from the corporate level.

Source: L. Chuanzhi, "Set Different Incentive Levels," *Harvard Business Review* 81, no. 1 (2003), p. 47.

A strong culture of trust has been the primary control mechanism at Semco, a Brazilian manufacturing equipment company that has been exceptionally successful throughout the last 20 years.[19] Employees are expected to make their own decisions about their work and form self-directed teams to pursue projects that they consider to be contributing to the firm's objectives; they are also rewarded for their accomplishments. All employees, including Ricardo Semler, the owner, belong to one of three layers; there are no titles, and responsibility is assigned on the basis of initiative. Semler suggests that adding rules to control the few who might abuse the situation would be pandering to the lowest common denominator and, in creating a culture of distrust, would diminish the sense of personal responsibility that each employee, today, feels toward the company. Problems would become the management's headache.

Motivating with Rewards and Incentives

Reward and incentive systems represent a powerful means of influencing an organization's culture as they work to focus efforts on high-priority tasks and motivate both individual and collective task performances.[20] Since much of culture deals with influencing beliefs, behaviours, and attitudes of people within an organization, the reward system—by specifying who gets rewarded and why—is an effective control mechanism.[21] Strategy Spotlight 10.2 discusses how the China-based Legend Group varies its incentives according to the different hierarchical levels in its organization.

To be effective, reward and incentive systems need to reinforce basic core values and enhance cohesion and commitment to goals and objectives. They must also be aligned with the organization's overall mission and purpose.[22]

Consider how incentives are used at General Mills. To ensure a manager's interest in the overall performance of his or her unit, half of a manager's annual bonus is linked to business-unit results and half to individual performance.[23] And, if a manager simply matches a rival manufacturer's performance, his or her salary will be roughly 5 percent lower than a peer's. However, if a manager's product ranks in the industry's top 10 percent in earnings growth and return on capital, that manager's total compensation can rise to nearly 30 percent beyond the industry norm.

Effective reward and incentive systems share a number of common characteristics:[24]

♦ Objectives are clear, well understood, and broadly accepted.
♦ Rewards are clearly linked to performance and desired behaviours.
♦ Performance measures are clear and highly visible.
♦ Feedback is prompt, clear, and unambiguous.
♦ The compensation "system" is perceived as fair and equitable.
♦ The structure is flexible: it can adapt to changing circumstances.

The perception that a plan is "fair and equitable" is critically important. Similarly, the firm must have the flexibility to respond to changing requirements as its direction and objectives change. Emerson Electric is one company that has shifted its emphasis from cost cutting to growth. To ensure that changes take hold, the management compensation formula has been changed from a largely bottom-line focus to one that emphasizes growth, new products, acquisitions, and international expansion. Discussions about profits are handled separately, and a culture of risk taking is encouraged.[25]

Setting Boundaries and Constraints

In an ideal world, a strong culture and effective rewards should be sufficient to ensure that all individuals and subunits work toward the common goals and objectives of the whole organization.[26] In the real world, however, this is not usually the case. Counterproductive behaviour can arise because of self-interest, lack of a clear understanding of goals and objectives, or outright malfeasance. Boundaries and constraints, when used properly, can serve many useful purposes for organizations, including

♦ focusing individual efforts on strategic priorities,
♦ providing short-term objectives and action plans to channel efforts, and
♦ minimizing improper and unethical conduct.

Focusing Efforts on Strategic Priorities Boundaries and constraints play a valuable role in focusing a company's strategic priorities. One well-known strategic boundary was Bombardier's intent to enter only those niches where it thought it had a good chance of being the number one or number two player in the world, a strategy also advocated by GE under the leadership of Jack Welch during the 1980s and 1990s. In a similar vein, Eli Lilly has reduced its research efforts to five broad areas of disease, down from eight or nine a decade ago.[27] This concentration of effort and resources provides the firm with greater strategic focus and the potential for stronger competitive advantages in the remaining areas.

Norman Augustine, Lockheed Martin's former chairman, provided four criteria for selecting candidates for diversification into "closely related" businesses.[28] They must be (1) high-tech, (2) systems oriented, (3) able to deal with large customers (either corporations or government) as opposed to consumers, and (4) involved in growth businesses. Augustine said, "We have found that if we can meet most of those standards, then we can move into adjacent markets and grow."

Boundaries also have a place in the non-profit sector. For example, a British relief organization uses a system to monitor strategic boundaries by maintaining a list of companies whose contributions it will neither solicit nor accept. Such boundaries go beyond simply taking the moral high road. Rather, they are essential for maintaining legitimacy with existing and potential benefactors.

Providing Short-Term Objectives and Action Plans In Chapter 1, we discussed the importance, for a firm, of having a vision, mission, and strategic objectives that are internally consistent and provide strategic direction. Together, these set clear choices for all employees within the organization with respect to what is desirable, what the priorities are, and what they should strive for; at the same time, they define what is not a priority and what would not be in line with the organization. For example, Canadian Tire's vision of being "a national champion and Canada's most trusted company" or Procter & Gamble's "provide quality products and services that improve the lives of the world's consumers" suggest the kind of action that all associates and employees should carry out, consistently contributing toward and providing a yardstick for making choices.[29] Short-term objectives and action plans provide similar benefits. Again, they represent boundaries that help to allocate resources in an optimal manner and to channel the efforts of employees at all levels throughout the organization.[30] To be effective, short-term objectives must have several attributes. They should

- be specific and measurable.
- include a specific time horizon for their attainment.
- be achievable, yet challenging enough to motivate managers who must strive to accomplish them.

Short-term objectives must provide proper direction while, at the same time, providing enough flexibility for the firm to keep pace with and anticipate changes in the external environment. Additionally, unexpected events within a firm may require it to make important adjustments in both strategic and short-term objectives.

Along with short-term objectives, action plans are critical to the implementation of chosen strategies. Unless action plans are specific, there may be little assurance that managers have thought through all of the resource requirements for implementing their strategies. In addition, without adequate specificity, managers may not understand what needs to be implemented or have a clear time frame for completion. Such information is essential for the scheduling of key activities. Finally, individual managers must be held accountable for the implementation of action plans. This helps to provide a "sense of ownership" and the necessary motivation to implement action plans on a timely basis. Strategy Spotlight 10.3 illustrates how an action plan fits into the mission statement and objectives of a small manufacturer of aircraft interior components.

Minimizing Improper and Unethical Conduct Guidelines can be useful in specifying proper relationships with a company's customers and suppliers.[31] For example, many companies have explicit rules regarding commercial practices, including the prohibition of any form of payment, bribe, or kickback. Cadbury Schweppes has followed a rather simple but effective step in controlling the use of bribes by specifying that all payments, no matter how unusual, be recorded on the company's books. Its chairman, Sir Adrian Cadbury, contended that such a practice causes managers to pause and consider whether a payment is a necessary and standard cost of doing business or simply a bribe.[32] Consulting companies, too, typically have strong rules and regulations directed at protecting client confidentiality and conflicts of interest.

To ensure fair and equitable treatment of its suppliers, Chemical Bank (now part of Chase Bank) forbids any review that determines whether suppliers are Chemical customers before the bank awards contracts. Regulations backed up with strong sanctions can also

Developing Meaningful Action Plans: MSA Aircraft Interior Products, Inc.

MSA Aircraft Interior Products Inc. is a manufacturing firm based in San Antonio, Texas, that was founded in 1983 by Mike Spraggins and Robert Plenge. With two key product lines, the firm fulfills a small but highly profitable niche in the aviation industry. Their Accordia line consists of patented, lightweight, self-contained window-shade assemblies. Interior cabin shells, MSA's other product, are state-of-the-art assemblies that include window panels, side panels, headliners, and suspension system structures. MSA's products have been installed on a variety of aircraft such as the Gulfstream series, Cessna Citation, and Boeing's 727, 737, 757, and 707.

Much of MSA's success can be attributed to carefully articulated action plans consistent with the firm's mission and objectives. During the past five years, MSA has increased its sales at an annual rate of 15 to 18 percent. It has also succeeded in adding many prestigious companies to its customer base. Below are excerpts from MSA's mission statement and objectives, as well as the action plan to achieve a 20 percent annual increase in sales.

Mission Statement

♦ Be recognized as an innovative and reliable supplier of quality interior products for the high-end, personalized transportation segments of the aviation, marine, and automotive industries.

♦ Design, develop, and manufacture interior fixtures and components that provide exceptional value to the customer through the development of innovative designs in a manner that permits decorative design flexibility while retaining the superior functionality, reliability, and maintainability of well-engineered, factory-produced products.

♦ Grow, be profitable, and provide a fair return, commensurate with the degree of risk, for owners and shareholders.

Objectives

1. Achieve sustained and profitable growth over the next three years:

   ♦ 20 percent annual growth in revenues
   ♦ 12 percent pretax profit margins
   ♦ 18 percent return on shareholder equity

2. Expand the company's revenues through the development and introduction of two or more new products capable of generating revenues in excess of $8 million a year by 2007.

3. Continue to aggressively expand market opportunities and applications for the Accordia line of window-shade assemblies, with the objective of sustaining or exceeding a 20 percent annual growth rate for at least the next three years.

help an organization to avoid conducting business in an unethical manner. In the wake of the corporate scandals of the early twenty-first century and the passing of the Sarbanes-Oxley Act (which, among other things, provides for stiffer penalties for financial reporting misdeeds), many chief financial officers (CFOs) have taken steps to ensure ethical behaviour in the preparation of financial statements. For example, Home Depot's CFO, Carol B. Tome, strengthened the firm's code of ethics and developed stricter guidelines. Now, all 25 of her subordinates must sign personal statements that all of their financial statements are correct—just as she and her boss, Home Depot's CEO, are directed to do by the legislation.[33]

Behavioural Control in Organizations: Situational Factors

Controls, especially behavioural controls, are put in place to ensure that the behaviour of individuals at all levels of an organization is directed toward achieving organizational goals and objectives. Typically, an organization pursues one or a combination of controls on the basis of a variety of internal and external factors. For example, in professional organizations, such as high-technology firms engaged in basic research, members may work under high levels of autonomy.[34] An individual's performance would generally

MSA's action plans are supported by detailed, month-by-month budgets and strong financial incentives for its executives. Budgets are prepared by each individual department and include all revenue and cost items. Managers are motivated by their participation in a profit-sharing program, and the firm's two founders each receive a bonus equal to 3 percent of total sales. Exhibit 10.2 details an "Action Plan" for Objective 3.

Exhibit 10.2
Action Plan for Objective 3

Description	Primary Responsibility	Target Date
1. Develop and implement 2004 marketing plan, including specific plans for addressing Falcon 20 retrofit programs and expanded sales of cabin shells.	R.H. Plenge (V.P. Marketing)	December 15, 2003
2. Negotiate new supplier agreement with Gulfstream Aerospace.	M. Spraggins (President)	March 1, 2004
3. Continue and complete the development of the UltraSlim window and have a fully tested and documented design ready for production at a manufacturing cost of less than $900 per unit.	D.R. Pearson (V.P. Operations)	June 15, 2004
4. Develop a window design suitable for L-1011 and similar wide-body aircraft, and have a fully tested and documented design ready for production at a manufacturing cost comparable to the current Boeing window.	D.R. Pearson (V.P. Operations)	September 15, 2004

Source: For purposes of confidentiality, some of the information presented in this spotlight has been disguised. We would like to thank company management and Joseph Picken, consultant, for providing us with the information used in this application.

be quite difficult to measure with precision because of the long lead times involved in research and development activities. Thus, internalized norms and values become very important.

In organizations where the measurement of an individual's output or performance is quite straightforward, control depends primarily on granting or withholding rewards. Frequently, a sales manager's compensation is in the form of a commission and bonus tied directly to his or her sales volume, which is relatively easy to determine. In such situations, behaviour is influenced more strongly by the attractiveness of the compensation than by the norms and values implicit in the organization's culture. Furthermore, the measurability of output lessens the need for an elaborate system of rules to control behaviour.

Control in bureaucratic organizations has long been recognized as dependent on members following a highly formalized set of rules and regulations. In such circumstances, most activities are routine, and the desired behaviour can be specified in a detailed manner because there is generally little need for innovative or creative activity. In business organizations, for example, managing an assembly plant requires strict adherence to many rules as well as exacting sequences of assembly operations. In the public sector, activities such as the issuance of driver licences, passports, and birth certificates follow clearly prescribed procedures, as do approvals of budgets and the funding of new programs.

Evolving from Boundaries to Rewards and Culture

In most environments, organizations should strive to provide a system of rewards and incentives, coupled with a culture strong enough that boundaries become internalized. This reduces the need for external controls such as rules and regulations. Several measures can move an organization in this direction.

First, it is essential to hire the right people—individuals who already identify with the organization's dominant values and have attributes consistent with them. Microsoft's David Pritchard is well aware of the consequences of failing to hire properly.

> If I hire a bunch of bozos, it will hurt us because it takes time to get rid of them. They start infiltrating the organization, and then they themselves start hiring people of lower quality. At Microsoft, we are always looking for people who are better than we are.

Second, training plays a key role. At the extreme, such as in elite military units, the training regimen leads to such internalization of the culture that individuals, in effect, lose their identity. The group becomes the overriding concern and focal point of their energies. At firms such as FedEx, training not only builds skills but also plays a significant role in building a strong culture on the foundation of the organization's dominant values.

Third, managerial role models are vital. Andy Grove at Intel doesn't need (or want) a large number of bureaucratic rules to determine who is responsible for what, who is supposed to talk to whom, or who gets to fly first class (he does not). He encourages openness by not having many of the trappings of success; he works in a cubicle like all the other professionals. Not surprisingly, no new manager ever asks whether he or she can fly first class. Grove's personal example eliminates such a need.

Fourth, reward systems must be clearly aligned with the organizational goals and objectives. An effective reward system, together with a strong culture, reduces the need for rules and regulations in places such as Home Depot—a company with very selective hiring and generous bonus and stock option plans.

LINKING STRATEGIC CONTROL TO BUSINESS-LEVEL AND CORPORATE-LEVEL STRATEGIES

There is no "one best way" to design strategic control systems for an organization. Effective controls are contingent on many factors and are related to the choices made by the organization regarding its business-level and corporate-level strategies. For example, firms competing on the basis of overall cost leadership must implement tight cost controls, frequent and comprehensive reports to monitor the costs associated with outputs, and highly structured tasks and responsibilities. Not surprisingly, incentives tend to be based on explicit financial targets since innovation and creativity are expensive and might tend to erode competitive advantages. On the other hand, firms pursuing a differentiation strategy would typically want to encourage the development of innovative products and services, requiring the employment of experts who can identify the crucial elements of intricate, creative designs and formulate innovative marketing decisions. Highly trained professionals, such as scientists and engineers, are essential for devising, assessing, implementing, and continually changing complex product designs. New product design also requires collaboration and co-operation among specialists and functional managers from different areas within a firm. Such individuals must, for example, evaluate and implement a new design, constantly bearing in mind marketing, financial, production, and engineering considerations.

Given the need for co-operation and coordination among professionals in many functional areas, it becomes important to be able to measure and assess such activity. Yet, it is difficult to evaluate individuals using hard-and-fast quantitative criteria. It is much more difficult to measure such efforts on an individual basis, or to attribute those outcomes to specific individuals. Thus, more behavioural measures (such as how effectively employees collaborate and share information) become necessary, as well as intangible incentives and rewards that aim to support a strong culture of collaboration.

In appreciating the relationship between strategy and evaluation and control systems, a key issue that becomes apparent is the need to foster *in*dependence versus *inter*dependence. In the cases of cost leadership strategies or unrelated diversification, there tends to be less need for interdependence. Thus, the reward and control systems focus more on the use of financial indicators because unit costs, profits, and revenues can be rather easily attributed to a given business unit or division.

By contrast, firms that follow differentiation or related diversification strategies have intense needs for tight interdependencies among the functional areas and business units within the corporation. In these firms, the sharing of resources, including raw materials, R&D knowledge, marketing information, and so on, is critical to organizational success. In other words, achieving synergies across value-creating activities and business units is more important than with cost leadership or unrelated strategies. To facilitate sharing and collaboration, reward and control systems tend to incorporate more behavioural indicators.

Finally, we must include an important caveat. In actual practice, organizations have combinations of financial and behavioural control systems. In fact, in both overall cost leadership and unrelated diversification strategies, there is a need for collaboration and the sharing of best practices across value-creating activities and business units. General Electric, for example, has developed many integrating mechanisms to enhance the sharing of "best practices" across what would appear to be rather unrelated businesses such as jet engines, appliances, and network television. And, for both differentiation and related diversification strategies, financial indicators, such as revenue growth and profitability, should not be overlooked at either the business-unit or corporate level.

THE ROLE OF CORPORATE GOVERNANCE

So far in this chapter, we addressed how management can exercise strategic control over the firm's overall operations through the use of informational and behavioural controls. But who should exercise control over management? Corporate governance addresses the need for shareholders (the owners of the corporation) and their elected representatives, the board of directors, to actively ensure that management fulfills its overriding purpose: increasing long-term shareholder value.

Robert Monks and Nell Minow, two leading scholars in corporate governance, define it as "the relationship among various participants in determining the direction and performance of corporations. The primary participants are (1) the shareholders, (2) the management (led by the chief executive officer), and (3) the board of directors." Consistent with Monks and Minow's definition, our discussion centres on how corporations can succeed (or fail) in aligning managerial motives with the interests of the shareholders and their elected representatives, the board of directors.[35] In Chapter 1, we discussed the important role of boards of directors and provided some examples of effective and ineffective boards.

There is little doubt that effective corporate governance can affect a firm's bottom line. Good corporate governance plays an important role in the investment decisions of major institutions, and a premium is often reflected in the price of securities of companies that practise it. The corporate governance premium is larger for firms in countries with sound corporate governance practices compared to countries with weaker corporate governance standards.[36] In addition, there is a strong correlation between strong corporate governance and superior financial performance. The following are some recent notable examples of flawed corporate governance.[37]

- Oracle CEO Larry Ellison exercised 23 million stock options for a record gain of more than $706 million—weeks before lowering earnings forecasts. (January 2001). The company's market value dropped precipitously soon after, erasing billions of dollars in value.
- Arthur Andersen, the accounting firm, agreed to pay $110 million to settle a shareholders suit for alleged fraud in its audit of Sunbeam. (May 2001)
- Former Sunbeam CEO Al Dunlap agreed to pay $15 million to settle a lawsuit from shareholders and bondholders alleging that he cooked the books of the maker of small appliances. (January 11, 2002)
- Global Crossing, once a high-flying telecom service provider, filed for Chapter 11. In the preceding three years, the company's insiders had cashed in $1.3 billion in stock. (January 28, 2002)
- Nortel's top executives received special bonuses during 2003 totalling $21 million, based on profits that were later called into question. The company admitted in 2004 that it had possessed no reliable financial statements since January 2001. This came on the heels of another scandal in which former CEO John Roth cashed in $135 million in stock options just months before the company's stock, together with much of the telecom sector, crashed from a high of $124 to a low of 75 cents. (2001 to March 2004)
- Board members of Nortel met with institutional investors to discuss possible changes to the board. This was after ten executives were fired for artificially boosting the company's 2003 financial results. (September 30, 2004)
- Tyco International disclosed that it paid a director $10 million in cash (and gave an additional $10 million to his favourite charity) in exchange for the director's help in closing an acquisition deal. (January 29, 2002)

The many lapses in corporate governance point to the real possibility for corporate managers to behave in their own self-interest, often to the detriment of shareholders. Scholars identify these lapses as direct implications of the separation of ownership and management in the modern corporation and suggest mechanisms that can be used to ensure consistency (or alignment) between the interests of shareholders and those of the managers, to minimize potential conflicts.

The Modern Corporation: The Separation of Owners (Shareholders) and Management

The corporation has been defined, in a general sense, as "a body of persons granted a charter legally recognizing them as a separate entity having its own rights, privileges, and liabilities distinct from those of its members" (*American Heritage Dictionary*). More specifically, the business corporation has been defined as:

> an instrument through which capital is assembled for the activities of producing and distributing goods and services and making investments. Accordingly, a basic premise of corporation law is that a business corporation should have as its objective the conduct of such activities with a view to enhancing the corporation's profit and the gains of the corporation's owners, that is, the shareholders. (Melvin Aron Eisenberg, *The Structure of Corporation Law*)

Each of these definitions has some validity and reflects a key feature of the corporate form of business organization—its ability to draw resources from a variety of groups as well as establish and maintain a persona that is separate from all of them.[38] As Henry Ford once said, "A great business is really too big to be human."

Simply put, a corporation is a mechanism created to allow different parties to contribute capital, expertise, and labour for the maximum benefit of each party. The shareholders (investors) are able to participate in the profits of the enterprise without taking direct responsibility for the operations. The management can run the company without the responsibility of personally providing the funds. And, in order to make both of these possible, the shareholders have limited liability as well as rather limited involvement in the company's affairs. However, they reserve the right to elect directors who have the fiduciary obligation to protect their interests.

Scholars have addressed the divergence of interests between the owners of the corporation and the professional managers who are hired to run it.[39] They warned that widely dispersed ownership "released management from the overriding requirement that it serve stockholders." The separation of ownership from management has given rise to a set of ideas called "agency theory." Central to agency theory is the relationship between two primary players—the *principals* who are the owners of the firm (shareholders) and *agents* who are the people paid by principals to perform a job on their behalf (management). The shareholders elect and are represented by a board of directors that is responsible for ensuring that management acts in the best interests of shareholders to ensure long-term financial returns for the firm.

Agency theory is concerned with resolving two problems that can occur in agency relationships. The first is the problem that arises when the goals of the principals and agents conflict, and when it is difficult or expensive for the principal to verify what the agent is actually doing. In a corporation, this means that the board of directors would be unable to confirm that the managers were actually acting in the shareholders' interests because, in most cases, managers are "insiders" with regard to the businesses they operate and, therefore, better informed than the principals. Thus, managers may act "opportunistically" in pursuing their own interests—to the detriment of the corporation.[40] They may, for example, spend corporate funds on expensive perquisites (e.g., company jets and expensive art), devote time and resources to pet projects (initiatives in which they have a personal interest but which have limited market potential), engage in power struggles (where they may fight over resources for their own betterment, disregarding what is best for the firm), and negate (or sabotage) attractive merger offers because they may result in increased employment risk.[41]

The second problem is that of risk sharing. This arises when the principal and the agent have different attitudes and preferences toward risk. For example, the executives in a firm may favour additional diversification initiatives because—by their very nature—they increase the size of the firm and, by extension, the level of executive compensation. At the same time, such diversification initiatives may erode shareholder value if they fail to achieve some of the synergies that we discussed in Chapter 6 (e.g., building on core competencies, sharing activities, or enhancing market power). In effect, agents (executives) may have a stronger preference toward diversification than shareholders because it reduces their personal risk of loss of employment. In contrast, research has shown that executives who have large holdings of stock in their firms were more likely to engage in diversification strategies that were more consistent with shareholder interests and with increasing long-term returns.[42]

Governance Mechanisms: Aligning the Interests of Owners and Managers

As noted above, a key characteristic of the modern corporation is the separation of ownership from control. To minimize the potential for managers to act in their own self-interest, or opportunistically, the owners can implement some governance mechanisms.[43] Among those, they can create (1) *a committed and involved board of directors* that acts in the best interests of the shareholders to create long-term value for shareholders; (2) *shareholder activism*, wherein the owners of the corporation view themselves as share*owners* instead of shareholders and become actively engaged in the governance of the corporation; and (3) *managerial rewards and incentives*, sometimes called "contract-based outcomes," which consist of reward and compensation agreements that align the interests of management with those of the shareholders.

A Committed and Involved Board of Directors The board of directors acts as a fulcrum between the owners and controllers of a corporation. In effect, they are the intermediaries who provide a balance between a small group of key managers in the firm, based at the corporate headquarters, and a sometimes vast group of shareholders, typically spread out all over the world. In the United States and Canada, relevant legislation imposes on the board a strict and absolute fiduciary duty to ensure that a company is run according to the long-term interests of the owners, or shareholders. The reality, as we have seen, is somewhat more ambiguous.[44]

The International Corporate Governance Network (ICGN), representing investors, companies, financial intermediaries, and other parties interested in the development of global corporate governance practices, describes the duties of an effective board as follows:[45]

♦ Reviewing, approving, and guiding corporate strategy, major plans of action, risk policy, annual budgets, and business plans; setting performance objectives; monitoring implementation and corporate performance; and overseeing major capital expenditures, acquisitions, and divestitures.

♦ Monitoring the effectiveness of the company's governance practices and making changes as needed to ensure the alignment of the corporation's governance system with current best practices.

♦ Selecting, compensating, monitoring and, when necessary, replacing key executives, and overseeing succession planning.

♦ Aligning key executive and board remuneration with the longer-term interests of the company and its shareholders.

♦ Ensuring a formal and transparent board nomination and election process.

♦ Monitoring and managing potential conflicts of interest of management, board members, shareholders, external advisors, and other service providers, including misuse of corporate assets and abuse in related party transactions.

♦ Ensuring the integrity of the corporation's accounting and financial reporting systems, including the independent audit, and that appropriate systems of control are in place—in particular, systems for risk management, financial and operational control, and compliance with the law and relevant standards.

♦ Overseeing the process of disclosure and communications.

Given these principles, what makes for a good board of directors? According to the ICGN as well as powerful institutional investors like the Ontario Teachers Pension Plan, the most important factor is a board of directors who are active, critical participants in determining a company's strategies.[46] That does not mean board members should micromanage or circumvent the CEO. Rather, they should provide strong oversight that goes beyond simply approving the chief executive's plans. Today, a board's primary responsibilities are to ensure that strategic plans undergo rigorous scrutiny, to evaluate managers against high performance standards, and to take control of the succession process.

Although boards in the past were often dismissed as the CEO's rubber stamps, increasingly they are playing a more active role by forcing out CEOs who cannot deliver on performance. According to a recent study by the consulting firm Booz Allen Hamilton, the rate of CEO departures for performance reasons has more than tripled, from 1.3 percent to 4.2 percent, between 1995 and 2002.[47] Well-known CEOs, like Gerald M. Levin of AOL Time Warner and Jack M. Greenberg of McDonald's, paid the price for poor financial performance by being forced to leave. Others, such as Bernard Ebbers of World-Com Inc. and Dennis Kozlowski of Tyco International, lost their jobs due to scandals. Don Carty of American Airlines was forced by the board to resign in 2003 for failure to disclose executive compensation plans during negotiations with unions. Frank Dunn, CEO of Nortel, was terminated in 2004 after the board determined that the company's reported financial performance for the previous three years could not be relied upon and a serious review of its books had to be undertaken. The firm was able to publish reliable financials for a number of years.

Board Composition Another key component of top-ranked boards is director independence. Governance experts believe that a majority of directors should be free of all ties to either the CEO or the company. That means a minimum of "insiders" (past or present members of the management team) should serve on the board and that directors and their firms should be barred from doing consulting, legal, or other work for the company.[48] Interlocking directorships in which CEOs and other top managers serve on each other's boards are not desirable. Perhaps the best guarantee that directors act in the best interests of shareholders is the simplest: most good companies now insist that directors own significant stock in the company they oversee.[49]

At times, though, it would appear that the practices of the boards of directors of some companies are the antithesis of such guidelines. Consider the case of Walt Disney Company. Over a recent five-year period, company CEO Michael Eisner pocketed an astonishing $531 million. Although Eisner had led Disney to provide shareholder returns of over 20 percent within a 10-year period, he likely had very little resistance from his board of directors. Many investors view the Disney board as an anachronism. Eisner's personal attorney was one of the company's 16 directors and for several years was also chairman of the company's compensation committee! The group also included the architect who designed Eisner's Aspen home and his parents' apartment. Joining them were the principal of an elementary school once attended by his children and the president of a university to which Eisner donated $1 million. The board also included the actor Sidney Poitier, seven current and former Disney executives, and an attorney who did business with Disney. Moreover, most of the outside directors owned little or no Disney stock. "It is an egregiously bad board—a train wreck waiting to happen," warned Michael L. Useem, a management professor at the University of Pennsylvania's Wharton School.[50] Indeed, soon after those issues came to light, Eisner was forced to resign from the helm of Disney, but without foregoing any of the compensation or perks that he had been granted by the board. Subsequently though, shareholders forced a complete revamping of the board, the adoption of solid board of governance guidelines, and the installation of truly independent directors. The Disney example also demonstrates that "outside directors" are only beneficial to strong corporate governance if they are engaged and vigilant in carrying out their responsibilities.[51] As Warren Buffett, founder and chairman of Berkshire Hathaway, observed, "The ratcheting up of compensation has been obscene. … There is a tendency to put cocker spaniels on compensation committees, not Doberman pinschers."[52]

Manulife Financial Corporation: an Exemplary Governance Structure

One of the best examples of governance guidelines is that of Manulife Financial. The country's largest insurance company's practices address some of the most important issues in governance, such as director independence, meetings of outside directors, evaluation and compensation of directors and executives, auditing, and succession planning. The guidelines are posted on the company's Web site for every one to see and represent another example of the board's commitment to communicate with shareholders in a timely, accurate, and straightforward fashion. Below are a few highlights:

Board Composition

- The board's independence is fundamental to its stewardship role and its effectiveness.

- All but one member (the current CEO) of the board are unrelated and independent.

- All committees of the board are comprised solely of unrelated and independent directors.

- The positions of chair and CEO are separate. The chair must be an unrelated and independent director.

Compensation

- The board, with the assistance of independent external advisors, undertakes a biennial review of director compensation.

- Directors are required to hold an equity position having a minimum value of $300,000 in the company.

- A Compensation Committee, established by the board and consisting of unrelated and independent directors, oversees the company's global human resource strategy, approves appointments of senior management, and provides proper development, review, and compensation of all senior management. It also approves the annual performance assessment and compensation of senior executives.

Board Meetings

- Each meeting of the board and of its committees is followed by an "in camera" meeting that excludes all members of management.

- Individual shareholders can directly contact both non-management directors and the chair.

- The board and its committees may retain any outside advisors at the company's expense. Individual directors may also retain outside advisors, at the company's expense, to provide independent advice on any matter before the board or a board committee.

Business Conduct

- A Code of Business Conduct and Ethics, established by the board, provides a set of guidelines for all employees, executives (including the CEO), and all members of the board of directors; they periodically sign an acknowledgement confirming their commitment to the Code.

- The CEO and CFO sign and certify the annual and quarterly financial statements.

- An Ethics Committee, established by the board and consisting exclusively of unrelated and independent directors, oversees items such as conflicts of interest, related party transactions, and confidential information. The Committee also reviews the company's compliance with legal requirements.

Sources: J. McFarland, and E. Church, "Do better boards make better companies?" *The Globe and Mail*, October 24, 2006, B1; www.manulife.com; MFC Proxy Circular 2005.

Many firms do have exemplary board practices. Strategy Spotlight 10.4 addresses some of the excellent practices at Manulife Financial Corporation, Canada's largest insurance company. In general, Canadian public firms have been urged to split the roles of CEO and chairman of the board. By 2004, 77 percent of S&P/TSX index corporations had already followed suit, a much higher percentage than their U.S. counterparts, in spite of the fact that many of Canada's public companies are still dominated by families and have dual-class share structures.

Shareholder Activism There are, in fact, so many owners of the largest corporations that it makes little sense to refer to all individuals as "owners." Moreover, substantial stock ownership comes through mutual funds, pension plans, and other means of institutional investing, further distancing the individual investor from the affairs of a public corporation. Nevertheless, every individual shareholder has several rights. These include (1) the right to sell the stock, (2) the right to vote the proxy (which includes the election of board members), (3) the right to bring suit for damages if the corporation's directors or managers fail to meet their obligations, (4) the right to certain information from the company, and (5) certain residual rights following the company's liquidation (or its filing for reorganization under bankruptcy laws), once creditors and other claimants are paid off.[53]

Collectively, shareholders have the power to direct the course of corporations.[54] This may involve acts such as being party to shareholder action suits and demanding that key issues be brought up for proxy votes at annual board meetings. The power of shareholders has intensified in recent years because of the increasing influence of large institutional investors such as mutual funds groups (e.g., AIC, CI, Fidelity, Investors Group, and Mackenzie) and retirement systems like the Ontario Teachers Pension Plan (OTPP).[55] Institutional investors hold over 50 percent of all listed corporate stock in the United States and a similar proportion in Canada.

Many institutional investors are aggressive in protecting and enhancing their investments. While shifting from traders to owners, they assume the role of permanent shareholders and rigorously analyze issues of corporate governance. In the process, they are reinventing terms of corporate monitoring and accountability.[56]

Consider the proactive behaviour of the Ontario Teachers Pension Plan, which manages approximately $85 billion in assets and is the largest pension fund in Canada and one of the largest in the world. Every year, OTPP reviews the performance of all companies in its stock portfolio and identifies those that are among the lowest long-term relative performers and whose governance structures do not ensure full accountability to company owners. OTPP meets with the directors and management to discuss performance and suggest specific governance reforms. It also follows a set of guidelines on all corporate governance issues and has frequently voted down items on shareholder annual meeting agendas or withheld its support for individual board members as well as entire boards of directors that do not conduct their affairs according to those guidelines. OTPP lists and explains, on its Web site, its voting decisions and principle of transparency and accountability toward the plan's beneficiaries, whom it sees as the ultimate owners of those public corporations.

Managerial Rewards and Incentives Incentive systems must be designed to help a company achieve its goals. Similarly, from the perspective of governance, one of the most critical roles of the board of directors is to create incentives that align the interests of the CEO and top executives with the interests of owners of the corporation—to ensure long-term shareholder returns.[57] After all, shareholders rely on CEOs to adopt policies and strategies that maximize the value of their shares. A combination of three basic policies may create the right monetary incentives enabling CEOs to maximize the value of their companies:

1. Boards can require that the CEOs become substantial owners of company stock.
2. Salaries, bonuses, and stock options can be structured so as to provide rewards for superior performance and penalties for poor performance.
3. Threat of dismissal for poor performance can be a realistic outcome.

In recent years, the granting of stock options has enabled top executives of publicly held corporations to earn enormous levels of compensation. In 2004, the CEOs of large corporations in Canada averaged $5.5 million, or 200 times as much as the average factory worker. Over the past decade, the wages of rank-and-file workers increased only 30 percent, while the pay of CEOs climbed 300 percent.[58] The lion's share of such increases came from exercising options. Stock options can be a valuable governance mechanism to align the CEO's interests with those of the shareholders, and the extraordinarily high level of compensation can often be grounded in sound governance principles.[59] For example, Robert Gratton, CEO of Power Financial Corporation, received a total compensation of $173.2 million in 2004 comprised of $3.5 million in salary and $169.3 million in stock options. During Gratton's tenure, the firm also did very well, and shareholders saw the price of their stock more than double. Another successful CEO, Bernard Isautier of PetroKazakhstan, received a total compensation of $93.1 million in 2004, including $493,850 in salary and $92.6 million in stock options exercised during the year. The shareholders also did well; the stock price more than tripled over the previous two years. And Isautier had not drawn even a base salary early in his tenure. The average annual stock market gain over the last five years for PetroKazakhstan had been 71.5 percent.

However, the pay for performance principle does not always hold. Consider, for example, that CoolBrands International's shares lost more than three-quarters of their value between 2004 and 2005—largely because of the loss of the contract to produce and sell Smart Ones, a frozen dessert, for the Weight Watchers brand name. At the same time, company president David Stein received a salary of $645,183 and exercised stock options worth $10.6 million, while the now deceased Richard Smith received a salary of $1,711,710 and $8.3 million in stock options. Over the next two years, CoolBrands sold off many of its remaining assets to cover debts and other obligations. From its position as the third-largest ice cream maker in North America, it was left with a small processing facility in Arkansas employing less than 40 people. Recently, CoolBrands was asked to delist its stock from the TSX for dropping below one dollar in value for an extended period of time; just a few short years ago the shares were at an all-time high of over $25.

There is a fundamental difference between investors, who risk their own money, and executives with stock options, who do not.[60] Good governance endeavours to balance the interests of executives with those of the corporation. On the one hand, this suggests that the board of directors' compensation committee should provide appropriate incentives for outstanding performance. On the other hand, corporate boards must use incentives to protect shareholder interests. However, boards of directors have often not upheld the interests of shareholders when they, in effect, have shielded top executives from a falling market and erosion of their firms' market values. Many boards have awarded huge option grants despite poor executive performance, and others have made performance goals easier to reach. In 2002, nearly 200 companies swapped or repriced options—all to enrich wealthy executives who are already among the country's richest people.

In addition to the granting of stock options, boards of directors are often failing to fulfill their fiduciary responsibilities to shareholders when they lower the performance targets that executives need to meet in order to receive millions of dollars. At General Motors, for example, CEO G. Richard Wagoner, Jr. and other top executives were entitled to a special performance bonus if the company's net profit margin reached 5 percent by the end of 2003. However, the 5 percent target was later lowered. And Coca-Cola's CEO, Douglas Daft, was scheduled to receive one million performance-based shares if the firm achieved 20 percent annual earnings growth over a five-year period. In 2001, this target was lowered to 16 percent. So much for sound corporate governance.

<table>
<tr>
<td>

Stock-based compensation plans are a critical element of most compensation programs and can provide opportunities for managers whose efforts contribute to the creation of shareholder wealth. In evaluating the suitability of these plans, consideration of reasonableness, scale, linkage to performance, and fairness to shareholders and all employees also apply. TIAA-CREF, the largest pension system in the world, has set forth guidelines for proper stock-based compensation. The plans should display the following characteristics:

- Allow for creation of executive wealth that is reasonable in view of the creation of shareholder wealth. Management should not prosper through stock while shareholders suffer.

- Have measurable and predictable outcomes that are directly linked to the company's performance.

- Be market oriented, within levels of comparability for similar positions in companies of similar size and business focus.

- Be straightforward and clearly described so that investors and employees can understand them.

- Be fully disclosed to the investing public and be approved by shareholders.

Source: www.tiaa-cref.org/pubs.

</td>
<td>

Exhibit 10.3
TIAA-CREF's Principles on the Role of Stock in Executive Compensation

</td>
</tr>
</table>

The Retirement Fund System of University Teachers and Administrators (TIAA-CREF) has provided several principles of corporate governance with regard to executive compensation.[61] These include the importance of aligning the rewards of all employees—rank and file as well as executives—to the long-term performance of the corporation; general guidelines on the role of cash compensation, stock, and "fringe benefits"; and the mission of a corporation's compensation committee. Exhibit 10.3 addresses TIAA-CREF's principles on the role of stock in managerial compensation.

External Governance Control Mechanisms

Our discussion so far has been on internal governance mechanisms. Internal controls, however, are not always enough to ensure good governance. The separation of ownership and control that we discussed earlier requires multiple control mechanisms, some internal and some external, to ensure that managerial actions lead to shareholder value maximization. Further, society wants some assurance that this goal is met without harming other stakeholder groups. In this section, we discuss several external control mechanisms that have developed in most modern economies. These include the market for corporate control, auditors, banks and analysts, governmental regulatory bodies, the media, and public activists.

The Market for Corporate Control Let us assume, for a moment, that internal control mechanisms in a company are failing. This means that the board is ineffective in monitoring managers and is not exercising the oversight required of them and that shareholders are not taking action to monitor or discipline managers. Theoretically, under these circumstances, managers may behave opportunistically.[62] Opportunistic behaviour can take many forms. First, managers can shirk their responsibilities, meaning they fail to exert themselves fully, as is required of them. Second, they can engage in on-the-job consumption. Examples of on-the-job consumption include possession of private jets, club memberships, and expensive art work for the offices. Each of these represents consumption by managers that does not in any way increase shareholder value. Instead, they actually diminish shareholder value. Third, managers may engage in excessive product-market diversification.[63] As we discussed in Chapter 6, such diversification serves to reduce only the employment risk of the managers rather than the financial risk of the shareholders, who can more cheaply diversify their risk by owning a portfolio of investments. Is there any external mechanism to stop managers from shirking, consumption on the job, and excessive diversification?

The market for corporate control is one such external mechanism that provides at least a partial solution to the problems described above. If internal control mechanisms fail and the management is behaving opportunistically, the likely response of most shareholders will be to sell their stock rather than engage in activism.[64] As more and more shareholders vote with their feet, the value of the stock begins to decline. As the decline continues, the market value of the firm eventually becomes attractive to a corporate raider who can take over the company for a price less than the underlying value of the assets of the company. The first thing that the raider may do, on assuming control of the company, is fire the underperforming management. The risk of being acquired by a hostile raider is often referred to as the *takeover constraint*. The takeover constraint deters management from engaging in excessive opportunistic behaviour.[65]

Although, in theory, the takeover constraint is supposed to limit managerial opportunism, its effectiveness has become diluted in recent years as a result of a number of defence tactics adopted by incumbent management. In Chapter 6, we discussed such tactics as poison pills and golden parachutes.

Auditors Even when there are stringent disclosure requirements, there is no guarantee that the information disclosed will be accurate. Managers may deliberately disclose false information or withhold negative financial information. It is also possible that they may use accounting methods that distort results based on highly subjective interpretations. Therefore, all accounting statements must be audited and certified for accuracy by external auditors. These auditing firms are independent organizations staffed by certified professionals who verify the books of accounts of the company. Audits can unearth financial irregularities and ensure that financial reporting by the firm conforms to standard accounting practices.

Recent developments leading to the bankruptcy of firms such as Enron and World-Com and a spate of earnings restatements raise questions about the failure of the auditing firms to act as effective external control mechanisms. Why did an auditing firm like Arthur Andersen, with a reputation based on decades in the auditing profession, fail to raise red flags about accounting irregularities? First, auditors are appointed by the firm that is being audited. The desire to continue that business relationship sometimes makes auditors overlook financial irregularities. Second, most auditing firms also do consulting work and often have lucrative consulting contracts with the firms that they audit. Understandably, some of them tend not to ask too many difficult questions for fear of jeopardizing the consulting business, which is often more profitable than the auditing work.

The recent restatement of earnings by Xerox is an example of the lack of independence of auditing firms. The Securities and Exchange Commission filed a lawsuit against KPMG, the world's third-largest accounting firm, in January 2003 for allowing Xerox to inflate its revenues by $3 billion between 1997 and 2000. Of the $82 million that Xerox paid KPMG during these four years, only $26 million was for auditing. The rest was for consulting services. When one of the auditors objected to Xerox's practice of booking revenues for equipment leases earlier than they should have been, Xerox asked KPMG to replace him, which they did.[66] As a result, the Ontario Teachers Pension Plan has used its proxy voting rights to refuse the appointment of KPMG as the external auditor to public companies in which it holds shares.

Banks and Analysts Two external groups that monitor publicly held firms are financial institutions and stock analysts. Commercial and investment banks do so because they have lent money to corporations and, therefore, have to ensure that the borrowing firm's finances are in order and that the loan covenants are being followed. Stock analysts conduct ongoing, in-depth studies of the firms that they follow and make recommendations to their clients to buy, hold, or sell. Their rewards and reputation depend on the quality of these recommendations. Their access to information, knowledge of the industry and the firm, and insights gained from interactions with the management of the company enable them to alert the investing community of both positive and negative developments relating to a company.

It is generally observed, however, that analyst recommendations are often more optimistic than warranted by facts. "Sell" recommendations tend to be exceptions rather than the norm. Many analysts seem to have failed to grasp the gravity of the problems surrounding companies like Enron and Global Crossing until the very end. Part of the explanation may lie in the fact that most analysts work for firms that also have investment banking relationships with the companies that they follow. Negative recommendations by analysts can displease the management, who may decide to take their investment banking business to a rival firm. Thus, otherwise independent and competent analysts may be pressured to overlook negative information or tone down their criticism. A recent settlement imposed on ten powerful Wall Street investment banks by the Securities and Exchange Commission and the New York State Attorney General office forced the banks to pay over $1.4 billion in penalties and to put in place mechanisms that would ensure independent research.[67]

Regulatory Bodies All corporations are subject to some regulation by the government. The extent of regulation is often a function of the type of industry. Banks, utilities, and pharmaceuticals, for example, are subject to more regulatory oversight because of their importance to society. Public corporations are subject to more regulatory requirements than private corporations. In fact, all public corporations are required to disclose a substantial amount of financial information. This information includes quarterly and annual filings of financial performance, stock trading by insiders, and details of executive compensation packages. There are two primary reasons behind such disclosure requirements. First, markets can operate efficiently only when the investing public has faith in the market system. In the absence of disclosure requirements, the average investor suffers from a lack of reliable information and may, therefore, stay away from the capital market. This will negatively impact an economy's ability to grow. Second, disclosure of information, such as insider trading, protects the small investor to some extent from the negative consequences of information asymmetry. Since the insiders and large investors typically have more information than the small investor, they may use that information to buy or sell before the information becomes public knowledge.

The failure of a variety of external control mechanisms led the U.S. Congress to pass the Sarbanes-Oxley Act in 2002. This act calls for many stringent measures that would ensure better governance of U.S. corporations and foreign companies listed in U.S. stock exchanges. Some of these measures include the following:[68]

- Auditors are barred from certain types of non-audit work. They are not allowed to destroy records for five years. Lead partners auditing a client should be changed at least every five years.

- CEOs and CFOs must fully reveal off–balance sheet finances and vouch for the accuracy of the information revealed.
- Executives must promptly reveal the sale of shares in firms they manage and are not allowed to sell when other employees cannot.
- Corporate lawyers must report to senior managers any violations of securities law lower down.

While the Sarbanes-Oxley Act has been a welcomed move to clean up corporate boards and reinstate confidence in public markets, it has also had unintended consequences. For example, in Canada, compliance with the relevant provisions of the Act is estimated to cost hundreds of millions of dollars for the affected firms and has spun a small industry of lawyers and accountants to guide corporations through the regulatory maze. In other countries, such as the United Kingdom, Germany, and Japan, some provisions conflict with their current corporate laws and customs, which is causing furor in Europe and Asia.[69] Nevertheless, regulators in each of those countries are looking for ways to strengthen corporate governance. Canadian regulators have introduced Rule 198 to address some of the same issues as those identified by the Sarbanes-Oxley Act. The Canadian Securities Administrators, an umbrella group for all provincial securities commissions, require CEOs not only to certify their financial statements but also to guarantee the internal processes, such as computer and accounting systems, used to create them. In Japan, legislation is promoting the importance of independent directors, and in Russia, extensive education on corporate governance is being promoted via a grant from the Canadian International Development Agency.

Media and Public Activists The press is not usually recognized as an external control mechanism in the literature on corporate governance. There is, however, no denying the fact that in all developed capitalist economies, the financial press and media play an important indirect role in monitoring the management of public corporations. In Canada, business magazines such as *Canadian Business*, the financial sections of national newspapers such as the Report on Business and Financial Post, as well as television networks like ROBTV, are constantly reporting on companies. Public perceptions about a company's financial prospects and the quality of its management are greatly influenced by the media. Bethany McLean of *Fortune* magazine is often credited as the first to raise questions about Enron's long-term financial viability.[70]

Similarly, consumer groups and activist individuals often take a crusading role in exposing corporate malfeasance. Well-known examples include organizations such as Pollution Probe in Canada and Ralph Nader and Erin Brockovich in the U.S., who played important roles in bringing to light such things as the safety issues related to GM's Corvair and environmental pollution issues concerning Pacific Gas and Electric Company of California.

Emerging Issues in Corporate Governance Countries besides the U.S. have also started addressing issues relating to corporate governance, whether it is because their companies have started venturing overseas or because they have come to recognize the economic benefits of liquid financial markets. Yet shareholders in those countries, Canada among them, face additional challenges with respect to the governance of their public corporations, in part due to the reality of concentrated ownership, extensive family ownership and control of public corporations, business group structures, sometimes weak legal protections of minority shareholders, and frequently even weaker enforcement mechanisms for existing legislation. The phenomenon often arises in the protection of the rights of minority shareholders. For example, Sears Holdings Corp., the majority owner of Sears

Canada, has repeatedly been accused of suppressing Sears' minority shareholders. In one case, the courts cited with the minority by forcing Sears to increase its offer when Sears Holdings wanted to acquire their stakes; the court agreed that management and the board acted, in statements and actions, to deflate the price of the stock before extending an offer for the 20 percent of the stock they did not control, in effect creating a situation where they could buy out the minority at below fair value.[71] In another case, the board added five new members, most of them current or former employees. The majority owner could easily force the slate of names through with little concern for the opinions of the minority. As long as it kept the legal minimum of three notionally independent directors, there was little the others could do to force its hand.

Magna International is another firm that has frequently been in the news for corporate mis-governance. For example, the loans and guarantees authorized by the board toward Magna Entertainment (MEC), the thoroughbred racing, race track, and slots business, are financial arrangements that are difficult to justify or explain to shareholders.[72] The horses and their affiliated operations have been losing truckloads of money for years, and without the backing of Magna International they would most certainly be facing bankruptcy. Although one would be very hard pressed to find any business connections, synergistic prospects, or complementary asset allocation benefits between MEC and the global automobile parts manufacturer, MEC is very dear to Frank Stronach and, as such, it is supported by the public corporation that Mr. Stronach controls. The board of Magna International has also authorized numerous consulting and other related contracts to companies that are controlled by Mr. Stronach and his family. Analysts have argued that such arrangements, common in many countries across the world and used by public firms that are effectively controlled by a family or an individual, cause a substantial discount to the underlying value of the stock and hurt the effectiveness of the financial markets.

Summary

For firms to be successful, they must practice effective strategic control and corporate governance. Without such controls, the firm will not be able to achieve competitive advantages and outperform rivals in the marketplace.

We began the chapter with a brief description of traditional feedback control systems, which rely on measuring outcomes of organizational efforts. We discussed how those control systems are still valid but often inadequate to help managers steer through the strategic challenges facing organizations today. In their place, managers increasingly rely on informational controls, which continuously monitor the internal and external environments, and adjust their assumptions, goals, and strategies to respond to unanticipated changes and surprises.

Behavioural controls are also a vital part of effective control systems. We argued that firms must develop the proper balance between culture, rewards and incentives, and boundaries and constraints. Where there are strong and positive cultures and rewards, employees tend to internalize the organization's strategies and objectives. This permits a firm to spend fewer resources on monitoring behaviour, and the firm is assured that the efforts and initiatives of employees are more consistent with the overall objectives of the organization.

We took a contingency approach to the subject of control systems, arguing that there is no one best way to design a strategic control system; rather, it is dependent on a variety of factors. The two that we discussed were the firm's business- and corporate-level strategies. We argued that with overall cost leadership strategies and unrelated diversification, it is appropriate to rely on cultures and reward systems that emphasize the production outcomes of the organization because it is rather easy to quantify such indicators. On the other hand, with differentiation strategies and related diversification, there must be culture and incentive systems that encourage and reward creativity initiatives as well as co-operation among professionals in many different functional areas. Here, it becomes more difficult to measure accurately each individual's contribution, and more subjective indicators become necessary.

In the final section of this chapter, we addressed corporate governance, which can be defined as the relationship between various participants in determining the direction and performance of the corporation. The primary participants include shareholders, management (led by the chief executive officer), and the board of directors. We noted that studies indicate a consistent relationship between effective corporate governance and financial performance. There are also several internal and external control mechanisms that can serve to align managerial interests and shareholder interests. The internal mechanisms include a committed and involved board of directors, shareholder activism, and effective managerial incentives and rewards. The external mechanisms include the market for corporate control, auditors, banks and analysts, regulatory bodies, the media, and public activists.

Summary Review Questions

1. Why are effective strategic control systems so important in today's economy?

2. What are the main advantages of "informational" control systems over "feedback" control systems? What are the main differences between these two systems?

3. Why is it important to have a balance between the three elements of behavioural control—culture, rewards and incentives, and boundaries?

4. Discuss the relationship between types of organizations and their primary means of behavioural control.

5. Boundaries become less important as a firm develops a strong culture and reward system. Explain.

6. Why is it important to avoid a "one best way" mentality concerning control systems? What are the consequences of applying the same type of control system to all types of environments?

7. What is the role of effective corporate governance in improving a firm's performance? What are some of the key governance mechanisms that are used to ensure that managerial and shareholder interests are aligned?

Experiential Exercise

Bombardier, the world's third-largest airplane manufacturer, with 2002 sales of $15 billion, has encountered declining shareholder value since the early 2000s. Using the Internet and library sources, evaluate the quality of the corporation in terms of management and the board of directors. Are the issues you list favourable or unfavourable for sound corporate governance?

Application Questions Exercises

1. Most of Nortel's problems may be attributed to a control system that failed to continuously monitor the environment and make necessary changes in the company's strategy and objectives. What companies are you familiar with that responded appropriately (or inappropriately) to environmental change?
2. How can a strong, positive culture enhance a firm's competitive advantage? How can a weak, negative culture erode competitive advantages? Explain and provide examples.
3. Use the Internet to research a firm that has an excellent culture and/or reward and incentive system. What are this firm's main financial and non-financial benefits?
4. Using the Internet, go to the Web site of a large, publicly held corporation in which you are interested. What evidence do you see of effective (or ineffective) corporate governance?

Ethics Questions

1. Strong cultures can have powerful effects on employee behaviour. How does this create inadvertent control mechanisms? Are strong cultures an ethical way to control behaviour?
2. Rules and regulations can help reduce unethical behaviour in organizations. To be effective, however, what other systems, mechanisms, and processes are necessary?
3. Some would argue that minority shareholders should not be afforded special protections; after all, they bought the stock in full knowledge of the disproportional power of the controlling shareholders or the family owners of the public corporation. Can you think of any financial and ethical implications of such "buyer beware" attitude and why indeed, a government might want to encourage or discourage these types of protections?

Chapter 11

Strategic Leadership:
Creating a Learning Organization and an Ethical Organization

LEARNING OBJECTIVES

After reading this chapter, you should have a good understanding of:

LO 1 → the three key activities in which all successful leaders must be continually engaged.

LO 2 → the importance of recognizing the interdependence of the three key leadership activities, and the power in overcoming resistance to change.

LO 3 → the crucial role of emotional intelligence (EI) in successful leadership.

LO 4 → the value of creating and maintaining a "learning organization" in today's global marketplace.

LO 5 → the importance of ethics in organizations and a leader's role in establishing an ethical organization.

In 1970, Vic De Zen, a Dutch immigrant with an engineering background, started a small extrusion die shop in Woodbridge, Ontario.[1] From the start, he showed dedication, hard work, keen insight into the demands of the market, and commitment to being an active contributor to the technological developments in the plastics industry. Within 30 years, his firm, Royal Group Technologies Ltd., became North America's largest PVC extruder with sales reaching $2 billion from products for the construction industry, housewares, furniture, and other consumer goods as well as building systems and window coverings.

De Zen was a workaholic by all accounts, and he demanded nothing less from his employees. The plastics industry was fiercely competitive with many small firms and large corporations fighting for slim margins on many commodity-type products. Royal Group invested heavily in research and development, to the tune of $30 million per year, and was delivering a number of new products with solid market potential. Among those promising lines were injection-moulded window frames, which have advantages over alternatives such as wood, aluminium, and vinyl windows due, in part, to their versatile large-span casement system.

Royal's commitment to the environment and sustainability were demonstrated by products such as deck boards produced from a substructure of recycled garbage made using a patented process, garage doors with a core of recycled garbage, and a siding product that looks like cement board.

The success in Canada supported the Royal Group's endeavours, first in the U.S. and later in opening operations in Mexico, China, Poland, Argentina, the Philippines, and Hawaii. By 2004, 60 percent of the group's sales came from the U.S., 30 percent from Canada, and the remaining from overseas.

Yet, 2004 also saw an extensive investigation of Royal Group and its bankers by the RCMP, the Ontario Securities Commission and the Securities and Exchange Commission, and the District Attorney's Office of Lower Manhattan. In addition, while the construction industry and all housing markets were registering healthy gains, the firm reported its first losses and was barely able to achieve the sales levels of the previous year. Soon after, the founder and his top two lieutenants were forced out and eventually the company was sold, but for only one quarter of what it had been worth just five years earlier.

What Went Wrong at Royal Group? The investigations zeroed in on many related-party transactions that spanned a number of years from the time the company had become a public corporation. Even though De Zen had retained 80 percent of the votes through control of all multiple shares, his holdings represented just 17 percent of the equity. Still, his control had effectively allowed him to appoint most of the members on the board of directors, and he had full control over the appointments of the senior management team.

The publicity around the investigations forced the independent directors to strike a review committee and consider the allegations. A forensic accounting firm was called to examine the firm's books and produce a report for the board and the firm's public shareholders. Soon, a number of revelations came to the surface. According to reports, related-party transactions between the public company and Vic De Zen, the minority owner but controlling shareholder (who, together with two senior executives, had participated in buying and selling deals, share exchanges, and the securing of personal loans and loans to companies they controlled), were not, or had only been partly, disclosed to the company's board and shareholders. The forensic accounting firm identified 13 real estate transactions totalling $41 million, six corporate acquisitions worth $34 million, a stock transaction that netted a profit of nearly $2 million, excessive bonuses, material sales to a Royal St. Kitts Beach Resort that was 60 percent owned by De Zen, and other transactions. In one particular deal, a numbered company owned by De Zen and others, including CEO Douglas Dunsmuir, acquired a property adjacent to Royal Group's main facilities for $20.5 million and immediately turned the property over to Royal Group for $27 million without disclosing the details to the board. Some of those transactions were facilitated by the company's CFO, who allegedly was fully aware of the details.

The things that went wrong at Royal Group could make a long list. Among them, one can identify the following factors:

◆ De Zen's obsession with controlling all activities of the corporation neither allowed for nor facilitated the development of competent executives who might have the integrity to block such alleged actions.

◆ Since De Zen was not willing to empower others and, subsequently, ran the firm as his own private fiefdom, he likely put together a team that he was certain would support his decisions, paying little attention to the financial and ethical ramifications.

◆ His leadership style did not allow much room for disagreement among the senior management ranks or the board. As a result, ideas about foreign expansion were likely not thoroughly vetted, and dissenting voices were muffled. Furthermore, much effort and investment to establish operations overseas had paid few dividends while having occupied a lot of management's time.

◆ Many of the related-party transactions were likely pursued to enrich certain individuals rather than for the benefit of the company. The preoccupation with covering those deals most likely further diminished management's attention to the competitive pressures mounting within the marketplace.

Vic De Zen led his company to great accomplishments through 30 years of hard work, but it seems that, at the same time, he failed to provide the kind of leadership that is demanded to compete in the global marketplace. In contrast to Vic De Zen at the Royal Group, effective leaders play an important and often pivotal role in the development and implementation of strategies as well as in providing ethical leadership to their organization.

Below, we define leadership and introduce what are considered to be the three most important leadership activities; then we discuss the important role of power. The second section focuses on a key trait, emotional intelligence, which has become increasingly recognized as critical to successful leadership. The third major section of the chapter, "Developing a Learning Organization," provides a useful framework for guiding leaders to help their firms learn and adapt in the face of accelerating change. Central to this contemporary idea is the concept of empowerment, wherein employees and managers throughout the organization truly come to have a sense of self-determination, meaning, competence, and impact. The fourth section addresses the leader's role in building an ethical organization. Here, we address both the value of an ethical culture for a firm as well as the key elements that it encompasses.

LEADERSHIP: THREE INTERDEPENDENT ACTIVITIES

In today's chaotic world, few would argue against the need for leadership—but how does one go about encouraging it? Is it enough to merely keep the organization afloat, or is it essential to make steady progress toward some well-defined objective? Custodial management is not leadership. Rather, leadership is proactive, goal-oriented, and focused on the creation and implementation of a unique vision. *Leadership is the process of transforming organizations from what they are to what the leader would have them become.* This definition implies a lot: *dissatisfaction* with the status quo, a *vision* of what should be, and a *process* for bringing about change.

There is substantial overlap between leadership and strategic management. In many respects, leadership is about managing strategically, and strategic management relies on leadership skills. Both deal with the process of guiding the organization to achieve its aspirations. Both leadership and strategic management are about identifying a vision—what the organization wants to become some time in the future. And they both also involve the process of helping the organization to get there. We have argued in this book that strategic management is the job of every manager in an organization. That is, every manager should think and act in ways that contribute to defining and accomplishing the strategic objectives set for the organization. Similarly, leadership, even though most of our discussion revolves around the top management team and the person in charge, is not the exclusive purview of the person at the top. Every employee looks to his or her boss to set a direction and provide guidance about his or her job; an effective manager provides subordinates with a sense of purpose and an identity, creates opportunities, motivates, and makes the resources available for all employees to achieve their best while contributing to the success of the whole organization. In essence, every manager is and needs to act as a leader for the group of people that report to him or her.

W. Glen Rowe distinguishes between managerial leaders and strategic leaders.[2] The former are concerned with preserving order, applying their expertise in a functional area, ensuring compliance with rules and procedures, creating new order, predictability, and efficiency in their area of responsibility. By contrast, strategic leaders are not only comfortable in overseeing their operating responsibilities but can also proactively look at situations, shape ideas, take risks, and make choices that can make a difference in their organizations. Rowe defines strategic leaders as those who are able to influence others to voluntarily make day-to-day decisions that enhance the long-term viability of their organizations; on the other hand, he suggests that managerial leaders only recognize rewards and punishments as tools to influence their subordinates' behaviours in conforming to predetermined rules. Strategic leaders make appropriate investments for the future while maintaining an appropriate level of stability in the present.

Doing the right thing is becoming increasingly important in today's competitive environment. After all, many industries are declining; the global village is becoming increasingly complex, interconnected, and unpredictable; and product and market life cycles are becoming increasingly compressed. Richard D'Aveni, author of *Hypercompetition*, argued that in a world where all dimensions of competition appear to be compressed in time and heightened in complexity, *sustainable* competitive advantages are no longer possible.[3]

Despite the importance of doing the "right thing," leaders must also be concerned about doing "things right." Charan and Colvin strongly argue in *Fortune* magazine that implementation (or execution) is also essential to success:

> Any way that you look at it, mastering execution turns out to be the odds-on best way for a CEO to keep his job. So what's the right way to think about that sexier obsession, strategy? It's vitally important—obviously. The problem is that our age's fascination feeds the mistaken belief that developing exactly the right strategy will enable a company to rocket past competitors. In reality, that's less than half the battle.[4]

Leaders are change agents whose success is measured by how effectively they define and implement a strategic vision and mission. Accordingly, many authors contend that successful leaders must recognize three interdependent activities that must be continually reassessed for organizations to succeed. As shown in Exhibit 11.1, these are: (1) determining a direction, (2) designing the organization, and (3) nurturing a culture dedicated to excellence and ethical behaviour.[5]

Exhibit 11.1
Three
Interdependent
Activities of
Leadership

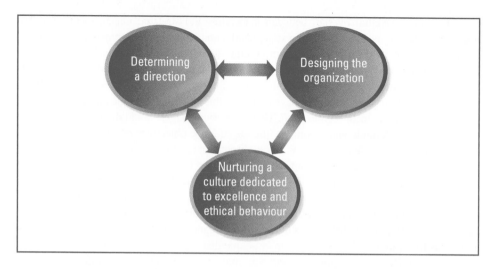

The interdependent nature of these three activities is self-evident. Consider an organization with a great mission and a super organizational structure and design but a culture that implicitly encourages shirking and unethical behaviour, or with a strong culture and organizational design but little direction and vision. Much of the failure of today's organizations can be attributed to a lack of equal consideration for these three activities. The metaphor of a three-legged stool is instructive: it will collapse if one leg is missing or broken. In the next section, we briefly look at each of these activities. We also address the important role of a leader's power in overcoming resistance to change.

Setting a Direction

Leaders need a holistic understanding of an organization's stakeholders. This requires an ability to scan the environment to develop knowledge of all of the company's stakeholders (e.g., customers, suppliers, shareholders) and other salient environmental trends and events and to integrate this knowledge into a vision of what the organization could become. It necessitates the capacity to solve increasingly complex problems, become proactive in approach, and develop viable strategic options. Developing a strategic vision provides many benefits: a clear future direction, a framework for the organization's mission and goals, and enhanced employee communication, participation, and commitment.

At times, the creative process involves what the CEO of Yokogawa, GE's Japanese partner in the Medical Systems business, called "bullet train" thinking.[6] That is, if you want to increase the speed by 10 miles per hour, you look for incremental advances. However, if you want to double the speed, you've got to think "out of the box" (e.g., widen the track, change the overall suspension system). In today's challenging times, leaders typically need to do more than just keep the same train with a few minor tweaks. Instead, they must come up with more revolutionary visions.

Consider how Robert Landry, CEO of Zurich North America, Canada, dramatically revitalized his firm by setting a clear and compelling direction. Zurich was a mid-size insurer, attempting to be all things to all people and competing with much larger domestic operators for small shares in a range of markets. Its performance was lacklustre, and during 2000 and 2001, it even posted some serious losses. Landry, after a candid assessment of the firm's strengths and prospects, decided to focus on a small but defensible niche, where he could develop a competitive edge, and to give up the struggle with personal insurance products, where the competition was eating his lunch. Zurich zeroed in on the middle-sized commercial market and the international corporate arena, where the company could leverage its connection with its giant parent Zurich Financial. In capitalizing on its far-flung global reach, it could then serve its customers more effectively. Zurich could handle the large risks that international operations of its clients entailed and price them for better margins. Within two short years, losses had been converted to generous gains for its shareholders and a return on equity of 13 percent.[7]

Designing the Organization

Almost all leaders, at some point, have difficulty implementing their vision and strategies. Such problems may stem from a variety of sources, including the following:

- A lack of understanding of responsibility and accountability among managers.
- Reward systems that do little to motivate individuals (or collectives such as groups and divisions) toward desired organizational goals.
- Inadequate or inappropriate budgeting and control systems.
- Insufficient mechanisms to coordinate and integrate activities across the organization.

Successful leaders are actively involved in building structures, teams, systems, and organizational processes that facilitate the implementation of their vision and strategies. To that end, we discussed the necessity for consistency between business-level and corporate-level strategies and organizational control in Chapter 9. A firm would generally be unable to attain an overall low-cost advantage without closely monitoring its costs through detailed and formalized cost and financial control procedures. In a similar vein, achieving a differentiation advantage would necessitate encouraging innovation, creativity, and sensitivity to market conditions. Such efforts would typically be impeded by the use of cumbersome rules, regulations, and highly centralized decision making. With regard to corporate-level strategy, we addressed, in Chapter 9, how a related diversification strategy would necessitate reward systems that emphasize behavioural measures to promote sharing across divisions within a firm; on the other hand, an unrelated strategy should rely more on financial (or objective) indicators of performance, such as revenue gains and profitability, since there is less need or likelihood for collaboration across business units.

Nurturing a Culture Dedicated to Excellence and Ethical Behaviour

In the previous chapter we discussed how organizational culture can be an effective and positive means of organizational control. Leaders play a key role in developing and sustaining—as well as changing, when necessary—an organization's culture. For example, Guy Laliberté has created a global sensation and a multi-billion dollar enterprise from the street performances of the old city of Montreal, while developing a strong organization dedicated to artistic excellence and social activism.[8]

In 20 short years, Cirque du Soleil has transformed the seedy circus business into a high-class, distinctive brand of live performances with elements of opera and theatre, lavish costumes, amazing sets, and spectacular high-tech special effects. Guy Laliberté has developed an almost mystical organization that still maintains a family atmosphere. At the same time, it has grown to over 3,500 people and has evolved into a multi-line company that has ventured into television, film, music, and merchandise. Still at the centre are four permanent and five touring shows in Europe, America, Asia, and Australia.

Laliberté once said, "to keep your edge, you have to feel insecure," and he has been pushing himself and his artistic talents to continuously experiment, innovate, and fuel

Strategic Leadership, One Store at a Time

Tim Hortons, the Canadian icon of coffee and doughnuts that has dominated rural and urban Canada for more than 30 years, has taken its winning recipe stateside. The U.S. is not only a much larger market with ten times as many coffee-drinking, doughnut-hungry, prospective customers, it is also the most saturated and competitive fast-food market in the world. Yet, it is in the U.S. that the Oakville, Ontario-based chain sees its future. With over 2,400 outlets in Canada, there is little room for growth at home. Tim Hortons has already opened 250 franchises in ten Northeast and Midwest states and is pushing to double that number within two years.

The legendary hockey player, Tim Horton, and his business partner, Ron Joyce, built the chain from what began as a single store in Hamilton back in 1964. Joyce, an ex-police officer, took over when Tim Horton died in a car accident in 1974. He was adamant from the start about the ingredients of a successful store: just coffee and doughnuts that are always fresh (although they have recently complemented the menu with lunch items that have augmented sales by 10 percent), clean stores, outstanding service, unpretentious managers, and an intimate connection to the local community. Franchisees brought the local community connections, and the fresh coffee brought the local customers. Ron Joyce made sure that he and his president, Paul House, knew every franchisee personally and that each one of them felt part of the family.

When Tim Hortons merged with Wendy's in 1995, Joyce and House's first concern was to meet each one of the 1,000 franchisees within the first three days and explain why this was a good move for the company and how it would help their business. They spent as much time as needed with each franchisee to answer all their questions and ensure that there were no lingering concerns. In turn, the franchisees have been extremely loyal, and the pride they and their staff feel is evident throughout each store so that it has spread to their millions of customers. This is not a small feat, considering that the average store serves some 1,500 customers each day, for a typical purchase of less than $3. Yet, average store sales reached $1.7 million in 2004 giving humble Tim's a share in the Canadian fast-food market that was larger than all-mighty McDonald's.

Sources: D. DeCloet, "A Better Way to Sell Doughnuts," *The Globe and Mail*, November 24, 2004, p. B13; B. McKenna, "Tim Hortons Filling U.S. Doughnut Holes," *The Globe and Mail*, March 28, 2005, p. B1; and www.timhortons.com.

the creative sparks that have brought much of the success to date. The latest show, a $170 million extravaganza, is slated to go up in another permanent home in Las Vegas, the fourth in that city.

Cirque du Soleil has a strong commitment to the community and is socially active in programs such as Cirque du Monde, which offers circus workshops for street children in countries spanning from Brazil to Mongolia. It allocates 1 percent of gross revenue to social projects, and its activism is shared among its performers, who are attracted to Cirque's concern with social responsibility as well as to its genuine focus on its staff. Laliberté has not only been able to guide Cirque to impressive financial results but has also strengthened its valuable human capital.

All managers and top executives must accept personal responsibility for developing and strengthening ethical behaviour throughout their organization. They must consistently demonstrate that such behaviour is central to the vision and mission of the organization. Several elements must be present and reinforced for a firm to become a highly ethical organization: role models, corporate credos and codes of conduct, reward and evaluation systems, and policies and procedures.

Strategy Spotlight 11.1 discusses how Ron Joyce, Tim Hortons's CEO, effectively performed all three leadership activities addressed in this section.

OVERCOMING BARRIERS TO CHANGE AND THE EFFECTIVE USE OF POWER

Now that we have discussed the three interdependent activities that leaders perform, we must address a key question: What are the barriers to change that leaders often encounter, and how can they use power to bring about meaningful change in their organizations? After all, people generally have some level of choice about how strongly they support a leader's change initiatives (or resist them, for that matter). Why is there often so much resistance? There are many reasons as to why organizations and managers at all levels are prone to inertia and slow to learn, adapt, and change.

1. *Vested interests in the status quo* People are comfortable with what they know and with things functioning a certain way; typically, they have worked hard to set up the routines around them. In general, people are not ready to jump at the first sight of change, nor do they see change as necessarily a good thing. There is a broad collection of organizational literature on the subject of "escalation," wherein individuals continue to throw "good money at bad decisions" despite negative performance feedback.[9]
2. *Systemic barriers* Here, the design of the organization's structure, information processing, reporting relationships, and so forth impede the proper flow and evaluation of information. A bureaucratic structure with multiple layers, onerous requirements for documentation, and rigid rules and procedures will often "insulate" the organization against change.
3. *Behavioural barriers* These are associated with the tendency of managers to look at issues from a biased or limited perspective. This can be attributed to their education, training, work experiences, or perceptions regarding the norms of the organization and what actions would be encouraged or discouraged within it.
4. *Political barriers* These refer to conflicts arising from power relationships. This can be the outcome of a myriad of symptoms such as vested interests (e.g., the aforementioned escalation problems), refusal to share information, conflicts over resources, conflicts between departments and divisions, and petty interpersonal differences.
5. *Personal time constraints* Gresham's law of planning states that operational decisions will drive out the time necessary for strategic thinking and reflection. This tendency is even more pronounced in organizations experiencing severe price competition or retrenchment, wherein managers and employees are spread rather thin.

Successful leadership requires effective use of power in overcoming barriers to change.[10] Power refers to a leader's ability to get things done in a way he or she wants them to be done. It is the ability to influence other people's behaviour—to persuade them to do things that they otherwise would not have done and to overcome their resistance and opposition to changing direction. Effective exercise of power is essential for successful leadership.

A leader derives his or her power from several sources, or bases. Numerous classifications of such sources, or bases, abound in the literature on power. However, the simplest way to understand the bases of power is by classifying them as organizational and personal bases of power, as shown in Exhibit 11.2.

Exhibit 11.2
A Leader's Bases of Power

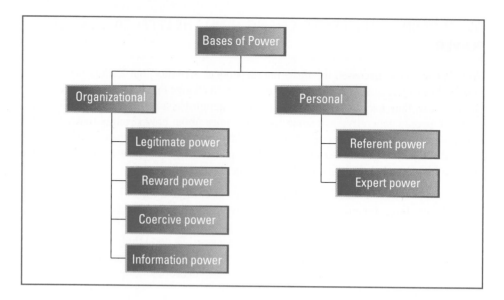

Organizational bases of power refer to the power that a person wields because of holding a formal management position. These include legitimate power, reward power, coercive power, and information power. *Legitimate power* is derived from organizationally conferred decision-making authority and is exercised by virtue of a manager's position in the organization. *Reward power* depends on the ability of the leader or manager to confer rewards for positive behaviours or outcomes. *Coercive power* is the power exercised by instilling fear of punishment for errors of omission or commission on the part of the employees. *Information power* arises from a manager's access, control, and distribution of information that is not freely available to everyone in an organization.

Apart from the organizationally derived power, a leader might be able to influence subordinates because of his of her personality and behaviour. These would be considered the personal bases of power, which consist of referent power and expert power. The source of *referent power* is a subordinate's identification with the leader. A leader's personal attributes or charisma might influence subordinates and make them devoted to that leader. On the other hand, the source of *expert power* is the leader's expertise and knowledge in a particular field. The leader is the expert on whom subordinates depend for information that they need to do their job successfully.

Successful leaders use the different bases of power, often a combination of them, as appropriate to meet the demands of a situation, including the specific nature of the task, the personality characteristics of the subordinates, the urgency of the issue, and other factors. They also recognize that virtually everybody has a need for power and endeavour to satisfy that need in the process of exercising their power effectively. An example of how Johnson & Johnson's CEO, William C. Weldon, exercised these different bases of power is addressed in Strategy Spotlight 11.2.

EMOTIONAL INTELLIGENCE: A KEY LEADERSHIP TRAIT

In the previous section, we discussed three of the salient activities of a strategic leader. In a sense, the focus was on "what leaders *do*." In this section, the issue becomes "who leaders *are*" and what the most important traits (or capabilities) of successful leaders are. Clearly, these two issues are related since successful leaders possess the valuable traits that, at the end of the day, enable them to engage in the activities that they must perform effectively in order to create value for their organization.

William C. Weldon: Utilizing Multiple Bases of Power

William C. Weldon, the CEO of Johnson & Johnson (J&J), is well known in the company for his charisma and powers of persuasion. He can convince, cajole, or sometimes even just sweet talk his colleagues into seeing things his way. A few years ago, the chief of pharmaceutical research and development of J&J, Dr. Per A. Peterson, was so disappointed with the personnel problems that he was contemplating leaving the company and told Weldon about it. The next morning, Weldon made a call to Dr. Peterson as early as 5:30 a.m. and invited him for breakfast. Well into the afternoon, the two men were still talking about Peterson's concerns. Eventually, Peterson agreed to remain in the company, and within a week, Weldon had made the changes that Peterson was asking for. Weldon used his charisma to get Peterson to agree with him.

Weldon has worked his way up from being a drug salesman to become the top executive in the company. He was head of Ethicon Endo Surgery, Inc., a J&J company that was supposed to establish itself in the emerging field of endoscopic surgery in the early 1990s. While there, he often set higher goals for his region than were set by the headquarters. He was always hungry for more. This, however, did not mean that Weldon did not understand the power of rewards or positive reinforcement. On at least two occasions, he gave higher bonuses to his managers than was normal at J&J. At another time, he closed shop for a day to give time off to his staff who had worked hard for a particularly difficult couple of months. Neither he nor his staff ever told this to executives at the corporate headquarters. According to Weldon, "Sometimes it is better to beg forgiveness than to ask permission."

For executives who fell short of expectations, Weldon made it clear that he did not like to be disappointed. When Centocor Inc., a new J&J drug business, did not meet the aggressive sales goals it set for the year 2000, Weldon was at their offices before the week was out. David Holveck, a former company group chairman of Centocor who now runs J&J's venture-capital arm, says, "He is a man of few words. But his body language was very clear: In the game there are two strikes. In 2001, we were expected to get it right." And they did it.

Source: A. Barret, "Staying on Top," *BusinessWeek*, May 5, 2003, pp. 60–68.

There exists, as one would expect, a huge literature exploring the traits of successful leaders—including business leaders at the highest level.[11] Characteristics of successful leaders include integrity, maturity, energy, judgment, motivation, intelligence, expertise, and so on. For simplicity, these traits may be grouped into three broad sets of capabilities:

- Purely technical abilities (like accounting or business planning)
- Cognitive abilities (like analytical reasoning or quantitative analysis)
- Emotional intelligence (such as the ability to work with others and a passion for work)

Emotional intelligence has been frequently identified as among the most consistent traits of successful managers.[12] Goleman defines emotional intelligence (EI) as the capacity for recognizing one's own emotions and those of others.[13] Findings indicate, for example, that EI is a better predictor of life success (economic well-being, satisfaction with life, friendship, family life), including occupational attainments, than IQ is.[14] This is not to say that IQ and technical skills are irrelevant. Obviously, they do matter, but they should be viewed as "threshold capabilities." That is, they are the necessary requirements for attaining higher-level managerial positions. EI, on the other hand, is essential for leadership success. Without it, Goleman has argued, a manager can have excellent training, an incisive and analytical mind, and many smart ideas but will still not be a great leader.

There are five components of EI: self-awareness, self-regulation, motivation, empathy, and social skill. We briefly discuss each below and summarize them in Exhibit 11.3.

Exhibit 11.3

The Five Components of Emotional Intelligence at Work

	Definition	Hallmarks
Self-management skills:		
Self-awareness	◆ The ability to recognize and understand one's moods, emotions, and drives as well as their effect on others.	◆ Self-confidence ◆ Realistic self-assessment ◆ Self-deprecating sense of humour
Self-regulation	◆ The ability to control or redirect disruptive impulses and moods. ◆ The propensity to suspend judgment—to think before acting.	◆ Trustworthiness and integrity ◆ Comfort with ambiguity ◆ Openness to change
Motivation	◆ A passion to work for reasons that go beyond money or status. ◆ A propensity to pursue goals with energy and persistence.	◆ Strong drive to achieve ◆ Optimism, even in the face of failure ◆ Organizational commitment
Managing relationships:		
Empathy	◆ The ability to understand the emotional makeup of other people. ◆ Skill in treating people according to their emotional reactions.	◆ Expertise in building and retaining talent ◆ Cross-cultural sensitivity ◆ Service to clients and customers
Social skill	◆ Proficiency in managing relationships and building networks. ◆ An ability to find common ground and build rapport.	◆ Effectiveness in leading change ◆ Persuasiveness ◆ Expertise in building and leading teams

Source: Adapted and reprinted by permission of *Harvard Business Review*. Exhibit from "What Makes a Leader," by D. Goleman, January 2004. Copyright © 2004 by the Harvard Business School Publishing Corporation; all rights reserved.

Self-Awareness   Self-awareness brings to mind that Delphic oracle who, thousands of years ago, gave the advice "know thyself." Self-awareness involves having a deep understanding of one's emotions, strengths, weaknesses, and drives. People with strong self-awareness are neither overly critical nor unrealistically optimistic. Instead, they are honest—with themselves and others.

People generally admire and respect candour. Further, leaders are constantly required to make judgment calls that require a candid assessment of capabilities—their own and those of others. People who assess themselves honestly (i.e., self-aware people) are well suited to do the same for the organizations they run.

Self-Regulation   Biological impulses drive our emotions. Although we cannot do away with them, we can strive to manage them. Self-regulation, which is akin to an ongoing inner conversation, frees us from being prisoners of our feelings. People engaged in such conversation feel bad moods and emotional impulses just as everyone else does. However, they find ways to control them and even channel them in useful ways.

People who are in control of their feelings and impulses are able to create an environment of trust and fairness. In such an environment, political behaviour and infighting are sharply reduced and productivity tends to be high. As well, people who have mastered their emotions are better able to bring about and implement change in an organization. When a new initiative is announced, they are less likely to panic; rather, they are able to suspend judgment, seek out information, and listen to executives explain the new program.

Motivation   Successful executives are driven to achieve beyond expectations—their own and everyone else's. Although many people are driven by external factors, such as money and prestige, those with leadership potential are driven by a deep-rooted desire to achieve for the sake of achievement.

How can one tell if one is motivated by a drive for achievement instead of external rewards? Look for a sign of passion for the work itself such as seeking out creative challenges, a love of learning, and taking pride in a job well done. Also, motivated people have a high level of energy and drive to do things better as well as a restlessness with the status quo. They are eager to explore new approaches to their work.

Empathy   Empathy is probably the component of EI that is most easily recognized. In a business setting, empathy means thoughtfully considering an employee's feelings—along with other factors—in the process of making intelligent decisions. Empathy is particularly important in today's business environment for at least three reasons: the increasing use of teams, the rapid pace of globalization, and the growing need to retain talent.

When leading a team, one is often charged with arriving at a consensus—often in the face of a high level of emotions. Empathy enables one to sense and understand the viewpoints of everyone around the table.

Globalization typically involves cross-cultural communication that can easily lead to miscues. Empathetic people are attuned to the subtleties of body language; they can hear the message beneath the words being spoken. In a more general sense, they have a deep understanding of the existence and importance of cultural and ethnic differences.

Empathy also plays a key role in retaining talent as empathetic leaders can appreciate, connect with, and create a work environment that high-performing knowledge workers find attractive to excel in.

Social Skill   While the first three components of emotional intelligence are all self-management skills, the last two—empathy and social skill—concern a person's ability to manage relationships with others. Social skill may be viewed as friendliness with a purpose: moving people in the desired direction, whether that's agreement on a new marketing strategy or enthusiasm about a new product.

Socially skilled people tend to have a wide circle of acquaintances as well as a knack for finding common ground and building rapport. They recognize that nothing gets done alone. Rather, one needs to have a network in place when the time for action comes.

Dan Goleman makes the following comments:

> It would be foolish to assert that good old-fashioned IQ and technical ability are not important ingredients to strong leadership. But the recipe would not be complete without emotional intelligence. It was once thought that the components of emotional intelligence were "nice to have" in business leaders. But now we know that, for the sake of performance, these are ingredients that leaders "need to have."

Emotional Intelligence: Gilles Lepage

Since becoming CEO of the Caraquet, New Brunswick-based Mouvement des Caisses Populaires Acadiennes (MCPA) in 1994, Gilles Lepage has doubled its workforce to 2,000 employees, doubled its asset base to over $2 billion, and more than quadrupled profitability, to $20.3 million in 2002. Member-owned co-operative style institutions are disappearing in most parts of Canada, but MCPA is thriving in New Brunswick's Acadian community, where some 200,000 people representing 60 percent of French-speaking households are Caisse members.

Lepage's secret is a pragmatic strategy that embraces the capitalist ethic of creating shareholder value while nurturing economic and social development for people still sorely lacking both. "We used to have a more passive approach," says Lepage, who has pushed his organization into everything from mutual funds and venture capital to administering corporate payrolls. The upshot is not just impressive financial performance. Caisse members are able to give back to their community as never before. Four percent of profits, double the rate before Lepage took over, are plowed directly into university scholarships, academic chairs, music festivals, theatre troupes, art galleries, hospitals, schools, and sports programs. A prime example is an annual $40,000 contribution that makes possible the Acadian Games, held every summer at a different location in the Maritimes. Lepage also points to the thousands of competitively paid jobs within the Caisse system itself that have slowed the exodus of the young and ambitious from the region. Growing bigger and more profitable, Lepage says, also allows Caisse branches to fund more companies, organizations, and individuals that traditional banks would never touch.

Source: J. DeMont, "Gilles Lepage," *Maclean's*, June 30, 2003, p. 46.

It is fortunate, then, that emotional intelligence can be learned. The process is not easy. It takes time and, most of all, commitment. But the benefits that come from having a well-developed emotional intelligence, both for the individual and for the organization, make it worth the effort.[15]

Strategy Spotlight 11.3 illustrates some of the components of emotional intelligence, such as self-regulation, motivation, empathy, and social skill that characterize Gilles Lepage, CEO of Mouvement des Caisses Populaires Acadiennes, a financial co-operative in New Brunswick.

Emotional Intelligence: Some Cautionary Notes While many strong leaders have great reserves of empathy, interpersonal astuteness, awareness of their own feelings, and awareness of their impact on others, there is always the danger of a leader becoming preoccupied with building and deploying these traits to the detriment of actually leading.[16] Managers may exhibit tremendous empathy for others but they must also be able to make tough decisions. It is easy to confuse empathy with sympathy and allow it to guide one's actions. Firing subordinates becomes impossible, and turning down proposals and projects becomes problematic as the manager is too concerned with hurting others' feelings. Similarly, overemphasis on social skills, team building, and consensus forming can get in the way of decisiveness and swift action. The opposite is also true as managers can be overzealous in their motivation, passion, and drive to achieve; they may become obsessed with their ideas and blind to other possibilities, or oblivious to signals for the need to re-evaluate and rethink the direction taken. Managers that get too close to everybody in the organization risk losing sight of the bigger picture and of the distance required in order to make objective and dispassionate decisions. Managers also may become preoccupied with self-awareness and self-management and as a result come across as stilted, inauthentic, and phoney. Finally, managers may end up using their emotional intelligence skills to manipulate others, increase their power, and feed their own self-worth.

The above observations suggest that emotional intelligence traits need to be balanced; excessive deployment of one capability to the detriment of others is likely to lead to failure rather than success. Moreover, emotional intelligence in and of itself is simply a set of capabilities that, in order to be effective, must be coupled with strong values and a moral compass to guide both the leader and the subordinates to the right direction. We will tackle the moral and ethical dimensions of leadership later on in this chapter.

DEVELOPING A LEARNING ORGANIZATION

Charles Handy, author of *The Age of Unreason* and *The Age of Paradox*, and one of today's most respected business visionaries, recently commented:

> The other day, a courier could not find my family's remote cottage. He called his base on his radio, and the base called us to ask directions. He was just around the corner, but his base managed to omit a vital part of the directions. So he called them again, and they called us again. Then the courier repeated the cycle a third time to ask whether we had a dangerous dog. When he eventually arrived, we asked whether it would not have been simpler and less aggravating to everyone if he had called us directly from the roadside telephone booth where he had been parked. "I can't do that," he said, "because they won't refund any money I spend." "But it's only pennies!" I exclaimed. "I know," he said, "but that only shows how little they trust us!"[17]

At first glance, it would appear that the story simply epitomizes the lack of empowerment granted to the hapless courier and the company's lack of trust: Don't ask questions, Do as you're told![18] However, implicit in this scenario is also the message that learning, information sharing, adaptation, decision making, and so on were *not* shared throughout the organization. By contrast, leading-edge organizations recognize the importance of having everyone involved in the process of actively learning and adapting. As noted by today's leading expert on learning organizations, MIT's Peter Senge, the days when Henry Ford, Alfred Sloan, and Tom Watson "learned *for* the organization are gone." As noted earlier, it is no longer possible in today's increasingly dynamic, interconnected, and unpredictable world for anyone to "figure it all out at the top." The old model, in which "the top thinks and the base acts," must give way to an integration of thinking and acting at all levels. "The person who figures out how to harness the collective genius of the people in his or her organization," according to former Citibank CEO Walter Wriston, "is going to blow the competition away."[19]

Learning and change typically involve the ongoing questioning of an organization's status quo and methods. This inevitably entails the imperative for individuals throughout the organization—not just those at the top—to reflect. Although this seems simple enough, it is easy to ignore. After all, organizations, especially successful ones, are so caught up in carrying out their day-to-day work that they rarely, if ever, stop to think objectively about themselves and their businesses. They often fail to ask the probing questions that might lead them to call into question their basic assumptions, to refresh their strategies, or to re-engineer their work processes. According to Michael Hammer and Steven Stanton, the pioneer consultants who touched off the re-engineering movement:

> Reflection entails awareness of self, of competitors, of customers. It means thinking without preconception. It means questioning cherished assumptions and replacing them with new approaches. It is the only way in which a winning company can maintain its leadership position, by which a company with great assets can ensure that they continue to be well deployed.[20]

Successful learning organizations create a proactive, creative approach to the unknown, actively solicit the involvement of employees at all levels, and enable all employees to use their intelligence and apply their imagination. Higher-level skills are required of everyone, not just those at the top. A learning environment involves organization-wide commitment to change, an action orientation, and applicable tools and methods.

A critical requirement of all learning organizations is that everyone feels and supports a compelling purpose. In the words of William O'Brien, CEO of Hanover Insurance, "Before there can be meaningful participation, people must share certain values and pictures about where we are trying to go. We discovered that people have a real need to feel that they're part of an enabling mission."[21]

Inspiring and motivating people by specifying a mission or purpose is a necessary but not a sufficient condition for developing an organization that can learn and adapt to a rapidly changing, complex, and interconnected environment. Four other critical, ongoing processes are needed to build learning organizations:

- Empowering employees at all levels
- Accumulating and sharing internal knowledge
- Gathering and integrating external information
- Challenging the status quo and enabling creativity

Empowering Employees at All Levels

"The great leader is a great servant," asserted Ken Melrose, CEO of Toro Company and author of *Making the Grass Greener on Your Side*.[22] A manager's role becomes creating an environment where employees can achieve their potential as they help move the organization toward its goals. Instead of viewing themselves as resource controllers and power brokers, leaders must truly envision themselves as flexible resources willing to assume numerous (and perhaps unfamiliar) roles—coaches, information providers, teachers, decision makers, facilitators, supporters, or listeners—depending on the needs of their employees.

The key to empowerment is effective leadership. Empowerment can't occur in a leadership vacuum. According to Melrose, "I came to understand that you best lead by serving the needs of your people. You don't do their jobs for them; you enable them to learn and progress on the job." Robert Quinn and Gretchen Spreitzer considered two diametrically opposite perspectives on empowerment that draw a sharp contrast in assumptions that people make about trust and control.[23] In the top-down perspective, empowerment is about delegation and accountability; senior management develops a clear vision and communicates specific plans to the rest of the organization. This strategy for empowerment encompasses the following:

- Start at the top.
- Clarify the organization's mission, vision, and values.
- Clearly specify the tasks, roles, and rewards for employees.
- Delegate responsibility.
- Hold people accountable for results.

By contrast, the bottom-up view looks at empowerment as concerned with risk taking, growth, and change. It involves trusting people to "do the right thing" and having a tolerance for failure. Employees would act with a sense of ownership and typically "ask for forgiveness rather than permission." Here, the salient elements of empowerment include the following:

- Start at the bottom by understanding the needs of employees.
- Teach employees skills of self-management and model desired behaviour.
- Build teams to encourage co-operative behaviour.
- Encourage intelligent risk taking.
- Trust people to perform.

Employee Empowerment at Dofasco

Hamilton, Ontario-based Dofasco is Canada's second largest steel maker. The non-unionized labour force of 7,300 has been credited for the company's success on many occasions and for being the basis of the advertising slogan, "Our product is steel. Our strength is people." The "Dofasco Way," as the company's culture has come to be known, has kept unions out and pays workers for productive ideas, includes training and education subsidies for employees and their families, and offers morale-boosting initiatives such as a recreation club, a pipe band, an annual picnic, and legendary Christmas parties.

Founded in 1912, Dofasco became the first Canadian company to offer profit sharing to its employees, in 1938. While the company always relied on and took care of its employees, drastic changes have occurred in the last 15 years. Coming out of a deep recession in the early 1990s, Dofasco, under its president and CEO John Mayberry, set a new strategy called "Solutions in Steel" that focused on three elements: operational excellence, technology and innovation, and intimate customer relationships. The restructuring process sought to engage employees and move away from a somewhat paternalistic culture of "entitlement" toward an "earnings" culture that involved linking the success of employees directly to the success of the company and the fortunes of the shareholders. It trained all employees in problem solving and customer service, and it began to involve them in initiatives that aimed to develop solutions to customers' problems. It de-layered management, established team-based manufacturing processes, gave more responsibility to cross-functional teams, and shared financial information with employees.

The changes paid off handsomely. Dofasco was named one of the world's most sustainable companies by the Dow Jones Sustainability World Index for three consecutive years (1999–2001), a ranking based on a combination of financial, social, and environmental performance. In 2001, Dofasco was the only steel company on the Index and one of only 15 Canadian companies listed. Dofasco did not forget its employees. In 1999, when Dow Jones named Dofasco the top global steel company, Hamilton saw the largest Christmas bash in the world, with more than 40,000 guests in attendance. Under a huge Christmas tree, some 7,000 full-time employees found an equal share from the record $53 million profit sharing, half of which went into their pension plan.

Sources: T. Watson, "Dofasco," *Canadian Business*, July 7–21, 2003, p. 84; and G. DiGiacomo, *Dofasco's Healthy Lifestyles Program*, A case for the Canadian Labour and Business Centre, March 2002.

Many leading-edge organizations are moving in the direction of the second perspective—recognizing the importance of trust, cultural control, and expertise at all levels over the extensive and cumbersome rules and regulations inherent in hierarchical control.[24] In the information economy, the strongest organizations are those that effectively use the talents of all the players on the team. Strategy Spotlight 11.4 illustrates how Dofasco empowers its employees.

Accumulating and Sharing Internal Knowledge

Effective organizations also redistribute *knowledge*, as well as *rewards*.[25] For example, a company might give front-line employees the power to act as "customer advocates," doing whatever is necessary to please the customers. These employees, however, also need to have the appropriate training to act as business people. The company needs to disseminate information by sharing customer expectations and feedback as well as financial information. The employees need to know about the goals and objectives of the business as well as how key value-creating activities in the organization are related to each other. Finally, organizations should allocate rewards on the basis of how effectively employees use information, knowledge, and power to improve customer service quality and the company's financial performance. Strategy Spotlight 11.5 helps point out both the motivational and utilitarian advantages of sharing company information.

Additional benefits of sharing of company information by management can be gleaned from a look at Whole Foods Market Inc., the largest natural foods grocer in

"Open-Book" Management

Jack Stack, president and CEO of Springfield ReManufacturing Corporation (SRC), is generally considered the pioneer of open-book management—an innovative way to gather and disseminate internal information. Implementing his system involved three core activities. First, results were generated daily for each of the company's employees—numbers that reflected the employee's work performance and production costs. Second, this aggregated information was shared once a week with all of the company's people, from secretaries to top management. Third, there was extensive training in how to use and interpret the numbers, how to understand balance sheets as well as cash flows and income statements.

In explaining why SRC embraces open-book management, Stack provided an insightful counter-perspective to the old adage "information is power":

> We are building a company in which everyone tells the truth every day—not because everyone is honest but because everyone has access to the same information: operating metrics, financial data, valuation estimates. The more people understand what's really going on in their company, the more eager they are to help solve its problems. Information isn't power. It's a burden. Share information, and you share the burdens of leadership as well.

Source: J. Stack, *The Great Game of Business*, New York: Doubleday/Currency.

North America.[26] Whole Foods uses an active process of *internal benchmarking*. Competition is intense at Whole Foods: teams compete against their own goals for sales, growth, and productivity; they compete against different teams in their stores; and they compete against similar teams at different stores and in different regions. Parallel to that, there is an elaborate system of peer reviews through which teams benchmark each other. The "Store Tour" is the most intense. Periodically, each Whole Foods store is toured by a group of as many as 40 visitors from another region. The tour is a mix of social interaction, reviews, performance audits, and structured feedback sessions. Lateral learning—discovering what your colleagues are doing right and carrying those practices into your organization—has become a driving force at Whole Foods.

In addition to enhancing the sharing of company information, both up and down as well as across the organization, leaders also have to develop means to tap into some of the more informal sources of internal information. In a survey of presidents, CEOs, board members, and top executives in a variety of non-profit organizations, respondents were asked what differentiated the successful candidates for promotion. The consensus was that the successful executive was a person who listens. According to Peter Meyer, the author of the study, "The value of listening is clear: You cannot succeed in running a company if you do not hear what your people, customers, and suppliers are telling you. Poor listeners do not survive. Listening and understanding well are key to making good decisions."[27]

John Chambers, president and CEO of Cisco Systems, the networking giant, also uses an effective vehicle for getting candid feedback from employees and for discovering potential problems.[28] Each year during their birthday month, employees at Cisco's corporate headquarters in San Jose, California, receive an email invitation to a birthday breakfast with Chambers. Each month at these events, several dozen of the employees fire some pretty tough questions, including bruising queries about partnering strategy and stark assessments of perceived management failings, at the CEO. Any question is fair game, and directors and vice presidents are strongly discouraged from attending.

Gathering and Integrating External Information

Recognizing new opportunities—as well as threats—in the external environment is vital to a firm's ongoing success. Focusing exclusively on internal operations may result in a firm becoming the world's most efficient producer of products that nobody wants and that are well past their prime time. Employees and managers can utilize numerous channels to ensure that, as organizations *and* environments become more complex and evolve more rapidly, they remain aware of environmental trends and events, as well as knowledgeable about their customers and competitors.

The Internet, trade and professional publications, books, business magazines such as *BusinessWeek*, *Canadian Business*, *Economist*, and *Fortune* represent invaluable sources for information about the industry, the economy and the marketplace. Other venues for gathering external information include membership in professional and trade organizations and attendance at meetings and conventions. Networking among colleagues inside and outside of one's industry is also a very useful means. Intel's legendary leader Andy Grove, famously sought out people like DreamWorks SKG's Steven Spielberg and Tele-Communications Inc.'s John Malone to gather information about the latest views on how to make personal computers more entertaining and better at communicating.[29]

Benchmarking can also be a useful structure for the gathering of external information. Here, managers seek out the best examples of a particular practice as part of an ongoing effort to improve the corresponding practice in their own organization.[30] With *competitive benchmarking*, the search focuses on the best practices of competitors, while *functional benchmarking* endeavours to determine best practices regardless of industry. Industry-specific standards (e.g., response times required to repair power outages in the electric utility industry) are typically best handled through competitive benchmarking, whereas more generic processes (e.g., answering 1–800 calls) lend themselves to functional benchmarking as the function is essentially the same in any industry.

Ford Motor Company benefited from benchmarking when it studied Mazda's accounts payable operations.[31] Soon, the initial goal of a 20 percent reduction in its 500-employee accounts payable staff was ratcheted up to 75 percent—and it was met. Ford's benchmarkers found that, unlike at Mazda, their own staff spent most of the time trying to match often conflicting data in a mass of paper that included purchase orders, invoices, and receipts. Mazda, instead, used an "invoiceless system" where payments to suppliers were simply triggered by the initial receipts without any loss of accountability.

It is often worthwhile to go directly to customers for information. For over 100 years, 3M has famously encouraged the sales force for its abrasives and other industrial products to go out to the shop floors and find out what the workers needed, instead of speaking only to purchasing managers and company executives.[32] More recently, Fred Taylor, senior vice president for global marketing at Gateway 2000, discussed the value of customer input in reducing response time, a critical success factor in the PC industry:

> We talk to 100,000 people a day—people calling to order a computer, shopping around, looking for tech support. Our website gets 1.1 million hits per day. The time it takes for an idea to enter this organization, get processed, and then go to customers for feedback is down to minutes. We've designed the company around speed and feedback.[33]

Challenging the Status Quo and Enabling Creativity

Earlier in this chapter, we discussed some of the barriers that leaders face when trying to bring about change in an organization. For a firm to become a "learning organization," it also must overcome barriers to fostering creativity. This becomes quite a challenge, of course, to the firm that is entrenched in a status quo mentality.

Perhaps the primary way to directly challenge the status quo is for the leader to forcefully create a sense of urgency. For example, Tom Kasten, the vice president at Levi Strauss who is charged with leading the campaign to transform the company for the twenty-first century, has a direct approach to initiating change:

> You create a compelling picture of the risks of not changing. We let our people hear directly from customers. We videotaped interviews with customers and played excerpts. One big customer said, "We trust many of your competitors implicitly. We sample their deliveries. We open all Levi's deliveries." Another said, "Your lead times are the worst. If you weren't Levi's, you'd be gone." It was powerful. I wish we had done more of it.[34]

Such initiative—if sincere and credible—establishes a sharing of mission and the need for major transformations. If effective, it can channel energies to bring about both change and creative endeavours.

Establishing a "culture of dissent" can be another effective means of questioning the status quo and spurring creativity. Here, norms are established whereby dissenters can openly question a superior's perspective without fear of retaliation or retribution. Consider the perspective of Steven Balmer, Microsoft's CEO:

> Bill [Gates] brings to the company the idea that conflict can be a good thing. … Bill knows it's important to avoid that gentle civility that keeps you from getting to the heart of an issue quickly. He likes it when anyone, even a junior employee, challenges him, and you know he respects you when he starts shouting back.[35]

Closely related to the culture of dissent is the fostering of a culture that encourages risk taking. "If you're not making mistakes, you're not taking risks, and that means you're not going anywhere," claimed John Holt, co-author of *Celebrate Your Mistakes*. "The key is to make errors faster than the competition, so you have more chances to learn and win."[36]

Companies that cultivate cultures of experimentation and curiosity make sure that *failure* is not, in essence, an obscene word. People who stretch the envelope and ruffle feathers are protected. More importantly, they encourage mistakes as a key part of their competitive advantage. Wood Dickinson, CEO of the Kansas City-based Dickinson movie theatre chain, told his property managers that he wanted to see them committing "intelligent failures in the pursuit of service excellence."[37] This philosophy was shared by Stan Shih, CEO of Acer, a Taiwan-based computer company. If a manager at Acer took an intelligent risk and made a mistake—even a costly one—Shih wrote off the loss as tuition payment for the manager's education.

CREATING AN ETHICAL ORGANIZATION

What are ethics?[38] Ethics may be defined as a system of right and wrong. Ethics assist individuals in deciding when an act is moral or immoral, socially desirable or not. There are many sources for an individual's ethics. These include religious beliefs, national and ethnic heritage, family practices, community standards and expectations, educational experiences, friends, and neighbours. Business ethics is the application of ethical standards to commercial enterprise.

Individual Ethics versus Organizational Ethics

Many leaders may think of ethics as a question of personal scruples, a confidential matter between employees and their consciences. Such leaders are quick to describe any wrong-doing as an isolated incident, the work of a rogue employee. They assume the company should not bear any responsibility for an individual's misdeeds. After all, in their view, ethics has nothing to do with leadership.

In fact, ethics has everything to do with leadership. Seldom does the character flaw of a lone actor completely explain corporate misconduct. Unethical business practices typically involve the tacit, if not explicit, co-operation of others and, therefore, reflect the values, attitudes, and behaviour patterns that define an organization's operating culture. Clearly, ethics is as much an organizational issue as a personal one. Leaders who fail to provide proper leadership to institute proper systems and controls that facilitate ethical conduct share responsibility with those who conceive, execute, and knowingly benefit from corporate misdeeds.

The ethical orientation of a leader is generally considered to be a key factor in promoting ethical behaviour among employees. Ethical leaders must take personal, ethical responsibility for their actions and decision making. Leaders who exhibit high ethical standards become role models for others in the organization and raise its overall level of ethical behaviour. In essence, ethical behaviour must start with the leader.

Over the last few decades, there has been a growing interest in corporate ethical performance. Some reasons for this trend may be the increasing lack of confidence regarding corporate activities, the growing emphasis on quality of life issues, and a spate of recent corporate scandals at such firms as Enron, Hollinger, and Tyco, as well as the excesses of Bay and Wall Streets that were largely responsible for the financial meltdown of 2008. Concerns about protecting the environment, fair employment practices, and the distribution of unsafe products have served to create powerful federal and provincial regulatory agencies such as Environment Canada, the Canadian Food Inspection Agency, and Equal Opportunity for Ontario. Recently, however, other concerns have come to the fore, including the problems associated with the use of fetal tissue for research, disproportionate executive pay levels, corporate crises such as those at Royal Group and Nortel, and the practices of major financial services institutions in the wake of the subprime lending crisis. Merely adhering to the minimum regulatory standards may not be enough to remain competitive in a world that is becoming more socially conscious.

Without a strong ethical culture, the chance of ethical crises occurring is increased. They can be very damaging in terms of financial costs, the erosion of human capital, and overall loss of reputation among firms. Consider the debacle at CIBC regarding its involvement with Enron and accusations that the bank helped the defunct energy firm raise money, hide debt, and inflate revenues. The bank had to settle some of its Enron litigation, without admitting any wrongdoing, for upward of $2.4 billion, while simultaneously announcing a series of retirements and departures among its senior management ranks. The settlement represented almost 25 percent of the bank's book value. Instantly, the stock lost more than 10 percent of its value, clipping away the same amount from thousands of its shareholders' pockets. While CIBC has, in the past, frequently been identified as a corporation with excellent governance, many have questioned the leadership and values of its CEO who chose to retire just days before the announcement, pocketing some $52 million in bonuses and pay.[39] Two short years later, CIBC again made the news by announcing billions of dollars in write-offs relating to its exposure in exotic financial products associated with subprime mortgages. In response, the bank's stock lost more than 40 percent of its value. Interestingly, this time neither the members of the board nor any of the senior managers saw fit to resign or retire.

The past several years have exposed numerous instances of unethical and illegal behaviour by many senior corporate executives. For example, Bernard Ebbers, CEO of WorldCom, obtained some $400 million in personal loans from the company and was convicted of massive accounting fraud to the tune of $9 billion, precipitating the largest bankruptcy in history, which wiped out $140 billion in market value. Enron's CEO Kenneth Lay, president Jeffrey Skilling, and CFO Andrew Fastow all led that company to a mega-scandal of inflated profits, money laundering, and accounting manipulations that destroyed one of the U.S.'s most admired companies and erased $67 billion of investor wealth. Tyco's CEO, Dennis Kozlowski, destroyed over $100 billion in market capitalization following revelations of accounting irregularities, questionable payments to supposedly independent directors, and personal spending excesses charged to the corporation. Conrad Black made headlines of his own after disclosures of diverting funds to himself and senior officers and directors of Hollinger International, while Frank Dunn of Nortel was terminated for cause in a deepening accounting scandal that saw the company's stock value drop by 50 percent in a single day.

The ethical organization is characterized by a commitment to ethical values and integrity as a driving force of the enterprise.[40] Ethical values shape the search for opportunities, the design of organizational systems, and the decision-making process used by individuals and groups. They provide a common frame of reference that serves as a unifying force across different functions, lines of business, and employee groups. Organizational ethics help define what a company is and what it stands for.

The potential benefits of ethical practice to an organization are many but often indirect. The literature has found somewhat inconsistent results concerning the overall relationship between ethical performance and measures of financial performance.[41] That is, the dictum that "ethics pays" cannot always be supported. Indeed, ethicists have told us that to behave ethically can cost dearly, and ethics and interests can and do conflict.[42] Sometimes, doing the right thing means walking away from a deal and not purchasing materials from the lowest cost producer. If anything, the conflicting interests among an organization's diverse stakeholders almost guarantee that, normally, it will be impossible to benefit everybody and not disadvantage somebody. While the concept of enlightened self-interest, which implies an instrumentalist view of ethical behaviour, suggests that corporate social responsibility should be easy to deliver, the reality is that it is not always the case that what is good will also necessarily be beneficial to the organization—in the short run or in the long run. Moreover, in today's diverse, multicultural world, what is considered "good" for some individuals, at a particular time and place, is not necessarily viewed as such by others. Norms, ethical values, and moral standards do vary and do change. Managers are called on to reconcile this complexity and make strategic decisions that are fraught with critical ethical dilemmas.

Positive relationships, though, have been found between ethical performance and strong organizational culture, along with increased employee motivation, lower turnover, higher organizational commitment, and enhanced social responsibility. These findings are particularly important in today's knowledge-intensive organizations, where human capital is critical in creating value and competitive advantages. As we discussed in Chapter 4, constructive relationships among individuals (i.e., social capital) are vital in leveraging human capital and other resources in an organization. There are many other potential benefits as well. Drawing on the concept of stakeholder management, which we discussed in Chapter 1, an ethically sound organization can also strengthen its bonds among its suppliers, customers, and governmental agencies. John E. Pepper, chairman of Procter & Gamble, addresses such a perspective in Strategy Spotlight 11.6.

Integrity-Based versus Compliance-Based Approaches to Organizational Ethics

Before discussing the key elements for building an ethical organization, it is important to understand the essential links between organizational integrity and the personal integrity of an organization's members.[43] There cannot be high-integrity organizations without high-integrity individuals. At the same time, individual integrity is rarely self-sustaining.

Procter & Gamble: Using Ethics to "Build the Spirit of the Place"

John Pepper, former CEO and chairman of Procter & Gamble Company, shares his perspective on ethics:

> Let me start by saying that while ethics may seem like a soft concept—not as hard, say, as strategy or budgeting or operations—it is, in fact, a very hard concept. It is tangible. It is crucial … it is good for business.
>
> There are several reasons for this.
>
> First, a company's values have a tremendous impact on who is attracted to your company and who will stay with it. We only have one life to live. All of us want to live it as part of an institution committed to high goals and high-sighted means of reaching these goals. This is true everywhere I've been. In our most mature countries and our newest.
>
> Strong corporate values greatly simplify decision making. It is important to know the things you won't even think about doing. Diluting a product. Paying a bribe. Not being fair to a customer or an employee.
>
> Strong values earn the respect of customers and suppliers and governments and other companies, too. This is absolutely crucial over the long term.
>
> A company which pays bribes in a foreign market becomes an open target for more bribes when the word gets out. It never stops.
>
> A company which is seen to be offering different trade terms to different customers based on how big they are or how hard they push will forever be beset by requests for special terms.
>
> A company which is seen by a government as having weak or varying standards will not be respected by that government.
>
> And more positively, governments and other companies really do want to deal with companies they feel are pursuing sound values because, in many, if not most cases, they believe it will be good for them.
>
> One final but very fundamental reason for operating ethically is that strong values create trust and pride among employees. Simply put, they build the spirit of the place.

Source: J. E. Pepper, "The Boa Principle: Operating Ethically in Today's Business Environment," speech presented at Florida A&M University, Tallahassee, January 30, 1997.

Even good people can lose their bearings when faced with pressures, temptations, and heightened performance expectations in the absence of organizational support systems and ethical boundaries. Organizational integrity, on the other hand, is beyond personal integrity. It rests on a concept of purpose, responsibility, and ideals for an organization as a whole. An important responsibility of leaders in building organizational integrity is to create this ethical framework and develop the organizational capabilities to make it operational.

It is also important to know the approaches organizations may adopt in dealing with ethics. Exhibit 11.4 compares the compliance-based approach to the integrity-based approach. They help make the distinction among ethics, moral standards, public norms, and the letter of the law. Faced with the prospect of litigation, several organizations reactively implement compliance-based ethics programs. Such programs are typically designed by a corporate counsel with the goal of preventing, detecting, and punishing legal violations. But being ethical is much more than being legal, and an integrity-based approach addresses the issue of ethics in a more comprehensive manner.

An integrity-based approach to ethics management combines a concern for law with an emphasis on managerial responsibility for ethical behaviour. This approach is broader, deeper, and more demanding than a legal compliance initiative. It is broader in that it seeks to enable responsible conduct. It is deeper in that it cuts to the ethos and operating systems of an organization and its members, their core guiding values, thoughts, and actions. And it is more demanding because it requires an active effort to define the responsibilities and aspirations that constitute an organization's ethical compass. Most importantly, in this

Exhibit 11.4

Approaches or Strategies for Ethics Management

Characteristics	Compliance-Based Approach	Integrity-Based Approach
Ethos	Conformity with externally imposed standards	Self-governance according to chosen standards
Objective	Prevent criminal misconduct	Enable responsible conduct
Leadership	Lawyer-driven	Management-driven with aid of lawyers, HR, and others
Methods	Education, reduced discretion, auditing and controls, penalties	Education, leadership, accountability, organizational systems and decision processes, auditing and controls, penalties
Behavioural assumptions	Autonomous beings guided by material self-interest	Social beings guided by material self-interest, values, ideals, peers

Source: Reprinted by permission of *Harvard Business Review*. Exhibit from "Managing Organizational Integrity," by L. S. Paine. Copyright 1994 by the Harvard Business School Publishing Corporation; all rights reserved.

approach, organizational ethics is seen as the work of management. A corporate counsel may play a role in designing and implementing integrity strategies, but it is managers at all levels and across all functions that are involved in the process. Once integrated into the day-to-day operations of an organization, such strategies can help prevent damaging ethical lapses, while tapping into powerful human impulses for moral thought and action. Ethics then become the governing ethos of an organization instead of burdensome constraints to be adhered to. Texas Instruments represents an example of an organization that goes beyond mere compliance to laws in building an ethical organization. In teaching ethics to its employees, Texas Instruments, the $8 billion chip and electronics manufacturer, asks them to consider an issue by asking the following questions: Is it legal? Is it consistent with the company's stated values? Will one feel bad doing it? What will the public think if the action is reported in the press? Does one think it is wrong? Further, if the employees are not sure of the ethicality of the issue, they are encouraged to ask someone until they are clear about it. In the process, employees can approach high-level personnel and the company's lawyers to seek advice.[44]

Compliance-based approaches are externally motivated; that is, they are based on the fear of punishment for doing something unlawful. On the other hand, integrity-based approaches are driven by a personal and organizational commitment to ethical behaviour.

Strategy Spotlight 11.7 presents examples from the financial sector, highlighting the range of behaviours that can traverse the legal and ethical divide.

A firm must have several key elements before it can become a highly ethical organization. These elements, which must be present and constantly reinforced in order for the firm to be successful, include

- role models,
- corporate credos and codes of conduct,
- reward and evaluation systems, and
- policies and procedures.

Ethics on Bay Street

Much has been said recently about the actions of some in the investment banking community on Toronto's Bay Street, the financial capital of Canada. Consider, for example, the actions of AGF Funds Inc., AIC Ltd., CI Mutual Funds Inc., and a unit of Investors Group Inc.—four of Canada's largest mutual fund companies. They all admitted that they routinely gave preferential treatment to a handful of sophisticated market professionals at the expense of their long-term investors. The Ontario Securities Commission fined them a total of $156 million for a practice called market timing. The four firms were accused of failing in their duty to protect the best interest of their funds and allowing trading that inflicted significant harm on the funds by reducing returns for long-term investors. Furthermore, four investment dealers—RBC Dominion Securities Inc., BMO Nesbitt Burns Inc., TD Waterhouse (Canada) Inc., and Investors Group Financial Services Inc., an arm of Investor Groups Inc., all belonging to some of Canada's largest financial institutions, were fined over $46 million by the Investment Dealers Association of Canada for failing to detect and prevent systemic market timing in mutual funds by some of their clients.

The settlements state that in the practice known as market timing, the firms allowed a small number of hedge funds and other professional traders to make very rapid in-and-out trades within particular mutual funds and thereby benefit from small differences in valuation. The practice not only increased the volatility of those funds but added to the cost of their management—a cost that was borne by all the other mutual fund holders. In one case, a bank's trading arm actively encouraged and promoted market timing activities, while an internal memo from its mutual fund unit explicitly cited its own analysis that showed rapid trading would have "a significant negative impact on the performance of the funds involved." Although the practice is not strictly illegal, it certainly flies in the face of the mutual fund firms' public pronouncements and the procedures many fund companies have in place to shield their unit holders from added costs and volatility. The regulators argued that the documented practices violated the principles of fairness to clients, raising serious questions about the appropriateness of the conduct of the mutual fund companies.

Sources: S. Stewart, P. Waldie, and K. Howlett, "Securities Probe," *The Globe and Mail*, February 10, 2005, pp. B1–B9; K. Howlett, and J. Saunders, "Fund Firms Admit Role in Market Timing Trades," *The Globe and Mail*, December 17, 2004, pp. B1–B4; and K. Damsell, "Dealers Slapped with Close to $50 Million in Penalties," *The Globe and Mail*, December 17, 2004, p. B4.

These elements are highly interrelated. For example, reward structures and policies will be useless if leaders throughout the organization are not sound role models. That is, leaders who implicitly say, "Do as I say, not as I do," will quickly have their credibility eroded and, in the process, will sabotage other elements that are essential to building an ethical organization.

Role Models

For good or for bad, leaders are role models in their organizations. As we noted in Chapter 9, leaders must "walk the talk"; that is, they must be consistent in their words and deeds. The values as well as the character of leaders become transparent to an organization's employees through their behaviours. In addition, when leaders do not believe in the ethical standards that they are trying to inspire, they will not be effective as role models. Being an effective leader often includes taking responsibility for ethical lapses within the organization—even if the executives themselves are not directly involved. Consider, for example, the perspective of Dennis Bakke, CEO of AES, a $9 billion global electricity company based in Arlington, Virginia:

> There was a major breach (in 1992) of the AES values. Nine members of the water treatment team in Oklahoma lied to the EPA about water quality at the plant. There was no environmental damage, but they lied about the test results. A new, young chemist at the plant discovered it, and she told a team leader, and, of course, we then were notified. Now, you could argue that the people who lied were responsible and were accountable, but the senior management team also took responsibility by taking pay cuts. My reduction was about 30 percent.[45]

Such action enhances the loyalty and commitment of employees throughout the organization. Many might believe that it would have been much easier (and personally less expensive!) for Bakke and his management team to merely take strong punitive action against the nine individuals who were acting in ways inconsistent with the behaviour expected in AES's ethical culture. However, by taking responsibility for the misdeeds, the top executives—through their highly visible action—made it very clear that responsibility and penalties for ethical lapses goes well beyond the "guilty" parties. Such courageous behaviour by leaders helps to strengthen an organization's ethical environment.

Corporate Credos and Codes of Conduct

Corporate credos or codes of conduct are another important element of an ethical organization. Such mechanisms provide a statement and guidelines for norms and beliefs as well as guidelines for decision making. They provide employees with a clear understanding of the organization's position regarding employee behaviour. Such guidelines also provide the basis for employees to refuse to commit unethical acts and help to make them aware of issues before they are faced with a difficult situation. For such codes to be truly effective, organization members must be aware of them and the behavioural guidelines they contain.

Large corporations are not the only ones to develop and use codes of conduct. Consider the example of Wetherill Associates (WAI), a small, privately-held supplier of electrical parts to the automotive market. Rather than a conventional code of conduct, WAI has a Quality Assurance Manual—a combination of philosophy text, conduct guide, technical manual, and company profile—that describes the company's commitment to honesty, ethical action, and integrity. Interestingly, WAI doesn't have a corporate ethics officer because the company's corporate ethics officer is top management. Marie Bothe, as WAI's chief executive officer, saw her main function as keeping the 350-employee company on the path of ethical behaviour and looked for opportunities to help the community. She delegated the "technical" aspects of the business—marketing, finance, personnel, and operations—to other members of the organization.[46]

Perhaps the best-known credo, a statement describing a firm's commitment to certain standards, is that of Johnson & Johnson (J&J). It is reprinted in Exhibit 11.5. The credo stresses honesty, integrity, superior products, and putting people before profits. What distinguishes the J&J credo from those of other firms is the amount of energy the company's top managers devote to ensuring that employees live by its precepts.

Over a three-year period, Johnson & Johnson undertook a massive effort to assure that its original credo, already decades old, was still valid. More than 1,200 managers attended two-day seminars in groups of 25, with explicit instructions to challenge the credo. The president or CEO of the firm personally presided over each session. In the end, the company came out of the process believing that its original document was still valid. However, the questioning process continues. Such "challenge meetings" are still replicated every other year for all new managers. These efforts force J&J to question, internalize, and then implement its credo. The investments paid off handsomely many times—most notably in 1982, when one of its flagship products, Tylenol, was laced with cyanide, unbeknownst to J&J, and eight people died as a result. Leaders such as Ralph Larsen made an across-the-board recall of the product, even though it affected only a limited number of untraceable units, thereby sending a strong message throughout the organization.

Reward and Evaluation Systems

It is entirely possible for a highly ethical leader to preside over an organization that commits several unethical acts. How? It may reflect a flaw in the organization's reward structure. A reward and evaluation system may inadvertently cause individuals to act in

Exhibit 11.5
Johnson & Johnson's
Credo

We believe our first responsibility is to the doctors, nurses and patients, to mothers and fathers and all others who use our products and services. In meeting their needs, everything we do must be of high quality. We must constantly strive to reduce our costs in order to maintain reasonable prices. Customers' orders must be serviced promptly and accurately. Our suppliers and distributors must have an opportunity to make a fair profit.

We are responsible to our employees, the men and women who work with us throughout the world. Everyone must be considered as an individual. We must respect their dignity and recognize their merit. They must have a sense of security in their jobs. Compensation must be fair and adequate, and working conditions clean, orderly, and safe. We must be mindful of ways to help our employees fulfill their family responsibilities. Employees must feel free to make suggestions and complaints. There must be equal opportunity for employment, development, and advancement for those qualified. We must provide competent management, and their actions must be just and ethical.

We are responsible to the communities in which we live and work and to the world community as well. We must be good citizens—support good works and charities and bear our fair share of taxes. We must encourage civic improvements and better health and education. We must maintain in good order the property we are privileged to use, protecting the environment and natural resources.

Our final responsibility is to our stockholders. Business must make a sound profit. We must experiment with new ideas. Research must be carried on, innovative programs developed, and mistakes paid for. New equipment must be purchased, new facilities provided, and new products launched. Reserves must be created to provide for adverse times. When we operate according to these principles, the stockholders should realize a fair return.

Source: Reprinted with permission of Johnson & Johnson Co.

an inappropriate manner if rewards are seen as being distributed on the basis of outcomes instead of on the basis of the means by which goals and objectives are achieved. Much of a company's illegal and unethical behaviour can result from the absence of rules and regulations to guide behaviour. When the message is, "Do whatever it takes to make the numbers," company reputations do suffer.

Consider, for example, Sears Canada Inc.'s recent brush with the Competition Bureau. Sears was ordered to pay a hefty fine for a series of ads that were promoting 45 percent savings on a line of all-season tires.[47] The Bureau concluded that the ads were deceptive since they did not represent actual prices; the tires were to be sold directly at the lower prices, and the consumers were not, in fact, receiving any discounts on their purchases. The Bureau determined that only 2 percent of the tires were sold at the original prices and that the message was purposefully misleading, ultimately hurting consumers and competitors.

Sears tried to convince the quasi-judicial tribunal that while most of the tires never sold for the full price mentioned in the ads, "the claims were simply commercial expressions." Chances are that aggressive Sears marketers had pushed the limits, which resulted in behaviour that cost the company some of its reputation.

The Sears example makes two important points. First, inappropriate reward systems may cause individuals at all levels throughout an organization to commit unethical acts that they might not otherwise engage in. Second, the penalties in terms of damage to reputations, human capital erosion, and financial loss—in the short run and long run—are typically much higher than any gains that could be obtained through the unethical behaviour.

Policies and Procedures

Many situations that a firm faces have regular, identifiable patterns. Typically, leaders tend to handle such routine by establishing a policy or procedure that can be applied rather uniformly to each occurrence. As we noted in Chapter 10, clear guidelines can be useful in specifying the proper relationships with a firm's customers and suppliers. We gave the example of Levi Strauss's global sourcing guidelines and Chemical Bank's policy of forbidding any review that would determine whether or not suppliers are Chemical customers when the bank awards contracts.

Clearly, it is important to carefully develop policies and procedures to guide behaviour so that all employees will be encouraged to behave in an ethical manner. However, it is not enough merely to have policies and procedures "on the books." Rather, they must be reinforced with effective communication and monitoring as well as sound corporate governance practices. In the U.S., the Sarbanes-Oxley Act provides considerable legal protection to employees of publicly-traded companies who report unethical or illegal practices. Canada still relies on related labour legislation but does not have explicit whistle-blower protection provisions. Some firms, though, such as Shell Canada, have gone beyond de facto legal and regulatory requirements and have created strong ethics codes or structures, such as an ombudsman office, to provide greater confidentiality in the case of complaints.[48]

Summary

Strategic leadership is vital in ensuring that strategies are formulated and implemented in an effective manner. Leaders must play a central role in performing three critical and interdependent activities: setting the direction, designing the organization, and nurturing a culture committed to excellence and ethical behaviour. In this chapter, we used the imagery of a "three-legged stool" to explain these activities. If leaders ignore or are ineffective in performing any one of the three, the organization will not be very successful. Leaders must also use power effectively to overcome barriers to change.

For leaders to effectively fulfill their activities, emotional intelligence (EI) is very important. Five elements that contribute to EI are self-awareness, self-regulation, motivation, empathy, and social skill. The first three elements pertain to self-management skills, whereas the last two are associated with a person's ability to manage relationships with others.

Leaders must also play a central role in creating a learning organization. Gone are the days when the top-level managers "think" and everyone else in the organization "does." With the rapidly changing, unpredictable, and complex competitive environments that characterize most industries, leaders must engage everyone in the ideas and energies of others throughout the organization. Great ideas can come from anywhere in the organization—from the executive suite to the factory floor. The five elements that we discussed as central to a learning organization are inspiring and motivating people through a mission or purpose, empowering people at all levels throughout the organization, accumulating and sharing internal knowledge, gathering external information, and challenging the status quo to stimulate creativity.

In the final section of the chapter, we addressed a leader's central role in instilling ethical behaviour in the organization. We discussed the enormous costs that firms face when ethical crises arise, including financial and reputational loss as well as the erosion of human capital and relationships with suppliers, customers, society at large, and governmental agencies. And, as one would expect, the benefits of having a strong ethical organization are also numerous. We contrasted compliance-based and integrity-based approaches to organizational ethics. Compliance-based approaches are largely externally motivated; that is, they are motivated by the fear of punishment for doing something that is unlawful. Integrity-based approaches, on the other hand, are driven by a personal and organizational commitment to ethical behaviour. We also addressed the four key elements of an ethical organization: role models, corporate credos and codes of conduct, reward and evaluation systems, and policies and procedures.

Summary Review Questions

1. Three key activities—setting a direction, designing the organization, and nurturing a culture and ethics—are all part of what effective leaders do on a regular basis. Explain how these three activities are interrelated.

2. Define emotional intelligence (EI). What are the key elements of EI? Why is EI so important to successful strategic leadership?

3. The knowledge a firm possesses can be a source of competitive advantage. Describe ways that a firm can continuously learn to maintain its competitive position.

4. How can the five central elements of "learning organizations" be incorporated into global companies?

5. What are the benefits to firms and their shareholders of conducting business in an ethical manner?

6. Firms that fail to behave in an ethical manner can incur high costs. What are these costs, and what is their source?

7. What are the most important differences between an "integrity organization" and a "compliance organization" in terms of a firm's approach to organizational ethics?

8. What are some of the important mechanisms for promoting ethics in a firm?

Experiential Exercise

Select two well-known business leaders—one you admire and one you do not. Evaluate each of them on the five characteristics of emotional intelligence.

Emotional Intelligence Characteristics	Admired Leader:	Leader Not Admired:
Self-awareness		
Self-regulation		
Motivation		
Empathy		
Social skill		

Application Questions Exercises

1. Identify two CEOs whose leadership you admire. What is it about their skills, attributes, and effective use of power that causes you to admire them?
2. Founders have an important role in developing their organization's culture and values. At times their influence persists for many years. Identify and describe two organizations in which the cultures and values established by the founder(s) continue to flourish. You may find research on the Internet helpful in answering these questions.
3. Some leaders place a great emphasis on developing superior human capital. In what ways does this help a firm to develop and sustain competitive advantages?
4. In this chapter, we discussed the five elements of a "learning organization." Select a firm with which you are familiar, and discuss whether or not it exemplifies some (or all) of these elements.

Ethics Questions

1. Sometimes organizations must go outside the firm to hire talent, thus bypassing employees already working for the firm. Are there conditions under which this might raise ethical considerations?
2. Ethical crises can occur in virtually any organization. Describe some of the systems, procedures, and processes that can help to prevent such crises.
3. The recent failures of large financial institutions have brought to light the exorbitant compensation packages of executives who have been walking away with millions of dollars in their pockets while the companies they led are suffering losses of billions of dollars. These executives have had legal contracts that entitle them to those payouts. Should companies or governments try to void those contracts? What may be the implications of those efforts?

Chapter 12 *Innovation and Growth:*
New Ventures and Organizational Renewal

Economic development makes a critical contribution to the prosperity of a society, and the engines of growth foster the betterment of both individuals and the collective. Growth results from the activities of established corporations and the creation of new firms. Companies often grow by commercializing new technologies, although novelty is frequently relative and new products in one market can be imitations of what has succeeded in another market. Nevertheless, new activities typically involve assuming additional risk as both established and new firms can only grow by embracing what is new and uncertain. Entrepreneurship, in the sense of identifying and pursuing a business opportunity to achieve a personal ambition, is at the heart of strategy and strategic management. Every organization started out as the idea or dream of a single individual or a small group of people pursuing an opportunity, capitalizing on some invention, and achieving some goal. Moreover, the entrepreneurial drive does not and should not cease after the first phase of an organization's existence. Thus, to the extent that strategy management is about the whole organization and organizational renewal, entrepreneurship is an integral part of strategic management. The success of an entrepreneurial venture—whether it is undertaken by a major corporation or a small start-up—depends on many factors. The right combination of resources, know-how, and strategic action can lead to above-average profitability and new advantages. However, many things can go wrong. To see how a firm's entrepreneurial efforts, even in the face of technological progress, can turn into failure, consider Digital Renaissance Inc.[1]

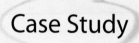

Case Study

From the very beginning in 1991, Digital Renaissance Inc. and its founder, Keith Kocho, attracted a lot of attention, along with numerous awards and recognitions. Among its many accomplishments, Digital Renaissance pioneered interactive television and produced some hip shows such as *Drop the Beat* and *Our Hero* for CBC, *Life 360* for PBS, and *Dish It Out* for Atlantis Communications—interactive programs that, among other things, invited viewers to purchase items they saw on TV by clicking their remotes or connecting through their PCs.

Some called the Oshawa-raised, Toronto-educated Kocho a visionary. Certainly, he had the ability to grasp and exploit people's fascination with technology and get them to believe that everything was possible. Before most people knew about email or the Web, he could excite them with descriptions of what the computer and the television could do together. The video capabilities of computers were still in their infancy, but Kocho could envision their vast potential. At one point, Kocho was seen as one of Canada's leaders of the New Economy; the financial markets took his predictions, no matter how outlandish, very seriously. His company became one of Canada's best-known multimedia design outfits and a global Internet powerhouse. His clients included blue-chip companies such as Bell, Nortel, Bank of Montreal, Rogers Communications, and Globemedia.

By the spring of 2000, following a deal with Los Angeles-based Creative Artists Agency, people were speculating that Kocho could soon become the Walt Disney of multimedia. Digital Renaissance had opened offices in Los Angeles and New York. In Toronto, the company had expanded into much larger space, taking over an old, 5,500 square metre factory. The space quickly became the talk of the town. It was converted into a digital paradise with no walls, fully-stocked bars, a pool table, and nap rooms for the more than 200 staffers who did not work normal hours but routinely gave up their weekends, had no business titles, and operated without management structures. They were all driven by a sense of mission and personal responsibility to push the limits of every new direction of the digital world, including interactive television, ecommerce, and technology convergence.

As for valuing the company, consider that in 1996 a 20 percent stake in Digital Renaissance was sold for $1 million. A year later, another 20 percent fetched $2.5 million. In 1999, warrants representing roughly a 20 percent stake were sold for $26.5 million, giving the company a valuation of over $120 million. Even though its sales had not yet exceeded

$8 million, it had accumulated losses of over $12 million, and most of the work was on specialized Web design rather than the easily scalable software programming that had commanded the stratospheric valuations on the Nasdaq. Soon after, Digital Renaissance changed its name to ExtendMedia and selected, among a number of firms courting it, its own investment bankers who would lead its IPO, which was expected to bring in twice as much as the company had raised to that point.

Yet, in the fall of 2000, everything unravelled. One hundred and eighty people had to be laid off, the Los Angeles and New York offices were closed, much of the factory space was put up for lease, and there were no investment dollars to keep the dream alight. Even more disheartening, the only people who would get severance packages were the corporate types, those brought in most recently to prepare the company for the IPO and who had employment contracts with rather generous termination clauses. The veterans and the creative people who fuelled the company had to leave unceremoniously and with little, if any, compensation. There was simply not much left to give them, even though Kocho would have liked nothing more than to be able to demonstrate that, as these people had put the company's interests ahead of their own, the company was not going to let them down.

What Went Wrong at Digital Renaissance? Kocho successfully foresaw the convergence of technologies and the capabilities afforded by the digitization of video images. Yet, the business model that he put in place to capitalize on those insights relied on high-priced talent, a market's appetite for products and services at prices that were not reasonably sustainable, and few entry barriers, as more and more computer "nerds" and designers were graduating from colleges and dreaming of their own high-tech success stories.

The company, designed on some New Age notions of corporate democracy (if not anarchy), had no clear leadership and, in spite of Kocho's visionary role, had no sense of who was in charge. Kocho wanted it this way, believing in an egalitarian ethic and no business titles. One thing was clear: the personal and professional lives of the 200 employees were expected to be intimately intertwined.

Upon reflecting on the highs and the lows, Kocho remarked, "I was totally focused, totally married to the business. I realize now that you have to keep it bracketed." There was no balance—only a relentless drive to define and explore the next new thing in the digital world in something that someone once referred to as corporate "attention deficit disorder." There were continuous shifts in emphasis—efforts at following the latest buzzword, the next big thing, and the next bold new idea. During the late 1990s, it seems that everybody had been inflicted by the same bug and was convinced that this was a new era in which the old rules of economics and business no longer applied.

Setting a vision and charting the firm's direction, organizational renewal, and managing change as we suggested in Chapter 11, are among the most important functions performed by strategic leaders. The transformative activity of bringing organizations "from what they are to what the leader would have them become" requires fresh ideas and a vision of the future. Most organizations want to grow. To do so, they must expand their product offering, reach into new markets, and obtain new customers. Sometimes, profitability can be increased by streamlining processes and operating more efficiently. These activities inevitably involve change, and a firm's leaders must be effective change agents.

Two options are available to individuals and organizations that conceive achievement of their mission through strategies of change and growth: innovation and entrepreneurship. These two activities go hand-in-hand because they have similar aims. Innovations help an organization stay fresh and reinvent itself as conditions in the business environment change. Innovative breakthroughs as well as new product concepts, evolving technologies, and shifting demand create opportunities for corporate venturing, corporate entrepreneurship, or intrapreneurship as some prefer to call it, as well as for the formation of new ventures and the establishment of new enterprises. They describe an organization's efforts to pursue new venture opportunities from within its boundaries and the efforts of individuals to pursue new venture opportunities outside the boundaries of established organizations. In this chapter, we explore how innovation can stimulate strategic renewal, how organizations foster corporate entrepreneurship, as well as how individuals and teams can recognize opportunities and create new ventures.

MANAGING INNOVATION

One of the most important sources of growth opportunities is innovation. Innovation involves using new knowledge to transform organizational processes or create commercially viable products and services. The sources of new knowledge may include the latest technology, the results of experiments, creative insights, or competitive information. However it comes about, innovation occurs when new combinations of ideas and information bring about positive change.

The emphasis on newness is a key point. The root of the word *innovation* is the Latin *novus*, which means new. Innovation involves introducing or changing to something new.[2] Among the most important sources of new ideas is new technology. Technology creates new possibilities. Technology provides the raw ingredient that firms use to make innovative new products and services. But technology is not the only source of innovations. There can be innovations in human resources, firm infrastructure, marketing, services, or in many other value-adding areas that have little to do with anything "high tech." Strategy Spotlight 12.1 highlights some of the many technological and marketing innovations that revolutionized radio technology and became the foundations of the Standard Radio Corporation, the forefather of today's Rogers Communications Inc., a multi-billion dollar cable, wireless, and media corporation, whose operations touch the everyday lives of most Canadians. As the Rogers example suggests, innovation can take many forms.

TYPES OF INNOVATION

Although innovations are not always high-tech, changes in technology can be an important source of change and growth. When an innovation is based on a sweeping new technology, it often has a more far-reaching impact. However, sometimes even a small innovation can add value and create competitive advantages. Innovation can and should be pursued throughout an organization—in every department and in all aspects of the value chain.

One way to view the impact of an innovation is in terms of its degree of innovativeness, which falls somewhere on a continuum that extends from incremental to radical.[3]

♦ *Radical innovations* produce fundamental changes by evoking major departures from existing practices. These breakthrough innovations usually occur because of technological change. They tend to be highly disruptive and can transform a company or even revolutionize a whole industry. They may lead to products or processes that can be patented, giving a firm a strong competitive advantage. Examples include electricity, telephones, transistors, desktop computers, fibre optics, artificial intelligence, and genetically engineered drugs.

Radio Wizard: Edward Samuel Rogers and the Revolution of Communications

Wireless radio communication was born at the beginning of the twentieth century. Although awkward and messy at first, its potential for relaying information and providing entertainment captured the imagination of young Edward Samuel Rogers. He had first become interested in wireless telegraphy at the age of 11 when he built a crystal set, a complex apparatus of coils and condensers that allowed him to monitor reports of such events as the sinking of RMS Titanic and the declaration of World War I.

By the age of 24, he had purchased the assets of a radio manufacturing company. All radios at the time ran on batteries, which were cumbersome, expensive, and continually leaked corrosive fluids. Rogers set about to create a batteryless radio tube and soon, defying the industry wisdom that the task was impossible, he developed a radio tube that could be operated, instead of from batteries, from an alternating current—the 110-volt current that was already providing lighting to most households. The tubes became the heart of the Rogers Batteryless Radio Receiver—the first all-electric radio in the world, launched at the 1925 Canadian National Exhibition in Toronto. Radio had entered a new age.

Rogers combined his interest in radio with an innate marketing ability. Rogers Radios soon became the leading manufacturer of radios in Canada and the United States. Rogers also started a companion radio station, CFRB (Canada's First Rogers Batteryless) in Toronto, the first all-electric radio station in the world, powered by Rogers AC tubes. The station's superb broadcasting capabilities were highlighted by extensive broadcasts of both live and recorded music, which were soon augmented by another first—regular news programming from the editorial room of *The Globe* newspaper. The station's activities stimulated more sales of radio receivers, which, in turn, increased advertising revenues.

Rogers was one of very few companies that continued to grow and provide new employment opportunities during the Great Depression. Its drive for innovation and growth continued unrelentingly. Among its many innovations, Rogers introduced the first dashboard-mounted radio receivers and secured exclusive agreements from both Ford Motor Company of Canada and General Motors of Canada. It also introduced many improvements to the original tube, automatic tuning and automatic voltage control of the radios, special microphones for commentators and broadcast studios, North America's tallest broadcast antennas, numerous programming innovations, and, finally, one of the first four licences to experiment with television.

Source: I. A. Anthony, *Radio Wizard, Edward Samuel Rogers and the Revolution of Communications* (Toronto: Gage Publishing, 2000).

♦ *Incremental innovations* enhance existing practices or make small improvements in products and processes. They may represent evolutionary applications within existing paradigms of earlier, more radical innovations. Because they often sustain a company by extending or expanding its product lines or manufacturing skills, incremental innovations can be a source of competitive advantage. They increase revenues by creating a new marketplace offering or reduce costs by providing new capabilities that lower expenses or speed up productivity. Examples include frozen food, sports drinks, steel-belted radial tires, electronic bookkeeping, shatterproof glass, and digital telephones.

Some innovations are highly radical; others are only slightly incremental. But most innovations fall somewhere between these two extremes. Exhibit 12.1 shows where several innovations fall along the radical-incremental continuum.

Christensen makes a further distinction by characterizing *disruptive technologies* as those innovations that bring to the market a very different value proposition than what the established firms had been making available previously.[4] While the products of disruptive technologies may underperform established products in mainstream markets, they offer features that are cheaper, simpler, smaller, and frequently more convenient to use, and they appeal, at least initially, to a few fringe and generally new customers. Examples of

Exhibit 12.1
Continuum of
Radical and
Incremental
Innovations

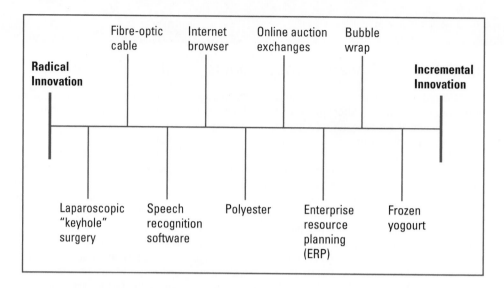

disruptive technologies are the personal desktop computer, mini-mill steelmaking, discount retailing, transistors, vacuum tubes, small off-road motorcycles, and certain Internet applications. While radical and incremental innovations typically enhance production efficiencies, improve product performance, and reinforce the dominance of leading firms by providing more of the features valued by mainstream customers in major markets, Christensen argues that, without exception, all disruptive technologies have led to the failure of leading firms.

Another distinction often used when discussing innovation is product innovation versus process innovation.[5] *Product innovation* refers to efforts to create product designs and applications of technology to develop new products for end users. Recall from Chapter 5 how generic strategies are typically different, depending on the stage of the industry life cycle. Product innovations tend to be more radical and are more common during the earlier stages of an industry's life cycle. As an industry matures, there are fewer opportunities for newness, so the innovations tend to be more incremental. Product innovations are also commonly associated with a differentiation strategy. Firms that differentiate by providing customers with new products or services that offer unique features or quality enhancements often engage in product innovation.

Process innovation, by contrast, is typically associated with improving the efficiency of an organizational process, especially manufacturing systems and operations. By drawing on new technologies and an organization's accumulated experience, firms can often improve materials utilization, shorten cycle time, and increase quality. Process innovations are more likely to occur in the later stages of an industry's life cycle as companies seek ways to remain viable in markets where demand has flattened out and competition is more intense. As a result, process innovations are often associated with overall cost leader strategies since the aim of many process improvements is to lower the costs of operations.

Challenges of Innovation

As you can see from the discussion of different types of innovation, the innovation process itself has numerous strategic implications. Innovation is a force in the external environment (technology, competition) and also a factor affecting a firm's internal choices (generic strategy, value-adding activities). Furthermore, innovation can be quite difficult for some firms to manage, especially those that have become comfortable with the status quo. Yet, as management guru Peter Drucker warned, "An established company which, in an age demanding innovation, is not capable of innovation is doomed to decline and extinction."[6] To put it simply, in today's competitive environment, most firms have only one choice: Innovate or die.

As with change, however, firms are often resistant to innovation. Only those companies that actively pursue innovation, even though it is often difficult and uncertain, will get a payoff from their innovation efforts.

What is it that makes innovation so difficult? Clearly the uncertainty about outcomes is one factor. Companies are often reluctant to invest time and resources into activities with an unknown future. Another factor is that the innovation process involves so many choices.[7] Most companies have an abundance of innovative ideas. They must decide which of these are most likely to bear fruit—the "Seeds"—and which should be cast aside—the "Weeds." This is an ongoing dilemma that is often complicated by the fact that some innovation projects require a considerable level of investment before a firm can fully evaluate whether they are worth pursuing. Firms must also manage the timing and scale of new innovation projects. An incremental launch is less risky because it requires fewer resources and serves as a market test. But a launch that is too tentative can undermine the project's credibility. It also opens the door for a competitive response. A large-scale launch requires more resources, but it can effectively pre-empt a competitive response.

Finally, innovation projects often require new sets of skills. Firms can seek help from partners that bring resources and experience and enable the sharing of costs of development. Innovation partners outside the firm can be from among its suppliers, customers, and competitors as well as non-business organizations such as research universities and the government. Bombardier is asking its potential suppliers to actively contribute in developing the next generation C-Series long-range jet. Chip-maker Intel has benefited from underwriting substantial amounts of university research. Rather than hand universities a blank cheque, Intel bargains for rights to patents that emerge from Intel-sponsored research. The university retains ownership of the patent, but Intel gets royalty-free use of it.[8] However, some caution is in order as such arrangements can create dependencies and inhibit internal skills development. Further, partners frequently end up disagreeing about the relative value of their respective contributions or how the benefits of the project are to be allocated.

Firms can address the challenges pertaining to innovation efforts by, among other things, defining the "strategic envelope"—that is, the scope of a firm's innovation efforts.[9] Firms can ensure that their innovation efforts are not wasted on projects that are highly uncertain or outside the firm's domain of interest. Strategic enveloping defines the range of acceptable projects. As Alistair Corbett, an innovation expert who directs the Toronto office of the global consulting firm Bain & Company, said, "One man's radical innovation is another man's incremental innovation."[10] Thus, a strategic envelope creates a firm-specific view of innovation that defines how a firm can create new knowledge and learn from an innovation initiative even if the project fails. Although such limitations might seem overly constraining, they also give direction to a firm's innovation efforts, which helps separate seeds from weeds and build internal capabilities.

Along with clarifying the scope of an innovation by defining a strategic envelope, firms also need to regulate the pace of innovation. An advantage of assessing the extent to which an innovation is radical or incremental is that it helps determine how long it will take for an innovation initiative to realistically come to fruition. The project timeline of an incremental innovation may be six months to two years, whereas a more radical innovation is typically long term—10 years or more.[11] Thus, radical innovations often begin with a long period of exploration in which experimentation makes strict timelines unrealistic. In contrast, firms that are innovating incrementally in order to exploit a window of opportunity may use a milestone approach that is more stringently driven by goals and deadlines.

NEW VENTURES BY LARGE AND SMALL BUSINESSES

No matter what the source and type of innovation is, growth and rewards come from converting innovations into successful business ventures. Large corporations pursue new business ventures through the creation of new divisions, introductions of new product lines and other activities associated with corporate entrepreneurship. Yet, the majority of new business creation is the result of entrepreneurial efforts by start-up firms and small businesses. Managing entrepreneurial firms can benefit greatly from applying the principles of strategic management as developed throughout the textbook. While entrepreneurial ventures can vary greatly, depending on such factors as the size, age, or growth goals of the firm, entrepreneurial activities will be more successful if strategic thinking guides decision making. It is worth noting that indeed, new ventures are risky undertakings. Even though thousands of small businesses are formed each year, thousands also close. In a recent year, a little over 60,000 businesses were formed in Canada. This translates into an annual business birth rate of 14 to 16 percent. But in the same year, 12 to 14 percent of existing businesses were terminated.[12]

We consider first the main categories of entrepreneurial ventures and then discuss what constitutes corporate entrepreneurship before proceeding to examine the steps and challenges to establishing a new venture.

Categories of Entrepreneurial Ventures

There are many ways to categorize entrepreneurial ventures. The term *entrepreneurship* itself has come to represent a wide array of meanings.[13] The following are some examples:

- Working for oneself rather than for someone else for a salary.
- Entering into a new or established market with new or existing products or services.
- Operating a firm in which there is no separation between ownership and management.
- Discovering, evaluating, and exploiting opportunities.
- Creating new organizations.

All of these definitions have been used to characterize entrepreneurial firms and small businesses.

For purposes of strategic analysis, it is useful to note three differences among entrepreneurial firms because these distinctions have strategic implications. The first of these is *size*. Small businesses, of course, are small. However, some ventures are small because they are new. This leads to the second factor, *age*. Start-ups and new ventures are often considered to be entrepreneurial simply because they are young; that is, size is often correlated with age. New ventures usually begin small and grow over time as their business activity increases. Thus, as the age of a firm increases, so does its size. There is a third factor, however, that may limit an entrepreneurial firm's size: its *growth goals*. Firms that do not aspire to grow usually don't. Therefore, a young firm's growth goals often determine whether it will remain small as it ages or grow large.

In fact, growth goals are one of the key factors used to distinguish between entrepreneurial firms and small businesses. Small businesses are generally thought to have low or modest growth goals. Because small business owners prefer to maintain control of their business, they are often unwilling to take steps that are considered necessary to grow, even though they may have growth potential. These steps include, most notably, borrowing heavily or going public in order to obtain the funding needed to finance growth. Not surprisingly, most remain small businesses.

By contrast, entrepreneurial firms generally favour growth. Because growth is a priority, founders with high-growth goals will often sell a share of the business (thus giving up some control) in order to finance growth. As a result, successful businesses founded by high-growth entrepreneurs develop a life of their own. For example, Hip Interactive Corp., a Mississauga, Ontario-based distributor of video games and other video entertainment products, started in 1999 as a distributor of DVDs, with sales of some $3 million. It soon was designing new video games and generating total sales of over $425 million.[14] Another Mississauga-based firm, Biovail Corp., was founded in the early 1990s as a contract research business for the development of drugs on the basis of novel delivery technologies. A little over 10 years later, it became a global pharmaceutical corporation with sales approaching one billion dollars for its own patented drugs as well as generic and new versions of other cardiovascular and nervous system drugs.[15]

Small businesses, on the other hand, are often associated so closely with their founders that when the founder is gone, the business ceases to operate. Of course, there may be intervening factors that affect growth outcomes unexpectedly—some entrepreneurs may want to grow large businesses but cannot; others may become bigger than they ever expected because market forces propel them onto a growth curve they did not anticipate. In general, though, the difference between entrepreneurial firms and small businesses is related to their path of growth. Nevertheless, even those distinctions sometimes get blurred. Consider the example of M.A.C, the cult cosmetics firm that was established in Toronto in 1985 and sought neither publicity nor glory. Its founders aspired only to create a line of makeup for artists and professionals, based on quality, and to sell the products directly out of an off-the-beaten-path store. They did no advertising, but word of mouth made them known among actors and actresses, fashion models, photographers, journalists, and professional makeup artists. Soon, their discerning clients had them shipping products to all the fashion capitals of the world. M.A.C still resisted pressures for expansion until 1998, when the Estée Lauder group of companies acquired the firm. Shortly thereafter, M.A.C could be found in upscale department stores and in its own free-standing boutiques in forty-five countries.[16]

Although technology is often a hot growth area, the majority of entrepreneurial firms are not high-tech leaders. Approximately 30 percent are in retail and wholesale trades (primarily low tech), and another 30 percent are in services (including both high and low tech).[17] Family businesses, home-based businesses, and franchises can also be the vehicles of entrepreneurial ventures. *Family businesses* can be broadly defined as privately held firms in which family members have some degree of effective control over the strategic direction of the firm, and they intend for the business to remain within the family. According to the Family Firm Institute, family-owned businesses comprise some 80 to 90 percent of all business enterprises in North America, 30 to 35 percent of the Fortune 500 companies, and the majority of enterprises internationally. Along with the thousands of "mom and pop" stores and small businesses, Rogers Communications Inc., Irving Oil Ltd., and McCain Foods are effectively controlled by a single family and belong to the ranks of family businesses.

A special category of family businesses constitutes *the home-based businesses*, also commonly referred to as SOHO (Small Office/Home Office), which consist of companies with 20 or fewer employees and include the self-employed, free agents, free-lancers, telecommuters, or other independent professionals working from a home-based setting. According to some estimates, half of all small businesses are home-based.

 Finally, individual entrepreneurs who want to mitigate the risk of starting a new venture from scratch frequently resort to *franchises*. A franchise exists when a firm that already has a successful product or service (the franchiser) contracts with another firm or an individual entrepreneur to be its dealer by using the franchiser's name, trademark, and business system in exchange of a fee, royalties, and commissions. There are several types of franchises, but the most common is the business format franchise, in which the fran-chiser provides a complete plan for managing the business. Americans dominate the world of franchising with some 320,000 businesses employing more than 8 million people in 75 different industries. McDonald's is the world's largest franchiser with over 30,000 restau-rants; some notable Canadian examples include Tim Hortons, with 2,400 franchise opera-tions, and Canadian Tire, with 450 dealers.

Corporate Entrepreneurship

Corporate entrepreneurship (CE) has two primary aims: the pursuit of new venture oppor-tunities and strategic renewal.[18] The innovation process keeps firms alert by exposing them to new technologies, making them aware of marketplace trends, and helping them evaluate new possibilities. Corporate entrepreneurship uses the fruits of the innovation process to help firms build new sources of competitive advantage and renew their value proposi-tions. Just as the innovation process helps firms to make positive improvements, corporate entrepreneurship helps firms identify opportunities and launch new ventures. In Chapter 6, we addressed corporate growth through mergers and acquisitions as well as through joint ventures and strategic alliances. Internal venture development represents the third avenue of growth. In a typical corporation, factors that determine whether and how entrepreneurial projects will be pursued include the following:

- corporate culture
- leadership
- structural features that guide and constrain action
- organizational systems that foster learning and manage rewards
- the use of teams in strategic decision making
- whether the company is product or service oriented

In other words, all of the factors that influence the strategy implementation process will also determine whether and how a corporation engages in internal venturing. Because these factors are different in every organization, some companies may be more involved than others in identifying and developing new venture opportunities. Moreover, these fac-tors also influence the nature of the CE process; in a *focused* corporate venturing approach, CE activities are isolated from a firm's existing operations and carried out by independent work units. In a *dispersed*, approach, all parts of the organization and every organization member are engaged in intrapreneurial activities.[19]

Corporate ventures may be developed internally, or via acquisition of existing start-ups. In other cases, firms may resort to external venture funding, which allows them to build a connection with a start-up by providing venture capital but without stifling its entrepreneurial drive by bringing the venture in-house. Many global corporations, such as Exxon Mobil, Intel, Siemens, and Deutsche Telekom, have invested in externally gener-ated business ideas in order to strengthen their innovation profile, cement business ties

Corporate Venture Capital and Ballard Power Systems Inc.

Ford Motor Co. and Daimler AG (formerly Daimler-Chrysler) hold large stakes in Ballard Power Systems Inc., the Burnaby, British Columbia-based company that is developing a commercially viable hydrogen fuel cell for automobiles. Although analysts do not expect fuel cell powered vehicles to become serious competitors to conventional cars for at least another 10 years, neither company can afford to not have its finger on the technology and to not work in parallel to develop hybrid cars.

Ballard was founded in 1979 to develop high-energy lithium batteries, but by 1983 it had directed its research efforts toward proton exchange membrane fuel cells, which promised to replace internal combustion engines with clean power generation and no emissions, without sacrificing performance. Although the technological challenges are still numerous, the company has already solved many problems and has achieved many milestones along the way

to developing a commercially viable hydrogen-fuel-cell-powered automobile.

Its corporate partners have also made major strides in their businesses. Daimler AG has introduced a fleet of fuel-cell buses and minivans; Ford recently unveiled a Ballard-powered Ford Focus; and Daimler AG is the largest contributor to a U.S. government-sponsored program that is putting a fleet of hydrogen-fuel vehicles into the hands of consumers, who use the cars in their daily lives and provide invaluable feedback on the vehicles' long-term performance. Collectively, they estimate that during 2004, buses, vans, and passenger vehicles powered by Ballard fuel cells were driven for a total of over 925,000 kilometres. A test engine was operated continuously for 2,200 hours until a 5 percent reduction in performance was observed. At an average speed of 50 kilometres per hour, this would translate to over 100,000 driving kilometres.

Sources: "Ballard Fuel Cells Set for U.S. Program," *The Globe and Mail*, March 31, 2005, p. B17; www.Ballard.com; and Ballard Power Systems Inc. annual reports.

with promising start-ups, and engage in market development.[20] Strategy Spotlight 12.2 describes the main corporate connections that have been at the root of the success of Ballard Power Systems Inc., a Burnaby, British Columbia, developer and manufacturer of fuel-cell products for power generation, with applications in various sectors such as the automotive industry. In contrast, Strategy Spotlight 12.3 describes Virgin's culture and a few of its start-up successes.

LAUNCHING A NEW VENTURE

No matter how a new idea comes to light, a new venture concept must pass through some critical tests in order to get off the ground. Entrepreneurs wishing to launch a new venture must first identify a promising business opportunity. What constitutes a good opportunity? How does one know that one opportunity is better than another? A promising opportunity must be justified in terms of its attractiveness in the marketplace. But this is not all. The readiness and skills of the entrepreneurial founder and his or her team must be evaluated. Do they have the necessary knowledge, skills, experience, and drive to make the venture successful? Moreover, the availability and access to resources needed for the launch of the venture must be considered. Start-up costs, operational expenses, and later-stage financing are among the requirements for a successful launch. Exhibit 12.2 identifies the three factors that are needed to successfully proceed. Both established firms and new ventures must do a good job of *opportunity* recognition in order to be successful. For the entrepreneurial start-up, though, the issue of availability of *resources* and a qualified and motivated *entrepreneurial team* are especially critical. Established firms are more likely to have access to resources and may already have key personnel on board. For them, the need for corporate support and the adoption of the idea by someone or a team who will champion the idea and

Growing New Ventures at Virgin Group

While most large companies have to work hard to stoke the fires of entrepreneurship, that fire burns with ferocious intensity at the Virgin Group. As a U.S.$4.25 billion company that has created nearly 200 businesses, Virgin stands as clear evidence that ideas, capital, and talent can flow as freely in big, far-flung organizations as they can among the start-ups of Silicon Valley.

The mix of businesses that Virgin has spawned is indicative of the fun-loving, eclectic culture that its chairman, Richard Branson, has developed. Branson and his deputies have worked hard to create a culture where employees speak up and share their ideas. There are no gleaming corporate headquarters or executive privileges, just a large house in London where meetings are held in a small room. "Rules and regulations are not our forte," Branson said. "Analyzing things to death is not our kind of thing."

There aren't even any job descriptions at Virgin because they are thought to place too many limits on what people can do. Instead, senior executives work shoulder to shoulder with first-line employees. Branson believes that

employees should be given top priority, and he has created a friendly, non-hierarchical, family-like environment in which people have fun and enjoy themselves. His advice to his employees reflects his personal philosophy: "Do things that you like. If your work and your hobby are the same, you will work long hours because you are motivated."

The result is that Virgin's businesses include entertainment megastores, cinemas, a fun-to-fly airline, an all-in-one consumer banking system, a hip radio station, and a passenger train service. Smaller ventures have also been launched by persistent employees with good ideas. A woman who believed the company's airline should offer passengers on-board massages camped on Branson's doorstep until she was allowed to give him a neck and shoulder rub. Now an inflight massage is a valued perk in Virgin Atlantic's Upper Class. On another occasion, a soon-to-be-married flight attendant came up with the idea of offering an integrated bridal-planning service—everything from wedding apparel and catering to limousines and honeymoon reservations. She became the first CEO of Virgin Bride.

Sources: G. Hamel, "Bringing Silicon Valley Inside," *Harvard Business Review* 77, no. 5 (1999), pp. 71–84; and M. F. R. Kets de Vries, "The Transformational Abilities of Virgin's Richard Branson and ABB's Percy Barnevik," *Organizational Dynamics* 26, no. 3 (1998), pp. 7–21.

Exhibit 12.2
Opportunity Analysis Framework

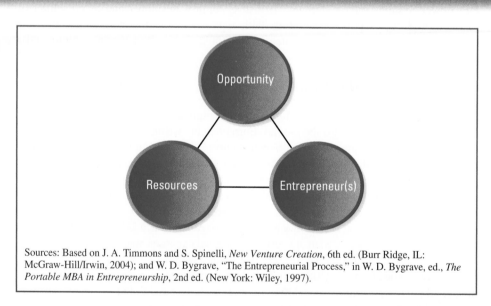

Sources: Based on J. A. Timmons and S. Spinelli, *New Venture Creation*, 6th ed. (Burr Ridge, IL: McGraw-Hill/Irwin, 2004); and W. D. Bygrave, "The Entrepreneurial Process," in W. D. Bygrave, ed., *The Portable MBA in Entrepreneurship*, 2nd ed. (New York: Wiley, 1997).

push it over the various corporate hurdles is equally critical for the idea to take form and become a business. For new business founders, starting a new venture presents formidable challenges in securing needed resources and developing entrepreneurial talent. For corporate entrepreneurs, legitimacy and approval are equally formidable hurdles.[21] We consider each of the three factors in turn.

Opportunity Recognition: Identifying and Developing Market Opportunities

The starting point for any new venture is the presence of an entrepreneurial opportunity. Where do opportunities come from? For new business start-ups, opportunities come from many sources: current or past work experiences, hobbies that grow into businesses or lead to inventions, suggestions by friends or family, or a chance event that makes an entrepreneur aware of an unmet need. For established firms, new business opportunities come from the needs of existing customers, suggestions by suppliers, or technological developments that lead to new advances.[22] For all types of firms, there is a major, overarching factor that is behind all viable opportunities that emerge in the business landscape: *change*. Change creates opportunities. Consider the following example of entrepreneurial activity that is related to some of the changes and trends we have come across in earlier chapters of this book.

In Chapter 7, we discussed the rapid pace of globalization. In Chapter 8, we saw how the Internet is changing the way new products enter the market. One company, Cove Bikes of Deep Cove, British Columbia, is capitalizing on both of these trends.[23] Free-riding is a particular kind of mountain biking enjoyed on the extreme terrain of dense woods and steep pitches such as those of the coast just north of Vancouver. The sport has quickly gained global appeal, and the North Shore has become synonymous with the genre. Recently, the highly respected UK magazine *Mountain Biking* even designed a competition for its readers to build a course that would resemble the landscape around North Shore. Cove Bikes is right there, at the heart of North Shore; enthusiasts call it the granddaddy of bike shops. It produces special bicycle frames that can take the beating that comes from the steep rocky descents and the thick overgrown roots. They sell for a steep $1,500 to $6,000 dollars each. In the spirit of true mountain-biking attitude, Cove Bikes only produces a limited number of frames, and its store is only open a few hours each day. But once its intriguing Web site went online, inquiries rolled in, and sales from overseas took off. Half of the company's annual sales of $2 million now come from outside North America.

The increasing concern of people and businesses about both the reality and the serious risks associated with global warming and our detrimental impact on the environment have spurred outfits such as Zerofootprint, a renewable-energy venture based in Toronto that wants to put geothermal heating and cooling systems in homes, shopping malls, and complexes, with the capital investment financed by the energy savings.[24] Clean Energy Developments is a designer and installer of solar-geothermal heating and cooling systems for new homes. Enwave Energy has developed a unique deep-lake cooling system that serves the air-conditioning needs of such building complexes as the Toronto City Hall and provides alternative heating and energy management to over one hundred buildings in downtown Toronto. All these companies are responding to the increasing pressure from individuals and corporate customers looking for renewable-energy options for their real estate facilities.

Each of these examples demonstrates how entrepreneurial firms respond to changes brought about by new technology, sociocultural trends, and shifts in consumer demand. Even death and tragedy stimulate business development. The Simple Alternative was set to capitalize on the frustrations and stress typically experienced by people purchasing funeral services, by promising a simple, no-sales-pitch, low-cost alternative to the high-priced traditional funerals.[25] Chasing the same opportunity, another company is now selling factory direct caskets at its eponymous Web page.

The Opportunity Recognition Process How do changes in the external environment lead to new business creation? They spark innovative new ideas. Business people often have ideas for entrepreneurial ventures. There are those "eureka" moments when a new idea is identified. Although such insights are often very important, not all are necessarily good ideas—that is, viable business opportunities. To determine which ideas are strong enough to become new ventures, entrepreneurs must go through a process that involves two phases of activity—discovery and formation—both of which lead to viable new venture opportunities.[26]

The *discovery* phase refers to the period when one becomes aware of a new business concept. Many entrepreneurs report that their idea for a new venture occurred to them in an instant, as a sort of "Aha!" experience; that is, they had some insight or epiphany, often based on their prior knowledge, that gave them an idea for a new business. This may occur unintentionally because the discovery of new opportunities is often spontaneous and unexpected. For example, Howard Schultz, CEO of Starbucks, was in Milan, Italy, when he suddenly realized that the coffee-and-conversation café model that was common in Europe would work in the United States as well. According to Schultz, he didn't need to do research to find out if Americans would pay $3 for a cup of coffee—he just *knew*. Starbucks was only a small business at the time, but Schultz reportedly began to shake with excitement about growing it into a bigger business.[27]

The discovery of opportunity may also occur as the result of a deliberate search for new venture opportunities or creative solutions to business problems. New venture ideas often emerge only after a concerted effort to identify good opportunities or realistic solutions. It is very similar to a creative process, which may be unstructured and "chaotic" at first but eventually leads to a practical solution or business innovation. To stimulate the discovery of new opportunities, companies often encourage creativity, out-of-the-box thinking, and brainstorming.

Michael Dell realized early on that personal computers would soon become a commodity, and he set up Dell Computers to manufacture and deliver PCs at the lowest possible cost rather than incorporate the newest technologies. In the process, he took on and won out against such powerhouses as IBM, HP, and Compaq, while revolutionizing the way people buy computers and all the peripherals. Similarly, Cognos Inc., the Ottawa-based technology firm, saw the need among corporations for software that would allow them to access their data. Thus, it created the now sought-after enterprise business intelligence software that, when combined with corporate performance management software, allows firms to search and manipulate information from multiple databases and use it to plan ahead.[28]

New ventures are often launched because founding entrepreneurs find innovative ways to apply new technologies. Indeed, the majority of patents and innovations come from small firms. Why is this so? Research suggests that entrepreneurial firms are often more successful at discovering radically different technology-based venture opportunities than large firms.[29] Young firms have a knack for seeing things differently. They approach problems with a fresh perspective. They are not burdened by old ways of thinking or beliefs about how things ought to be. They are also not encumbered by existing facilities, relationships, and committed investments that still have more value under the old paradigm. Entrepreneurial firms often have the freedom to see the big picture as well as the component parts. Managers in large firms tend to be driven by the specialist perspective of the division or department in which they belong and are typically rewarded based on the performance of their unit, not the whole organization. Even when that is not the case, a large organization is generally complex, and the individual manager seldom has the capacity to comprehend the connections between all the constituent components.

Opportunity *formation*, which occurs after an opportunity has been identified, involves evaluating an opportunity to determine whether it is viable and strong enough to be developed into a full-fledged new venture. Ideas that have been developed by new-product groups or in brainstorming sessions are tested by various methods, including talking to potential target customers and discussing operational requirements with production or logistics managers. A technique known as feasibility analysis is used to evaluate these and other critical success factors. This type of analysis often leads to the decision that a new venture project should be discontinued. If the venture concept continues to seem viable, a more formal business plan may be developed.

Among the most important factors to evaluate is the market potential for the product or service. Established firms tend to operate in established markets. They have to adjust to market trends and to shifts in consumer demand, of course, but they usually have a customer base for which they are already filling a marketplace need. New ventures, in contrast, must first determine whether a market exists for the product or service they are contemplating. Thus, a critical element of opportunity recognition is assessing the extent to which the opportunity is viable *in the marketplace*. Most definitions of entrepreneurial opportunity suggest that, to be a true opportunity, it must be viable in terms of its potential to earn a profit.

Several of the techniques suggested in Chapters 2 and 3 can be used to assess the market potential of a business concept. Questions that might emerge in a test of the market for a new product or service include the following:

- Do market forces support the introduction of it? For example, is market demand growing because of shifting demographics or sociocultural trends?
- How is the need that it addresses currently being met?
- What firms would be the closest competitors?
- How are competitive products priced?
- What is its value proposition? That is, in what ways does it add value relative to products or services already being sold?
- Can its value be enhanced by combining it with other value-adding activities?

For a more complete assessment of how well a new business concept would be received, marketing techniques, such as product concept testing, focus groups, and/ or extended trial runs with end users, are often necessary. In some respects, assessing marketability is as much an art as it is a science. Nevertheless, it is essential to create a structured model of how the product or service will perform in the marketplace in order to develop a plan for launching it. In effect, the aim of the opportunity recognition process is to explore and test a new venture concept in order to determine whether it is a viable opportunity.

Characteristics of Good Opportunities The opportunity recognition process involves discovering and forming business concepts into realistic business opportunities. To be viable, an opportunity needs to have four qualities.[30]

- *Attractive* The opportunity must be attractive in the marketplace; that is, there must be market demand for the new product or service. Motorola spent $2.5 billion on Iridium, a global satellite phone system. However, customers didn't like the heavy and bulky phones that could only be used outdoors and cost $1,500 each, so the project was abandoned.[31]

- *Achievable* The opportunity must be practical and possible. Round-trip vacations to the moon might sell really well, but they remain unrealistic. (Orbiting the earth by tourists, however, may be closer than we think. A company called Space Adventures is promising to provide joyrides into space for around $90,000 a trip. It's a service the company cannot even provide yet, but it already has 144 reservations!)[32]

- ◆ **Durable** The opportunity must be attractive long enough for the development and deployment to be successful; that is, the window of opportunity must be open long enough for it to be worthwhile. Toy-maker Playing Mantis figured out that retro toys have an enduring appeal. After buying the rights to Johnny Lightning die-cast cars (a Hot Wheels knock-off from the 1960s), founder Tom Lowe generated millions in sales to baby boomers who still loved the toy cars they had as kids.[33]

- ◆ **Value creating** The opportunity must be potentially profitable; that is, the benefits must surpass the cost of development by a significant margin. Kingsley Management LLC thinks it has found a profitable niche in the crowded car wash business. Using state-of-the-art equipment that adjusts to the dimensions of each car, its "Swash" car washes are cheaper than full service but more convenient than self-wash. Kingsley is building stand-alone units in high-traffic areas, and gas stations are buying in because they need the high-margin car washes to improve profitability.[34]

Entrepreneurial Resources

One of the major challenges that entrepreneurial firms face is a lack of resources. For start-ups, the most important resource is usually money. A new firm typically has to expend large sums just to open the door for business. However, financial resources are not the only kind of resource a young firm needs. Human capital and social capital are also important during the early days of a new venture and throughout the life of a small business. Some small firms also rely on government resources to help them thrive.

Young and small firms have many of the same needs as larger firms—financial resources, skilled and experienced workers, and the ability to operate in a network of beneficial relationships. But they also have unique needs that stem from being young or small. Nearly all young firms face the liability of newness.[35] This phrase refers to the vulnerability that most new firms face because they lack experience, are unknown in their industry, and are unfamiliar to customers. Until they have proven themselves, young firms lack credibility; banks often will not lend them money, and suppliers may not extend them credit. Tim Demello, chairman and CEO of Internet start-up Streamline, summed it up this way:

> Here I am, the budding entrepreneur. I have next to nothing. No money, no credibility. I also have a big challenge: I have to get people to understand who I am, what my company does, what we have to offer. I not only have to sell my product or service, I also have to sell my company to the people I want to work for me—people who will have to give up really good careers for this unknown start-up. I also have to sell my company to people who will invest capital in it. I have to sell my company to vendors, to get them to extend me credit. The point is that in the early stages of my start-up, I have absolutely no credibility. So my challenge becomes, How do I use somebody else's credibility?[36]

 To overcome the liability of newness and build credibility, founders must, in effect, find practical ways to obtain financial as well as other resources.

New-Venture Financing Along with the importance of markets (and marketing) to new-venture creation, start-up firms must also have financing. In fact, the level of available financing is often a strong determinant of how the business is launched and of its eventual success. Cash finances are, of course, highly important. But access to capital, such as a line of credit or favourable payment terms with a supplier, can also help a start-up to succeed. The vast majority of new firms are low-budget start-ups launched with personal savings and the contributions of family and friends.[37] Although bank financing, public financing, and venture capital are important sources of small business finance, these types of financial support are typically available only after a company has started to conduct business and generate sales. Therefore, the founders usually carry the initial burden of financing most new firms.

Bootstrapping may shift a start-up's priorities. To successfully bootstrap, a new firm may have to get cash-generating products or services to market quickly in order to jump-start cash flow. As a result, the new firm may postpone development activities or investments in technology. Consider the example of Stacy's Pita Chip Co.[38] In 1996, founders Mark and Stacy Andrus were operating a successful pita-wrap sandwich business that was ready to grow. But customers kept asking for the baked chips they made every night from leftover pita bread and handed out free to customers waiting in line. "We thought we could get bigger faster with the chips," said Stacy. The couple, who were still paying off six-figure student loans, decided to take their chips nationwide. The business they created is a model of bootstrapping efficiency. The paper sign on the door, folding tables, and used-dining room chairs are the first signs of their spartan approach to business. They also saved over $250,000 buying used equipment. "Everything goes into the business," said Stacy, who takes home a scavenger-level salary. But it has paid off. Their baked pita chips annual revenues recently hit $1.3 million, with sales in 37 states.

If personal savings and bootstrapping efforts are insufficient to finance the business, entrepreneurs must turn to other sources of funds. One of the most common mistakes business founders make is trying to launch a business with insufficient capital. Seeking external sources of financing is often essential for start-up success. There are many possible sources of external funding. One of the most important sources is family and friends. They can be especially helpful during the very early stages of a new venture. This type of financing may be in the form of either debt or equity. To preserve cash, other techniques that start-up businesses use involve unconventional or creative financing sources such as equipment leasing, barter transactions and exchanges of products and services, supplier financing, and selling accounts receivables.

Later-Stage Financing Once an entrepreneur has a going concern, certain types of financing become more readily available. Young firms that have contracted with a first customer or can demonstrate several months of sales are considered a better risk by investors and creditors. Even "angel" investors—private individuals who provide seed capital during the early stages of a new venture—favour companies that already have a winning business model and dominance in a market niche.[39] According to Cal Simmons, co-author of *Every Business Needs an Angel*, "I would much rather talk to an entrepreneur who has already put his money and his effort into proving the concept. And I think most angels I know feel the same way right now."[40]

Angel investors are an important source of equity investment for many entrepreneurial firms. They often invest modest amounts—under $1 million—and help firms that are trying to grow beyond their initial start-up success. Angels also provide mentoring and contacts for young firms that are trying to become established.

Opportunities that involve large capital investments or extensive development costs, such as manufacturing or engineering firms that are trying to commercialize an innovative product, may, soon after they are founded, have high cash requirements that go beyond the risk appetite of angels and the self-financing capabilities of the entrepreneurs. To obtain additional funding, entrepreneurial firms often seek venture capital. Venture capital is a form of private equity financing through which entrepreneurs raise money by selling shares in the new venture. In contrast to angel investors, who are actively engaged in investing their own money, venture capital companies are organized to place the funds of private investors into lucrative business opportunities.

Equity financing, however, often comes with strings attached. On the one hand, venture capitalists often have high performance expectations and demand a regular accounting. On the other hand, sometimes these strings can enhance a firm's chances for success. Venture capital groups often provide important managerial advice, links to key contacts in an industry, and the peace of mind of knowing that financial backers support the project. But founders who use venture capital forfeit part of the payoff if the venture succeeds. Further, they must agree to let the venture capitalists influence management decisions. For Phil Trubey, founder of Netpartners Internet Solutions, it meant losing his job. The Morgan Stanley venture partners who agreed to back his start-up became powerful members of his board of directors. Four months after putting up $6 million in equity, they informed Trubey that his company had outgrown him.[41]

Venture capital groups also help start-ups by sponsoring independent business incubators to help facilitate the growth of both start-up and later-stage companies. The venture capital groups provide management assistance; the incubators provide office space, technology infrastructure, and business support services. Another example is a kind of business accelerator such as the not-for-profit MaRS in downtown Toronto. It brings together the traditional elements of an incubator with venture capitalists, support in the form of consulting, legal services, administrative and regulatory services, office and laboratory space at below market rates, as well as proximity to the research and science of the University of Toronto.[42]

Another important source of funding is debt. The primary providers of debt financing for new ventures are commercial banks. Although credit cards often represent an important source of funding for very young firms, banks frequently provide ongoing funding. Businesses with a track record of generating revenues are more likely to get bank loans. Besides cash flow, banks are also interested in collateral—assets that an entrepreneurial firm could sell to repay its loan in the event of a default. As a result, one of the ways that young firms often get start-up capital is through a home equity loan; a house provides valuable collateral that, in the event that the entrepreneur fails to make payments, the bank could force the homeowner to sell to satisfy its debt.

Other Entrepreneurial Resources Whether an entrepreneur starts by bootstrapping or bringing a large sum of assets to a new venture, founders often turn to three other types of resources that were discussed in Chapter 4: human capital, social capital, and government resources. Young and small firms have many of the same needs as larger firms—skilled and experienced workers and the ability to operate in a network of beneficial relationships. But they also have unique needs that stem from being young or small. By relying on the talents of other people, their network of contacts, and support services provided by government programs, entrepreneurial firms can often strengthen their ability to survive and succeed.

Human Capital The most important human capital may be in the founding team. Bankers, venture capitalists, and angel investors who invest in start-up firms and small businesses agree that the most important asset an entrepreneurial firm can have is strong and skilled management. According to Stephen Gaal, founding member of Walnut Venture Associates, venture investors do not invest in businesses, "We invest in people ... very smart people with very high integrity." Managers need to have a strong base of experience and extensive domain knowledge as well as an ability to make rapid decisions and change direction as shifting circumstances may require. Additionally, among start-ups, more is better. New ventures that are started by teams of three, four, or five entrepreneurs are more likely to succeed in the long run than ventures launched by "lone wolf" entrepreneurs.[43]

Social Capital New ventures founded by entrepreneurs who have extensive social contacts are more likely to succeed than ventures started without the support of a social network.[44] This is one of the major avenues for overcoming the problem of the liability of newness. Even though a firm may be new, if the founders have contacts who will vouch for them, they gain exposure and build legitimacy faster. This support can come from several sources: prior jobs, industry organizations, and local business groups such as the chamber of commerce. These contacts can all contribute to a growing network that provides support for the young or small firm. Janina Pawlowski, co-founder of the online lending company E-Loan, attributed part of her success to the strong advisors she persuaded to serve on her board of directors, including Tim Koogle, CEO of Yahoo![45]

Government Resources In Canada, the federal and provincial governments are an important resource for many young and small businesses. They provide support for entrepreneurial firms in two key arenas: financing and government contracting. Small business loan programs offer several loan guarantees designed to support the growth and development of entrepreneurial firms. The government itself does not lend money but underwrites loans made by banks to small businesses, thus reducing the risk associated with lending to firms that have unproven records. All three levels of government also offer training, counselling, and other support services through local offices and Canada Business Service Centres.[46]

Another key area of support is in government contracting. Programs sponsored by the various government agencies ensure that small businesses have the opportunity to bid on contracts to provide goods and services to the government.

Local governments also have hundreds of programs to provide funding, contracts, and other support for new ventures and small businesses. Local economic development initiatives are often designed specifically to stimulate small business activity. State-sponsored micro-enterprise funds, such as Aboriginal Business Canada, provide funding as well as training for companies established in aboriginal reserves or that are to be launched by aboriginal entrepreneurs.

The government provides numerous funding opportunities for small business and new ventures. Although working with the government sometimes has drawbacks in terms of issues of regulation and time-consuming decision making, programs to support young and small firms constitute an important resource for firms during the start-up and growth process. Yet, the Canadian Federation of Independent Business reports that many small businesses do not take advantage of most government programs. The reasons could include excessive red tape, lack of awareness, lack of trust, and, once again, time delays.

Entrepreneurial Leadership

Whether a venture is launched from within a large corporation or by an individual entrepreneur, effective leadership is needed. Launching a new venture requires a special kind of leadership. It involves courage, belief in one's convictions, and the energy to work hard even in difficult circumstances. Corporate entrepreneurs typically work on the fringe of the corporation and are frequently either ignored or resented by the mainstream. Entrepreneurs and small business owners work for themselves. They don't have bosses to inspire them or tell them what to do. Their next paycheque will arrive only as a result of their own efforts. They must oversee all aspects of a company's operations as well as monitor quality and performance. Yet, these are the very challenges that motivate most

← LO 6

business owners. Entrepreneurs put themselves to the test and get their satisfaction from acting independently, overcoming obstacles, and thriving financially. To do so, they must embody the characteristics of leadership—vision, dedication, and drive—and pass these on to all those who work with them.

Vision Vision may be an entrepreneur's most important asset. The entrepreneur has to envision realities that do not yet exist. This may consist of a new product or a unique service. It may include a competitive goal such as besting a close competitor. Entrepreneurs must exercise a kind of transformational leadership that aims to create something new and, in some way, change their world. Not all founders of new ventures succeed. Indeed, the majority fail. But without a vision, most entrepreneurs would never even get a new business off the ground.

The idea of creating something new is captured in the vision of Paul Robbins, founder of Caribbean Shipping & Cold Storage, who saw opportunity in a rundown part of Jacksonville, Florida. Where others saw a stretch of ramshackle houses, a lot strewn with rubble, and an abandoned warehouse, Robbins saw promise and profits. Caribbean Shipping and Cold Storage handles food products that need cold storage on their way to Puerto Rico and other Caribbean islands. In the past, shipments from far-flung U.S. locations might be transferred from truck to train to ship as many as six times. Instead of making arrangements with all those carriers, customers such as Outback Steakhouse and the Ritz-Carlton have Robbins handle the entire shipment. So why the rundown lot in Jacksonville? Because it's one block from Interstate 95 and only half a mile from Interstate 10. CSX train lines are so close that train whistles interrupt meetings. And the lot is adjacent to Jacksonville's shipping port. In other words, it's a crossroads—one that has paid off. Caribbean Shipping's revenues rose from $3.5 million to $20 million in just four years.[47]

By itself, however, having a vision is not enough. The new venture idea must be effectively articulated as well. To develop support, get financial backing, and attract employees, entrepreneurial leaders must share their vision with others. The following leadership skills are needed to enact an entrepreneurial vision:[48]

- ◆ **The ability to communicate with a wide audience.** Entrepreneurial founders must reach a diverse collection of stakeholders. Understanding how these constituencies differ and fitting the vision message with their concerns is an important element of good leadership.
- ◆ **The willingness to make unpopular decisions.** As the new venture concept is developed, tough decisions will have to be made that define and shape the boundaries of the vision. Good leaders realize their decisions will not please everyone, but they still have to make them and move on.
- ◆ **The determination to make sure the message gets through.** Employees of a venture start-up must have a clear sense of the leader's vision. It's not enough to just make a vision statement. Good leaders must demonstrate how it is defining the direction of the company so the employees internalize it.
- ◆ **The ability to create and implement quality systems and methods that will survive.** For a vision to be meaningful on a daily basis, leaders need to think of it as a tool. As such, it can be used to identify benchmarks that are necessary for maintaining quality, controlling outcomes, and measuring success.

Creating and articulating a vision provide an essential starting point for an entrepreneurial venture. But, as noted, the vision itself is not enough. Without enthusiasm and perseverance, many ventures never get off the ground. Next, we turn to the important qualities of dedication and drive.

Dedication and Drive Dedication and drive are key success factors for the start-up entrepreneur. Dedication and drive are reflected in hard work. They require patience, stamina, and a willingness to work long hours. One of the key reasons that start-up businesses fail is that the founders lack commitment and neglect the business. Drive involves internal motivation, while dedication calls for an intellectual commitment to the enterprise that keeps the entrepreneur going even in the face of bad news or poor luck. Entrepreneurs typically have a strong enthusiasm, not just for their venture but for life in general. In fact, their dedication and drive are like a magnet that draws people to the business and builds confidence in what the entrepreneurs are doing. Consider the example of Bill Nguyen, founder and CEO of Seven Networks, a wireless software development start-up. Nguyen, who is only 30 years old and sleeps just three hours a night, has already been a part of six high-tech start-ups. One month after selling his previous start-up, One-box.com, to Openwave Systems for $850 million, Nguyen launched Seven Networks and started raising venture capital. Initially, the venture capital firm Ignition and Greylock told him, "Bill, we love you, but it's not going to work." This didn't stop Nguyen. He went home and worked on the technical problems for three days straight with no sleep. When he showed up at Ignition's offices with a revised plan, he had solved the problem. Soon thereafter, the venture capitalists pledged $34 million to Nguyen's Seven Networks venture. According to Brad Silverberg, CEO at Ignition, "He's a rocket; you just strap in and try to hold on."[49]

Clearly, Nguyen is an example of a driven entrepreneur who has used his personal example and sheer stamina to make his businesses succeed. Such dedication may be more important for some entrepreneurial firms than for others. However, a business built on the heroic efforts of one person may also suffer in the long run—especially if something happens to that person. The entrepreneurial leader as "anti-hero" represents a very valuable alternative to the traditional notions of a charismatic leader, a larger-than-life figure who is supposed to inspire dedication and solve all problems. Instead, an entrepreneurial leader knows how to rely on others to execute the vision, creates room in the organization for other members to make contributions, share responsibilities, find meaningful ways to have an impact, and to become part of a community dedicated to a cause greater than the business itself.[50]

In his book *Good to Great*, Jim Collins makes an important point: great companies are typically not led by lone-wolf leaders. Building a start-up on the vision or charisma of a single person can hinder a young firm because when that person leaves there is a vacuum that may be hard to fill. In fact, the reason some companies never go from good to great is that they never fill the void left by the founder. Business leaders with a commitment to excellence recognize that skilled and experienced people are needed to make the business successful. Such people are themselves leaders who attract other top-quality people to the organization.[51]

Entrepreneurs sometimes launch businesses without understanding what it will take to succeed. One of the major causes of business failure is managerial incompetence; too many business owners don't have a serious appreciation of the strategic implications of their behaviour. Others are insensitive to the needs of customers and other stakeholders. To succeed, entrepreneurs need to develop sensitivity to how the elements of their value chain fit together and contribute to overall success. Having this type of whole-organization perspective can help a venture founder manage the synergies that might exist between different value-adding functions in a firm's value chain. For the firm to survive and become successful, the entrepreneurial leader must manage a firm's value proposition and set high standards for quality and customer service.

Another important practice is to let people go when they don't fit with the company's culture. Even a skilled person can create problems for a firm if he or she does not embrace the company's goals and work ethic. Poor performers or laggards must also be proactively dismissed. Success requires focused and disciplined action. In the case of employees, that means leaders must have a willingness to get rid of people who are not working out. In an excellent company, says Collins, "Those people who do not share the company's core values find themselves surrounded by corporate antibodies and ejected like a virus."[52]

ENTREPRENEURIAL ORIENTATION

Entrepreneurial leadership is critical to the success of a new venture. However, especially for large firms, a frame of mind and a perspective toward entrepreneurship that is reflected in a firm's ongoing processes and corporate culture is also needed to overcome the bureaucracy, relative inflexibility and slow decision making that typically characterizes established corporations.[53]

An entrepreneurial orientation (EO) has five dimensions that characterize the decision-making styles and practices of the firm's members. These are autonomy, innovativeness, proactiveness, competitive aggressiveness, and risk taking. These factors can work together to enhance a firm's entrepreneurial performance. But even those firms that are strong in only a few aspects of EO can be very successful.[54]

Autonomy refers to a willingness to act independently in order to carry forward an entrepreneurial vision or opportunity. It applies to both individuals and teams that operate outside an organization's existing norms and strategies. In the context of corporate entrepreneurship, autonomous work units are often used to leverage existing strengths in new arenas, identify opportunities that are beyond the organization's current capabilities, and encourage development of new ventures or improved business practices.[55] Sometimes, corporations need to do more than create independent think-tanks to help stimulate new ideas. Unique organizational structures may also be necessary. Magna International is structured as a series of small autonomous units that can operate with the speed and flexibility of a start-up. Other organizational structures may also help promote autonomy, such as virtual organizations that allow people to work independently and communicate via the Web.

Innovativeness refers to a firm's attitude toward innovation and willingness to innovate, as well as its efforts to find new opportunities and novel solutions. At the beginning of this chapter, we discussed innovation; here, the focus is on innovativeness—that is, a firm's. It involves fostering creativity and experimentation that result in new products, new services, or improved technological processes. To innovate successfully, firms seek ways to break out of the moulds that have shaped their thinking. They create avenues for employees to express themselves openly and encourage them to develop breakthrough ideas that could change the playing field. Employees learn how to engage in non-linear thinking, uncover new opportunities, and challenge industry conventions.

Many corporations owe their success to an active program of innovation-based corporate venturing. Few, however, have a more exemplary reputation for effective entrepreneurship than Minnesota Mining & Manufacturing Co. (3M). With its overarching philosophy of entrepreneurship, 3M is a strong example of how a corporate strategy can induce internal venture development. Every aspect of 3M's management approach is aimed at entrepreneurial development. Exhibit 12.3 describes the policies that create a climate of innovativeness at 3M.

Rule	Implications
Don't kill a project.	Managers exhibit patience in nurturing projects. An idea can be kept alive by individual staffers who believe in a project, even if it can't find a home in one of 3M's divisions.
Tolerate failure.	If at first you don't succeed, 3M believes that you should be able to try and try again. Thus, it encourages experimentation and risk taking on projects, even when the outcome is unclear. This strategy has helped 3M achieve one of its key objectives: obtain 25–30 percent of sales from products introduced in the past five years.
Keep divisions small.	Divisions are split up if they get too big (e.g., over $250 million in sales). 3M believes its divisions should be granted autonomy and that division managers should know staffers by their first names.
Motivate the champions.	Product champions are challenged to be innovative. When successful, they are rewarded with salaries and promotions. If a product takes off, a champion forms an action team and may get to run his or her own product group.
Stay close to customers.	Product development is not conducted in isolation. Customers are often invited to join 3M researchers and marketers to brainstorm uses for technology and new product concepts.
Share the wealth.	Divisions and product groups do not have an exclusive claim on the technologies they develop. An atmosphere of open communication helps everyone benefit from the technological insights and breakthroughs that others at 3M discover.

Sources: P. Lukas, "3M: The Magic of Mistakes," *Fortune*, April 18, 2003, www.fortune.com; J. C. Collins and J. I. Porras, *Built to Last* (New York: HarperBusiness, 1997); R. Mitchell, "Masters of Innovation," *BusinessWeek*, April 10, 1989, pp. 58–63.

Exhibit 12.3
3M's Rules for Fostering Innovativeness

Proactiveness refers to a firm's efforts to seize new opportunities. Proactive organizations monitor trends, identify the future needs of existing customers, and anticipate changes in demand or emerging problems that can lead to new venture opportunities. Proactiveness involves not only recognizing changes but being willing to act on those insights ahead of the competition. Strategic managers who practice proactiveness have their eye on the future in a search for new possibilities for growth and development.[56] Proactiveness is especially effective in creating competitive advantages and building on the benefit gained by firms that are the first to enter new markets, establish brand identity, implement administrative techniques, and adopt new operating technologies.[57]

First movers usually have several advantages. First, industry pioneers, especially in new industries, often capture unusually high profits because there are no competitors to

The Wonderful World of BlackBerry

Research In Motion (RIM) was founded in 1984 by Mike Lazaridis and Douglas Fregin and has always had strong connections with the engineering school at the University of Waterloo in Ontario. From the beginning, RIM focused on applications of leading-edge radio technology. RIM had a rather successful evolution, and by 1998 it employed 200 people, mostly engineers, and had revenues of $33 million. Its IPO prospectus, during the previous year, emphasized the promise of emerging markets for two-way pagers and the benefits offered to that market by RIM's appliance, the Inter@ctive Pager. A second product line consisted of a series of OEM radio modems to be integrated into products that required wireless capabilities. They had found applications in mobile computing, ruggedized terminals, ATMs, vehicle location, remote meter-reading, vending machines, and point-of-sale devices. Admittedly, the lack of both a single technological standard and a dominant wireless network had given rise to many diverse offerings by a range of small- and medium-sized firms across the spectrum. RIM had responded with flexible design and universal network access capabilities.

Around the same time, the market began recognizing the importance of wireless email. Within months, RIM's emphasis had shifted to two-way messaging and promoting the capabilities of BlackBerry, a device based on the same Inter@ctive Pager hardware but combined with different software. It was RIM's offer of a wireless email solution to corporate customers who were using Microsoft Outlook® on their desktops. In May 1999, a *BusinessWeek* high-tech commentator wrote, "I have long been on a quest for the perfect mobile email reader ... it's getting closer, courtesy of Research in Motion. [BlackBerry] is the first wireless message device that I've found to be practical enough that I really want to carry it around."

Within a short, three-year period, RIM had expanded its distribution with a number of telephone carriers and had enlisted many third-party software developers and cellular phone licensors to develop new applications for its technology and the BlackBerry wireless platform. It had developed a second generation BlackBerry device that offered seamless access to time-sensitive information, including email, phone, messaging, and Internet-based applications. By 2005, RIM had grown to over 3,500 employees and had offices in North America, Europe, Asia, and Australia. Its revenues surpassed $1.3 billion from some 3 million subscribers in over 40 countries. Although some patent litigation issues had clouded the sky, BlackBerry was recognized as the world's most advanced mobile email and connectivity platform. Sony, Ericsson, Nokia, and Siemens were among the companies that had launched BlackBerry-enabled devices for their customers, and many more were waiting to sign up. By the end of 2007, RIM had surpassed 10 million subscribers and had inked deals to distribute BlackBerries in China and other countries in the fast growing regions of Asia.

Sources: *BusinessWeek*, May 3, 1999; J. Kapica, "RIM Suit Shows Perils of Patent Registration," *The Globe and Mail*, February 24, 2005, p. B9; www.rim.net; www.rim.com; RIM regulatory submissions and annual reports.

drive prices down. Second, first movers who establish brand recognition are often able to retain their image and hold on to the market-share gains they earned by being first. Sometimes these benefits also accrue to other early movers in an industry, but, generally speaking, first movers have an advantage that can be sustained until firms enter the maturity phase of an industry's life cycle.[58] Strategy Spotlight 12.4 describes the strategy of Research In Motion (RIM) and the proactiveness that has characterized the firm throughout its 20-year history—a proactiveness that is largely responsible for the phenomenal success of RIM as a provider of innovative wireless solutions.

Companies with an *aggressive* orientation are willing to "do battle" with competitors. They might slash prices and sacrifice profitability to gain market share, or spend aggressively to obtain manufacturing capacity. WestJet entered the Canadian airline industry with a distinct business model that was designed around drastically lower prices and a very efficient cost structure. It was able to develop a toehold in the Calgary–Edmonton and Calgary–Vancouver routes and subsequently expanded into the rest of the country, most notably east into the Toronto and Montreal markets. In a short period of time, the upstart airline was able to wrestle a substantial share of the market from the dominant player, Air Canada, which was saddled with heavy debt and legacy costs from a unionized labour force. Later in the chapter, Strategy Spotlight 12.5 outlines the course of WestJet's success.

Finally, entrepreneurship is closely intertwined with *risk taking* and a firm's willingness to seize a venture opportunity even though it does not know whether the venture will be successful—their inclination to act boldly without knowing the consequences. Successful firms usually take on riskier alternatives, even if it means foregoing the methods or products that have worked in the past. To obtain high financial returns, firms take risks such as assuming high levels of debt, committing large amounts of firm resources, introducing new products into new markets, and investing in unexplored technologies. In some ways, all of the approaches to internal development that we have discussed are potentially risky. Whether they are being aggressive, proactive, or innovative, firms on the path of corporate entrepreneurship act without knowing how their actions will turn out.

Even though risk taking involves taking chances, it is not gambling. The best-run companies investigate the consequences of various risks and create scenarios of likely outcomes. Their goal is to reduce the riskiness of business decision making; they evaluate new venture opportunities thoroughly enough to reduce the uncertainty surrounding them. Risk taking, by its nature, involves potential dangers and pitfalls. Only carefully managed risk is likely to lead to competitive advantages. Actions that are taken without sufficient forethought, research, and planning may prove to be very costly. Strategic managers always remain mindful of potential risks. In his book *Innovation and Entrepreneurship*, Peter Drucker argued that successful entrepreneurs are typically not risk takers. Instead, they take steps to minimize risks by carefully understanding them. That is how they remain focused on opportunity rather than risk.[59] Companies that choose to grow through internal corporate venturing must remember that entrepreneurship always involves embracing what is new and uncertain.

ENTREPRENEURIAL STRATEGY

Successfully creating new ventures requires several ingredients. As indicated in Exhibit 12.2, three factors are necessary: a viable opportunity, sufficient resources, and a skilled and dedicated entrepreneur or entrepreneurial team. The previous three sections addressed these requirements. Once these elements are in place, the new venture needs a strategy. For any given venture, the best strategy for the enterprise will be determined, to some extent, by the unique features of the opportunity, the resources, and the entrepreneur(s) in combination with other conditions in the business environment. But there are still numerous strategic choices to be made. The tools and techniques introduced in this text, such as five-forces and value-chain analysis, can also be used to guide decision making among new ventures. In this section, we consider several different strategic factors that are unique to new ventures and also the ways in which the generic strategies introduced in Chapter 5 can be applied to entrepreneurial firms. We also indicate how combination strategies might benefit young and small firms, and we address the potential pitfalls associated with launching new venture strategies.

As noted earlier, identifying strong opportunities is an important first step for any company that wants to launch an entrepreneurial venture. In addition to opportunity recognition, young and small businesses can benefit from strategically analyzing the situation surrounding a venture. To be successful, new ventures must evaluate industry conditions, the competitive environment, and market opportunities in order to position themselves strategically.

The new entrant needs to examine barriers to entry. If the barriers are too high, the potential entrant may decide not to enter or to gather more resources before attempting to do so. Compared to an older firm with an established reputation and available resources, the barriers to entry may be insurmountable for an entrepreneurial start-up. Therefore, understanding the force of these barriers is critical in making a decision to launch. Second, and especially important to a young or small firm, is the threat of retaliation by incumbents. In many cases, entrepreneurial ventures *are* the new entrants that pose a threat to incumbent firms. Therefore, in applying the five-forces model to young firms, the threat of retaliation by established firms needs to be considered. This threat can be deadly for a young start-up.

New ventures often face challenges that threaten their survival. They tend to have less power than large firms, which can put them at a disadvantage. To overcome this problem, small firms and start-ups must look for a strategic opportunity to offer a unique value proposition to potential customers. Part of any decision about what opportunity to pursue is a consideration of how a new entrant will actually enter a new market.

Entry Strategies

One of the most challenging aspects of launching a new venture is finding a way to begin doing business that generates cash flow, builds credibility, attracts good employees, and overcomes the liability of newness. A critical aspect of that effort is the initial decision about how to get a foothold in the market. The idea of an entry strategy or "entry wedge" involves several approaches that firms may take.[60] A number of factors discussed earlier will affect this decision:

- Does the entrepreneur prefer control or growth?
- Is the product/service high-tech or low-tech?
- What resources are available for the initial launch?
- What are the industry and competitive conditions?
- What is the overall market potential?

In some respects, any type of entry into a market for the first time may be considered entrepreneurial. But the entry strategy will vary, depending on how risky and innovative the new business concept is. New-entry strategies typically fall into one of three categories: pioneering new entry, imitative new entry, or adaptive new entry.

Pioneering New Entry A young firm with a radical new product or highly innovative service may change the way business is conducted in an industry. Creating new ways to solve old problems or meeting customers' needs in a unique new way is referred to as pioneering new entry. If the product or service is unique enough, a pioneering new entrant may actually have little direct competition. The first personal computer was a pioneering product; there had never been anything quite like it, and it revolutionized computing. The first Internet browser provided a type of pioneering service. These breakthroughs created whole new industries and changed the competitive landscape. Breakthrough innovations continue to inspire pioneering entrepreneurial efforts.

The pitfalls associated with pioneering new entry are numerous. For one thing, there is a strong risk that the product or service will not be accepted by consumers. The history of entrepreneurship is littered with new ideas that never got off the launching pad. Take, for example, Smell-O-Vision, an invention designed to pump odours into movie theatres from the projection room at pre-established moments in a film. It was tried only once (for the film *Scent of a Mystery*) before it was declared a major flop. Innovative? Sure. But, apparently, not a very good idea at the time.[61]

Pioneering new entry is disruptive to the status quo of an industry. It is similar to a radical innovation and may actually be based on a technological breakthrough, as was the personal computer, for example. If it is successful, other competitors will rush in to copy it. This can create issues of sustainability for an entrepreneurial firm, especially if a larger company with greater resources introduces a similar product. For a new entrant to sustain its pioneering advantage, it may, then, be necessary to protect its intellectual property, advertise heavily to build brand, form alliances with businesses that will adopt its products or services, and offer exceptional customer service.

Imitative New Entry　In many respects, an imitative new-entry strategy is the opposite of entering by way of pioneering. Entrepreneurs who start imitative businesses have a very different perspective. Whereas pioneers are often inventors or people who like to tinker with new technology, imitators usually have a strong marketing orientation. They look for opportunities to capitalize on proven market successes. An imitation strategy is used by entrepreneurs who identify products or business concepts that have been successful in one market niche or physical locale and who then introduce the same basic product or service in another segment of the market.

Sometimes, the key to success with an imitative strategy is to fill a market space where the need had previously been filled inadequately. Entrepreneurs are prompted to be imitators when they realize that they have the resources or skills to do a job better than an existing competitor. Franchising is a very successful imitative new-entry strategy. Franchising provides the opportunity to own a business and work independently while benefiting from the accumulated success of others. Entrepreneurs sign up with corporations that have proven concepts and multiple successful outlets already operating in other locations. The entrepreneur imitates the existing business model in a new location and takes advantage of the corporation's reputation and size as well as brand name recognition. Competitive advantages accrue from the size of the large corporation and the individualistic dedication of the franchisee/owner/entrepreneur.

Adaptive New Entry　Most new entrants use a strategy somewhere between "pure" imitation and "pure" pioneering. That is, they offer a product or service that is somewhat new and sufficiently different to create new value for customers and capture market share. Such firms are adaptive in the sense that they are aware of marketplace conditions and conceive entry strategies to capitalize on current trends. Some would argue that "every new idea is merely a spin of an old idea." An entrepreneur does not have to be totally creative. Sometimes a slight twist to an old idea makes all the difference."[62] Consider the example of Green Mountain Coffee Roasters (GMCR), a Vermont-based distributor of specialty coffees. While the coffee business is not new and is dominated by global powerhouses such as Starbucks, Kraft, and Procter & Gamble, GMCR has found a niche and has become a tremendously successful enterprise. In the meantime, it has also become a leading advocate for fair trade practices and for providing financial support for local coffee growers. GMCR purchases coffee exclusively from small farm cooperatives in Peru, Mexico, and Sumatra. It provides micro-loans to agricultural family businesses that are trying to create more diverse local economies, and it sells its roasted beans in upscale stores, side by side with Starbucks, Nabob, Maxwell House, and Folgers.[63]

There are several pitfalls that might limit the success of an adaptive new entrant. First, the value proposition set forth by the new entrant firm must be perceived as unique. Unless potential customers believe a new product or service does a superior job of meeting their needs, they will have little motivation to try it out. Second, there is nothing to prevent a close competitor from mimicking the new firm's adaptation as a way to hold on to its customers. Notice how today, very much every coffee company touts its own fair trade beans. Third, once an adaptive entrant achieves initial success, the challenge is to keep the idea fresh. If the attractive features of the new business wear off or are copied, the entrepreneurial firm must find ways to adapt and improve the product or service offering.

Generic Strategies

A new entrant must decide not only the best way to enter into business for the first time but also what type of strategic positioning will work best as the business goes forward. Early on in the life of a new venture, the entrepreneur faces strategic choices that would place the business to stand as the overall cost leader, as a differentiator, or with a focused strategy. These choices can be informed by the guidelines suggested for the generic strategies, although an entrepreneur may also consider some unique combination strategies that blend elements of cost leadership and differentiation.

Overall Cost Leadership One of the ways entrepreneurial firms achieve success is by doing more with less. That is, by holding down costs or making more efficient use of resources than larger competitors do, new ventures are often able to offer lower prices and still be profitable. Thus, under the right circumstances, a low-cost leader strategy is a viable alternative for some new ventures. The way new ventures achieve low-cost leadership, however, often differs from their established counterparts. Recall from Chapter 5 that three of the features of a low-cost approach included operating at a large enough scale to spread costs over many units of production (i.e., economies of scale), making substantial capital investments in order to increase scale economies, and using knowledge gained from experience to make cost-saving improvements. These elements of a cost-leadership strategy may be unavailable to new ventures. Because new ventures are typically small, they usually don't have high economies of scale relative to competitors. Because they are usually cash strapped, they can't make large capital investments to increase their scale advantages. And because they are young, they often don't have a wealth of accumulated experience to draw on to achieve cost reductions.

Compared to large firms, though, new ventures often have simple organizational structures, which mean decision making is both easier and faster. The smaller size also helps young firms change more quickly when upgrades in technology or feedback from the marketplace indicate that improvements are needed. New ventures are also able to make decisions at the time they are founded that help them deal with the issue of controlling costs. For example, they may source materials from a supplier that provides them more cheaply, or they may set up manufacturing facilities in another country where labour costs are especially low. The Internet offers other potential cost-saving alternatives. Firms may choose to manage supplier relations through a Web site and sell products online, achieving savings and expanding their reach.[64]

Whatever methods young firms use to realize a low-cost advantage, this has always been a way that entrepreneurial firms take business away from incumbents. Strategy Spotlight 12.5 describes how WestJet was able to find its place in the middle of a highly competitive domestic airline industry, dominated by Air Canada, by offering comparable services at lower prices.

Differentiation Both pioneering and adaptive entry strategies involve some degree of differentiation. That is, the new entry is based on being able to offer a differentiated value proposition. Clearly, in the case of pioneers, the new venture is attempting to do something strikingly different, either by using a new technology or deploying resources in a way that radically alters the way business is conducted. Often, entrepreneurs do both. A classic example is FedEx founder Fred Smith, who combined delivery, air transportation, and

Finally, an Airline that Makes Money!

WestJet was founded in 1996 as a low-frills, service-oriented airline that initially operated on the Calgary–Edmonton and Calgary–Vancouver corridors. Its simple business formula relied upon online reservations, which reduced the need for commissioned travel agents or telephone operators, as well as on the elimination of "frills" such as expensive airport lounges, frequent miles programs, and on-board free amenities like meals and drinks. It employed non-union staff and operated the industry's fuel-efficient workhorse, the venerable Boeing 737 in a network of point-to-point routes that maximized the in-air time of the planes. Short domestic flights also meant quick turnaround at the airport gates to facilitate the maximum number of flights by each plane within the normal 16- to 18-hour workday.

Within a short period, the airline had gained the respect of travellers for its friendly and efficient service and its reliability as well as their admiration for its low fares. Following the absorption of Canadian Airlines by Air Canada in early 2000, WestJet saw the opportunity to expand further as the federal government was determined not to allow the dominant national carrier to harm the small upstart. Notwithstanding the government's help, WestJet's lower adjusted unit costs allowed it to undercut Air Canada's fares and gain market share while remaining profitable. Soon, WestJet was flying east, and before long, it was touching down at the country's busiest airport, Pearson International in Toronto. By 2004, WestJet controlled a 28 percent domestic market share and had a fleet of 54 planes. The airline's next big move was to launch selected flights into the United States. WestJet has carved a strong position as a low-cost competitor in the cutthroat airline industry.

Sources: K. McArthur, "Rivals Grab Bigger Piece of Air Canada's Market Share," *The Globe and Mail*, April 21, 2004, p. B1; B. Jang, "WestJet Soars on the Wings of Expansion," *The Globe and Mail*, April 7, 2005, p. B4; www.westjet.ca.

some innovative tracking technology to revolutionize the overnight delivery business. He literally created demand with his suggestive ad campaign that asked customers what to do "when it absolutely, positively has to be there overnight."

More recently, Jeff Bezos set out to use Internet technology to revolutionize the way books are sold. He garnered the ire of other booksellers and the attention of the public by making bold claims about being the world's largest bookseller. As a bookseller, Bezos was not doing anything that had not been done before, but two key differentiating features—doing it on the Internet and offering extraordinary customer service—have made Amazon a differentiated success.

Even though the Internet and new technologies have provided many opportunities for entrepreneurs, differentiators don't have to be highly sophisticated or high-tech to succeed. Consider, for example, Rainbow/Magic Lantern, the Edmonton-based artsy movie house for purists who are indifferent to theatre glitz, megaplexes, food courts, game arcades, and extravagant exteriors. According to its owner, Tom Hutchinson, purists want to go to a movie, not an amusement park.[65] For them, Magic Lantern offers both first-run and alternative films in simple settings for reasonable ticket prices. Its 17 theatres have weathered the big swings that have consumed the industry during the last 20 years.

Similarly, Cora Tsouflidou of Montreal embarked on making one thing right in the highly competitive industry of quick restaurants.[66] Her venture focused exclusively on breakfast and giving its busy and health conscious customers heaping mounds of fresh fruit with a wholesome staple of omelettes, pancakes, and waffles. Ten years later, Cora's restaurant chain of over 100 franchise stores is among the biggest players in the breakfast sector across the country and has been approached by investors from around the world for licensing rights and a global expansion.

There are several factors that make it more difficult for young firms to be successful as differentiators. For one thing, the strategy is generally thought to be expensive to enact.

For example, differentiation is often associated with strong brand identity, and establishing a brand is usually expensive because of the costs: advertising and promotion, paid endorsements, exceptional customer service, aggressive warranties and return guarantees, and other expenses typically associated with building a brand. Differentiation successes are sometimes built on superior innovation or use of technology. These are also areas in which it may be challenging for young firms to excel relative to established competitors.

On the other hand, all of these areas—innovation, technology, customer service, distinctive branding—are arenas where new ventures have sometimes made a name for themselves even though they must operate with limited resources and experience. To be successful, according to Garry Ridge, CEO of the WD-40 Company, "You need to have a great product, make the end user aware of it, and make it easy to buy."[67]

Focus Because of the competitive environment facing most ventures, focus or niche strategies provide one of the most effective entry strategies for any new firm. A niche represents a small segment within a market. A young or small firm can play an important role in such a market space if there is an opportunity to thrive in that environment. Typically, a focus strategy is used to pursue a niche. Focus strategies are associated with small businesses because there is a natural fit between the narrow scope of the strategy and the small size of the firm. As we learned earlier, a focus strategy may include elements of differentiation and overall cost leadership as well as combinations of these approaches. But to be successful within a market niche, the key strategic requirement is to stay focused. Here's why.

Despite all the attention given to fast-growing new industries, most start-ups enter industries that are mature.[68] In mature industries, growth in demand tends to be slow, and there are usually many competitors. Therefore, if a start-up wants to get a piece of the action, it often has to take business away from an existing competitor. If a start-up enters a market with a broad or aggressive strategy, it is likely to evoke retaliation from a more powerful competitor. Young firms can often succeed best by finding a market niche where they can get a foothold and make small advances that erode the position of existing competitors.[69] From this position, they can build a name for themselves and grow. Abebooks, the online bookseller from British Columbia has set itself right in the middle, or perhaps more appropriately, in the fringe, of the multi-billion dollar market dominated by the likes of Amazon and Indigo.[70] Abebooks specializes in used and rare books, antiquarian editions, and hard-to-find titles. Abebooks is neither Amazon nor eBay but a unique player in a narrow niche that serves book enthusiasts who don't like the auction process of the latter and are looking for titles too much on the fringe for the former.

Many small businesses are very successful even though their share of the market is quite small. Giant companies, such as Procter & Gamble, Johnson & Johnson, and Ford, are often described in terms of their market share—that is, their share of sales in a whole market. But many of the industries that small firms participate in have thousands of participants that are not direct competitors. Small restaurants and auto repair shops in British Columbia don't compete with those in Ontario or Quebec. These industries are considered "fragmented" because no single company is strong enough to have power over other competitors. Small firms focus on building market share only in their trade area, which may be defined as a geographical area or a small segment of a larger product group.

Combination Strategies

Although each of the three strategies holds promise as well as pitfalls for new ventures and small businesses, firms that can make unique combinations of the generic approaches may have the greatest chances of success. By combining the best features of low-cost, differentiation, and focus strategies, young firms can often achieve something that is truly distinctive.

Entrepreneurial firms are often in a strong position to offer a combination strategy because they have the flexibility to approach situations uniquely. For example, holding down expenses can be difficult for big firms because each layer of bureaucracy adds to the cost of communicating and doing business. To get a part made or to outsource it may be complicated and expensive for many large firms. In contrast to that situation, the Nartron Corporation, a small engineering firm whose innovations include the first keyless-automobile entry system, solves that problem by building everything in-house. By engineering its own products from its own designs, it not only saves money but also creates better parts. "Our parts look different from other people's because we keep adding functionality," says Nartron CEO Norman Rautiola. According to Rautiola, this capability allows the company to "run rings" around its competitors, which include Texas Instruments and Motorola.[71]

Similarly, large firms often find it difficult to offer highly specialized products or superior customer services. Entrepreneurial firms, by contrast, can create high-value products and services through their unique differentiating efforts and attention to a small number of unique clients.

For nearly all small firms, one of the major dangers is that a large firm with more resources will copy what they are doing. That is, well-established larger competitors that observe the success of a new entrant's product or service may copy it and use their market power to overwhelm the smaller firm. Although this happens frequently, the threat may be lessened for firms that use combination strategies. Because of the flexibility and quick decision-making ability of entrepreneurial firms, they can often enact their combination strategies in ways that the large firms cannot copy. This makes the strategies much more sustainable.

Perhaps more threatening than large competitors for many entrepreneurial firms are other small firms that are close competitors. Because they have similar structural features that help them adjust quickly and be flexible in decision making, close competitors are often a danger to young and small firms. Here again, a carefully crafted and executed combination strategy may be the best way for an entrepreneurial firm to thrive in a competitive environment.

Summary

New ventures and small businesses that capitalize on marketplace opportunities make an important contribution to the economy. They are leaders in terms of implementing new technologies and introducing innovative products and services. They generate the bulk of new jobs in an economy and are sources of creativity and new ideas. To remain competitive in today's economy, corporations must also find new avenues for development and growth. Yet, both large established firms and small start-ups face unique challenges as they try to grow and prosper.

This chapter addressed how innovation and entrepreneurship can be a means of venture creation and strategic renewal and how an entrepreneurial orientation can help corporations enhance their competitive position. Innovation is one of the primary means by which corporations grow and strengthen their strategic position. Innovations can take several forms, ranging from radical breakthrough innovations to incremental improvement innovations. Often, innovations are used to update products and services or to improve organization processes.

To successfully launch new ventures or implement new technologies, firms must first be able to recognize viable opportunities. Opportunity recognition is a process of determining which venture ideas are, in fact, promising business opportunities and proceeding with feasibility plans and assessment of the risks and rewards. In addition to strong opportunities, entrepreneurial firms need sufficient resources and entrepreneurial leadership to succeed. The resources that start-ups need include financial resources as well as human capital and social capital. Many small firms also benefit from government programs that support their development and growth. Various avenues for obtaining resources are available to start-ups, ranging from personal savings and financial support from family and friends to borrowing and extending equity stakes to early investors. Most start-ups can also benefit from bootstrapping—that is, operating economically and relying on as few outside resources as possible. Bank financing and venture capital are often used by entrepreneurial firms in later stages of development.

New ventures thrive best when they are led by individuals who have vision, dedication and drive, and an entrepreneurial orientation. Vision provides entrepreneurial leaders with an ability to conceive of realities that do not yet exist. Dedication and drive are needed in order to persist in the face of difficulties and keep up the level of motivation necessary to succeed. Entrepreneurial orientation steers them toward methods, practices, and decision-making styles that strategic managers use to act entrepreneurially and led the new ventures to success. Five dimensions of entrepreneurial orientation are found in firms that pursue corporate venture strategies. Autonomy, innovativeness, proactiveness, competitive aggressiveness, and risk taking each make a unique contribution to the pursuit of new opportunities.

New ventures face numerous strategic challenges. However, many of the tools of strategic management can be applied to respond effectively and proceed with the promising venture. Decisions about the strategic positioning of young firms can be enhanced through applying the five-forces analysis and evaluating the requirements of niche markets. Entry strategies used by new ventures take several forms, including pioneering new entry, imitative new entry, and adaptive new entry. Entrepreneurial firms can benefit from using overall low-cost, differentiation, and focus strategies, although each of these approaches has pitfalls that are unique to young and small firms. Entrepreneurial firms are also in a strong position to benefit from combination strategies.

Summary Review Questions

1. What is meant by the concept of a continuum of radical and incremental innovations?

2. What are the dilemmas that organizations face when deciding what innovation projects to pursue? What steps can organizations take to effectively manage the innovation process?

3. Explain how an entrepreneurial firm's size, age, and growth goals help determine its character and strategic direction.

4. What is the difference between discovery and formation in the process of opportunity recognition? Give an example of each.

5. How can bootstrapping help a young start-up or small business minimize its resource requirements? How might bootstrapping efforts affect decisions about strategic positioning?

6. Describe the characteristics of entrepreneurial leadership: vision, dedication and drive.

7. Why is entrepreneurial orientation necessary for fostering entrepreneurship in an established corporation? What are the dimensions of entrepreneurial orientation?

8. Explain the difference between proactiveness and competitive aggressiveness in terms of achieving and sustaining competitive advantage.

9. Briefly describe the three types of entrepreneurial entry strategies: pioneering, imitative, and adaptive.

10. Explain why entrepreneurial firms are often in a strong position to use combination strategies.

Experiential Exercises

1. Select two different major corporations from two different industries (you might use Report on Business 1000 companies to make your selection). Compare and contrast these organizations in terms of their entrepreneurial orientation.

Entrepreneurial Orientation	Company A:	Company B:
Autonomy		
Innovativeness		
Proactiveness		
Competitive Aggressiveness		
Risk Taking		

Answer the following based on your above comparison,

a. How is the corporation's entrepreneurial orientation reflected in its strategy?

b. Which corporation would you say has the stronger entrepreneurial orientation?

c. Is the corporation with the stronger entrepreneurial orientation also stronger in terms of financial performance?

2. Pick the most recent issue of *The Globe and Mail's* Report on (small) Business magazine. Select two entrepreneurial stories and use the information provided to evaluate the qualities of the opportunity identified in terms of the four characteristics. In each category, complete the following:
   a. Evaluate the extent to which they met the criteria (using high, medium, or low).
   b. Explain your rationale. That is, what features of the opportunity account for the score you gave them?

Characteristics	High/Medium/Low	Rationale
1. Attractive		
2. Achievable		
3. Durable		
4. Value Creating		

Application Questions Exercises

1. Select a firm known for its corporate entrepreneurship activities. Research the company, and discuss how it has positioned itself relative to its close competitors. Does it have a unique strategic advantage? disadvantage? Explain.
2. Using the Internet, select a company that is listed on the Toronto Stock Exchange. Research the extent to which the company has an entrepreneurial culture. Does the company use product champions? Does it have a corporate venture capital fund? Do you believe its entrepreneurial efforts are sufficient to generate sustainable advantages?
3. Using the Internet, research the Web site of the Canada Business Service Centres (www.bsa.cbsc.org). What different types of financing are available to small firms? Besides financing, what other programs are available to support the growth and development of small businesses?
4. Think of an entrepreneurial firm that has been successfully launched in the last 10 years. What are the characteristics of the entrepreneur(s) who launched the firm?

5. Select a small business, which you are familiar with, in your local community. Research the company, and discuss how it has positioned itself relative to its close competitors. Does it have a unique strategic advantage? disadvantage? Explain.

6. Using the Internet, find an example of a young entrepreneurial firm (founded within the last five years). What kind of entry strategy did it use—pioneering, imitative, or adaptive? Since the firm's initial entry, how has it used or combined overall low-cost, differentiation, and/or focus strategies?

Ethics Questions

1. Innovation activities are often aimed at making a discovery or commercializing a technology ahead of the competition. What are some of the unethical practices that companies could engage in during the innovation process? What are the potential long-term consequences of such actions?

2. Imitation strategies entail copying another firm's idea and using it for one's own purposes. Is this unethical or simply a smart business practice? What may be some ethical implications of this practice?

3. The prices of some foreign products that enter Canada are regulated to keep prices high, and "dumping" laws have been established to prevent some foreign companies from selling below wholesale prices. Should price wars that drive small businesses or new entrants out of business be illegal? What ethical considerations are raised (if any)?

4. Discuss the ethical implications of using "vaporware" to signal competitors and potential customers about software products that have not yet been released.

Appendix

Analyzing Strategic Management Cases

WHY ANALYZE STRATEGIC MANAGEMENT CASES?

It is often said that the key to finding good answers is to ask good questions. Strategic managers and business leaders are required to evaluate options, make choices, and find solutions to the challenges they face every day. To do so, they must learn to ask the right questions. The process of analyzing, decision making, and implementing strategic actions raises many good questions:

- Why do some firms succeed and others fail?
- Why are some companies higher performers than others?
- What information is needed in the strategic planning process?
- How do competing values and beliefs affect strategic decision making?
- What skills and capabilities are needed to implement a strategy effectively?

How does a student of strategic management learn to ask the right questions? Case studies can be a tremendous tool in developing the discipline to ask good questions and in mastering the tools to answer those questions. Case analysis simulates the real-world experience that strategic managers and company leaders face as they try to determine how best to run their companies. It places students in the middle of an actual situation and challenges them to figure out what to do.[1]

Asking the right questions is just the beginning of case analysis. Throughout the chapters of the book, we have discussed issues and challenges that managers face and provided analytical frameworks for understanding the situation. But, once the analysis is complete, decisions have to be made. Case analysis forces us to choose among different options and set forth a plan of action based on our choices. But even then the job is not done. Strategic case analysis also requires that we address how we will implement the plan and the implications of choosing one course of action over another.

A strategic management case is a detailed description of a challenging situation faced by an organization.[2] It usually includes a chronology of events and extensive support materials such as financial statements, product lists, and transcripts of interviews with employees. Although names or locations are sometimes disguised to provide anonymity, cases usually report the facts of a situation as authentically as possible.

One of the main reasons to analyze strategic management cases is to develop an ability to evaluate business situations critically. In case analysis, memorizing key terms and conceptual frameworks is not enough. To analyze a case, it is important that we go beyond textbook prescriptions and quick answers. It requires that we look deeply into the information provided and root out the essential issues and causes of a company's problems.

The types of skills that are required to prepare an effective strategic case analysis can benefit you in actual business situations. Case analysis adds to the overall learning experience by helping you acquire or improve skills that may not be taught in a typical lecture course. Three capabilities that can be learned by conducting case analysis are especially useful to strategic managers—the ability to differentiate, speculate, and integrate.[3] Here's how case analysis can enhance those skills.

1. ***Differentiate*** Effective strategic management requires that many different elements of a situation be evaluated at once. This is also true in case analysis. When analyzing cases, it is important to isolate critical facts, evaluate whether assumptions are useful or faulty, and distinguish between good and bad information. Differentiating between the factors that are influencing the situation presented by a case is necessary for making a good analysis. Strategic management also involves understanding that problems are often complex and multi-layered. This applies to case analysis as well. Ask whether the case deals with operational, business-level, or corporate issues. Do the problems stem from weaknesses in the internal value chain or threats in the external environment? Dig deep. Being too quick to accept the easiest or least controversial answer will usually fail to get to the heart of the problem.

2. ***Speculate*** Strategic managers need to be able to use their imagination to envision an explanation or solution that might not readily be apparent. The same is true with case analysis. Being able to imagine different scenarios or contemplate the outcome of a decision can aid the analysis. Managers also have to deal with uncertainty since most decisions are made without complete knowledge of the circumstances. This is also true in case analysis. Case materials often seem to be missing data, or the information provided is contradictory. The ability to speculate about details that are unknown or the consequences of an action can be helpful.

3. ***Integrate*** Strategy involves looking at the big picture and having an organization-wide perspective. Strategic case analysis is no different. Even though the chapters in this textbook divide the material into various topics that may apply to different parts of an organization, all of this information must be integrated into one set of recommendations that will affect the whole company. A strategic manager needs to comprehend how all the factors that influence the organization will interact. This also applies to case analysis. Changes made in one part of the organization affect other parts. Thus, a holistic perspective that integrates the impact of various decisions and environmental influences on all parts of the organization is needed.

In business, these three activities sometimes "compete" with each other for a manager's attention. For example, some decision makers may have a natural ability to differentiate among elements of a problem but are not able to integrate them very well. Others have enough innate creativity to imagine solutions or fill in the blanks when information is missing. But they may have a difficult time when faced with hard numbers or cold facts. Even so, each of these skills is important. It is the ability to simultaneously make distinctions and envision the whole, as well as to imagine a future scenario while staying focused on the present, that is the mark of a good strategic manager. Thus, another reason to conduct case analysis is to practise developing and exercising the ability to differentiate, speculate, and integrate.

Case analysis takes the student through the whole cycle of activity that a manager would face. Beyond the textbook descriptions of concepts and examples, case analysis requires "walking a mile in the shoes" of the strategic decision maker and learning to evaluate situations critically. Executives and owners must make decisions every day, with limited information and a swirl of business activity going on around them. Businesses are often faced with immediate challenges that threaten their life. Case studies illustrate how the strategic management process can help many of them survive. Students are called to put themselves in the manager's shoes and, first, realistically assess the environment, evaluate the marketplace, and analyze the company's resources. Then, they are asked to make tough decisions, which include shifting the market focus, hiring and firing, and redeploying the company's assets.

HOW TO CONDUCT A CASE ANALYSIS

The process of analyzing strategic management cases involves several steps. In this section, we will review the mechanics of preparing a case analysis. Before beginning, though, there are two things to keep in mind that will help make your understanding of the process more clear and the results of the process more meaningful.

First, unless you prepare for a case discussion, there is little you can gain from the discussion and even less that you can offer. Effective strategic managers don't enter into problem-solving situations without doing some homework—investigating the situation, analyzing and researching possible solutions, and sometimes gathering the advice of others. Good problem solving often requires that decision makers be immersed in the facts, options, and implications surrounding the problem. In case analysis, this means reading and thoroughly comprehending the case materials before trying to make an analysis.

The second point is related to the first. To get the most out of a case analysis, you must place yourself "inside" the case—that is, think like an actual participant in the case situation. However, there are several positions you can take. These are discussed below.

- *Strategic decision maker* This is the position of the senior executive responsible for resolving the situation described in the case. It may be the CEO, the business owner, or a strategic manager in a key executive position.
- *Board of directors* Since the board of directors represents the owners of a corporation, it has a responsibility to step in when a management crisis threatens the company. As a board member, you may be in a unique position to solve problems.
- *Outside consultant* Either the board or top management may decide to bring in outsiders. Consultants often have an advantage because they can look at a situation objectively. But they may also be at a disadvantage, since they have no power to enforce changes.

Before beginning the analysis, it may be helpful to envision yourself assuming one of these roles. Then, as you study and analyze the case materials, you can make a diagnosis and recommend solutions in a way that is consistent with your position. Try different perspectives. You may find that your view of the situation changes, depending on the role you play. As an outside consultant, for example, it may be easy for you to conclude that certain individuals should be replaced in order to solve a problem presented in the case. However, if you take the role of the CEO who knows the individuals and the challenges they have been facing, you may be reluctant to fire them and will seek another solution instead.

The idea of assuming a particular role is similar to the real world in various ways. In your career, you may work in an organization where outside accountants, bankers, lawyers, or other professionals are advising you about how to resolve business situations or improve your practices. Their perspective will be different from yours, but it is useful to understand things from their point of view. Conversely, you may work as a member of the audit team of an accounting firm or the loan committee of a bank. In those situations, it would be helpful if you understood the situation from the perspective of the business

Using a Business Plan Framework to Analyze Strategic Cases

Established businesses often have to change what they are doing in order to improve their competitive position or sometimes simply to survive. To make the changes effectively, businesses usually need a plan. Business plans are no longer just for entrepreneurs. The kind of market analysis, decision making, and action planning that are considered standard practice among new ventures can also benefit going concerns that want to make changes, seize an opportunity, or head in a new direction.

The best business plans, however, are not those loaded with decades of month-by-month financial projections or that depend on rigid adherence to a schedule of events that is impossible to predict. The good ones are focused on four factors that are critical to new-venture success. These factors are important in case analysis as well, because they get to the heart of many of the problems found in strategic cases.

1. *People* "When I receive a business plan, I always read the resumé section first," says Harvard Professor William Sahlman. The people questions that are critically important to investors include the following: What are their skills? How much experience do they have? What is their reputation? Have they worked together as a team? These same questions may also be used in case analysis to evaluate the role of individuals in the strategic case.

2. *Opportunity* Business opportunities come in many forms. They are not limited to new ventures. The chance to enter new markets, introduce new products, or merge with a competitor provides many of the challenges that are found in strategic management cases. What are the consequences of such

actions? Will the proposed changes affect the firm's business concept? What factors might stand in the way of success? The same issues are also present in most strategic cases.

3. *Context* Things happen in contexts that cannot be controlled by a firm's managers. This is particularly true of the general environment where social trends, economic changes, or events, such as terrorist attacks, can change business overnight. When evaluating strategic cases, ask these questions: Is the company aware of the impact of context on the business? What will it do if the context changes? Can it influence the context in a way that favours the company?

4. *Risk and Reward* With a new venture, the entrepreneurs and investors take the risks and get the rewards. In strategic cases, the risks and rewards often extend to many other stakeholders—employees, customers, suppliers, and so on. When analyzing a case, ask these questions: Are the managers making choices that will pay off in the future? Are the rewards evenly distributed? Will some stakeholders be put at risk if the situation in the case changes? What if the situation remains the same—could that be even more risky?

Whether a business is growing or shrinking, large or small, industrial or service oriented, the issues of people, opportunities, context, and risks and rewards will have a large impact on its performance. Therefore, you should always consider these four factors when evaluating strategic management cases.

Sources: E. Wasserman, "A Simple Plan," *MBA Jungle*, February 2003, pp. 50–55; C. A. DeKluyver, *Strategic Thinking: An Executive Perspective* (Upper Saddle River, NJ: Prentice Hall, 2000); and W. A. Sahlman, "How to Write a Great Business Plan," *Harvard Business Review* 75, no. 4 (1997), pp. 98–108.

leader who must weigh your views against all the other advice that he or she receives. Case analysis can help develop an ability to appreciate such multiple perspectives.

One of the most challenging roles to play in business is business founder or owner. For small businesses or entrepreneurial start-ups, the founder may wear all hats at once—key decision maker, primary shareholder, and CEO. Hiring an outside consultant may not be an option. However, the issues faced by young firms and established firms are often not that different, especially when it comes to formulating a plan of action. Business plans that entrepreneurial firms use to raise money or propose a business expansion typically revolve around a few key issues that must be addressed no matter what the size or age of the business. Strategy Spotlight A.1 reviews business planning issues that are most important to consider when evaluating any case, especially from the perspective of the business founder or owner.

Conducting a strategic management case analysis can be organized in five easy steps: becoming familiar with the material, identifying the problems, analyzing the strategic issues using the tools and insights of strategic management, proposing alternative solutions, and making recommendations.[4]

Become Familiar with the Material

Written cases often include a lot of material. They may be complex and include detailed financials or long passages. Even so, to understand a case and its implications, you must become familiar with its content. Sometimes, key information is not immediately apparent. It may be contained in the footnotes to an exhibit or an interview with a lower-level employee. In other cases, the important points may be difficult to grasp because the subject matter is so unfamiliar. When you approach a strategic case, try the following technique to enhance comprehension:

- ◆ Read quickly through the case to get an overall sense of the material.
- ◆ Use the initial read-through to assess possible links to strategic concepts.
- ◆ Read through the case again, in depth. Make written notes as you read.
- ◆ Evaluate how strategic concepts might inform key decisions, or suggest alternative solutions.
- ◆ After formulating an initial recommendation, thumb through the case again quickly to help assess the consequences of the actions you propose.

Identify Problems

When conducting case analysis, one of your most important tasks is to identify the problem. Earlier, we noted that one of the main reasons to conduct case analysis was to find solutions. But you cannot find a solution unless you know the problem. A good diagnosis is half the cure is well-known dictum in medicine and equally applies here. In other words, once you have determined what the problem is, you are well on your way to identifying a reasonable solution.

Some cases involve more than one problem. But the problems are usually related. Consider the following case: Company A was losing customers to a new competitor. Upon analysis, it was determined that the competitor had a 50 percent faster delivery time even though its product was of lower quality. The managers could not understand why customers would settle for an inferior product. It turns out that no one was marketing to the company's customers that its product was superior. A second problem was that falling sales resulted in cuts in company A's sales force. Thus, there were two related problems: inferior delivery technology and insufficient sales effort.

When trying to determine the problem, avoid getting hung up on symptoms. Zero in on the problem. For example, in the situation above, losing customers was the symptom. The problems were an underfunded, understaffed sales force combined with outdated delivery technology. Try to see beyond the immediate symptoms to the more fundamental problems.

Another tip when preparing a case analysis is to articulate the problem.[5] Writing down a problem statement gives you a reference point to turn to as you proceed through the case analysis. This is important because the process of formulating strategies or evaluating implementation methods may lead you away from the initial problem. Make sure your recommendation actually addresses the problem you have identified.

There is one more thing about identifying problems. Sometimes problems are not apparent until *after* you do the analysis. In some cases, the problem will be presented plainly, perhaps in the opening paragraph or on the last page of the case. But in other cases, the problem does not emerge until after the issues in the case have been analyzed.

Conduct Strategic Analyses

This textbook has presented numerous analytical tools (e.g., five-forces analysis and value-chain analysis), contingency frameworks (e.g., when to use related rather than unrelated diversification strategies), and other techniques that can be used to evaluate strategic situations. The 12 chapters have addressed practices that are common in strategic management, but only so much can be learned by studying the practices and concepts. The best way to understand these methods is to apply them by conducting analyses of specific cases.

The first step is to determine which strategic issues are involved. Is there a problem in the company's competitive environment? Or is it an internal problem? If it is internal, does it have to do with organizational structure? strategic controls? uses of technology? Or perhaps the company has overworked its employees or underutilized its intellectual capital. Has the company mishandled a merger? chosen the wrong diversification strategy? botched a new product introduction? Each of these issues is linked to one or more of the concepts discussed earlier in the text. Determine what strategic issues are associated with the problems you have identified. Remember also that most real-life case situations involve issues that are highly interrelated. Even in cases where there is only one major problem, the strategic processes required to solve it may involve several parts of the organization.

Once you have identified the issues that apply to the case, conduct the analysis. You may need to conduct a five-forces analysis or dissect the company's competitive strategy. Perhaps you need to evaluate whether its resources are rare, valuable, difficult to imitate, or difficult to substitute. Financial analysis may be needed to assess the company's economic prospects. Perhaps the international entry mode needs to be re-evaluated because of changing conditions in the host country. Employee empowerment techniques may need to be improved to enhance organizational learning. Whatever the case, all the strategic concepts introduced in the text include insights for assessing their effectiveness. Determining how well a company is doing these things is central to the case analysis process.

Financial analysis is one of the primary tools used to conduct case analyses. The second section of this Appendix, Financial Ratio Analysis, includes a discussion and examples of the financial ratios that are often used to evaluate a company's performance and financial well-being. Exhibit A.1 provides a summary of the financial ratios presented in that section.

In this part of the overall strategic analysis process, it is also important to test your own assumptions about the case.[6] First, what assumptions are you making about the case materials? It may be that you have interpreted the case content differently from your team members or classmates. Being clear about these assumptions will be important in determining how to analyze the case. Second, what assumptions have you made about the best way to resolve the problems? Ask yourself why you have chosen one type of analysis over another. This process of assumption checking can also help determine if you have gotten to the heart of the problem or are still just dealing with symptoms.

As mentioned earlier, sometimes the critical diagnosis in a case can only be made after the analysis is conducted. However, by the end of this stage in the process, you should know the problems and have completed a thorough analysis of them. You can now move to the next step: finding solutions.

Exhibit A.1

Summary of Financial Ratio Analysis Techniques

Ratio	What It Measures
Short-term solvency, or liquidity, ratios:	
Current ratio	Ability to use assets to pay off liabilities
Quick ratio	Ability to use liquid assets to pay off liabilities quickly
Cash ratio	Ability to pay off liabilities with cash on hand
Long-term solvency, or financial leverage, ratios:	
Total debt ratio	How much of a company's total assets are financed by debt
Debt-equity ratio	The amount of the company financed by debt compared to the amount financed by equity
Equity multiplier	How much debt is being used to finance assets
Times interest earned ratio	How well a company has its interest obligations covered
Cash coverage ratio	A company's ability to generate cash from operations
Asset utilization, or turnover, ratios:	
Inventory turnover	How many times each year a company sells its entire inventory
Days' sales in inventory	How many days, on average, inventory is at hand before it is sold
Receivables turnover	How frequently each year a company collects on its credit sales
Days' sales in receivables	How many days on average it takes to collect on credit sales (average collection period)
Total asset turnover	How much of sales is generated for every dollar in assets
Capital intensity	The dollar investment in assets needed to generate $1 of sales
Profitability ratios:	
Profit margin	How much profit is generated by every dollar of sales
Return on assets (ROA)	How effectively assets are being used to generate a return
Return on equity (ROE)	How effectively amounts invested in the business by its owners are being used to generate a return
Market value ratios:	
Price-earnings ratio	How much investors are willing to pay per dollar of current earnings
Market-to-book ratio	Compares market value of the company's investments to the cost of those investments

Propose Alternative Solutions

It is important to remember that in strategic management cases there is rarely one right answer or one best way. Even when members of a class or a team agree on what the problem is, you may not agree upon how to solve the problem. Therefore, it is helpful to consider several different solutions.

    After conducting strategic analysis and identifying the problem, develop a list of options. What are the possible solutions? What are the alternatives? Generate a list first, noting all of the options you can think of without prejudging any one of them. Remember that not all cases call for dramatic decisions or sweeping changes. Some companies just need to make small adjustments. In fact, "Do nothing" may be a reasonable alternative in some cases. Although that is rare, it might be useful to consider what would happen if the company did nothing. This point illustrates the purpose of developing alternatives: to evaluate what is likely to happen if a company chooses one solution over another.

Thus, during this step of a case analysis, you will evaluate choices and the implications of those choices. One aspect of any business that is likely to be highlighted in this part of the analysis is strategy implementation. Ask how the choices made will be implemented. It may be that what seems like an obvious choice for solving a problem creates an even bigger problem when implemented. Remember that no strategy or strategic "fix" is going to work if it cannot be implemented. Once a list of alternatives is generated, ask the following:

- Can the company afford it? How will it affect the bottom line?
- Is the solution likely to evoke a competitive response?
- Will employees throughout the company accept the changes? What impact will the solution have on morale?
- How will the decision affect other stakeholders? Will customers, suppliers, and others buy into it?
- How does this solution fit with the company's vision, mission, and objectives?
- Will the culture or values of the company be changed by the solution? Is it a positive change?

The point of this step in the case analysis process is to find a solution that both solves the problem and is realistic. A consideration of the implications of various alternative solutions will generally lead you to a final recommendation that is more thoughtful and complete.

Make Recommendations

The basic aim of case analysis is to find solutions. Your work is not complete until you have recommended a course of action. In this step, the task is to make a set of recommendations that your analysis supports. Describe exactly what needs to be done. Explain why this course of action will solve the problem. The recommendation should also include suggestions for how best to implement the proposed solution because the recommended actions and their implications for the performance and future of the firm are interrelated.

The solution you propose must solve the problem you identified. This point cannot be overemphasized; too often, students make recommendations that treat only symptoms or fail to tackle the central problems in the case. Make a logical argument that shows how the problem led to the analysis and how the analysis led to the recommendations you are proposing. Remember, an analysis is not an end in itself; it is useful only if it leads to a solution.

The actions you propose should describe the very next steps that the company needs to take. Don't say, for example, "If the company does more market research, then I would recommend the following course of action … ." Instead, make conducting the research part of your recommendation. If you also want to suggest subsequent actions that may be different *depending on* the outcome of the market research, that's OK. But don't make your initial recommendation conditional on actions the company may or may not take.

In summary, case analysis can be a very rewarding process but, as you might imagine, it can also be frustrating and challenging. If you follow the steps described above, you will address the different elements of a thorough analysis. This approach can give your analysis a solid footing. Then, even if there are differences of opinion about how to interpret the facts, analyze the situation, or solve the problems, you can feel confident that you have not missed any important steps in finding the best course of action.

ORAL PRESENTATION

Students are often asked to prepare oral presentations of the information in a case and their analysis of the best remedies. This is frequently assigned as a group project. Or you may be called upon in class to present your ideas about the circumstances or solutions for a case the class is discussing. Exhibit A.2 provides some tips for preparing an oral case presentation.

Exhibit A.2
Preparing an Oral
Case Presentation

Rule	Description
Organize your thoughts	Begin by becoming familiar with the material. If you are working with a team, compare notes about the key points of the case, and share insights that other team members may have gleaned from tables and exhibits. Then, make an outline. This is one of the best ways to organize the flow and content of the presentation.
Emphasize strategic analysis	The purpose of case analysis is to diagnose problems and find solutions. In the process, you may need to unravel the case material as presented and reconfigure it in a fashion that can be more effectively analyzed. Present the material in a way that lends itself to analysis—don't simply restate what is in the case. This involves three major categories, each representing a different degree of emphasis: Background/Problem Statement 10–20% Strategic Analysis/Options 50–75% Recommendations/Action Plan 10–25% As you can see, the emphasis of your presentation should be on analysis. This will probably require you to reorganize the material so that the tools of strategic analysis can be applied.
Be logical and consistent	A presentation that is rambling and hard to follow may confuse the listener and fail to evoke a good discussion. Present your arguments and explanations in a logical sequence. Support your claims with facts. Include financial analysis where appropriate. Be sure that the solutions you recommend address the problems you have identified.
Defend your position	Usually an oral presentation is followed by a class discussion. Anticipate what others might disagree with, and be prepared to defend your views. This means being aware of the choices you made and the implications of your recommendations. Be clear about your assumptions. Be able to expand on your analysis.
Share presentation responsibilities	Strategic management case analyses are often conducted by teams. Each member of the team should have a clear role in the oral presentation, preferably a speaking role. It's also important to coordinate the different parts of the presentation into a logical, smooth-flowing whole. How well a team works together is usually very apparent during an oral presentation.

HOW TO GET THE MOST FROM CASE ANALYSIS

One of the reasons case analysis is so enriching as a learning tool is that it draws on many resources and skills besides what is in the textbook. This is especially true in the study of strategy. Strategic management itself is a highly integrative task that draws on many areas of specialization at several levels, from the individual to the whole of society. You can get the most out of case analysis if you expand your horizons beyond the concepts in this text and seek insights from your own reservoir of knowledge. Here are some tips for how to do that.[7]

- *Keep an open mind.* Like any good discussion, a case analysis discussion often evokes strong opinions and emotions. But it's the variety of perspectives that makes case analysis so valuable: many viewpoints usually lead to a more complete analysis. Therefore, avoid letting an emotional response to another person's style or opinion keep you from hearing what he or she has to say. Once you evaluate what is said, you may disagree with it or dismiss it as faulty. But unless you keep an open mind in the first place, you may miss the importance of the other person's contribution. Also, people often place a higher value on the opinions of those they consider to be good listeners.

- *Take a stand for what you believe.* Although it is vital to keep an open mind, it is also important to state your views proactively. Don't try to figure out what your friends or the instructor wants to hear. Analyze the case from the perspective of your own background and belief system. For example, perhaps you feel that a decision is unethical or that the managers in a case have misinterpreted the facts. Don't be afraid to assert that in the discussion. For one thing, when a person takes a strong stand, it often encourages others to evaluate the issues more closely. This can lead to a more thorough investigation and a more meaningful class discussion.

- *Draw on your personal experience.* You may have experiences from work or as a customer that can shed light on some of the issues in a case. Even though one of the purposes of case analysis is to apply the analytical tools from this text, you may be able to add to the discussion by drawing on your outside experiences and background. Of course, you need to guard against carrying that to extremes. Don't think that your perspective is the only viewpoint that matters! Simply recognize that first-hand experience usually represents a welcome contribution to the overall quality of case discussions.

- *Participate and persuade.* People who are persuasive and speak their mind can often influence the views of others. But to do so, you have to be prepared and convincing. Being persuasive is more than being loud or long-winded. It involves understanding all sides of an argument and being able to overcome objections to your own point of view. These efforts can make a case discussion more lively. And they parallel what happens in the real world; in business, people frequently share their opinions and attempt to persuade others to see things their way.

- *Be concise and to the point.* In addition to speaking up and "selling" your ideas to others in a case discussion, you must be clear about what you are selling. Make your arguments in a way that is explicit and direct. Zero in on the most important points. Be brief. Don't try to make a lot of points at once by jumping around between topics. Avoid trying to explain the whole case situation at once. Remember, a sure way to lose your audience is to go on and on, take up a lot of "air time," or be unnecessarily repetitive. The best way to avoid this is to stay focused and be specific.

- ◆ *Think outside of the box.* It's OK to be a little provocative; sometimes that is the consequence of taking a stand on issues. In fact, it may be equally important to be imaginative and creative when making a recommendation or determining how to implement a solution. Albert Einstein once stated, "Imagination is more important than knowledge." Managing strategically requires more than memorizing concepts. Strategic management insights must be applied to each case differently—just knowing the principles is not enough. Imagination and out-of-the-box thinking help to apply strategic knowledge in novel and unique ways.

- ◆ *Learn from the insights of others.* Before you make up your mind about a case, hear what other students have to say. Of course, in a situation where you have to put your analysis in writing, you may not be able to learn from others ahead of time. But in a case discussion, observe how various students attack the issues and engage in problem solving. Such observation skills may also be a key to finding answers within the case. For example, people tend to believe authority figures, so they would place a higher value on what a company president says. In some cases, however, the statements of middle managers may represent a point of view that is even more helpful for finding a solution to the problems presented by the case.

- ◆ *Apply insights from other case analyses.* Throughout the text, we have used examples of actual businesses to illustrate strategy concepts. The aim has been to show you how firms think about and deal with business problems. During the course, you may be asked to conduct several case analyses as part of the learning experience. Once you have performed a few case analyses, you will see how the concepts from the text apply in real-life business situations. Incorporate the insights learned from the text examples and your own previous case discussions into each new case that you analyze.

- ◆ *Critically analyze your own performance.* Performance appraisals are a standard part of many workplace situations. They are used to determine promotions, raises, and work assignments. The same can be applied to your performance in a case analysis situation. Ask yourself, were my comments insightful? Did I make a good contribution? Am I being effective? How might I improve next time? Use the same criteria on yourself that you use to evaluate others. What grade would you give yourself? This technique will not only make you more fair in your assessment of others but also indicate to you how your own performance can improve.

- ◆ *Conduct outside research.* Many times you can enhance your understanding of a case situation by investigating sources outside the case materials. For example, you may want to study an industry more closely or research a company's close competitors. Recent moves, such as mergers and acquisitions or product introductions, may be reported in the business press. The company itself may provide useful information on its Web site or in its annual reports. Such information can usually spur additional discussion and enrich the case analysis. (Caution: It is best to check with your instructor in advance to be sure this kind of additional research is encouraged. Incorporating outside research may conflict with the instructor's learning objectives.)

Several of the points suggested above for how to get the most out of case analysis apply to an open discussion of a case, like that in a classroom setting. Exhibit A.3 provides some additional guidelines for preparing a written case analysis.

Rule	Description
Be thorough	Many of the ideas presented in Exhibit A.2 about oral presentations also apply to written case analysis. However, a written analysis typically has to be more complete. This means writing out the problem statement and articulating assumptions. It is also important to provide support for your arguments and reference case materials or other facts.
Coordinate team efforts	Written cases are often prepared by small groups. Within a group, just as in a class discussion, you may disagree about the diagnosis or the recommended plan of action. This can be healthy if it leads to a richer understanding of the case material. But before committing your ideas to writing, make sure you have coordinated your responses. Don't prepare a written analysis that appears contradictory or looks like a patchwork of disconnected thoughts.
Avoid restating the obvious	There is no reason to restate material that everyone is familiar with already—namely, the case content. It is too easy for students to use up space in a written analysis with a recapitulation of the details of the case; this accomplishes very little. Stay focused on the key points. Only restate the information that is most central to your analysis.
Present information graphically	Tables, graphs, and other exhibits are usually one of the best ways to present factual material that supports your arguments. For example, financial calculations, such as break-even analysis, sensitivity analysis, or return on investment, are best presented graphically. Even qualitative information, such as product lists or rosters of employees, can be summarized effectively and viewed quickly by using a table or graph.
Exercise quality control	When presenting a case analysis in writing, it is especially important to use good grammar, avoid misspelling words, and eliminate typos and other visual distractions. Mistakes that can be glossed over in an oral presentation or class discussion are often conspicuous when they appear in writing. Make your written presentation appear as professional as possible. Don't let the appearance of your written case keep the reader from recognizing the importance and quality of your analysis.

USING CONFLICT-INDUCING DECISION-MAKING TECHNIQUES IN CASE ANALYSIS

We would now like to address some techniques to use in order to improve case analyses that involve the constructive use of conflict. In the classroom—as well as in the business world—you will frequently be analyzing cases or solving problems in groups. While the word *conflict* often has a negative connotation, it can be very helpful in arriving at better solutions to cases. It can provide an effective means for realizing new insights as well as for rigorously questioning and analyzing assumptions and strategic alternatives. In fact, if you don't have constructive conflict, you may only get consensus. When this happens, decisions tend to be based on compromise rather than collaboration.

In your organizational behaviour classes, you probably learned the concept of "group-think," a condition in which group members strive to reach agreement or consensus without realistically considering other viable alternatives.[8] Group norms bolster morale at the expense of critical thinking, and effective decision making processes are impaired.[9]

Many of us have probably been "victims" of groupthink at one time or another in our life. We may be confronted with situations in which social pressure, politics, or "not wanting to stick out" may prevent us from voicing our concerns about a chosen course of action.

Let's first look at some of the symptoms of groupthink and suggest ways of preventing it. Then, we will suggest some conflict-inducing decision-making techniques—devil's advocacy and dialectical inquiry—that can help to prevent groupthink and lead to better decisions.

Symptoms of Groupthink and How to Prevent It

Irving Janis identified several symptoms of groupthink. These include the following:

- *An illusion of invulnerability.* This reassures people about possible dangers and leads to over-optimism and failure to heed warnings of danger.
- *A belief in the inherent morality of the group.* Because individuals think that what they are doing is right, they tend to ignore ethical or moral consequences of their decisions.
- *Stereotyped views of members of opposing groups.* Members of other groups are viewed as weak or not intelligent.
- *The application of pressure to members who express doubts about the group's shared ideas or question the validity of arguments proposed.*
- *The practice of self-censorship.* Members keep silent about their opposing views and downplay to themselves the value of their own perspectives.
- *An illusion of unanimity.* People assume that judgments expressed by members are shared by all.
- *The appointment of mindguards.* People sometimes appoint themselves as mind-guards to protect the group from adverse information that might break the climate of consensus (or agreement).

Groupthink is an undesirable and negative phenomenon that can lead to poor decisions. Irving Janis considers it to be a key contributor to such faulty decisions as the failure to prepare for the attack on Pearl Harbor and the escalation of the Vietnam conflict. Many instances of the same type of flawed decision-making process occur in business organizations. Janis has provided several suggestions for preventing groupthink that can be used as valuable guides in decision making and problem solving:

◆ Leaders must encourage group members to express their concerns and objectives.

◆ When higher-level managers assign a problem for a group to solve, they should adopt an impartial stance—not mention their preferences.

◆ Before a group reaches its final decision, the leader should encourage members to discuss their deliberations with trusted associates and then report the perspectives back to the group.

◆ The group should invite outside experts and encourage them to challenge the group's viewpoints and positions.

◆ The group should divide into subgroups, meet at various times under different chairpersons, and then get together to resolve differences.

◆ After reaching a preliminary agreement, the group should hold a "second chance" meeting that provides members a forum to express any remaining concerns and rethink the issue prior to making a final decision.

Using Conflict to Improve Decision Making

In addition to the above suggestions, the effective use of conflict can be a means of improving decision making. Conflict can have negative outcomes such as ill will, anger, tension, and lowered motivation, but leaders and group members can use it in a constructive manner if they ensure that it is managed properly.

Two conflict-inducing decision-making approaches that have become quite popular are *devil's advocacy* and *dialectical inquiry*. Both approaches incorporate conflict into the decision-making process through formalized debate.

Devil's Advocacy An individual or a small group is asked to serve as a critic to the plan. The devil's advocate tries to identify problems with the proposed alternative and suggest reasons as to why it should not be adopted. The role of the devil's advocate is to create dissonance. This ensures that the group will take a hard look at its original proposal or alternative. By having a group (or individual) assigned the role of devil's advocate, it becomes clear that such an adversarial stance is legitimate. It brings out criticisms that might otherwise not be made.

The use of a devil's advocate can be very helpful in encouraging groups, task forces, and others, such as boards of directors, to ensure that decisions are addressed comprehensively and that groupthink is avoided.[10] Charles Elson, a director of Sunbeam Corporation, made the following argument:

> Devil's advocates are terrific in any situation because they help you to figure a decision's numerous implications … . The better you think out the implications prior to making the decision, the better the decision ultimately turns out to be. That's why a devil's advocate is always a great person, irritating sometimes, but a great person.

As one might expect, there can be some potential problems with using the devil's advocate approach. If one's views are constantly criticized, one may become demoralized. That person may come up with "safe solutions" in order to minimize embarrassment or personal risk and become less subject to criticism. Additionally, even if the devil's advocate is successful with finding problems with the proposed course of action, there may be no new ideas or counterproposals to take its place. The approach frequently focuses on what is wrong without suggesting other ideas.

Dialectical Inquiry Dialectical inquiry is a technique whereby a problem is approached from two alternative points of view. Out of a critique of the opposing perspectives—a

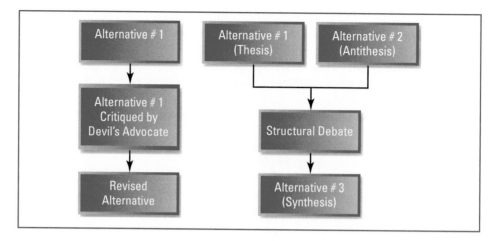

thesis and an antithesis—a creative synthesis can occur. Dialectical inquiry involves the following steps:

1. Identify a proposal and the information that was used to derive it.
2. State the underlying assumptions of the proposal.
3. Identify a counter plan (antithesis) that is believed to be feasible, viable, and generally credible— but rests, however, on assumptions that are opposite to the original proposal.
4. Engage in a debate in which individuals favouring each plan provide their arguments and support.
5. Identify a synthesis which, ideally, includes the best components of each alternative.

There are some potential downsides associated with dialectical inquiry. It can be quite time consuming and may require a good deal of training. Further, it may result in a series of compromises between the initial proposal and the counter plan. In cases where the original proposal was the best approach, this would be unfortunate. People may also identify too strongly with one solution and resent their work being compromised.

Despite some possible limitations associated with these conflict-inducing decision-making techniques, they have many benefits. Both techniques force debate about underlying assumptions, data, and recommendations between subgroups. Such debate tends to prevent the uncritical acceptance of a plan that may seem to be satisfactory after a cursory analysis. They serve to tap the knowledge and perspectives of group members and continue until group members agree on both assumptions and recommended actions. Given that both approaches serve to use, rather than minimize or suppress, conflict, higher quality decisions should result. Exhibit A.4 depicts these techniques.

FOLLOWING THE ANALYSIS-DECISION-ACTION CYCLE IN CASE ANALYSIS

In Chapter 1, we defined strategic management as the analysis, decisions, and actions that organizations undertake to create and sustain competitive advantages. It is no accident that we chose that sequence of words, because it corresponds to the sequence of events that typically occurs in the strategic management process. In case analysis, as in the real world, this cycle of events can provide a useful framework. First, an analysis of the case in terms of the business environment and current events is needed. To carry out such an analysis, the case background must be considered. Next, based on that analysis, decisions must be made. This may involve formulating a strategy, choosing between difficult options, moving forward aggressively, or retreating from a bad situation. There are many possible decisions, depending on the case situation. Finally, action is required. Once decisions are made and plans are set, the action begins. The recommended action steps and understanding the consequences of implementing these actions are the final stage.

Each of the 12 chapters of this book includes techniques and information that may be useful in a case analysis. However, not all of the issues presented will be important in every case. As noted earlier, one of the challenges of case analysis is to identify the most critical points and sort through material that may be ambiguous or unimportant.

In this section, we draw on the material presented in each of the 12 chapters to show how it informs the case analysis process. The ideas are linked sequentially and in terms of an overarching strategic perspective. One of your jobs when conducting case analysis is to see how the parts of a case fit together and how the insights from the study of strategy can help you understand the case situation.

1. ***Analyzing organizational goals and objectives.*** A company's vision, mission, and objectives keep organization members focused on a common purpose. They also influence how an organization deploys its resources, relates to its stakeholders, and matches its short-term objectives with its long-term goals. The goals may even impact how a company formulates and implements strategies. When exploring issues of goals and objectives, consider the following:

   ♦ Has the company developed short-term objectives that are inconsistent with its long-term mission? If so, how can management realign its vision, mission, and objectives?

   ♦ Has the company considered all of its stakeholders equally in making critical decisions? If not, should the views of all stakeholders be treated the same or are some stakeholders more important than others?

   ♦ Is the company being faced with an issue that conflicts with one of its long-standing policies? If so, how should it relate its existing policies to the potential new situation?

2. ***Analyzing the external environment.*** The business environment has two components. The general environment consists of demographic/psychographic, sociocultural, political/legal, technological, economic, and global conditions. The competitive environment includes rivals, suppliers, customers, and other factors that may directly affect a company's success. Strategic managers must monitor the external environment to identify opportunities and threats that may have an impact on performance. When investigating a firm's external environment, you might ask the following series of questions:

   ♦ Does the company follow trends and events in the general environment? If not, how can these influences be made part of the company's strategic analysis process?

   ♦ Is the company effectively scanning and monitoring the competitive environment? If so, how is it using the competitive intelligence it is gathering to enhance its competitive advantage?

   ♦ Has the company correctly analyzed the impact of the competitive forces in its industry on profitability? If so, how can it improve its competitive position relative to these forces?

3. *Analyzing the internal environment.* A firm's internal environment consists of its resources and other value-adding capabilities. Value-chain analysis and a resource-based approach to analysis can be used to identify a company's strengths and weaknesses and determine how they are contributing to its competitive advantages. Evaluating firm performance can also help make meaningful comparisons with competitors. Consider these aspects when researching a company's internal environment:

   ♦ Does the company know how the various components of its value chain are adding value to the firm? If not, what internal analysis is needed to determine its strengths and weaknesses?

   ♦ Has the company accurately analyzed the sources and vitality of its resources? If so, is it deploying its resources in a way that contributes to competitive advantages?

   ♦ Is the company's financial performance as good as or better than that of its close competitors? If so, has it balanced its financial success with the performance criteria of other stakeholders such as customers and employees?

4. *Assessing a firm's intellectual assets.* Human capital is a major resource in today's knowledge economy. As a result, attracting, developing, and retaining talented workers is a key strategic challenge. Other assets, such as patents and trademarks, are also critical. How companies leverage their intellectual assets through social networks and strategic alliances and how technology is used to manage knowledge may be a major influence on a firm's competitive advantage. When analyzing a firm's intellectual assets, you might ask these questions:

   ♦ Does the company have underutilized human capital? If so, what steps are needed to develop and leverage its intellectual assets?

   ♦ Is the company missing opportunities to forge strategic alliances? If so, how can it use its social capital to network more effectively?

   ♦ Has the company developed knowledge-management systems that capture what it learns? If not, what technologies can it employ to retain new knowledge?

5. *Formulating business-level strategies.* Firms use the competitive strategies of differentiation, focus, and overall cost leadership as a basis for overcoming the five competitive forces and developing sustainable competitive advantages. Combinations of these strategies may work best in some competitive environments. Additionally, an industry's life cycle is an important contingency that may affect a company's choice of business-level strategies. There are some questions to consider when assessing business-level strategies:

   ♦ Has the company chosen the correct competitive strategy given its industry environment and competitive situation? If not, how should it use its strengths and resources to improve its performance?

   ♦ Does the company use combination strategies effectively? If so, what capabilities can it cultivate to further enhance profitability?

   ♦ Is the company using a strategy that is appropriate for the industry life cycle in which it is competing? If not, how can it realign itself to match its efforts to the current stage of industry growth?

6. *Formulating corporate-level strategies.* Large firms often own and manage portfolios of businesses. Corporate strategies address methods for achieving synergies among these businesses. Related and unrelated diversification techniques

are alternative approaches to deciding which business should be added to or removed from a portfolio. Companies can diversify by means of mergers, acquisitions, joint ventures, strategic alliances, and internal development. When analyzing corporate-level strategies, ask the following:

- Is the company competing in the right businesses given the opportunities and threats that are present in the environment? If not, how can it realign its diversification strategy to achieve competitive advantages?
- Is the corporation managing its portfolio of businesses in a way that creates synergies among the businesses? If so, what additional business should it consider adding to its portfolio?
- Are the motives of the top corporate executives who are pushing diversification strategies appropriate? If not, what action can be taken to curb their activities or align them with the best interests of all stakeholders?

7. ***Formulating international-level strategies.*** Foreign markets provide both opportunities and potential dangers for companies that want to expand globally. To decide which entry strategy is most appropriate, companies have to evaluate the trade-offs between two factors that firms face when entering foreign markets: cost reduction and local adaptation. To achieve competitive advantages, firms will typically choose one of three strategies: global, multidomestic, or transnational. When evaluating international-level strategies, ask these questions:

- Is the company's entry into an international marketplace threatened by the actions of local competitors? If so, how can cultural differences be minimized to give the firm a better chance of succeeding?
- Has the company made the appropriate choices between cost reduction and local adaptation to foreign markets? If not, how can it adjust its strategy to achieve competitive advantages?
- Can the company improve its effectiveness by embracing one international strategy over another? If so, how should it choose between a global, multidomestic, or transnational strategy?

8. ***Creating effective organizational designs.*** Organizational designs that align with competitive strategies can enhance performance. As companies grow and change, their structures must also evolve to meet new demands. In today's economy, boundaries of firms must be flexible and permeable to facilitate smoother interactions with external parties such as customers, suppliers, and alliance partners. New forms of organizing are becoming more common. When evaluating the role of organizational structure on strategy implementation, consider the following:

- Has the company implemented organizational structures that are suited to the type of business it is in? If not, how can it alter the design in ways that enhance its competitiveness?
- Is the company employing boundaryless organizational designs where appropriate? If so, how are senior managers maintaining control of lower-level employees?
- Does the company use outsourcing to achieve the best possible results? If not, what criteria should it use to decide which functions can be outsourced?

9. ***Achieving effective strategic control.*** Strategic controls enable a firm to implement strategies effectively. Informational controls involve comparing performance to stated goals and scanning, monitoring, and being responsive to the environment.

Behavioural controls emerge from a company's culture, reward systems, and organizational boundaries. Consider these issues when assessing the impact of strategic controls on implementation:

♦ Is the company employing the appropriate informational control systems? If not, how can it implement a more interactive approach to enhance learning and minimize response times?

♦ Does the company have a strong and effective culture? If not, what steps can it take to align its values and rewards system with its goals and objectives?

♦ Has the company implemented control systems that match its strategies? If so, what additional steps can be taken to improve performance?

10. ***Creating a learning organization and an ethical organization.*** Strong leadership is essential for achieving competitive advantages. Two leadership roles are especially important. The first is creating a learning organization by harnessing talent and encouraging the development of new knowledge. Second, leaders play a vital role in motivating employees to achieve excellence and in inspiring ethical behaviour. When exploring the impact of effective strategic leadership, you might ask the following:

♦ Do company leaders promote excellence as part of the overall culture? If so, how has this influenced the performance of the firm and the individuals in it?

♦ Is the company committed to being a learning organization? If not, what can it do to capitalize on the individual and collective talents of organizational members?

♦ Have company leaders exhibited an ethical attitude in their own behaviour? If not, how has their behaviour influenced the actions of other employees?

11. ***Fostering corporate entrepreneurship.*** Many firms continually seek new growth opportunities and avenues for strategic renewal. In some corporations, autonomous work units, such as business incubators and new-venture groups, are used to focus corporate venturing activities. In other corporate settings, product champions and other firm members provide companies with the impetus to expand into new areas. When investigating the impact of entrepreneurship on strategic effectiveness, consider the following:

♦ Has the company resolved the dilemmas associated with managing innovation? If so, is it effectively defining and pacing its innovation efforts?

♦ Has the company developed autonomous work units that have the freedom to bring forth new product ideas? If so, has it used product champions to implement new-venture initiatives?

♦ Does the company have an entrepreneurial orientation? If not, what can it do to encourage entrepreneurial attitudes in the strategic behaviour of its organizational members?

12. ***Creating new ventures.*** Young and small firms launch ventures that add jobs and create new wealth. In order to do so, they must identify opportunities that will be viable in the marketplace. The strategic management concepts introduced in this text can guide new ventures and small businesses in their efforts to identify

markets, obtain resources, and create effective strategies. Consider these issues when examining the role of strategic thinking on the success of small business management and new-venture creation:

- Is the company engaged in an ongoing process of opportunity recognition? If not, how can it enhance its ability to recognize opportunities?
- Do the entrepreneurs who are launching new ventures have vision, dedication and drive, and a commitment to excellence? If so, how have these affected the performance and dedication of other employees involved in the venture?
- Have strategic principles been used in the process of obtaining valuable resources and crafting effective entrepreneurial strategies? If not, how can the venture apply the tools of five-forces and value-chain analysis to improve its strategy making and performance?

Financial Ratio Analysis

Standard Financial Statements

One obvious thing we might want to do with a company's financial statements is to compare them to those of other, similar companies. We would immediately have a problem, however. It's almost impossible to directly compare the financial statements for two companies because of differences in size.

For example, Oracle and IBM are obviously serious rivals in the computer software market, but IBM is much larger (in terms of assets), so it is difficult to compare them directly. For that matter, it's difficult to even compare financial statements from different points in time for the same company if the company's size has changed. The size problem is compounded if we try to compare IBM and, say, SAP (of Germany). If SAP's financial statements are denominated in German marks, then we have a size *and* a currency difference.

To start making comparisons, we will need to somehow standardize the financial statements. One very common and useful way of doing this is to work with percentages instead of total dollars. The resulting financial statements are called *common-size statements*. We consider these next.

Common-Size Balance Sheets

For easy reference, Prufrock Corporation's 2006 and 2007 balance sheets are provided in Exhibit A.5. Using these, we construct common-size balance sheets by expressing each item as a percentage of total assets. Prufrock's 2006 and 2007 common-size balance sheets are shown in Exhibit A.6.

Notice that some of the totals don't check exactly because of rounding errors. Also notice that the total change has to be zero since the beginning and ending numbers must add up to 100 percent.

In this form, financial statements are relatively easy to read and compare. For example, just looking at the two balance sheets for Prufrock, we see that current assets were 19.7 percent of total assets in 2006, up from 19.1 percent in 2007. Current liabilities declined from 16.0 percent to 15.1 percent of total liabilities and equity over that same time. Similarly, total equity rose from 68.1 percent of total liabilities and equity to 72.2 percent.

	2006	2007
Assets		
Current assets		
Cash	$ 84	$ 98
Accounts receivable	165	188
Inventory	393	422
Total	$ 642	$ 708
Fixed assets		
Net plant and equipment	$2,731	$2,880
Total assets	$3,373	$3,588
Liabilities and Owners' Equity		
Current liabilities		
Accounts payable	$ 312	$ 344
Notes payable	231	196
Total	$ 543	$ 540
Long-term debt	$ 531	$ 457
Owners' equity		
Common stock and paid-in surplus	$ 500	$ 550
Retained earnings	1,799	2,041
Total	$2,299	$2,591
Total liabilities and owners' equity	$3,373	$3,588

Exhibit A.5
Prufrock Corporation
Balance Sheets as of December 31, 2006 and 2007
($ in millions)

Overall, Prufrock's liquidity, as measured by current assets compared to current liabilities, increased over the year. Simultaneously, Prufrock's indebtedness diminished as a percentage of total assets. We might be tempted to conclude that the balance sheet has grown "stronger."

Common-Size Income Statements

A useful way of standardizing the income statement, shown in Exhibit A.7, is to express each item as a percentage of total sales, as illustrated for Prufrock in Exhibit A.8.

This income statement tells us what happens to each dollar in sales. For Prufrock, interest expense eats up $.061 out of every sales dollar and taxes take another $.081. When all is said and done, $.157 of each dollar flows through to the bottom line (net income), and that amount is split into $.105 retained in the business and $.052 paid out in dividends.

These percentages are very useful in comparisons. For example, a relevant figure is the cost percentage. For Prufrock, $.582 of each $1.00 in sales goes to pay for goods sold. It would be interesting to compute the same percentage for Prufrock's main competitors to see how Prufrock stacks up in terms of cost control.

Exhibit A.6
Prufrock Corporation
Common-Size Balance Sheets as of December 31, 2006 and 2007 (%)

	2006	2007	Change
Assets			
Current assets			
Cash	2.5%	2.7%	+ .2%
Accounts receivable	4.9	5.2	+ .3
Inventory	11.7	11.8	+ .1
Total	19.1	19.7	+ .6
Fixed assets			
Net plant and equipment	80.9	80.3	− .6
Total assets	100.0%	100.0%	.0%
Liabilities and Owners' Equity			
Current liabilities			
Accounts payable	9.2%	9.6%	+ .4%
Notes payable	6.8	5.5	− 1.3%
Total	16.0	15.1	− .9
Long-term debt	15.7	12.7	− 3.0%
Owners' equity			
Common stock and paid-in surplus	14.8	15.3	+ .5%
Retained earnings	53.3	56.9	+ 3.6%
Total	68.1	72.2	+ 4.1%
Total liabilities and owners' equity	100.0%	100.0%	+ .0%

Note: Numbers may not add up to 100.0% due to rounding.

Exhibit A.7
Prufrock Corporation
2007 Income Statement ($ in millions)

Sales		$2,311
Cost of goods sold		1,344
Depreciation		276
Earnings before interest and taxes		$ 691
Interest paid		141
Taxable income		$ 550
Taxes (34%)		187
Net income		$ 363
Dividends	$121	
Addition to retained earnings	242	

Sales		100.0%
Cost of goods sold		58.2
Depreciation		11.9
Earnings before interest and taxes		29.9
Interest paid		6.1
Taxable income		23.8
Taxes (34%)		8.1
Net income		15.7%
Dividends	5.2%	
Addition to retained earnings	10.5	

Exhibit A.8

Prufrock Corporation

2007 Common-Size Income Statement (%)

Ratio Analysis

Another way of avoiding the problems involved in comparing companies of different sizes is to calculate and compare *financial ratios*. Such ratios are ways of comparing and investigating the relationships between different pieces of financial information. We cover some of the more common ratios next, but there are many others that we don't touch on.

One problem with ratios is that different people and different sources frequently don't compute them in exactly the same way, and this leads to much confusion. The specific definitions we use here may or may not be the same as others you have seen or will see elsewhere. If you ever use ratios as a tool for analysis, you should be careful to document how you calculate each one, and, if you are comparing your numbers to those of another source, be sure you know how its numbers are computed.

For each of the ratios we discuss, several questions come to mind:

1. How is it computed?
2. What is it intended to measure, and why might we be interested?
3. What is the unit of measurement?
4. What might a high or low value be telling us? How might such values be misleading?
5. How could this measure be improved?

Financial ratios are traditionally grouped into the following categories:

1. Short-term solvency, or liquidity, ratios.
2. Long-term solvency, or financial leverage, ratios.
3. Asset management, or turnover, ratios.
4. Profitability ratios.
5. Market value ratios.

We will consider each of these in turn. In calculating these numbers for Prufrock, we will use the ending balance sheet (2007) figures unless we explicitly say otherwise. The numbers for the various ratios come from the income statement and the balance sheet.

Short-Term Solvency, or Liquidity, Measures

As the name suggests, short-term solvency ratios as a group are intended to provide information about a firm's liquidity, and these ratios are sometimes called *liquidity measures*. The primary concern is the firm's ability to pay its bills over the short run without undue stress. Consequently, these ratios focus on current assets and current liabilities.

For obvious reasons, liquidity ratios are particularly interesting to short-term creditors. Since financial managers are constantly working with banks and other short-term lenders, an understanding of these ratios is essential.

One advantage of looking at current assets and liabilities is that their book values and market values are likely to be similar. Often (though not always), these assets and liabilities just don't live long enough for the two to get seriously out of step. On the other hand, like any type of near cash, current assets and liabilities can and do change fairly rapidly, so today's amounts may not be a reliable guide to the future.

Current Ratio One of the best-known and most widely used ratios is the *current ratio*. As you might guess, the current ratio is defined as follows:

$$\text{Current ratio} = \frac{\text{Current assets}}{\text{Current liabilities}}$$

For Prufrock, the 2007 current ratio is:

$$\text{Current ratio} = \frac{\$708}{\$540} = 1.31 \text{ times}$$

Because current assets and liabilities are, in principle, converted to cash over the following 12 months, the current ratio is a measure of short-term liquidity. The unit of measurement is either dollars or times. So, we could say Prufrock has $1.31 in current assets for every $1 in current liabilities, or we could say Prufrock has its current liabilities covered 1.31 times over.

To a creditor, particularly a short-term creditor such as a supplier, the higher the current ratio, the better. To the firm, a high current ratio indicates liquidity, but it also may indicate an inefficient use of cash and other short-term assets. Absent some extraordinary circumstances, we would expect to see a current ratio of at least 1, because a current ratio of less than 1 would mean that net working capital (current assets less current liabilities) is negative. This would be unusual in a healthy firm, at least for most types of businesses.

The current ratio, like any ratio, is affected by various types of transactions. For example, suppose the firm borrows over the long term to raise money. The short-run effect would be an increase in cash from the issue proceeds and an increase in long-term debt. Current liabilities would not be affected, so the current ratio would rise.

Finally, note that an apparently low current ratio may not be a bad sign for a company with a large reserve of untapped borrowing power.

Quick (or Acid-Test) Ratio Inventory is often the least liquid current asset. It's also the one for which the book values are least reliable as measures of market value, since the quality of the inventory isn't considered. Some of the inventory may later turn out to be damaged, obsolete, or lost.

More to the point, relatively large inventories are often a sign of short-term trouble. The firm may have overestimated sales and overbought or overproduced as a result. In this case, the firm may have a substantial portion of its liquidity tied up in slow-moving inventory.

To further evaluate liquidity, the *quick*, or *acid-test*, *ratio* is computed just like the current ratio, except inventory is omitted:

$$\text{Quick ratio} = \frac{\text{Current assets} - \text{Inventory}}{\text{Current liabilities}}$$

Notice that using cash to buy inventory does not affect the current ratio, but it reduces the quick ratio. Again, the idea is that inventory is relatively illiquid compared to cash.

For Prufrock, this ratio in 2007 was:

$$\text{Quick ratio} = \frac{\$708 - 422}{\$540} = .53 \text{ times}$$

The quick ratio here tells a somewhat different story than the current ratio, because inventory accounts for more than half of Prufrock's current assets. To exaggerate the point, if this inventory consisted of, say, unsold nuclear power plants, then this would be a cause for concern.

Cash Ratio A very short-term creditor might be interested in the *cash ratio:*

$$\text{Cash ratio} = \frac{\text{Cash}}{\text{Current liabilities}}$$

You can verify that this works out to be .18 times for Prufrock.

Long-Term Solvency Measures

Long-term solvency ratios are intended to address the firm's long-run ability to meet its obligations, or, more generally, its financial leverage. These ratios are sometimes called *financial leverage ratios* or just *leverage ratios*. We consider three commonly used measures and some variations.

Total Debt Ratio The *total debt ratio* takes into account all debts of all maturities to all creditors. It can be defined in several ways, the easiest of which is:

$$\text{Total debt ratio} = \frac{\text{Total assets} - \text{Total equity}}{\text{Total assets}}$$

$$= \frac{\$3,588 - 2,591}{\$3,588} = .28 \text{ times}$$

In this case, an analyst might say that Prufrock uses 28 percent debt.[11] Whether this is high or low or whether it even makes any difference depends on whether or not capital structure matters.

Prufrock has $.28 in debt for every $1 in assets. Therefore, there is $.72 in equity ($1 − .28) for every $.28 in debt. With this in mind, we can define two useful variations on the total debt ratio, the *debt-equity ratio* and the *equity multiplier:*

$$\text{Debt-equity ratio} = \text{Total debt/Total equity}$$

$$= \$.28/\$.72 = .39 \text{ times}$$

$$\text{Equity multiplier} = \text{Total assets/Total equity}$$

$$= \$1/\$.72 = 1.39 \text{ times}$$

The fact that the equity multiplier is 1 plus the debt-equity ratio is not a coincidence:

$$\text{Equity multipler} = \text{Total assets/Total equity} = \$1/\$.72 = 1.39$$

$$= (\text{Total equity} + \text{Total debt})/\text{Total equity}$$

$$= 1 + \text{Debt-equity ratio} = 1.39 \text{ times}$$

The thing to notice here is that given any one of these three ratios, you can immediately calculate the other two, so they all say exactly the same thing.

Times Interest Earned Another common measure of long-term solvency is the *times interest earned* (TIE) *ratio*. Once again, there are several possible (and common) definitions, but we'll stick with the most traditional:

$$\text{Times interest earned ratio} = \frac{\text{EBIT}}{\text{Interest}}$$

$$= \frac{\$691}{\$141} = 4.9 \text{ times}$$

As the name suggests, this ratio measures how well a company has its interest obligations covered, and it is often called the interest coverage ratio. For Prufrock, the interest bill is covered 4.9 times over.

Cash Coverage A problem with the TIE ratio is that it is based on earnings before interest and taxes (EBIT), which is not really a measure of cash available to pay interest. The reason is that depreciation, a noncash expense, has been deducted. Since interest is most definitely a cash outflow (to creditors), one way to define the *cash coverage ratio* is:

$$\text{Cash coverage ratio} = \frac{\text{EBIT} + \text{Depreciation}}{\text{Interest}}$$

$$= \frac{\$691 + 276}{\$141} = \frac{\$967}{\$141} = 6.9 \text{ times}$$

The numerator here, EBIT plus depreciation, is often abbreviated EBDIT (earnings before depreciation, interest, and taxes). It is a basic measure of the firm's ability to generate cash from operations, and it is frequently used as a measure of cash flow available to meet financial obligations.

Asset Management, or Turnover, Measures

We next turn our attention to the efficiency with which Prufrock uses its assets. The measures in this section are sometimes called *asset utilization ratios*. The specific ratios we discuss can all be interpreted as measures of turnover. What they are intended to describe is how efficiently, or intensively, a firm uses its assets to generate sales. We first look at two important current assets: inventory and receivables.

Inventory Turnover and Days' Sales in Inventory During the year, Prufrock had a cost of goods sold of $1,344. Inventory at the end of the year was $422. With these numbers, *inventory turnover* can be calculated as:

$$\text{Inventory turnover} = \frac{\text{Cost of goods sold}}{\text{Inventory}}$$

$$= \frac{\$1,344}{\$422} = 3.2 \text{ times}$$

In a sense, we sold off, or turned over, the entire inventory 3.2 times. As long as we are not running out of stock and thereby foregoing sales, the higher this ratio is, the more efficiently we are managing inventory.

If we know that we turned our inventory over 3.2 times during the year, then we can immediately figure out how long it took us to turn it over, on average. The result is the average *days' sales in inventory:*

$$\text{Days's sales in inventory} = \frac{365 \text{ days}}{\text{Inventory turnover}}$$

$$= \frac{365}{3.2} = 114 \text{ days}$$

This tells us that, on average, inventory sits 114 days before it is sold. Alternatively, assuming we used the most recent inventory and cost figures, it will take about 114 days to work off our current inventory.

For example, we frequently hear things like "Majestic Motors has a 60 days' supply of cars." This means that, at current daily sales, it would take 60 days to deplete the available inventory. We could also say that Majestic has 60 days of sales in inventory.

Receivables Turnover and Days' Sales in Receivables Our inventory measures give some indication of how fast we can sell products. We now look at how fast we collect on those sales. The *receivables turnover* is defined in the same way as inventory turnover:

$$\text{Receivables turnover} = \frac{\text{Sales}}{\text{Accounts receivable}}$$

$$= \frac{\$2,311}{\$188} = 12.3 \text{ times}$$

Loosely speaking, we collected our outstanding credit accounts and reloaned the money 12.3 times during the year.[12]

This ratio makes more sense if we convert it to days, so the *days' sales in receivables* is:

$$\text{Days' sales in receivables} = \frac{365 \text{ days}}{\text{Receivables turnover}}$$

$$= \frac{365}{12.3} = 30 \text{ days}$$

Therefore, on average, we collect on our credit sales in 30 days. For obvious reasons, this ratio is very frequently called the *average collection period* (ACP).

Also note that if we are using the most recent figures, we can also say that we have 30 days' worth of sales currently uncollected.

Total Asset Turnover Moving away from specific accounts like inventory or receivables, we can consider an important "big picture" ratio, the *total asset turnover ratio*. As the name suggests, total asset turnover is:

$$\text{Total asset turnover} = \frac{\text{Sales}}{\text{Total assets}}$$

$$= \frac{\$2,311}{\$3,588} = .64 \text{ times}$$

In other words, for every dollar in assets, we generated $.64 in sales.

A closely related ratio, the *capital intensity ratio*, is simply the reciprocal of (i.e., 1 divided by) total asset turnover. It can be interpreted as the dollar investment in assets needed to generate $1 in sales. High values correspond to capital intensive industries (e.g., public utilities). For Prufrock, total asset turnover is .64, so, if we flip this over, we get that capital intensity is $1/.64 = $1.56. That is, it takes Prufrock $1.56 in assets to create $1 in sales.

Profitability Measures

The three measures we discuss in this section are probably the best known and most widely used of all financial ratios. In one form or another, they are intended to measure how efficiently the firm uses its assets and how efficiently the firm manages its operations. The focus in this group is on the bottom line, net income.

Profit Margin Companies pay a great deal of attention to their *profit margin:*

$$\text{Profit margin} = \frac{\text{Net income}}{\text{Sales}}$$

$$= \frac{\$363}{\$2,311} = 15.7\%$$

This tells us that Prufrock, in an accounting sense, generates a little less than 16 cents in profit for every dollar in sales.

All other things being equal, a relatively high profit margin is obviously desirable. This situation corresponds to low expense ratios relative to sales. However, we hasten to add that other things are often not equal.

For example, lowering our sales price will usually increase unit volume, but will normally cause profit margins to shrink. Total profit (or, more importantly, operating cash flow) may go up or down; so the fact that margins are smaller isn't necessarily bad. After all, isn't it possible that, as the saying goes, "Our prices are so low that we lose money on everything we sell, but we make it up in volume!"[13]

Return on Assets *Return on assets* (ROA) is a measure of profit per dollar of assets. It can be defined several ways, but the most common is:

$$\text{Return on assets} = \frac{\text{Net income}}{\text{Total assets}}$$

$$= \frac{\$363}{\$3,588} = 10.12\%$$

Return on Equity *Return on equity* (ROE) is a measure of how the stockholders fared during the year. Since benefiting shareholders is our goal, ROE is, in an accounting sense, the true bottom-line measure of performance. ROE is usually measured as:

$$\text{Return on equity} = \frac{\text{Net income}}{\text{Total equity}}$$

$$= \frac{\$363}{\$2,591} = 14\%$$

For every dollar in equity, therefore, Prufrock generated 14 cents in profit, but, again, this is only correct in accounting terms.

Because ROA and ROE are such commonly cited numbers, we stress that it is important to remember they are accounting rates of return. For this reason, these measures should properly be called *return on book assets* and *return on book equity*. In addition, ROE is sometimes called *return on net worth*. Whatever it's called, it would be inappropriate to compare the results to, for example, an interest rate observed in the financial markets.

The fact that ROE exceeds ROA reflects Prufrock's use of financial leverage. We will examine the relationship between these two measures in more detail below.

Market Value Measures

Our final group of measures is based, in part, on information not necessarily contained in financial statements—the market price per share of the stock. Obviously, these measures can only be calculated directly for publicly traded companies.

We assume that Prufrock has 33 million shares outstanding and the stock sold for $88 per share at the end of the year. If we recall that Prufrock's net income was $363 million, then we can calculate that its earnings per share were:

$$\text{EPS} = \frac{\text{Net income}}{\text{Shares outstanding}} = \frac{\$363}{33} = \$11$$

Price-Earnings Ratio The first of our market value measures, the *price-earnings*, or PE, *ratio* (or multiple), is defined as:

$$\text{PE ratio} = \frac{\text{Price per share}}{\text{Earnings per share}}$$

$$= \frac{\$85}{\$11} = 8 \text{ times}$$

In the vernacular, we would say that Prufrock shares sell for eight times earnings, or we might say that Prufrock shares have, or "carry," a PE multiple of 8.

Since the PE ratio measures how much investors are willing to pay per dollar of current earnings, higher PEs are often taken to mean that the firm has significant prospects for future growth. Of course, if a firm had no or almost no earnings, its PE would probably be quite large; so, as always, be careful when interpreting this ratio.

Market-to-Book Ratio A second commonly quoted measure is the *market-to-book ratio:*

$$\text{Market-to-book ratio} = \frac{\text{Market value per share}}{\text{Book value per share}}$$

$$= \frac{\$88}{(\$2,591/33)} = \frac{\$88}{\$78.5} = 1.12 \text{ times}$$

Notice that book value per share is total equity (not just common stock) divided by the number of shares outstanding.

Since book value per share is an accounting number, it reflects historical costs. In a loose sense, the market-to-book ratio therefore compares the market value of the firm's investments to their cost. A value less than 1 could mean that the firm has not been successful overall in creating value for its stockholders.

Exhibit A.9

A Summary of Five Types of Financial Ratios

I. Short-term solvency, or liquidity, ratios

$$\text{Current ratio} = \frac{\text{Current assets}}{\text{Current liabilities}}$$

$$\text{Quick ratio} = \frac{\text{Current assets} - \text{Inventory}}{\text{Current liabilities}}$$

$$\text{Cash ratio} = \frac{\text{Cash}}{\text{Current liabilities}}$$

II. Long-term solvency, or financial leverage, ratios

$$\text{Total debt ratio} = \frac{\text{Total assets} - \text{Total equity}}{\text{Total assets}}$$

$$\text{Debt-equity ratio} = \text{Total debt/Total equity}$$

$$\text{Equity multiplier} = \text{Total assets/Total equity}$$

$$\text{Times interest earned ratio} = \frac{\text{EBIT}}{\text{Interest}}$$

$$\text{Cash coverage ratio} = \frac{\text{EBIT} + \text{Depreciation}}{\text{Interest}}$$

III. Asset utilization, or turnover, ratios

$$\text{Inventory turnover} = \frac{\text{Cost of goods sold}}{\text{Inventory}}$$

$$\text{Days' sales in inventory} = \frac{365 \text{ days}}{\text{Inventory turnover}}$$

$$\text{Receivables turnover} = \frac{\text{Sales}}{\text{Accounts receivable}}$$

$$\text{Days' sales in receivables} = \frac{365 \text{ days}}{\text{Receivables turnover}}$$

$$\text{Total asset turnover} = \frac{\text{Sales}}{\text{Total assets}}$$

$$\text{Capital intensity} = \frac{\text{Total assets}}{\text{Sales}}$$

IV. Profitability ratios

$$\text{Profit margin} = \frac{\text{Net income}}{\text{Sales}}$$

$$\text{Return on assets (ROA)} = \frac{\text{Net income}}{\text{Total assets}}$$

$$\text{Return on equity (ROE)} = \frac{\text{Net income}}{\text{Total equity}}$$

$$\text{ROE} = \frac{\text{Net income}}{\text{Sales}} \times \frac{\text{Sales}}{\text{Assets}} \times \frac{\text{Assets}}{\text{Equity}}$$

V. Market value ratios

$$\text{Price-earnings ratio} = \frac{\text{Price per share}}{\text{Earnings per share}}$$

$$\text{Market-to-book ratio} = \frac{\text{Market value per share}}{\text{Book value per share}}$$

Conclusion

This completes our definition of some common ratios. Exhibit A.9 summarizes the ratios we've discussed.

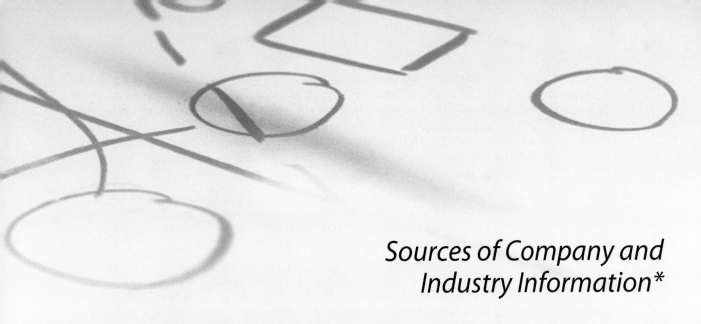

Sources of Company and Industry Information*

For business executives to make the best decisions when developing strategy, it is critical for them to be knowledgeable about their competitors and about the industries in which they compete. We offer below an overview of important sources of information that may be useful in conducting company and industry analysis. Much information of this nature is available in libraries, article databases, business reference books, and on Web sites. This list recommends a variety of them. Ask a librarian for assistance because library collections and resources vary.

The information sources are organized into 10 categories: competitive intelligence; public or private, subsidiary or division, domestic or foreign, annual report collections—public companies; guides and tutorials; corporate disclosure reports, filings and submissions, SEC/SEDAR filings; company rankings; business metasites and portals; strategic and competitive analysis—information sources; sources for industry research and analysis; and search engines.

Competitive Intelligence

Students and other researchers who want to learn more about the value and process of competitive intelligence should see three recent books on this subject:

> Craig S. Fleisher and Babette Bensoussan. *Business and Competitive Analysis: Effective Applications of New and Classic Methods*. Philadelphia, PA: Wharton School, 2007.

> David Blenkhorn and Craig S. Fleisher, eds. *Competitive Intelligence and Global Business*. Westport, CT: Praeger, 2005.

> Conor Vibert, ed. *Competitive Intelligence: A Framework for Web-based Analysis and Decision Making*. Mason, OH: Thomson, South-Western Publishing, 2004.

Public or Private, Subsidiary or Division, Domestic or Foreign?

Companies traded on stock exchanges are required to file a variety of reports that disclose information about the company. This begins the process that produces a wealth of data

*This information was compiled by Ruthie Brock and Carol Byrne, Business Librarians at the University of Texas at Arlington and Elizabeth Watson, Business Librarian at the Schulich School of Business, York University. We greatly appreciate their valuable contribution.

on public companies and, at the same time, distinguishes them from private companies that often lack available data. Similarly, financial data of subsidiaries and divisions are typically filed in a consolidated financial statement by the parent company, rather than treated independently, thus limiting the kind of data available on them. Additional filing regiments provide useful sources of information. For example, foreign companies that trade on U.S. stock exchanges are required to file 20F reports, similar to the 10-K for U.S. companies, the most comprehensive of the required reports.

Corporate Directory of U.S. Public Companies. San Mateo, CA: Walker's Research, LLC, 2007. The Corporate Directory provides company profiles of more than 9,000 publicly traded companies in the United States, including 1,200 foreign companies trading on U.S. exchanges (American depositary receipts, or ADRs).

Corporate Affiliations. New Providence, NJ: National Register Publishing, A Lexis-Nexis Group Company, 2006 edition. This directory features brief profiles, identifying major U.S. and foreign corporations, both public and private, as well as their subsidiaries, divisions, and affiliates. The directory also indicates hierarchies of corporate affiliation for each firm.

Ward's Directory of Public and Private Companies. Detroit, MI: Gale Group, 2007. (8 volumes). This directory lists brief profiles on more than 110,000 public and private companies and indicates whether they are public or private, a subsidiary or a division. Two volumes of the set are arranged using the Standard Industrial Classification (SIC) and the North American Industry Classification System (NAICS) and feature company rankings within industries.

Hoovers database contains both public and private company information for thousands of Canadian and international firms and can be accessed from your library.

Scott's Directories. Toronto, ON: Business Information Group, 2008. There is a directory for each region of Canada and a three-volume set for the Greater Toronto Area. A brief profile of both public and private companies is provided, along with contact information.

Financial Post Advisor (sometimes referred to as FPinformat). This is a comprehensive resource for Canadian public companies. Within FP Advisor, you can also find and additional database called Profile Canada, which contains directory listings for Canadian private companies.

Canadian Company Capabilities database contains extensive information on private companies at http://www.ic.gc,ca/epic/site/ccc-rec.nsf/en/home.

Canadian Key Business Directory, and D & B Billion Dollar Directory. Toronto, ON: D&B Canada, 2008. These two directories provide profiles of Canadian companies and can be accessed online from your library.

Annual Report Collections—Public Companies

A growing number of companies have their annual report to shareholders and other financial reports available on corporate Web sites. A few "aggregators" have cumulated links to many of these Web sites for Canadian, U.S., and international corporations.

Annual Reports.com. IR Solutions, Weston, FL. This Web site contains annual reports in both HTML and PDF formats with additional links to company Web sites. Reports can be retrieved by company name, ticker symbol, exchange, industry or sector. http://www.annualreports.com

Company Annual Reports Online (CAROL). This Web site is based in the United Kingdom; therefore, many reports are European. Links are also provided for companies in

Asia and the United States. A pull-down menu allows users to select companies within an industry. http://www.carol.co.uk/

Public Register's Online Annual Report Service. Baytact Corp. Woodstock Valley, CT. Visitors to this Web site may choose from more than 4,500 company annual reports and 10-K filings to view online or order a paper copy. http://www.annualreportservice.com/

Mergent Online. New York: Mergent, Inc. The Mergent Online site provides company financial data for public companies headquartered in the United States as well as those headquartered in other countries, including a large collection of corporate annual reports in portable document format (PDF). Industry reports are available as a subscription add-on. Library subscriptions to Mergent Online may vary.

Guides and Tutorials

Guide to Understanding Financials. This guide gives basic information on how to read the financial statements in a company's annual report. http://www.ibm.com/investor/financialguide/

Researching Companies Online. Debbie Flanagan, Fort Lauderdale, FL. This site provides a step-by-step process for finding free company and industry information on the Web. www.learnwebskills.com/company

Researching Information on Companies. This Web-based guide highlights key print and electronic resources for finding company and competitive information. http://www.library.yorku.ca/ccm/BG/guides/companyresearch.htm/

Annual Reports and Financial Statements: An introduction. IBM. Armonk, NY. These educational guides, located on IBM's Web site, provide basic information on how to read financial statements and other information in annual reports. http://www.ibm.com/investor/

Locating Industry Information. Tutorial. William and Joan Schreyer Business Library, Penn State University, University Park, PA. Created by librarians at Penn State, this tutorial provides suggestions for online and print resources for company information. Click on "how to" links for each item to view a brief instruction vignette. http://www.libraries.psu.edu/business/about.htm

Competitive Edge – Industry Research and Company Research. Peter Bronfman Business Library, York University. Two online guides for doing business research and analysis using library sources; they contain explanations of common terms and direct links to hundreds of sources from Canada and around the world.

Corporate Disclosure Reports, Filings and Submissions, SEC/SEDAR Filings

SEC filings are the various reports that publicly traded companies must file with the Securities Exchange Commission to disclose information about themselves. These are often referred to as EDGAR filings, the acronym for the Electronic Data Gathering, Analysis and Retrieval System. Some Web sites and commercial databases improve access to these reports by offering additional retrieval features not available on the official (www.sec.gov) Web site. Although SEC filings pertain exclusively to public corporations listed in U.S. stock exchanges, much of the information below is relevant to anyone conducting research on companies.

Companies traded on Canadian stock exchanges are required to file all public documents, such as annual reports, financial statements, prospectuses, etc., with SEDAR, a subsidiary of The Canadian Depository for Securities Limited. http://www.sedar.com

Academic Universe—SEC Filings and Reports. Lexis-Nexis. EDGAR filings and reports are available through the "Business" option of the Academic Universe Web site. These reports and filings can be retrieved by company name, industry code (Standard Industrial Classification, or SIC), or ticker symbol for a particular time period or by a specific report. Proxy, prospectus, and registration filings are also available.

EDGAR Database—Securities Exchange Commission. The 10-K reports and other corporate documents are made available in the EDGAR database within 24 hours after being filed. Annual reports, on the other hand, are sent to shareholders and are not required as part of EDGAR by the SEC, although some companies voluntarily provide them. Both 10-Ks and shareholders' annual reports are considered basic sources of company research. http://www.sec.gov/edgar.shtml

EdgarScan—an Intelligent Interface to the SEC EDGAR Database. (PricewaterhouseCoopers). Using filings from the SEC's servers, EdgarScan's intelligent interface parses the data automatically to a common format that is comparable across companies. A small Java applet called the "Benchmarking Assistant" performs graphical financial benchmarking interactively. Extracted financial data from the 10-K includes ratios with links to indicate where the data was derived and how it was computed. Tables showing company comparisons can be downloaded as Excel charts. http://www.edgarscan.pwcglobal.com/servlets/edgarscan

Mergent Online—EDGAR. Mergent, Inc. (formerly Moody's). From the "EDGAR Search" tab within Mergent Online, EDGAR SEC filings and reports can be searched by company name or ticker symbol, filing date range, and file type (e.g., 10-K, 8-K, ARS). The reports are available in HTML or MS word format. Using the "Find in Page" option from the browser provides the capability of jumping to specific sections of an SEC report.

SEDAR contains all Canadian regulatory submissions such as annual reports, IPOs filings, and management discussion documents. http://www.sedar.com

Company Rankings

Fortune 500. Time Warner, New York. The *Fortune* 500 list and other company rankings are available at the *Fortune* magazine Web site. http://www.money.cnn.com/magazines/fortune/fortune500/

Global 500. Time Warner, New York. The Global 500 list and other company rankings are available at the *Fortune* magazine Web site. http://www.money.cnn.com/magazines/fortune/global500/

Report on Business 1000. Toronto, ON: *The Globe and Mail*, 2008. This special issue of *The Globe and Mail* ranks the top 1,000 Canadian companies and also provides industry sector rankings.

Market Share Reporter provides information and rankings of companies and can be searched by brand, product or company name.

FP500. Toronto, ON: National Post Business, 2008. This supplement of the *National Post* ranks the top 500 Canadian companies and also provides industry sector rankings.

Ward's Directory of Public and Private Companies. Detroit, MI: Gale Group, 2003. (8 volumes). *Ward's Business Directory* is one of the few directories to rank both public and private companies together by sales within an industry, using both the Standard Industrial Classification (SIC) system (in volume 5 only) and the North American Industry Classification system (in volume 8 only). With this information, it is easy to spot who the big "players" are in a particular product or industry category. Market share within an industry group can be calculated by determining a company's percentage of sales from the total given by Ward's for that industry group.

Business Metasites and Portals

@Brint.com, The Biz Tech Network. Syracuse, NY: Brint Institute. Brint's business metasite has a concentration of Web links related to ebusiness, knowledge management, and technology. http://www.brint.com/

Strategis. Industry Canada's business and consumer Web site provides access to industry data and research reports as well as company directories, an importers database and export/import data, along with guides to starting a business. http://strategis.ic.gc.ca/eng-doc/main.html

Financial Post Advisor. A wealth of information on Canadian publicly traded companies is included. It is organized by key product category, including company snapshots, companies by industry, corporate surveys, predecessor & defunct, analyzer search, investor reports (formerly blue sheets), historical reports (formerly yellow cards), dividends, new issues, and additional databases (e.g., directory of directors).

Yahoo Finance, Sunnyvale, CA: Yahoo! Inc. This metasite links to information on U.S. markets, world markets, data sources, finance references, investment editorials, financial news, and other helpful Web sites.

CI—CorporateInformation. Milford, CT: Winthrop Corporation. The CorporateInformation Web site includes information on public and private companies, both in the United States and worldwide. It also provides access to company profiles and research reports alphabetically, geographically by specific countries or U.S. states, and by industry sector. Each interactive research report analyzes sales, dividends, earnings, profit ratios, research and development, and inventory and allows up to three companies to be compared to the company selected. http://www.corporateinformation.com/

Hoover's Online. Short Hills, NJ: Hoover's Inc., Dun & Bradstreet Corporation. Hoover's Online includes capsules of over 50,000 companies with links to corporate Web sites. Some information is free and some is available only to member subscribers. (The lock symbol indicates members only.) http://www.hoovers.com/free

Strategic and Competitive Analysis—Information Sources

Analyzing a company can take the form of examining its internal and external environment. In the process, it is useful to identify the company's strengths, weaknesses, opportunities, and threats (SWOT). Sources for this kind of analysis are varied, but perhaps the best approach would be to locate articles from *The Globe and Mail*, *Report on Business*, business magazines, and industry trade publications. Publications such as these can be found in the following databases available at many public and academic libraries. When using a database that is structured to allow it, try searching the company name combined with one or more key words, such as "Air Canada and competition" or "Hollinger and courts" or "Brascan and acquisition" to retrieve articles relating to the external environment.

ABI/Inform. Ann Arbor, MI: ProQuest Information & Learning. ABI/Inform provides abstracts and full-text articles covering management, law, taxation, human resources, and company and industry information from more than 1,000 business and management journals. *ABI/Inform* includes market condition reports, case studies, and executive profiles.

MarketLine (formerly Datamonitor). The Datamonitor Business Information Center database is divided into company, industry, and country sections and includes 10,000 company profiles, 2,500 market profiles, 1,000 SWOT analyses, more than 50 country profiles, and over 150 industry rankings, along with news, comments, and analysis.

Factiva. Coverage of approximately 300,000 companies, worldwide, is featured on this Web site. It provides company and industry intelligence as well as news and articles from sources such as Reuters, Dow Jones, and *The Globe and Mail.*

Business & Company Resource Center. Detroit, MI: Gale Group. Business & Company Resource Center site provides company and industry intelligence for a selection of public and private companies. Company profiles include parent-sibling relationships, industry rankings, products and brands, current investment ratings, and financial ratios. Use the geographic search to locate company contact information.

Business Source Premier. Ispswich, MA: EBSCO Publishing. Business Source Premier is a full-text database with over 2,800 scholarly business journals covering management, economics, finance, accounting, international business, and more. Contact information is available from an expansive company directory. Business Source Premier contains over 900 peer-reviewed business journals.

Investext Plus. Detroit, MI: Thomson Gale. Investext Plus offers full-text analytical reports on more than 11,000 public and private companies and 54 industries. Developed by a global roster of brokerage, investment banking, and research firms, these full-text investment reports include a wealth of hard-to-find private company data. Investext is also a component of the Gale Group's Business & Company Resource Center a subsidiary of Thomson Reuters, based in Toronto, the world's leading source of intelligence information for businesses.

International Directory of Company Histories. Detroit, MI: St. James Press, 1988–present. (84 volumes to date). This directory covers more than 4,500 multinational companies. Each company history is approximately three to four pages in length and provides a summary of the company's mission, goals, and ideals, followed by company milestones, principal subsidiaries, and competitors. Strategic decisions made during the company's period of existence are usually noted. This series covers public and private companies and non-profit entities. Entry information includes a company's legal name, headquarters information, URL, incorporation date, ticker symbol, stock exchange prices, sales figures, and the primary North American Industry Classification System (NAICS) code. Further reading selections complete the entry information.

LexisNexis Academic. Bethesda, MD: LexisNexis. The "business" category in LexisNexis Academic provides access to a wide range of business information. Timely business articles can be retrieved from newspapers, magazines, journals, wires, and broadcast transcripts. Other information available in this section includes detailed company financials, company comparisons, and industry and market information for over 25 industries.

LexisNexis Statistical. Bethesda, MD: LexisNexis. LexisNexis Statistical provides access to a variety of statistical publications indexed in the American Statistics Index (ASI), Statistical Reference Index (SRI), and the Index to International Statistics (IIS). Use the PowerTables search to locate historical trends, future projections, industry or demographic information. LexisNexis Statistical provides links to originating government Web sites when available.

Notable Corporate Chronologies. Julie A. Mitchell, ed., Detroit, MI: Gale Group, 2002. This two-volume set provides chronologies for over 1,800 corporations that operate in the United States and abroad. Each company entry includes the company address, phone and fax numbers, a timeline, and a further-reading selection. The timeline explains the major events that affected the company's history. Dates of mergers and acquisitions, product introductions, financial milestones, and major stock offerings are also included in the chronologies. The Chronology Highlights in volume 2 provide a historical snapshot of major events for the companies listed.

CorpTech EXPLORE Database. Concord, MA: OneSource Information Services. The CorpTech CD-ROM database covers over 50,000 U.S. technology-related companies, both public and private, headquartered in the United States or affiliated with a foreign parent company. Narrative descriptions of each company, along with sales, number of employees, and other details are provided by the database. CorpTech can be searched by industry, product, geographic location, sales category, size, and so forth to create lists of companies that meet certain criteria. The percentage of employment growth compared with the prior year is stated. Web site addresses, toll-free numbers, or fax numbers are frequently provided. CorpTech is one of the best sources for information on private companies, as long as the company is in some way related to technology.

Wall Street Journal. Dow Jones Reuters Business Interactive. This respected business newspaper is available in searchable full text from 1984 to the present in the Factiva database. The "News Pages" link provides access to current articles and issues of the *Wall Street Journal.*

The Globe and Mail. This respected Canadian newspaper is also available in searchable full text in the Factiva database. The "News Pages" link provides access to current articles and issues of *The Globe and Mail.*

Scott's Directories, Toronto, ON: Business Information Group, 2008, is a Canadian source that provides regional directories and company listings classified geographically and by SIC code. Regional directories include *Ontario Manufacturers, Ontario Business Directory, Western Industrial Directory, Quebec Manufacturers,* and *Atlantic Manufacturers.*

Sources for Industry Research and Analysis

CI—CorporateInformation. This is a meta Web site, covering over 65 industry sectors as well as company and country information. http://www.corporateinformation.com

Factiva. New York: Dow Jones Reuters Business Interactive. The Factiva database has several options for researching an industry. One would be to search the database for articles in the business magazines and industry trade publications. A second option in Factiva would be to search the "Companies/Markets" category for company/industry comparison reports. Factiva also contains coverage of approximately 300,000 companies, worldwide. It provides company and industry intelligence as well as news and articles from sources such as Reuters, Dow Jones, and *The Globe and Mail.*

F & S Index, United States. Detroit, MI: Gale Group, 2003. *F & S Index* provides a compilation of company, product, and industry information from more than 750 financial publications, business-oriented newspapers, special reports, and trade magazines. Volume 1, *Industries & Products,* uses a modified seven-digit SIC product code to organize, by industry, articles on new products, market data, plant capacities, equipment expenditure, and technologies. Volume 2 provides articles accessed by company name. Companies are arranged alphabetically, and topics include mergers and acquisitions, corporate announcements, profits, and sales information. *F&S Index Europe* and *F&S Index International* are companion services.

Strategis. Industry Canada's business and consumer Web site provides access to industry data and research reports as well as company directories, an importers database and export/import data, along with guides to starting a business. http://strategis.ic.gc.ca/eng-doc/main.html

Financial Post Advisor. A wealth of information on Canadian publicly traded companies is included. It is organized by key product category, including company snapshots, companies by industry, corporate surveys, predecessor & defunct, analyzer search, investor reports (formerly blue sheets), historical reports (formerly yellow cards), dividends, new issues, and additional databases (e.g., directory of directors).

MarketLine (formerly Datamonitor). The Datamonitor Business Information Center database is divided into company, industry, and country sections and includes 10,000 company profiles, 2,500 market profiles, 1,000 SWOT analyses, more than 50 country profiles, and over 150 industry rankings, along with news, comments, and analysis.

Mergent Online. New York: Mergent, Inc. In Mergent Online, the "advanced" search option has a feature for searching by industry codes (either SIC or NAICS). Once the search is executed, a list of companies in that industry should be listed. A custom or standard peer group analysis can be created to compare companies in the same industry on various criteria.

Industry Norms and Key Business Ratios. New York: Dun & Bradstreet, 2005. *Industry Norms and Key Business Ratios* provides key financial measures and business ratios, based on efficiency, profitability, and solvency, which are used as a benchmark to compare the performance of a company with the industry average. Industries are presented by the four-digit Standard Industrial Classification (SIC) code and cover agriculture, mining, construction, transportation, communication, utilities, manufacturing, wholesaling, retailing, financial, real estate, and services.

Researching Information on Industries. This Web-based guide highlights key print and electronic resources for finding industry information. http://www.library.yorku.ca/ccm/BG/guides/industryresearch.htm

Standard & Poor's Industry Surveys. New York: Standard & Poor's, 2005. (3 volumes.) *S&P's Industry Surveys* provides an overview of 52 U.S. industries. Each industry report includes a table of contents, narrative description, history, trends, financial and company information, glossary of terms, and a section on how to perform an analysis of the industry. Industry references (associations, periodicals, and Web sites), composite industry data (industry norms and ratios), and comparative company analysis (comparison of 50 major companies, their operating ratios, P/E, revenue, and so forth) complete the industry report section.

Search Engines

Google. Mountain View, CA: Google, Inc. Recognized for its advanced technology, quality of results, and simplicity, the search engine Google is highly recommended by librarians and other expert Web "surfers." http://www.google.com

Vivisimo. Pittsburgh, PA: Vivisimo, Inc. One of the newer search engines, Vivisimo not only finds relevant results but organizes them in logical subcategories. http://www.vivisimo.com.

Endnotes

Chapter 1

1. This example draws on Boisseau, P., 2000, Nortel Network Corp. chief executive John Roth, *CanWest News*, October 14: 1; Time names Nortel Networks CEO John Roth Canadian newsmaker of the year, 2000, *Canada NewsWire*, December 17: 1; Kari, S., 2001, An unapologetic John Roth, *CanWest News*, February 18: 1; Macklem, K., 2001, Plunge from grace, *Maclean's*, March 5: 41; Wahl, A., 2001, Warning? What Warning? *Canadian Business*, March 19: 46; Macklem, K., 2001, The trials of John Roth: Nortel's chief, like his stock, fights an image problem, *Maclean's*, April 9: 24, Avery, S., Perkins, T., & Blackwell, R., 2008, White-collar crime: arrests made nearly five years after tech firm's bubble burst, *The Globe and Mail*, June 20, B1.

2. For a discussion of the "romantic" versus "external control" perspective, refer to Meindl, J. R., 1987, The romance of leadership and the evaluation of organizational performance, *Academy of Management Journal* 30: 92–109; and Pfeffer, J., & Salancik, G. R., 1978, *The External Control of Organizations: A Resource Dependence Perspective* (New York: Harper & Row).

3. For an interesting perspective on the need for strategists to maintain a global mind-set, refer to Begley, T. M., & Boyd, D. P., 2003, The need for a global mind-set, *MIT Sloan Management Review* 44 (2): 25–32.

4. Porter, M. E., 1996, What is strategy?, *Harvard Business Review* 74 (6): 61–78.

5. See, for example, Barney, J. B., & Arikan, A. M., 2001, The resource-based view: Origins and implications, in Hitt, M. A., Freeman, R. E., & Harrison, J. S., eds., *Handbook of Strategic Management* (Malden, MA: Blackwell Business), 124–89.

6. Barney, J., 1991, Firm resources and sustained competitive advantage, *Journal of Management* 17 (1): 99–120.

7. Much of Gary Hamel's work advocates the importance of not focusing on incremental change. For example, refer to Hamel, G., & Prahalad, C. K., 1994, *Competing for the Future* (Boston: Harvard Business School Press); see also Christensen, C. M., 2001, The past and future of competitive advantage, *Sloan Management Review* 42 (3): 105–9.

8. Porter, M. E., 1996, What is strategy? *Harvard Business Review* 74 (6): 61–78; and Hammonds, K. H., 2001, Michael Porter's big ideas, *Fast Company*, March: 55–56.

9. This section draws on Dess, G. G., & Miller, A., 1993, *Strategic Management* (New York: McGraw-Hill).

10. See, for example, Hrebiniak, L. G., & Joyce, W. F., 1986, The strategic importance of managing myopia, *Sloan Management Review* 28 (1): 5–14.

11. For an insightful discussion on how to manage diverse stakeholder groups, refer to Rondinelli, D. A., & London, T., 2003, How corporations and environmental groups cooperate: Assessing cross-sector alliances and collaborations, *Academy of Management Executive* 17 (1): 61–76.

12. Senge, P., 1996, Leading learning organizations: The bold, the powerful, and the invisible, in Hesselbein, F., Goldsmith, M., & Beckhard, R., eds., *The Leader of the Future* (San Francisco: Jossey Bass), 41–58.

13. For another interesting perspective on this issue, refer to Abell, D. F., 1999, Competing today while preparing for tomorrow, *Sloan Management Review* 40 (3): 73–81.

14. Loeb, M., 1994, Where leaders come from, *Fortune*, September 19: 241 (quoting Warren Bennis).

15. Address by Norman R. Augustine at the Crummer Business School, Rollins College, Winter Park, FL, October 20, 1989.

16. Mintzberg, H., 1985, Of strategies: Deliberate and emergent, *Strategic Management Journal* 6: 257–72.

17. Monks, A. G., & Minow, N., 2001, *Corporate Governance*, 2nd ed. (Malden, MA: Blackwell).

18. Intel Corp., www.intel.com/intel/finance/corp_gov.html.

19. For example, see The best (& worst) managers of the year, 2003, *BusinessWeek*, January 13: 58–92; and Lavelle, M., 2003, Rogues of the year, *Time*, January 6: 33–45.

20. Handy, C., 2002, What's a business for? *Harvard Business Review* 80 (12): 49–55.

21. Stakeholder symbiosis, 1998, *Fortune*, March 30: S2.

22. For a definitive, recent discussion of the stakeholder concept, refer to Freeman, R. E., & McVae, J., 2001, A stakeholder approach to strategic management, in Hitt, M. A., Freeman, R. E., & Harrison, J. S., eds., *Handbook of Strategic Management* (Malden, MA: Blackwell), 189–207.

23. Atkinson, A. A., Waterhouse, J. H., & Wells, R. B., 1997, A stakeholder approach to strategic performance measurement, *Sloan Management Review* 39 (3): 25–38.

24. For an insightful discussion on the role of business in society, refer to Handy, op. cit.

25. Stakeholder symbiosis. op. cit., p. S3.

26. Rucci, A. J., Kirn, S. P., & Quinn, R. T., 1998, The employee-customer-profit chain at Sears, *Harvard Business Review* 76 (1): 82–97.

27. An excellent theoretical discussion on stakeholder activity is Rowley, T. J., & Moldoveanu, M., 2003, When will stakeholder groups act? An interest and identity-based model of stakeholder group mobilization, *Academy of Management Review* 28 (2): 204–19. A comprehensive work on current debates in CSR can be found in, Crane, A., McWilliams, A., Matten, D., Moon, J., & Siegel, D.S., eds., 2008, *The Oxford Handbook of Corporate Social Responsibility* (Oxford University Press).

28. Thomas, J. G., 2000, Macroenvironmental forces, in Helms, M. M., ed., *Encyclopedia of Management*, 4th ed. (Farmington Hills, MI: Gale Group), 516–20.

29. This discussion draws on Austin, J. E., 2000, Measuring a triple bottom line, *Leader to Leader*, Fall: 51.

30. Funk, K., 2003, Sustainability and performance, *MIT Sloan Management Review* 44 (2): 65–70.

31. The company's website, www.suncor.ca, reports on a range of social and environmental initiatives.

32. Senge, P. M., 1990, The leader's new work: Building learning organizations, *Sloan Management Review* 32 (1): 7–23.

33. Barkema, G. G., Baum, A. C., & Mannix, E. A., 2002, Management challenges in a new time, *Academy of Management Journal* 45 (5): 916–30.

34. This section draws on a variety of sources, including Tetenbaum, T. J., 1998, Shifting paradigms: From Newton to chaos, *Organizational Dynamics* 26 (4): 21–33; Ulrich, D., 1998, A new mandate for human resources, *Harvard Business Review* 76 (1): 125–35; and Hitt, M. A., 2000, The new frontier: Transformation of management for the new millennium, *Organizational Dynamics* 28 (2): 7–17.

35. Garten, J. E., 2001, *The Mind of the C.E.O.* (New York: Basic Books).

36. An interesting discussion on the impact of AIDS on the global economy is found in Rosen, S., 2003, AIDS *is* your business, *Harvard Business Review* 81 (2): 80–87.

37. Ulrich, D., 1998, Intellectual capital: Competence 3 commitment, *Strategic Management Journal* 39 (2): 15–26.

38. Rivette, K. G., & Kline, D., 2000, Discovering new value in intellectual property, *Harvard Business Review* 78 (1): 54–66.

39. For an interesting perspective on the role of middle managers in the strategic management process, refer to Huy, Q. H., 2001, In praise of middle managers, *Harvard Business Review* 79 (8): 72–81.

40. Senge, 1996, op. cit., pp. 41–58.

41. Helgesen, S., 1996, Leading from the grass roots, in Hesselbein, F., Goldsmith, M., & Beckhard, R., eds., *The Leader of the Future* (San Francisco: Jossey-Bass), 19–24.

42. Wetlaufer, S., 1999, Organizing for empowerment: An interview with AES's Roger Sant and Dennis Blake, *Harvard Business Review* 77 (1): 110–26.

43. Kets de Vries, M. F. R., 1998, Charisma in action: The transformational abilities of Virgin's Richard Branson and ABB's Percy Barnevik, *Organizational Dynamics* 26 (3): 7–21.

44. Hammonds, K. H., 2000, The next agenda, *Fast Company*, April: 140.

45. Our discussion draws on a variety of sources. These include Lipton, M., 1996, Demystifying the development of an organizational vision, *Sloan Management Review* 37 (4): 83–92; Bart, C. K., 2000, Lasting inspiration, *CA Magazine*, May: 49–50; and Quigley, J. V., 1994, Vision: How leaders develop it, share it, and sustain it, *Business Horizons*, September–October: 37–40.

46. Lipton, op. cit.

47. Quigley, op. cit.

48. Ibid.

49. Lipton, op. cit. Additional pitfalls are addressed in this article.

50. Company records.

51. Lipton, op. cit.

52. Sexton, D. A., & Van Aukun, P. M., 1985, A longitudinal study of small business strategic planning, *Journal of Small Business Management*, January: 8–15, cited in Lipton, op. cit.

53. Ibid.

Chapter 2

1. Lumber industry information gathered from the following sources: Ebner, D., 2008, Forestry returns suffer, *The Globe and Mail*, July 2008: B6; Ebner, D., Ease obstacles to consolidation, report urges, *The Globe and Mail*, June 4: B5; Meissner, D., 2008, Mill closings sap lifeblood from towns, *The Globe and Mail*, June 23: A5; Forest Products Association of Canada website and company annual reports.

2. Hamel, G., & Prahalad, C. K., 1994, *Competing for the Future* (Boston: HBS Press).

3. Drucker, P. F., 1994, Theory of the business, *Harvard Business Review* 72: 95–104.

4. The example of Novell draws on Pickering, C. I., 1998, Sorry … Try again next year, *Forbes ASAP*, February 23: 82–83.

5. For an insightful discussion on managers' assessment of the external environment, refer to Sutcliffe, K. M., & Weber, K., 2003, The high cost of accurate knowledge, *Harvard Business Review* 81 (5): 74–86.

6. Charitou, C. D., & Markides, C. C., 2003, Responses to disruptive strategic innovation, *MIT Sloan Management Review* 44 (2): 55–64.

7. Our discussion of scanning, monitoring, competitive intelligence, and forecasting concepts draws on several sources. These include Fahey, L., & Narayanan, V. K., 1983, *Macroenvironmental Analysis for Strategic*

Management (St. Paul, MN: West); Lorange, P., Scott, F. S., & Ghoshal, S., 1986, *Strategic Control* (St. Paul, MN: West); Ansoff, H. I., 1984, *Implementing Strategic Management* (Englewood Cliffs, NJ: Prentice Hall); and Schreyogg, G., & Stienmann, H., 1987, Strategic control: A new perspective, *Academy of Management Review* 12: 91–103.

8. Elenkov, D. S., 1997, Strategic uncertainty and environmental scanning: The case for institutional influences on scanning behavior, *Strategic Management Journal* 18: 287–302.

9. For an interesting perspective on environmental scanning in emerging economies, see May, R. C., Stewart, W. H., & Sweo, R., 2000, Environmental scanning behavior in a transitional economy: Evidence from Russia, *Academy of Management Journal* 43 (3): 403–27.

10. Browne, Sir John, The new agenda, Keynote speech delivered to the World Petroleum Congress in Calgary, Alberta, June 13, 2000.

11. Bowles, J., 1997, Key issues for the automotive industry CEOs, *Fortune*, August 18: S3.

12. Walters, B. A., & Priem, R. L., 1999, Business strategy and CEO intelligence acquisition, *Competitive Intelligence Review* 10 (2): 15–22.

13. Prior, V., 1999, The language of competitive intelligence, Part 4, *Competitive Intelligence Review* 10 (1): 84–87.

14. Zahra, S. A., & Charples, S. S., 1993, Blind spots in competitive analysis, *Academy of Management Executive* 7 (2): 7–27.

15. Wolfenson, J., 1999, The world in 1999: A battle for corporate honesty, *The Economist Publications* 38: 13–30.

16. Drucker, P. F., 1997, The future that has already happened, *Harvard Business Review* 75 (6): 22.

17. Evans, P. B., & Wurster, T. S., 1997, Strategy and the new economics of information, *Harvard Business Review* 75 (5): 71–82.

18. Fahey & Narayanan, op. cit., p. 41.

19. Courtney, H., Kirkland, J., & Viguerie, P., 1997, Strategy under uncertainty, *Harvard Business Review* 75 (6): 66–79.

20. Odlyzko, A., 2003, False hopes, *Red Herring*, March: 31.

21. Martin, R., 2002, The oracles of oil, *Business 2.0*, January: 35–39; and Epstein, J., 1998, Scenario planning: An Introduction, *The Futurist*, September: 50–52.

22. Colvin, G., 1997, How to beat the boomer rush, *Fortune*, August 18: 59–63.

23. Grant, P., 2000, Developing plans to serve a graying population, *The Wall Street Journal*, October 18: B12; and Rostoks, L., 2003, The changing profile of the consumer, *Canadian Grocer*, March: 32.

24. Walgreen's, Inc., 2000, annual report, 20.

25. Foot, D., & Stoffman, D., 1996, *Boom, Bust & Echo: How to Profit from the Coming Demographic Shift* (Toronto: Macfarlane Walter & Ross).

26. Peterson, R., 1999, *Global Entrepreneurship Monitor*, Canadian National Executive Report.

27. Challenger, J., 2000, Women's corporate rise has reduced relocations, *Lexington* (KY) *Herald-Leader*, October 29: D1.

28. Peterson, op. cit.; Challenger, op. cit.; and OECD Conference on women Entrepreneurs in SMEs: A Major Force in Innovation and Job Creation, Paris, 1998.

29. Watkins, M. D., 2003, Government games, *MIT Sloan Management Review* 44 (2): 91–95.

30. Gillies, J., 2001, Globalization and Canadian economic and industrial strategy in the twenty-first century, in Wesson, T., ed., *Canada and the New World Economic Order* (Toronto: Captus Press), 178–201.

31. Business ready for Internet revolution, 1999, *Financial Times*, May 21: 17.

32. The Internet example draws on Bernasek, A., 2000, How the broadband adds up, *Fortune*, October 9: 28, 30; and Kromer, E., B2B or not B2B? *UW Alumni Magazine:* 10–19.

33. Ginsburg, J., 2000, Letting the free market clear the air, *BusinessWeek*, November 6: 200, 204.

34. Smith, G., Wheatley, J., & Green, J., 2000, Car power, *BusinessWeek*, October 23: 72–80.

35. Mellgren, D., 2000, Norwegian ships relied on in global disasters, *Lexington* (KY) *Herald-Leader*, November 6: A8.

36. Goll, I., & Rasheed, M. A., 1997, Rational decision-making and firm performance: The moderating role of environment, *Strategic Management Journal* 18: 583–91.

37. This discussion draws heavily on Porter, M. E., 1980, *Competitive Strategy* (chap. 1) (New York: Free Press).

38. Ibid.

39. Fryer, B., 2001, Leading through rough times: An Interview with Novell's Eric Schmidt, *Harvard Business Review* 78 (5): 117–23.

40. Wise, R., & Baumgarter, P., 1999, Go downstream: The new profit imperative in manufacturing, *Harvard Business Review* 77 (5): 133–41.

41. Salman, W. A., 2000, The new economy is stronger than you think, *Harvard Business Review* 77 (6): 99–106; The B2B Tool That Really Is Changing the World., Time Inc.

42. Mudambi, R., & Helper, S., 1998, The "close but adversarial" model of supplier relations in the U.S. auto industry, *Strategic Management Journal* 19: 775–92.

43. Tischler, L., 2002. IBM: Manager Jam, *Fast Company*, October: 48.

44. Kumar, N., 1996, The power of trust in manufacturer-retailer relationship, *Harvard Business Review* 74 (6): 92–110.

45. Brandenburger, A., & Nalebuff, B. J., 1995, The right game: Use game theory to shape strategy, *Harvard Business Review* 73 (4): 57–71.

46. The discussion draws heavily on McGahan, A., 2004. How industries change, *Harvard Business Review*, 82 (10): 87–94.

47. Peteraf, M., & Shanly, M., 1997, Getting to know you: A theory of strategic group identity, *Strategic Management Journal* 18 (Special Issue): 165–86.

48. An interesting scholarly perspective on strategic groups may be found in Dranove, D., Perteraf, M., & Shanly, M., 1998, Do strategic groups exist? An economic framework for analysis, *Strategic Management Journal* 19 (11): 1029–44.

49. This section draws on several sources, including Kerwin, K. R., & Haughton, K., 1997, Can Detroit make cars that baby boomers like? *BusinessWeek*, December 1: 134–48; and Taylor, A., III, 1994, The new golden age of autos, *Fortune*, April 4: 50–66.

50. Csere, C., 2001, Supercar supermarket, *Car and Driver*, January: 118–27.

51. Healey, J. R., 1999, Groomed so as not to marry, *USA Today*, August 6: B1.

52. Csere, op. cit.; and Pandolfi, A., 2003, Auto and truck industry, *Value Line*, March 7: 101.

Chapter 3

1. Keenan, G., 2005, Auto parts makers heading for a fiscal smash-up, *The Globe and Mail*, March 11: B1; GM scraps new car platform intended for Oshawa plant, *The Globe and Mail*, March 22: B1; Linamar revs up for five-year spending blitz, *The Globe and Mail*, April 8: B1; and Canada's auto labour advantage evaporates, *The Globe and Mail*, May 27: B1.

2. Our discussion of the value chain will draw on Porter, M. E., 1985, *Competitive Advantage* (New York: Free Press), chap. 2.

3. Dyer, J. H., 1996, Specialized supplier networks as a source of competitive advantage: Evidence from the auto industry, *Strategic Management Journal* 17: 271–91.

4. For an insightful perspective on value-chain analysis, refer to Stabell, C. B., & Fjeldstad, O. D., 1998, Configuring value for competitive advantage: On chains, shops, and networks, *Strategic Management Journal* 19: 413–37. The authors develop concepts of value chains, value shops, and value networks to extend the value-creation logic across a broad range of industries. Their work builds on the seminal contributions of Porter, 1985, op. cit. and others who have addressed how firms create value through key interrelationships among value-creating activities.

5. Ibid.

6. Maynard, M., 1999, Toyota promises custom order in 5 days, *USA Today*, August 6: B1.

7. Shaw Industries, 1999, annual report, pp. 14–15.

8. Fisher, M. L., 1997, What is the right supply chain for your product? *Harvard Business Review* 75 (2): 105–16.

9. Jackson, M., 2001, Bringing a dying brand back to life, *Harvard Business Review* 79 (5): 53–61.

10. Anderson, J. C., & Nmarus, J. A., 2003, Selectively pursuing more of your customer's business, *MIT Sloan Management Review* 44 (3): 42–50.

11. Berggren, E., & Nacher, T., 2000, Why good ideas go bust, *Management Review*, February: 32–36.

12. Brown, J., 2000, Service, please, *BusinessWeek* E. Biz, October 23: EB 48–50.

13. Imperato, G., 1998, How to give good feedback, *Fast Company*, September: 144–56.

14. Bensaou, B. M., & Earl, M., 1998, The right mindset for managing information technology, *Harvard Business Review* 96 (5): 118–28.

15. Williams, D.H., 2004, The strategic implication of Wal-Mart's RFID mandate, *Directions Magazine*, July 29; Wal-Mart RFID plans change, *RFid Gazette*, February 27, 2007.

16. Ulrich, D., 1998, A new mandate for human resources, *Harvard Business Review* 96 (1): 124–34.

17. Wood, J., 2003, Sharing jobs and working from home: The new face of the airline industry, *AviationCareer.net*, February 21.

18. Follow AT&T's lead in this tactic to retain "plateaued" employees, n.d., *Recruitment & Retention:* 1.

19. For a cautionary note on the use of IT, refer to McAfee, A., 2003, When too much IT knowledge is a dangerous thing, *MIT Sloan Management Review* 44 (2): 83–90.

20. Rivette, K. G., & Kline, D., 2000, Discovering new value in intellectual property, *Harvard Business Review* 78 (1): 54–66.

21. Collis, D. J., & Montgomery, C. A., 1995, Competing on resources: Strategy in the 1990's, *Harvard Business Review* 73 (4): 119–28; and Barney, J., 1991, Firm resources and sustained competitive advantage, *Journal of Management* 17 (1): 99–120.

22. Barney, 1991, op. cit.; Collis, D. J., & Montgomery, C. A., 2005, *Corporate Strategy* (Boston: McGraw-Hill); and Grant, R., 1991, *Contemporary Strategy Analysis* (Cambridge: Blackwell Business).

23. Barney, J. B., 1986, Types of competition and the theory of strategy: Towards an integrative framework, *Academy of Management Review* 11 (4): 791–800.

24. Harley-Davidson, 1993, annual report.

25. Dutta, S., Narasimhan, O., & Rajiv S., 2005, Conceptualizing and measuring capabilities: Methodology and empirical application, *Strategic Management Journal*, 26 (3): 277–286; Lorenzoni, G., & Lipparini, A., 1999, The leveraging of interfirm relationships as a distinctive organizational capability: A longitudinal study, *Strategic Management Journal* 20: 317–38.

26. Collins, J., 1997, The most creative product ever, *Inc.*, May: 75–78.

27. Barney, 1991, op. cit.

28. Barney, 1986, op. cit. Our discussion of inimitability and substitution draws on this source.

29. Deephouse, D. L., 1999, To be different, or to be the same? It's a question (and theory) of strategic balance, *Strategic Management Journal* 20: 147–66.

30. Yeoh, P. L., & Roth, K., 1999, An empirical analysis of sustained advantage in the U.S. pharmaceutical industry: Impact of firm resources and capabilities, *Strategic Management Journal* 20: 637–53.

31. Robins, J. A., & Wiersema, M. F., 2000, Strategies for unstructured competitive environments: Using scarce resources to create new markets, in Bresser, R. F., et al., eds.,

Winning Strategies in a Deconstructing World (New York: John Wiley), 201–20.

32. Amit, R., & Schoemaker, J. H., 1993, Strategic assets and organizational rent, *Strategic Management Journal* 14 (1): 33–46; Collis & Montgomery, 1995, op. cit.; Coff, R. W., 1999, When competitive advantage doesn't lead to performance: The resource-based view and stakeholder bargaining power, *Organization Science* 10 (2): 119–33; and Blyler, M., & Coff, R. W., in press, Dynamic capabilities, social capital, and rent appropriation: Ties that split pies, *Strategic Management Journal*.

33. Munk, N., 1998, The new organization man, *Fortune*, March 16: 62–74.

34. Coff, R. W., op. cit.

35. We have focused our discussion on how internal stakeholders (e.g., employees, managers, and top executives) may appropriate a firm's profits (or rents). For an interesting discussion of how a firm's innovations may be appropriated by external stakeholders (e.g., customers, suppliers) as well as competitors, refer to Grant, R. M., 2002, *Contemporary Strategy Analysis*, 4th ed. (Malden, MA: Blackwell Business), 335–40.

36. Luehrman, T. A., 1997, What's it worth? A general manager's guide to valuation, *Harvard Business Review* 45 (3): 132–42.

37. See, for example, Kaplan, R. S., & Norton, D. P., 1992, The balanced scorecard—Measures that drive performance, *Harvard Business Review* 69 (1): 71–79.

38. Hitt, M. A., Ireland, R. D., & Stadter, G., 1982, Functional importance of company performance: Moderating effects of grand strategy and industry type, *Strategic Management Journal* 3: 315–30.

39. Home Depot, 2007, annual report.

40. Berner, R., 2000, Procter & Gamble: Just say no to drugs, *BusinessWeek*, October 9: 128.

41. Kaplan & Norton, op. cit.

42. Ibid.

43. Rucci, A. J., Kirn, S. P., & Quinn, R. T., 1998, The employee-customer-profit chain at Sears, *Harvard Business Review* 76 (1): 82–97.

Chapter 4

1. Drucker, P., 1992, The new society of organizations, *Harvard Business Review 70* (4): 44–52.

2. Swap, W., & Leonard, D., 2000, Gurus in the garage, *Harvard Business Review* 78 (6): 71–82; Hamel, G., 1999, Bringing Silicon Valley inside, *Harvard Business Review* 77 (5): 71–84; and Alley, J., 1997, Silicon Valley is the intellectual incubator of the digital age, *Fortune*, July 7: 67–74.

3. Keenan, G., Pitts, G., & Scoffield, H., 2006, A place that does not hold back its best, *The Globe and Mail*, April 25: B10.

4. Gunning for KPMG, 2003, *The Economist*, February 1: 63; Bianco, A., & Moore, P. L., 2001, Downfall: The inside story of the management fiasco at Xerox, *BusinessWeek*, May 5: 82–92; Deutsch, C. H., 2000, Moody's puts Xerox

below investment grade, *New York Times*, December 2: A1; Deutsch, C. H., 2000, The fading copier king: Xerox has failed to capitalize on its own innovations, *New York Times*, October 19: B6.

5. An acknowledged trend: The world economic survey, 1996, *The Economist*, September 28: 25–28.

6. Quinn, J. B., Anderson, P., & Finkelstein, S., 1996, Leveraging intellect, *Academy of Management Executive* 10 (3): 7–27.

7. Hamel, G., & Prahalad, C. K., 1996, Competing in the new economy: Managing out of bounds, *Strategic Management Journal* 17: 238.

8. Stewart, T. A., 1997, *Intellectual Capital: The New Wealth of Organizations* (New York: Doubleday/Currency); and Conley, J. G., & Szobocsan, J., 2001, Snow White shows the way, *Managing Intellectual Property*, June: 15–25.

9. Thomas Stewart has suggested this formula in his book *Intellectual Capital*. He provides an insightful discussion on pages 224–25, including some of the limitations of this approach to measuring intellectual capital. We recognize, of course, that during the late 1990s and in early 2000, there were some excessive market valuations of high-technology and Internet firms. For an interesting discussion of the extraordinary market valuation of Yahoo!, an Internet company, refer to Perkins, A. B., 2001, The Internet bubble encapsulated: Yahoo! *Red Herring*, April 15: 17–18.

10. Roberts, P. W., & Dowling, G. R., 2002, Corporate reputation and sustained superior financial performance, *Strategic Management Journal* 23 (12): 1077–95.

11. Conley, J. G., 2005, Intellectual capital management, Kellogg School of Management and Schulich School of Business, York University, Toronto, KS '03.

12. One of the seminal contributions on knowledge management is Becker, G. S., 1993, *Human Capital: A Theoretical and Empirical Analysis with Special Reference to Education*, 3rd ed. (Chicago: University of Chicago Press).

13. For an excellent discussion of social capital and its impact on organizational performance, refer to Nahapiet, J., & Ghoshal, S., 1998, Social capital, intellectual capital, and the organizational advantage, *Academy of Management Review* 23: 242–66.

14. Polanyi, M., 1967, *The Tacit Dimension* (Garden City, NY: Anchor Publishing).

15. Conley & Szobocsan, op. cit.

16. Barney, J. B., 1991, Firm resources and sustained competitive advantage, *Journal of Management* 17: 99–120.

17. Some of the notable books on this topic include Edvisson, L., & Malone, M. S., 1997, *Intellectual Capital: Realizing Your Company's True Value by Finding Its Hidden Brainpower* (New York: HarperBusiness); Stewart, op. cit.; and Nonaka, I., & Takeuchi, I., 1995, *The Knowledge Creating Company* (New York: Oxford University Press).

18. Stewart, T. A., 2000, Taking risk to the marketplace, *Fortune*, March 6: 424.

19. Dutton, G., 1997, Are you technologically competent? *Management Review*, November: 54–58.

20. Dess, G. G., & Picken, J. C., 1999, *Beyond Productivity* (New York: AMACOM).

21. Webber, A. M., 1998, Danger: Toxic company, *Fast Company*, November: 152–61.

22. Key to success: People, people, people, 1997, *Fortune*, October 27: 232.

23. Martin, J., 1998, So, you want to work for the best … , *Fortune*, January 12: 77.

24. Carbonara, P., 1997, Hire for attitude, train for skill, *Fast Company*, August–September: 66–67.

25. Stewart, T. A., 1996, Why value statements don't work, *Fortune*, June 10: 138.

26. Carbonara, op. cit.

27. Martin, op. cit.; Henkoff, R., 1993, Companies that train best, *Fortune*, March 22: 53–60.

28. Bartlett, C. A., & Ghoshal, S., 2002, Building competitive advantage through people, *MIT Sloan Management Review* 43 (2): 34–41.

29. Stewart, T. A., 1998, Gray flannel suit? moi? *Fortune*, March 18: 80–82.

30. Key to success: People, people, people, 1997, *Fortune*, October 27: 232.

31. The discussion of the 360-degree feedback system draws on UPS, 1997, 360-degree feedback: Coming from all sides, *Vision* (a UPS Corporation internal company publication), March: 3; Slater, R., 1994, *Get Better or Get Beaten: Thirty-one Leadership Secrets from Jack Welch* (Burr Ridge, IL: Irwin); Nexon, M., 1997, General Electric: The secrets of the finest company in the world, *L'Expansion*, July 23: 18–30; and Smith, D., 1996, Bold new directions for human resources, *Merck World* (internal company publication), October: 8.

32. Kets de Vries, M. F. R., 1998, Charisma in action: The transformational abilities of Virgin's Richard Branson and ABB's Percy Barnevik, *Organizational Dynamics*, Winter: 20.

33. One has only to consider Air Canada's pending lawsuit against WestJet or the most celebrated case of industrial espionage in recent years, wherein José Ignacio Lopez was indicted in a German court for stealing sensitive product planning documents from his former employer, General Motors, and sharing them with his executive colleagues at Volkswagen. The lawsuit was dismissed by the German courts, but Lopez and his colleagues were investigated by the U.S. Justice Department. Also, consider the recent litigation involving non-compete employment contracts and confidentiality clauses of *International Paper v. Louisiana-Pacific, Campbell Soup v. H. J. Heinz Co., and PepsiCo v. Quaker Oats's Gatorade*. In addition to retaining valuable human resources and often their valuable network of customers, firms must also protect proprietary information and knowledge. For interesting insights, refer to Carley, W. M., 1998, CEO gets hard lesson in how not to keep his lieutenants, *Wall Street Journal*, February 11: A1, A10; and Lenzner, R., &

34. Shhok, C., 1998, Whose Rolodex is it, anyway? *Forbes*, February 23: 100–103.

34. DesMarteau, K., 1999, Magna: Master of automotive innovation, *Columbia*, April: 58–60.

35. Sutherland, J., 2005, Unbeatable, Report on Business, January: 47.

36. The examples in this section draw on a variety of sources, including Lubove, S., 1998, New age capitalist, *Forbes*, April 6: 42–43; Kets de Vries, op. cit.; Pfeffer, J., 1995, Producing sustainable competitive advantage through the effective management of people, *Academy of Management Executive* 9 (1): 55–69; Vlasic, B., 2008, Honda stays true to efficient driving, *The New York Times*, August 26, C1. The concept of strategic intent is generally credited to Hamel, G., & Prahalad, C. K., 1989, Strategic intent, *Harvard Business Review* 67: 63–76.

37. Kets de Vries, op. cit., pp. 73–92.

38. Amabile, T. M., 1997, Motivating creativity in organizations: On doing what you love and loving what you do, *California Management Review*, Fall: 39–58.

39. The discussion of internal markets for human capital draws on Hamel, op. cit.

40. Pfeffer, J., 2001, Fighting the war for talent is hazardous to your organization's health, *Organizational Dynamics* 29 (4): 248–59.

41. For an insightful discussion on strategies for retaining and developing human capital, refer to Coff, R. W., 1997, Human assets and management dilemmas: Coping with hazards on the road to resource-based theory, *Academy of Management Review* 22 (2): 374–402.

42. Reguly, E., 2005, David versus the Goliaths, Report on Business, January: 19.

43. Galt, V., 2005, Babysitting service pays off for CIBC, *The Globe and Mail*, February 16: B10. The statistics on child care trends are drawn from Bubbar, S. E., & Aspelin, D. J., 1998, The overtime rebellion: Symptom of a bigger problem? *Academy of Management Executive* 12: 68–76. The other examples in this section are drawn from various sources, including Munk, N., 1998, The new organization man, *Fortune*, March 16: 68–72; and Hammonds, K. H., Furchgott, R., Hamm, S., & Judge, P. C., 1997, Work and family, *BusinessWeek*, September 15: 96–104.

44. The discussion draws on Adler, P. S., & Kwon, S. W., 2002, Social capital: Prospects for a new concept, *Academy of Management Review* 27 (1): 17–40.

45. Capelli, P., 2000, A market-driven approach to retaining talent, *Harvard Business Review* 78 (1): 103–13.

46. This hypothetical example draws on Peteraf, M., 1993, The cornerstones of competitive advantage, *Strategic Management Journal* 14: 179–91.

47. Wernerfelt, B., 1984, A resource-based view of the firm, *Strategic Management Journal* 5: 171–80.

48. Wysocki, B., Jr., 2000, Yet another hazard of the new economy: The Pied Piper effect, *Wall Street Journal*, March 20: A1–A16.

49. McMillan, C. J., & Jasson, E. M. V., 2001, Technology and the new economy: A Canadian strategy,

in Wesson, T., ed., *Canada and the New World Economic Order* (Toronto: Captus Press).

50. Buckman, R. C., 2000, Tech defectors from Microsoft resettle together, *Wall Street Journal*, October: B1–B6.

51. For an insightful discussion on the creation of social capital, see Bolino, M. C., Turnley, W. H., & Bloodgood, J. M., 2002, Citizenship behavior and the creation of social capital in organizations, *Academy of Management Review* 27 (4): 505–22.

52. An insightful discussion of the interorganizational aspects of social capital can be found in Dyer, J. H., & Singh, H., 1998, The relational view: Cooperative strategy and sources of interorganizational competitive advantage, *Academy of Management Review* 23: 66–79.

53. Prusak, L., & Cohen, D., 2001, How to invest in social capital, *Harvard Business Review* 79 (6): 86–93.

54. Leonard, D., & Straus, S., 1997, Putting your company's whole brain to work, *Harvard Business Review* 75 (4): 110–22.

55. Leana, C. R., & Van Buren, H. J., III, 1999, Organizational social capital and employment practices, *Academy of Management Review* 24: 538–55.

56. Prusak & Cohen, op. cit., pp. 86–93.

57. Lei, D., Slocum, J., & Pitts, R. A., 1999, Designing organizations for competitive advantage: The power of unlearning and learning, *Organizational Dynamics*, Winter: 24–38.

58. For an innovative study on how firms share knowledge with competitors and the performance implications, read Spencer, J. W., 2003, Firms' knowledge sharing strategies in the global innovation system: Empirical evidence from the flat panel display industry, *Strategic Management Journal* 24 (3): 217–35.

59. The examples of Accenture and Access Health draw on Hansen, M. T., Nohria, N., & Tierney, T., 1999, What's your strategy for managing knowledge? *Harvard Business Review* 77 (2): 106–18.

60. Ibid.; and Magretta, J., 1998, The power of virtual integration: An interview with Dell Computer's Michael Dell, *Harvard Business Review* 76 (3): 73–84.

61. Capelli, op. cit.

62. Koudsi, S., 2000, Actually, it is brain surgery, *Fortune*, March 20: 233.

63. The ensuing discussion draws on Conley, 2005, op. cit.; Conley & Szobocsan, 2001, op. cit.; Greenspan, A., 2004, Intellectual property rights, The Federal Reserve Board, Remarks by the chairman, February 27; and Teece, D. J., 1998, Capturing value from knowledge assets, *California Management Review* 40 (3): 54–79.

Chapter 5

1. Davis, J. E., 1994, Can The Limited fix itself? *Fortune*, October 17: 161–72.

2. The discussion draws on Cott Corporation: Private label in the 1990s, Harvard Business School Case #9-594-031; Cott Corporation, *News Releases*, March 18, 1999;

May 3, 2000; November 12, 2001; Bloom, R., 2005, Cott can't handle high demand, sees profit fizzle, *The Globe and Mail*, February 3: B7; Bnoguore, T., 2006, Cott hopes shakeup gives shares some fizz; analysts divided on impact of changes, *The Globe and Mail*, August 10: B11; Georgiades, A., 2007, Cott shares dive to 52-week low after firm cuts profit forecast, *The Globe and Mail*, September 21: B14; and Partridge, J., 2008, Cott stock surges on latest CEO shuffle, *The Globe and Mail*, March 25: B3;

3. For a perspective on the need for adapting competitive strategies to competitive conditions, refer to Christenson, C. M., 2001, The past and the future of competitive strategy, *Harvard Business Review* 42 (2): 105–9; and D'Aveni, R. A., 1999, Strategic supremacy through disruption and dominance, *Sloan Management Review* 40 (3): 117–35.

4. An excellent overview of the various schools of strategic management is provided in Mintzberg, H., Ahlstrand, B., & Lampel, J., 1998, *Strategy Safari: A Guided Tour through the Wilds of Strategic Management* (New York: The Free Press).

5. Porter, M. E., 1980, *Competitive Strategy* (New York: McGraw-Hill). For a recent perspective by Porter on competitive strategy, refer to Porter, M. E., 1996, What is strategy? *Harvard Business Review* 74 (6): 61–78.

6. Miller, A., & Dess, G. G., 1993, Assessing Porter's model in terms of its generalizability, accuracy, and simplicity, *Journal of Management Studies* 30 (4): 553–85.

7. For a scholarly discussion and analysis of the concept of competitive parity, refer to Powell, T. C., 2003, Varieties of competitive parity, *Strategic Management Journal* 24 (1): 61–86.

8. Rao, A. R., Bergen, M. E., & Davis, S., 2000, How to fight a price war, *Harvard Business Review* 78 (2): 107–20.

9. Whalen, C. J., Pascual, A. M., Lowery, T., & Muller, J., 2001, The top 25 managers, *BusinessWeek*, January 8: 63.

10. For an interesting perspective on the need for creative strategies, refer to Hamel, G., & Prahalad, C. K., 1994, *Competing for the Future* (Boston: Harvard Business School Press).

11. Symonds, W. C., Arndt, M., Palmer, A. T., Weintraub, A., & Holmes, S., 2001, Trying to break the choke hold, *BusinessWeek*, January 22: 38–39.

12. For a perspective on the sustainability of competitive advantages, refer to Barney, J., 1995, Looking inside for competitive advantage, *Academy of Management Executive* 9 (4): 49–61.

13. Thornton, E., 2001, Why e-brokers are broker and broker, *BusinessWeek*, January 22: 94.

14. Koretz, G., 2001, E-commerce: The buyer wins, *BusinessWeek*, January 8: 30.

15. MacMillan, I., & McGrath, R., 1997, Discovering new points of differentiation, *Harvard Business Review* 75 (4): 133–45; Wise, R., & Baumgarter, P., 1999, Beating the clock: Corporate responses to rapid change in the PC industry, *California Management Review* 42 (1): 8–36.

16. For a discussion on quality in terms of a company's software and information systems, refer to Prahalad, C. K., & Krishnan, M. S., 1999, The new meaning of quality in the information age, *Harvard Business Review* 77 (5): 109–18.

17. Taylor, A., III, 2001, Can you believe Porsche is putting its badge on this car? *Fortune*, February 19: 168–72.

18. Ward, S., Light, L., & Goldstine, J., 1999, What high-tech managers need to know about brands, *Harvard Business Review* 77 (4): 85–95.

19. Zesiger, S., 1999, Silicon speed, *Fortune*, September 13: 120.

20. Whalen et al., op. cit.

21. Rosenfeld, J., 2000, Unit of one, *Fast Company*, April: 98.

22. Markides, C., 1997, Strategic innovation, *Sloan Management Review* 38 (3): 9–23.

23. Dess, G. G., & Picken, J. C., 1997, *Mission Critical* (Burr Ridge, IL: Irwin Professional Publishing), 84.

24. The authors would like to thank Scott Droege, a faculty member at Mississippi State University, for providing this example.

25. Symonds, W. C., 2000, Can Gillette regain its voltage? *BusinessWeek*, October 16: 102–4.

26. Gadiesh, O., & Gilbert, J. L., 1998, Profit pools: A fresh look at strategy, *Harvard Business Review* 76 (3): 139–58.

27. Colvin, G., 2000, Beware: You could soon be selling soybeans, *Fortune*, November 13: 80.

28. Straus, M., 2005, Staples courts small business with more value, less Britney, *The Globe and Mail*, February 7: B6.

29. Whalen et al., op. cit., p. 63.

30. Bloom, R., 2005, Keg chews up competition even as industry sales drop, *The Globe and Mail*, February 7: B5.

31. Hall, W. K., 1980, Survival strategies in a hostile environment, *Harvard Business Review* 58: 75–87; on the paint and allied products industry, see Dess, G. G., & Davis, P. S., 1984, Porter's (1980) generic strategies as determinants of strategic group membership and organizational performance, *Academy of Management Journal* 27: 467–88; for the Korean electronics industry, see Kim, L., & Lim, Y., 1988, Environment, generic strategies, and performance in a rapidly developing country: A taxonomic approach, *Academy of Management Journal* 31: 802–27; Wright, P., Hotard, D., Kroll, M., Chan, P., & Tanner, J., 1990, Performance and multiple strategies in a firm: Evidence from the apparel industry, in Dean, B. V., & Cassidy, J. C., eds., *Strategic Management: Methods and Studies* (Amsterdam: Elsevier-North Holland), 93–110; and Wright, P., Kroll, M., Tu, H., & Helms, M., 1991, Generic strategies and business performance: An empirical study of the screw machine products industry, *British Journal of Management* 2: 1–9.

32. Gilmore, J. H., & Pine, B. J., II, 1997, The four faces of customization, *Harvard Business Review* 75 (1): 91–101.

33. Ibid.

34. Goodstein, L. D., & Butz, H. E., 1998, Customer value: The linchpin of organizational change, *Organizational Dynamics*, Summer: 21–34.

35. Gadiesh & Gilbert, op. cit., pp. 139–58.

36. This example draws on Dess, G. G., & Picken, J. C., 1999, Creating competitive (dis)advantage: Learning from Food Lion's freefall, *Academy of Management Executive* 13 (3): 97–111.

37. Mintzberg et al., op. cit.

38. Dickson, P. R., 1994, *Marketing Management* (Fort Worth, TX: Dryden Press), 293; Day, G. S., 1981, The product life cycle: Analysis and application, *Journal of Marketing Research* 45: 60–67.

39. Bearden, W. O., Ingram, T. N., & LaForge, R. W., 1995, *Marketing Principles and Practices* (Burr Ridge, IL: Irwin).

40. MacMillan, I. C., 1985, Preemptive strategies, in Guth, W. D., ed., *Handbook of Business Strategy* (Boston: Warren, Gorham & Lamont), 9-1–9-22; Pearce, J. A., & Robinson, R. B., 2000, *Strategic Management*, 7th ed. (New York: McGraw-Hill); Dickson, op. cit., pp. 295–96.

41. Bartlett, C. A., & Ghoshal, S., 2000, Going global: Lessons for late movers, *Harvard Business Review* 78 (2): 132–42.

42. Berkowitz, E. N., Kerin, R. A., & Hartley, S. W., 2000, *Marketing*, 6th ed. (New York: McGraw-Hill).

43. MacMillan, op. cit.

44. Brooker, K., 2001, A game of inches, *Fortune*, February 5: 98–100.

45. MacMillan, op. cit.

46. Berkowitz et al., op. cit.

47. Bearden et al., op. cit.

48. The discussion of these four strategies draws on MacMillan, op. cit.; Berkowitz et al., op. cit.; and Bearden et al., op. cit.

49. Augustine, N. R., 1997, Reshaping an industry: Lockheed Martin's survival story, *Harvard Business Review* 75 (3): 83–94.

50. Hambrick, D. C., & Schecter, S. M., 1983, Turnaround strategies for mature industrial product business units, *Academy of Management Journal* 26 (2): 231–48.

51. Mullaney, T. J., 2002, The wizard of Intuit, *BusinessWeek*, October 28: 60–63.

Chapter 6

1. The discussion on BCE draws on Willis, A., 2007, Michael Sabia's Legacy, *The Globe and Mail*, September 22: B7; Laver, R., 2000, BCE divides to conquer, *Maclean's*, February 7: 38–39; Avery, S., 2004, Sabia lays out a new BCE: Lower costs, more wireless, *The Globe and Mail*, December 16: B1–B7; Financial Post 500, 1999, *Financial Post*, June; and Avery, S., 2004, Bell Canada boosts consolidated revenue, *The Globe and Mail*, November 4: B1, B24.

2. Pare, T. P., 1994, The new merger boom, *Fortune*, November 28: 96.

3. The relationship and divergence of interests between individual shareholders and managers have attracted significant attention and have yielded many powerful insights through what has been called "agency theory." (Jensen, M., & Meckling, W., 1976, Theory of the firm:

Managerial behavior, agency costs, and ownership structure, *Journal of Financial Economics* 3: 305–60; Fama, E., 1980, Agency problems and the theory of the firm, *Journal of Political Economy* 88: 288–307.) Briefly, agency theory considers the reality that frequently, if not always, the interests of managers (i.e., agents) deviate from those of owners/shareholders (i.e., principals). Diversification serves those interests differently. Growth, expansion, and diversification create a larger firm (whether more or less profitable), higher salaries and other forms of compensation, more prestige, more perks, and even less probability of loss of employment for its managers. Whether the owners/shareholders would undertake many of those ventures, given their risk profiles, is questionable; typically, the shareholders do not possess the means or the information to properly assess the merits of each proposed venture nor the time to closely monitor managers, who are better informed about the affairs of the business. Diversification can provide managers with substantial personal benefits while causing declines in shareholders' wealth.

4. Our discussion draws on a variety of sources, including Goold, M., & Campbell, A., 1998, Desperately seeking synergy, *Harvard Business Review* 76 (5): 131–43; Porter, M. E., 1987, From competitive advantage to corporate strategy, *Harvard Business Review* 65 (3): 43–59; and Hitt, M. A., Ireland, R. D., & Hoskisson, R. E., 2001, *Strategic Management: Competitiveness and Globalization*, 4th ed. (Cincinnati, OH: South-Western).

5. Collis, D. J., & Montgomery, C. A., 1987, *Corporate Strategy: Resources and the Scope of the Firm* (New York: McGraw-Hill).

6. This imagery of the corporation as a tree and related discussion draws on Prahalad, C. K., & Hamel, G., 1990, The core competence of the corporation, *Harvard Business Review* 68 (3): 79–91. Parts of this section also draw on Picken, J. C., & Dess, G. G., 1997, *Mission Critical* (Burr Ridge, IL: Irwin Professional Publishing), chap. 5.

7. This section draws on Prahalad & Hamel, op. cit.; and Porter, op. cit.

8. Harley-Davidson, 1993, annual report.

9. Collis, D. J., & Montgomery, C. A., 1998, Creating corporate advantage, *Harvard Business Review* 76 (3): 70–83.

10. Henricks, M., 1994, VF seeks global brand dominance, *Apparel Industry Magazine*, August: 21–40; VF Corporation, 1993, 1st quarter, corporate summary report, 1993 VF Annual Report.

11. Lowry, T., 2001, Media, *BusinessWeek*, January 8: 100–1.

12. The Tribune Company, 1999, annual report.

13. Hill, A., & Hargreaves, D., 2001, Turbulent times for GE-Honeywell deal, *Financial Times*, February 28: 26.

14. This discussion draws on Hrebiniak, L. G., & Joyce, W. F., 1984, *Implementing Strategy* (New York: MacMillan); Oster, S. M., 1994, *Modern Competitive Analysis* (New York: Oxford University Press); and Hax, A. C., & Majluf, N. S., 1991, *The Strategy Concept and Process: A Pragmatic Approach* (Englewood Cliffs, NJ: Prentice Hall), 139.

15. Anwar, H., 2005, Diamond firm's results shine with newly acquired retailer, *The Globe and Mail*, March 10: B5.

16. This discussion draws on Oster, S. M., 1994, *Modern Competitive Analysis*, 2nd ed. (New York: Oxford University Press); and Harrigan, K., 1986, Matching vertical integration strategies to competitive conditions, *Strategic Management Journal* 7 (6): 535–56.

17. Bettis, R. A., Bradley, S. P., & Hamel, G., 1992, Outsourcing and industrial decline, *Academy of Management Executive* 6 (1): 7–22.

18. For a scholarly explanation on how transaction costs determine the boundaries of a firm, see Oliver E. Williamson's pioneering books *Markets and Hierarchies: Analysis and Antitrust Implications* (New York: Free Press, 1975) and *The Economic Institutions of Capitalism* (New York: Free Press, 1985).

19. Campbell, A., Goold, M., & Alexander, M., 1995, Corporate strategy: The quest for parenting advantage, *Harvard Business Review* 73 (2): 120–32; and Picken & Dess, op. cit.

20. Anslinger, P. A., & Copeland, T. E., 1996, Growth through acquisition: A fresh look, *Harvard Business Review* 74 (1): 126–35.

21. Willis, A., 2005, Boeing play will follow Onex's familiar script, *The Globe and Mail*, February 24: B15; and Kalawsky, K., & Kirby, J., 2005, Onex buys Boeing plants for $1.5B, *National Post*, February 23: FP1–FP16.

22. This section draws on Porter, op. cit.; and Hambrick, D. C., 1985, Turnaround strategies, in Guth, W. D., ed., *Handbook of Business Strategy* (Boston: Warren, Gorham & Lamont), 10-1–10-32.

23. There is an important difference between companies that are operated for a long-term profit and those that are bought and sold for short-term gains. The latter are sometimes referred to as "holding companies" and are generally more concerned about financial issues than strategic issues.

24. Casico, W. F., 2002, Strategies for responsible restructuring, *Academy of Management Executive* 16 (3): 80–91; and Singh, H., 1993, Challenges in researching corporate restructuring, *Journal of Management Studies* 30 (1): 147–72.

25. Strauss, M., 2008, Shoppers shrugs off recession worries; Drugstore chain posts record profit gains, issues bullish forecast for 2008, *The Globe and Mail*, February 6: B6; Reguly, E., 2007, A peek into the pages of KKR's playbook, *The Globe and Mail*, April 27, B8; www.kkr.com; www.shoppersdrugmart.ca;.

26. Hax & Majluf, op. cit. By 1979, 45 percent of Fortune 500 companies employed some form of portfolio analysis, according to Haspelagh, P., 1982, Portfolio planning: Uses and limits, *Harvard Busines Review* 60: 58–73. A later study conducted in 1993 found that over 40 percent of the respondents used portfolio analysis techniques, but the level of usage was expected to increase to more than 60 percent in the near future: Rigby, D. K., 1994, Managing the management tools, *Planning Review*, September–October: 20–24.

27. Goold, M., & Luchs, K., 1993, Why diversify? Four decades of management thinking, *Academy of Management Executive* 7 (3): 7–25.

28. Other approaches include the industry attractiveness–business strength matrix developed jointly by General Electric and McKinsey and Company, the life-cycle matrix developed by Arthur D. Little, and the profitability matrix proposed by Marakon. For an extensive review, refer to Hax & Majluf, op. cit., pp. 182–94.

29. Porter, op. cit., pp. 49–52.

30. Collis, D. J., 1995, Portfolio planning at Ciba-Geigy and the Newport investment proposal, Harvard Business School Case No. 9-795-040. Novartis AG was created in 1996 by the merger of Ciba-Geigy and Sandoz.

31. Buzzell, R. D., & Gale, B. T., 1987, *The PIMS Principles: Linking Strategy to Performance* (New York: Free Press); and Miller, A., & Dess, G. G., 1996, *Strategic Management*, 2nd ed. (New York: McGraw-Hill).

32. Seeger, J., 1984, Reversing the images of BCG's growth share matrix, *Strategic Management Journal* 5 (1): 93–97.

33. Picken & Dess, op. cit.; Cabot Corporation, 2001, 10-Q filing, Securities and Exchange Commission, May 14.

34. Koudsi, S., 2001, Remedies for an economic hangover, *Fortune*, June 25: 130–39.

35. Perkins, T., 2007, CEO urges action on takeover frenzy, *The Globe and Mail*, May 4: B5; Martin, R. & Nixon, G., 2007, Whoa, Canada: More must be done to protect companies from foreign takeovers. The country's place in the world depends on it, *The Globe and Mail*, July 2: B1.

36. Carey, D., moderator, 2000, A CEO roundtable on making mergers succeed, *Harvard Business Review* 78 (3): 146.

37. Shinal, J., 2001, Can Mike Volpi make Cisco sizzle again? *BusinessWeek*, February 26: 102–4; Kambil, A., Eselius, E. D., & Monteiro, K. A., 2000, Fast venturing: The quick way to start web businesses, *Sloan Management Review* 41 (4): 55–67; and Elstrom, P., 2001, Sorry, Cisco: The old answers won't work, *BusinessWeek*, April 30: 39.

38. Like many high-tech firms during the economic slump that began in mid-2000, Cisco Systems has experienced declining performance. On April 16, 2001, it announced that its revenues for the quarter closing April 30 would drop 5 percent from a year earlier—and a stunning 30 percent from the previous three months—to about $4.7 billion. Furthermore, Cisco announced that it would lay off 8,500 employees and take an enormous $2.5 billion charge to write down inventory. By late October 2002, its stock was trading at around $10, down significantly from its 52-week high of $70. Elstrom, op. cit., p. 39.

39. Barrett, A., 2001, Drugs, *BusinessWeek*, January 8: 112–13.

40. McArthur, K., 2005, Coors' toughest tasks are only just beginning, *The Globe and Mail*, February 2: B4.

41. Muoio, A., ed., 1998, Unit of one, *Fast Company*, September: 82.

42. This section draws on Anard, B. N., & Khanna, T., 2000, Do firms learn to create value? *Strategic Management Journal* 12 (3): 295–317; Vermeulen, F., & Barkema, H. P., 2001, Learning through acquisitions, *Academy of Management Journal* 44 (3): 457–76; Hutt, M. D., Stafford, E. R., Walker, B. A., & Reingen, P. H., 2000, Case study: Defining the strategic alliance, *Sloan Management Review* 41 (2): 51–62; and Walters, B. A., Peters, S., & Dess, G. G., 1994, Strategic alliances and joint ventures: Making them work, *Business Horizons*, 4: 5–10.

43. Leitch, C., 2005, Master of the impulse-buy attacks investors with strategic purchases, *The Globe and Mail*, February 10: B16.

44. Edmondson, G., & Reinhardt, A., 2001, From niche player to Goliath, *BusinessWeek*, March 12: 94–96.

45. Anonymous, 2006, Magna to work with IBM to create really smart cars, *Toronto Star*, September 14: C2.

46. Anonymous, 2006 Tim Hortons raises C783 million in initial offering, *Bloomberg News*, March 23; company annual reports and www.timhortons.ca.

47. Waldie, P. & Straus, M., 2007, Lululemon supplier navigates rocky shoals, *The Globe and Mail*, November 16:B3.

48. Hoskin, R. E., 1994, *Financial Accounting* (New York: Wiley).

49. We know stock options as derivative assets, i.e., "an asset whose value depends on or is derived from the value of another, the underlying asset" (Amram, M., & Kulatilaka, N., 1999, *Real Options: Managing Strategic Investment in an Uncertain World* [Boston: Harvard Business School Press], 34).

50. de Neufville, R., 2001, Real options: Dealing with uncertainty in systems planning and design, paper presented to the Fifth International Conference on Technology Policy and Innovation at the Technical University of Delft, Delft, Netherlands, June 29.

51. For an interesting discussion on why it is difficult to "kill options," refer to Royer, I., 2003, Why bad projects are so hard to kill, *Harvard Business Review* 81 (2): 48–57.

52. Triantis, A., et al., 2003, University of Maryland roundtable on real options and corporate practice, *Journal of Applied Corporate Finance* 15 (2): 8–23.

53. For a more in-depth discussion of ROA, refer to Copeland, T. E., & Keenan, P. T., 1998, Making real options real, *McKinsey Quarterly* 3; and Luehrman, T. A., 1998, Strategy as a portfolio of real options, *Harvard Business Review*, September–October.

54. Janney, J.J., Dess, G.G., 2004, Can real options analysis improve decision making? Promises and pitfalls, *Academy of Management Executive* 18 (4): 60–75.

55. Porter, op. cit., pp. 43–59.

56. Editors, 2003, The fallen, *BusinessWeek*, January 13: 80–82.

57. The Jack Welch example draws on Sellers, P., 2001, Get over yourself, *Fortune*, April 30: 76–88.

58. Polek, D., 2002, The rise and fall of Dennis Kozlowski, *BusinessWeek*, December 23: 64–77.

59. DeCloet, D., 2008, The cost of playing backup to Stronach, *The Globe and Mail*, August 12: B1.

60. This section draws on Weston, J. F., Besley, S., & Brigham, E. F., 1996, *Essentials of Managerial Finance*, 11th ed. (Fort Worth, TX: Dryden Press, Harcourt Brace), 18–20; Chakraborty, A., & Baum, C. F., 1998, Poison pills, optimal contracting and the market for corporate control: Evidence from Fortune 500 firms, *International Journal of Finance* 10 (3): 1120–38; Sundramurthy, C., 1996, Corporate governance within the context of antitakover provisions, *Strategic Management Journal* 17: 377–94; and Vicente, J. P., 2001, Toxic treatment: Poison pills proliferate as internet firms worry they've become easy marks, *Red Herring*, May 1–15: 195.

61. DeCloet, D., 2005, Ottawa urged to tie Bombardier aid, *The Globe and Mail*, March 18: B1.

Chapter 7

1. Based on information from annual reports of the companies cited; Bloom, R., 2005, Molson-Coors marriage hits the rocks fast, *The Globe and Mail*, April, 29:A1; McArthur, K., 2004, Heineken to write down value of stake in Brazilian brewery, *The Globe and Mail*, November 4: B17; and McArthur, K., 2005, Coors' toughest tasks are only just beginning, *The Globe and Mail*, February 2: B4.

2. Our discussion of globalization draws on Engardio, P., & Belton, C., 2000, Global capitalism: Can it be made to work better? *BusinessWeek*, November 6: 72–98.

3. Ibid.

4. The above discussion draws on Clifford, M. L., Engardio, P., Malkin, E., Roberts, D., & Echikson, W., 2000, Up the ladder, *BusinessWeek*, November 6: 78–84.

5. For another interesting discussion on a country perspective, refer to Makino, S., 1999, MITI Minister Kaora Yosano on reviving Japan's competitive advantages, *Academy of Management Executive* 13 (4): 8–28.

6. The following discussion draws heavily on Porter, M. E., 1990, The competitive advantage of nations, *Harvard Business Review*, March–April: 73–93.

7. Landes, D. S., 1998, *The Wealth and Poverty of Nations* (New York: W. W. Norton).

8. Part of our discussion of the motivations and risks of international expansion draws on Gregg, F. M., 1999, International strategy, in Helms, M. M., ed., *Encyclopedia of Management* (Detroit: Gale Group), 434–38.

9. These two examples are discussed, respectively, in Dawar, N., & Frost, T., 1999, Competing with giants: Survival strategies for local companies in emerging markets, *Harvard Business Review* 77 (2): 119–29; and Prahalad, C. K., & Lieberthal, K., 1998, The end of corporate imperialism, *Harvard Business Review* 76 (4): 68–79.

10. This discussion draws on Gupta, A. K., & Govindarajan, V., 2001, Converting global presence into global competitive advantage, *Academy of Management Executive* 15 (2): 45–56.

11. Stross, R. E., 1997, Mr. Gates builds his brain trust, *Fortune*, December 8: 84–98.

12. For a good summary of the benefits and risks of international expansion, refer to Bartlett, C. A., & Ghoshal, S., 1987, Managing across borders: New strategic responses, *Sloan Management Review* 28 (5): 45–53; and Brown, R. H., 1994, *Competing to Win in a Global Economy* (Washington, DC: U.S. Department of Commerce).

13. For an interesting insight into rivalry in global markets, refer to MacMillan, I. C., van Putten, A. B., & McGrath, R. G., 2003, Global gamesmanship, *Harvard Business Review* 81 (5): 62–73.

14. For a discussion of the political risks in China for U.S. companies, refer to Garten, J. E., 1998, Opening the doors for business in China, *Harvard Business Review* 76 (3): 167–75.

15. Shari, M., 2001, Is a holy war brewing in Indonesia? *BusinessWeek*, October 15: 62.

16. Gikkas, N. S., 1996, International licensing of intellectual property: The promise and the peril, *Journal of Technology Law & Policy* 1 (1): 1–26.

17. For an excellent theoretical discussion of how cultural factors can affect knowledge transfer across national boundaries, refer to Bhagat, R. S., Kedia, B. L., Harveston, P. D., & Triandis, H. C., 2002, Cultural variations in the cross-border transfer of organizational knowledge: An integrative framework, *Academy of Management Review* 27 (2): 204–21.

18. Berkowitz, E. N., 2000, *Marketing*, 6th ed. (Burr Ridge, IL: McGraw-Hill).

19. Levitt, T., 1983, The globalization of markets, *Harvard Business Review* 61 (3): 92–102.

20. Our discussion of these assumptions draws on Douglas, S. P., & Wind, Y., 1987, The myth of globalization, *Columbia Journal of World Business*, Winter: 19–29.

21. Wetlaufer, S., 1999, Driving change: An interview with Ford Motor Company's Jacques Nasser, *Harvard Business Review* 77 (2): 76–81.

22. Ghoshal, S., 1987, Global strategy: An organizing framework, *Strategic Management Journal* 8: 425–40.

23. Bartlett, C. A., & Ghoshal, S., 1989, *Managing across Borders: The Transnational Solution* (Boston: Harvard Business School Press).

24. Bartlett & Ghoshal ibid.; for insights on global branding, refer to Aaker, D. A. & Joachimsthaler, E., 1999, The lure of global branding, Harvard Business Review, 77 (6): 137–146.

25. For an interesting perspective on how small firms can compete in their home markets, refer to Dawar & Frost, op. cit., pp. 119–29.

26. Hout, T., Porter, M. E., & Rudden, E., 1982, How global companies win out, *Harvard Business Review* 60 (5): 98–107.

27. Fryer, B., 2001, Tom Siebel of Siebel Systems: High tech the old-fashioned way, *Harvard Business Review* 79 (3): 118–30.

28. The risks that are discussed for the global, multidomestic, and transnational strategies draw on Gupta & Govindarajan, op. cit.

29. Sigiura, H., 1990, How Honda localizes its global strategy, *Sloan Management Review* 31: 77–82.

30. Prahalad & Lieberthal, op. cit., pp. 68–79. Their article also discusses how firms may have to reconsider their brand management, costs of market building, product design, and approaches to capital efficiency when entering foreign markets.

31. Hofstede, G., 1980, *Culture's Consequences: International Differences in Work- Related Values* (Beverly Hills, CA: Sage); Hofstede, G., 1993, Cultural constraints in management theories, *Academy of Management Executive* 7 (1): 81–94; Kogut, B., & Singh, H., 1988, The effect of national culture on the choice of entry mode, *Journal of International Business Studies* 19: 411–32; and Usinier, J. C., 1996, *Marketing across Cultures* (London: Prentice Hall).

32. This discussion draws on Bartlett, C. A., & Ghoshal, S., 1991, *Managing across Borders: The Transnational Solution* (Boston: Harvard Business School Press); and Raisinghani, M., 2000, Transnational organization, in Helms, M. M., ed., *Encyclopedia of Management*, 4th ed. (Detroit: Gale Group), 968–69.

33. Prahalad, C. K., & Doz, Y. L., 1987, *The Multinational Mission: Balancing Local Demands and Global Vision* (New York: Free Press).

34. Kidd, J. B., & Teramoto, Y., 1995, The learning organization: The case of Japanese RHQs in Europe, *Management International Review* 35 (Special Issue): 39–56.

35. Gupta, A. K., & Govindarajan, V., 2000, Knowledge flows within multinational corporations, *Strategic Management Journal* 21 (4): 473–96.

36. Wetlaufer, S., 2001, The business case against revolution: An interview with Nestlé's Peter Brabeck, *Harvard Business Review* 79 (2): 112–21.

37. Nobel, R., & Birkinshaw, J., 1998, Innovation in multinational corporations: Control and communication patterns in international R&D operations, *Strategic Management Journal* 19 (5): 461–78.

38. For a rigorous analysis of performance implications of entry strategies, refer to Zahra, S. A., Ireland, R. D., & Hitt, M. A., 2000, International expansion by new venture firms: International diversity, modes of entry, technological learning, and performance, *Academy of Management Journal* 43 (6): 925–50.

39. Li, J. T., 1995, Foreign entry and survival: The effects of strategic choices on performance in international markets, *Strategic Management Journal* 16: 333–51.

40. For a discussion of how home-country environments can affect diversification strategies, refer to Wan, W. P., & Hoskisson, R. E., 2003, Home country environments, corporate diversification strategies, and firm performance, *Academy of Management Journal* 46 (1): 27–45. For further discussion on entry mode, refer to Sharma, A.,

1998, Mode of entry and ex-post performance, *Strategic Management Journal* 19 (9): 879–900.

41. Arnold, D., 2000, Seven rules of international distribution, *Harvard Business Review* 78 (6): 131–37.

42. This section draws on Arnold, op. cit., pp. 131–37; and Berkowitz, op. cit.

43. Kline, D., 2003, Strategic licensing, *MIT Sloan Management Review* 44 (3): 89–93.

44. Arnold, op. cit.; and Berkowitz, op. cit.

45. Martin, J., 1999, Franchising in the Middle East, *Management Review*, June: 38–42.

46. Manufacturer-supplier relationships can be very effective in global industries such as automobile manufacturing. Refer to Kotabe, M., Martin, X., & Domoto, H., 2003, Gaining from vertical partnerships: Knowledge transfer, relationship duration, and supplier performance improvement in the U.S. and Japanese automotive industries, *Strategic Management Journal* 24 (4): 293–316.

47. For a good discussion, refer to Merchant, H., & Schendel, D., 2000, How do international joint ventures create shareholder value? *Strategic Management Journal* 21 (7): 723–38.

48. This discussion draws on Walters, B. A., Peters, S., & Dess, G. G., 1994, Strategic alliances and joint ventures: Making them work, *Business Horizons* 37 (4): 5–11.

49. For a rigorous discussion of the importance of information access in international joint ventures, refer to Reuer, J. J., & Koza, M. P., 2000, Asymmetric information and joint venture performance: Theory and evidence for domestic and international joint ventures, *Strategic Management Journal* 21 (1): 81–88.

50. Treece, J., 1991, Why Daewoo wound up on the road to nowhere, *BusinessWeek*, September 23: 55.

51. Dyer, J. H., Kale, P., & Singh, H., 2001, How to make strategic alliances work, *MIT Sloan Management Review* 42 (4): 37–43.

52. For a discussion of some of the challenges in managing subsidiaries, refer to O'Donnell, S. W., 2000, Managing foreign subsidiaries: Agents of headquarters, or an independent network? *Strategic Management Journal* 21 (5): 525–48.

53. Won, S., 2005, Edmonton design firm targets spot in global top 10, *The Globe and Mail*, January 8: B4.

Chapter 8

1. www.abebooks.com; www.amazon.com; Bennett, R., 2005, Friendly, knowledgeable staff make little stores a haven for bibliophiles, *National Post*, June 20: A13; and Greenwood, J., 2005, Selling books online: Chapter 2, *Financial Post*, June 20: FP1. Teicher, C. M., 2007, March of the small presses. *Publishers Weekly*, www.publishersweekly.com, March 26.

2. Walczak, L., 2001, The mood now, *BusinessWeek*, August 27: 74–78.

3. *CyberAtlas*, Harris Interactive and *Computer Industry Almanac*.

4. Data and conclusions drawn from Mandel, M. J., & Hof, R. D., 2001, Rethinking the Internet, *BusinessWeek*, March 26: 117–22; Ipsos Reid, Online shopping survey, Calgary, Alberta, January 2005; TNS Canadian Facts, February 2005; www.shop.org; Mulaney, T. J., 2003, At last the Web hits 100 mph, *BusinessWeek*, June 23: 80–81; and BPO market to reach $122B in 2003, *CyberAtlas*, June 11, 2003, www.cyberatlas.com.

5. Evans, P., & Wurster, T. S., 2000, *Blown to Bits* (Cambridge, MA: Harvard Business School Press); and Negroponte, N., 1995, *Being Digital* (New York: Alfred A. Knopf).

6. Oliver, R. W., 2000, The seven laws of e-commerce strategy, *Journal of Business Strategy* 21 (5): 8–10.

7. Porter, M. E., 2001, Strategy and the Internet, *Harvard Business Review*, March: 63–78.

8. Prahalad, C. K., & Ramaswamy, V., 2004, *The Future of Competition*, (Boston, MA: Harvard Business School Press).

9. www.consumerreports.org.

10. Siegel, D., 1999, *Futurize Your Enterprise* (New York: Wiley), 5.

11. For an alternative perspective on the role of customers in an Internet environment, refer to Nambisan, S., 2002, Designing virtual customer environments for new product development: Toward a theory, *Academy of Management Review* 27 (3): 392–413.

12. Time to rebuild, 2001, *The Economist*, May 19: 55–56.

13. For more on the role of the Internet as an electronic intermediary, refer to Carr, N. G., 2000, Hypermediation: Commerce as clickstream, *Harvard Business Review* 78 (1): 46–48.

14. Downes, L., & Mui, C., 1998, *Unleashing the Killer App* (Boston: Harvard Business School Press), 45–46.

15. Poe, R., 2001, Tickets to go, *Business 2.0*, March 20: 60–61.

16. Lelii, S. R., 2001, Free online storage a thing of the past? *eWEEK*, April 22.

17. McKay, N., 2000, Ballpark figures, *Red Herring*, May: 360; and www.insightexpress.com.

18. www.privacy.net; and www.epic.org.

19. www.mysimon.com; and www.pricescan.com.

20. www.cnet.com; and www.gomez.com.

21. Hanrahan, T., 1999, Price isn't everything, *Wall Street Journal*, July 12: R20.

22. For a discussion of strategic implications of partnering and competing, refer to Gulati, R., Nohria, N., & Zaheer, A., 2000, Strategic networks, *Strategic Management Journal* 21: 203–15.

23. www.bestbookbuys.com.

24. The ideas in this section draw on several sources, including Zeng, M., & Reinartz, W., 2003, Beyond online search: The road to profitability, *California Management Review*, Winter: 107–30; and Stabell, C. B., & Fjeldstad, O. D., 1998, Configuring value for competitive advantage: On chains, shops, and networks, *Strategic Management Journal* 19: 413–37.

25. Hardy, Q., 2003, All eyes on Google, *Forbes*, May 26, www.forbes.com.

26. Breen, B., 2002, Lilly's R&D prescription, *Fast Company* 57: 44; and www.inocentive.com.

27. Bayers, C., 2002, The last laugh, *Business 2.0*, September: 86–93.

28. Yamada, K., 2001. Web trails, *Forbes*, December 3.

29. Greenspan, R., 2003, Internet not for everyone, *CyberAtlas*, April 16, www.cyberatlas.com.

30. Afuah, A., & Tucci, C. L., 2003, *Internet Business Models and Strategies*, 2nd ed. (Burr Ridge, IL: McGraw-Hill); and Timmers, P., 1999, *Electronic Commerce* (New York: Wiley).

31. Big, boring, booming, 1998, *The Economist*, July 18: 15–16; Madden, J., & Shein, E., 1998, Web purchasing attracts more pioneers, *PC Week Online*, March 6; see www. tpn.geis.com and www.ge.com/news/welch/index.htm.

32. For an interesting discussion of the cost and pricing implications of Internet technology, refer to Sinha, I., 2000, Cost transparency: The net's real threat to prices and brands, *Harvard Business Review* 78 (2): 43–51.

33. Evans, P., & Wurster, T. S., 2000, *Blown to Bits* (Boston: Harvard Business School Press), 82–83.

34. Over the counter e-commerce, 2001, *The Economist*, May 26, 77–78; Collett, S., 1999, Nike offers mass customization online, *ComputerWorld*, November 23.

35. McHugh, J., 2000, Will online publishing ever fly? *Business 2.0*, July; Mullaney, T. J., 2001, Sites worth paying for? *BusinessWeek e.biz*, May 14: EB10–EB12; and Mount, I., 2003, If they have to pay, will they come? *Business 2.0*, February: 45.

36. Seybold, P., 2000, Niches bring riches, *Business 2.0*, June 13: 135.

37. Hof, R. D., 2001, Those mighty mini-dots, *BusinessWeek e.biz*, February 9: 56.

38. Miller, M. J., 2001, A tangled, wireless web, *PC Magazine*, February 2.

39. Porter, op. cit.

40. Downes & Mui, op. cit.

Chapter 9

1. The Power Corporation of Canada, 2000, *Seventy-Five Years of Growth 1925–2000: The Power Corporation of Canada;* www.powercorporation.com; Annual Reports 2000, 2004, 2007, Power Corporation of Canada and Power Financial Corporation; Pitts, G., 2004, Underdogs at heart, Report on (Small) Business, Fall: 14–19; and Damsell, K., 2005, A Canadian conglomerate just keeps on compounding, *The Globe and Mail*, March 15: B19.

2. This introductory discussion draws on Hall, R. H., 2002, *Organizations: Structures, Processes, and Outcomes*, 8th ed. (Upper Saddle River, NJ: Prentice-Hall); and Duncan, R. E., 1979, What is the right organization structure? Decision-tree analysis provides the right answer,

Organizational Dynamics 7 (3): 59–80. For an insightful discussion of strategy-structure relationships in the organization theory and strategic management literatures, refer to Keats, B., & O'Neill, H. M., 2001, Organization structure: Looking through a strategy lens, in Hitt, M. A., Freeman, R. E., & Harrison, J. S., eds., *The Blackwell Handbook of Strategic Management* (Malden, MA: Blackwell Publishers Ltd.), 520–42.

3. This discussion draws on Chandler, A. D., 1962, *Strategy and Structure* (Cambridge, MA: MIT Press); Galbraith, J. R., & Kazanjian, R. K., 1986, *Strategy Implementation: Structure, Systems, and Process* (St. Paul, MN: West Publishing); and Scott, B. R., 1971, Stages of corporate development, Intercollegiate Case Clearinghouse, 9-371-294, BP 998, Harvard Business School.

4. Our discussion of the different types of organizational structures draws on a variety of sources, including Galbraith & Kazanjian, op. cit.; Hrebiniak, L. G., & Joyce, W. F., 1984, *Implementing Strategy* (New York: Macmillan); Distelzweig, H., 2000, Organizational structure, in Helms, M. M., ed., *Encyclopedia of Management* (Farmington Hills, MI: Gale), 692–99; Dess, G. G., & Miller, A., 1993, *Strategic Management* (New York: McGraw-Hill); McDougall, P. P., & Oviatt, B. M., 1996, New venture internationalization, strategic change and performance: A follow up study, *Journal of Business Venturing* 11: 23–40; and McDougall, P. P., & Oviatt, B. M., eds., 2000, The special research forum on international entrepreneurship, *Academy of Management Journal*, October: 902–6.

5. Collis, D. J., & Montgomery, C. A., 1998, Creating corporate advantage, *Harvard Business Review* 76 (3): 70–83.

6. Schein, E. H., 1996, Three cultures of management: The key to organizational learning, *Sloan Management Review* 38 (1): 9–20.

7. For a discussion of performance implications, refer to Hoskisson, R. E., 1987, Multidivisional structure and performance: The contingency of diversification strategy, *Academy of Management Journal* 29: 625–44.

8. For a thorough and seminal discussion of the evolution toward the divisional form of organizational structure in the United States, refer to Chandler, op. cit. A rigorous empirical study of the strategy and structure relationship is found in Rumelt, R. P., 1974, *Strategy, Structure, and Economic Performance* (Cambridge: Harvard Business School Press).

9. See, for example, Hill, C. W. L., Hitt, M. A., & Hoskisson, R. E., 1988, Declining U.S. competitiveness: Reflections on a crisis, *Academy of Management Executive* 2 (1): 51–60.

10. Ghoshal, S., & Bartlett, C. A., 1995, Changing the role of management: Beyond structure to processes. *Harvard Business Review* 73 (1): 88.

11. Bloom, R., 2005, Weston's new, lean diet: Stick to the basics, *The Globe and Mail*, February 15: B1–B9.

12. Pitts, R. A., 1977, Strategies and structures for diversification, *Academy of Management Journal* 20 (2): 197–208.

13. Daniels, J. D., Pitts, R. A., & Tretter, M. J., 1984, Strategy and structure of U.S. multinationals: An exploratory study, *Academy of Management Journal* 27 (2): 292–307.

14. Habib, M. M., & Victor, B., 1991, Strategy, structure, and performance of U.S. manufacturing and service MNCs: A comparative analysis, *Strategic Management Journal* 12 (8): 589–606.

15. Our discussion of global start-ups draws from Oviatt, B. M., & McDougall, P. P., 2005, The internationalization of entrepreneurship, *Journal of International Business Studies*, 36 (1) 2–8; Oviatt, B. M., & McDougall, P. P., 1995, Global start-ups: Enrepreneurs on a worldwide stage, *Academy of Management Executive*, 9 (2): 30–43; Oviatt, B. M., & McDougall, P. P., 1994, Toward a theory of international new ventures, *Journal of International Business Studies*, 25 (1): 45–64. and Kuemmerle, W. 2005, The entrepreneur's path for global expansion, *MIT Sloan Management Review*, 46 (2): 42–50.

16. See, for example, Miller, D., & Friesen, P. H., 1980, Momentum and revolution in organizational structure, *Administrative Science Quarterly* 13: 65–91.

17. Many authors have argued that a firm's structure can influence a firm's strategy and performance. These include Amburgey, T. L., & Dacin, T., 1995, As the left foot follows the right? The dynamics of strategic and structural change, *Academy of Management Journal* 37: 1427–52; Dawn, K., & Amburgey, T. L., 1991, Organizational inertia and momentum: A dynamic model of strategic change, *Academy of Management Journal* 34: 591–612; Fredrickson, J. W., 1986, The strategic decision process and organization structure, *Academy of Management Review* 11: 280–97; Hall, D. J., & Saias, M. A., 1980, Strategy follows structure!, *Strategic Management Journal;* and Burgelman, R. A., 1983, A model of the interaction of strategic behavior, corporate context, and the concept of strategy, *Academy of Management Review* 8: 61–70.

18. Ashkenas, R., 1977, The organization's new clothes, in Hesselbein, F., Goldsmith, M., & Beckhard, R., eds., *The Organization of the Future* (San Francisco: Jossey Bass) 104–6. An interesting discussion on how the Internet has affected the boundaries of firms can be found in Afuah, A., 2003, Redefining firm boundaries in the face of the Internet: Are firms really shrinking? *Academy of Management Review* 28 (1): 34–53.

19. Collis & Montgomery, op. cit.

20. Pfeffer, J., 1998, *The Human Equation: Building Profits by Putting People First* (Cambridge: Harvard Business School Press).

21. For a discussion on how functional area diversity affects performance, see Bunderson, J. S., & Sutcliffe, K. M., 2002, *Academy of Management Journal* 45 (5): 875–93.

22. Augustine, N. R., 1983, *Augustine's Laws* (New York: Viking Press).

23. See, for example, Hoskisson, R. E., Hill, C. W. L., & Kim, H., 1993, The multidivisional structure: Organizational fossil or source of value? *Journal of Management* 19 (2): 269–98.

24. Kuedtjam, H., Haskins, M. E., Rosenblum, J. W., & Weber, J., 1997, The generative cycle: Linking knowledge and relationships, *Sloan Management Review* 39 (1): 47–58.

25. Thompson, L., 2003, Improving the creativity of organizational work groups, *Academy of Management Executive* 17 (1): 96–111.

26. Pottruck, D. A., 1997, speech delivered by the co-CEO of Charles Schwab Co., Inc., to the Retail Leadership Meeting, San Francisco, CA, January 30; and Miller, W., 1999, Building the ultimate resource, *Management Review*, January: 42–45.

27. Magretta, J., 1998, The power of virtual integration: An interview with Dell Computer's Michael Dell, *Harvard Business Review* 76 (2): 75.

28. Forster, J., 2001, Networking for cash, *BusinessWeek*, January 8: 129.

29. Dess, G. G., Rasheed, A. M. A., McLaughlin, K. J., & Priem, R., 1995, The new corporate architecture, *Academy of Management Executive* 9 (3): 7–20.

30. Barnes, C., 1998, A fatal case, *Fast Company*, February–March: 173.

31. Handy, C., 1989, *The Age of Unreason* (Boston: Harvard Business School Press); Ramstead, E., 1997, APC maker's low-tech formula: Start with the box, *Wall Street Journal*, December 29: B1; Mussberg, W., 1997, Thin screen PCs are looking good but still fall flat, *Wall Street Journal*, January 2: 9; Brown, E., 1997, Monorail: Low cost PCs, *Fortune*, July 7: 106–8; and Young, M., 1996, Ex-Compaq executives start new company, *Computer Reseller News*, November 11: 181.

32. Tully, S., 1993, The modular corporation, *Fortune*, February 8: 196.

33. For a recent review of the relationship between outsourcing and firm performance, see Gilley, K. M., & Rasheed, A., 2000, Making more by doing less: An analysis of outsourcing and its effects on firm performance, *Journal of Management* 26 (4): 763–90.

34. Quinn, J. B., 1992, *Intelligent Enterprise: A Knowledge and Service Based Paradigm for Industry* (New York: Free Press).

35. This discussion draws on Quinn, J. B., & Hilmer, F. C., 1994, Strategic outsourcing, *Sloan Management Review* 35 (4): 43–55.

36. See also Stuckey, J., & White, D., 1993, When and when not to vertically integrate, *Sloan Management Review*, Spring: 71–81; Harrar, G., 1993, Outsource tales, *Forbes ASAP*, June 7: 37–39, 42; and Davis, E. W., 1992, Global outsourcing: Have U.S. managers thrown the baby out with the bath water?, *Business Horizons*, July–August: 58–64.

37. The discussion of virtual organizations draws on Doz, Y., & Hamel, G., 1998, *Alliance Advantage: The Art of Creating Value through Partnering* (Boston: Harvard Business School Press); Miles, R. E., & Snow, C. C., 1986, Organizations: New concepts for new forms, *California Management Review*, Spring: 62–73; Miles, R. E., & Snow, C. C., 1999, Causes of failure in network organizations, *California Management Review*, Summer: 53–72; and Bahrami, H., 1991, The emerging flexible organization: Perspectives from Silicon Valley, *California Management Review*, Summer: 33–52.

38. DeSanctis, G., Glass, J. T., & Ensing, I. M., 2002, Organizational designs for R&D, *Academy of Management Executive* 16 (3): 55–66.

39. Barringer, B. R., & Harrison, J. S., 2000, Walking a tightrope: Creating value through interorganizational alliances, *Journal of Management* 26: 367–403.

40. Davis, E., 1997, Interview: Norman Augustine, *Management Review*, November: 14.

41. One contemporary example of virtual organizations is R&D consortia. For an insightful discussion, refer to Sakaibara, M., 2002, Formation of R&D consortia: Industry and company effects, *Strategic Management Journal* 23 (11): 1033–50.

42. Bartness, A., & Cerny, K., 1993, Building competitive advantage through a global network of capabilities, *California Management Review*, Winter: 78–103. For an insightful historical discussion of the usefulness of alliances in the computer industry, see Moore, J. F., 1993, Predators and prey: A new ecology of competition, *Harvard Business Review* 71 (3): 75–86.

43. See Lorange, P., & Roos, J., 1991, Why some strategic alliances succeed and others fail, *Journal of Business Strategy*, January–February: 25–30; and Slowinski, G., 1992, The human touch in strategic alliances, *Mergers and Acquisitions*, July–August: 44–47. A compelling argument for strategic alliances is provided by Ohmae, K., 1989, The global logic of strategic alliances, *Harvard Business Review* 67 (2): 143–54.

44. Some of the downsides of alliances are discussed in Das, T. K., & Teng, B. S., 2000, Instabilities of strategic alliances: An internal tensions perspective, *Organization Science* 11: 77–106.

45. This section draws on Dess, G. G., & Picken, J. C., 1997, *Mission Critical* (Burr Ridge, IL: Irwin Professional Publishing).

46. Katzenbach, J. R., & Smith, D., 1994, *The Wisdom of Teams: Creating the High Performance Organization* (New York: HarperBusiness).

47. Hammer, M., & Champy, J., 1993, *Reengineering the Corporation: A Manifest for Business Revolution* (New York: HarperCollins).

Chapter 10

1. Based on accounts of the Hollinger International legal filings and other sources: McClearn, M., 2004, The verdict, *Canadian Business*, March 1: 22–25; Lavelle, L., 2004, Lessons of the Hollinger chronicles, *BusinessWeek*,

September 13: 42; McKenna, B., & Howlett, K., 2004, Are criminal, civil charges next? *The Globe and Mail*, September 1: B1–B6; and Blackwell, R., 2005, OSC vetoes Black's Hollinger plan, *The Globe and Mail*, March 29: B1–B8; Waldie, P., 2008, Appeals court rejects all arguments for Black; His lawyer not conceding defeat, but others say "realistically it's over" *The Globe and Mail*, June 26: A19.

2. McFarland, J., & Church, E., 2004, Board games, Canada's definitive corporate governance rankings, *The Globe and Mail*, Report on Business, October 12.

3. This chapter draws on Picken, J. C., & Dess, G. G., 1997, *Mission Critical* (Burr Ridge, IL: Irwin Professional Publishing); Simons, R., 1994, How new top managers use control systems as levers of strategic renewal, *Strategic Management Journal* 15: 169–89; and Simons, R., 1995, Control in an age of empowerment, *Harvard Business Review* 73: 80–88.

4. Good, M., & Quinn, J. B., 1990, The paradox of strategic controls, *Strategic Management Journal* 11 (1): 43–57.

5. Mintzberg, H., 1987, Crafting strategy, *Harvard Business Review* 65 (4): 66–75.

6. Quinn, J. B., 1980, *Strategies for Change* (Homewood, IL: Richard D. Irwin).

7. Weston, J. S., 1992, Soft stuff matters, *Financial Executive*, July–August: 52–53.

8. Argyris, C., 1977, Double-loop learning in organizations, *Harvard Business Review* 55: 115–25.

9. This discussion of control systems draws on Simons, R., 1995, Control in an age of empowerment, *Harvard Business Review* 73: 80–88.

10. For an interesting perspective on this issue and how a downturn in the economy can reduce the tendency toward "free agency" by managers and professionals, refer to Morris, B., 2001, White collar blues, *Fortune*, July 23: 98–110.

11. Ouchi, W., 1981, *Theory Z* (Reading, MA: Addison-Wesley); Deal, T. E., & Kennedy, A. A., 1982, *Corporate Cultures* (Reading, MA: Addison-Wesley); Peters, T. J., & Waterman, R. H., 1982, *In Search of Excellence* (New York: Random House); and Collins, J., 2001, *Good to Great* (New York: HarperCollins).

12. Collins, J. C., & Porras, J. I., 1994, *Built to Last: Successful Habits of Visionary Companies* (New York: HarperBusiness).

13. Lee, J., & Miller, D., 1999, People matter: Commitment to employees, strategy, and performance in Korean firms, *Strategic Management Journal* 6: 579–94.

14. For an insightful discussion of IKEA's unique culture, see Kling, K., & Goteman, I., 2003, IKEA CEO Anders Dahlvig on international growth and IKEA's unique corporate culture and brand identity, *Academy of Management Executive* 17 (1): 31–37.

15. For a discussion of how professionals inculcate values, refer to Uhl-Bien, M., & Graen, G. B., 1998, Individual self-management: Analysis of professionals' self-managing activities in functional and cross-functional work teams, *Academy of Management Journal* 41 (3): 340–50. For a discussion about the connection between culture and performance, see Barney, J., 1986, Organizational culture: Can it be a source of sustained competitive advantage? *Academy of Management Review* 11 (3): 656–65.

16. A perspective on how certain behaviour can erode a firm's culture can be found in Robinson, S. L., & O'Leary-Kelly, A. M., 1998, Monkey see, monkey do: The influence of work groups on the antisocial behavior of employees, *Academy of Management Journal* 41 (6): 658–72.

17. Mitchell, R., 1989, Masters of innovation, *BusinessWeek*, April 10: 58–63.

18. Sellers, P., 1993, Companies that serve you best, *Fortune*, May 31: 88.

19. Semler, R., 1989, Managing without managers, *Harvard Business Review* 67 (5): 76–84; Killian, K., Perez, F., & Siehl, C., 2001, Ricardo Semler and Semco S. A., American Graduate School of International Management, August: 1-12; and Mann, D. T., 2001, *Maverick: The Success behind the World's Most Unusual Workplace* (New York: Warner Books).

20. Kerr, J., & Slocum, J. W., Jr., 1987, Managing corporate culture through reward systems, *Academy of Management Executive* 1 (2): 99–107.

21. For a unique perspective on leader challenges in managing wealthy professionals, refer to Wetlaufer, S., 2000, Who wants to manage a millionaire? *Harvard Business Review* 78 (4): 53–60.

22. For a discussion of the benefits of stock options as executive compensation, refer to Hall, B. J., 2000, What you need to know about stock options, *Harvard Business Review* 78 (2): 121–29.

23. Tully, S., 1993, Your paycheck gets exciting, *Fortune*, November 13: 89.

24. For a recent discussion linking pay to performance, refer to Rappaport, A., 1999, New thinking on how to link pay to performance, *Harvard Business Review* 77 (2): 91–105.

25. Zellner, W., Hof, R. D., Brandt, R., Baker, S., & Greising, D., 1995, Go-go goliaths, *BusinessWeek*, February 13: 64–70.

26. This section draws on Dess, G. G., & Picken, J. C., 1997, *Beyond Productivity* (New York: AMACOM).

27. Simons, op. cit.

28. Davis, E., 1997, Interview: Norman Augustine, *Management Review*, November: 11.

29. www.canadiantire.ca; and www.pandg.com.

30. This section draws on Dess, G. G., & Miller, A., 1993, *Strategic Management* (New York: McGraw-Hill). For a good review of the goal-setting literature, refer to Locke, E. A., & Latham, G. P., 1990, *A Theory of Goal Setting and Task Performance* (Englewood Cliffs, NJ: Prentice Hall).

31. Weaver, G. R., Trevino, L. K., & Cochran, P. L., 1999, Corp. ethics programs as control systems: Influences of executive commitment and environmental factors, *Academy of Management Journal* 42 (1): 41–57.

32. Cadbury, S. A., 1987, Ethical managers make their own rules, *Harvard Business Review* 65: 69–73.

33. Weber, J., 2003, CFOs on the hot seat, *BusinessWeek*, March 17: 66–70.

34. William Ouchi has written extensively about the use of clan control (which is viewed as an alternate to bureaucratic or market control). As in a clan, a powerful culture results in people aligning their individual interests with those of the firm. Refer to Ouchi, W. C., 1981, *Theory Z* (Reading, MA: Addison-Wesley). This section also draws on Hall, R. H., 2002, *Organizations: Structures, Processes, and Outcomes*, 8th ed. (Upper Saddle River, NJ: Prentice Hall).

35. Monks, A. G., & Minow, N., 2001, *Corporate Governance*, 2nd ed. (Malden, MA: Blackwell). Management, of course, cannot ignore the demands of other important firm stakeholders such as creditors, suppliers, customers, employees, and government regulators. For a seminal discussion on stakeholder management, refer to Freeman, R. E., 1984, *Strategic Management: A Stakeholder Approach* (Boston: Pitman).

36. Pound, J., 1995, The promise of the governed corporation, *Harvard Business Review* 73 (2): 89–98.

37. Byrne, J. A., Lavelle, L., Byrnes, N., Vickers, M., & Borrus, A., 2002, How to fix corporate governance, *BusinessWeek*, May 6: 44–52.

38. This discussion draws on Monks & Minow, op. cit.

39. Eisenhardt, K. M., 1989, Agency theory: An assessment and review, *Academy of Management Review* 14 (1): 57–74. Some of the seminal contributions to agency theory include Jensen, M., & Meckling, W., 1976, Theory of the firm: Managerial behavior, agency costs, and ownership structure, *Journal of Financial Economics* 3: 305-60; Fama, E., & Jensen, M., 1983, Separation of ownership and control, *Journal of Law and Economics* 26: 301, 325; and Fama, E., 1980, Agency problems and the theory of the firm, *Journal of Political Economy* 88: 288–307.

40. Managers may also engage in "shirking," that is, reducing or withholding their efforts. See, for example, Kidwell, R. E., Jr., & Bennett, N., 1993, Employee propensity to withhold effort: A conceptual model to intersect three avenues of research, *Academy of Management Review* 18 (3): 429–56.

41. For an interesting perspective on agency and clarification of many related concepts and terms, visit the following website: www.encycogov.com.

42. Argawal, A., & Mandelker, G., 1987, Managerial incentives and corporate investment and financing decisions, *Journal of Finance* 42: 823–37.

43. For an insightful, recent discussion of the academic research on corporate governance, in particular, the role of boards of directors, refer to Chatterjee, S., & Harrison, J. S., 2001, Corporate governance, in Hitt, M. A., Freeman, R. E., & Harrison, J. S., eds., *Handbook of Strategic Management* (Malden, MA: Blackwell), 543–63.

44. This opening discussion draws on Monks & Minow, op. cit, pp. 164, 169; see also Pound, op. cit.

45. International Corporate Governance Network, *ICGN Statement on Global Corporate Governance Principles*, revised July 8, 2005 at the Annual Conference in London.

46. Byrne, J. A., Grover, R., & Melcher, R. A., 1997, The best and worst boards, *BusinessWeek*, November 26: 35–47. The three key roles of boards of directors are monitoring the actions of executives, providing advice, and providing links to the external environment to provide resources. See Johnson, J. L., Daily, C. M., & Ellstrand, A. E., 1996, Boards of directors: A review and research agenda, *Academy of Management Review* 37: 409–38; and the Ontario Teachers Pension Plan Governance Principles listed on www.otpp.com.

47. McGeehan, P., 2003, More chief executives shown the door, study says, *New York Times*, May 12: C2.

48. There are benefits, of course, to having some insiders on the board of directors. Inside directors would be more aware of the firm's strategies. Additionally, outsiders may rely too often on financial performance indicators because of information asymmetries. For an interesting discussion, see Baysinger, B. D., & Hoskisson, R. E., 1990, The composition of boards of directors and strategic control: Effects on corporate strategy, *Academy of Management Review* 15: 72–87.

49. Hambrick, D. C., & Jackson, E. M., 2000, Outside directors with a stake: The linchpin in improving governance, *California Management Review* 42 (4): 108–27.

50. Ibid.

51. Disney has begun to make many changes to improve its corporate governance such as assigning only independent directors to important board committees, restricting directors from serving on more than three boards, and appointing a lead director who can convene the board without approval by the CEO. In recent years, the Disney Co. has shown up on some "best" board lists.

52. Talk show, 2002, *BusinessWeek*, September 30: 14.

53. Monks and Minow, op. cit., p. 93.

54. A discussion of the factors that lead to shareholder activism is found in Ryan, L. V., & Schneider, M., 2002, The antecedents of institutional investor activism, *Academy of Management Review* 27 (4): 554–73.

55. There is strong research support for the idea that the presence of large block shareholders is associated with value-maximizing decisions. For example, refer to Johnson, R. A., Hoskisson, R. E., & Hitt, M. A., 1993, Board of director involvement in restructuring: The effects of board versus managerial controls and characteristics, *Strategic Management Journal*, 14: 33–50.

56. For an interesting perspective on the impact of institutional ownership on a firm's innovation strategies, see Hoskisson, R. E., Hitt, M. A., Johnson, R. A., & Grossman, W., 2002, *Academy of Management Journal* 45 (4): 697–716.

57. Jensen, M. C., & Murphy, K. J., 1990, CEO incentives—It's not how much you pay, but how, *Harvard Business Review* 68 (3): 138–49.

58. All figures on executive compensation are drawn from the Special Report on Compensation, 2005, *The Globe and Mail*, May 4: B1, B9; The Top 1000, 2005, Report on Business, July-August: 43–100; and closing prices quoted in the daily stock tables.

59. Research has found that executive compensation is more closely aligned with firm performance in companies with compensation committees and boards dominated by outside directors. See, for example, Conyon, M. J., & Peck, S. I., 1998, Board control, remuneration committees, and top management compensation, *Academy of Management Journal* 41: 146–57.

60. Byrne, Lavelle, et al., op. cit; and Lavelle, L., Jespersen, F. F., & Arndt, M., 2002, Executive pay, *BusinessWeek*, April 15: 66–72.

61. www.tiaa-cref.org/pubs.

62. Such opportunistic behaviour is common in all principal-agent relationships. For a description of agency problems, especially in the context of the relationship between shareholders and managers, see Jensen, M. C., & Meckling, W. H., 1976, Theory of the firm: Managerial behavior, agency costs, and ownership structure, *Journal of Financial Economics* 3: 305–60.

63. Hoskisson, R. E., & Turk, T. A., 1990, Corporate restructuring: Governance and control limits of the internal market, *Academy of Management Review* 15: 459–77.

64. For an insightful perspective on the market for corporate control and how it is influenced by knowledge intensity, see Coff, R., 2003, Bidding wars over R&D-intensive firms: Knowledge, opportunism, and the market for corporate control, *Academy of Management Journal* 46 (1): 74–85.

65. Walsh, J. P., & Kosnik, R. D., 1993, Corporate raiders and their disciplinary role in the market for corporate control, *Academy of Management Journal* 36: 671–700.

66. Gunning for KPMG, 2003, *The Economist*, February 1: 63.

67. Timmons, H., 2003, Investment banks: Who will foot their bill? *BusinessWeek*, March 3: 116.

68. Wishy-washy: The SEC pulls its punches on corporate-governance rules, 2003, *The Economist*, February 1: 60.

69. Lavelle, L., & McNamee, M., 2002, Will overseas boards play by American rules? *BusinessWeek*, December 16: 35; and Kemp, S., U.S. laws to hinder SA companies, CFOweb, November 2002.

70. McLean, B., 2001, Is Enron overpriced? *Fortune*, March 5: 122–25.

71. Erman, B., 2006, Shareholders quash takeover bid by Sears, *The Globe and Mail*, November 15: B6; Church, E., & McFarland, J., 2006, *The Globe and Mail*, Corporate governance winners and losers, October 24: B8.

72. DeCloet, D., 2008, The cost of playing back up to Stronach, *The Globe and Mail*, August 12: B1.

Chapter 11

1. Bogomolny, L., 2003, Timing is everything, *Canadian Business*, November 24: 11; De Zen passes the reins at Royal Technologies, 2003, *Plastics in Canada*, December: 5; Royal rebounds, 2003, *Canadian Plastics*, January: 9; Howlett, K., 2008, Royal Group founder stunned by charges, *The Globe and Mail*, June 20, B1; Waldie, P., 2005, De Zen cuts deal, gives up control of Royal Group, *The Globe and Mail*, March 25: B1; and Royal Group Technologies, Annual Reports.

2. Rowe, W. G., 2001, Creating wealth in organizations: The role of strategic leadership, *Academy of Management Executive* 15 (1): 81–94.

3. D'Aveni, R., 1994, *Hypercompetition* (New York: Free Press).

4. Charan, R., & Colvin, G., 1999, Why CEOs fail, *Fortune*, June 21: 68–78.

5. These three activities and our discussion draw on Kotter, J. P., 1990, What leaders really do, *Harvard Business Review* 68 (3): 103–11; Pearson, A. E., 1990, Six basics for general managers, *Harvard Business Review* 67 (4): 94–101; and Covey, S. R., 1996, Three roles of the leader in the new paradigm, in *The Leader of the Future*, Hesselbein, F., Goldsmith, M., & Beckhard, R., eds. (San Francisco: Jossey-Bass), 149–60. Some of the discussion of each of the three leadership activity concepts draws on Dess, G. G., & Miller, A., 1993, *Strategic Management* (New York: McGraw-Hill), 320–25.

6. Day, C., Jr., & LaBarre, P., 1994, GE: Just your average everyday $60 billion family grocery store, *Industry Week*, May 2: 13–18.

7. Aarsteinsen, B., 2004, Regaining momentum, *Canadian Insurance*, May: 10.

8. Face value: Lord of the rings, 2005, *The Economist*, February 5: 61.

9. For insightful perspectives on escalation, refer to Brockner, J., 1992, The escalation of commitment to a failing course of action, *Academy of Management Review* 17 (1): 39–61; and Staw, B. M., 1976, Knee-deep in the big muddy: A study of commitment to a chosen course of action, *Organizational Behavior and Human Decision Processes* 16: 27–44. The discussion of systemic, behavioural, and political barriers draws on Lorange, P., & Murphy, D., 1984, Considerations in implementing strategic control, *Journal of Business Strategy* 5: 27–35. In a similar vein, Noel M. Tichy has addressed three types of resistance to change in the context of General Electric: technical resistance, political resistance, and cultural resistance. See Tichy, N. M., 1993, Revolutionalize your company, *Fortune*, December 13: 114–18. Examples draw on O'Reilly, B., 1997, The secrets of America's most admired corporations: New ideas and new products, *Fortune*, March 3: 60–64.

10. This section draws on Champoux, J. E., 2000, *Organizational Behavior: Essential Tenets for a New Millennium* (London: South-Western); and The mature

use of power in organizations, 2003, *RHR International-Executive Insights*, May 29, http://12.19.168.197/execinsights/8-3.htm.

11. For a review of this literature, see Daft, R., 1999, *Leadership: Theory and Practice* (Fort Worth, TX: Dryden Press).

12. This section draws on Luthans, F., 2002, Positive organizational behavior: Developing and managing psychological strengths, *Academy of Management Executive* 16 (1): 57–72; and Goleman, D., 1998, What makes a leader? *Harvard Business Review* 76 (6): 92–105.

13. EI has its roots in the concept of "social intelligence" that was first identified by E. L. Thorndike in 1920 (Intelligence and its uses, *Harper's Magazine* 140: 227–35). Psychologists have been uncovering other intelligences for some time now and have grouped them into such clusters as abstract intelligence (the ability to understand and manipulate with verbal and mathematical symbols), concrete intelligence (the ability to understand and manipulate with objects), and social intelligence (the ability to understand and relate to people). See Ruisel, I., 1992, Social intelligence: Conception and methodological problems, *Studia Psychologica* 34 (4–5): 281–96.

14. See, for example, Luthans, op. cit.; Mayer, J. D., Salvoney, P., & Caruso, D., 2000, Models of emotional intelligence, in Sternberg, R. J., ed., *Handbook of Intelligence* (Cambridge, UK: Cambridge University Press); and Cameron, K., 1999, Developing emotional intelligence at the Weatherhead School of Management, *Strategy: The Magazine of the Weatherhead School of Management*, Winter: 2–3.

15. Goleman, op. cit., p. 102.

16. Insightful perspectives on some of the concerns with emotional intelligence are drawn from Mayer, J. D., et. al. 2004, Leading by feel, *Harvard Business Review* 82 (1): 27–37; Heifetz, R., 2004, Question authority, *Harvard Business Review* 82 (1: 37; and Goleman, D., Boyztzis, R., & McKee, A., 2002, *Primal Leadership: Realizing the power of emotional intelligence* (Boston: Harvard Business School.)

17. Handy, C., 1995, Trust and the virtual organization, *Harvard Business Review* 73 (3): 40–50.

18. This section draws on Dess, G. G., & Picken, J. C., 1999, *Beyond Productivity* (New York: AMACOM). The elements of the learning organization in this section are consistent with the work of Dorothy Leonard-Barton. See, for example, Leonard-Barton, D., 1992, The factory as a learning laboratory, *Sloan Management Review* 11: 23–38.

19. Senge, P. M., 1990, The leader's new work: Building learning organizations, *Sloan Management Review* 32 (1): 7–23.

20. Hammer, M., & Stanton, S. A., 1997, The power of reflection, *Fortune*, November 24: 291–96.

21. Covey, S. R., 1989, *The Seven Habits of Highly Effective People: Powerful Lessons in Personal Change* (New York: Simon & Schuster).

22. Melrose, K., 1995, *Making the Grass Greener on Your Side: A CEO's Journey to Leading by Servicing* (San Francisco: Barrett-Koehler).

23. Quinn, R. C., & Spreitzer, G. M., 1997, The road to empowerment: Seven questions every leader should consider, *Organizational Dynamics* 25: 37–49.

24. Helgesen, S., 1996, Leading from the grass roots, in *Leader of the Future*, Hesselbein, F., Goldsmith, M., & Beckhard, R., eds. (San Francisco: Jossey-Bass), 19–24.

25. Bowen, D. E., & Lawler, E. E., III, 1995, Empowering service employees, *Sloan Management Review* 37: 73–84.

26. Schafer, S., 1997, Battling a labor shortage? It's all in your imagination, *Inc.*, August: 24.

27. Meyer, P., 1998, So you want the president's job ... , *Business Horizons*, January– February: 2–8.

28. Goldberg, M., 1998, Cisco's most important meal of the day, *Fast Company*, February–March: 56.

29. Novicki, C., 1998, The best brains in business, *Fast Company*, April: 125.

30. The introductory discussion of benchmarking draws on Miller, A., 1998, *Strategic Management* (New York: McGraw-Hill), 142–43.

31. Port, O., & Smith, G., 1992, Beg, borrow—and benchmark, *BusinessWeek*, November 30: 74–75.

32. Main, J., 1992, How to steal the best ideas around, *Fortune*, October 19: 102–6.

33. Taylor, W. C., 1997, What happens after what comes next? *Fast Company*, December– January: 84–85.

34. Sheff, D., 1996, Levis changes everything, *Fast Company*, June–July: 65–74.

35. Isaacson, W., 1997, In search of the real Bill Gates, *Time*, January 13: 44–57.

36. Holt, J. W., 1996, *Celebrate Your Mistakes* (New York: McGraw-Hill).

37. Harari, O., 1997, Flood your organization with knowledge, *Management Review*, November: 33–37.

38. The discussion draws on Conley, J. H., 2000, Ethics in business, in Helms, M. M., ed., *Encyclopedia of Management*, 4th ed. (Farmington Hills, MI: Gale Group), 281–85; Crane, A, & Matten, D., 2007, *Business Ethics*, 2e, (Oxford: Oxford University Press); Crane, A., & Matten, D., 2004, Questioning the domain of business ethics curriculum, *Journal of Business Ethics* 54 (4): 357–369; Paine, L. S., 1994, Managing for organizational integrity, *Harvard Business Review* 72 (2): 106–17; Jennings, M. M., 1999, *Business Ethics*, 3rd ed. (Cincinnati, OH: West Educational Publishing); and Carlson, D. S., & Perrewe, P. L., 1995, Institutionalization of organizational ethics through transformational leadership, *Journal of Business Ethics* 14: 829–38.

39. Stewart, S., 2005, CIBC's Enron bombshell, *The Globe and Mail*, July 3: B1–B16; and Stewart, S., 2005, Investors want Hunkin to share CIBC pain, *The Globe and Mail*, July 4: B1–B2.

40. Soule, E., 2002, Managerial moral strategies—in search of a few good principles, *Academy of Management Review*

27 (1): 114–24; Lavelle, M., 2002, Rogue of the year, *Time*, December 30: 32–45; The best and worst managers of the year, 2003, *BusinessWeek*, January 13; Bianco, A., Symonds, W., & Byrnes, N., 2002, The rise and fall of Dennis Kozlowski, *BusinessWeek*, December 23; and Ebner, D., & Howlett, K., 2004, The bombshell, *The Globe and Mail*, April 4: B1.

41. Carlson & Perrewe, op. cit.

42. Jennnings, op. cit.; and Stark, A., 1993, What's the matter with business ethics? *Harvard Business Review* 71 (3): 38–48.

43. This discussion is based on Paine, L. S., 1994, Managing for organizational integrity, *Harvard Business Review*, March–April: 106–17; Paine, L. S., 1997, *Cases in Leadership, Ethics, and Organizational Integrity: A Strategic Approach* (Burr Ridge, IL: Irwin); and Fontrodone, J., Business ethics across the Atlantic, Business Ethics Direct, www.ethicsa.org/BED_art_fontrodone.html.

44. www.ti.com/corp/docs/company/citizen/ethics/benchmark.shtml; and www.ti.com/corp/ docs/company/citizen/ethics/quicktest.shtml.

45. Wetalufer, S., 1999, Organizing for empowerment: An interview with AES's Roger Sant and Dennis Bakke, *Harvard Business Review* 77 (1): 110–26.

46. Paine, 1994, op. cit.

47. Competition Bureau fines Sears for deceptive ads, *Toronto Star*, April 1, 2005, www.thestar.com.

48. McClearn, M., 2004, A snitch in time, *Canadian Business*, January: 61; and Bogomolny, L., 2004, Good housekeeping, *Canadian Business*, March 1: 87.

Chapter 12

1. Shulgan, C., 2005, Survivor, Report on Business, Spring: 28–33; and various listings and press releases within www.extendmedia.com.

2. For an interesting discussion, see Johannessen, J.-A., Olsen, B., & Lumpkin, G. T., 2001, Innovation as newness: What is new, how new, and new to whom? *European Journal of Innovation Management* 4 (1): 20–31.

3. The discussion of radical and incremental innovations draws on Leifer, R., McDermott, C. M., Colarelli, G., O'Connor, G. C., Peters, L. S., Rice, M. P., & Veryzer, R. W., 2000, *Radical Innovation: How Mature Companies Can Outsmart Upstarts* (Boston: Harvard Business School Press); Damanpour, F., 1996, Organizational complexity and innovation: Developing and testing multiple contingency models, *Management Science* 42 (5): 693–716; and Hage, J., 1980, *Theories of Organizations* (New York: Wiley).

4. Christensen, C. M., 1997, *The Innovator's Dilemma: When New Technologies Cause Great Firms to Fail* (Cambridge, MA: Harvard Business School Press).

5. The discussion of product and process innovation is based on Roberts, E. B., ed., 2002, *Innovation: Driving Product, Process, and Market Change* (San Francisco: Jossey-Bass); Hayes, R., & Wheelwright, S., 1985, Competing through manufacturing, *Harvard Business Review* 63 (1): 99–109; and Hayes, R., & Wheelwright, S., 1979, Dynamics of product-process life cycles, *Harvard Business Review* 57 (2): 127–36.

6. Drucker, P. F., 1985, *Innovation and Entrepreneurship* (New York: Harper & Row).

7. Morrissey, C. A., 2000, Managing innovation through corporate venturing, *Graziadio Business Report*, Spring, gbr.pepperdine.edu; and Sharma, A., 1999, Central dilemmas of managing innovation in large firms, *California Management Review* 41 (3): 147–64.

8. Chesbrough, H., 2003, *Open Innovation: The New Imperative for Creating and Profiting from Tecnology*, (Cambridge, MA: Harvard Business School Press).

9. Sharma, op. cit.

10. Canabou, C., 2003, Fast ideas for slow times, *Fast Company*, May: 52.

11. Leifer et al., op. cit.

12. *Report on Trade* (Toronto, ON: Canadian Federation of Independent Business, 2004); and The importance of small business in Canada, Industry Canada, http://strategis.ic.gc.ca.

13. Shane, S., & Venkataraman, S., 2000, The promise of entrepreneurship as a field of research, *Academy of Management Review* 25 (1): 217–26; Lumpkin, G. T., & Dess, G. G., 1996, Clarifying the entrepreneurial orientation construct and linking it to performance, *Academy of Management Review* 21 (1): 135–72; and Gartner, W. B., 1988, Who is an entrepreneur? is the wrong question, *American Journal of Small Business* 12 (4): 11–32.

14. Partridge, J., 2005, Hip interactive game to raise stakes, *The Globe and Mail*, January 24: B1; Mayer, A., 2004, Can't stop starting, Report on (small) Business, Fall: 23–27; and www.hipinteractive.com.

15. www.biovail.com.

16. www.elcompanies.com; and www.maccosmetics.com.

17. Case, op. cit.

18. Guth, W. D., & Ginsberg, A., 1990, Guest editor's introduction: Corporate entrepreneurship, *Strategic Management Journal* 11: 5–15.

19. Pinchot, G., 1985, *Intrapreneuring* (New York: Harper & Row).

20. Stein, T., 2002, Rip cord, *Red Herring*, November 28, www.redherring.com; Franzke, E., 2001, Four keys to corporate venturing success, *European Venture Capital Journal*, June 1: 36–37; Letzelter, J., 2000, The new venture capitalists: Utilities go shopping for deals, *Public Utilities Fortnightly*, December: 34–38; and Rabinovitz, J., 2000, Venture capital, Inc., *Industry Standard*, April 17: 88–90.

21. Timmons, J. A., & Spinelli, S., 2004, *New Venture Creation*, 6th ed. (Burr Ridge, IL: McGraw-Hill/Irwin); and Bygrave, W. D., 1997, The entrepreneurial process, in W. D. Bygrave, ed., *The Portable MBA in Entrepreneurship*, 2nd ed. (New York: Wiley), 1–26.

22. Fromartz, S., 1998, How to get your first great idea, *Inc. Magazine*, April 1: 91–94; and Vesper, K. H., 1990, *New Venture Strategies*, 2nd ed. (Englewood Cliffs, NJ: Prentice Hall).

23. Patriquin, M., 2005, The secret of my address, Report on (small) Business, Spring: 16–21; www.covebike.com; and www.mntbikehalloffame.com.

24. Hamilton, T, 2006, Greening the machine, *Toronto Star*, August 21: D1; www.enwave.com; www.toronto.ca/ewmo.

25. www.simplealternative.com; and www.casketsdirect.com.

26. Gaglio, C. M., 1997, Opportunity identification: Review, critique and suggested research directions, in J. A. Katz, ed., *Advances in Entrepreneurship, Firm Emergence and Growth*, vol. 3 (Greenwich, CT: JAI Press), 139–202; Hills, G. E., Shrader, R. C., & Lumpkin, G. T., 1999, Opportunity recognition as a creative process, in *Frontiers of Entrepreneurship Research, 1999* (Wellesley, MA: Babson College), 216–27; and Long, W., & McMullan, W. E., 1984, Mapping the new venture opportunity identification process, in *Frontiers of Entrepreneurship Research, 1984* (Wellesley, MA: Babson College), 567–90.

27. Stewart, T. A., 2002, How to think with your gut, *Business 2.0*, November: 99–104.

28. www.cognos.com; and Avery, S., 2004, Little guy Cognos nears big time, *The Globe and Mail*, October 2: B3.

29. Christensen, C. M., 1997, *The Innovator's Dilemma: When New Technologies Cause Great Firms to Fail* (Cambridge, MA: Harvard Business School Press).

30. Timmons, J. A., 1997, Opportunity recognition, in W. D. Bygrave, ed., *The Portable MBA in Entrepreneurship*, 2nd ed. (New York: Wiley), 26–54.

31. Finkelstein, S., & Sanford, S. H., 2000, Learning from corporate mistakes: The rise and fall of Iridium, *Organizational Dynamics* 29 (2): 138–48.

32. Schonfeld, E., 2000, Going long, *Fortune*, March 20: 172–92.

33. Warshaw, M., 2000, The thing that would not die, *Inc. Tech* 1: 89–100.

34. Welles, E. O., 2001, Hell-bent for lather, *Inc. Magazine*, September: 50–52.

35. Stinchcombe, A. L., 1965, Social structure in organizations, in J. G. March, ed., *Handbook of Organizations* (Chicago: Rand McNally), 142–93.

36. Fast Pack 1999, 1999, *Fast Company*, February–March: 139.

37. Small business 2001: Where are we now? 2001, *Inc. Magazine*, May 29: 18–19; and Zacharakis, A. L., Bygrave, W. D., & Shepherd, D. A., 2000, *Global Entrepreneurship Monitor—National Entrepreneurship Assessment: United States of America 2000 Executive Report* (Kansas City, MO: Kauffman Center for Entrepreneurial Leadership).

38. Stuart, A., 2001, The pita principle, *Inc. Magazine*, August: 58–64.

39. Seglin, J. L., 1998, What angels want, *Inc. Magazine* 20 (7): 43–44.

40. Torres, N. L., 2002, Playing an angel, *Entrepreneur*, May: 130–38.

41. Osborne, D. M., 2001, Dear John, *Inc. Magazine*, May: 45–48.

42. www.marsdd.com.

43. Eisenhardt, K. M., & Schoonhoven, C. B., 1990, Organizational growth: Linking founding team, strategy, environment, and growth among U.S. semiconductor ventures, 1978–1988, *Administrative Science Quarterly* 35: 504–29.

44. Dubini, P., & Aldrich, H., 1991, Personal and extended networks are central to the entrepreneurship process, *Journal of Business Venturing* 6 (5): 305–33.

45. Vogel, C., 2000, Janina Pawlowski, *Working Woman*, June: 70.

46. For more information, go to the Canada Business Service Centres Web site at www.bsa.cbsc.org.

47. Tanner, J., 2000, Meals on wheels (and rails and water), *Inc. Magazine*, May: 124–26.

48. Based on Kurlantzick, J., 2003, Got what it takes? *Entrepreneur*, March: 52.

49. Briody, D., 2001, Top ten entrepreneurs: Bill Nguyen, *Red Herring*, August 1: 58–60.

50. Hopkins, M. S., 2003, Why Leadership Is the Most Dangerous Idea in American Business, *Inc. Magazine*, June, pp. 87–94.

51. Collins, J., 2001, *Good to Great* (New York: HarperBusiness).

52. Collins, ibid.; and Collins, J., 2003, Bigger, better, faster, *Fast Company*, June: 74–78.

53. Covin, J. G., & Slevin, D. P., 1991, A conceptual model of entrepreneurship as firm behavior, *Entrepreneurship Theory and Practice* 16 (1): 7–24; Lumpkin, G. T., & Dess, G. G., 1996, Clarifying the entrepreneurial orientation construct and linking it to performance, *Academy of Management Review* 21 (1): 135–72; and McGrath, R. G., & MacMillan, I., 2000, *The Entrepreneurial Mindset* (Boston: Harvard Business School Press).

54. Lumpkin, G. T., & Dess, G. G., 2001, Linking two dimensions of entrepreneurial orientation to firm performance: The moderating role of environment and life cycle, *Journal of Business Venturing* 16: 429–51.

55. For an interesting discussion, see Day, J. D., Mang, P. Y., Richter, A., & Roberts, J., 2001, The innovative organization: Why new ventures need more than a room of their own, *McKinsey Quarterly* 2: 21–31.

56. Evans, P., & Wurster, T. S., 2000, *Blown to Bits* (Boston: Harvard Business School Press).

57. Lieberman, M. B., & Montgomery, D. B., 1988, First mover advantages, *Strategic Management Journal* 9 (Special Issue): 41–58.

58. The discussion of first mover advantages is based on several articles, including Lambkin, M., 1988, Order of entry

and performance in new markets, *Strategic Management Journal* 9: 127–40; Lieberman & Montgomery, op. cit., pp. 41–58; and Miller, A., & Camp, B., 1985, Exploring determinants of success in corporate ventures, *Journal of Business Venturing* 1 (2): 87–105.

59. Drucker, op. cit., pp. 109–10.
60. The idea of entry wedges was discussed by Vesper, K., 1990, *New Venture Strategies*, 2nd ed. (Englewood Cliffs, NJ: Prentice Hall); and Drucker, P. F., 1985, *Innovation and Entrepreneurship* (New York: HarperBusiness).
61. Maiello, M., 2002, They almost changed the world, *Forbes*, December 22: 217–20.
62. Williams, G., 2002, Looks like rain, *Entrepreneur*, September: 104–11.
63. Asmus, P, 2005, 100 best corporate citizens for 2005, *Business Ethics*, www.business-ethics.com
64. Burrows, P., 2003, Ringing off the hook in China, *BusinessWeek*, June 9: 80–82.
65. Lorinc, J., 2004, The niche play, Report on (small) Business, Fall: 28–33.
66. Shaw, H, 2008, Diner eats into breakfast market, *National Post*, June 16: FP4.
67. Barrett, A., 2003, Hot growth companies, *BusinessWeek*, June 9: 74–77.
68. Dennis, W. J., Jr., 2000, *NFIB Small Business Policy Guide* (Washington, DC: National Federation of Independent Business); *The State of Small Business: A Report of the President, 1992* (Washington, DC: U.S. Government Printing Office), 65–90.
69. Romanelli, E., 1989, Environments and strategies of organization start-up: Effects on early survival, *Administrative Science Quarterly* 34 (3): 369–87.
70. Lorinc, op. cit.
71. Buchanan, L., 2003, The innovation factor: A field guide to innovation, *Forbes*, April 21, www.forbes.com.

Appendix

1. The material in this appendix is based on several sources, including Barnes, L. A., Nelson, A. J., & Christensen, C. R., 1994, *Teaching and the Case Method: Text, Cases and Readings* (Boston: Harvard Business School Press); Guth, W. D., 1985, Central concepts of business unit and corporate strategy, in W. D. Guth, ed., *Handbook of Business Strategy* (Boston: Warren, Gorham & Lamont), 1–9; Lundberg, C. C., & Enz, C., 1993, A framework for student case preparation, Case Research Journal 13 (Summer): 129–40; and Ronstadt, R., 1980, *The Art of Case Analysis: A Guide to the Diagnosis of Business Situations* (Dover, MA: Lord Publishing).
2. Edge, A. G., & Coleman, D. R., 1986, *The Guide to Case Analysis and Reporting*, 3rd ed. (Honolulu, HI: System Logistics).
3. Morris, E., 1987, Vision and strategy: A focus for the future, *Journal of Business Strategy* 8: 51–58.
4. This section is based on Lundberg & Enz, op. cit.; and Ronstadt, op. cit.
5. The importance of problem definition was emphasized in Mintzberg, H., Raisinghani, D., & Theoret, A., 1976, The structure of "unstructured" decision processes, *Administrative Science Quarterly* 21 (2): 246–75.
6. Drucker, P. F., 1994, The theory of the business, Harvard Business Review 72 (5): 95–104.
7. This section draws on Edge & Coleman, op. cit.
8. Irving Janis is credited with coining the term groupthink, and he applied it primarily to fiascos in government (such as the Bay of Pigs incident in 1961). Refer to Janis, I. L., 1982, *Victims of Groupthink*, 2nd ed. (Boston: Houghton Mifflin).
9. Much of our discussion is based on Finkelstein, S., & Mooney, A. C., 2003, Not the usual suspects: How to use board process to make boards better, *Academy of Management Executive* 17 (2): 101–13; Schweiger, D. M., Sandberg, W. R., & Rechner, P. L., 1989, Experiential effects of dialectical inquiry, devil's advocacy, and consensus approaches to strategic decision making, *Academy of Management Journal* 32 (4): 745–72; and Aldag, R. J., & Stearns, T. M., 1987, *Management* (Cincinnati: South-Western Publishing).
10. Finkelstein and Mooney, op. cit.
11. Total equity here includes preferred stock, if there is any. An equivalent numerator in this ratio would be (Current liabilities + Long-term debt).
12. Here we have implicitly assumed that all sales are credit sales. If they were not, then we would simply use total credit sales in these calculations, not total sales.
13. No, it's not; margins can be small, but they do need to be positive!

Company Index

Subject Index